PROGRAMMING MULTICORE AND MANY-CORE COMPUTING SYSTEMS

Wiley Series on Parallel and Distributed Computing

Series Editor: Albert Y. Zomaya

A complete list of the titles in this series appears at the end of this volume.

PROGRAMMING MULTICORE AND MANY-CORE COMPUTING SYSTEMS

Edited by

Sabri Pllana
Fatos Xhafa

Published by John Wiley & Sons, Inc., Hoboken, New Jersey
Published simultaneously in Canada

For general information on our other products and services or for technical support, please contact our Customer Care Department within the United States at (800) 762-2974, outside the United States at (317) 572-3993 or fax (317) 572-4002.

Wiley also publishes its books in a variety of electronic formats. Some content that appears in print may not be available in electronic formats. For more information about Wiley products, visit our web site at www.wiley.com.

Library of Congress Cataloguing-in-Publication Data

Names: Pllana, Sabri, editor. | Xhafa, Fatos, editor.
Title: Programming multicore and many-core computing systems / edited by
    Sabri Pllana, Fatos Xhafa.
Description: First edition. | Hoboken, New Jersey : John Wiley & Sons, [2017]
    | Includes bibliographical references and index.
Identifiers: LCCN 2016038244| ISBN 9780470936900 (cloth) | ISBN 9781119332008
    (epub) | ISBN 9781119331995 (Adobe PDF)
Subjects: LCSH: Parallel programming (Computer science) |
    Coprocessors–Programming.
    Classification: LCC QA76.642 .P767 2017 | DDC 005.2/75–dc23 LC record available at
https://lccn.loc.gov/2016038244

Cover Image: Creative-idea/Gettyimages
Cover design by Wiley

Set in 10/12pt, TimesLTStd by SPi Global, Chennai, India.

Printed in the United States of America

10 9 8 7 6 5 4 3 2 1

CONTENTS

LIST OF CONTRIBUTORS

MARCO ALDINUCCI, Computer Science Department, University of Torino, Corso Svizzera 185, 10149 Torino, Italy. [email: aldinuc@di.unito.it]

JØRN AMUNDSEN, Norwegian University of Science and Technology, SemSælandsvei 7-9, NO-7491 Trondheim, Norway. [email: jorn.amundsen@ntnu.no]

EDUARD AYGUADE, Barcelona Supercomputing Center, Nexus-2 Building, 3rd Floor, Jordi Girona 29, 08034 Barcelona, Spain. [email: eduard.ayguade@bsc.es]

ROSA M. BADIA, Barcelona Supercomputing Center, Nexus-2 Building, 3rd Floor, Jordi Girona 29, 08034 Barcelona, Spain. [email: rosa.m.badia@bsc.es]

HENRI E. BAL, Department of Computer Science, Vrije Universiteit, De Boelelaan 1081A,1081 HV, Amsterdam, The Netherlands. [email: bal@cs.vu.nl]

DENIS BARTHOU, INRIA Bordeaux Sud-Ouest, 200 avenue de la Vieille Tour 33405 Talence Cedex, France. [email: denis.barthou@labri.fr]

PIETER BELLENS, Barcelona Supercomputing Center, Nexus-2 Building, 3rd Floor, Jordi Girona 29, 08034 Barcelona, Spain. [email: pieter.bellens@bsc.es]

SIEGFRIED BENKNER, Faculty of Computer Science, University of Vienna, Wahringer-strasse29, A-1090 Vienna, Austria. [email: sigi@par.univie.ac.at]

DANIEL RUBIO BONILLA, Department for Intelligent Service Infrastructures, HLRS, University of Stuttgart, Nobelstr. 19, 70569 Stuttgart, Germany. [email: rubio@hlrs.de]

JAVIER BUENO, Barcelona Supercomputing Center, Nexus-2 Building, 3rd Floor, Jordi Girona 29, 08034 Barcelona, Spain. [email: javier.bueno@bsc.es]

ALI R. BUTT, Virginia Tech, 2202 Kraft Drive (0106), Blacksburg, VA 24061, USA. [email: butta@cs.vt.edu]

DANIEL CEDERMAN, Department of Computer Science and Engineering, Chalmers University of Technology, SE-412 96 Göteborg, Sweden. [email: cederman @chalmers.se]

PIERRE COLLET, Strasbourg University, Pole API BdSébastien Brant BP 10413 67412 Illkirch CEDEX France. [email: pierre.collet@unistra.fr]

HERBERT CORNELIUS, Intel Gmbh, DornacherStrasse 1, D-85622 Feldkirchen, Germany. [email: herbert.cornelius@intel.com]

TOMMASO CUCINOTTA, Retis Lab, ScuolaSuperioreSant'Anna CEIICP, Att.NeFrancesca Gattai, Via Moruzzi 1, 56124 Pisa, Italy. [email: tommaso .cucinotta@sssup.it]

MARCO DANELUTTO, Computer Science Department, University of Pisa, Largo Pontecorvo3, 56127 Pisa, Italy. [email: marcod@di.unipi.it]

USMAN DASTGEER, IDA, Linköping University, S-58183 Linköping, Sweden. [email: usman.dastgeer@liu.se]

PABLO DE OLIVEIRA CASTRO, CEA, LIST, Université De Versailles, 45, Avenue DesÉtats Unis, Versailles, 78035 France. [email: pablo.oliveira@exascale-computing.eu]

ALEJANDRO DURAN, Barcelona Supercomputing Center, Nexus-2 Building, 3rd Floor, Jordi Girona 29, 08034 Barcelona, Spain. [email: alex.duran@bsc.es]

MUJAHED ELEYAT, University of Science and Technology (NTU), SemSælandsvei 7-9, NO-7491 Trondheim, Norway. [email: mujahed.eleyat@miriam.as]

JOHAN ENMYREN, IDA, Linköping University, S-58183 Linköping, Sweden. [email: x10johen@ida.liu.se]

YOAV ETSION, Barcelona Supercomputing Center, Nexus-2 Building, 3rd Floor, Jordi Girona 29, 08034 Barcelona, Spain. [email: yoav.etsion@bsc.es]

EITAN FARCHI, IBM, 49 Hashmonaim Street, Pardes Hanna 37052, Israel. [email: farchi@il.ibm.com]

MONTSE FARRERAS, Barcelona Supercomputing Center, Nexus-2 Building, 3rd Floor, Jordi Girona 29, 08034 Barcelona, Spain. [email: mfarrera@ac.upc.edu]

MIN FENG, Department of Computer Science, The University of California At Riverside, Engineering Bldg. Unit 2, Rm. 463, Riverside, CA 92521, USA. [email: mfeng@cs.ucr.edu]

ROGER FERRER, Barcelona Supercomputing Center, Nexus-2 Building, 3rd Floor, Jordi Girona 29, 08034 Barcelona, Spain. [email: roger.ferrer@bsc.es]

ANDERS GIDENSTAM, School of Business and Informatics, Högskolan I Borås, S-50190 Borås, Sweden. [email: anders.gidenstam@hb.se]

SERGEI GORLATCH, FB10, Universität Münster, D-48149 Münster, Germany. [email: gorlatch@uni-muenster.de]

VINCENT GRAMOLI, LPD, EPFL IC, Station 14, CH-1015 Lausanne, Switzerland. [email: vincent.gramoli@epfl.ch]

RACHID GUERRAOUI, LPD, EPFL IC, Station 14, CH-1015 Lausanne, Switzerland. [email: rachid.guerraoui@epfl.ch]

NEIL GUNTHER, Performance Dynamics Company, 4061 East Castro Valley Blvd. Suite 110, Castro Valley, CA 95954, USA. [email: njgunther@perfdynamics.com]

RAJIV GUPTA, Department of Computer Science, The University of California at Riverside, Engineering Bldg. Unit 2, Rm. 408, Riverside, CA 92521, USA. [email: gupta@cs.ucr.edu]

PHUONG HA, Department of Computer Science, Faculty of Science, University of Tromsø, NO-9037 Tromsø, Norway. [email: phuong@cs.uit.no]

PIETER HIJMA, Department of Computer Science, Vrije Universiteit, De Boelelaan1081A, 1081 HV, Amsterdam, The Netherlands. [email: pieter@cs.vu.nl]

ALEXANDRU IORDAN, University of Science and Technology (NTU), SemSælandsvei 7-9, NO-7491 Trondheim, Norway. [email: iordan@idi.ntnu.no]

MAGNUS JAHRE, University of Science and Technology (NTU), SemSælandsvei 7-9, NO-7491 Trondheim, Norway. [email: jahre@idi.ntnu.no]

MAHMUT KANDEMIR, The Pennsylvania State University, 111 IST Building, University Park, PA 16802, USA. [email: kandemir@cse.psu.edu]

PHILIPP KEGEL, FB10, Universität Münster, D-48149 Münster, Germany. [email:philipp.kegel@uni-muenster.de]

CHRISTOPH KESSLER, IDA, Linköping University, S-58183 Linköping, Sweden. [email: christoph.kessler@liu.se]

PETER KILPATRICK, School of Electronics, Electrical Engineering and Computer Science, Queen's University Belfast, Belfast BT7 1NN, UK. [email: p.kilpatrick@qub.ac.uk]

JESUS LABARTA, Barcelona Supercomputing Center, Nexus-2 Building, 3rd Floor, Jordi Girona 29, 08034 Barcelona, Spain. [email: jesus.labarta@bsc.es]

NICOLAS LACHICHE, Strasbourg University, Pole API BdSébastien Brant BP 10413 67412 Illkirch CEDEX France. [email: nicolas.lachiche@unistra.fr]

GIUSEPPE LIPARI, Real-Time Systems Laboratory, ScuolaSuperioreSant'Anna, Pisa, Italy. [email: g.lipari@sssup.it]

STÉPHANE LOUISE, CEA, LIST, Gif-Sur-Yvette, 91191 France. [email: stephane.louise@cea.fr]

EMILIO LUQUE, Computer Architecture and Operating System Department, Universitat Autonoma De Barcelona, 08193, Barcelona, Spain. [email: emilio.luque@uab.es]

OGIER MAITRE, Strasbourg University, Pole API BdSébastien Brant BP 10413 67412 Illkirch CEDEX France. [email: ogier.maitre@unistra.fr]

SANDYA MANNARSWAMY, Xerox Research Centre India, 225 1st C Cross, 2nd Main, Kasturi Nagar, Bangalore, India. 560043. [email: sandya@hp.com]

VLADIMIR MARJANOVIC, Barcelona Supercomputing Center, Nexus-2 Building, Jordi Girona 29, 08034 Barcelona, Spain. [email: vladimir.marjanovic@bsc.es]

LLUIS MARTINELL, Barcelona Supercomputing Center, Nexus-2 Building, 3rd Floor, Jordi Girona 29, 08034 Barcelona, Spain. [email: luis.martinell@bsc.es]

XAVIER MARTORELL, Barcelona Supercomputing Center, Nexus-2 Building, Jordi Girona 29, 08034 Barcelona, Spain. [email: xavim@ac.upc.edu]

DAVID MOLONEY, Movidius Ltd., Mountjoy Square East 19, D1 Dublin, Ireland. [email: david.moloney@movidius.com]

RONAL MURESANO, Computer Architecture and Operating System Department, Universitat Autonoma De Barcelona, 08193, Barcelona, Spain. [email: rmuresano@caos.uab.es]

M. MUSTAFA RAFIQUE, Virginia Tech, 2202 Kraft Drive (0106), Blacksburg, Virginia 24061, USA. [email: mustafa@cs.vt.edu]

RAYMOND NAMYST, Institut National De Recherche En Informatique Et En Automatique (INRIA), Bordeaux Sud-Ouest, Cours De La Liberation 351, F-33405 Talence Cedex, France. [email: raymond.namyst@labri.fr]

LASSE NATVIG, University of Science and Technology (NTU), Semsælandsvei 7-9, NO-7491 Trondheim, Norway. [email: lasse@idi.ntnu.no]

DIMITRIOS S. NIKOLOPOULOS, FORTH-ICS, N. Plastira 100, VassilikaVouton, Heraklion, Crete, Greece. [email: dsn@ics.forth.gr]

FRANK OTTO, Institute for Program Structures and Data Organization, Karlsruhe Institute of Technology, Am Fasanengarten 5, 76131 Karlsruhe, Germany. [email: frank.otto@kit.edu]

OZCAN OZTURK, Department of Computer Engineering, Engineering Building, EA 407B, Bilkent University, Bilkent, 06800, Ankara, Turkey. [email: ozturk@cs.bilkent.edu.tr]

MARINA PAPATRIANTAFILOU, Department of Computer Science and Engineering, Chalmers University of Technology, SE-412 96 Göteborg, Sweden. [email: ptrianta@chalmers.se]

STEFAN PARVU, Nokia Group, Espoo, Karakaari 15, Finland. [email: stefan.parvu@nokia.com]

JOSEP M. PEREZ, Barcelona Supercomputing Center, Nexus-2 Building, 3rd Floor, Jordi Girona 29, 08034 Barcelona, Spain. [email: josep.m.perez@bsc.es]

JUDIT PLANAS, Barcelona Supercomputing Center, Nexus-2 Building, 3rd Floor, Jordi Girona 29, 08034 Barcelona, Spain. [email: judit.planas@bsc.es]

SABRI PLLANA, Department of Computer Science, Linnaeus University, SE-351 95 Vaxjo, Sweden. [email: sabri.pllana@lnu.se]

STEPHANE QUERRY, Pole API BdSébastien Brant BP 10413 67412 Illkirch CEDEX France. [email: stephane.querry@unistra.fr]

ALEX RAMIREZ, Barcelona Supercomputing Center, Nexus-2 Building, 3rd Floor, Jordi Girona 29, 08034 Barcelona, Spain. [email: alex.ramirez@bsc.es]

DOLORES REXACHS, Computer Architecture and Operating System Department, Universitat Autonoma De Barcelona, 08193, Barcelona, Spain. [email: dolores.rexachs@uab.es]

ANDREW RICHARDS, Codeplay Software Limited, York Place 45, EH1 3HP Edinburgh, United Kingdom. [email: andrew@codeplay.com]

ANTÓNIO RODRIGUES, TU Lisbon/IST/INESC-ID, Rua Alves Redol 9, 1000-029Lisboa, Portugal. [email: antonio.c.rodrigues@ist.utl.pt]

NUNO ROMA, TU Lisbon/IST/INESC-ID, Rua Alves Redol 9, 1000-029 Lisboa, Portugal. [email: nuno.roma@inesc-id.pt]

PETER SANDERS, KarlsruherInstitut Für Technologie, Amfasanengarten 5, D-76128Karlsruhe, Germany. [email: sanders@kit.edu]

LUTZ SCHUBERT, Department for Intelligent Service Infrastructures, HLRS, University of Stuttgart, Nobelstr. 19, 70569 Stuttgart, Germany. [email: schubert@hlrs.de]

HAZIM SHAFI, One Microsoft Way, Redmond, WA 98052, USA. [email: hshafi@microsoft.com]

DEEPAK SHARMA, Pole API BdSébastien Brant BP 10413 67412 Illkirch CEDEX, France. [email: deepak.sharma@unistra.fr]

LEONEL SOUSA, TU Lisbon/IST/INESC-ID, Rua Alves Redol 9, 1000-029 Lisboa, Portugal. [email: leonel.sousa@inesc-id.pt]

MICHEL STEUWER, FB10, Universität Münster, D-48149Münster, Germany. [email:michel.steuwer@uni-muenster.de]

SHANTI SUBRAMANYAM, Yahoo! Inc., 701 First Ave, Sunnyvale, CA 94089. [email: shantis@yahoo-inc.com]

HÅKAN SUNDELL, School of Business and Infomatics, Högskolan I Borås, S-501 90BorâĂăs, Sweden. [email: hakan.sundell@hb.se]

XAVIER TERUEL, Barcelona Supercomputing Center, Nexus-2 Building, 3rd Floor, Jordi Girona 29, 08034 Barcelona, Spain. [email: xavier.teruel@bsc.es]

CHEN TIAN, Department of Computer Science, The University of California at Riverside, Engineering Bldg. Unit 2, Rm. 463, Riverside, CA 92521, USA. [email: tianc@cs.ucr.edu]

WALTER F. TICHY, Institute for Program Structures and Data Organization, Karlsruhe Institute of Technology, Am Fasanengarten 5, 76131 Karlsruhe, Germany. [email: tichy@kit.edu]

MASSIMO TORQUATI, Computer Science Department, University of Pisa, Largo Pontecorvo3, 56127 Pisa, Italy. [email: torquati@di.unipi.it]

JESPER LARSSON TRÄFF, Research Group Parallel Computing, Vienna University of Technology, Favoritenstrasse 16/184-5, A-1040 Vienna, Austria. [email: traff@par.tuwien.ac.at]

IOANNA TSALOUCHIDOU, Barcelona Supercomputing Center, Nexus-2 Building, 3rdFloor, Jordi Girona 29, 08034 Barcelona, Spain. [email: ioanna.tsalouchidou @bsc.es]

PHILIPPAS TSIGAS, Department of Computer Science and Engineering, Chalmers University of Technology, SE-412 96 Göteborg, Sweden. [email: philippas.tsigas@chalmers.se]

PHILIPPAS TSIGAS, Department of Computer Science and Engineering, Chalmers Tekniska Höogskola, SE-41296 Göteborg, Sweden. [email: tsigas@chalmers.se]

MATEO VALERO, Barcelona Supercomputing Center, Nexus-2 Building, 3rd Floor, Jordi Girona 29, 08034 Barcelona, Spain. [email: mateo.valero@bsc.es]

ROB V. VAN NIEUWPOORT, Department of Computer Science, Vrije Universiteit, De Boelelaan 1081A, 1081 HV, Amsterdam, The Netherlands. [email: rob@cs.vu.nl]

ANA LUCIA VARBANESCU, Department of Software Technologies, Delft University of Technology, Delft, The Netherlands Mekelweg 4, 2628 CD, Delft, The Netherlands. [email: a.l.varbanescu@tudelft.nl]

STEFAN WESNER, HLRS, Department of Applications and Visualization, University of Stuttgart, Nobelstr. 19, 70569 Stuttgart, Germany. [email: wesner@hlrs.de]

PREFACE

Multicore and many-core computing systems have emerged as an important paradigm in high-performance computing (HPC) and have significantly propelled development of advanced parallel and distributed applications as well as of embedded systems. Multicore processors are now ubiquitous, indeed, from processors with 2 or 4 cores in the 2000s, the trend of increasing the number of cores keeps the pace, and processors with hundreds or even thousands of (lightweight) cores are becoming commonplace to optimize not only performance but also energy. However, this disruptive technology (also referred to as 'continuum computing paradigm') presents several major challenges such as increased effort and system-specific skills for porting and optimizing application codes, managing and exploiting massive parallelism and system heterogeneity to achieve increased performance, innovative modeling strategies for low-power simulation, etc. Among these, we would distinguish the challenge of mastering the multicore and many-core and heterogeneous systems – this is precisely the focus of this book!

The emergence of multicore processors has helped in addressing several problems that are related to single-core processors – known as memory wall, power wall and instruction-level parallelism wall – but they pose several other 'walls' such as the programmability wall or the coherency wall. Among these, programmability wall is a long-standing challenge. Indeed, on the one hand, program development for multicore processors, especially for heterogeneous multicore processors, is significantly more complex than for single-core processors. On the other hand, programmers have been traditionally trained for the development of sequential programs, and only a small percentage of them have experience with parallel programming.

In fact, in the past only a relatively small group of programmers interested in HPC was concerned with the parallel programming issues; the situation has changed dramatically with the appearance of multicore processors in commonly used computing systems. Traditionally parallel programs in HPC community have been developed by heroic programmers using a simple text editor as programming environment, programming at a low level of abstraction and doing manual performance optimization. It is expected that with the pervasiveness of multicore processors, parallel programming will become mainstream, but it cannot be expected that a mainstream programmer will prefer to use the traditional HPC methods and tools.

The main objective of this book is to present a comprehensive view of the state-of-the-art parallel programming methods, techniques and tools to aid the programmers in mastering the efficient programming of multicore and many-core systems. The book comprises a selection of twenty-two chapter contributions by experts in the field of multicore and many-core systems that cover fundamental techniques and algorithms, programming approaches, methodologies and frameworks, task/application scheduling and management, testing and evaluation methodologies and case studies for programming multicore and many-core systems. Lessons learned, challenges and road map ahead are also given and discussed along the chapters.

The content of the book is arranged into five parts:

Part I: Foundations

The first part of the book covers fundamental issues in programming of multicore and many-core computing systems. Along four chapters the authors discuss the state of the art on multi- and many-core architectures, programming models, concurrent data structures and memory allocation, scheduling and management.

Natvig et al. in the first chapter, '*Multi- and many-cores, architectural overview for programmers*', provide a broad overview of the fundamental parallel techniques, parallel taxonomies and various 'walls' in programming multicore/many-core computing systems such as 'power wall', 'memory wall' and 'ILP (instruction level parallelism) wall'. The authors also discuss the challenges of the heterogeneity in multicore/many-core computing systems. They conclude by stressing the need for more research in parallel programming models to meet the five P's of parallel processing – performance, predictability, power efficiency, programmability and portability – when building and programming multicore and many-core computing systems.

Varbanescu et al. in the second chapter, '*Programming models for multicore and many-core computing systems*', survey a comprehensive set of programming models for most popular families of many-core systems, including both specific and classical parallel models for multicore and many-core platforms. The authors have introduced four classes of reference features for model evaluation: usability, design support, implementation support and programmability. Based on these features, a multidimensional comparison of the surveyed models is provided aiming to identify the essential characteristics that separate or cluster these models. The authors conclude by emphasizing the influence that the choice of a programming model can have on the application design and implementation and give a few guidelines for finding a programming model that matches the application characteristics.

The third chapter by **Cederman et al.**, '*Lock-free concurrent data structures*', deals with the use of concurrent data structures in parallel programming of multicore and many-core systems. Several issues such as maintaining consistency in the presence of many simultaneous updates are discussed and lock-free implementations of data structures that support concurrent access are given. Lock-free concurrent data structures are shown to support the design of lock-free algorithms that scale much better when the number of processes increases. A set of fundamental synchronization primitives is also described together with challenges in managing dynamically allocated memory in a concurrent environment.

Mannarswamy in the fourth chapter, '*Software transactional memory*', addresses the main challenges in writing concurrent code in multicore and many-core computing systems. In particular, the author focuses on the coordinating access to shared data, accessed by multiple threads concurrently. Then, the software transactional memory (STM) programming paradigm for shared memory multithreaded programs is introduced. STM is intended to facilitate the development of complex concurrent software as an alternative to conventional lock-based synchronization primitives by reducing the burden of programming complexity involved in writing concurrent code. The need for addressing performance bottlenecks and improving the application performance on STM is also discussed as a major research issue in the field.

Part II: Programming Approaches

The second part of the book is devoted to programming approaches for multicore and many-core computing systems. This part comprises seven chapters that cover a variety of programming approaches including heterogeneous programming, skeleton programming, DSL and object-oriented stream programming and programming with transactional memory.

The fifth chapter, '*Heterogeneous programming with OMPSs and its implications*', by **Ayguadé et al.** discusses on programming models for heterogeneous architectures aiming to ease the asynchrony and to increment parallelization, modularity and portability of applications. The authors present the OmpSs model, which extends the OpenMP 3.0 programming model, and show how it leverages MPI and OpenCL/CUDA, mastering the efficient programming of the clustered heterogeneous multi-/many-core systems. The implementation of OmpSs as well as a discussion on the intelligence needed to be embedded in the runtime system to effectively lower the programmability wall and the opportunities to implement new mechanisms and policies is also discussed and some overheads related with task management in OmpSs are pointed out for further investigation.

Kessler et al. in the sixth chapter, '*Skeleton programming for portable many-core computing*', consider skeleton programming ('data parallel skeletons') as a model to solve the portability problem that arises in multi-and many-core programming and to increase the level of abstraction in such programming environment. After overviewing the concept of algorithmic skeletons, the authors give a detailed description of two recent approaches for programming emerging heterogeneous many-core systems, namely, SkePU and SkelCL. Some other skeleton programming frameworks, which share ideas with SkePU and SkelCL but address a more narrow range of architectures or are used in industrial application development, are also discussed. Adding support for portable task parallelism, such as farm skeletons, is pointed out as an important research issue for future research.

In the seventh chapter, *'DSL stream programming on multicore architectures'*, by **de Oliveira Castro et al.**, the authors present a novel approach for stream programming, considered a powerful alternative to program multi-core processors by offering a deterministic execution based on a sound mathematical formalism and the ability to implicitly express the parallelism by the stream structure, which leverages compiler optimizations that can harness the multicore performance without having to tune the application by hand. Two families of stream programming languages are analyzed, namely, languages in which the data access patterns are explicitly described by the programmer through a set of reorganization primitives and those in which the data access patterns are implicitly declared through a set of dependencies between tasks. Then, the authors expose the principle of a two-level approach combining the advantages and expressivity of both types of languages aiming to achieve both the expressivity of high-level languages such as Array-OL and Block Parallel and the rich optimization framework, similar to StreamIT and Brook.

The eighth chapter, *'Programming with transactional memory'*, by **Gramoli and Guerraoui** addresses similar issues as in Chapter 4, namely, the use of transactional memory to remedy numerous concurrency problems arising in multicore and many-core programming. The chapter analyzes the state-of-the-art concurrent programming advances based on transactional memory. Several programming languages that support TM are considered along with some TM implementations and a running example for software support. The causes for performance limitations that TMs may suffer from and some recent solutions to cope with such limitations are also discussed.

Otto and Tichy in the ninth chapter, *'Object-oriented stream programming'*, present an approach unifying the concepts of object orientation (OO) and stream programming aiming to take advantage of features of both paradigms. Aiming for better programmability and performance gains, the object-oriented stream programming (OOSP) is introduced as a solution. The benefits of OO and stream programming are exemplified with XJava, a prototype OOSP language extending Java. Other issues such as potential conflicts between tasks, run-time performance tuning and correctness, allowing for interprocess application optimization and faster parameter adjustments are also discussed.

The tenth chapter, *'Software-based speculative parallelization'*, by **Tian et al**. studies the thread level speculative parallelization (SP) approach for parallelizing sequential programs by exploiting dynamic parallelism that may be present in a sequential program. As SP is usually applied to loops and performed at compile time, it requires minimal help from the programmer who may be required to identify loops to which speculative parallelization is to be applied. The authors have discussed several issues in SP, such as handling misspeculations, recovery capabilities and techniques for identifying parallelizable regions. Some ongoing projects that focus on SP techniques are also briefly discussed along with direction on future research issues comprising energy efficiency in SP, using SP for heterogeneous processors and 3D multicore processors, etc.

Schubert et al. in the eleventh chapter, '*Autonomic distribution and adaptation*', describe an approach for increasing the scalability of applications by exploiting inherent concurrency in order to parallelize and distribute the code. The authors focus more specifically on concurrency, which is a crucial part in any parallelization approach, in the sense of reducing dependencies between logical parts of an application. To that end, the authors have employed graph analysis methods to assess the dependencies on code level, so as to identify concurrent segments and relating them to the specific characteristics of the (heterogeneous, large-scale) environment. Issues posed to programming multicore and many-core computers by the high degree of scalability and especially the large variance of processor architectures are also discussed.

Part III: Programming Frameworks

The third part of the book deals with methodologies, frameworks and high programming tools for constructing and testing software that can be ported between different, possibly in themselves heterogeneous many-core systems under preservation of specific quantitative and qualitative performance aspects.

The twelfth chapter, '*PEPPHER: Performance portability and programmability for heterogeneous many-core architectures*', by **Benkner et al**. presents PEPPHER framework, which introduces a flexible and extensible compositional metalanguage for expressing functional and nonfunctional properties of software components, their resource requirements and possible compilation targets, as well as providing abstract specifications of properties of the underlying hardware. Also, handles for the run-time system to schedule the components on the available hardware resources are provided. Performance predictions can be (automatically) derived by combining the supplied performance models. Performance portability is aided by guidelines and requirements to ensure that the PEPPHER framework at all levels chooses the best implementation of a given component or library routine among the available variants, including settings for tunable parameters, prescheduling decisions and data movement operations.

Aldinucci et al. in the thirteenth chapter, '*Fastflow: high level and efficient streaming on multicore*', consider, as in other chapters, the difficulties of programmability of multicore and many-core systems, but from the perspective of two interrelated needs, namely, that of efficient mechanisms supporting correct concurrent access to shared-memory data structures and of higher-level programming environments capable of hiding the difficulties related to the correct and efficient use of shared-memory objects by raising the level of abstraction provided to application programmers. To address these needs the authors introduce and discuss FastFlow, a programming framework specifically targeting cache-coherent shared-memory multicores. The authors show the suitability of the programming abstractions provided by the top layer of FastFlow programming model for application programmers. Performance and efficiency considerations are also given along with some real-world applications.

In the fourteenth chapter, Roma et al., '*Programming framework for H.264/AVC video encoding in multicore systems*', the authors bring the example of usefulness of multicore and many-core computing for the video encoding as part of many multimedia applications. As video encoding distinguishes for being highly computationally demanding, to cope with the real-time encoding performance concerns, parallel approaches are envisaged as solutions to accelerate the encoding. The authors have presented a new parallel programming framework, which allows to easily and efficiently implementing high-performance H.264/AVC video encoders. The modularity and flexibility make this framework particularly suited for efficient implementations in either homogeneous or heterogeneous parallel platforms, providing a suitable set of fine-tuning configurations and parameterizations that allow a fast prototyping and implementation, thus significantly reducing the developing time of the whole video encoding system.

The fifteenth chapter, '*Parallelizing evolutionary algorithms on GPGPU cards with the EASEA platform*', by **Maitre et al**. presents the EASEA (EAsy Specification of Evolutionary Algorithm) software platform dedicated to evolutionary algorithms that allows to exploit parallel architectures, that range from a single GPGPU equipped machine to multi-GPGPU machines, to a cluster or even several clusters of GPGPU machines. Parallel algorithms implemented by the EASEA platform are proposed for evolutionary algorithms and evolution strategies, genetic programming and multiobjective optimization. Finally, a set of problems is presented that contains artificial and real-world problems, for which performance evaluation results are given. EASEA is shown suitable to efficiently parallelize generic evolutionary optimization problems to run on current petaflop machines and future exaflop ones.

Part IV: Testing, Evaluation and Optimization

The forth part of the book covers testing, evaluation and optimization of parallel programs, with special emphasis for multicore and many-core systems. Techniques, methodologies and approaches are presented along four chapters.

Farchi in the sixteenth chapter, '*Smart interleavings for testing parallel programs*', discusses the challenges of testing parallel programs that execute several parallel tasks, might be distributed on different machines, under possible node or network failures and might use different synchronization primitives. Therefore, the main challenge is of parallel program testing resides in the definition and coverage of the rather huge space of possible orders of tasks and environment events. The author has presented state-of-the-art testing techniques including parallel bug pattern-based reviews and distributed reviews. The later techniques enable the design of a test plan for the parallel program that is then implemented in unit testing. Coping with the scaling is envisaged as a main challenge for future research.

In the seventeenth chapter by **Shafi**, '*Parallel performance evaluation and optimization*', are covered important aspects of shared-memory parallel programming that impact performance. Guidance and mitigation techniques for diagnosing performance issues applicable to a large spectrum of shared-memory multicore programs in order to assist in performance tuning are also given. Various overheads in parallel programs including thread overheads, cache overheads and synchronization overheads are discussed and mitigation techniques analyzed. Also, optimization-related issues such as nonuniform access memory and latency are described. The chapter overviews diagnostic tools as critical means to achieving good performance in parallel applications.

The eighteenth chapter, '*A methodology for optimizing multithreaded system scalability on multicores*', by **Gunther et al**. presents a methodology which combines controlled measurements of the multithreaded platform together with a scalability modeling framework within which to evaluate performance measurements for multithreaded programs. The authors show how to quantify the scalability using the Universal Scalability Law (USL) by applying it to controlled performance measurements of memcached, J2EE and WebLogic. The authors advocate that system performance analysis should be incorporated into a comprehensive methodology rather than being done as an afterthought. Their methodology, based on the USL, emphasizes the importance of validating scalability data through controlled measurements that use appropriately designed test workloads. Some results from quantifying GPU and many-core scalability using the USL methodology are also reported.

Ozturk and Kandemir in the nineteenth chapter, '*Improving multicore system performance through data compression*', consider some important issues related to accessing off-chip memory in a multicore architecture. Such issues include off-chip memory latencies, large performance penalties, bandwidth limitations between the multicore processor and of the off-chip memory, which may not be sufficient to handle simultaneous off-chip access requests coming from multiple processors. To tackle these issues the authors propose an on-chip memory management scheme based on data compression, aiming to reduce access latencies, reduce off-chip bandwidth requirements and increase the effective on-chip storage capacity. Results are exemplified with empirical data from an experimental study. Building an optimization framework to find the most suitable parameters in the most effective way is planned for future research direction.

Part V: Scheduling and Management

The last part of the book deals with scheduling and resource management in multicore and many-core computing systems. The chapters discuss many-core accelerators as catalysts for HPC systems, nodes management, configuration, efficient allocation and scheduling in multicore clusters as well as operating systems and scheduling support for multicore systems and accelerator-based clusters.

In the twentieth chapter, '*Programming and managing resources on accelerator enabled clusters*', **Rafique et al**. study the use of computational accelerators as catalysts for HPC systems and discuss the challenges that arise in accelerator-based systems (specifically the case of accelerators on clusters), large-scale parallel systems with heterogeneous components for provisioning general-purpose resources and custom accelerators to achieve a balanced system. The study is exemplified with a study on the implementation of MapReduce, a high-level parallel programming model for large-scale data processing, on asymmetric accelerator-based clusters. Empirical results are presented from an experimental test-bed using three representative MapReduce benchmarks, which shed light on overall system performance.

Muresano et al. in the twenty-first chapter, '*An approach for efficient execution of SPMD applications on multicore clusters*', describe an efficient execution methodology for multicore clusters, which is based on achieving a suitable application execution with a maximum speedup achievable while the efficiency is maintained over a defined threshold. The proposed methodology enables calculating the maximum number of cores that maintain strong application scalability while sustaining a desired efficiency for SPMD applications. The ideal number of tiles that have to be assigned to each core with the objective of maintaining a relationship between speedup and efficiency can also be calculated. It was shown, by experimental evaluation tests using various scientific applications, that the execution methodology can reach an improvement of around 40% in efficiency.

The last chapter, '*Operating system and scheduling for future multicore and many-core platforms*', by **Cucinotta et al**. analyzes the limitations of the nowadays operating system support for multicore systems, when looking at future and emerging many-core, massively parallel and distributed platforms. Therefore, most promising approaches in the literature dealing with such platforms are discussed. The discussion is mainly focused on the kernel architecture models and kernel-level mechanisms, and the needed interface(s) toward user-level code and more specifically on the problem of scheduling in multiprocessor and distributed systems, comprising scheduling of applications with precise timing requirements.

ACKNOWLEDGEMENTS

The editors of the book would like to sincerely thank the authors for their contributions and their patience during the preparation and publication of the book. We would like to appreciate the reviewers' constructive feedback that helped improve the content of the chapters. We would like to express our gratitude to Prof. Albert Y. Zomaya, Founding Editor-in-Chief of the Wiley Book Series on Parallel and Distributed Computing, for his encouragement and the opportunity to edit this book. The help and support from Wiley editorial and publishing team are highly appreciated!

Fatos Xhafa's work is partially supported by research projects from the Spanish Ministry for Economy and Competitiveness (MINECO) and the European Union (FEDER funds) under grant COMMAS (ref. TIN2013-46181-C2-1-R).

ACRONYMS

ACML	AMD core math library
ALU	arithmetic logic unit
AMP	asymmetric multicore processor
API	application programming interface
ASF	advanced synchronization facility
ASIC	application-specific integrated circuit
ATLAS	automatically tuned linear algebra software
BE	best effort
BLAS	basic linear algebra subprograms
BLI	bilinear interpolation
BSP	bulk synchronous parallel
CABAC	context-adaptive binary arithmetic coding
CAS	compare-and-swap
CAVLC	context-adaptive variable-length coding
CBS	constant bandwidth server

ccNUMA	cache-coherent nonuniform memory access architecture
Cell/B.E.	cell broadband engine
CellSs	cell superscalar
CG	conjugate gradient
CMP	chip multiprocessor
CorD	copy or discard
COTS	commercial off-the-shelf
CPU	central processing unit
Ct	intel C for throughput
cuBLAS	CUDA BLAS
CUDA	compute unified device architecture
D & C	divide and conquer
DCT	discrete cosine transform
DES	data encryption standard
DMA	direct memory access
DPB	decoded picture buffer
DRAM	dynamic random-access memory
DSL	domain-specific language
DSP	digital signal processor
DTMC	dresden transactional memory compiler
EA	evolutionary algorithm
EASEA	EAsy Specification of Evolutionary Algorithms
EC2	elastic compute cloud
EIB	element interconnect bus
ES	evolution strategy
FFT	fast fourier transform
FIFO	first in, first out
FIR	finite impulse response
FOSS	free open-source software
FPGA	field-programmable gate array
FS	file system
GA	genetic algorithm
GCC	GNU compiler collection

GOP	group of pictures
GP	genetic programming
GP	general-purpose
GPGPU	general-purpose computing on graphics processing units
GPMC	general-purpose multicore
GPOS	general-purpose operating system
GPP	general-purpose processor
GPU	graphics processing units
GPUSs	GPU superscalar
HPC	high-performance computing
HPL	high-performance linpack
HT	hyper-threading
HW	hardware
ILP	instruction-level parallelism
IOIF	input/output interface
IPC	interprocess communications
ISA	instruction set architecture
J2EE	Java 2 platform, enterprise edition
JVM	Java virtual machine
KOPS	kilo operations per second
KPN	Kahn process networks
LAN	local area network
LL/SC	Load-linked/store-conditional
LOC	lines of code
LS	local storage
MB	macroblock
MCD	memcached
MCSTL	multi-core standard template library
ME	motion estimation
MFC	memory flow controller
MG	multigrid
MIC	memory interface controller
MIMD	multiple instruction, multiple data

MKL	math kernel library
MOEA	multiobjective evolutionary algorithm
MP	multiprocessor
MPI	message passing interface
MPMC	multiproducer/multiconsumer
MPMD	multiple process, multiple data
MPSC	multiproducer/single-consumer
MPSoC	multiprocessor system-on-chip
NAS	NASA Advanced Supercomputing
NB-FEB	nonblocking full/empty bit
NFS	network file system
NIC	network Interconnect
NUMA	nonuniform memory access
ODE	ordinary differential equation
OmpSs	openMP superscalar
OO	object-orientation
OOSP	object-oriented stream programming
OpenCL	open computing language
OpenMP	open multiprocessing
OS	operating system
PCIe	PCI express (peripheral component interconnect express)
PEPPHER	performance portability and programmability for heterogeneous many-core architectures
PGAS	partitioned global address space
POSIX	portable operating system interface
PPE	power processing element
PPU	power processing unit
PS3	PlayStation 3
PSNR	peak signal-to-noise ratio
PU	processing unit
QoS	quality of service
RAM	random-access memory
RISC	reduced instruction set computing

RT	real time
RTOS	real-time operating system
SAD	sum of absolute differences
SDF	synchronous data flow
SDK	software development kit
SGL	single global lock
SIMD	single instruction, multiple data
SIMT	single instruction, multiple threads
SISD	single instruction, single data
SIU	system interface unit
SM	streaming multiprocessor
SMP	symmetric multiprocessors
SMPSs	SMP superscalar
SMT	simultaneous multithreading
SoC	system on chip
SP	streaming processor
SP	speculative parallelization
SPE	synergistic processing element
SPM	Scratchpad memory
SPMD	single program, multiple data
SPSC	single producer, single consumer
SPU	synergistic processing unit
SSI	single system image
ST	supertile
STAPL	Standard Template Adaptive Parallel Library
STL	Standard Template Library
STM	software transactional memory
SW	Software
TBB	Threading Building Blocks
TBD	total bandwidth server
TLP	thread-level parallelism
TLS	thread-level speculation
TM	transactional memory
TPA	thread processor array

TPC	thread processing cluster
UMA	uniform memory access
USL	universal scalability law
VLIW	very long instruction word
VLSI	very-large-scale integration

PART I

FOUNDATIONS

CHAPTER 1

MULTI- AND MANY-CORES, ARCHITECTURAL OVERVIEW FOR PROGRAMMERS

LASSE NATVIG, ALEXANDRU IORDAN, MUJAHED ELEYAT, MAGNUS JAHRE AND JORN AMUNDSEN

1.1 INTRODUCTION

1.1.1 Fundamental Techniques

Parallelism has been used since the early days of computing to enhance performance. From the first computers to the most modern sequential processors (also called *uniprocessors*), the main concepts introduced by von Neumann [20] are still in use. However, the ever-increasing demand for computing performance has pushed computer architects toward implementing different techniques of parallelism. The von Neumann architecture was initially a sequential machine operating on scalar data with bit-serial operations [20]. *Word-parallel* operations were made possible by using more complex logic that could perform binary operations in parallel on all the bits in a computer word, and it was just the start of an adventure of innovations in parallel computer architectures.

Programming Multicore and Many-core Computing Systems,
First Edition. Edited by Sabri Pllana and Fatos Xhafa.

Prefetching is a 'look-ahead technique' that was introduced quite early and is a way of parallelism that is used at several levels and in different components of a computer today. Both data and instructions are very often accessed sequentially. Therefore, when accessing an element (instruction or data) at address k, an automatic access to address $k+1$ will bring the element to where it is needed *before* it is accessed and thus eliminates or reduces waiting time. Many clever techniques for *hardware prefetching* have been researched [5, 17] and can be exploited in the context of the new multicore processors. However, the opportunities and challenges given by the new technology in multicores require both a review of old techniques and a development of new ones [9, 21]. *Software prefetching* exploits sequential access patterns in a similar way but either it is controlled by the compiler inserting prefetch operations or it can be explicitly controlled by the programmer [10].

Block access is also a fundamental technique that in some sense is a parallel operation. Instead of bringing one word closer to the processor, for example, from memory or cache, a *cache line* (block of words) is transferred. Block access also gives a prefetching effect since the access to the first element in the block will bring in the succeeding elements. The evolution of processor and memory technology during the last 20 years has caused a large and still increasing gap between processor and memory speed-making techniques such as prefetching and block access even more important than before. This *processor–memory gap*, also called the *memory wall*, is further discussed in Section 1.2.

Functional parallelism is a very general technique that has been used for a long time and is exploited at different levels and in different components of almost all computers today. The principle is to have different functional units in the processor that can operate concurrently. Consequently, more than one instruction can be executed at the same time, for example, one unit can execute an arithmetic integer operation while another unit executes a floating-point operation. This is to exploit what has later been called *instruction level parallelism* (ILP).

Pipelining is one main variant of functional parallelism and has been used extensively at different levels and in different components of computers to improve performance. It is perhaps most widely known from the *instruction pipeline* used in almost all contemporary processors. Instructions are processed as a sequence of steps or stages, such as instruction fetch, instruction decoding, execution and write back of results. Modern microprocessors can use more than 20 pipeline stages so that more than 20 instructions are being processed concurrently. Pipelining gives potentially a large performance gain but also added complexity since interdependencies between instructions must be handled to ensure correct execution of the program.

The term *scalar processor* denotes computers that operate on one computer word at a time. When functional parallelism is used as described in the preceding text to exploit ILP, we have a *superscalar processor*. A *k-way superscalar* processor can issue up to k instructions at the same time (during one clock cycle). Also instruction fetching, decoding and other nonarithmetic operations are parallelized by adding more functional units.

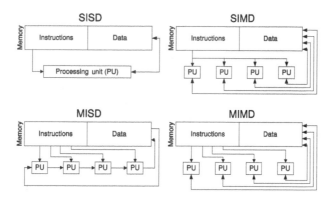

Figure 1.1 Flynn's taxonomy.

1.1.2 Multiprogramming, Multiprocessors and Clusters

Multiprogramming is a technique invented in the 1960s to interleave the execution of the programs and I/O operations among different users by time multiplexing. In this way many users can share a single computer and get acceptable response time, and the concept of a *time-sharing operating system* controlling such a computer was a milestone in the history of computers.

Multiprocessors are computers with two or more distinct physical processors, and they are capable of executing real parallel programs. Here, at the cost of additional hardware, a performance gain can be achieved by executing the parallel processes in different processors.

Many multiprocessors were developed during the 1960s and early 1970s, and in the start most of the commercial multiprocessors had only two processors. Different research prototypes were also developed, and the first computer with a large number of processors was the Illiac IV developed at the University of Illinois [6]. The project development stretched roughly 10 years, and the computer was designed to have 256 processors but was never built with more than 64 processors.

1.1.2.1 *Flynn's Taxonomy* Flynn divided multiprocessors into four categories based on the multiplicity of instruction streams and data streams – and this has become known as the famous *Flynn's taxonomy* [14, 15] illustrated in Figure 1.1.

A conventional computer (uniprocessor or von Neumann machine) is termed a *Single Instruction Single Data (SISD)* machine. It has one execution or processing unit (PU) that is controlled by a single sequence of instructions, and it operates on a single sequence of data in memory. In the early days of computing, the control logic needed to decode the instructions into control signals that manage the execution and data traffic in a processor was a costly component. When introducing parallel processing, it was therefore natural to let multiple execution units operate on different data (multiple data streams) while they were controlled by the same single *control unit*, that is, a single instruction stream. A fundamental limitation of these *SIMD archi-*

tectures is that different PUs cannot execute different instructions and, at the same time, they are all bound to one single instruction stream.

SIMD machines evolved in many variants. A main distinction is between SIMD with shared memory as shown in Figure 1.1 and SIMD computers with distributed memory. In the latter variant, the main memory is distributed to the different PUs. The advantage of this architecture is that it is much easier to implement compared to multiple data streams to one shared memory. A disadvantage is that it gives the need for some mechanism such as special instructions for communicating between the different PUs.

The *Multiple Instruction Single Data (MISD)* category of machines has been given a mixed treatment in the literature. Some textbooks simply say that no machines of this category have been built, while others present examples. In our view MISD is an important category representing different parallel architectures. One of the example architectures presented in the classical paper by Flynn [14] is very similar to the variant shown in Figure 1.1. Here a source data stream is sent from the memory to the first PU, then a *derived* data stream is sent to the next PU, where it is processed by another program (instruction stream) and so on until it is streamed back to memory. This kind of computation has by some authors been called a *software pipeline* [26]. It can be efficient for applications such as real-time processing of a stream of images (video) data, where data is streamed through different PUs executing different image processing functions (e.g. filtering or feature extraction).

Another type of parallel architectures that can be classified as MISD is *systolic arrays*. These are specialized hardware structures, often implemented as an application specific integrated circuit (ASIC), and use highly pipelined and parallel execution of specific algorithms such as pattern matching or sorting [36, 22].

The *Multiple Instruction Multiple Data (MIMD)* category comprises most contemporary parallel computer architectures, and its inability to categorize these has been a source for the proposal of different alternative taxonomies [43]. In a MIMD computer, every PU has its own control unit that reads a separate stream of instructions dictating the execution in its PU. Just as for SIMD machines, a main subdivision of MIMD machines is into those having shared memory or distributed memory. In the latter variant each PU can have a local memory storing both instructions and data. This leads us to another main categorization of multiprocessors, –shared memory multiprocessors and message passing multiprocessors.

1.1.2.2 *Shared Memory versus Message Passing*   When discussing communication and memory in multiprocessors, it is important to distinguish the *programmers view* (logical view or *programming model*) from the actual implementation (physical view or *architecture*). We will use Figure 1.2 as a base for our discussion.

The programmers, view of a *shared memory multiprocessor* is that all processes or threads share the same single main memory. The simplest and cheapest way of building such a machine is to attach a set of processors to one single memory through a bus. A fundamental limitation of a bus is that it allows only one transaction (communication operation or memory access) to be handled at a time. Consequently, its performance does not scale with the number of processors. When multiproces-

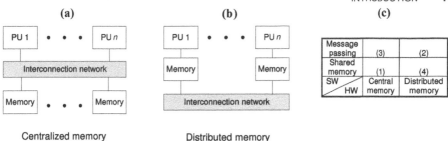

Figure 1.2   Multiprocessor memory architectures and programming models.

sors with higher number of processors were built – the bus was often replaced by
an interconnection network that could handle several transactions simultaneously.
Examples are a crossbar switch (all-to-all communication), multistage networks, hy-
percubes and meshes (see [23] Appendix E for more details). The development
of these parallel interconnection networks is another example of increased use of
parallelism in computers, and they are highly relevant also in multi- and many-core
architectures.

When attaching many processors to a single memory module through a parallel interconnection network, the memory could easily become a bottleneck. Consequently,
it is common to use several physical memory modules as shown in Figure 1.2(a).
Although it has multiple memory modules, this architecture can be called a
centralized memory system since the modules (memory banks) are assembled as
one subsystem that is equally accessible from all the processors. Due to this uni-
formity of access, these systems are often called *symmetric multiprocessors (SMP)*
or *uniform memory access (UMA)* architectures. This programming model (SW)
using shared memory implemented on top of centralized memory (HW) is marked
as alternative (1) in Figure 1.2(c).

The parallel interconnection network and the multiplicity of memory modules
can be used to let the processors work independently and in parallel with different
parts of the memory, or a single processor can distribute its memory accesses across
the memory banks. This latter technique was one of the early methods to exploit
parallelism in memory systems and is called *memory interleaving*. It was motivated
by memory modules being much slower than the processors and was together with
memory pipelining used to speed up memory access in early multiprocessors [26]. As
seen in the next section, such techniques are even more important today.

The main alternative to centralized memory is called *distributed memory* and is
shown in Figure 1.2(b). Here, the memory modules are located together
with the processors. This architecture became popular during the late 1980s
and 1990s, when the combination of the RISC processor and VLSI technology made it
possible to implement a complete processor with local memory and network interconnect (NIC) on a single board. The machines typically ran multiprocessor variants
of the UNIX operating system, and parallel programming was facilitated by *message
passing libraries*, standardized with the message passing interface (MPI) [47]. Typical for these machines is that access to a processors local memory module is much

faster than access to the memory module of another processor, thus giving the name *NonUniform Memory Access (NUMA)* machines. This multiprocessor variant with message passing SW and a physically distributed memory is marked as (2) in the right part of Figure 1.2(c).

The distributed architectures are generally easier to build, especially for computers designed to be scalable to a large number of processors. When the number of processors grows in these machines either the cost of the interconnection network will increase rapidly (as with crossbar) or it will become both more costly and slower (as with multistage network). A slower network will make every memory access slower if we use centralized memory.

However, with distributed memory, a slower network can to some extent be hidden if a large fraction of the accesses can be directed to the local memory module. When this design choice is made, we can use cheaper networks and even a hierarchy of interconnection networks, and the programmer is likely to develop software that exploits the given NUMA architecture. A disadvantage is that the distribution and use of data might become a crucial factor to achieve good performance – and in that way making programming more difficult. Also, the ability of porting code to other architectures without loosing performance is reduced.

Shared memory is generally considered to make parallel programming easier compared to message passing, since cooperation and synchronization between the processors can be done through shared data structures, explicit message passing code can be avoided, and memory access latency is relatively uniform. In such *distributed shared memory (DSM)* machines, the programmers view is one single address space, and the machine implements this using specialized hardware and/or system software such as message passing. The last alternative (3) – to offer message passing on top of centralized memory-is much less common but can have the advantage of offering increased portability of message passing code. As an example, MPI has been implemented on multicores with shared memory [42].

The term *multicomputer* has been used to denote parallel computers built of autonomous processors, often called nodes [26]. Here, each node is an independent computer with its own processor and address space, but message passing can be used to provide the view of *one* distributed memory to the multicomputer programmer. The nodes normally also have I/O units, and today the mostly used term for these parallel machines is *cluster*. Many clusters are built of commercial-off-the -shelf (COTS) components, such as standard PCs or workstations and a fast local area network or switch. This is probably the most cost-efficient way of building a large supercomputer if the goal is maximum compute power on applications that are easy to parallelize. However, although the network technology has improved steadily, these machines have in general a much lower internode communication speed and capacity compared to the computational capacity (processor speed) of the nodes. As a consequence, more tightly coupled multiprocessors have often been chosen for the most communication intensive applications.

1.1.2.3 Multithreading *Multithreading* is quite similar to multiprogramming, that is, multiple processes or threads share the functional units of one processor by using overlapped execution. The purpose can be to execute several programs on one processor as in multiprogramming or can be to execute a single application organized as a multithreaded program (real parallel program). The threads in multithreading are sometimes called HW threads, while the threads of an application can be called SW threads or processes. The HW threads are under execution in the processor, while SW threads can be waiting in a queue outside the processor or even swapped to disk.

When implementing multithreading in a processor, it is common to add internal storage making it possible to save the current architectural state of a thread in a very fast way, making rapid switches between threads possible.

A switch between processes, normally denoted *context switch* in operating systems terminology, can typically use hundreds or even thousands of clock cycles, while there is multithreaded processors that can switch to another thread within one clock cycle. Processes can belong to different users (applications) while threads belong to the same user (application). The use of multithreading is now commonly called *thread-level parallelism (TLP),* and it can be said to be a higher level of parallelism than ILP since the execution of each single thread can exploit ILP.

Fine-grained multithreading denotes cases where the processor switches between threads at every instruction, while in *coarse grained multithreading* the processor executes several instructions from the same thread between switches, normally when the thread has to wait for a lengthy memory access. Both ILP and TLP can be combined as in *simultaneous multithreading (SMT)* processors where the k issue slots of a k-way superscalar processor can be filled with instructions from different threads. In this way, it offers 'real parallelism' in the same way as a multiprocessor. In a SMT processor, the threads will compete for the different subcomponents of the processor, and this might at first sight seem to be a poor solution compared to a multiprocessor where a process or thread can run at top speed without competition from other threads. The advantage of SMT is the good resource utilization of such architectures – very often the processor will stall on lengthy memory operations, and more than one thread is needed to fill in the execution gap. *Hyper-threading* is Intel's terminology (officially called hyper-threading technology) and corresponds to SMT [48].

1.2 WHY MULTICORES?

In recent years, general-purpose processor manufacturers have started to provide chips with multiple processor cores. This type of processor is commonly referred to as a *multicore architecture* or a *chip multiprocessor (CMP)* [38]. Multicores have become a necessity due to four technological and economical constraints, and the purpose of this section is to give a high-level introduction to these.

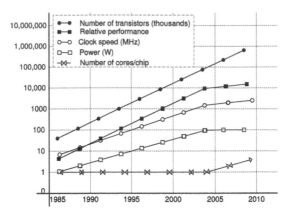

Figure 1.3   Technological trends for microprocessors. Simplified version of Figure 1 in [18].

1.2.1   The Power Wall

High-performance single-core processors consume a great deal of power, and high power consumption necessitates expensive packaging and powerful cooling solutions. During the 1990s and into the 21st century, the strategy of scaling down the gate size of integrated circuits, reducing the supply voltage and increasing the clock rate, was successful and resulted in faster single-core processors. However, around year 2004, it became infeasible to continue reducing the supply voltage, and this made it difficult to continue increasing the clock speed without increasing power dissipation. As a result, the power dissipation started to grow beyond practical limits [18], and the single-core processors were said to hit the *power wall*. In a CMP, multiple cores can cooperate to achieve high performance at a lower clock frequency.

Figure 1.3 illustrates the evolution of processors and the recent shift toward multicores. First, the figure illustrates that Moore's law still holds since the number of transistors is increasing exponentially. However, the relative performance, clock speed and power curves have a distinct knee in 2004 and has been flat or slowly increasing since then. As these curves flatten, the number of cores per chip curve has started to rise. The *aggregate* chip performance is the product of the relative performance per core and the number of cores on a chip, and this scales roughly with Moore's law. Consequently, Figure 1.3 illustrates that multicores are able to increase aggregate performance without increasing power consumption. This exponential performance potential can only be realized for a single application through scalable parallel programming.

1.2.2   The Memory Wall

Processor performance has been improving at a faster rate than the main memory access time for more than 20 years [23]. Consequently, the gap between processor performance and main memory latency is large and growing. This trend is referred to as the *processor–memory gap* or *memory wall*. Figure 1.4 contains the classical plot by Hennessy and Patterson that illustrates the memory wall. The effects of the

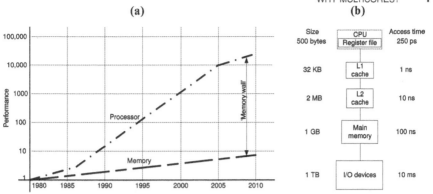

Figure 1.4   The processor–memory gap (a) and a typical memory hierarchy (b).

memory wall have traditionally been handled with latency hiding techniques such as pipelining, out-of-order execution and multilevel caches. The most evident effect of the processor–memory gap is the increasing complexity of the memory hierarchy, shown in Figure 1.4(b). As the gap increased, more levels of cache were added. In recent years, it has been common with a third level of cache, L3 cache. The figure gives some typical numbers for storage capacity and access latency at the different levels [23].

The memory wall also affects multicores, and they invest a significant amount of resources to hide memory latencies. Fortunately, since multicores use lower clock frequencies, the processor–memory gap is growing at a slower rate for multi-cores than for traditional single cores. However, *aggregate* processor performance is growing at roughly the same rate as Moore's Law. Therefore, multicores to some extent transform a latency hiding problem into an increased bandwidth demand. This is helpful because off-chip bandwidth is expected to scale significantly better than memory latencies [29, 40]. The multicore memory system must provide enough bandwidth to support the needs of an increasing number of concurrent threads. Therefore, there is a need to use the available bandwidth in an efficient manner [30].

1.2.3   The ILP Wall and the Complexity Wall

It has become increasingly difficult to improve performance with techniques that exploit ILP beyond what is common today. Although there is a considerable ILP available in the instruction stream [55], extracting it has proven difficult with current process technologies [2]. This trend has been referred to as the *ILP wall*. Multicores alleviate this problem by shifting the focus from transparently extracting ILP from a serial instruction stream to letting the programmer provide the parallelism through TLP.

Designing and verifying a complex out-of-order processor is a significant task. This challenge has been referred to as the *complexity wall*. In a multicore, a processor core is designed once and reused as many times as there are cores on the chip.

These cores can also be simpler than their single-core counterparts. Consequently, multicores facilitate design reuse and reduce processor core complexity.

1.3   HOMOGENEOUS MULTICORES

Contemporary multicores can be divided into two main classes. This section introduces *homogeneous multicores* that are processors where all the cores are similar, that is, they execute the same instruction set, they run on the same clock frequency and they have the same amount of cache resources. Conceptually, these multicores are quite similar to SMPs. The section starts by introducing a possible categorization of such multicores, before we describe a selected set of modern multicores at a high level. All of these are rather complex products, and both *the scope of this chapter and the space available make it impossible to give a complete and thorough description. Our goal is to introduce the reader to the richness and variety of the market – motivating for further studies.* The other mainclass, heterogeneous multicores, is discussed in the next section. A tabular summary of a larger number of commercial multicores can be found in a recent paper by Sodan et-al. [48].

1.3.1   Early Generations

In the paper *Chip Multithreading: Opportunities and Challenges* by Spracklen and Abraham [50], the authors introduced a categorization of what they called chip multi threaded processors (CMT processors) that also can be used to categorize multicore architectures. As shown in Figure 1.5, the first generation multicores typically had processor cores that did not share any on-chip resources except the off-chip datapaths. It was normally two cores per chip and they were derived from earlier uniprocessor designs. Also the PUs used in the second generation multicores were from earlier uniprocessor designs, but they were more tightly integrated through use of a *shared L2 cache*. It could be more than two processors, and the shared L2 made intracore communication very fast. The cores sometimes run the same program (SPMD), so the demand for cache capacity for storing instructions can be reduced. Both these advantages of the shared L2 cache can reduce the demand of off-chip bandwidth. However, more than one core using the L2 cache introduce new challenges such as cache partitioning, fairness and quality of service (Qos) [12, 11, 30].

The third generation multicores can be said to be those using cores that are designed from the ground up and optimized to sit in a multicore processor. These may typically be simpler cores running at a lower frequency and hence with a much lower power consumption. Further, they are typically using SMT. Olukotun and Hammond [37] call these three generations for simple CMP, shared-cache CMP and multithreaded shared-cache CMP, respectively.

(a)   (b)   (c)

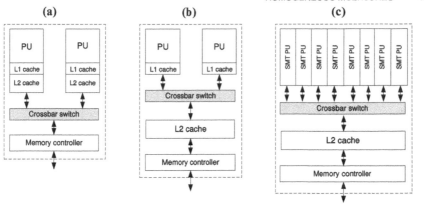

Figure 1.5   Multicore processor generations: first (a), second (b), third (c).

1.3.2   Many Thin Cores or Few Fat Cores?

The choice between a few powerful and many less powerful processors or cores has been discussed widely both during the multiprocessor era and the multicore era. In his classical paper Amdahl [3] gave a simple formula explaining how the serial fraction of an application severely constraints the maximum speedup that can be achieved by a multiprocessor. The serial fraction is a code that cannot be parallelized, and Amdahl's law might motivate for having at least one core that is faster than the others, that is, go for a heterogeneous multicore. For executing the so-called *embarrassingly parallel applications*, that is, applications that are very easy to parallelize since they have no or a very tiny serial part – a multicore with a large number of small cores might be most efficient, especially if power efficiency is in focus. However, if there is significant serial fraction, a smaller number of more powerful cores might be best. A recent paper by Hill and Marty [24] titled *Amdahl's Law in the Multicore Era* demonstrates the influence of Amdahl's law on this trade-off in an elegant way.

1.3.3   Example Multicore Architectures

1.3.3.1   IBM(R) Power(R)   Performance Optimization With Enhanced RISC (POWER) is an IBM processor architecture for technical computing workloads implementing superscalar RISC. The POWER architecture was the starting point in 1991 of the Apple®, IBM and Motorola® (now Freescale Semiconductor®) joint effort to develop a new RISC processor architecture, the PowerPC® architecture [49]. The design goals of PowerPC were to create a single chip providing multiprocessing extensions and 64-bit support (addressing and operations). It was later expanded with vector instructions, originally trademarked AltiVec™. In 2006, POWER and PowerPC was unified into a new brand, the *Power Architecture*, owned by Power.org.

The POWER*n* series of processors are IBM's main product line implementing the Power architecture. The first product in this series was the multichip, superscalar and out-of-order POWER1 processor, introduced in 1990. The POWER7®, introduced in 2010, is the latest development in this series and is also the processor to power the first DARPA High Productivity Computing System (HPCS) petaflops computer. A stripped-down POWER7-core is expected to be used in the Blue Gene®/Q system, replacing the BlueGene/P massively parallel supercomputer in 2012.

The POWER7 processor provides 4, 6 or 8 cores per chip, each with 4-way hardware multithreading (SMT) [1]. A core might under software control be set to

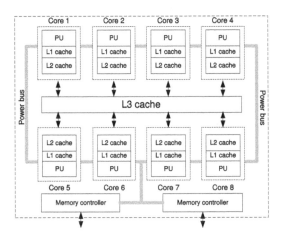

Figure 1.6   Power 7 multicore, simplified block diagram.

operate at different degrees of multithreading from single-threaded mode (ST) to 4-ways SMT.

The chip is implemented in 45 nm technology, with cores running at a nominal frequency of 3.0 – 4.14 GHz, depending on the configuration. The cache hierarchy consists of 32K 4-way L1 data and instruction caches, a 256K 8-way L2 cache and 32 MB shared L3 cache, partitioned into 8 × 4 MB 8-way partitions. The L3 cache is implemented with embedded DRAM technology (eDRAM). The chip is organized as 8 cores (called *chiplets*), each containing the PU, L1 and L2 caches and one of the 8 L3-cache partitions (Fig. 1.6). A consequence of this design is that the L3 has a nonuniform latency. A pair of DDR3 DRAM controllers, each with four 6.4 GHz channels provides a sustained main memory bandwidth of over 100 GB/s.

In addition to POWER6® VMX (AltiVec) and decimal floating point (DFU), the POWER7 core provides the new VSX vector facility. VSX is mainly an extension for 64-bit vector floating-point arithmetic; it does not provide 64-bit integer arithmetic like Intel® and AMD processors.

Energy efficiency is implemented at the core or chiplet level where each core frequency might be individually changed. The modes *sleep*, *nap* and *turbo* allows dynamic voltage and frequency adjustment, from off, to −50% and +10% for maximum performance.

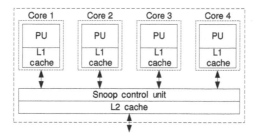

Figure 1.7   ARM Cortex A15, simplified block diagram.

1.3.3.2   ARM(R) Cortex™-A15 MPCoreTM Processor

ARM became one of the first companies to implement multicore technology with the launch of the ARM11™ MPCore™ processor in 2004. The latest version of the ARM MPCore technology is the ARM Cortex™-A15 MPCore processor, targeting markets ranging from mobile computing, high-end digital home, servers and wireless infrastructure.

The processor can be implemented to include up to four cores (see Figure 1.7). The multicore architecture enables the processor to exceed the performance of single-core high-performance embedded devices while consuming significantly less power. Every Cortex-A series processor has power management features including dynamic voltage and frequency scaling and the ability for each core to go independently into standby, dormant or power off energy management states. Like its predecessors Cortex-A15 is based on the ARMv7A processor architecture giving full application compatibility with all ARM Cortex-A processors. This compatibility enables access to an established developer and software ecosystem.

Each processor core has an out-of-order superscalar pipeline and low-latency access through a bus to a shared L2 cache that can be up to 4 MB. The cores provide floating-point support and special SIMD instructions for media performance [4].

1.3.3.3   Sun UltraSPARC(R) T2

Sun's UltraSPARC T2 is a homogeneous multithreaded multicore specially designed to exploit the TLP present in almost every server type application. Sun introduced its first multicore, multithreaded microprocessor the UltraSPARC T1 (codenamed Niagara) in November 2005 [33]. The UltraSPARC T1 uses the SPARC V9® instruction set and was available with 4, 6 and 8 processing cores, each able to execute four threads simultaneously [48]. The UltraSPARC T2 includes a network interface unit and a PCI express interface unit, and this is why the T2 is sometimes referred to as a system on chip [45]. It was available in October 2007 and produced in 65 nm technology.

The UltraSPARC T2 is comprised of 8 64-bit cores, and each core can execute 8 independent threads. Thus, T2 is able to execute 64 threads simultaneously. The cores are connected by a crossbar to an 8-banked shared L2 cache, 4 DRAM controllers and 2 interface units (Fig. 1.8).

In order to minimize power requirements and to meet temperature constraints, the UltraSPARC T2 uses a core frequency of only 1.4 GHz. A complete implementation of the UltraSparc T2 processor in Verilog™ (a HW description language) along

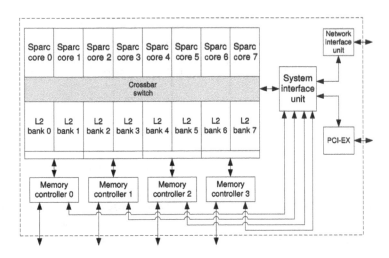

Figure 1.8   Sun UltraSPARC T2 architecture, simplified block diagram.

with tools is freely available from the OpenSPARC® project [54]. This gives the interested researcher a rare opportunity to study the inner details of a modern multi-core processor.

In autumn 2010, Oracle launched the SPARC T3, previously known as Ultra-SPARC T3. It has 16 cores each capable of 8-way SMT giving a total of 128-way multithreading [39].

1.3.3.4 AMD Istanbul

The Istanbul processor is the first 6-core AMD Opteron™ processor and is available for 2-, 4- and 8-socket systems, with clock speeds ranging from 2.0 to 2.8 GHz. It was introduced in June 2009 and is manufactured in a 45 nm process and based on the AMD 64-bit K10 architecture. The K10 architecture supports the full AMD64 instruction set and SIMD instructions for both integer and floating-point operations [25].

Figure 1.9 shows a simplified block diagram. The processor has six cores, three levels of cache, a crossbar connecting the cores, the system request interface, the memory controller and the three HyperTransport™ 3.0 links. The memory controller supports DDR2 memory with a bandwidth of up to 12.8 GB/s. In addition, the HyperTransport 3.0 links provide an aggregate bandwidth of 57.6 GB/s and are used to allow communication between different Istanbul processors.

The 6 MB of L3 cache is shared among the 6 cores: there are a 512 KB L2 cache per core and 64 KB L1 data cache and a 64 KB L1 instruction cache for each core.

1.3.3.5 Intel(R) Nehalem

In November 2008, with the release of Core™ i7, Intel introduced the new microprocessor architecture Nehalem [28]. The Nehalem architecture (Fig. 1.10) has been used in a large number of processor variants in the mobile, desktop and servers markets and is mainly produced in 45 nm technology. The core count is typically 2 for mobile products, 2 – 4 cores for desktop and 4,

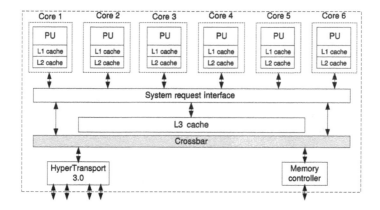

Figure 1.9 AMD Opteron Istanbul processor, simplified block diagram.

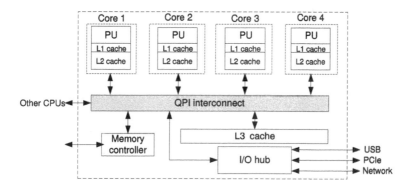

Figure 1.10 Intel Nehalem architecture – 4 cores, simplified block diagram.

6 or 8 for servers. At the high end, the Nehalem architecture shrinked to 32 nm technology (also called Westmere) has been announced to provide a 10-core chip.

Intel introduced with Nehalem the *turbo boost technology* (TBT) to allow adjustments of core frequency at runtime [27]. Considering the number of active cores, estimated current usage, estimated power requirements and CPU temperature, TBT determines the maximum frequency that the processor can run at. Core frequency can be increased in steps of 133 MHz and to a higher level if few cores are active. This allows for a boost in performance while still maintaining the power envelope. To save energy, it is possible to power down cores when they are idle, but when needed again they are turned on, and the frequency of the processor is reduced accordingly [52].

The *QuickPath interconnect* (QPI) was introduced in Nehalem to provide high speed, point-to-point connections between all cores, the I/O hub, the memory controller and the large shared L3 cache (Fig. 1.10). The L3 cache is inclusive. Nehalem-based processors have up to 3.5 times more memory bandwidth than previous generation processors.

The Nehalem architecture reintroduced hyper-threading, a technique that allows each core to run two threads simultaneously, improving on resource utilization and reducing latency. Although it was introduced in Intel processors as early as in 2002, it was not used in the *Intel core* architecture that preceded Nehalem.

For faster computation of media applications, the Nehalem architecture supports the SSE4 instruction set introduced in the previous generation processors. SSE is an abbreviation for *streaming SIMD extensions* and is an SIMD instruction set extension to the $\times 86$ architecture that is used by compilers and assembly coders for vectorization.

1.3.3.6 *Tilera(R) TILE64 TM* Tilera [53] has developed and is currently shipping the TILEPro36™ and TILEPro64™ series of embedded many-core processors. The Tilera devices may contain up to 64 individual 32-bit processors on a single silicon device and are targeted at embedded markets which require programmability, high performance and demanding power constraints. All Tilera devices contain numerous integrated IO interfaces, allowing system designers to save board real estate and complexity by integrating the IO and processing into a single device. Current target markets for the TILEPro™ family of devices include video and network processing. The TILEPro family of devices is fabricated in TSMC's 90 nm technology and comes in 700 and 866 MHz frequency grades.

Each Tilera device contains multiple individual processor cores. Each core supports the TILE instruction set architecture (ISA), a Tilera proprietary ISA sharing many similarities with modern RISC ISAs. The Tilera ISA is a 3-wide VLIW format, where each 64-bit VLIW instruction encodes three operations. Correspondingly, there are three execution pipelines per processor core, two arithmetic pipelines and one load/store pipeline. When running at 866 MHz, a TILEPro64 is capable of 166 billion 32-bit operations per second. Additionally, the Tilera ISA contains SIMD operations, enabling 32b, 16b and 8b arithmetic. The physical address of the TILEPro devices is 36 bits, giving a TILEPro device access to up to 64 GB of memory. The TILEPro processor is an in-order machine, issuing 64-bit VLIW instructions in program order. However, the TILEPro cache subsystem is out of order, allowing the processor to continue to fetch, issue and execute instructions in the presence of multiple cache misses. The TILE cores do not have HW FPU support.

The TILEPro device is a complete system on a chip, containing multiple integrated IO interfaces. TILEPro64 contains four integrated DDR2 memory controllers, capable of supporting 800 MHz operation. Memory space may be configured to be automatically interleaved across the four controllers or programmatically assigned on a page-by-page mapping from page to controller.

A TILEPro processor core contains a 16 KB L1 instruction cache, an 8 KB L1 data cache and a 64 KB unified L2 cache (used for both instructions and data). All processor cores on a TILEPro device are cache coherent, enabling running of standard, shared-memory programs such as POSIX threads across the entire device. The cores may be configured into multiple coherence domains, allowing a single SMP Linux image to run across all cores within the system, or only a subset. Tilera hypervisor technology enables the ability to run multiple Linux images in parallel. Coherency is maintained between the processor cores via a unique directory-based coherency protocol, called dynamic distributed cache (DDC). The DDC protocol tracks address sharers within the system via a distributed directory and maintains coherence by properly invalidating/updating shared data upon modification. Additionally, the Tilera cache subsystem provides the ability for one core's L2 cache to serve as a backing L3 cache for another core within the system. In this context, the L2 storage structures may contain both L2 and L3 cache blocks.

The TILEPro processor cores communicate with each other and the IO interfaces via multiple on-chip, packet-switched networks. These networks, called the iMesh™, are proprietary interconnects used to carry communication within the system such as memory read requests, memory read responses, tile-to-tile read responses, etc. The networks are configured in a mesh topology, providing performance scalability as the number of cores is increased. The TILEPro devices contain three separate mesh networks for memory and cache communication, as well as two networks for user-level messaging. These networks are synchronous with the processor cores and run at the same frequency, and the latency for a message through the mesh networks is one processor cycle per node.

1.4 HETEROGENEOUS MULTICORES

This section introduces *heterogeneous multicores* – processors where one or some of the cores are significantly different than the others. The difference can be as fundamental as the instruction set used, or it can be the processor speed or cache/memory capacity of the different cores. We start by introducing some of the main types of heterogeneity, before we present three different contemporary products in this category of processors.

1.4.1 Types of Heterogeneity in Multicores

Single-ISA heterogeneous multicores are processors where all the cores have the same ISA, that is, they can execute the same instructions, but they can have different clock frequencies and/or cache sizes. Also, the cores might have different architectures implementing the same ISA. Typically there is one or a few high-performance cores (fat cores) that are superscalar out-of-order processors and a larger number of smaller and simpler cores that can be in-order processors with a shorter pipeline [34]. As discussed in Section 1.3.2, this can be beneficial for speeding up applications where there is a significant part of the computation that is serial or if some of the threads put more demand on the memory system. This kind of multicores is called by some authors *asymmetric multicore processors (AMP)*. They have gained increased interest lately since they potentially can be more energy efficient than conventional homogeneous multicores [13].

Multiple-ISA multicores such as the Cell/BE™ microprocessor presented in Section 1.4.2.1 have two or more different instruction sets. They require a toolchain for each core type and are in general harder to program. In addition, many of these processors, including Cell[TM], have explicitly managed memory hierarchies where the programmer is responsible for placement and transfer of data. This will in general increase programmer effort and code complexity compared to a cache-based system that are automatic and hidden from the programmer. Recent research has shown that comparable performance can be achieved through programming environments where compiler and runtime support implicitly manage locality [44].

In the embedded systems market, there is a long tradition of using highly heterogeneous multicores with different kinds of simple or complex cores and HW units integrated on a single chip. These *multiprocessor system-on-chip* (MPSoC) systems often achieve a very high level of power efficiency through specialization [35], but again the price to pay is often more difficult programming. MPSoC systems have been available as commercial products for longer than multicores, and some few MPSoCs are homogeneous. We refer the reader to a recent survey of MPSoCs by Wolf, Jerraya and Martin for this rich branch of multicore processors [57].

Graphics processing units (GPU) and accelerators are also considered examples of heterogeneous multicores, even though in most cases they in general need a host processor to be able to run a complete application. The principle of *hardware acceleration* – adding a special purpose HW unit to off load the processor or to speed up computation by doing specific functions in HW instead of software - has a long history. About 30 years ago, a common practice for speeding up floating-point operations in a PC was to add a floating-point coprocessor unit (FPU). Today, the inclusion of different accelerator subunits in a CMP is becoming increasingly popular, and IBM has recently announced a processor architecture where processing cores and hardware accelerators are closely coupled [16].

Similarly, the GPU was added to accelerate the processing of graphics. GPUs have during the last two decades been through a substantial development from specialized units for graphics processing only to more programmable units being popular for general-purpose GPU (GPGPU). Their programming has become substantially improved through languages such as CUDA[TM] and OpenCL[TM] [32, 8].

1.4.2 Examples of Multicore Architectures

1.4.2.1 The Cell[TM] Processor Architecture The Cell Broadband Engine[TM]
(Cell/BE) is a heterogeneous processor that was jointly developed by Sony®, Toshiba® and IBM®. As shown in Figure 1.11, it is mainly composed of one main core (power processing element (PPE)), 8 specialized cores (called synergistic processing elements (SPEs)), an on-chip memory controller and a controller for a configurable I/O interface, all linked together by an element interconnection bus (EIB) [46]. The main core is a 64-bit Power processor with vector processing extensions and two levels of hardware-managed caches, a 32 KB L1 data cache and a 512 KB L2 cache. In addition, it is a dual-issue, dual-threaded processor that has a single-precision peak of 25.6 Gflops/s and a double-precision peak of 6.4 Gflops/s.

The 8 SPEs are SIMD cores (SPU) which each possess a 256 KB local store (LS) for storing both data and instructions, a 128 × 128-bit register file and a memory flow controller (MFC). MFC has the capability to move code and data between main

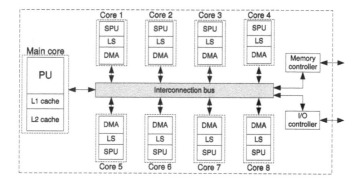

Figure 1.11 Simplified block diagram of Cell/BE.

memory and LS using a direct memory access (DMA) controller. Moreover, each SPE has a single-precision peak of 25.6 Gflops/s and a double-precision peak of only 1.83 Gflops/s. The EIB is composed of 4 unidirectional rings that are used as a communication bus between elements that are connected to it, and it can deliver 25.6 GB/s to each of them.

The memory controller is used to connect to a dual-channel Rambus extreme data rate (XDR) memory which can deliver a bandwidth of 25.6 GB/s. In addition, the Cell has an I/O controller which can be dedicated to connect up to two separate logical interfaces [31]. These interfaces provide chip-to-chip connections and can be used to design an efficient dual-processor system.

The main core (PPE) is usually responsible for running the operating system and controlling the other cores (SPEs); it can start, stop, interrupt and schedule processes running on them. In fact, SPEs achieve their work only by following PPE commands. The PPE can read and write the main memory and the local memories of SPEs through the standard load/store instructions. However, data movement to and from an SPE (LS) is achieved explicitly using DMA commands. The explicit transfer of data and limited size of SPE LS poses a major challenge to software development on the Cell/BE processor.

The *PowerXCell*^{TM} *8i* is a revised variant of the Cell/BE processor that was announced by IBM in 2008 and made available in IBM QS22 blade servers. The SPEs in the new variant have a much better double-precision floating-point peak performance (102.4 GFLOPS) compared to the previous one (14.64 GFLOPS). In addition, it has support for up to 32 GB of slotted DDR2 memory. The PowerXCell 8i processor has been used in several supercomputers. For example, the Roadrunner supercomputer, the world's fastest in 2008–2009, has 12,240 PowerXCell 8i processors in addition to 6562 AMD Opteron processors. PoweXCell 8i supercomputers have also occupied many of the top positions on the Green500 list of the most energy-efficient supercomputers in the world [51].

1.4.2.2 NVIDIA(R) Fermi   The GPU is a highly specialized PU dedicated to execute or accelerate video applications. Since these applications have an increased

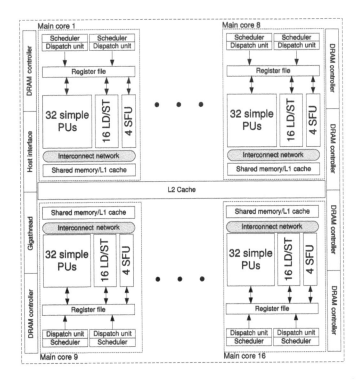

Figure 1.12   NVIDIA Fermi, simplified block diagram.

degree of parallelism, GPUs use tens to hundreds of cores to perform the advanced floating-point operations specific to video rendering. With the introduction of NVIDIA's *unified shader architecture* in 2006 and CUDA in 2007, the potential performance of GPU's massively parallel architecture was also made available to other fields, like high-performance computing (HPC) [19].

Fermi (or GeForce®400) is the latest architecture from NVIDIA [19]. It has up to 512 PUs distributed among 16 main cores, which NVIDIA calls *streaming multiprocessors*. It has a two-level cache hierarchy and very fast double-precision floating-point math operations [56]. Fermi is a good fit for some HPC applications, and NVIDIA offers the Tesla line of products as dedicated GPGPUs to be used as accelerators in HPC supercomputers. In October 2010, after being upgraded with more than 7000 Fermi-based Tesla GPGPUs, Tianhe-1A became the fastest supercomputer in the world, as ranked by the TOP500 list.

Fermi has a transistor count of more than 3 billions that are used to create 16 main cores, a shared L2 cache, 6 memory (DRAM) controllers, a hardware thread scheduler (called GigaThread) and the host interface (Fig. 1.12). However, not all of these resources are always activated.

Each main core consists of 32 very simple PUs, capable of performing integer or floating-point operations. All PUs share a single-register file, 16 load/store units, 4

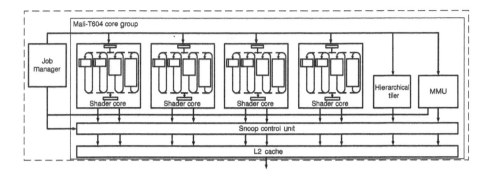

Figure 1.13   ARM Mali T604, simplified block diagram.

special function units (for advanced math like square root or sine), 2 thread schedulers and dispatch units and an L1 cache. The main core can been seen as a 32-issue superscalar processor. This main core design, coupled with the GigaThread scheduler, allows a Fermi-class GPU to switch very fast between threads and to handle more than 24.000 parallel threads in an efficient way.

In order to improve the HPC performance, Fermi uses a more standard memory hierarchy which includes a shared L2 cache. Since the memory penalty is greater with GPUs than with CPUs, NVIDIA added new keywords to its CUDA implementation that allow a programmer to specify where data will be stored. Also, in order to make it more programmer friendly, NVIDIA improved Fermi's ISA (improved atomic integer instructions [41]) and added support for C++ object-oriented programming.

1.4.2.3 ARM(R)Mali TM-T604 GPU   The ARM Mali-T604 GPU is a licensable, low-power multicore GPU targeting system-on-chip (SoC) providers and a broad range of applications including mobile, digital TV, gaming and navigation. It is the first GPU from ARM with an architecture designed to enhance GPU computing through, for example, the Khronos^{TM} OpenCL^{TM} API. This is in addition to graphics standards such as Khronos OpenGL ES^{TM} and OpenVG^{TM}.

The ARM multicore design philosophy previously used with CPUs has been applied to ARM Mali GPUs, and the result is the Mali-T604. This multicore GPU has a customer-configurable number of cores that share a coherent Level 2 memory subsystem. A single job manager handles the host CPU interface and load balancing on the GPU, while a hierarchical tiler (HT) accelerates the tile-based graphics processing and a memory management unit (MMU) handles virtual address translation and processes separation (see Fig. 1.13).

The Level 2 memory subsystem can maintain full coherency between cores through a Snoop Control Unit (SCU). This approach is inspired by ARM multiprocessor CPUs and is different from traditional GPUs where local memory is noncoherent. Each shader core is a multipipeline, multithreaded unit with the ability to execute hundreds of threads simultaneously. This is particularly beneficial for throughput-oriented computing with an abundance of data-level parallelism. The processor supports a wide range of data types, including integer and IEEE-754 floationg point up to 64-bit allowing for algorithms requiring single and double precision. Support for 64-bit integer arithmetic is provided.

Computing on the Mali-T604 GPU is highly efficient compared to high-end desktop or server GPUs. The moving of data between CPU and GPU memory is avoided by the use of a unified memory system coherent between the GPU and CPU, such as the ARM Cortex™-A15 CPU. Fast atomic operations with Mali-T604 mean that algorithms requiring interthread communication will be much more efficient than on a traditional GPU.

1.5 CONCLUDING REMARKS

Current trends in multi- and many-core architectures are increased parallelism, increased heterogeneity, use of accelerators and energy efficiency as a first-order design constraint. The '5 P's of parallel processing: performance, predictability, power efficiency, programmability and portability' are all important goals that we strive to meet when we build or program multicore systems. To meet the challenge of partly conflicting goals, we need more research in parallel programming models that adopts a holistic view – covering aspects from hardware and power consumption through system software and up to the programmers wish for programmability and portability.

A challenge is that optimizing for one of these goals very often will reduce the possibility of achieving some of the others. The present state of the art is very diverse and dynamic and in many ways less stable than 10 years ago. As an example, heterogeneous processors with explicitly managed memories like the Cell processor have achieved outstanding results for power efficiency [51] at the cost of reduced programmability. However, researchers are continuously looking for ways to achieve many of these goals at the same time. Power efficiency innovations in runtime systems is one of the many promising directions. Borkar and Chien [7] outline a hypothetical heterogeneous processor consisting of a few large cores and many small cores, where the supply voltage and frequency of each core are controlled individually. This fine-grained power management improves energy efficiency without burdening the application programmer, since it is controlled by the runtime system. However, significant breakthroughs are needed on the software level to make such systems practical.

To end the chapter, we would like to quote the recent and highly motivating paper *Computing Performance: Game Over or Next Level?* [18]: the era of sequential computing must give way to an era in which parallelism holds the forefront.

Trademark Notice

Product or corporate names may be trademarks or registered trademarks and are used only for identification and explanation without intent to infringe.

REFERENCES

1. J. Abeles et al. Performance Guide For HPC Applications On IBM Power 755 System. http://power.org, 2010.

2. V. Agarwal, M. S. Hrishikesh, S. W. Keckler, and D. Burger. Clock rate versus IPC: the end of the road for conventional microarchitectures. *ACIM SIGARCH Computer Architecture News*, 28(2):248–259, 2000.

3. G. M. Amdahl. Validity of the single processor approach to achieving large scale computer capabilities. In *AFIPS Joint Computer Conference Proceedings*, volume 30, pages 483–485, 1967.

4. ARM website. http://www.arm.com.

5. J. L. Baer and T. F. Chen. Effective hardware-based data prefetching for high–performance processors. *IEEE Transactions on Computers*, 44:609–623, May 1995.

6. G. H. Barnes, R. M. Brown, M. Kato, D. J. Kuck, D. L. Slotnick, and R. A. Stokes. The ILLIAC IV Computer. *IEEE Transactions on Computers*, C-17(8):746 – 757, August 1968.

7. S. Borkar and A. A. Chien. The future of microprocessors. *Communications of the ACM*, 54:67–77, May 2011.

8. A. R. Brodtkorb, C. Dyken, T. R. Hagen, J. M. Hjelmervik, and O. O. Storaasli. State-of-the-art in heterogeneous computing. *Scientific Programming*, 18:1–33, January 2010.

9. S. Byna, Y. Chen, and X. H. Sun. Taxonomy of data prefetching for multicore processors. *Journal of Computer Science and Technology*, 24:405–417, 2009.

10. D. Callahan, K. Kennedy, and A. Porterfield. Software prefetching. In *Proceedings of the 4th International Conference on Architectural Support for Programming Languages and Operating Systems*, ASPLOS-IV, pages 40–52, New York, NY, USA, 1991. ACM.

11. H. Dybdahl. *Architectural Techniques to Improve Cache Utilization*. PhD thesis, Norwegian University of Science and Technology, Trondheim, Norway, 2010.

12. H. Dybdahl, P. Stenstrom, and L. Natvig. A cache-partitioning aware replacement policy for chip multiprocessors. In Y. Robert et al., editor, *High Performance Computing – HiPC 2006*, volume 4297 of *LNCS*, pages 22–34. Springer Berlin / Heidelberg, 2006.

13. A. Fedorova, J. C. Saez, D. Shelepov, and M. Prieto. Maximizing power efficiency with asymmetric multicore systems. *Communications of the ACM*, 52:48–57, December 2009.

14. M. J. Flynn. Very high-speed computing systems. In *Proceedings of the IEEE*, volume 54, pages 1901–1909, December 1966.

15. M. J. Flynn. Some computer organizations and their effectiveness. *IEEE Transactions on Computers*, C-21(9):948 –960, September 1972.

16. H. Franke, J. Xenidis, C. Basso, B. M. Bass, S. S. Woodward, J. D. Brown, and C. L. Johnson. Introduction to the wire-speed processor and architecture. *IBM Journal of Research and Development*, 54(1):3:1 –3:11, January–February 2010.

17. J. W. C. Fu, J. H. Patel, and B. L. Janssens. Stride directed prefetching in scalar processors. In *Proceedings of the 25th annual International Symposium on Microarchitecture*, MICRO 25, pages 102–110. IEEE Computer Society Press, Los Alamitos, CA, USA, 1992.

18. S. H. Fuller and L. I. Millett. Computing performance: game over or next level? *Computer*, 44(1):31–38, January 2011.

19. P. N. Glaskowsky. NVIDIA's Fermi: The First Complete GPU Computing Architecture. http://www.nvidia.com/content/PDF/fermi_white_papers/P. Glaskowsky_NVIDIA's_Fermi-The_First_Complete_GPU_Architecture. pdf 2009.

20. M. D. Godfrey and D. F. Hendry. The computer as von Neumann planned it. *IEEE Annals of the History of Computing,* 15(1):11–21, 1993.

21. M. Grannaes. *Reducing Memory Latency by Improving Resource Utilization.* PhD thesis, Norwegian University of Science and Technology, Trondheim, Norway, 2010.

22. A. Halaas, B. Svingen, M. Nedland, P. Saetrom, O. Snoeve Jr., and O.R. Birkeland. A recursive MISD architecture for pattern matching. *IEEE Transactions on Very Large Scale Integration (VLSI) Systems*, 12(7):727 – 734, July 2004.

23. J. L. Hennessy and D. A. Patterson. *Computer Architecture: A Quantitative Approach.* Morgan Kaufmann, fourth edition, 2006.

24. M. D. Hill and M. R. Marty. Amdahl's law in the multicore era. *Computer*, 41(7):33 –38, July 2008.

25. P. G. Howard. Six-Core AMD Opteron Processor Istanbul. http://www.microway. com/pdfs/microway_istanbul_whitepaper_2009-07.pdf, 2009.

26. K. Hwang. *Advanced Computer Architecture: Parallelism, Scalability, Programmability.* McGraw-Hill Higher Education, first edition, 1992.

27. Intel corp. 2nd Generation Intel Core Processor Family Desktop. http://download. intel.com/design/processor/datashts/324641.pdf.

28. Intel corp. First the Tick, Now the Tock – Intel Microarchitecture (Nehalem). http:// www.intel.com/technology/architecture-silicon/next-gen/ 319724.pdf.

29. ITRS. International Technology Roadmap for Semiconductors. http://www.itrs. net/, 2006.

30. M. Jahre. *Managing Shared Resources in Chip Multiprocessor Memory Systems.* PhD thesis, Norwegian University of Science and Technology, Trondheim, Norway, 2010.

31. J. A. Kahle, M. N. Day, H. P. Hofstee, C. R. Johns, T. R. Maeurer, and D. Shippy. Introduction to the cell multiprocessor. *IBM Journal of Research and Development.*, 49: 589–604, July 2005.

32. D. B. Kirk and Wen-mei W. Hwu. *Programming Massively Parallel Processors: A Hands-on Approach.* Morgan Kaufmann Publishers Inc., first edition, 2010.

33. P. Kongetira, K. Aingaran, and K. Olukotun. Niagara: a 32-way multithreaded sparc processor. *IEEE Micro*, 25(2):21 – 29, 2005.

34. R. Kumar, K. I. Farkas, N. P. Jouppi, P. Ranganathan, and D. M. Tullsen. Single-ISA heterogeneous multicore architectures: the potential for processor power reduction. *IEEE/ACM International Symposium on Microarchitecture*, pages 81–92, 2003.

35. R. Kumar, D. M. Tullsen, N. P. Jouppi, and P. Ranganathan. Heterogeneous chip multiprocessors. *Computer*, 38(11):32 – 38, November 2005.

36. H. T. Kung. Why systolic architectures? *Computer*, 15:37–46, 1982.

37. K. Olukotun and L. Hammond. The future of microprocessors. *Queue*, 3:26–29, September 2005.

38. K. Olukotun, B. A. Nayfeh, L. Hammond, K. Wilson, and K. Chang. The case for a single-chip multiprocessor. In *Proceedings of the 7th International Conference on Architectural Support for Programming Languages and Operating Systems*, ASPLOS-VII, pages 2–11. ACM, New York, NY, USA, 1996.

39. Oracle Unveils SPARC T3 Systems and Storage Appliances. http://www.oracle.com/us/corporate/features/sparc-t3-feature-173454.html.

40. D. A. Patterson. Latency lags bandwith. *Communications of the ACM*, 47:71–75, October 2004.

41. D. A. Patterson. The Top 10 Innovations in the New NVIDIA Fermi Architecture, and the Top 3 Next Challenges. http://www.nvidia.com/content/PDF/fermi_white_papers/D.Patterson_Top10InnovationsInNVIDIAFermi.pdf, 2009.

42. J. Psota and A. Agarwal. rMPI: message passing on multicore processors with on-chip interconnect. In P. Stenstrom et al., editor, *High Performance Embedded Architectures and Compilers*, volume 4917 of *LNCS*, pages 22–37. Springer Berlin Heidelberg, 2008.

43. M. J. Quinn. *Designing Efficient Algorithms for Parallel Computers*. McGraw-Hill Book Company, New York, 1987.

44. S. Schneider, J. S. Yeom, and D. S. Nikolopoulos. Programming multiprocessors with explicitly managed memory hierarchies. *Computer*, 42:28–34, 2009.

45. M. Shah et al. UltraSPARC T2 – a highly-threaded, power-efficient, SPARC SOC. In *Solid-State Circuits Conference, ASSCC '07. IEEE Asian*, pages 22–25, November 2007.

46. G. Shi, V. V. Kindratenko, I. S. Ufimtsev, T. J. Martinez, J. C. Phillips, and S. A. Gottlieb. Implementation of scientific computing applications on the cell broadband engine. *Scientific Programming*, 17:135–151, January 2009.

47. M. Snir et al. *MPI – The Complete Reference, Volume 1, The MPI Core*, volume 1. The MIT Press, second edition, 1999.

48. A.C.Sodan, J. Machina, A. Deshmeh, K. Macnaughton, and B. Esbaugh. Parallelism via multithreaded and multicore CPUs. *Computer*, 43(3):24–32, march 2010.

49. F. Soltis. When Is PowerPC Not PowerPC? http://systeminetwork.com, 2002.

50. L. Spracklen and S.G. Abraham. Chip multithreading: opportunities and challenges. In *11th International Symposium on High-Performance Computer Architecture, HPCA-11*, pages 248 – 252, 2005.

51. The Green 500 List. http://www.green500.org/.

52. M. E. Thomadakis. The Architecture of the Nehalem Processor and Nehalem-EP SMP Platforms. http://www.ece.tamu.edu/~tex/manual/node24.html, 2011.

53. Tilera website. http://www.tilera.com.

54. UltraSPARC T2 architecture and performance modelings software tools. http://www.opensparc.net/opensparc-t2/index.html.

55. D. W. Wall. Limits of Instruction-Level Parallelism. Technical report, Digital Western Research Laboratory, 1993.

56. White paper. Looking Beyond Graphics. http://www.nvidia.com/content/PDF/fermi_white_papers/T.Halfhill_Looking_Beyond_Graphics.pdf.

57. W. Wolf, A. A. Jerraya, and G. Martin. Multiprocessor system-on-chip (MPSoC) technology. *IEEE Transactions on Computer-Aided Design of Integrated Circuits and Systems*, 27(10):1701 –1713, october 2008.

CHAPTER 2

PROGRAMMING MODELS FOR MULTICORE AND MANY-CORE COMPUTING SYSTEMS

ANA LUCIA VARBANESCU, ROB V. VAN NIEUWPOORT, PIETER HIJMA, HENRI E. BAL, ROSA M. BADIA AND XAVIER MARTORELL

2.1 INTRODUCTION

Writing massively parallel applications for many-cores is difficult because it is a problem with multiple constraints: we want applications to deliver great performance, to be easy to program and to be portable between architectures. The perceived levels of these parameters – performance, productivity and portability – combine into a measure of platform programmability, which is a good indicator for the success of an architecture. In reality, the programmability gap (i.e. the difference between the theoretical performance offered by the platform and the performance achieved when programming it) remains the major concern for the use of many cores.

Many hardware and software vendors, as well as many groups in academia, are actively working on programming models able to cope with the diversity of platforms and applications. These efforts have generated a large variety of programming

Programming Multicore and Many-core Computing Systems,
First Edition. Edited by Sabri Pllana and Fatos Xhafa.
© 2017 John Wiley & Sons, Inc. Published 2017 by John Wiley & Sons, Inc.

models, each with its own characteristics. This makes the search for a suitable programming model for a specific workload a very difficult task.

In this work, we discuss a comprehensive set of programming models currently used for the most popular families of many-cores. Our survey includes both models specifically developed for many-cores (thus addressing specific architectural concerns), as well as classical parallel models that are also used to develop parallel applications for these platforms. To evaluate these models, we introduce four classes of reference features: usability, design support, implementation support and programmability. Thus, for each model, we discuss how the model is used for parallel application development, what type of support it offers to the user, and how it addresses performance, portability and productivity concerns, and finally, we evaluate its overall impact on platform programmability.

Using this detailed analysis, we provide a multidimensional comparison of the surveyed models. Our goal is not to determine a 'best' programming model for many-core platforms but rather to identify the essential characteristics that separate or cluster these models. To conclude, we comment on the influence that the choice of a programming model can have on the application design and implementation, and we give a few guidelines for finding a programming model that matches the application characteristics.

This chapter is organized as follows. In Section 2.2, we introduce the classes of many-core platforms we target in this work. Section 2.3 introduces the features we use to evaluate the programming models. Section 2.4 presents an overview of the programming models. Section 2.5 presents a multidimensional overview of the presented models, while Section 2.6 presents our conclusions and sketches the future work directions.

2.2   A COMPARATIVE ANALYSIS OF MANY-CORES

In this section we discuss three classes of many-core architectures used for high performance computing: general purpose multicore processors (GPMCs),[1] graphical processing units (GPUs) and the Cell Broadband Engine (Cell/B.E.) processor. We briefly highlight the key differences between the architectures. Our final goal is to demonstrate which architectural properties impact the accompanying programming models (Section 2.4) and how.

Since 2006, GPMCs have been replacing traditional single-core CPUs in both personal computers and servers. GPMCs are homogeneous platforms with complex cores, based on traditional processor architectures. They are typically shared memory architectures, with multiple levels of caches. We emphasize the diversity of the spectrum of GPMCs by showing the characteristics of multi cores from different vendors in Tables 2.1 and 2.2: the Intel Nehalem EX (Xeon 7500 series), the AMD Magny-Cours, the IBM POWER7 and the Sun Niagara II

---

[1]We generically call all these platforms 'many-cores' due to their relatively large numbers of hardware threads. However, we preserve the name 'multicores' as traditional for general purpose many-cores.

(UltraSPARC T2+). Many-core programming models should be retargetable to all these architectures.

The large-scale use of GPUs for general purpose computing started in 2006. Since then, the state-of-the-art GPU architectures target HPC markets directly, by adding computation-only features to their graphics pipelines. GPUs are shared memory machines, with a complex memory hierarchy, combining different types of caches and scratchpads at each level. Because they are typically used as computational accelerators (linked to the host system via the PCI express bus), GPUs have fairly simple control flow hardware but provide high memory throughput and massive computation capabilities. We show properties of GPUs from NVIDIA (the Fermi architecture) and AMD/ATI (the Cypress).

Finally, the Sony, Toshiba and IBM (STI) Cell/B.E. is a hetero geneous architecture with one general purpose processor (the power processing element (PPE)) and eight compute processors (the synergestic processing elements (SPEs)), each one with its own private local memory (local store (LS)). Each one of the nine Cell cores can be programmed independently. Physically, the Cell/B.E. is a distributed memory machine, as SPEs can access only their own local memories and have to program DMA transfers to fetch data from or send data to the main memory. This combination of heterogeneous cores and fullyuser-managed memory makes Cell a real challenge in terms of programmability.

Table 2.1 Computing properties of many-core hardware.

Platform	Cores/threads	Vectors	ALUs	Types	Scheduling	Par levels
Intel Nehalem EX	8/16	4 wide	64	HO	OS	2
AMD Magny-Cours	12/12	4 wide	48	HO	OS	2
IBM POWER 7	8/64	4 wide	256	HO	OS	2
Sun Niagara II	8/64	No	64	HO	OS	1
NVIDIA Fermi	16 × 32	No	512	HO + host	Hardware	3
ATI Cypress	20 × 16	4 wide	1600	HO + host	Hardware	4
Cell/B.E.	9/10	4 wide	36	HE	User/app	5

Note: HO = homogeneous; HE = heterogeneous.

Table 2.1 focuses on the computing properties of the many-core hardware, that is, how the parallelism is achieved. The table clearly shows that each processor has – relative to its own architecture – a large number of hardware parallelism available. Programming models can handle this explicitly or implicitly, trading performance for programmability. We will come back to this in Section 2.4.

In Table 2.2, we summarize the memory properties of the many-cores. The memory subsystems of many-cores are increasing in complexity. This happens because they have to compensate for the inherent decrease in memory bandwidth *per core* with the increase in the number of cores and ALUs. More and more complex memory and caching hierarchies are needed to solve this problem. One of the key differences between multicore CPUs on the one hand and the GPUs and the Cell/B.E. on the other is that the memory hierarchy is more exposed and often explicitly handled in the latter. This has a clear impact on the programming effort that is needed to achieve good performance.

Table 2.2   Memory properties of many-core hardware.

Platform	Space(s)	Access	Cache
Intel Nehalem EX	Shared	R/W	Transparent L1-3
AMD Magny-Cours	Shared	R/W	Transparent L1-3
IBM POWER7	Shared	R/W	Transparent L1-3
Sun Niagara II	Shared	R/W	Transparent L1-2
NVIDIA Fermi	Shared; device; host	R/W; R/W; DMA	App-controlled shared store; transparent L1-2
ATI Cypress	Shared; device; host	R/W; R/W; DMA	App-controlled shared store; transparent L1-2
Cell/B.E.	PPU, SPU	R/W; DMA	App-controlled local store

2.3   PROGRAMMING MODELS FEATURES

This section discusses the features we use to evaluate programming models. Our goal is to define programmability in terms of productivity, portability and performance and further extract the features that programming models use to improve platform programmability.

2.3.1   Programmability

The programmability gap is the difference between the theoretical performance of a platform and the observed performance of the applications running on that platform. The advent of many-cores widens the programmability gap because platform peak performance is only achievable if applications are able to extract and express multiple layers of parallelism, at par with those offered by the hardware platform. In this context, platform programmability is a measure of how easy it is for (generic) applications to express enough parallelism to match the hardware offer.

Typically, the native programming model of a platform exposes its 'bare' programmability, as it provides users with the means to express parallelism in a platform -specific form, and it has minor limitations on achievable performance. Higher-level programming models aim to improve programmability, by (i) offering users easier abstractions for designing and building parallelism and (ii) building better back-end components (i.e. compilers and runtime systems) to minimize the impact on performance.

We judge the impact a programming model can have on platform programmability as a combination of its *productivity*, *portability* and *performance*. Productivity is a measure of the development effort (typically, the time spent by the user when designing and developing the application). A model's portability indicates the potential reusability of the solutions built using it. A model's performance indicates the achievable performance of a solution; from the model's perspective, the performance potential is usually measured as efficiency (i.e. how much of the platform's peak performance is achievable when using the chosen model).

Note that productivity, portability and performance are strongly interconnected. For example, obtaining maximum performance might increase development time, thus decreasing productivity; similarly, a highly portable solution can use no hardware-specific optimizations, thus limiting achievable performance. Therefore, a programming model has a positive impact on platform programmability if it can increase productivity and portability without (negatively) affecting the achievable performance.

2.3.2 Classes of Models

Based on their approach to application parallelization, we define three different classes of models:

Parallelism-centric models are built to allow users to express typical parallelism constructs in a simple and effective way and at various levels of abstraction. The higher the level of abstraction is, the less (explicit) parallelism constructs are available, and the less the flexibility and expressibility of the model are. Parallelism-centric models are typically used to express complex parallel algorithms (i.e. the design of the parallel solution for the application and its implementation are decoupled).

Hardware-centric models are designed to replace native platform programming (typically supported by a low-level programming model) with higher-level, user-friendly solutions. These models aim to hide some of the low-level peculiarities of platforms, offering a clearer interface to the programmer. These models are typically used when the platform is chosen and portability (which may or may not be supported by the model) is of less importance compared with the potential performance. These models require users to understand the chosen platform and parallelize applications for it.

Application-centric models tackle application parallelization from design to implementation. Some of them also include several generic optimizations. These models have less explicit parallelism constructs. Their goal is to help users to find an effective, (partially) platform-agnostic parallel solutions for their applications, and implement them using a limited set of concurrency, granularity and parallelism constructs.

2.3.3 Features

We discuss three categories of features we use to evaluate the programming models: usability, design support and implementation support. The following paragraphs briefly explain the features we consider representative for each category, as well as their expected impact on platform programmability (if any):

Usability   We include here a set of practical features that programming models offer; these features are linked to the ease of use of a programming model, ultimately aiming at increased programmer productivity:

Class Models are parallelism-centric, hardware-centric or application-centric. A model's class can have impact on productivity because the initial application has to be expressed differently depending on the chosen class. For example, to use parallelism-centric models, one needs to parallelize applications in such a way that they use the right parallel constructs.

Problem specification Programming models require different ways of exposing the problem to be solved. We distinguish here models that start from the sequential code (typically enhanced with parallelism by the programmer), models that start from an algorithm and apply model-specific parallelization (this usually requires finding a new, parallel algorithm) and models that start from application specification. Note that for hierarchical models (e.g. CUDA), the problem specification may differ between layers.

Problem specification is important for productivity: using the right initial description helps with correct solution design and minimizes the time spent in design, thus making the process more efficient. For example, if sequential code is not available for a given application, choosing a model that requires the sequential code algorithm to design the parallel version is counterproductive.

Actions The actions to be performed to transform the problem specification into a parallel solution, as well as the way they are done (by the user or (semi-) automated), are essential in increasing productivity. Typical actions are specific parallelization, where the user parallelizes the given algorithm to fit the target model; loop-level parallelization, usually done by the compiler; kernel isolation and fine-grain parallelization, where the users need to isolate the highly parallel regions in the code and exploit loop-like parallelism within the model space and data clustering, where users specify collections of data to be processed in parallel, and a compiler or runtime system uses these elements as concurrency units.

Note that models that require a detailed application specification and complex actions to be performed by the user have good performance potential, but their impact on productivity is negative; by contrast, models that rely on automated transformations of application specification typically show both improved productivity and performance limitations.

Implementation Programming models may be constructed as programming languages (and using compilers) or as collections of keywords or pragmas added to existing languages (and using preprocessors and libraries for implementation). Some models also include runtime systems, allowing more control over the parallel execution of their concurrency units. The implementation of a model does not necessarily have an objective impact on programmability. However, models that are based on known programming languages or use familiar programming constructs, as well as models that use libraries of pre-optimized components, are proven to be more productive than models that use new abstractions and languages.

Design support   We investigate four features that programming models offer to their users for designing parallel applications:

Algorithm view   The *algorithm view* [9] of a programming model can be fragmented or global. The parallelism constructs of a fragmented-view model are usually explicit and interleaved with the processing constructs. In this case, the processing appears as fragmented, like in the classical example of Message Passing Interface (MPI) [22]. In contrast, a global-view model typically uses implicit communication and synchronization constructs, resulting in little interference with the processing, thus preserving the global view of the algorithm. Examples of such models are OpenMP [2] and Cilk [23]. The model's *algorithm view* [9] influence on programmability is application specific: applications with complex synchronization patterns usually benefit from fragmented-view solution, while applications with massive data parallelism are more suitable for mixed- or even global-view models. Overall, global-view algorithms are easier to reason about, while fragmented-view models make debugging slightly easier.

Parallelism   A model can support multiple *types of parallelism*. At a lower level, models can offer support for single instruction, multiple data (SIMD) (typically known as vectorization) or single instruction, multiple thread (SIMT) (–also known as lock-step execution), targeting fine-grain parallelism. At a higher level, models can offer single process, multiple data/multiple process, multiple data (SPMD or MPMD) [11] – targeting coarse-grain parallelism. Finally, at the highest level, models can offer one or several patterns for both SPMD and MPMD, such as divide-and-conquer, map/reduce, pipelining or streaming. The influence of the supported types of parallelism on productivity is application dependent. Therefore, a good match of the application parallelism with the programming model parallelism leads to a programmability boost, while a mismatch typically requires a lot of empirical changes on the algorithm, decreasing productivity.

Concurrency units and granularity   The *control over granularity of the concurrency units* can contribute not only to performance but also to portability. A model that allows explicit granularity definition without changing the program may contribute to performance. In addition, applications can be ported to an architecture which needs more fine-grained or coarse-grained parallelism. Available models range from those which do not have abstractions for granularity control, other than changing the program (the majority), to programming models that offer automatic and/or dynamic granularity control.

Data layout   A model can provide ways to specify the *data layout*, thus increasing productivity. A model that allows users to define how data is partitioned or distributed among the concurrency units can reduce unneeded communication and simplify future mapping and scheduling decisions.

Implementation support   There are several features that offer implementation -level support and impact overall platform programmability. We discuss here four such features:

Mapping and scheduling By mapping and scheduling, we refer to the way the concurrency units are 'placed' on the platform resources and executed to improve concurrency. Using explicit mapping and scheduling increases solution complexity, while the implicit alternatives typically affect performance. Therefore, models choose one of the following solutions: (i) require users to make an explicit mapping, (ii) determine the mappings automatically or even dynamically (using their own runtime system) or (iii) rely on either the operating system (OS) or the hardware schedulers for a 'default' mapping.

Data transfers Due to their complex memory hierarchies, many-cores need *data transfers* between memory levels. The way data transfers between concurrency units (and, eventually, concurrency layers) are done impacts both performance and productivity. Requiring data transfers to be made explicitly affects portability and increases the complexity of the solution, while making them implicit (i.e. transparent) without performance penalties requires the programming model to know the concurrency units mapping. Due to the large variety in memory hierarchies, hybrid solutions (where some transfers are explicit, while the rest are taken care of by either the hardware (shared memories) or a runtime system) are likely to prevail.

Communication and synchronization Transparent communication between cores reduces development time, but explicit communication enables overlapping of computation and communication which may improve performance.

Optimizations Programming models can simplify certain types of optimizations. If such optimizations can be performed automatically (without users tweaking the code), their positive influence on performance translates into a positive impact on programmability. However, optimizations are typically low level and platform specific (see memory coalescing for GPUs and SIMD extensions for the Cell/B.E. or the GPMCs), requiring user's intervention and diminishing solution portability and productivity.

Among the models that require users' intervention for optimization are those models that encourage the users to freely apply low-level optimizations (by simply altering the code) and those which limit or even obstruct this action – mainly because such interventions on code lower the ability of the model's analyzers to parse and extract other parameters and/or parallelization opportunities.

2.4 PROGRAMMING MODELS FOR MANY-CORES

In this section, we present a survey of representative multicore programming models for each of the three classes of platforms discussed in Section 2.3.2.

2.4.1 Parallelism-Centric Programming Models

We list here four traditional models which have been adapted and adopted for many-core processors: threads, MPI, OpenMP and Cilk, together with Intel Threading Building Blocks (TBB), a newer, multicore-induced model that started as a hardware-centric approach and evolved into a parallelism-centric one.

Note that two other classes of programming models – namely, partitioned global address space (PGAS) models and high-productivity languages – can be considered of interest in the context of parallelism-centric programming. However, these target first and foremost large-scale distributed systems and are only recently starting to respond to the requirements of multi- and many-cores [38, 37, 39]. Therefore, they are not part of our study. However, more details about such models can be found in [30].

2.4.1.1 Threads with Shared Memory Threading libraries such as POSIX threads [21] or the Java thread class extend the sequential imperative programming model in a natural way to obtain parallelism. Functions are spawned as new threads that globally share data.

Threads provide mechanisms on the lowest level of abstraction of parallel programming and are very flexible. It is natural to spawn threads with different functions to obtain task parallelism, but threads can also be spawned in a loop, with the same function operating on different data, which results in data parallelism. There is extensive synchronization support, such as joins, barriers and condition variables. Threads offer a fragmented view as programmers need to divide data among threads and join for the results. Algorithms expressed in this model are not portable to other architectures, and there is no concept of tasks that can be sized or resized other than functions. Users have no control over mapping and scheduling, and the model has no specific means to change the data layout. Threads do allow other low-level optimizations.

The flexibility of threads provides programmers lots of control over task creation and synchronization. Threads are well suited for coarse-grained tasks that need much synchronization. Because threads are so low-level, programmers have many opportunities to optimize on for example synchronization.

2.4.1.2 MPI MPI [22] targets both distributed memory systems and shared memory machines but is normally used for distributed memory. An application consists of multiple processes that communicate with messages. MPI gives much control due to the strong separation of communication and computation and is not suitable for fine-grain parallelism.

MPI is the typical example of a fragmented-view programming model. The user is responsible for all communication and synchronization. Explicitly parallel algorithms are needed, which result in algorithms being not easily portable to another family of platforms or even other platforms of the same family. There is no way to size MPI tasks other than changing the program. Data transfer and layout is explicit but only on a high granularity. Communication and synchronization is explicit by means of messages, and the user has no control over how processes are scheduled. However, it allows other optimizations at a later stage. For example, MPI can be mixed with OpenMP [2].

MPI is well suited for applications where the input and communication is static, for example, a regular data structure that can be divided in regular coarse-grained blocks that each are computed on different processors.

2.4.1.3 OpenMP OpenMP [2] comprises a set of compiler directives and a library. Programmers can annotate sequential C, C++ or Fortran code for parallel execution on a shared memory machine. It originally targeted structured parallelism in for loops, but as of version 3.0, it also supports the concept of tasks, making it easier to walk lists and trees and to deal with parallelism in recursive functions. OpenMP uses a relaxed consistency model in which each thread has its own temporary view of shared variables.

OpenMP offers a global-view programming model. Algorithms remain general as sequential algorithms are parallelized incrementally with compiler directives. OpenMP supports both task and data parallelism and focuses on parallelization of loops. Granularity can be controlled manually by adjusting loop chunks in combination with a scheduling type, such as `static` or `dynamic`. Communication and synchronization is mostly implicit, and OpenMP does not provide anything to adjust the data layout. It obstructs other optimizations as this can break the parallelization.

OpenMP is mainly used for parallelizing loops in an already existing sequential program. The goal is to parallelize an application by adding only compiler directives and without restructuring the application.

2.4.1.4 Cilk The language Cilk [23] allows programmers to write parallel divide-and-conquer programs. It extends C and C++ with keywords such as `spawn` and `sync`. A `spawn` in front of a function call creates a nonblocking function call that is executed in its own thread and may spawn other (possibly recursive) functions. Multiple consecutive spawn function calls create parallelism in the program. The keyword `sync` blocks the calling thread until the results of the spawned function calls are available.

Cilk offers a global view of the algorithm. Syntactically, a sequential divide-and-conquer algorithm is very similar to a parallel divide-and-conquer algorithm. The language is limited to divide-and-conquer parallelism. The model gives no control over tasks. Programmers often control the granularity of the recursive task by manually choosing between a sequential version or parallel version based on the size of the data that needs to be processed.

Data is communicated to threads by using parameters of spawn function calls. The model offers several ways to obtain more control over synchronization. For example, the `abort` keyword aborts other spawned threads. A typical use case is a parallel search where one thread finds an item and aborts the others. Another example is the use of inlets that guarantee that results of spawned threads are treated atomically with respect to the other spawned threads.

The Cilk system dynamically schedules threads and dynamically maps them to hardware.

2.4.1.5 *Intel Threading Building Blocks (TBB)*   Intel TBB [31, 16] is a C++ library with a strong focus on data parallelism. It centers around the concept of tasks instead of threads where tasks are performed on data in parallel. The library provides scalability by means of recursive subdivision of data and tasks that perform work stealing. It is flexible enough to allow building higher-level languages such as concurrent collections [14, 7]. The library has three types of building blocks. It contains built-in constructs like `parallel_reduce` that can be composed recursively, container classes that are thread-safe and locking classes (although the usage of these is discouraged).

With the predefined constructs, TBB offers a global view, and ensures that algorithms remain general. TBB is rather flexible and offers both task and data parallelism and good control over task creation and granularity. TBB does not offer mechanisms to specify data layout, task mapping or data transfers, but it is possible to control task scheduling. It is also possible to perform communication and synchronization by hand, but it is not recommended. The model allows other optimizations at a later stage.

TBB can be used to parallelize parts of an existing C++ program. It provides parallelism at a level of abstraction that is above threads, with support for concurrent container classes and reduction constructs. However, it is still a flexible framework where programmers can also use lower-level constructs.

2.4.2 Hardware-Centric Programming Models

We further discuss these models per platform, according to the original platform they have been designed for. We include here models for GPMCs, GPUs and Cell/B.E. processor.

2.4.2.1 *GPMC Programming Models*   The native parallelism model of GPMCs is symmetrical multithreading as we deal with homogeneous architectures. GPMCs target coarse-grain MPMD or SPMD workloads. Programmers cannot control scheduling and mapping; this is typically done by the OS. Memory consistency and contention are other problems. Consistency problems may impact correctness, and memory contention often limits performance.

Given the generic nature of GPMCs, many of the programming models they use are actually at the border between hardware-centric and parallelism-centric – see, for example, pthreads or Intel TBB. Therefore, we only include here Intel Array Building Blocks (ArBB), and we mention that Intel TBB can also be seen as GPMC-centric, but due to its comprehensive parallelism constructs, we have chosen to list it among the parallelism-centric models (see Section 2.4.1).

Intel Array Building Blocks   ArBB [15] is a continuation of C for throughput (Ct [12]) with some features from RapidMind. It extends C++ with a library, JIT compiler and ArBB-specific constructs such as special for and while statements. The programming model centers around special data containers with support for regular data (dense or sparse) and irregular data. Through the use of these data types, ArBB supports data and nested data parallelism. Operations, such as reductions on these data types, are logically performed in a separate memory space and garbage collected to obtain a deterministic programming model. ArBB targets GPMCs using vector instructions and aims to be scalable when the number of cores on a chip increases or vector instructions becomes wider.

There are special copy in and copy out instructions to logically define the data in the ArBB memory space. This does not mean that the data is actually copied, but from the programming model point of view, this results in a fragmented view of algorithms. The users have no control of task granularity as the dynamic compilation phase of ArBB operations takes care of this. Users have control over data layout by specifying their data structures in a different way.

ArBB is well suited to parallelize data intensive parts with numerical computations in an existing C++ program.

2.4.2.2 *GPGPU Programming Models*   Programming GPUs is based on offloading and fine-grain mass parallelism: the host CPU offloads the data-parallel *kernels* as large collections (blocks) of threads on the GPU. GPUs are typically used for highly data-parallel workloads, where hundreds to thousands of threads can compute concurrently.

The most common parallelism models are SIMD/SIMT, with medium and low granularity. For GPUs, the features with the highest impact on programmability are the very large number of threads, the uncontrollable hardware-based mapping and scheduling, the limited amount of fast memory, the different types of memories and their large performance imbalance (orders of magnitude) and the different memory spaces (host and device). Finally, since registers are dynamically partitioned between running threads, there is a trade-off between using more registers per thread and more threads with less local data stored in registers.

NVIDIA CUDA   NVIDIA's native programming model is called CUDA [25]. Based on C, CUDA uses language extensions for separating device (i.e. GPU) from host code and data, as well as for launching CUDA kernels. An advantage of NVIDIA hardware and CUDA is that the application does not have to do vectorization, since all cores have their own address generation units. All data parallelism is expressed by using threads. The programmer has to explicitly group threads in thread blocks. All threads in a block run on the same streaming multiprocessor. Thread blocks are in turn grouped in a grid.

While considered a fairly simple programming model, CUDA is still a low-level tool and requires a lot of programmer's insight and experience to claim impressive performance results. With CUDA, one essentially explicitly subdivides the work over the streaming multiprocessors and has to define correct and suitable grid configurations. In addition, the programmer has to consider many details such as memory coalescing, the texture cache, etc.

CUDA allows for a global algorithm view, while kernels need to be separated (using special constructs) from the host code and explicitly launched. The model uses kernels as the main concurrency unit for the overall application and data elements for the SIMT/SIMD parallelization of the kernels themselves (finer granularity). The application data layout is also specified in two layers: the data structures used by the kernels are simply moved when and where they are needed, and for the kernels themselves, the data layout results from the access patterns of the threads. Mapping and scheduling are performed by the hardware, and the data transfers from host to device are explicit. Low-level optimizations are left to the user.

Stanford Brook/AMD Brook+   In terms of workloads, ATI GPUs are targeting similar applications as NVIDIA's processors: highly data-parallel applications, with medium and low granularity. Therefore, choosing between the two becomes a matter of performance and ease of programming. For high-level programming, ATI adopted *Brook*, which was originally developed at Stanford [6]. ATI's extended version is called *Brook+* [1]. In contrast to CUDA, Brook+ offers a programming model that is based on streaming. Therefore, a paradigm shift is needed to port CPU applications to Brook+, making this a more difficult task than porting applications to CUDA.

With Brook+, the programmer has to do the vectorization, unlike with NVIDIA GPUs. Brook+ provides a feature called *swizzling*, which is used to select parts of vector registers in arithmetic operations, improving readability.

Brook is a fragmented-view model, which uses explicit data transfers between host and device and implicit data layouts and transfers on the device itself. The concurrency units are kernels (coarse granularity) and stream elements (fine granularity). These are both controllable through the code, using language constructs. Mapping and scheduling are implicit. The model allows low-level optimizations.

In our experience, the high-level Brook+ model does not achieve acceptable performance. The low-level CAL model that AMD also provides does, but it is difficult to use. Recently, AMD adopted OpenCL as a high-level programming model not only for their GPUs but also for the CPUs.

PGI Fortran and C Accelerator Programming Model   Using PGI Accelerator compilers [32], programmers can accelerate applications by adding OpenMP-like compiler directives to existing high-level Fortran and C programs. In this respect, PGI's programming model is similar to PathScale's. Compute-intensive kernels are offloaded to the GPU, using two levels of explicit parallelism. There is an outer *forall* loop and an inner synchronous SIMD loop level.

Based on sequential code reuse, PGI Accelerator is a global-view model which uses pragmas to separate the potential kernels (its main concurrency units). Data layouts and transfers are both implicit, as kernels are automatically offloaded and parallelized. As the model uses CUDA as back end, most of the implementation features – hardware-based mapping and synchronization, SIMT-based granularity etc. – are inherited from CUDA. Still, the model does not allow hand-tuning or architecture-specific optimizations on potential kernel code, as these interfere with the ability of the compiler to automatically parallelize the kernel loops.

PathScale ENZO   The PathScale compiler company [29] has recently released a GPU software suite called ENZO. Although the programming model is device independent, it initially targets NVIDIA GPUS and GPMCs, as well as hybrid combinations between these two. ENZO comes with its own hardware device drivers, which focus on computing and do not support graphics. This way, PathScale expects to achieve better performance than CUDA.

With ENZO, programmers annotate their code with directives to indicate which code regions should be parallelized on the GPU. The C with annotations approach is similar to the OpenMP and PGI Accelerator models, preserving their advantages (e.g. portability, relatively high level and starting from sequential code), as well as their drawbacks (e.g. important architecture-specific optimizations cannot be expressed).

ENZO is a global-view model, using pragmas for kernels' granularity control and mapping/scheduling. It relies on hardware-based mapping and scheduling at kernel level. Data transfers are automatically generated and performed, and there are no special constructs for data layouts. To compensate for the lack of low-level optimizations, the model uses preoptimized libraries, code generators and autotuning to improve kernel performance.

2.4.2.3   *Cell/B.E. Programming Models*   Cell/B.E. programming is based on a simple multithreading model: the PPE spawns threads that execute asynchronously on SPEs, until interaction and/or synchronization is required. The communication between the SPEs and the PPE is bidirectional and on demand. The difficulty of programming the Cell/B.E. resides in its multiple layers of parallelism. The architecture is suitable for coarse-parallel workloads, allowing both SPMD and MPMD parallelism; additionally, to achieve peak performance, the SPEs require SIMD parallelism.

Cell's performance depends mainly on the way an application is partitioned and on how the SPE's potential is leveraged. The platform's features with the highest impact on programmability are the heterogeneous cores, the intercore communication and synchronization, the work and data distribution, the task scheduling (including thread management), the vectorization for the PPE and especially for the SPEs and the DMA operations.

IBM Cell SDK   The SDK [5, 17] is the native Cell/B.E. programming model, developed to allow full flexibility for any workload. The model offers all the needed constructs to define the PPE and the SPE codes and their interaction. With the SDK, programmers design and develop the main control flow on the PPE (using simple C or C++ code) and the computation kernels for the SPEs (using C and special intrinsics for optimized processing). Both SPMD and MPMD executions are supported for the SPE kernels. The SPE kernels are managed and coordinated by the PPE. Data layout is implicit – the SPEs and the PPE collaborate in data transfers. There are no special constructs for data layouts, as most of these are settled through programmed DMA to the main memory.

To summarize, the SDK is a fragmented-view model, with kernels as main concurrency units. Granularity is derived from code (no special constructs are provided), and concurrency is achieved by running different threads on the SPEs. Data transfers are all explicit and programmed by the user using DMAs so are synchronization and communication, which use special channels, but still require code to manage the protocol. Mapping and scheduling are performed by the user via the PPE code. Low-level optimizations (mostly vectorization and SIMD operations) are also explicitly performed by the user.

ALF   Accelerated Library Framework [13, 8] (ALF) provides a set of functions/APIs for the development of data-parallel applications following an SPMD model on a (multilevel) hierarchical host-accelerators system (PPE-SPEs and/or host Cell's). In ALF, the *host* runs the control task and the *accelerators* run the compute tasks. The same program runs on all accelerators at one level. ALF provides data-transfer management, task management, double buffering support and data partitioning. Further, the model uses three types of code: (i) accelerator-optimized code (compute tasks optimized for a specific accelerator), (ii) accelerated libraries (kernels and their interfaces, including the data management and buffering) and (iii) applications (user-defined aggregation of compute tasks).

ALF is also a fragmented-view model, with coarse, task-level granularity. The model is hierarchical but focuses on SPMD parallelism. Kernels are defined by the programmer as concurrency units. Kernel mapping and scheduling are solved transparently by the runtime system; the same holds for communication and synchronizations. Data layout can be preset for the SPMD tasks, and data transfers, communication and synchronization are implicit. Mapping and scheduling are performed by the runtime system. Optimizations are typically performed by the user in the kernel code, but the model can use imported kernel from preoptimized libraries. Overall, ALF is an elegant high-level model which offers high productivity and, provided with the right libraries, also very good performance.

Cell Superscalar   CellSs (short for Cell Superscalar) is a pragmatic model, suitable for quick porting of existing sequential applications to the Cell/B.E. [4]. CellSs uses a compiler and a runtime system. The compiler separates an annotated sequential application in two: a PPE part (the main application thread) and the SPEs part (a collection of functions to be offloaded as SPE tasks). The runtime system maintains a dynamic data dependency graph with all active tasks. When the PPE reaches a task invocation, it requests the CellSs runtime to add a new task to the execution list.

When a task is ready for execution (i.e. all its data dependencies are satisfied and there is an SPE available), the DMA transfers are transparently started (and optimized), and the task itself is started on the available SPE. Various scheduling optimizations are performed to limit communication overhead. Additionally, CellSs provides execution tracing, a mechanism included in the runtime system to allow performance debugging by inspecting the collected traces.

When starting from suitable sequential code, CellSs is a very productive global view model for first-order implementations of Cell applications. As mapping and scheduling are dynamically optimized, the performance depends on the kernels' performance. As kernels are generated from sequential user-written functions, low-level optimizations need to be performed by hand, and some manual (re)sizing might be needed to avoid task imbalance.

Note that CellSs is a flavor of OmpSs for the Cell/B.E. – see Section 2.4.3 for more details.

2.4.3   Application-Centric Programming Models

Finally, we discuss six application-centric models, which run on more than one family of many-core processors. These models start with a clear design phase that transforms a generic application into a parallel one. The implementation phase which follows uses dedicated or generic back ends:

SP@CE   SP@CE [35, 24] is a generic model that targets streaming applications. The SP@CE framework is composed from an application design front end, an intermediate representation of the expanded application dependency graph and a runtime system with various back ends. A SP@CE application is designed as a graph of computation kernels, connected by data streams (the only data communication mechanism). Kernels are sensitive to events, and the overall graph can be reconfigured at runtime. This graph is expanded into a complete application dependency graph, optimized and dynamically scheduled (using a job queue) on the hardware platform by the runtime system.

The low-level code optimizations are left to the programmer, but optimized kernels can be easily added to the already provided library of functions and/or reused. Using SP@CE for streaming applications boosts productivity, but its restricted applicability domain diminishes its portability. Performance-wise, both the SPE runtime system and the SP@CE scheduler are competitive.

SP@CE is a fragmented-view model. Its design phase requires the applications to be expressed in streaming fashion, using kernels and data streams. Parallelization is based on components, which are typically kernels or agglomerations of kernels which work on the same data instance from a stream. Components are controllable at design time and can be resized and removed from or added to the application at runtime. Data layout is implicit, as it is automatically generated by the streaming discipline. Mapping and scheduling are solved dynamically by the runtime and optimized for data reuse. Optimizations at kernel level are allowed and encouraged, while data transfer optimizations are performed automatically.

Sequoia   Sequoia [10] is a model that requires the programmer to reason about a parallel application focusing on memory locality. A Sequoia application is a tree-like hierarchy of parametrized tasks; running tasks concurrently leads to parallelism. A tree has two different types of tasks: inner nodes, which spawn children threads, and leaf nodes, which run the computation itself. The task hierarchy has to be mapped on the memory hierarchy of the target machine by the programmer. Tasks run in isolation, using only their local memory, while data movement is exclusively done by passing arguments (no shared variables). One task can have multiple implementation versions, which can be used interchangeably; each implementation uses both application and platform parameters, whose values shall be fixed during the mapping phase. For the Cell/B.E. processor, all inner nodes run on the PPE, while the leaf nodes are executed by the SPEs. The PPE runs the main application thread and handles the SPE thread scheduling. Each SPE uses a single thread for the entire lifespan of the application, and it continuously waits, idle, for the PPE to asynchronously request the execution of a computation task.

As a generic model, Sequoia uses a fragmented algorithm view. Based on coarse-level granularity SPMD parallelism, the model requires applications to be designed using a divide-and-conquer approach. The granularity can be controlled at both compile time and runtime. Data transfers are implicit. The special feature of the model is its user-defined mapping and scheduling (by user file), which also results in implicit yet automated data layouts. Optimizations are allowed as different versions of the same kernel can be used interchangeably during the lifespan of the application.

Still, Sequoia has limited productivity, as the model is difficult to use for non -divide-and-conquer applications. The application and machine decompositions are independently reusable. The manual application-to-machine mapping offers a flexible environment for tuning and testing application performance.

Charm++ and the Offload API   Charm++ [19, 20] is an existing parallel programming model adapted to run on accelerator-based systems. A Charm++ program consists of a number of *chares* (i.e. the equivalents of tasks) distributed across the processors in the parallel machine. These chares can be dynamically created and destroyed at runtime and can communicate with each other using messages. For the Cell/B.E. processor, a chare can offload *work requests*, which are computation-intensive kernels to be accelerated by the SPEs. On the PPE side, the Offload API manages each work request, coordinating data movement to/from the SPE, execution and completion notifications. Each SPE runs an *SPE Runtime*, which handles the work requests it receives and optimizes their execution order.

Charm++ is a fragmented view-model, with coarse parallelism expressed by chares. The model supports both SPMD and MPMD. The granularity is controlled at design time, by defining the chares; data distribution is implicitly defined by the data usage of these chares, and data transfers are automated. The dynamic mapping and scheduling, together with the highly optimized data transfers, contribute to high performance potential.

OmpSs   OmpSs [3] addresses the programmability of heterogeneous architectures extending task-level parallelism of OpenMP with task dependencies. Based on pragmas, the model uses a source-to-source translator to separate the code in dedicated kernels for the different components of the heterogeneous system. The runtime system maintains a dynamic data dependency graph with all active tasks; furthermore, the runtime system schedules tasks to execution, preserving and optimizing the dependencies among tasks.

The system is based on incremental parallelization of a single-source code, allowing step-by-step restructuring and optimization, and a separation of the implementation from the platform-specific details (which are, of course, encapsulated in the runtime system). OmpSs is also portable, as the same code (typically, a sequential C/C++ or FORTRAN application with pragmas) runs on any machine where the back end is ported. Programmers may choose to apply platform-specific optimizations (i.e. design and implement platform-specific versions of the tasks), but they may also choose to ignore them, preserving portability at the expense of performance.

For heterogeneous systems, data transfers are transparently managed by the run time system. Other type of optimizations include locality-aware scheduling policies that reduce the amount of data that needs to be transferred or data prefetching. Additionally, OmpSs provides execution tracing, a mechanism included in the runtime system to allow performance analysis and debugging.

To summarize, OmpSs is a global-view model with coarse granularity, MPMD (and SPMD) parallelism, implicit data transfers, pragmas for data distribution and runtime-based dynamic mapping and scheduling. High-level optimizations (i.e. at the level of the sequential code) are not encouraged, to prevent them from interfering with the automated parallelization, but low-level (i.e. kernel-level) optimizations can and should be applied to improve the overall performance of the application.

Pattern-Based Models: OPL   Pattern-based models allow users to focus entirely on application analysis. An application is built as a composition of nested patterns. Once all these patterns are available for each platform, their composition, also a pattern, leads to a complete application. Pattern languages are composed from different classes of patterns, applied at different stages of application design. First, the high-level application structure is described in terms of structural patterns – its task graph is mapped on a collection of task-graph patterns – and computational patterns. Further, the tasks are mapped on existing computational patterns.

Once the parallel design of the application has been established, the algorithm strategies patterns are required – essentially, these patterns identify and exploit the application concurrency. The way the program and data are organized is specified by implementation strategies patterns, which are ways of implementing each algorithmic pattern. Finally, the low-level parallelism support, matching both the application and the target architecture, is included in the so-called parallel execution patterns.

To extend to new platforms, these languages have to implement/retarget the platform-specific pattern implementations to the new platforms. Based on the assumption that the number of patterns used often is limited to less than 20, the effort might not be very large. Overall, pattern-based models are very elegant, generic, systematic and allow feedback loops and incremental redesign. However, the first and last categories of patterns – the structural and the parallel execution – are not trivial to apply. Structural mistakes can significantly affect both productivity and performance.

One example of a pattern-based language is Our Pattern Language (OPL) [28], developed at Berkeley. OPL has five categories of patterns: (i) structural patterns, which describe the overall organization of the application and the way the computational elements that make up the application interact; (ii) computational patterns, which describe the essential classes of computations that make up the application; (iii) algorithm strategies, which define the high-level strategies to exploit concurrency; (iv) implementation strategies, which show how the program itself is organized and written; and (v) parallel execution patterns, which support the execution itself. Details on the way these patterns can be further detailed and used are presented in [18], but real implementation details are currently missing; therefore, we consider that the practical side of this solution is yet to be proven.

OpenCL   OpenCL [26, 27] was proposed as a standard in 2008 (by the Khronos group), aiming to tackle the platform diversity problem by proposing a common hardware model for all multicore platforms. The user programs this 'virtual' platform, and the resulting source code is portable on any OpenCL compliant platform.[2]

The OpenCL platform model consists of a host connected to one or more OpenCL compute devices. A compute device is divided into multiple compute units (CUs); CUs are divided into multiple processing elements (PEs); PEs perform the computations. Each PE can behave either as a SIMD or as a SPMD unit. The main difference between SIMD and SPMD is whether a kernel is executed concurrently on multiple PEs each with its own data and a shared program counter or each with its own data but its program counter. In the SIMD case all PEs execute a strictly identical set of instructions which cannot be always true for the SPMD case due to possible branching in a kernel. Each OpenCL application runs on a host according to the hosting platform models and submits commands from the host to be executed on the PEs within a device.

An OpenCL program has two parts: the compute kernels that will be executed on one or more OpenCL devices and a host program that defines the context for the kernels and initiates and manages their execution.

Kernels can run either in order or out of order, depending on the parameters passed to the system when submitting the kernel for execution. Events allow checking the status of outstanding kernel execution requests and other runtime requests. The execution domain of a kernel is defined by an N-dimensional computation domain. This lets the system know how large of a problem the user would like the kernel to be applied to. Each element in the execution domain is a work item, and

---

[2]Currently (July 2010), these devices have hardware drivers and compiler back ends: ATI's and NVIDIA's GPUs, AMD's multicores, and the Cell/B.E.

OpenCL provides the ability to group together work-items into work-groups for synchronization and communication purposes.

OpenCL defines a multilevel shared memory model, featuring four distinct memory spaces: private, local, constant and global. Depending on the hardware memory subsystem, different memory spaces are allowed to be collapsed together. Private memory is memory that can only be used by a single CU. This is similar to registers in a single CU or a single CPU core. Local memory is memory that can be used by the work-items in a work-group. This is similar to the local data share that is available on the current generation of AMD GPUs. Constant memory is memory that can be used to store constant data for read-only access by all of the CUs in the device during the execution of a kernel. The host processor is responsible for allocating and initializing the memory objects that reside in this memory space. This is similar to the constant caches that are available on AMD GPUs. Finally, global memory is memory that can be used by all the CUs on the device. This is similar to the off-chip GPU memory that is available on AMD GPUs.

OpenCL supports two main programming models: the data-parallel programming model and the task parallel programming model. Hybrids of the two models are allowed, though the driving one remains the data parallel. OpenCL maps data to work-items and work-items to work-groups. The data-parallel model is implemented in two possible ways. The first or explicit model lets the programmer define both the number of work-items to execute in parallel and how work-items are divided among work-groups. The second (implicit) model requires the programmer to specify the number of work-items but OpenCL to manage the division into work-groups.

In summary, OpenCL provides a fragmented view of the algorithm (it needs to express it in kernels). The model supports both data and task parallelism, at virtually any granularity set by the programmer. Mapping is done in two steps: it is explicit between the application and the virtual OpenCL platform and implicit (i.e. performed by the driver) between the OpenCL platform and the real hardware. Following this final mapping, scheduling is automatic and transparent to the user. OpenCL provides no data distribution constructs – all data transfers and mappings are done by coding. However, there are various efforts to improve on OpenCL's front end, and it is expected that data distribution would be addressed with priority.

Overall, despite its CUDA resemblance, we believe OpenCL is an application-centric model because of its approach to parallelization: while CUDA programmers need to think of their application as mapping on the NVIDIA hardware (thus expressing the code in platform-specific elements), OpenCL allows its users to express the application in parallelism units. In practical terms, for the moment, these parallelism items, as given by the OpenCL model, and the hardware parallelism, as given by the NVIDIA platforms, are very similar. However, OpenCL has multiple opportunities to raise the level of abstraction (i.e. by tuning the underlying virtual platform), while CUDA, in its current approach, is inseparable from the machine it runs on.

2.5 AN OVERVIEW OF MANY-CORE PROGRAMMING MODELS

In this section, we present the overall evaluation of all surveyed programming models. For this comprehensive evaluation, we use the features described in Section 2.3.3. Our results are presented in the form of several tables, each focused on one class of features: usability, design-level support and implementation-level support. Finally, we add a brief qualitative comparison of the model encountered so far from the perspective of their impact on programmability.

2.5.1 A Pragmatic View on Usability

Table 2.3 presents an overview of the practical, usability-related features of the surveyed models. 'Class' specifies the class of model: parallelism-centric, hardware-centric or application-centric (P, H and A, respectively). 'Platform' indicates the family of platform for which the model is available. 'Starts from' describes the starting point the model takes for solving a problem: when a model starts from an 'Algorithm,' programmers need to design a model-specific parallelization; when a model starts from any type of 'Sequential code,' the code needs to be available; finally, models that start from application specification require, in theory, only a high-level description of the application functionality. The column 'Action' lists the main actions required for parallelization in the studied model, and 'Performed by' specifies who is doing these actions. Finally, 'Implementation' describes the components used to 'build' the programming model: language, library, preprocessor, compiler and runtime (L, lib, pP, C and RT, respectively); NA stands for 'Not Applicable.'

Based on the results presented in the previous table, we make the following observations:

1. The starting point for most models is either an algorithm or simply sequential source code; a notable exception is OPL, which uses real application specification.

2. The user is always responsible for the design phase of the complete parallel application, while lower-level parallelization can be done/aided by tools.

3. In terms of usability, the surveyed models differ in the action the user must perform to design a parallel solution that matches the problem and the platform.

2.5.2 An Overview of Design-Support Features

Table 2.4 presents an overview of the design-support features offered by the programming models under survey. The column 'Algo view' shows whether the model provides a global or fragmented view of the algorithm (see Section 2.3.3). 'Parallelization support' shows how does the model expose parallelism, while the 'Parallelism' column lists the types of parallelism the programming model supports. The 'Granularity' column lists the granularity of the parallelism, and the 'Concurrency

Table 2.3   An overview of the usability-related features of the programming models.

Model	Type	Supported platform(s)	Starts from	Action	Performed by	Implementation
Threads	P	GPMCs,Cell	Algorithm	Specific parallelization	User	L,lib
MPI	P	GPMCs,Cell	Algorithm	Specific parallelization	User	lib,RT
OpenMP	P	GPMCs,Cell	Sequential code	Loop parallelization	User,compiler	lib,C
Cilk	P	GPMCs	Sequential code	Recursive division of work	Runtime	L,C,RT
TBB	H	GPMCs	Algorithm	Loop parallelization,	User,compiler	C,RT
				Data clustering (containers)	User	
ArBB	H	GPMCs	Algorithm	Data clustering	User	L,RT
CUDA	H	GPUs	Algorithm	Kernel isolation	User	L,lib,C
		(NVIDIA)	Sequential kernel code	Fine-grain parallelization	User	
Brook+	H	GPUs	Algorithm	Kernel isolation	User	L,lib,C
		(AMD/ATI)	Sequential kernel code	Fine-grain parallelization	User	
				Data clustering (in streams)	User	
PGI accelerate	H	GPUs	Sequential code	Kernel isolation	User	pP,C
		(NVIDIA)	Sequential kernel code	Fine-grain parallelization	Compiler	
ENZO	H	GPU+GPMC	Sequential code	Kernel isolation	User	pP,C
			Sequential kernel code	Fine-grain parallelization	Generator	
SDK	H	Cell	Algorithm	Specific parallelization	User	lib,C
ALF	H	Cell+GPMC	Algorithm	Task isolation	User	lib,C,RT,
			Sequential task code	Fine-grain parallelization	User	lib
CellSs	H	Cell	Sequential code	Task isolation	User	lib,RT
SP@CE	A	Cell,GPMCs	Algorithm	Filter,streams isolation	User	pP
			Sequential filter code	SPMD parallelization	RT	
Sequoia	A	Cell,GPMCs	Algorithm	Task definition and mapping	User	L,C
				Task interconnection	Compiler	
Charm++	A	Cell,GPMCs	Algorithm	Chares definition/isolation	User	lib,RT
			Chare code	SPMD parallelization	User	
OmpSs	A	Cell,GPMCs,GPUs	Sequential code	Task isolation	User	lib,RT
			Task code	Parallelization	User	
OPL	A	[any]	Application	Identify patterns	User	NA
(pattern-based)			Patterns	Pattern implementation	User	NA
OpenCL	A	Cell,GPMCs, GPUs	Algorithm	Kernel isolation	User	lib,C
			Sequential kernel code	Fine-grain parallelization	User	

units' lists the name of the concurrency units each model uses, while the 'Control' column specifies if and how does a model allow the user to control granularity at compile time or at runtime.

Finally, 'Data distribution' specifies if and how the data distribution needed for an application is specified in a programming model. If a model offers no explicit data layout primitives, we list 'none' in this column. For models with explicit data distributions (i.e. models where programmers need to explicitly define the data layout), we differentiate the models by the way the data layout can be specified.

Our results can be summarized in the following observations:

1. The diversity of the parallelization support values shows that multiple parallel solutions can be designed for the same application, by simply choosing a different parallelization dimension: some models focus on computation-based parallelization (see MPI, Cilk or OmPSs), while others focus on data-driven parallelization (see ArBB or Sequoia).

2. The concurrency units are fairly diverse, ranging for one data collection element (for models like OpenMP and CUDA) to whole functions (for threads and OmPSs) and tasks (MPI).

3. The granularity control is not strictly defined by any of the models – rather, they seem to rely on the underlying hardware for finding out its limitations.

Table 2.4 An overview of the design-support features that the models under survey have (see Section 2.3.3 for more explanations).

Model	Algo view	Parallelization support	Parallelism	Granularity	Concurrency units	Granularity control	Data distribution
Threads	Fragmented	In language; in library	MPMD,SPDM	Coarse, no restrictions	Functions	No constructs	No constructs, explicit in the code
MPI	Fragmented	In library	SPMD,MPMD	Coarse, no restrictions	Processes	No constructs	Implicit with pragmas
OpenMP	Global	Pragmas for loops	SPMD, MPMD	Coarse	Loop iterations, tasks	Constructs + automatic	
Cilk	Global	Keywords in language	Divide-and-conquer	Coarse	Recursive function	No constructs	
TBB	Global	Library constructs	SPMD, MFMD	Coarse	Tasks	Constructs + auto	
ArBB	Global	Data containers	SPMD	Fine	Items in data containers	Automatic	Explicit w
CUDA	Global	Kernels	SIMT	Fine	Data elements	No constructs	Grid/block size specification
Brook+	Fragmented	Streams	SPMD/SIMD	Fine	Data elements	Streams	Streams constru
PGI	Global	Pragmas for kernels, loops, data	SPMD, SIMT	Coarse (kernels), fine (threads)	Functions Functions	Implicit with pragmas	Implicit,
ENZO	Global	Pragmas for kernels loops	SPMD, SIMT SPMD, SIMT	Coarse (kernels), fine (threads)	Functions Functions	Explicit	Explicit,
SDK	Fragmented	Kernels	MPMD, SPMD	Coarse	Kernels	No constructs	
ALF	Fragmented	Hierarchy of kernels	SFMD, MPMD	Coarse	Kernels	No constructs	
CellSs	Global	Pragmas for kernels	MPMD, SPMD	Coarse	Kernels	Implicit with pra	
SP@CE	Fragmented	Streams, filters	Streaming, SPMD, MPMD	Coarse	Components	Resizing constructs	Special constructs
Sequoia	Fragmented	Tasks hierarchy	Divide-and-conquer SPMD	Coarse	Tasks	Versions	Configuration file
Charm++	Global	Chares	MPMD, SPMD	Coarse	Chares	Resizing constructs	I
OmpSs	Global	Pragmas for kernels	MPMD, SPMD	Coarse	Kernels	Constructs	E
OPL (pattern based)	Global	Patterns	Any	Coarse, fine	Any (pattern dependent)	NA	
OpenCL	Fragmented	Kernels	MPMD, SPMD	Coarse, fine	Kernels	No constructs	Patterns for explicit placement

4. Several models (SP@CE, Sequoia and Cilk) offer higher-level parallelism (streaming and divide-and-conquer). Most of the models that work at coarse granularity allow both SPMD and MPMD parallelism. Models that work at fine granularity focus on SIMD and/or SIMT parallelism and provide no support (other than the typical offload) for coarser parallelism.

5. The data distribution features of programming models are difficult to evaluate, as they are highly dependent on the chosen parallelism, on the assumed memory model (shared or distributed) and on the granularity of the concurrency units. Note, however, that most languages do not have explicit constructs for data layout (in the traditional way of HPF) but allow for simple data distribution techniques, either explicitly (indicated by the programmers using pragmas) or implicitly (generated by the SPMD/MPMD parallelization).

Overall, we conclude that there is significant overlap in the way various models approach parallel application design, but there are no two models, from the one presented here, that match completely. We also note that in terms of parallel design, application-centric models can offer more flexibility and higher-level abstractions than the hardware-centric ones (see Sequoia and OPL). An exception is OpenCL which, despite its application-centric view, is a low-level, fragmented model that requires significant algorithmic transformation in the design phase.

2.5.3 An Overview of Implementation-Support Features

Table 2.5 presents an overview of the implementation-support features that the studied models offer. 'Mapping' indicates how do programming models map the concurrency units of the parallel solution on the hardware platform. The notation is as follows: I and E stand for implicit and explicit, respectively; 'unitA:unitB' indicates what concurrency unit is mapped on what hardware parallelism unit. For example, 'E→ processes:nodes' means that the model requires explicit mapping of processes to nodes. 'Scheduling' indicates how are the parallel units scheduled for concurrent execution. Here, 'OS' stands for the operating system, 'HW' indicates mapping done by a hardware engine, 'RT' indicates dynamic mapping at runtime, 'C' indicates static mapping at compile time and 'user' indicates that mapping is left to be done explicitly by the user. The 'Data transfer' column indicates whether the data transfers have to be programmed or they are generated from the parallel design and the implicit/explicit mapping. The 'Comm/Sync' mentions how are the communication and synchronization among the concurrency units performed: I (implicit) is used when the model generate the required code, while E (explicit) is used to mark that users need to explicitly address the issue. Finally, 'Optimizations' includes information on how models address low-level optimizations.

The evaluation of the implementation support for the surveyed programming models leads us to the following observations:

1. Mapping and scheduling support are very hardware dependent. Therefore, the models map concurrency units with some sort of abstraction of an execution

Table 2.5 An overview of the implementation-support features that the models under survey offer (see Section 2.3.3 for more explanations).

Model	Mapping	Scheduling	Data transfer	Comm/Sync	Optimizations
Threads	E→ functions:threads	OS	NA (shared memory)	E/E	Allows
MPI	E→ processes:nodes	OS	Programmed	E/E	Allows
OpenMP	I→ iteration:threads (C)	OS	NA (shared memory)	I/I	Limits
Cilk	I→ tasks:threads (RT)	OS	NA (shared memory)	E/E	Limits
TBB	I→ tasks:threads (RT)	OS	NA	I/I	Allows
ArBB	I→ items:threads (RT)	OS	Generated	I/E	Limits
CUDA	I→ elements:threads	HW	Programmed	Host-device/E	Allows
Brook+	I→ elements:threads	HW	Generated	Host-device/E	Limits
PGI	I→ tasks:accelerators	RT	Generated	I/I	Limits
ENZO	I→ tasks:accelerators	RT	Generated	I/I	Limits
SDK	E→ kernels:threads	User	Programmed	E/E	Allows
ALF	E→ kernels:threads	RT	Generated	I/I	Supports
CellSs	I→ kernels:threads	RT	Generated	I/I	Limits
SP@CE	E→ components:threads	RT	Generated	I/I	Allows
Sequoia	E→ tasks:threads	User	Generated	I/I	Limits
Charm++	I→ chares:nodes	RT	Programmed	E/E	Supports
OmpSs	I→ kernels:threads	RT	Generated	I/I	Limits
OPL	E→ patterns:threads	User	Generated	Patterns	Preoptimized
OpenCL	E→ elements:threads	HW	Programmed	E/I	Supports

unit (typically a thread or a processor), allowing scheduling to work more or less independently with a unique abstraction. The exception is the Cell SDK – which requires the users to map and schedule the threads on the cores explicitly.

2. The models auto-generate the bulk data transfers inferred by mapping and scheduling – the exceptions are the native programming models (CUDA, SDK and OpenCL) which require these transfers to be explicitly programmed.

3. Communication and synchronization show the largest variety among the studied models: some models choose to leave these operations to be explicitly performed by the user, while others (especially higher-level models) prefer to hide these error-prone operations and generate them implicitly. Note that some many-core architectures (like the GPUs and the Cell) use multiple synchronization layers, with different performance consequences; for those, applications that require fine-grain synchronization (like linked lists or graph traversals) often need explicit synchronization and communication tricks, or they simply require different hardware targets.

4. Low-level optimizations are not really part of the programming model concerns – they are usually left to the user and/or to the compiler without any incentive from the programming model itself. The only minor exception is ENZO, which includes kernel code generators and auto tuning as part of the model.

2.5.4 Impact on Programmability

Table 2.6 presents a qualitative view on the way the models under study influence portability, performance and productivity and what is their impact on platform portability. The estimation is based on the assessments given by the programming model designers, the inspection and benchmarking of available sample codes (released as part of the models themselves), and independent application studies using various models and developed by medium and expert programmers (e.g. studies like [34, 36, 33]).

Table 2.6 A qualitative comparison of the surveyed programming models. For each feature, we use one of five qualifiers, $++$ (very good) to $--$ (very bad).

Model	Productivity	Portability	Performance	Programmability impact
Threads	$--$	$--$	$+$	$-$
MPI	$--$	$+$	$+$	$-$
OpenMP	$+$	$\sim$	$+$	$+$
Cilk	$+$	$-$	$+$	$\sim$
TBB	$\sim$	$-$	$+$	$-$
ArBB	$+$	$\sim$	$+$	$+$
CUDA	$\sim$	$-$	$++$	$\sim$
Brook+	$+$	$\sim$	$\sim$	$\sim$
PGI accelerate	$\sim$	$+$	$\sim$	$+$
ENZO	$+$	$-$	$+$	$+$
SDK	$--$	$--$	$++$	$--$
ALF	$+$	$\sim$	$+$	$\sim$
CellSs	$++$	$+$	$\sim$	$+$
SP@CE	$+$	$\sim$	$+$	$+$
OmpSs	$++$	$+$	$\sim$	$++$
Sequoia	$\sim$	$+$	$+$	$\sim$
Charm++	$\sim$	$\sim$	$+$	$\sim$
OPL (pattern-based)	$+$	$++$	$?$	$++$
OpenCL	$\sim$	$++$	$++$	$+$

This qualitative analysis leads us to the following observations:

1. None of the models we have studied seem to deteriorate the achievable performance of the (application, platform) pair. Even the usual suspects – the application-centric models, built for platform-agnostic parallel application development – allow users to tweak the code (or use preoptimized code) and gain the performance from low-level, hardware-specific optimizations.

2. In terms of productivity, some of the models are able to simplify the job of the programmer, while others make it slightly more difficult (e.g. SDK, TBB or even OpenCL), as they require significant changes at the algorithm level in order to make use of the abstractions that the programming model uses.

3. Most models do not score high for portability. The best cases are OPL (which has no real implementation, and therefore it is only evaluated on paper) and

OpenCL (which enables portability by using common platform models as virtual intermediate hardware) – these two models promise to be portable by construction. Models that score + are models based on runtime which are (or could be) easily ported on other architectures – this is the case of OpenMP, OmPSs and Sequoia. The other models, scoring ~ and below, might require not only changes in the back end of the programming model but also significant changes for the application parallel design or implementation. These models are not considered portable.

4. In terms of programmability impact, the few models which score below ~ should be avoided (unless very high performance is the overall goal of the application) – these are threads, MPI, SDK and TBB. Other models, such as CUDA, Brook, Sequoia, Charm++ and ALF are usable, but their programmability boost is not significant. Languages like OpenMP, ENZO, OmPSs and CellSs offer a significant boost to platform programmability, but they are all based on available sequential code – if such code is not available, writing it might become an expensive detour. OpenCL is a good alternative in case an application needs to be developed from scratch.

2.6 CONCLUDING REMARKS

Many-core processors are here to stay, bringing along a huge demand for parallel applications. The software community is (suddenly) faced with a large problem: virtually every application will have to run on a parallel machine, rather sooner than later. Trying to use native programming models for each platform or even each family of platforms might deliver the expected performance, but it will never deliver the required productivity. The alternative solution is to use high-level many-core programming models that are able to increase programmers' productivity and applications' portability, without affecting the achievable platform performance. Such models have a positive impact on platform programmability, ultimately leading to quicker many-core adoption and faster application development.

In this chapter, we presented a comprehensive set of many-core programming models belonging to three classes: parallelism-centric, hardware-centric and application-centric. For each class, we have presented several instances, briefly describing their architecture, parallelism model and functionality. Furthermore, to provide a clear overview of all these models, we focused on three categories of features: usability, design-support features and implementation-support features. We provide a clear overview of these features for all surveyed models and discuss our findings for each category of features. We show that the diversity of models covers a lot of design cases, but we were unable to find a model that excels for all categories. Therefore, choosing the matching platform(s) and programming model(s) remains an important first step when a new application needs a many-core port.

Finally, we have summarized all the results of our analysis in a qualitative analysis, aiming to determine how do these models respond to the challenges of portability, productivity and performance; our end goal was to determine how do these models impact platform programmability. We see that none of the studied models significantly deteriorate the achievable performance of the (application, platform) pair. However, only some of the models are able to simplify the job of the programmer, while others make it slightly more difficult (e.g. SDK, TBB or even OpenCL). In terms of portability, only OPL and OpenCL are portable by construction; others score reasonably well due to portable back ends. In terms of programmability impact, low-level programming models score pretty bad (but compensate with performance), models based on sequential code are very productive, and OpenCL is a good alternative in case an application needs to be developed from scratch.

Overall, we conclude that available programming models cover a large variety of feature and combinations thereof – in fact, we could not find a desirable combination of features that is not yet covered by an existing model. In this context, building new programming models from scratch does not seem entirely justified – we believe a more focused approach toward improving existing models (e.g. OpenCL, OPL, ENZO or Sequoia), port and runtime systems, compilers, and debugging/ profiling/analysis tools will give better results in the near future.

REFERENCES

1. Advanced Micro Devices Corporation (AMD). *AMD Stream Computing User Guide*, August 2008. Revision 1.1.

2. E. Ayguade, N. Copty, A. Duran, J. Hoeflinger, Y. Lin, F. Massaioli, X. Teruel, P. Unnikrishnan, and G. Zhang. The design of openmp tasks. *IEEE Transactions on Parallel and Distributed Systems*, 20:404–418, 2009.

3. E. Ayguade, R. M. Badia, P. Bellens, D. Cabrera, A. Duran, M. Gonzalez, F. Igual, D. Jimenez-Gonzalez, J. Labarta, L. Martinell, X. Martorell, R. Mayo, J. M. Perez, J. Planas, and E. S. Quintana-Orti. Extending OpenMP to Survive the heterogeneous multi-core era. *International Journal of Parallel Programming,* 38(5–6):440–459, June 2010.

4. P. Bellens, J. M. Perez, R. M. Badia, and J. Labarta. CellSS: A programming model for the Cell BE architecture. In *SC'06*. IEEE Computer Society Press, November 2006.

5. N. Blachford. Programming The Cell Processor (white paper). http://www.blachford.info/computer/articles/CellProgramming1.html.

6. I. Buck, T. Foley, D. Horn, J. Sugerman, K. Fatahalian, M. Houston, and P. Hanrahan. Brook for GPUs: Stream Computing on Graphics Hardware. In *ACM Transactions on Graphics, Proceedings of SIGGRAPH 2004*, pages 777–786, Los Angeles, California, August 2004.

7. Z. Budimlic, A. Chandramowlishwaran, K. Knobe, G. Lowney, V. Sarkar, and L. Treggiari. Multi-core implementations of the Concurrent Collections programming model. In *CPC*. Springer, January 2009.

8. A. Buttari, P. Luszczek, J. Kurzak, J. Dongarra, and G. Bosilca. A rough guide to scientific computing on the playstation 3. Technical Report UT-CS-07-595, ICL, University of Tennessee Knoxville, May 2007.

9. B. L. Chamberlain, D. Callahan, and H. P. Zima. Parallel programmability and the chapel language. *International Journal of High Performance Computing Applications*, 21(3):291–312, 2007.

10. K. Fatahalian, T. J. Knight, M. Houston, M. Erez, D. Reiter Horn, L. Leem, J. Young Park, M. Ren, A. Aiken, W. J. Dally, and P. Hanrahan. Sequoia: Programming the memory hierarchy. In *SC'06*. ACM Press, November 2006.

11. M. J. Flynn. Some computer organizations and their effectiveness. *IEEE Transactions on computers*, C-21(9):948 –960, 1972.

12. A. Ghuloum, T. Smith, G. Wu, X. Zhou, J. Fang, P. Guo, B. So, M. Rajagopalan, Y. Chen, and B. Chen. Future-proof data parallel algorithms and software on intel multi-core architecture. *Intel Technology Journal*, 11(4):333–348, 2007.

13. IBM. *Cell Broadband Engine Programming Tutorial*, 2.0 edition, December 2006.

14. Intel. Concurrent collections for C/C++. `http://software.intel.com/en-us/articles/intel-concurrent-collections-for-cc`.

15. Intel. Intel Array Building Blocks. `http://software.intel.com/en-us/articles/intel-array-building-blocks/`.

16. Intel. Intel Threading Building Blocks. `http://threadingbuildingblocks.org/`.

17. J. A. Kahle, M. N. Day, H. P. Hofstee, C. R. Johns, T. R. Maeurer, and D. Shippy. Introduction to the cell multiprocessor. *IBM Journal of Research and Development*, 49 (4-5):589–604, July–September 2005.

18. K. Keutzer and T. Mattson. Opl: Our pattern language. `http://parlab.eecs.berkeley.edu/wiki/_media/patterns/opl-new_with_appendix-20091014.pdf`, October 2009.

19. D. Kunzman. CHARM++ on the Cell Processor. Master's thesis, Dept. of Computer Science, University of Illinois, 2006.

20. D. M. Kunzman and L. V. Kalé. Towards a framework for abstracting accelerators in parallel applications: experience with cell. In *SC '09: Proceedings of the Conference on High Performance Computing Networking, Storage and Analysis*, pages 1–12. ACM, New York, NY, USA, 2009.

21. LLNL. POSIX Threads Programming. `https://computing.llnl.gov/tutorials/pthreads`

22. Message Passing Interface Forum. MPI: A Message-Passing Interface standard, 1994.

23. MIT. The Cilk Project. `http://supertech.csail.mit.edu/cilk/`.

24. M. Nijhuis, H. Bos, and H. Bal. Supporting reconfigurable parallel multimedia applications. In *EuroPAR'06*, August 2006.

25. nVidia. *CUDA-Compute Unified Device Architecture Programming Guide*, 2007.

26. OpenCL committee. OpenCL 1.0 standard. `http://www.khronos.org/opencl`, December 2008.

27. OpenCL committee/KHRONOS Group. OpenCL 1.1 standard. `http://www.khronos.org/opencl`, June 2010.

28. ParLab – UC Berkeley. Our pattern language. `http://parlab.eecs.berkeley.edu/wiki/patterns/patterns`.

29. PathScale. ENZO 2011. http://www.pathscale.com/enzo.

30. pgas.org. PGAS: Partitioned Global Address Space. http://www.pgas.org.

31. J. Reinders. *Intel Threading building blocks.* O'Reilly & Associates, Inc. Sebastopol, CA, USA, 2007.

32. The Portland Group. *PGI Fortran & C Accelerator Programming Model white paper*, version 1.2 edition, March 2010. http://www.pgroup.com/lit/whitepapers/pgi_accel_prog_model_1.2.pdf.

33. A. S. van Amesfoort, A. L. Varbanescu, H. J. Sips, and R. V. van Nieuwpoort. Evaluating multi-core platforms for HPC data-intensive kernels. In *CF '09: Proceedings of the 6th ACM conference on Computing frontiers*, pages 207–216. ACM, New York, NY, USA, May 2009.

34. R. V. van Nieuwpoort and J. W. Romein. Using many-core hardware to correlate radio astronomy signals. In *ICS*, pages 440–449. ACM, March 2009.

35. A. L. Varbanescu, M. Nijhuis, A. Gonzalez-Escribano, H. J. Sips, H. Bos, and H. A. Bal. SP@CE – an SP-based programming model for consumer electronics streaming applications. In *LCPC 2006*, LNCS 4382. Springer, November 2006.

36. A. L. Varbanescu, A. S. van Amesfoort, T. Cornwell, G. van Diepen, R. van Nieuwpoort, B. G. Elmegreen, and H. Sips. Building high-resolution sky images using the Cell/B.E. *Scientific Programming*, 17(1–2):113–134, 2009.

37. W. Zhao and Z. Wang. Scaleupc: A upc compiler for multi-core systems. In *Proceedings of the Third Conference on Partitioned Global Address Space Programing Models*, PGAS '09, pages 11:1–11:8. ACM, New York, NY, USA, 2009.

38. Y. Zheng. Optimizing UPC programs for multi-core systems. *Scientific Programming*, 18(3–4):183–191, February 2011.

39. Y. Zheng, F. Blagojevic, D. Bonachea, P. H. Hargrove, S. Hofmeyr, C. Iancu, S.-J. Min, and K. Yelick. Getting multicore performance with UPC. In *SIAM* In *SIAM Conference on Parallel Processing for Scientific Computing*, February 2010.

CHAPTER 3

LOCK-FREE CONCURRENT DATA STRUCTURES

DANIEL CEDERMAN, ANDERS GIDENSTAM, PHUONG HA, HÅKAN SUNDELL,
MARINA PAPATRIANTAFILOU AND PHILIPPAS TSIGAS

Algorithms + Data Structures = Programs

—Niklaus Wirth

3.1 INTRODUCTION

Concurrent data structures are the data sharing side of parallel programming. Data structures not only give the means to the program to store data but also provide operations to the program to access and manipulate these data. These operations are implemented through algorithms that have to be efficient. In the sequential setting, data structures are crucially important for the performance of the respective computation. In the parallel programming setting, their importance becomes more crucial because of the increased use of data and resource sharing for utilizing parallelism. In parallel programming, computations are split into subtasks in order to introduce parallelization at the control/computation level. To utilize this opportunity of concurrency, subtasks share data and various resources (dictionaries, buffers and so forth). This makes it possible for logically independent programs to share various resources and data structures. In a subtask that wants to update a data structure, say, add an element into a dictionary, that operation may be logically independent of other subtasks that use the same dictionary.

Concurrent data structure designers are striving to maintain consistency of data structures while keeping the use of mutual exclusion and expensive synchronization to a minimum, in order to prevent the data structure from becoming a sequential bottleneck. Maintaining consistency in the presence of many simultaneous updates is a complex task. Standard implementations of data structures are based on locks in order to avoid inconsistency of the shared data due to concurrent modifications. In simple terms, a single lock around the whole data structure may create a bottleneck in the program where all of the tasks serialize, resulting in a loss of parallelism because too few data locations are concurrently in use.   Deadlocks, priority inversion and convoying are also side effects of locking. The risk for deadlocks makes it hard to compose different blocking data structures since it is not always possible to know how closed source libraries do their locking. It is worth noting that in graphics processing units (GPUs), locks are not recommended for designing concurrent data structures. GPUs prior to the NVIDIA Fermi architecture do not have writable caches, so for those GPUs, repeated checks to see if a lock is available or not require expensive repeated accesses to the GPU's main memory. While Fermi GPUs do support writable caches, there is no guarantee that the thread scheduler will be fair, which can make it difficult to write deadlock-free locking code. OpenCL explicitly disallows locks for these and other reasons.

Lock-free implementations of data structures support concurrent access. They do not involve mutual exclusion and make sure that all steps of the supported operations can be executed concurrently. Lock-free implementations employ an optimistic conflict control approach, allowing several processes to access the shared data object at the same time. They suffer delays only when there is an actual conflict between operations that causes some operations to retry. This feature allows lock-free algorithms to scale much better when the number of processes increases.

An implementation of a data structure is called *lock-free* if it allows multiple processes/threads to access the data structure concurrently and also guarantees that at least one operation among those finishes in a finite number of its own steps regardless of the state of the other operations. A consistency (safety) requirement for lock-free data structures is *linearizability* [45], which ensures that each operation on the data appears to take effect instantaneously during its actual duration, and the effect of all operations is consistent with the object's sequential specification. Lock-free data structures offer several advantages over their blocking counterparts, such as being immune to deadlocks, priority inversion and convoying, and have been shown to work well in practice in many different settings [92, 84]. They have been included in Intel's threading building blocks framework [75], the NOBLE library [84] and the Java concurrency package [57] and will be included in the forthcoming parallel extensions to the Microsoft. NET framework [69]. They have also been of interest to designers of languages such as C++ [12] and Java [57].

This chapter has two goals. The first and main goal is to provide a sufficient background and intuition to help the interested reader to navigate in the complex research area of lock-free data structures. The second goal is to offer the programmer familiarity to the subject that will allow her to use truly concurrent methods.

The chapter is structured as follows: First we discuss the fundamental and commonly–supported synchronization primitives on which efficient lock-free data structures rely. Then we give an overview of the research results on lock-free data structures that appeared in the literature with a short summary for each of them. The problem of managing dynamically allocated memory in lock-free concurrent data structures and general concurrent environments is discussed separately. Following this is a discussion on the idiosyncratic architectural features of graphics processors that are important to consider when designing efficient lock-free concurrent data structures for this emerging area.

3.2 SYNCHRONIZATION PRIMITIVES

To synchronize processes efficiently, multi-/many-core systems usually support certain synchronization primitives. This section discusses the fundamental synchronization primitives, which typically read the value of a *single* memory word, modify the value and write the new value back to the word *atomically*.

3.2.1 Fundamental Synchronization Primitives

The definitions of the primitives are described in Figure 3.1, where x is a memory word, v, *old and new* are values and *op* can be operators *add*, *sub*, *or*, *and* and *xor*. Operations between angle brackets $\langle \rangle$ are executed atomically.

TAS(x) /* *test-and-set, init: $x \leftarrow 0$* */
$\quad \langle oldx \leftarrow x; x \leftarrow 1; \textbf{return } oldx; \rangle$

FAO(x, v) /* *fetch-and-op* */
$\quad \langle oldx \leftarrow x; x \leftarrow op(x, v); \textbf{return } oldx; \rangle$

CAS(x, old, new) /* *compare-and-swap* */
$\quad \langle \textbf{ if}(x = old) \; \{x \leftarrow new; \textbf{return}(true); \}$
$\quad \textbf{else return}(false); \rangle$

LL(x) /* *load-linked* */
$\quad \langle return \; the \; value \; of \; x \; so \; that$
$\quad it \; may \; be \; subsequently \; used$
$\quad with \; \textbf{SC} \; \rangle$

SC(x, v) /* *store-conditional* */
$\quad \langle \textbf{ if} \; (no \; process \; has \; written \; to \; x$
$\quad since \; the \; last \; \textbf{LL}(x)) \; \{x \leftarrow v;$
$\quad \textbf{return}(true)\};$
$\quad \textbf{else return}(false); \rangle$

Figure 3.1   Synchronization primitives.

Note that there is a problem called the *ABA problem* that may occur with the *Compare-And-Swap (CAS)* primitive. The reason is that the *CAS* operation cannot detect if a variable was read to be A and then later changed to B and then back to A by some concurrent processes. The *CAS* primitive will perform the update even though this might not be intended by the algorithm's designer. The *Load-Linked/ Store-Conditional (LL/SC)* primitives can instead detect any concurrent update on the variable between the time interval of an *LL/SC* pair, independent of the value of the update.

3.2.2 Synchronization Power

The primitives are classified according to their synchronization power or *consensus number* [42], which is, roughly speaking, the maximum number of processes for which the primitives can be used to solve a *consensus problem* in a fault tolerant manner. In the consensus problem, a set of n asynchronous processes, each with a given input, communicate to achieve an agreement on one of the inputs. A primitive with a consensus number n can achieve consensus among n processes even if up to $n - 1$ processes stop [93].

According to the consensus classification, read/write registers have consensus number 1, that is, they cannot tolerate any faulty processes in the consensus setting.

There are some primitives with consensus number 2 (e.g. *test-and-set (TAS)* and *fetch-and-op (FAO)*) and some with infinite consensus number (e.g. *CAS* and *LL/SC*). It has been proven that a primitive with consensus number n cannot implement a primitive with a higher consensus number in a system of more than n processes [42]. For example, the *TAS* primitive, whose consensus number is two, cannot implement the *CAS* primitive, whose consensus number is unbounded, in a system of more than two processes.

3.2.3 Scalability and Combinability

As many-core architectures with thousands of cores are expected to be our future chip architectures [5], synchronization primitives that can support scalable thread synchronization for such large-scale architectures are desired. In addition to synchronization power criterion, synchronization primitives can be classified by their scalability or *combinability* [55]. Primitives are combinable if their memory requests to the same memory location (arriving at a switch of the processor-to-memory interconnection network) can be combined into *only one* memory request. Separate replies to the original requests are later created from the reply to the combined request (at the switch). The combining technique has been implemented in the NYU Ultracomputer [30] and the IBM RP3 machine [73] and has been shown to be a scalable technique for large-scale multiprocessors to alleviate the performance degradation due to a synchronization 'hot spot' . The set of combinable primitives includes *TAS*, *FAO* (where *op* is an associative operation or boolean operation), blocking full–empty bits [55] and nonblocking full–empty bits [36]. For example, two consecutive requests *fetch-and-add*(x, a) and *fetch-and-add*(x, b) can be combined into a *single* request *fetch-and-add*$(x, a + b)$. When receiving a reply *oldx* to the combined request *fetch-and-add*$(x, a + b)$, the switch, at which the requests were combined, creates a reply *oldx* to the first request *fetch-and-add*(x, a) and a reply $(oldx + a)$ to the successive request *fetch-and-add* (x, b).

The CAS primitives are not combinable since the success of a $CAS(x, a, b)$ primitive depends on the current value of the memory location x. For m-bit locations (e.g. 64-bit words), there are 2^m possible values, and therefore, a combined request that represents $k\ CAS(x, a, b)$ requests, $k < 2^m$, must carry as many as k different checking-values a and k new values b. The LL/SC primitives are not combinable either since the success of an SC primitive depends on the state of its reservation bit at the memory location that has been set previously by the corresponding LL primitive. Therefore, a combined request that represents $k\ SC$ requests (from different processes/processors) must carry as many as k store values.

3.2.4 Multiword Primitives

Although the *single-word* hardware primitives are conceptually powerful enough to support higher-level synchronization, from the programmer's point of view, they are not as convenient as *multiword* primitives. The multiword primitives can be built in hardware [53, 16, 11] or in software (in a lock-free manner) using single-word hardware primitives [3, 20, 34, 51, 71, 79]. Sun's third-generation chip-multithreading (CMT) processor called Rock is the first processor supporting transactional memory in hardware [11]. The transactional memory is supported by two new instructions *checkpoint* and *commit*, in which *checkpoint* denotes the beginning of a transaction and *commit* denotes the end of the transaction. If the transaction succeeds, the memory accesses within the transaction take effect atomically. If the transaction fails, the memory accesses have no effect.

Another emerging construct is the advanced synchronization facility (ASF), an experimental AMD64 extension that AMD's Operating System Research Center develops to support lock-free data structures and software transactional memory [16]. ASF is a simplified hardware transactional memory in which all memory objects to be protected should be statically specified before transaction execution. Processors can protect and speculatively modify up to eight memory objects of cache line size. There is also research on new primitives aiming at identifying new efficient and powerful primitives, with the nonblocking full/empty bit (NB-FEB) being an example that was shown to be as powerful as CAS or LL/SC [36].

3.3 LOCK-FREE DATA STRUCTURES

The main characterization on which one can classify the various implementations of lock-free data structures available in the literature is what *abstract data type* that it intends to implement. For each abstract data type, there are usually numerous implementations, each motivated by some specific targeted purposes, where each implementation is characterized by the various properties that it fulfills to different amounts. As many of these properties are orthogonal, for each specific implementation, one or more properties are often strengthened at the cost of some others. Some of the most important properties that differentiate the various lock-free data structure implementations in the literature are:

Semantic fulfillments Due to the complexity of designing lock-free data structures, it might not be possible to support all operations normally associated with a certain abstract data type. Hence, some algorithms omit a subset of the normally required operations and/or support operations with a modified semantics.

Time complexity Whether an operation can terminate in a time (without considering concurrency) that is linearly or logarithmically related to, for example, the size of the data structure, can have significant impact on performance. Moreover, whether the maximum execution time can be determined at all or if it can be expected in relation to the number of concurrent threads is of significant importance to time-critical systems (e.g. real-time systems).

Scalability Scalability means showing some performance gain with increasing number of threads. Synchronization primitives are normally not scalable in themselves; therefore it is important to avoid unnecessary synchronization. Israeli and Rappoport [51] have defined the term *disjoint-access parallelism* to identify algorithms that do not synchronize on data that is not logically involved simultaneously in two or more concurrent operations.

Dynamic capacity In situations where it can be difficult to determine the maximum number of items that will be stored in a data structure, it is necessary that the data structure can dynamically allocate more memory when the current capacity is about to be exceeded. If the data structure is based on statically allocated storage, capacity is fixed throughout the lifetime of the data structure.

Space complexity Some algorithms can guarantee an upper bound of memory required, while some others can transiently need an indefinite amount depending on the concurrent operations' invocation order and can thus not be deterministically determined.

Concurrency limitations Due to the limitations (e.g. consensus number) of the chosen synchronization primitives, some or all operations might not allow more than a certain number of concurrent invocations.

Synchronization primitives Contemporary multicore and many-core systems typically only support single-word *CAS* or weak and nonnestable variants of *LL/SC* (cf. Section 3.2). However, many algorithms for lock-free data structure depend on more advanced primitives as, for example, double-word *CAS* (called e.g. *DCAS* or *CAS2*), ideal *LL/SC* or even more complex primitives. These algorithms then need (at least) one additional abstraction layer for actual implementation, where these more advanced primitives are implemented in software using another specific algorithm. The *LL/SC* primitives can be implemented, for example, by *CAS* [51, 3, 70, 52, 65]. Multiword *CAS* (called e.g. *MWCAS* or *CASN*) can be implemented, for example, by *CAS* [38, 82] or by *LL/SC* [51, 3, 79, 71, 34].

Reliability Some algorithms try to avoid the ABA problem by the means of, for example, version counters. As these counters are bounded and can overflow, there is a potential risk of the algorithm to actually perform incorrectly and possibly cause inconsistencies. Normally, by design this risk can be kept low enough that it fits for practical purposes, although the risk increases as the computational speed increases. Often, version counters can be removed altogether by the means of proper memory management.

Compatibility and Dependencies Some algorithms only work together with certain memory allocators and reclamation schemes, specific types (e.g. real time) of system-level process scheduler, or require software layers or semantic constructions only found in certain programming languages (e.g. Java).

3.3.1 Overview

The following sections include a systematic overview of the research result in the literature. For a more in-depth look and a case study in the design of a lock-free data structure and how it can be used in practice, we would like to refer the reader to our chapter in 'GPU Computing Gems' [10], which describes in detail how to implement a lock-free work-stealing deque and the reasoning behind the design decisions.

3.3.2 Producer–Consumer Collections

A common approach to parallelizing applications is to divide the problem into separate threads that act as either producers or consumers. The problem of synchronizing these threads and streaming of data items between them can be alleviated by utilizing a shared collection data structure.

Bag The bag abstract data type is a collection of items in which items can be stored and retrieved in any order. Basic operations are *Add* (add an item) and *TryRemoveAny* (remove an arbitrary chosen item). TryRemoveAny returns the item removed. Data structures with similar semantics are also called *buffer*, unordered collection, unordered queue, pool and pile in the literature.

All lock-free stacks, queues and deques implicitly implements the selected bag semantics. Afek et al. [1] presented an explicit pool data structure. It is lock-free, although not linearizable, utilizes distributed storage and is based on randomization to establish a probabilistic level of disjoint-access parallelism.

In [26, 27] a data structure called *flat sets* was introduced and used as a building block in the concurrent memory allocation service. This is a bag-like structure that supports lock-free insertion and removal of items as well as an 'interobject' operation, for moving an item from one flat set to another in a lock-free and linearizable manner, thus offering the possibility of combining data structures.

In [83] a lock-free bag implementation is presented; the algorithm supports multiple producers and multiple consumers, as well as dynamic collection sizes. To handle concurrency efficiently, the algorithm was designed to optimize for disjoint -access parallelism for the supported semantics.

Stack The stack abstract data type is a collection of items in which only the most recently added item may be removed. The latest added item is at the top. Basic operations are *Push* (add to the top) and *Pop* (remove from the top). Pop returns the item removed. The data structure is also known as a 'last-in, first-out' or LIFO buffer.

Treiber presented a lock-free stack (aka IBM freelist) based on linked lists, which was later efficiently fixed from the ABA problem by Michael [64]. Also

Valois [95] presented a lock-free implementation that uses the *CAS* atomic primitive. Hendler et al. [41] presented an extension where randomization and elimination are used for increasing scalability when contention is detected on the *CAS* attempts.

Queue   The queue abstract data type is a collection of items in which only the earliest added item may be accessed. Basic operations are *Enqueue* (add to the tail) and *Dequeue* (remove from the head). Dequeue returns the item removed. The data structure is also known as a 'first-in, first-out' or FIFO buffer.

Lamport [56] presented a lock-free (actually wait-free) implementation of a queue based on a static array, with a limited concurrency supporting only one producer and one consumer. Giacomoni et al. [23] presented a cache-aware modification which, instead of using shared head and tail indices, synchronizes directly on the array elements. Herman and Damian-Iordache [47] outlined a wait-free implementation of a shared queue for any number of threads, although nonpractical due to its high time complexity and limited capacity.

Gong and Wing [29] and later Shann et al. [78] presented a lock-free shared queue based on a cyclic array and the *CAS* primitive, though with the drawback of using version counters, thus requiring double-width *CAS* for storing actual items. Tsigas and Zhang [90] presented a lock-free extension of [56] for any number of threads where synchronization is done both on the array elements and the shared head and tail indices using *CAS*, and the ABA problem is avoided by exploiting two (or more) null values.

Valois [94, 95] makes use of linked lists in his lock-free implementation which is based on the *CAS* primitive. Prakash et al. [74] also presented an implementation using linked lists and the *CAS* primitive, although with the drawback of using version counters and having low scalability. Michael and Scott [68] presented a lock-free queue that is more efficient, synchronizing via the shared head and tail pointers as well via the next pointer of the last node. Moir et al. [72] presented an extension where elimination is used as a back-off strategy when contention on *CAS* is noticed, although elimination is only possible when the queue contains very few items. Hoffman et al. [48] take another approach for a back-off strategy by allowing concurrent *Enqueue* operations to insert the new node at adjacent positions in the linked list if contention is noticed. Gidenstam et al. [28] combine the efficiency of using arrays and the dynamic capacity of using linked lists, by providing a lock-free queue based on linked lists of arrays, all updated using *CAS* in a cache-aware manner.

Deque   The deque (or doubly ended queue) abstract data type is a combination of the stack and the queue abstract data types. The data structure is a collection of items in which the earliest as well as the latest added item may be accessed. Basic operations are *PushLeft* (add to the head), *PopLeft* (remove from the head), *PushRight* (add to the tail) and *PopRight* (remove from the tail). PopLeft and PopRight return the item removed.

Large efforts have been put on the work on so-called work-stealing deques. These data structures only support three operations and with a limited level of concurrency and are specifically aimed for scheduling purposes. Arora et al. [4] presented a lock-free work-stealing deque implementation based on the *CAS* atomic primitive. Hendler et al. [40] improved this algorithm to also handle dynamic sizes.

Several lock-free implementations of the deque abstract data type for general purposes, although based on the nonavailable *CAS2* atomic primitive, have been published in the literature [31, 2, 13, 58, 6]. Michael [63] presented a lock-free deque implementation based on the *CAS* primitive, although not supporting any level of disjoint-access parallelism. Sundell and Tsigas [88] presented a lock-free implementation that allows both disjoint-access parallelism and dynamic sizes using the standard *CAS* atomic primitive.

Priority Queue   The priority queue abstract data type is a collection of items which can efficiently support finding the item with the highest priority. Basic operations are *Insert* (add an item), *FindMin* (finds the item with minimum (or maximum) priority) and *DeleteMin* (removes the item with minimum (or maximum) priority). DeleteMin returns the item removed.

Israeli and Rappoport [50] have presented a wait-free algorithm for a shared priority queue that requires the nonavailable multiword *LL/SC* atomic primitives. Greenwald [31] has presented an outline for a lock-free priority queue based on the nonavailable *CAS2* atomic primitive. Barnes [7] presented an incomplete attempt for a lock-free implementation that uses atomic primitives available on contemporary systems. Sundell and Tsigas [87] presented the first lock-free implementation of a priority queue based on skip lists and the *CAS* atomic primitive.

3.3.3   Lists

The list abstract data type is a collection of items where two items are related only with respect to their relative position to each other. The data structure should efficiently support traversals among the items. Depending on what type of the underlying data structure, for example, *arrays* or *linked lists*, different strengths of traversal functionality are supported.

Array   List implementations based on the fundamental array data structure can support traversals to absolute index positions. Higher-level abstractions as extendable arrays are in addition supporting stack semantics. Consequently, the array abstract data type would support the operations *ReadAt* (read the element at index), *WriteAt* (write the element at index), *Push* (add to the top) and *Pop* (remove from the top). Pop returns the item removed.

A lock-free extendable array for practical purposes has been presented by Dechev et al. [12].

Linked List   In a concurrent environment with list implementations based on linked lists, traversals to absolute index positions are not feasible. Consequently, traversals are only supported relatively to a current position. The current position is maintained by the cursor concept, where each handle (i.e. thread or process) maintains one independent cursor position. The first and last cursor positions do not refer to real items but are instead used as end markers, that is, before the first item or after the last item. Basic operations are *InsertAfter* (add a new item after the current), *Delete* (remove the current item), *Read* (inspect the current item), *Next* (traverse to the item after the current) and *First* (traverse to the position before the first item). Additional operations are *InsertBefore* (add a new item before the current), *Previous* (traverse to the item before the current) and *Last* (traverse to the position after the last item).

Lock-free implementations of the singly linked list based on the *CAS* atomic primitive and with semantics suitable for the dictionary abstract type rather than the list have been presented by Harris [39], Michael [61] and Fomitchev and Ruppert [18]. Greenwald [32] presented a doubly linked list implementation of a dictionary based on the nonavailable *CAS2* atomic primitive. Attiya and Hillel [6] presented a *CAS2*-based implementation that also supports disjoint-access parallelism. Valois [95] outlined a lock-free doubly linked list implementation with all list semantics except delete operations. A more general doubly linked list implementation supporting general list semantics was presented by Sundell and Tsigas [88].

3.3.4   Sets and Dictionaries

The set abstract data type is a collection of special items called *keys*, where each key is unique and can have at most one occurrence in the set. Basic operations are *Add* (adds the key), *ElementOf* (checks if key is present) and *Delete* (removes the key).

The dictionary abstract data type is a collection of items where each item is associated with a unique key. The data structure should efficiently support finding the item associated with the specific key. Basic operations are *Insert* (add an item associated with a key), *Find* (finds the item associated with a certain key) and *Delete* (removes the item associated with a certain key). Delete returns the item removed. In concurrent environments, an additional basic operation is the *Update* (reassign the association of a key with another item) operation.

Implementations of sets and dictionaries are often closely related in a way that most implementations of a set can be extended to also support dictionary semantics in a straightforward manner. However, the *Update* operation mostly needs specific care in the fundamental part of the algorithmic design to be linearizable. Nonblocking implementations of sets and dictionaries are mostly based on hash tables or linked lists as done by Valois [95]. The path using concurrent linked lists was improved by Harris [39]. Other means to implement sets and dictionaries are the skip list and tree data structures.

Skip List   Valois [95] outlined an incomplete idea of how to design a concurrent skip list. Sundell and Tsigas presented a lock-free implementation of a skip list in the scope of priority queues [85, 87] as well as dictionaries [86, 81] using the *CAS* primitive. Similar constructions have appeared in the literature by Fraser [19] and Fomitchev and Ruppert [18].

Hash Table   Michael [61] presented a lock-free implementation of the set abstract data type based on a hash table with its chaining handled by an improved linked list compared to [39]. To a large part, its efficiency is high thanks to the memory management scheme applied. The algorithm was improved by Shalev and Shavit [77] to also handle dynamic sizes of the hash table's underlying array data structure. Greenwald [32] has presented a dictionary implementation based on chained hash tables and the nonavailable *CAS2* atomic primitive.

Gao et al. [21] presented a lock-free implementation of the dictionary abstract data type based on a hash table data structure using open addressing. The hash table is fully dynamic in size, although its efficiency is limited by its relatively complex memory management.

Tree Tsay and Li [89] present an approach for designing lock-free implementations of a tree data structure using the *LL/SC* atomic primitives and extensive copying of data. However, the algorithm is not provided with sufficient evidence for showing linearizability. Ellen et al. [17] presented a lock-free implementation of the set abstract data type based on a binary tree data structure using the *CAS* atomic primitive. Spiegel and Reynolds [80] present a lock-free implementation of the set abstract data type based on a skip tree and the *CAS* atomic primitive.

3.4 MEMORY MANAGEMENT FOR CONCURRENT DATA STRUCTURES

The problem of managing dynamically allocated memory in a concurrent environment has two parts, keeping track of the free memory available for allocation and safely reclaim allocated memory when it is no longer in use, that is, memory allocation and memory reclamation.

3.4.1 Memory Allocation

A memory allocator manages a pool of memory (heap), for example, a contiguous range of addresses or a set of such ranges, keeping track of which parts of that memory are currently given to the application and which parts are unused and can be used to meet future allocation requests from the application. A traditional (such as the 'libc' malloc) general-purpose memory allocator is not allowed to move or otherwise disturb memory blocks that are currently owned by the application.

Some of the most important properties that distinguish memory allocators for concurrent applications in the literature are

Fragmentation To minimize fragmentation is to minimize the amount of free memory that cannot be used (allocated) by the application due to the size of the memory blocks.

False-sharing False sharing is when different parts of the same cache line are allocated to separate objects that end up being used by threads running on different processors.

Efficiency and scalability The concurrent memory allocator should be as fast as a good sequential one when executed on a single processor, and its performance should scale with the load in the system.

Here we focus on lock-free memory allocators, but there is also a considerable number of lock-based concurrent memory allocators in the literature.

Early work on lock-free memory allocation is the work on nonblocking operating systems by Massalin and Pu [60, 59] and Greenwald and Cheriton [33, 31].

Dice and Garthwaite [15] presented LFMalloc, a memory allocator based on the architecture of the hoard lock-based concurrent memory allocator [8] but with reduced use of locks. Michael [66] presented a fully lock-free allocator, also loosely based on the hoard architecture. Gidenstam et al. [26] presented NBmalloc, another lock-free memory allocator loosely based on the hoard architecture. NBmalloc is designed from the requirement that the first-remove-then-insert approach to moving references to large internal blocks of memory (superblocks) around should be avoided, and therefore introduces and uses a move operation that can move a reference between different internal data structures atomically. Schneider et al. [76] presented streamflow, a lock-free memory allocator that has improved performance over previous solutions due to allowing thread local allocations and deallocations without synchronization.

3.4.2 Memory Reclamation

To manage dynamically allocated memory in nonblocking algorithms is difficult due to overlapping operations that might read, change or *dereference* (i.e. follow) references to dynamically allocated blocks of memory concurrently. One of the most problematic cases is when a slow process dereferences a pointer value that it previously read from a shared variable. This dereference of the pointer value could occur an arbitrarily long time after the shared pointer holding that value was overwritten, and the memory designated by the pointer removed from the shared data structure. Consequently it is impossible to safely free or reuse the block of memory designated by this pointer value until we are sure that there are no such slow processes with pointers to that block.

There are several reclamation schemes in the literature with a wide and varying range of properties:

I. Safety of local references For local references, which are stored in private variables accessible only by one thread, to be safe, the memory reclamation scheme must guarantee that a dynamically allocated node is never reclaimed while there still are local references pointing to it.

II. Safety of shared references Additionally, a memory reclamation scheme could also guarantee that it is always safe for a thread to dereference any shared references located within a dynamic node the thread has a local reference to. Property I alone does not guarantee this, since for a node that has been deleted but cannot be reclaimed, yet any shared references within it could reference nodes that have been deleted and reclaimed since the node was removed from the data structure.

III. Automatic or explicit deletion A dynamically allocated node could either be reclaimed automatically when it is no longer accessible through any local or shared reference, that is, the scheme provides *automatic garbage collection*, or the user algorithm or data structure could be required to explicitly tell the memory reclama-

Table 3.1   Properties of different approaches to nonblocking memory reclamation.

	Property II	Property III	Property IV	Property V
Michael [62, 64]	No	Explicit	Yes	Yes
Herlihy et al. [44]	No	Explicit	Yes	No
Valois et al. [95, 67]	Yes	Automatic	No	Yes
Detlefs et al. [14]	Yes	Automatic	Yes	No
Herlihy et al. [43]	Yes	Automatic	Yes	No
Gidenstam et al. [24, 25]	Yes	Explicit	Yes	Yes
Fraser [19]	Yes	Explicit	Yes	Yes
Herlihy et al. [46]	Yes	Automatic	Integrated	Yes
Gao et al. [22]	Yes	Automatic	Integrated	Yes

tion scheme, when a node is removed from the active data structure and should be reclaimed as soon as it has become safe. While automatic garbage collection is convenient for the user, explicit deletion by the user gives the reclamation scheme more information to work with and can help to provide stronger guarantees, for example, bounds on the amount of deleted but yet unreclaimed memory.

IV. Requirements on the memory allocator Some memory reclamation schemes require special properties from the memory allocator, for example, that each allocable node has a permanent (i.e. for the rest of the system's lifetime) reference counter associated with it. Other schemes are compatible with the well-known and simple *allocate/free* allocator interface where the node has ceased to exist after the call to *free*.

V. Required synchronization primitives Some memory reclamation schemes are defined using synchronization primitives that few if any current processor architectures provide in hardware, for example, *double-word CAS*, which then have to be implemented in software often adding considerable overhead. Other schemes make do with *single-word CAS*, *single-word LL/SC* or even just reads and writes alone.

The properties of the memory reclamation schemes discussed here are summarized in Table 3.1. One of the most important is Property II, which many lock-free algorithms and data structures need. Among the memory reclamation schemes that guarantee Property II, we have the following ones, all based on reference counting: Valois et al. [95, 67], Detlefs et al. [14], Herlihy et al. [43] and Gidenstam et al. [24, 25] and the potentially blocking epoch-based scheme by Fraser [19].

On the other hand, for data structures that do not need Property II, for example, stacks, the use of a reclamation scheme that does not provide this property has significant potential to offer reduced overhead compared with the stronger schemes. Among these memory reclamation schemes, we have the nonblocking ones by Michael [62, 64] and Herlihy et al. [44].

Fully Automatic Garbage Collection.   A fully automatic garbage collector provides Property I, II and III with automatic deletion.

There are some lock-free garbage collectors in the literature. Herlihy and Moss presented a lock-free copying garbage collector in [46]. Gao et al. [22] presented a lock-free mark and sweep garbage collector, and Kliot et al. [54] presented a lock-free stack scanning mechanism for concurrent garbage collectors.

3.5   GRAPHICS PROCESSORS

Currently the two most popular programming environments for general-purpose computing for graphics processors are CUDA and OpenCL. Neither provides any direct support for locks, and it is unlikely that this will change in the future. Concurrent data structures that are used on graphics processors will therefore have to be lock-free.

While graphics processors share many features with conventional processors, and many lock-free algorithms can be ported directly, there are some differences that are important to consider, if one also wants to maintain or improve the scalability and throughput of the algorithms.

3.5.1   Data Parallel Model

A graphics processor consists of a number of multiprocessors that can execute the same instruction on multiple data, known as SIMD computing. Concurrent data structures are, as the name implies, designed to support multiple concurrent operations, but when used on a multiprocessor, they also need to support concurrent instructions within an operation. This is not straightforward, as most have been designed for scalar processors. Considering that SIMD instructions play an instrumental role in the parallel performance offered by the graphics processor, it is imperative that this issue be addressed.

Graphics processor has a wide memory bus and a high memory bandwidth, which makes it possible to quickly transfer data from the memory to the processor and back. The hardware is also capable of coalescing multiple small memory operations into a single large atomic memory operation. As a single large memory operation can be performed faster than many small, this should be taken advantage of in the algorithmic design of the data structure.

The cache in graphics processors is smaller than on conventional SMP processors and in many cases nonexistent. The memory latency is instead masked by utilizing thousands of threads and by storing data temporally in a high-speed multiprocessor local memory area. The high number of threads reinforces the importance of the data structure being highly scalable.

The scheduling of threads on a graphics processor is commonly being performed by the hardware. Unfortunately, the scheme used is often undocumented; thus there is no guarantee that it will be fair. This makes the use of algorithms with blocking behavior risky. For example, a thread holding a lock could be indefinitely swapped out in favor of another thread waiting for the same lock, resulting in a livelock situation. Lock-freeness is thus a must.

Of a more practical concern is the fact that a graphics processor often lacks stacks, making recursive operations more difficult. The lack of a joint address space between the GPU and the CPU also complicates the move of data from the CPU to the graphics processor, as all pointers in the data structure have to be rebased when moved to a new address.

3.5.2 New Algorithmic Design

The use of SIMD instructions means that if multiple threads write to the same memory location, only one (arbitrary) thread can succeed. Thus, allowing threads that will be combined to an SIMD unit by the hardware to concurrently try to enqueue an item to the same position in a queue will with all likelihood be unnecessarily expensive, as only one thread can succeed in enqueing its item. Instead, by first combining the operations locally and then trying to insert all elements in one step, this problem can be avoided. This is a technique used by XMalloc, a lock-free memory allocator for graphics processors [49]. On data structures with more disjoint memory access than a queue, the problem is less pronounced, as multiple operations can succeed concurrently if they access different parts of the memory.

An example of a way to take advantage of the SIMD instructions and memory coalescing is to allow each node in a tree to have more children. Allowing a node in a tree to have more children will have the effect of making the tree shallower and lower the number of nodes that needs to checked when searching for an item. As a consequence, the time spent in each node will increase, but with coalesced memory access and SIMD instructions, this increase in time spent can be limited by selecting the number of children to suit the SIMD instruction size. The node can then be read in a single-memory operation, and the correct child can be found using just two SIMD compare instructions.

Another suggestion is to use memory coalescing to implement lazy operations, where larger read and write operations replace a percentage of expensive CAS operations. An array-based queue, for example, does not need to update its tail pointer using CAS every time an item is inserted. Instead it could be updated every x:th operation, and the correct tail could be found by quickly traversing the array using large memory reads and SIMD instructions, reducing the traversal time to a low static cost. This type of lazy updating was used in the queue by Tsigas and Zhang [91].

The coalescing memory access mechanism also directly influences the synchronization capabilities of the graphics processor. It has, for example, been shown that it can be used to facilitate wait-free synchronization between threads, without the need of synchronization primitives other than reads and writes [35, 37].

When it comes to software-controlled load balancing, there have been experiments made comparing the built-in hardware scheduler with a software managed work-stealing approach [9]. It was shown that lock-free implementations of data structures worked better than lock based and that lock-free work stealing could outperform the built-in scheduler.

The lack of a stack can be a significant problem for data structures that require recursive helping for lock-freeness. While it is often possible to rewrite recursive code to work iteratively instead, it requires that recursive depth can be bounded to lower the amount of memory that needs to be allocated.

REFERENCES

1. Y. Afek, G. Korland, M. Natanzon, and N. Shavit. Scalable producer-consumer pools based on elimination-diffraction trees. In *Euro-Par 2010*, volume 6272 of *Lecture Notes in Computer Science*, pages 151–162. Springer, 2010.

2. O. Agesen, D. Detlefs, C. H. Flood, A. Garthwaite, P. Martin, N. Shavit, and G. L. Steele Jr. DCAS-based concurrent deques. In *ACM Symposium on Parallel Algorithms and Architectures*, pages 137–146, 2000.

3. J. H. Anderson and M. Moir. Universal constructions for multi-object operations. In *Proceedings of the 14th Annual ACM Symposium on the Principles of Distributed Computing*, August 1995.

4. N. S. Arora, R. D. Blumofe, and C. G. Plaxton. Thread scheduling for multiprogrammed Multiprocessors. In *ACM Symposium on Parallel Algorithms and Architectures*, pages 119–129, 1998.

5. K. Asanovic, R. Bodik, B. C. Catanzaro, J. J. Gebis, P. Husbands, K. Keutzer, D. A. Patterson, W. L. Plishker, J. Shalf, S. W. Williams, and K. A. Yelick. The Landscape of Parallel Computing Research: A View from Berkeley. *TR No. UCB/EECS-2006-183, University of California, Berkeley*, 2006.

6. H. Attiya and E. Hillel. Built-in coloring for highly-concurrent doubly-linked lists. In *Proceedings of the 20th International Symposium of Distributed Computing*, pages 31–45, 2006.

7. G. Barnes. Wait-Free Algorithms for Heaps. Technical report, Computer Science and Engineering, University of Washington, February 1992.

8. E. Berger, K. McKinley, R. Blumofe, and P. Wilson. Hoard: A scalable memory allocator for multithreaded applications. In *9th International Conference on Architectural Support for Programming Languages and Operating Systems*, pages 117–128, November 2000.

9. D. Cederman and P. Tsigas. On dynamic load balancing on graphics processors. In *Proceedings of the 23rd ACM SIGGRAPH/EUROGRAPHICS symposium on Graphics hardware*, pages 57–64, 2008.

10. D. Cederman and P. Tsigas. Dynamic load balancing using work-stealing. In W.-M. Hwu, editor, *GPU Computing Gems Jade Edition*. Morgan Kaufmann, 2011.

11. S. Chaudhry, R. Cypher, M. Ekman, M. Karlsson, A. Landin, S. Yip, H. Zeffer, and M. Tremblay. Rock: A high-performance sparc CMT processor. *IEEE Micro*, 29(2):6 –16, 2009.

12. D. Dechev, P. Pirkelbauer, and B. Stroustrup. Lock-free dynamically resizable arrays. In *Proceedings of the 10th International Conference on Principles of Distributed Systems*, Lecture Notes in Computer Science, pages 142–156. Springer Verlag, 2006.

13. D. Detlefs, C. H. Flood, A. Garthwaite, P. Martin, N. Shavit, and G. L. Steele Jr. Even better DCAS-based concurrent deques. In *International Symposium on Distributed Computing*, pages 59–73, 2000.

14. D. L. Detlefs, P. A. Martin, M. Moir, and G. L. Steele, Jr. Lock-free reference counting. In *Proceedings of the 20th annual ACM symposium on Principles of Distributed Computing*, pages 190–199. ACM, 2001.

15. D. Dice and A. Garthwaite. Mostly lock-free malloc. In *Proceedings of the 3rd International Symposium on Memory Management*, pages 163–174. ACM Press, 2002.

16. S. Diestelhorst and M. Hohmuth. Hardware acceleration for lock-free data structures and software transactional memory. In *Proceedings of the Workshop on Exploiting Parallelism with Transactional Memory and other Hardware Assisted Methods*, pages 1–8, 2008.

17. F. Ellen, P. Fatourou, E. Ruppert, and F. van Breugel. Non-blocking binary search trees. In *Proceeding of the 29th ACM SIGACT-SIGOPS symposium on Principles of Distributed Computing*, pages 131–140. ACM, 2010.

18. M. Fomitchev and E. Ruppert. Lock-free linked lists and skip lists. In *Proceedings of the 23rd annual symposium on Principles of Distributed Computing*, pages 50–59, 2004.

19. K. A. Fraser. *Practical Lock-Freedom*. PhD thesis, University of Cambridge, 2003.

20. K. Fraser and T. Harris. Concurrent programming without locks. *ACM Transactions on Computer Systems*, 25, May 2007.

21. H. Gao, J. F. Groote, and W. H. Hesselink. Lock-free dynamic hash tables with open addressing. *Distributed Computing*, 18(1):21–42, 2005.

22. H. Gao, J. F. Groote, and W. H. Hesselink. Lock-free parallel and concurrent garbage collection by Mark&Sweep. *Science of Computer Programming*, 64(3):341–374, 2007.

23. J. Giacomoni, T. Moseley, and M. Vachharajani. Fastforward for efficient pipeline parallelism: a cache-optimized concurrent lock-free queue. In *Proceedings of the 13th ACM SIGPLAN Symposium on Principles and practice of parallel programming*, pages 43–52. ACM, 2008.

24. A. Gidenstam, M. Papatriantafilou, H. Sundell, and P. Tsigas. Efficient and reliable lock-free memory reclamation based on reference counting. In *Proceedings of the 8th International Symposium on Parallel Architectures, Algorithms and Networks, pages 202–207. IEEE, 2005.

25. A. Gidenstam, M. Papatriantafilou, H. Sundell, and P. Tsigas. Efficient and reliable lock-free memory reclamation based on reference counting. *IEEE Transactions on Parallel and Distributed Systems*, 20(8):1173–1187, 2009.

26. A. Gidenstam, M. Papatriantafilou, and P. Tsigas. Allocating memory in a lock-free manner. In *Proceedings of the 13th Annual European Symposium on Algorithms*, pages 329–242. LNCS vol. 3669, Springer Verlag, 2005.

27. A. Gidenstam, M. Papatriantafilou, and P. Tsigas. NBmalloc: Allocating memory in a lock-free manner. *Algorithmica*, 58:304–338, 2010.

28. A. Gidenstam, H. Sundell, and P. Tsigas. Cache-aware lock-free queues for multiple producers/consumers and weak memory consistency. In *Proceedings of the 14th International Conference on Principles Of Distributed Systems*, pages 302–317, 2010.

29. C. Gong and J. M. Wing. A Library of Concurrent Objects and Their Proofs of Correctness. Technical Report CMU-CS-90-151, Computer Science Department, Carnegie Mellon University, 1990.

30. A. Gottlieb, R. Grishman, C. P. Kruskal, K. P. McAuliffe, L. Rudolph, and M. Snir. The NYU ultracomputer–designing a MIMD, shared-memory parallel machine (Extended Abstract). In *Proceedings of the 9th annual symposium on Computer Architecture*, ISCA '82, pages 27–42. IEEE Computer Society Press, 1982.

31. M. Greenwald. *Non-Blocking Synchronization and System Design*. PhD thesis, Stanford University, 1999.

32. M. Greenwald. Two-handed emulation: how to build non-blocking implementations of complex data-structures using DCAS. In *Proceedings of the 21st annual symposium on Principles of Distributed Computing*, pages 260–269. ACM Press, 2002.

33. M. Greenwald and D. Cheriton. The synergy between non-blocking synchronization and operating system structure. In *Proceedings of the 2nd Symposium on Operating System Design and Implementation*, pages 123–136, 1996.

34. P. H. Ha and P. Tsigas. Reactive multi-word synchronization for multiprocessors. *Journal of Instruction-Level Parallelism*, 6, April 2004.

35. P. H. Ha, P. Tsigas, and O. J. Anshus. Wait-free programming for general purpose computations on graphics processors. In *Proceedings of the IEEE International Parallel and Distributed Processing Symposium*, pages 1–12, 2008.

36. P. H. Ha, P. Tsigas, and O. J. Anshus. NB-FEB: a universal scalable easy-to-use synchronization primitive for manycore architectures. In *Proceedings of the International Conference on Principles of Distributed Systems*, pages 189–203, 2009.

37. P. H. Ha, P. Tsigas, and O. J. Anshus. The synchronization power of coalesced memory accesses. *IEEE Transactions on Parallel and Distributed Systems*, 21(7):939–953, 2010.

38. T. Harris, K. Fraser, and I. Pratt. A practical multi-word compare-and-swap operation. In *Proceedings of the 16th International Symposium on Distributed Computing*, 2002.

39. T. L. Harris. A pragmatic implementation of non-blocking linked lists. In *Proceedings of the 15th International Symposium of Distributed Computing*, pages 300–314, 2001.

40. D. Hendler, Y. Lev, M. Moir, and N. Shavit. A Dynamic-Sized Nonblocking Work Stealing Deque. *Distributed Computing*, 18(3):189–207, 2006.

41. D. Hendler, N. Shavit, and L. Yerushalmi. A scalable lock-free stack algorithm. *Journal of Parallel and Distributed Computing*, 70(1):1–12, 2010.

42. M. Herlihy. Wait-free synchronization. *ACM Transactions on Programming Languages and Systems*, 11(1):124–149, January 1991.

43. M. Herlihy, V. Luchangco, P. Martin, and M. Moir. Nonblocking memory management support for dynamic-sized data structures. *ACM Transactions on Computer Systems*, 23:146–196, May 2005.

44. M. Herlihy, V. Luchangco, and M. Moir. The repeat offender problem: a mechanism for supporting dynamic-sized, lock-free data structure. In *Proceedings of 16th International Symposium on Distributed Computing*, October 2002.

45. M. Herlihy and J.Wing. Linearizability: a correctness condition for concurrent objects. *ACM Transactions on Programming Languages and Systems*, 12(3):463–492, 1990.

46. M. P. Herlihy and J. E. B. Moss. Lock-free garbage collection for multiprocessors. *IEEE Transactions on Parallel and Distributed Systems*, 3:304–311, May 1992.

47. T. Herman and V. Damian-Iordache. Space-optimal wait-free queues. In *Proceedings of the 16th Annual ACM Symposium on Principles of Distributed Computing*, page 280. ACM Press, 1997.

48. M. Hoffman, O. Shalev, and N. Shavit. The baskets queue. In *Proceedings of the 11th International Conference on Principles of Distributed Systems*, pages 401–414, 2007.

49. X. Huang, C. I. Rodrigues, S. Jones, I. Buck, and W. Hwu. XMalloc: a scalable lock-free dynamic memory allocator for many-core machines. *International Conference on Computer and Information Technology*, 0:1134–1139, 2010.

50. A. Israeli and L. Rappoport. Efficient wait-free implementation of a concurrent priority queue. In *Proceedings of the 7th International Workshop on Distributed Algorithms*, volume 725 of *Lecture Notes in Computer Science*, pages 1–17. Springer Verlag, September 1993.

51. A. Israeli and L. Rappoport. Disjoint-access-parallel implementations of strong shared memory primitives. In *Proceedings of the 13th annual ACM symposium on Principles of Distributed Computing*, 1994.

52. P. Jayanti and S. Petrovic. Efficient and practical constructions of LL/SC variables. In *Proceedings of the 22nd Annual Symposium on Principles of Distributed Computing*, pages 285–294. ACM Press, 2003.

53. S. Kelly-Bootle and B. Fowler. *68000, 68010, 68020 Primer*. Howard W. Sams & Co., 1985.

54. G. Kliot, E. Petrank, and B. Steensgaard. A lock-free, concurrent, and incremental stack scanning for garbage collectors. In *Proceedings of the 2009 ACM SIGPLAN/ SIGOPS International Conference on Virtual Execution Environments*, pages 11–20. ACM, 2009.

55. C. P. Kruskal, L. Rudolph, and M. Snir. Efficient synchronization of multiprocessors with shared memory. *ACM Transactions on Programming Languages and Systems*, 10:579–601, October 1988.

56. L. Lamport. Specifying concurrent program modules. *ACM Transactions on Programming Languages and Systems*, 5(2):190–222, 1983.

57. D. Lea. The Java Concurrency Package (JSR-166), 2009.

58. P. Martin, M. Moir, and G. Steele. DCAS-based Concurrent Deques Supporting Bulk Allocation. Technical Report TR-2002-111, Sun Microsystems, 2002.

59. H. Massalin. *Synthesis: An Efficient Implementation of Fundamental Operating System Services*. PhD thesis, Columbia University, 1992.

60. H. Massalin and C. Pu. A Lock-Free Multiprocessor OS Kernel. Technical Report CUCS-005-91, Computer Science Department, Columbia University, June 1991.

61. M. M. Michael. High performance dynamic lock-free hash tables and list-based sets. In *Proceedings of the 14th ACM Symposium on Parallel Algorithms and Architectures*, pages 73–82, 2002.

62. M. M. Michael. Safe memory reclamation for dynamic lock-free objects using atomic reads and writes. In *Proceedings of the 21st ACM Symposium on Principles of Distributed Computing*, pages 21–30, 2002.

63. M. M. Michael. CAS-based lock-free algorithm for shared deques. In *Proceedings of the 9th International Euro-Par Conference*, LNCS. Springer Verlag, August 2003.

64. M. M. Michael. Hazard pointers: safe memory reclamation for lock-free objects. *IEEE Transactions on Parallel and Distributed Systems*, 15(8), August 2004.

65. M. M. Michael. Practical lock-free and wait-free LL/SC/VL implementations using 64-bit CAS. In *Proceedings of the 18th International Conference on Distributed Computing*, pages 144–158, 2004.

66. M. M. Michael. Scalable lock-free dynamic memory allocation. In *Proceedings of the 2004 ACM SIGPLAN Conference on Programming Language Design and Implementation*, pages 35–46, June 2004.

67. M. M. Michael and M. L. Scott. Correction of a Memory Management Method for Lock-Free Data Structures. Technical report, Computer Science Department, University of Rochester, 1995.

68. M. M. Michael and M. L. Scott. Simple, fast, and practical non-blocking and blocking concurrent queue algorithms. In *Proceedings of the 15th annual ACM Symposium on Principles of Distributed Computing*, pages 267–275, 1996.

69. Microsoft. Parallel Computing Developer Center, 2009.

70. M. Moir. Practical implementations of non-blocking synchronization primitives. In *Proceedings of the 15th Annual ACM Symposium on the Principles of Distributed Computing*, August 1997.

71. M. Moir. Transparent support for wait-free transactions. In *Proceedings of the 11th International Workshop on Distributed Algorithms*, volume 1320, pages 305–319, September 1997.

72. M. Moir, D. Nussbaum, O. Shalev, and N. Shavit. Using elimination to implement scalable and lock-free FIFO queues. In *Proceedings of the 17th annual ACM Symposium on Parallelism in Algorithms and Architectures*, pages 253–262. ACM, 2005.

73. G. F. Pfister, W. C. Brantley, D. A. George, S. L. Harvey, W. J. Kleinfelder, K. P. McAuliffe, E. S. Melton, V. A. Norton, and J. Weiss. The IBM research parallel processor prototype (RP3): introduction and architecture. In *ICPP*, pages 764–771, 1985.

74. S. Prakash, Y. H. Lee, and T. Johnson. A nonblocking algorithm for shared queues using compare-and-swap. *IEEE Transactions on Computers*, 43(5):548–559, 1994.

75. J. Reinders. *Intel Threading Building Blocks: Outfitting C++ for Multi-core Processor Parallelism*. O'Reilly Media, 2007.

76. S. Schneider, C. D. Antonopoulos, and D. S. Nikolopoulos. Scalable locality-conscious multithreaded memory allocation. In *Proceedings of the 5th International Symposium on Memory Management*, pages 84–94. ACM, 2006.

77. O. Shalev and N. Shavit. Split-ordered lists: lock-free extensible hash tables. In *Proceedings of the 22nd Annual Symposium on Principles of Distributed Computing*, pages 102–111. ACM Press, 2003.

78. C. Shann, T. Huang, and C. Chen. A practical nonblocking queue algorithm using compare-and-swap. In *Proceedings of the Seventh International Conference on Parallel and Distributed Systems*, pages 470–475, 2000.

79. N. Shavit and D. Touitou. Software transactional memory. In *Proceedings of the fourteenth annual ACM symposium on Principles of distributed computing*, pages 204–213. ACM Press, 1995.

80. M. Spiegel and P. F. Reynolds Jr. Lock-free multiway search trees. In *Proceedings of the 39th International Conference on Parallel Processing*, pages 604–613, 2010.

81. H. Sundell. *Efficient and Practical Non-Blocking Data Structures*. PhD thesis, Chalmers University of Technology, 2004.

82. H. Sundell. Wait-free multi-word compare-and-swap using greedy helping and grabbing. In *Proceedings of the International Conference on Parallel and Distributed Processing Techniques and Applications*, pages 494–500, 2009.

83. H. Sundell, A. Gidenstam, M. Papatriantafilou, and P. Tsigas. A lock-free algorithm for concurrent bags. In *Proceedings of the 23rd ACM Symposium on Parallelism in Algorithms and Architectures*. ACM, 2011.

84. H. Sundell and P. Tsigas. NOBLE: a non-blocking inter-process communication library. In *Proceedings of the 6th Workshop on Languages, Compilers and Run-time Systems for Scalable Computers*, 2002.

85. H. Sundell and P. Tsigas. Fast and lock-free concurrent priority queues for multithread systems. In *Proceedings of the 17th International Parallel and Distributed Processing Symposium*, page 11. IEEE press, 2003.

86. H. Sundell and P. Tsigas. Scalable and lock-free concurrent dictionaries. In *Proceedings of the 19th ACM Symposium on Applied Computing*, pages 1438–1445. ACM press, 2004.

87. H. Sundell and P. Tsigas. Fast and lock-free concurrent priority queues for multithread systems. *Journal of Parallel and Distributed Computing*, 65(5):609–627, May 2005.

88. H. Sundell and P. Tsigas. Lock-free deques and doubly linked lists. *Journal of Parallel and Distributed Computing*, 68(7):1008–1020, July 2008.

89. J. Tsay and H.-C. Li. Lock-free concurrent tree structures for multiprocessor systems. In *Proceedings of the International Conference on Parallel and Distributed Systems*, pages 544–549, 1994.

90. P. Tsigas and Y. Zhang. A simple, fast and scalable non-blocking concurrent FIFO queue for shared memory multiprocessor systems. In *Proceedings of the 13th annual ACM Symposium on Parallel Algorithms and Architectures*, pages 134–143, 2001.

91. P. Tsigas and Y. Zhang. Evaluating the performance of non-blocking synchronization on shared-memory multiprocessors. In *Proceedings of the International Conference on Measurement and Modeling of Computer Systems*, pages 320–321. ACM Press, 2001.

92. P. Tsigas and Y. Zhang. Integrating non-blocking synchronisation in parallel applications: performance advantages and methodologies. In *Proceedings of the 3rd ACM Workshop on Software and Performance*, pages 55–67. ACM Press, 2002.

93. J. Turek and D. Shasha. The many faces of consensus in distributed systems. *IEEE Computer*, 25(2):8–17, 1992.

94. J. D. Valois. Implementing lock-free queues. In *Proceedings of the 7th International Conference on Parallel and Distributed Computing Systems*, pages 64–69, 1994.

95. J. D. Valois. *Lock-Free Data Structures*. PhD thesis, Rensselaer Polytechnic Institute, Troy, New York, 1995.

CHAPTER 4

SOFTWARE TRANSACTIONAL MEMORY

Sandya Mannarswamy

4.1 INTRODUCTION

One of the most serious challenges in writing concurrent code is coordinating access to shared data accessed by multiple threads concurrently. Mutual exclusion in the form of locks has been used in shared-memory parallel programming to prevent the concurrent use of shared data, and thus locks remain among the fundamental building blocks of concurrent programs. However lock-based synchronization has proven to be complicated and error prone. Furthermore, lock-based synchronization mechanisms lack composability, which often precludes the modular design of concurrent components.

Software transactional memory (STM) has been proposed as a promising programming paradigm for shared-memory multithreaded programs as an alternative to conventional lock-based synchronization primitives. STM is intended to facilitate the development of complex concurrent software by reducing the burden of programming complexity involved in writing concurrent code. STM is an active and evolving

Programming Multicore and Many-core Computing Systems,
First Edition. Edited by Sabri Pllana and Fatos Xhafa.
© 2017 John Wiley & Sons, Inc. Published 2017 by John Wiley & Sons, Inc.

area of research with a large number of STM implementations having been proposed and evaluated over the past twenty years. In this chapter, we provide a background on STM. First we examine STM from a programmer's perspective. We then discuss briefly the different semantic models associated with some of the current STM proposals. We then provide a quick overview of the various STM design dimensions, and the evolution of STM over the years followed by a short overview of STM performance.

4.2   STM: A PROGRAMMER'S PERSPECTIVE

4.2.1   Atomic Sections

STM allows programmers to express synchronization at higher level of abstraction than traditional locks [14]. Programmers can specify what code has to execute atomically by simply enclosing the desired block of code with the keyword *atomic*. The atomic section delimits a block of code that should execute in a transaction. Using STM relieves the programmer from explicitly having to remember which locks protect what shared data. The programmer simply encloses the code block which needs to be executed atomically inside an atomic block as a transaction. He does not need to explicitly name the locks that need to be acquired when this block of code is executed. This shifts considerable programming complexity from programmer to the underlying STM system which ensures that the locks associated with the shared data accessed inside the atomic section are acquired and released accordingly without having to be specified explicitly. This allows STM implementations to support higher levels of abstraction than lock-based synchronization.

From the perspective of the programmer, the code specified inside the atomic block executes as a transaction. Hence from his/her perspective, a transaction can have one of the three possible outcomes. A terminating transaction either completes successfully in entirety making its state changes visible to the rest of the program known as a *transactional commit* or aborts, leaving the program state unchanged known as a *transactional abort*. If the transaction does not terminate, its behavior is undefined.

While code within an atomic region is being executed, we refer to the dynamic instance of the atomic section as an active transaction. When the thread leaves the atomic region, the transaction is considered as committed. If two active transactions attempt to access the same data and at least one active transaction is attempting to write that data, then there is a conflict between the two transactions. Conflicts impose an ordering on the transactions that are involved in the conflict. Conflicts are dynamically detected and resolved by the underlying TM runtime, either by means of appropriately reordering the transactions if they are serializable (in informal terms, serializable means that the execution of a set of concurrent transactions is equivalent to some serial order of execution of the transactions. We discuss serializability in detail later) or if they are not serializable, by allowing only one out of the group of conflicting transactions to proceed while aborting all the other conflicting trans-actions. When a transaction aborts, the STM runtime will roll back the transaction's local state and restart execution from the beginning of the atomic block.

4.2.2 Optimistic versus Pessimistic Concurrency Control

A pessimistic concurrency control (PCC) implemented using lock-based pro-gramming is based on the premise that shared data accessed/updated within the critical section is expected to be nondisjoint across threads. Hence it is nec-essary to obtain exclusive ownership of the data before executing the critical section since conflicts are definitely expected during the data accesses. PCC and optimistic concurrency control (OCC) are similar to asking permission (exclu-sive ownership before entering the atomic section) and *apologizing if there is a conflict* (execute assuming data is disjoint; if conflict occurs apologize , and retry) [12].

STM systems are typically optimistic: they achieve concurrency by pursuing transactions in parallel and then aborting and rolling back in the event of conflict. This is unlike lock-based programming where a critical section protected by a lock is entered only after obtaining exclusive ownership of the lock, which means that no two threads could be inside the same critical section at the same time. Optimistic concurrency is driven by the assumption of disjoint access parallelism among con-currently executing transactions. It supposes that shared data accessed/updated by concurrent transactions are expected to be disjoint, and hence conflicts among threads in accessing shared data is typically infrequent.

An atomic section which exhibits disjoint access parallelism is executed by con-currently executing transactions as long as there are no conflicts among the transac-tions. On the other hand, if the concurrently executing transactions often access/up-date data which is not disjoint access parallel, then the data accesses conflict with each other. Transactional conflicts require the conflicting concurrent transactions to be serialized if they are serializable. If the concurrent conflicting transactions are not serializable, it leads to aborts for all conflicting transactions except one which commits. Aborting transactions lead to wasted work and hence are a major source of performance overheads in STM systems.

Aborts can be triggered in two ways, either by the STM runtime or by the appl-ication program itself. STM runtime typically triggers a transactional abort if a trans-action's access to a resource conflicts with another concurrently executing transac-tion or if the transaction deadlocks waiting to acquire a resource. In such a case, the STM runtime aborts the transaction and reexecutes it. These aborts are invisible to the programmer except for their impact as lowered STM performance. It is also possible for the STM application to invoke abort programmatically or through an exception in the program. Such application program-induced aborts, control passes to the statement after the atomic block or to an exception handler.

4.2.3   Properties of Transactions

Code enclosed inside the atomic sections and hence executed transactionally is guaranteed to have the following three properties satisfied by the underlying STM implementation without any effort from the programmer:

Failure atomicity: This property guarantees that a transaction either executes to completion successfully or appears not to have executed at all to the rest of the program.

Consistency: This property guarantees that a transaction always leaves the program in a consistent state. Consistency is an inherent property of the program and hence is an application-dependent characteristic. STM guarantees to the programmer that a transaction operates on a consistent application state and leaves the resulting application state also consistent.

Isolation: This property guarantees that an executing transaction does not appear to have any effect on any other transactions which are executing concurrently. This allows the programmer to reason about a transaction as if it executes in isolation with respect to any other transaction thereby reducing the complexity; hence he can reason locally without having to worry about the effects due to any other concurrent transactions.

Guaranteeing of the atomicity, consistency and isolation (ACI) properties by the underlying STM implementation simplifies writing concurrent code for the programmer while shifting the burden to the underlying STM implementations. Next we discuss the transactional semantics supported by the various STM implementations.

4.3   TRANSACTIONAL SEMANTICS

Transactional memory semantics describe the expected or allowed outcomes of various memory operations on shared data accessed by concurrent threads of a transactional memory application. Unlike database transactions where shared data in the database is exclusively accessed through transactions, STM systems do not explicitly forbid the access of the shared data outside of transactions in nontransactional code regions. Therefore any transactional semantic specification of the STM also needs to cover the behavior of the STM with respect to interaction of shared data accesses both inside transactional code and outside transactional code.

While a clean and simple semantics facilitates easy adoption of the STM by the programmer due to its ability to support simpler reasoning, it is also important that the semantics supported should allow efficient implementation. While there has been no standard STM specification published nor has there been a de facto STM standard so far, there has been some attempts on formalizing the semantics that need to be supported by an STM implementation [18, 13, 9, 8 and 22]. Next we discuss a few of the popular semantic models for STMs.

4.3.1 Serializability

Since STM has its roots in database transactions, many of the STM implementations simply adopt the correctness criteria from the database world, namely, serializability [1]. Serializability means that the result of executing a set of concurrent transactions must be identical and equivalent to an execution in which the transactions are executed and committed serially one after another. Guaranteeing the ACI properties in an STM implementation ensures that the serializability criterion is satisfied. Note that while serializability is a useful model for understanding the behavior of transactional code, it falls short of completely specifying the complete STM semantics since it does not specify the interaction of transactional code and nontransactional code. Also it does not say anything about the state accessed by live (or aborted) transactions and considers only the committed transactions.

4.3.2 Single Global Lock (SGL) Semantics

One of the simplest and most intuitive STM semantics is to consider transactions as if executed under a single global lock (SGL) [18]. With this model, we can define the semantics of a transactional program to be equivalent to a corresponding nontransactional program where every transactional region is converted such that it is protected by a single global program-wide lock, which needs to be acquired before the transactional region can be entered and released at the end of the transactional region. Therefore from the SGL perspective, it is as if only one atomic block can be executed transactionally at a time, which means that the total number of concurrent transactions at any time is only one.

SGL semantics is appealing and intuitive because it matches our natural understanding of transactions. It provides complete isolation and serializability over all transactions. However it does not explicitly capture the failure atomicity property of the transactions. Also this model cannot be directly employed as an STM implementation strategy since it precludes any concurrency. SGL semantics can be used to reason about the interaction between transactional and non transactional code. Under this semantic model, the SGL enforces synchronization among transactions. Nontransactional code does not acquire the global lock. Therefore there can be data races between transactional and nontransactional code if they contain conflicting data accesses. The behavior of a program that uses transactions is well defined if the program does not exhibit data races when the transactions are expressed using a SGL semantic model. The behavior of program containing data races is undefined. Data races in a transactional memory program can expose details of the transactional memory implementation and so may produce different results on different systems.

4.3.3 Linearizability

Linearizability is another alternate correctness criterion that has been used for STM implementations [13]. While serializability criterion is described in terms of low-level memory accesses, linearizability is defined at the higher-level abstraction in terms of operations on an abstract data type. Linearizability means that, intuitively, every transaction should appear as if it took place at some single, unique point in time during its lifespan.

Linearizability can be applied as a correctness criterion for transactional memory by defining transaction method operations on a logical object representing the shared memory. Linearizability guarantees that the state of the concurrent system after the execution of transactions is equivalent to a state wherein the trans actions had been executed one after the other in some serial order. However, this serial order should match the actual execution order of transactions at runtime. That is, if a transaction *Tx1* completes before another transaction *Tx2* starts executing, the final state of the execution should be equivalent to a serial execution of transactions in which *Tx1* comes before *Tx2*.

Serializability provides the same guarantees as linearizability; however, it does not impose any restrictions based on the execution order of transactions. That is, the final state of the execution can be equivalent to any serial execution of transactions, no matter which transaction completes earlier. Also note that linearizability is restricted to the specification of the semantics of the transactional code regions and does not specify the interaction between transactional and nontransactional code.

While linearizability would be appropriate as a TM correctness criterion if the transactions were external to the application executing to them in the sense that only the end result of a transaction is significant, in real life, it is not so. A transaction does not appear as a black box to the application containing it, but instead every operation performed inside the transaction on a shared object is accessible and accessible to the user. Hence it has been suggested that linearizability is not very useful as a correctness criterion for TM since it is prone to division by zero errors. A detailed discussion on why linearizability is not very useful as a TM correctness criterion can be found in [9].

4.3.4 Opacity

The various correctness criteria we have discussed previously suffer from a major shortcoming. None of them captures exactly the important requirement that every transaction including those that are live (i.e. not yet completed) accesses only a consistent state, that is, a state produced by a sequence of previously committed transactions. Opacity is an STM correctness criterion proposed to address this issue [9]. In simple terms, opacity can be considered as an extension of the database serializability property with the additional requirement that even noncommitted transactions are prevented from accessing inconsistent states.

Many of the current STM implementations satisfy the opacity criterion. They ensure this by combining traditional database concurrency and recovery control schemes with additional validation strategies. These validation strategies ensure that each operation of a transaction does not access an inconsistent STM state and that each return value of an operation inside a transaction is consistent with the return values of all previous operations of the same transaction aborting the transaction in case this condition cannot be met. A detailed description of opacity can be found in [9].

4.4   STM DESIGN SPACE

Over the past decade, a number of STM implementations have been developed, each with different design choices. A wide variety of STM techniques, mainly inspired by database algorithms, have been explored in order to determine the right combination of strategies that suit the requirements of concurrent applications. Next we present a brief overview of the various design dimensions of modern STM implementations.

4.4.1   Strong versus Weak Transactional Isolation

Strong transactional isolation means that nontransactional memory accesses are analogous to single-instruction transactions and are prevented from violating the isolation of transactions. In this model, transactions are strictly more restrictive than locks and, thus, provide programmers with sufficiently strong guarantees. However, strong isolation typically requires either specialized hardware support available on existing systems, a sophisticated type system that may not be easily integrated with languages such as Java or C++, or runtime barriers on nontransactional reads or writes that can incur substantial cost on programs that do not use transactions [14].

An alternative to strong isolation is weak isolation where there is no general guarantee made on nontransactional code. In such a case, a shared data access occurring inside nontransactional code and conflicting with a concurrent correctly coded transaction can return an inconsistent value or result in incorrect transaction behavior. The exact behavior is implementation dependent. However many of the STM implementations which support weak isolation ensure that well-known programming idioms such as publication and privatization behave as they would behave in a lock-based implementation to help ease programming effort [14]. Note that many of the STM papers use the terms *strong atomicity* and *weak atomicity* instead of the terms *strong isolation* and *weak isolation*.

4.4.2   Nonblocking versus Blocking (Lock-Based) STM Implementation

Since initial research on transactional memory grew out of nonblocking atomic operations, early STM implementations were nonblocking implementations based on nonblocking atomic operations such as *compare-and-swap* (CAS). A couple of the popular state-of-the-art nonblocking STMs are *RSTM* [17] and *ASTM* [16]. In nonblocking STMs, arbitrary delays in some transactions in the system would not interfere with forward progress of other transactions. They do not use any blocking mechanisms such as locks and guarantee progress even when some of the transactions are delayed. Nonblocking STMs avoid various problems such as delays due to preemption, priority inversion and thread faults associated with lock-based implementations. However nonblocking STM implementations also have considerable performance overheads, and, hence of late, there has been considerable focus on developing lock-based STM implementations.

Lock-based STMs implement some variant of the two-phase locking protocol. Lock-based STMs use time-outs to detect and abort deadlocked or blocked transactions. Lock-based STMs, while themselves being prone to the various pitfalls associated with lock-based synchronization, are quite complex to build and reason about for STM implementers. Nevertheless they can provide higher performance while maintaining strong forward progress guarantees for users of an STM system. Two of the state-of-the-art popular STMs *TL2* [3] and *TinySTM* [6] are lock-based STM implementations.

4.4.3 Lazy-versus Eager Update STMs

There are two major classes of STM implementations based on their update policy, namely, *lazy update* versus *eager update*. *Eager update* STM is also referred to as *direct or in-place update STM*, whereas *lazy update* STM is referred to as *deferred-update* STM. In an *eager update* STM, the transaction directly modifies the shared data object itself, and the STM uses contention management mechanisms to prevent other concurrent transactions from either concurrently modifying the object or committing if they have read the updated value. If the transaction which has modified the object in place needs to abort, then the original value of the shared data object needs to be restored. Hence *eager update* STM typically maintains an *undo* log where the old values of the modified objects are recorded during the transaction and are used to restore the program state in case the application rolls back.

In a *lazy update* STM, the transaction modifies a private copy of the shared data object, and the modifications are updated to the actual shared data object only at the time of commit. Hence no other concurrent transactions can see the modified values from an uncommitted transaction. The updates made by the transaction are maintained in a *redo* log which is used to apply the modifications to the shared copy at the time of commit. On an abort, a transaction simply discards the local modifications it has made.

As can be seen from our previous discussion, an *eager update* STM increases the amount of work that needs to be done on an abort (since it needs to undo its changes), whereas a *lazy update* STM increases the amount of work that needs to be done on a commit (since it needs to apply the changes from the *redo* log to the shared object). On the other hand, an *eager update* STM performs less work on a commit, whereas a *lazy update* STM performs less work on an abort.

Also maintaining *undo* or *redo* logs can have subtle issues in enforcing transactional correctness in weakly isolated STM systems [14]. For example, a lazy update weakly isolated STM on a commit needs to ensure that the modified locations are updated in the same program order as they were encountered in the transactional execution. Else it is possible that a nontransactional conflicting access can see inconsistent values. A similar issue occurs for an eager update weakly isolated STM during a transactional abort.

4.4.4 Eager versus Lazy Locking

STMs allow for optimistic execution by permitting multiple atomic sections to run concurrently assuming they will not conflict. However, in case a conflict does occur, STMs employ a mechanism to detect and recover from such conflicts. Most STMs employ the single-writer-multiple-readers strategy; two concurrent transactions conflict when they access the same location and at least one of the accesses is a write (update). In order to commit, a transaction must eventually acquire write locks for every memory location that is written by it.

Locks can be acquired eagerly, that is, at the time of the first update operation by the transaction on the memory location, or lazily, that is, when the transaction is about to commit. Eager locking is also known as encounter time locking, whereas lazy locking is also referred to as commit time locking. Encounter time locking facilitates early conflict detection, whereas commit time locking facilitates late conflict detection.

Detecting conflicts eagerly helps avoid wasting work of transactions that are doomed to abort after a conflict. Lazy conflict detection, however, is more optimistic and gives transactions more possibilities to commit. While early STMs favored either a wholly eager locking or lazy locking, of late there has been work on using mixed mode locking policies [5]. For instance SwissTM [5] applies a combination of both strategies. SwissTM detects write/write conflicts eagerly and read/write conflicts lazily. This combined strategy is beneficial for complex workloads with long transactions because it prevents transactions with write/write conflicts from running for a long time before detecting the conflict while at the same time it allows short transactions having a read/write conflict with longer ones to proceed, thus increasing parallelism. However for mostly read-dominated STM workloads, it has been shown that a lazy locking policy is effective in handling conflicts [3].

4.4.5 Visible versus Invisible Reads

In an STM transactions execute speculatively. Reads and writes done by the transaction are speculative and can be rolled back if the transaction aborts. Reads done by STM transactions are typically optimistic in that the transaction may proceed with execution without performing locking for the read objects, under the assumption that transactional conflicts for the read objects will be rare. Reads to shared data can be either visible or invisible to other transactions accessing the same data.

In an STM which supports *invisible reads*, a transaction reading a shared datum x needs to detect any possible conflicts on x with other transactions that write x concurrently, that is, validating its read-set. Validation is the process of verifying that no object in its read-set has been modified by a concurrent transaction; if validation fails, the transaction must abort. Thus, reads are essentially *invisible* to concurrent transactions at runtime, and such transactions with *invisible reads* must explicitly bear the cost of validation of their read-set.

It is also possible for STMs to support *visible reads* wherein readers of a shared data are tracked explicitly and informed by any concurrent writing transaction which conflicts with it. While *visible reads* avoid the read-set validation cost penalty paid by the transactions, tracking the readers for each shared data objects imposes high overheads, leading to significant cache contention in multiprocessor systems and thus impacting scalability [15]. Most of the state-of-the-art STMs [3, 6, 5] therefore employ *invisible reads*.

4.4.6   Time Stamp-Based versus Value-Based Validation Mechanisms

Ensuring consistency in an STM with invisible reads requires the system to validate the read-set during transactional execution in order to prevent it from observing inconsistent states. To avoid entering an inconsistent state, a transaction needs to validate the objects it has read at appropriate times in program execution. Validation ensures that the object that has been previously read is still valid and has not been modified by a concurrent committed transaction at the point of validation. Validation can be done based on the value held by the object in question known as value-based validation or by associating a timestamp/version with each modification of the shared object and using a global timestamp or version clock [3] known as time stamp-based validation.

Incremental validation is a value-based validation strategy that validates all past invisible reads every time the transaction reads a new object. If any change in the past is detected, the validation fails. This strategy guarantees a consistent state but imposes a substantial overhead, since it is essentially an $O(n^2)$ operation where n is the number of objects newly read in a transaction.

Timestamp-based validation strategies guarantee the consistency of the past reads by simply checking whether the timestamp of the object being read is in the transaction's validity range. Each transaction reads the global timestamp counter at the start of the transaction. If the timestamp of the object being currently read is larger than the transaction's starting timestamp, then read-set validation fails, and the transaction aborts. This reduces the validation to a couple of comparisons, greatly reducing the overhead introduced by incremental validation.

4.4.7   Access Tracking Granularity of STM

To enable conflict detection, STMs associate metadata/locks for shared data accessed inside an atomic section. Conflict detection consists of examining the metadata/locks corresponding to the shared reads and writes to check if there has been a read–write or write–write conflict. Each lock typically contains a bit indicating whether the shared data associated with the given lock has been locked, and the remaining bits are used to represent a version number for the associated shared data. STMs typically support a global fixed-size lock table, and shared data is tracked/mapped to the lock table elements using a hash function [3].

The granularity at which shared data is tracked/mapped to the metadata/locks is the access tracking granularity for an STM implementation. This is basically the number of consecutive words of shared data that map to a single lock entry in the STM's global lock table and is the basic unit of tracking shared data items by the STM. Shared data items which fall within a single unit of access tracking granularity are treated as a single entity by the STM for conflict detection and validation since a single lock covers all the data items lying within a unit granularity region. Access tracking granularity can be a word, a strip of memory region or an object. Many of the state-of-the-art STMs such as *TL2* [3] and *TinySTM* [6] are word-based STMs.

Increasing the access tracking granularity reduces locking and validation time, due to the data access locality, but increases abort rates by introducing false conflicts due to multiple shared data items located contiguously getting mapped to the same lock. A false conflict occurs in an STM when two different addresses are mapped to the same metadata or lock, and this results in two transactions which are accessing truly disjoint data, getting falsely diagnosed as conflicting when they are not. Hence the selection of access tracking granularity that results in higher performance needs to factor in these complex and conflicting requirements while taking into account the data access patterns of a given STM application.

4.4.8 Contention Management

The main task of an STM is to detect conflicts among concurrent transactions and resolve them. If a transaction *Tx1* encounters a conflict with a concurrent transaction *Tx2*, it can either wait for *Tx2* to complete, abort itself or abort *Tx2*. The STM runtime can consult a contention manager to make an informed decision. STMs typically provide a contention manager which decides what to do when transactional conflicts arise. Contention manager implements contention resolution policies that decide which one of the conflicting transactions should be allowed to proceed while aborting others. A wide variety of contention managers have been proposed and evaluated in STM literature [20].

4.4.9 Handling of Nested Transactions

A nested transaction is a transaction whose dynamic execution is properly contained in the dynamic extent of another transaction. STMs support nested transactions in three different ways, namely:

Flattened nesting The simplest form of transaction nesting is flat nesting. When a TM uses flat nesting, operations of child transactions of a transaction T_k become part of T_k, and an abort of any child transaction of T_k results in T_k being also aborted. However committing of a child transaction has no impact until the outer transaction commits at which point all the modifications made by the outer transaction and all its children become visible to all other concurrent transactions. Flattened transactions are quite easy to implement. However they deprive the programmer from easily expressing composition and can impact performance since aborting an inner transaction leads to aborting all surrounding outer transactions.

Open nesting In an open nesting model STM, when an open-nested transaction commits, its changes become visible to all other transactions in the system, even if the enclosing transaction is still executing. Moreover, even if the enclosing transaction aborts, the results of the nested, open transactions will still remain committed. Open transactions permit a transaction to make permanent modifications to a program's state, which are not rolled back if a surrounding transaction aborts. In addition, they permit unrelated code, such as a garbage collector, to execute in the middle of a transaction and make permanent changes that are unaffected by the surrounding transactions. These uses of open transactions can help improve performance of applications on STM.

Closed nesting In a closed nesting model STM, a closed-nested transaction aborts without terminating its enclosing transaction. When a closed inner transaction commits or aborts, control passes to its enclosing transaction. If the inner transaction commits, its modifications become visible to the surrounding transaction. However, nonenclosing transactions see these changes only when the outermost enclosing transaction commits.

4.4.10   Programming Language Support for Transactions

Some of the STM systems are implemented as an external library whose interfaces can be invoked from within programs just as an external library function calls, while other STM systems integrate transactions in to the syntax of the programming language. One of the state-of-the-art STMs, namely, *TL2* [3] simply provides transactional support through an external library, whereas Intel C/C++ compiler provides language-level support for transactions with an STM-aware compiler and runtime. A closer integration between the language, compiler and STM runtime enables to provide of cleaner STM semantics and allow for language and compiler-specific optimizations which can help enhance application performance on STMs.

4.5   STM: A HISTORICAL PERSPECTIVE

A large number of STM implementations exist today [14]. Since it would be impossible for us to describe here the complete history of STM evolution due to space constraints, we restrict ourselves to a brief description of the evolution of STM pointing out some of the major STM proposals over this period. A detailed history of the STM evolution and the operational details of each of the STMs can be found in [14].

Shavit and Touitou proposed a software equivalent of transactional memory, the STM [21], in the year 1995. They used the term transaction for a nonblocking operation. In their system, threads may access shared memory using transactions. Each word in the shared memory is protected by a unique ownership record. A transaction must have predetermined knowledge of the set of locations it will access. These locations are accessed in some global total order. A transaction may modify a location by acquiring exclusive ownership of that location, via its ownership record. Ownership acquisition of locations is also done in the global total order. On completion, the transaction releases all acquired ownership records. A transaction aborts whenever it comes across a location whose ownership record has been acquired by another transaction.

The disadvantages of the static STM were overcome in the dynamic software transactional memory system (DSTM) [11]. DSTM did not require a programmer to specify a transaction's memory usage in advance. DSTM was a nonblocking STM implementation which used obstruction freedom as the nonblocking progress condition for transactions. Obstruction freedom criterion guarantees that a halted thread does not prevent active threads from making progress. At a conflict, the STM system has the freedom to choose which of the two conflicting transactions should be terminated (or delayed) and which transaction should be allowed to allow to continue. DSTM provides a general interface that allows a contention manager to implement a wide variety of policies. DSTM supported deferred updates, eager locking and object-based access granularity tracking with a flattened transaction model. DSTM was a library-based STM implementation for usage in C++/Java programs.

DSTM also proposed an *early release* mechanism which allows the transaction to release an object from its read-set before committing so that it need not be considered for further read-set validations. This requires programmer support, since the programmer decides whether an object in the read-set can be released early. Early release mechanism can help in reducing the read-set validation costs since it shrinks the size of the read-set.

WSTM described in [10] was the first STM implementation to be closely integrated with a programming language, namely, Java. ASTM [16] is a nonblocking object-based STM which uses a deferred update policy. It has an explicit contention manager which is based on DSTM [11]. ASTM also adapts its conflict resolution at runtime from *eager acquire* to *lazy acquire* for transactions with a small number of memory writes and a large number of reads. RSTM [17] is a nonblocking obstruction-free STM system implemented as a C++ class library with early or late conflict detection selectable by the programmer. It is an object-based STM with an explicit contention manager and a flattened transaction model. RSTM has support for both visible and invisible readers.

In 2006, Dice and Shavit proposed a lockbased blocking STM implementation known as transactional locking 2 (also known as TL2) [3]. TL2 is a state-of-the-art librarybased STM implementation supporting unmanaged environments like C/C++. TL2 is a deferred update STM, with support for flattened transaction model. TL2 uses the simple and passive contention management scheme, wherein *the requester always aborts* on a conflict. TL2 also uses a simple back-off scheme, wherein an aborting transaction has a short time delay before it is restarted. TL2 supports invisible reads with global version number (timestamp)-based validation. It uses versioned write locks to protect shared-memory locations. TinySTM [6] and SwissTM [5] are a couple of other lock-based STM implementations proposed recently.

McRT-STM is another popular lock-based STM which supports C/C++ and Java [19]. Unlike other popular lock-based STMs like TL2, McRT-STM is a direct update STM with an undo log to roll back the transactional updates in case of an abort. McRT-STM supports both object and cache line granularity access tracking. McRT-STM exports interfaces that can be used from C/C++ programs directly or as a target for compilers translating higher-level linguistic constructs.

Our discussion so far on the evolution of STMs has briefly touched upon some of the significant STM proposals over the past 20 years. However there are various other important and novel STM proposals that we do not discuss here due to space constraints. A detailed survey of the different STM implementations can be found in [14].

4.6 APPLICATION PERFORMANCE ON STM

There has been considerable research into developing STMs for unmanaged environments like C/C++, since much of the performance-critical enterprise applications are still written in them. State-of-the-art STM implementations for unmanaged environments have been developed [3, 6]. However adoption of STM in mainstream software has been quite low. The overheads incurred by STMs are often quoted as the main reasons for the above view. While STM offers the promise of being a programming paradigm which is less error prone and more programmer friendly compared to traditional lock-based synchronization, it also needs to be competitive in performance in order for it to be adopted in mainstream software.

4.6.1 Factors Impacting STM Performance

There has been considerable work in understanding the factors which impact the application performance on STM [4, 2]. The major factors impacting application performance on STM adversely are as follows:

Transactional conflicts Conflicts are a major source of overheads in STM implementations. Since transactions execute optimistically and typically roll back if a conflict is detected, there may be lot of wasted work done by transactions which eventually abort. Aborted transactions reduce performance, scalability and waste computing resources. Therefore reducing transactional aborts is an important consideration in improving the performance of the STMs. Conflicts can be either true data conflicts or false conflicts. While true data conflicts are an application artifact, STMs can also suffer from *false conflicts*. A *false conflict* occurs in an STM when two different addresses are mapped to the same metadata or lock, and this results in two transactions which are accessing truly disjoint data, getting falsely diagnosed as conflicting when they are not. Such false conflicts result in increased number of aborts/rollbacks and hence can impact the performance.

Based on how false conflicts occur, they are classified into two types, namely, *intraconflicts* and *interconflicts*. Intraconflicts occur wherein two different data items getting accessed in independent transactions are mapped to the same lock due to both of them falling within the same unit granularity region which gets mapped to a single lock. *Interconflicts* occur wherein two different data items getting accessed in independent transactions are mapped to the same lock, even when they are not in the same unit granularity region. This happens due to the limited size of the lock table. Since the number of locks is often fewer than the numbers of shared data (grouped at a fixed access tracking granularity), multiple uncorrelated data items can get mapped to the same lock. This is known as lock aliasing. When such uncorrelated data items which have been mapped to the same lock are accessed in concurrently executing transaction, they cause *interconflicts* between the transactions.

Poor cache behavior While STMs support increased parallelism by their basic performance premise of OCC, supporting optimistic concurrency can have significant impact on the cache behavior of applications running on STM. Fine-grained locking employed by the STM while improving concurrency impacts the cache behavior adversely due to the increased number of lock accesses required. An atomic section which accesses N words of shared data will contain an additional programmer invisible N lock word accesses on a word-based STM, increasing the pressure on the cache. To support optimistic concurrency, STMs also need to perform considerable book-keeping activity such as maintenance of read/write sets, maintenance of the global version clock to enable validation of transactional data, redo/undo logs and so on. Such activities being memory intensive can also impact the cache behavior adversely.

Overinstrumentation Overinstrumentation occurs when the compiler generates excessive read/write shared data references due to its lack of application level knowledge. This in turn results in many data references which are private being treated as shared data references and hence requiring lock accesses associated with them. In general, excessive lock accesses incur more false conflicts (due to the limited size of lock table), which again brings about significant performance degradation.

Transaction start-up and termination overheads There are fixed costs associated with supporting transactions such as transaction start-up and termination costs. Start-up costs occur due to STM library having to initialize various bookkeeping data structures associated with that transaction, whereas transaction termination costs occur due to commit time activities such as updating the global timestamp or abort time activities such as releasing the resources associated with the transaction. When transactions are extremely short, these fixed costs of transaction startup and termination are poorly amortized over the length of the transaction, adversely impacting performance.

4.6.2   Techniques to Improve STM Performance

There has been considerable work on addressing the various performance bottlenecks [3, 15, 17]. Since conflicts and the resulting transactional aborts are a major contributor to poor STM performance, there has been considerable work on reducing the transactional abort overheads [20, 7]. Contention management schemes have been studied widely in the context of improving the performance of STM implementations in order to reduce the number of aborts caused by data conflicts encountered in high-contention scenarios. Contention managers try to maximize the performance by effectively handling the contention after it has been detected. Rather than to take action after the contention has been detected, techniques have been proposed to perform proactive transaction scheduling to prevent transactional conflicts [24]. In order to reduce false conflicts, a number of improvements to STM's lock assignment schemes have been proposed [4].

Other than false conflicts, true data conflicts can also impact adversely STM performance in case of atomic sections with low or zero disjoint access parallelism. In applications which were written without keeping OCC in mind, there may exist certain data structures or constructs which do not exhibit disjoint access parallelism. Such data structures can be accessed inside atomic sections whose instances when executed concurrently by more than one thread always conflict. Executing such atomic sections using OCC has a negative impact on performance because of increased aborts due to conflicting transactions. Regions of low or zero disjoint access parallelism are better served by PCC since it avoids wasteful work due to aborting transactions. A number of techniques have been proposed to perform selective execution of atomic sections under PCC in order to reduce transactional conflicts [23].

4.7   CONCLUDING REMARKS

While there are considerable performance overheads associated with STM implementations, their most notable attraction lies in the fact that they simplify writing concurrent software by shifting the burden of programming complexity from the programmer to the STM runtime library. The various pitfalls associated with conventional lock-based programming such as data races, atomicity violations, deadlocks and poor scalability are no longer an issue in programming with STM. STM offers a mechanism that allows portions of a program to execute in isolation, without regard to other concurrently executing tasks. This facilitates local reasoning. Unlike locks, transactions are composable [14].

Addressing the performance bottlenecks and improving the application performance on STM continue to be a major focus for STM researchers. While STM is a programmer friendly and less error-prone alternative to lock-based synchronization, it is not a single panacea to all the concurrency issues. STM is still evolving and has a number of issues to overcome such as the high-performance overheads and low industry adoption. However given the fact that multicore revolution is well on its way, STM is here to stay coexisting with traditional lock-based synchronization mechanisms.

REFERENCES

1. U. Aydonat and T. Abdelrahman. Serializability of transactions in software transactional memory. In *TRANSACT '08: 3rd Workshop on Transactional Computing*, February 2008.

2. C. Cascaval, C. Blundell, M. Michael, H. W. Cain, P. Wu, S. Chiras, and S. Chatterjee. Software transactional memory: why is it only a research toy? *Communications of the ACM*, 51(11):40–46, November 2008.

3. D. Dice, O. Shalev, and N. Shavit. Transactional locking II. In *DISC '06: Proceedings of the. 20th International Symposium on Distributed Computing*, volume 4167, pages 194–208. Springer-Verlag Lecture Notes in Computer Science, September 2006.

4. D. Dice and N. Shavit. Understanding tradeoffs in software transactional memory. In *CGO '07: Proceedings of the International Symposium on Code Generation and Optimization*, pages 21–33, March 2007.

5. A. Dragojević, R. Guerraoui, and M. Kapalka. Stretching transactional memory. *SIGPLAN Not.*, 44:155–165, June 2009.

6. P. Felber, C. Fetzer, and T. Riegel. Dynamic performance tuning of word-based software transactional memory. In *Proceedings of the 13th ACM SIGPLAN Symposium on Principles and practice of parallel programming*, PPoPP '08, pages 237–246. ACM, New York, NY, USA, 2008.

7. P. Felber, V. Gramoli, and R. Guerraoui. E. transactions. In *Proceedings of the 23rd international conference on Distributed computing*, DISC '09, pages 93–107. Spriner-Verlag, Berlin, Heidelberg, 2009.

8. R. Guerraoui, T. A. Henzinger, and V. Singh. Software transactional memory on relaxed memory models. In *Proceedings of the 21st International Conference on Computer Aided Verification*, CAV '09, pages 321–336. Springer-Verlag, Berlin, Heidelberg, 2009.

9. R. Guerraoui and M. Kapalka. On the correctness of transactional memory. In *Proceedings of the 13th ACM SIGPLAN Symposium on Principles and practice of parallel programming*, PPoPP '08, pages 175–184. ACM, New York, NY, USA, 2008.

10. T. Harris and K. Fraser. Language support for lightweight transactions. In *Object-Oriented Programming, Systems, Languages, and Applications*, pages 388–402. ACM, October 2003.

11. M. Herlihy, V. Luchangco, M. Moir, and W. N. Scherer III. Software transactional memory for dynamic-sized data structures. In *PODC '03: Proceedings of the. 22nd ACM Symposium on Principles of Distributed Computing*, pages 92–101, July 2003.

12. M. Herlihy and J. E. B. Moss. Transactional memory: architectural support for lock-free data structures. In *Proceedings of the 20th Annual International Symposium on Computer Architecture*, pages 289–300. ACM, May 1993.

13. M. P. Herlihy and J. M. Wing. Linearizability: a correctness condition for concurrent objects. *ACM Transactions on Programming Languages and Systems,* 12:463–492, July 1990.

14. J. R. Larus and R. Rajwar. *Transactional Memory*. Morgan and Claypool, 2006.

15. Y. Lev, V. Luchangco, V. Marathe, M. Moir, D. Nussbaum, and M. Olszewski. Anatomy of a scalable software transactional memory. In *TRANSACT '09: 4th Workshop on Transactional Computing*, February 2009.

16. V. J. Marathe, W. N. Scherer III, and M. L. Scott. Adaptive software transactional memory. In *Proceedings of the 19th International Symposium on Distributed Computing*, Cracow, Poland, September 2005. Earlier but expanded version available as TR 868, University of Rochester Computer Science Dept., May 2005.

17. V. J. Marathe, M. F. Spear, C. Heriot, A. Acharya, D. Eisenstat, W. N. Scherer III, and M. L. Scott. Lowering the overhead of software transactional memory. Technical Report TR 893, Computer Science Department, University of Rochester, March 2006. Condensed version submitted for publication.

18. V. Menon, S. Balensiefer, T. Shpeisman, A.-R. Adl-Tabatabai, R. Hudson, B. Saha, and A. Welc. Single global lock semantics in a weakly atomic stm. In *TRANSACT '08: 3rd Workshop on Transactional Computing*, February 2008.

19. B. Saha, A.-R. Adl-Tabatabai, R. L. Hudson, C. C. Minh, and B. Hertzberg. Mcrt-stm: a high performance software transactional memory system for a multi-core runtime. In *Proceedings of the 11th ACM SIGPLAN Symp. on Principles and Practice of Parallel Programming (PPoPP '06)*, pages 187–197. ACM, March 2006.

20. W. N. Scherer III and M. L. Scott. Advanced contention management for dynamic software transactional memory. In *Proceedings of the 24th ACM Symposium on Principles of Distributed Computing*, Las Vegas, NV, July 2005.

21. N. Shavit and D. Touitou. Software transactional memory. In *Proceedings of the 14th ACM Symposium on Principles of Distributed Computing*, pages 204–213. ACM, August 1995.

22. T. Shpeisman, A.-R. Adl-Tabatabai, R. Geva, Y. Ni, and A. Welc. Towards transactional memory semantics for C++. In *SPAA '09: Proceedings. 21st Symposium on Parallelism in Algorithms and Architectures*, August 2009.

23. T. Usui, R. Behrends, J. Evans, and Y. Smaragdakis. Adaptive locks: combining transactions and locks for efficient concurrency. *Journal of Parallel and Distributed Computing*, 70:1009–1023, October 2010.

24. R. M. Yoo and H.-H. S. Lee. Adaptive transaction scheduling for transactional memory systems. In *SPAA '08: Proceedings of the Twentieth Annual Symposium on Parallelism in Algorithms and Architectures*, pages 169–178, June 2008.

PART II

PROGRAMMING APPROACHES

CHAPTER 5

HYBRID/HETEROGENEOUS PROGRAMMING WITH OMPSS AND ITS SOFTWARE/HARDWARE IMPLICATIONS

EDUARD AYGUADÉ, ROSA M. BADIA, PIETER BELLENS, JAVIER BUENO, ALEJANDRO DURAN, YOAV ETSION, MONTSE FARRERAS, ROGER FERRER, JESUS LABARTA, VLADIMIR MARJANOVIC, LLUIS MARTINELL, XAVIER MARTORELL, JOSEP M. PEREZ, JUDIT PLANAS, ALEX RAMIREZ, XAVIER TERUEL, IOANNA TSALOUCHIDOU AND MATEO VALERO

5.1 INTRODUCTION

Multicore architectures alleviate several problems that are related to single-core processors but at the same time raise the programmability wall: experienced application developers find it hard to extract reasonable performance from shared memory homogeneous multicore architectures, and the situation is even worse when considering heterogeneous multicore architectures, distributed memories and explicitly managed memory hierarchies. In order to overcome the new programming challenges, programming models need to evolve to include features that offer a simple and portable path to migrate applications to homogeneous and heterogenous architectures.

The majority of proposals for heterogeneous architectures assume a host-directed programming and execution model with attached accelerator devices. The bulk of a user application executes on the host, while user-specified code regions are offloaded to the accelerators. In general, the specifics of the different accelerators make programming extremely difficult (and nonportable) if one plans to use the vendor-

Programming Multicore and Many-core Computing Systems,
First Edition. Edited by Sabri Pllana and Fatos Xhafa.

provided SDKs (CUDA ^{TM} for Nvidia® GPUs, libspe for Cell/B.E.^{TM}, etc.). The attempt of OpenCL^{TM} to unify the programming models for accelerator-based architectures tries to ensure portability, low-level access to the hardware and performance portability. However, OpenCL still exposes much of the low-level details, making it cumbersome to use for nonexperts.

Our thesis is based on the key importance of asynchrony as well as incremental parallelization, modularity and portability of applications. The programmer should only be concerned with decomposing the application into tasks and describing the usage pattern of the variables in that task. It should be the responsibility of the runtime system to orchestrate the execution of tasks, dynamically detecting dependencies, scheduling work to the heterogeneous set of processors and managing the memory hierarchy in a transparent and portable way. Our proposal in this direction is the OmpSs programming model, an evolution of the current OpenMP® 3.0 standard with ideas inherited from the StarSs concept, a dataflow set of extensions which have been demonstrated with mature implementations for different target architectures (SMPSs [8] for homogeneous shared memory and ccNUMA architectures, CellSs [10] for the IBM® Cell/B.E. and GPUSs [2] for Nvidia GPUs).

This chapter describes how OmpSs extends the OpenMP 3.0 node programming model and how it leverages MPI and OpenCL/CUDA, mastering the efficient programming of the clustered heterogeneous multi-/many-core systems that will be available in current and future computing systems. A clean way to express the dataflow requirements for tasks [5] is the basis for deriving task dependencies at runtime and to implement locality-aware dataflow scheduling policies, in which data movement between different levels of the memory hierarchy or different address spaces is optimized. Also, the programming model allows [1] a portable and incremental specification of architecture (and code) heterogeneity which provides enough information to the runtime to take scheduling decisions with different trade-offs in mind (core heterogeneity, availability of resources and data being accessed, etc.). The hybrid use of OmpSs and OpenCL/CUDA allows the portable specification of computational kernels to be executed on accelerators, using the high-level data types and operators to achieve portable performance. The hybrid use of MPI and OmpSs achieves a global asynchronous dataflow execution of both communication and computation tasks, allowing the programmer to both easily introduce the asynchrony necessary to overlap communication and computation and accelerate the execution of the computation critical path.

In addition to describing the language extensions, this chapter describes the implementation of OmpSs, focusing on the intelligence that needs to be embedded in the runtime system to effectively lower the programmability wall and the opportunities to implement new mechanisms and policies. Finally this chapter reasons about the overheads related with task management (detecting intertask data dependencies, identifying task-level parallelism and executing tasks out of order) in OmpSs examining how far a software implementation can go to cope with fine-grain parallelism and opening the door to novel hardware mechanisms for emerging multicore architectures.

5.2 THE OMPSS PROPOSAL

This section first provides a brief description of the OmpSs execution model, necessary to understand the programming model extensions that are proposed afterward. A two-dimensional (2D) FFT code illustrates the use of the programming model. Additional details about the implementation of the execution model in the supporting runtime library are described later in Section 5.3.

5.2.1 Execution Model

Rather than implementing the basic OpenMP fork–join model, OmpSs defines a thread-pool model where all the threads exist from the beginning of the execution. Of these threads, only one, the master thread, starts executing the code in the main function, while the other threads remain ready to execute work when available. The pool, which is still considered a team of threads in the OpenMP sense, is the enabler for implementing asynchronous dataflow execution engines that hide the complexities and dynamic heterogeneities in the core and memory architectures, as well as adapt to dynamic changes in resource availability and workloads.

Since the team of threads exists from the beginning of the execution, there is no need for an explicit **parallel** construct. The master thread can generate work for the other threads by means of the regular OpenMP worksharing or task constructs. Another difference with OpenMP is that these work generation constructs can be nested, so all threads can eventually become work generators; therefore there is no need for nested teams of threads. The **parallel** construct is deprecated in OmpSs.

5.2.2 Dataflow Extensions

The original OpenMP 3.0 **task** construct:

```
#pragma omp task [omp_clauses] [ss_clauses]
task_block
```

is leveraged with **ss_clauses** that express the intended usage of data in the task: **input**, **output**, **inout** and **concurrent**. In OmpSs, functions can be annotated to be a task, *a la Cilk* [3]. In this case, any call to the function is treated as spawning a task that will execute the task code:

```
#pragma omp task [omp_clauses] [ss_clauses]
function definition | function header
```

The four **ss_clauses** accept a list of expressions that must evaluate to a set of *lvalues*[1] and that is used by the runtime system to build the task dependency graph:

- If a created task has an **input** clause that evaluates to a given *lvalue*, then the task will not be eligible to run as long as a *previously created* task with an **output** clause applying to the same *lvalue* has not finished its execution.

[1] An lvalue is an expression that refers to an object, that is, a named region of storage.

- If a created task has an **output** clause that evaluates to a given *lvalue*, then the task will not be eligible to run as long as a *previously created* task with an **input** or **output** clause applying to the same *lvalue* has not finished its execution. This is in fact a false dependence that could be removed using object renaming, as later described in Section 5.3.3.

- If a created task has an **inout** clause that evaluates to a given *lvalue*, then it is considered as if it had an **input** clause and an **output** clause that evaluated to that same *lvalue*.

- If a created task has a **concurrent** clause that evaluates to a given *lvalue*, then it is considered as if it had an **inout** clause that evaluated to that same *lvalue* "except" to it will not create dependences with other tasks with a **concurrent** clause evaluating to the same *lvalue*.

The C/C++ expressions in these new clauses are extended inside the context of the clause to allow other forms: array ranges and shaping expressions. Since neither C nor C++ has any way to express ranges of an array, we have borrowed the *array-section* syntax from Fortran 90. These array sections, with syntax a[e1:e2], designate all elements from a[e1] to a[e2] (both ends are included and e1 shall yield a lower or equal value than e2). Multidimensional arrays are eligible for multidimensional array sections (like a[1:2][3:4]). While not technically naming a subobject, nonmultidimensional array-section syntax can also be applied to pointers (i.e. pA[1:2] is valid for int *pA, but note that pB[1:2][3:4] is invalid for int **pB (because the size of the inner dimension is not known at compile time). Also note that pC[1:2][3:4] is valid for int (*a)[N], and so it is pD[1:2][3:4][5:6] for int (*a)[N][M]).

Shaping expressions are a sequence of dimensions, enclosed in square brackets, and a data reference that should refer to a pointer type (like [10][20] p). These shaping expressions are aimed at those scenarios where an array-like structure has been allocated but only a pointer to its initial element is available. The goal of shaping expressions is to return such unavailable structural information back to the compiler.

Figure 5.1 shows the skeleton of a sequential 2D FFT in which the main functions are annotated as OmpSs tasks with the appropriate dependence clauses (lines 1, 3, 7, 9 and 11). Figure 5.2 shows the blocks and the order they are accessed by the tasks of each phase, assuming the matrix is divided in 4 by 4 blocks (i.e. FFT_BS = TR_BS = N/4). Colors represent tasks, and numbers represent their sequential instantiation order. The transpositions have been implemented in place by blocks. The *trsp_blk* tasks transpose the contents of a block in the diagonal, while the rest are transposed in opposite pairs by the *trsp_swap* task. The merged twiddle and transpose phase (*tw_trsp_blk*) has the same structure as the transposition phases, but the tasks also multiply by the twiddle factors. The *fft1d* task performs in-place FFTs over the rows of a horizontal panel. Figure 5.3 shows the task graph dynamically generated by the OmpSs runtime system for the same problem size.

```
1   #pragma omp task inout([N][N] blk [0:TR_BS-1][0:TR_BS-1])
2   void trsp_blk(double _Complex blk[N][N]);
3   #pragma omp task inout([N][N] blk1 [0:TR_BS-1][0:TR_BS-1], \
4   [N][N] blk2 [0:TR_BS-1][0:TR_BS-1])
5   void trsp_swap (double _Complex blk1[N][N],
6   double _Complex blk2[N][N]);
7   #pragma omp task inout(panel)
8   void fft1d (double _Complex panel[FFT_BS][N]);
9   #pragma omp task input(I) inout([N][N] panel [0:TR_BS-1][0:TR_BS-1])
10  void tw_trsp_blk(long I, double _Complex panel[N][N]);
11  #pragma omp task input (I, J) inout([N][N] blk1 [0:TR_BS-1][0:TR_BS-1],
                                                                          \
12  [N][N] blk2 [0:TR_BS-1][0:TR_BS-1])
13  void tw_trsp_swap (long I, long J, double _Complex blk1[N][N],
14  double _Complex blk2[N][N]);
15  void fft (double _Complex A[N][N]) {
16  // 1. Transpose
17  for (i=0; i<N; i+=TR_BS) {
18  trsp_blk (&A[i][i]);
19  for (j=i+TR_BS; j<N; j+=TR_BS)
20  trsp_swap (&A[i][j], &A[j][i]);
21  }
22  // 2. First FFT round
23  for (j=0; j<N; j+=FFT_BS)
24  fft1d(&A[j][0]);
25  // 3 & 4. Twiddle and Transpose
26  for (i=0; i<N; i+=TR_BS) {
27  tw_trsp_blk (i, &A[i][i]);
28  for (j=i+TR_BS; j<N; j+=TR_BS)
29  tw_trsp_swap (i, j, &A[i][j], &A[j][i]);
30  }
31  // 5. Second FFT round
32  for (j=0; j<N; j+=FFT_BS)
33  fft1d(&A[j][0]);
34  // 6. Transpose
35  for (i=0; i<N; i+=TR_BS) {
36  trsp_blk (&A[i][i]);
37  for (j=i+TR_BS; j<N; j+=TR_BS)
38  trsp_swap (&A[i][j], &A[j][i]);
39  }
40  }
```

Figure 5.1   FFT example with OmpSs task dependencies.

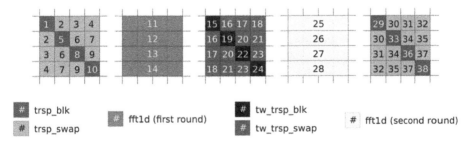

Figure 5.2   Block distribution for the arrays in the FFT example (4 × 4 blocks) with task instantiation numbers.

Figure 5.4 shows a trace for the execution of this code with 8 threads and a matrix divided in 16 by 16 blocks (i.e., FFT_BS = TR_BS = N/16). Task colors match those of Figure 5.2. Note that the different phases which are separated in the code actually overlap during the execution, escaping from the barrier synchronization that would be needed, for example, in OpenMP and reducing the potential load unbalance that could occur.

These same clauses can also be applied to OpenMP loop worksharings. When the expression in the dependence clause is not dependent on the loop induction variable, then, it applies to loop as a whole, and it will be considered *as if* the whole loop was a task for this matter. However, if the expression is dependent on the induction variable, then, the expression applies per iteration, and it will be evaluated *as if* each chunk of the loop was a task with the dependence expressions being evaluated with the appropriate chunk ranges. When a loop worksharing has any of the dependence clauses expressing *output*, it will be considered as if it had an OpenMP **nowait** clause on it:

```
#pragma omp for [omp_clauses] [ss_clauses]
for_block
```

Figure 5.5 shows a fragment of the same FFT shown in Figure 5.1. Some of the **inout** dependences in the loop in the first FFT phase match with the **inout** dependence of the task that executes *trsp_blk* and some with the **inout** dependence in the loop in the transpose phase; since these dependences in the loops involve the induction variable, finishing the execution of chunks in the first loop will release the execution of chunks of the second loop. So, the single *trsp_blk* and the different chunks of the first and second loop can be executed concurrently.

5.2.3 Heterogeneity Extensions

To support heterogeneity OmpSs introduces the **target** construct, which can be applied to either **task** or worksharing constructs or functions:

```
#pragma omp target [clauses]
task construct | worksharing construct |
function definition | function header
```

The intent of the **target** is to specify that a given computation can be run in a set of devices (core types, accelerators, etc.), the data movement necessary to offload that computation and possible optimized implementations for the devices. The valid clauses for the **target** construct are:

device It allows to specify on which devices should be targeting the construct (e.g. **cell**, **cuda**, **smp**, etc.). If no **device** clause is specified, then the target devices are decided by the implementation.

copy_in It specifies that a set of shared data may be needed to be transferred to the device before the associated code can be executed.

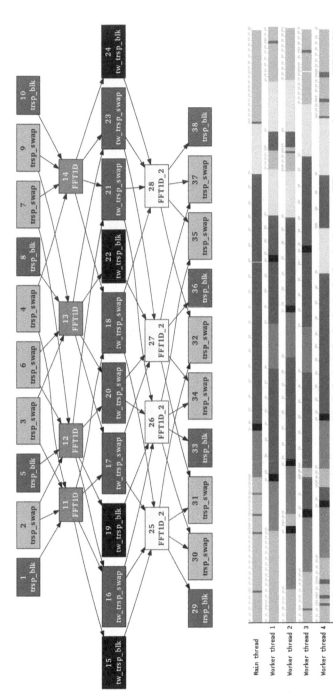

Figure 5.3 Dynamically generated task graph for the FFT example (4 × 4 blocks).

Figure 5.4 Task execution timeline for the FFT (16×16 blocks) example with 8 threads.

```
1    #pragma omp task inout([N][N] blk [0:TR_BS−1][0:TR_BS−1])
2    void trsp_blk(double _Complex blk[N][N]);
3
4    void trsp_swap (double _Complex blk1[N][N], double
5    _Complex blk2[N][N]);
6    void fft1d (double _Complex panel[FFT_BS][N]);
7    ...
8
9    void fft (double _Complex A[N][N]) {
10   // 1. Transpose
11   for (i=0; i<N; i+=TR_BS) {
12   trsp_blk (&A[i][i]);
13   #pragma omp for schedule(static,1) \
14   inout([N][N] A [i:i+TR_BS−1][j:j+TR_BS−1], \
15   [N][N] A [j:j+TR_BS−1][i:i+TR_BS−1])
16   for (j=i+TR_BS; j<N; j+=TR_BS)
17   trsp_swap (&A[i][j], &A[j][i]);
18   }
19   // 2. First FFT round
20   #pragma omp for schedule(static,1) \
21   inout([N][N] A [j:j+FFT_BS−1][0:N−1])
22   for (j=0; j<N; j+=FFT_BS)
23   fft1d(&A[j][0]);
24   ...
25   }
```

Figure 5.5   Example of OmpSs task and loop worksharing dependencies.

copy_out   It specifies that a set of shared data may be needed to be transferred from the device after the associated code is executed.

copy_inout   This clause is a combination of **copy_in** and **copy_out**.

copy_deps   It specifies that if the attached construct has any dependence clauses, then they will also have copy semantics (i.e. **input** will also be considered **copy_in**, **output copy_out** and **inout copy_inout**).

implements   It specifies that the code is an alternative implementation for the target devices of the function name specified in the clause. This alternative implementation can be used instead of the original one if the runtime considers it appropriate.

Figure 5.6 shows, for the same FFT example in Figure 5.1, the specialization of the task computing the *fft1d*. In this case, the programmer has chosen to use the CUFFT library and build an alternate implementation for this task. Since its execution targets a device with private memory, the **copy_*** clause is also used, in this case the shortcut to indicate the natural data movement implied by the dataflow clauses in the original **task** pragma.

The different **copy_*** clauses are advisory and not mandatory. This allows the implementation to take advantage of devices with access to the shared memory or implement different caching techniques. To make sure that data, which could have moved to a device, is valid again in the host, the SMP code must also use the **copy** clauses or appear after an OpenMP **flush** (either explicit or implicit). These clauses

```
1   #pragma omp task inout(panel)
2   void fft1d (double _Complex panel[FFT_BS][N]);
3
4   #pragma omp target device(cuda) copy_deps implements(fft1d)
5   void fft1d_specialized (double _Complex panel[FFT_BS][N]) {
6     cufftHandle plan;
7     CufftPlan1d (&plan, FFT_BS*B, CUFFT_C2C, 1);
8     CufftExecC2C (plan, CufftComplex *)panel,
9     CufftComplex *)panel, CUFFT_FORWARD);
10    CufftDestroy (plan);
11  }
```

Figure 5.6   FFT example with specialized task using CUFFT library for Nvidia GPUs.

can be checked at runtime for debugging purposes. We are developing a Valgrind-based tool to help programmers verify their correctness.

5.2.4 Hybrid MPI/OmpSs

OmpSs can also be used to leverage existing MPI codes so that the dataflow execution model in OmpSs can also be effectively used to exploit the distant parallelism that may exist between tasks in different regions separated by MPI calls. In order to achieve this, MPI calls need to be encapsulated in OmpSs tasks. From the local point of view of a process, tasks sending data to another process should receive the buffer as an input argument. Tasks receiving data from other processes should specify the buffer as an output of the task. With this encapsulation, the OmpSs scheduler is able to reorder the execution of communication tasks relative to the computational tasks, just guaranteeing that the dependences are fulfilled. In this way, the programmer is relieved from the responsibility to schedule the communication requests. At the global application level, MPI will impose synchronization between matching communication tasks. The fact that each of these tasks can be reordered with respect to the computation tasks enables the propagation of the asynchronous dataflow execution within each node to the whole MPI program.

Figure 5.7 shows two MPI communication calls encapsulated as OmpSs tasks and annotated with **device(comm_thread)**; this informs the runtime about the possible blocking nature of the code executed inside the task. Section 5.3 provides additional details about how these tasks are handled.

5.3 IMPLEMENTATION

Our implementation of OmpSs is built on two components: the Mercurium source-to-source compiler and the Nanos++ runtime library. In this section we provide the general idea for these two components and provide additional insight into the key modules in the runtime library (dependences detection, scheduler and the memory coherence) and their implementation for different architectures.

```
1    #pragma omp   target device(comm_thread)
2    #pragma omp task input(buf, count)
3    void send (double buf[count], int count)
4    {
5    MPI_Send(buf, count, MPI_DOUBLE, next_proc ,....);
6    }
7
8    #prama omp target device(comm_thread)
9    #pragma omp task input(count) output(buf)
10   void recv (double buf[count], int count)
11   {
12   MPI_Recv (buf, count, MPI_DOUBLE, prev_proc ,....)
13   }
```

Figure 5.7   Hybrid MPI/OmpSs example.

5.3.1   Mercurium Compiler

The compiler plays a relatively minor role on the implementation of the OmpSs model. On one side, the compiler recognizes the constructs and transforms them into calls to the Nanos++ runtime library. The dataflow clauses are transformed by generating a set of expressions that will be evaluated when the application is executed. These expressions will generate addresses of memory that will be passed to the runtime library to build the task dependency graph.

On the other side, the compiler manages code restructuring for different target devices. When the compiler is going to generate the code for a **task** construct, it look as if it were prepended with a **target** directive or if another **target** directive were linked to this task construct by means of an **implement** clause. If so, then the appropriate internal representation for the task is passed onto a device-specific 'handler' for each non-SMP device.

These 'handlers'generate the device-dependent data that must go associated with the task. They also, if necessary, generate a specialized outline for the device which may need to be generated in a separate file. This additional file is reintroduced in the compiler pipeline usually following a different compilation profile that will invoke different backend tools (e.g. the *nvcc* for *cuda* devices).

The binary output for these different files are merged together into a single object file that contains additional information about the different subobjects. This allows the compiler to maintain the traditional behavior of generating one object file per source file to enable compatibility with other tools (i.e. makefiles). The information is recovered at the linkage step to generate the final binary with all the objects.

5.3.2   Nanos++ Runtime Library

The Nanos++ runtime library is an extensible library for task-based programming models. The basic unit of work is called *work descriptor*. Both tasks and workshar-ing constructs are translated into *work descriptors*.

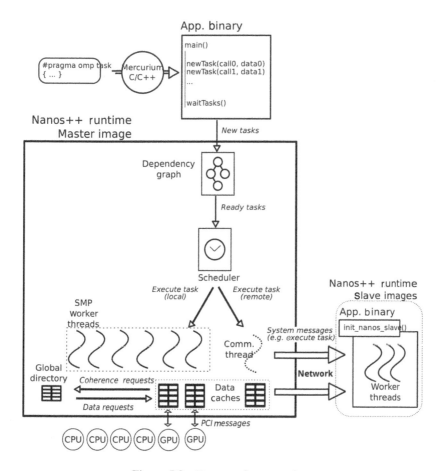

Figure 5.8   Nanos++ flow overview.

Figure 5.8 shows an overview of the flow of execution of a *work descriptor*. When created by the compiler generated code, *work descriptors* are composed of the following independent data: a data environment for its execution (including data that must be copied in/out the device before/after the task is executed), a list of data dependences and some properties (e.g. whether the task is tied [2] or not, etc.). Each *work descriptor* is attached with a list of device-dependent data. The list has as many elements as the number of devices where the task can run on. The information that each element contains depends on the specific device, but in general it contains the information needed to run the code associated to the *work descriptor* in the given device (e.g. a pointer to an outlined function). The runtime is oblivious to the contents of this list until it gets to the architecture-dependent layers where it is adequately

---

[2] An OpenMP tied task will keep executing on the same thread context after its first execution.

interpreted. This allows most of the policies and methods of the runtime system to be architecture-independent.

5.3.3 Detection of Task Dependencies

After creation, *work descriptors* are submitted into the runtime library. The first thing to be done is dependence checking. For this, the runtime maintains a directed acyclic graph where existing tasks are linked together based on the data dependences they have. For efficiency, instead of a global dependency graph, each task has a graph where dependencies of its children tasks are recorded (dependencies between tasks not related by a parental relation may result in deadlock and are explicitly forbidden in OmpSs).

To detect dependencies, the runtime computes the addresses of all arguments in the dependency clauses. The current implementation of dependency tracking for Nanos++ creates a graph edge for read after write (RAW), write after read (WAR) and write after write (WAW) dependencies that result from the evaluation of the addresses specified in the dependency clauses. WAW and WAR dependencies are false dependencies resulting from storage reuse. Both the compiler and the runtime system can eliminate such false dependencies. It is our decision to do this at runtime. The runtime system detects and removes them by allocating additional storage and making each *work descriptor* work with a different storage location. This is the same technique used in current superscalar processors and optimizing compilers to remove false dependencies due to the reuse of registers. In OmpSs the renaming may apply to whole regions of memory passed as arguments to a *work descriptor*. The runtime is responsible for properly handling the actual storage instance passed to each *work descriptor*. Also if necessary, it copies back the data to its original position. This renaming mechanism has the potential to use available memory to increase the actual amount of parallelism detected. An excessive use of renaming may result in swapping and may introduce a high-performance penalty. A parameter in a configuration file limits the size of memory that can be used for renaming.

Currently, the Nanos++ runtime does not support dependence checking between disjoint array sections. But this support has already been developed in other environments [9]. For contiguous data objects, checking dependencies is as easy as comparing their initial address and size. However, when discontiguous data objects are considered, this check may become very complex. A naive solution based on an address-by-address comparison would give exact answer although it would be unmanageable in terms of space and time. A compact representation for a set of addresses is proposed [9]. This solution consists of a linearized representation based on the actual addresses of the covered elements. This representation is not exact and will represent only with total precision certain sets of addresses (e.g. regions aligned and with dimensions with sizes power of two). Generating this low-level compact representation can be very time consuming as well; for this reason an algorithm with linear cost is proposed.

To represent regions, a low-level representation is used. This representation is an ordered sequence of digits such that the value of each digit can be either 0, 1 or

X [9]. To give an idea, the low-level representation is a superset of the addresses contained in the region. Another data structure important in this approach is the region tree [9] that contains information for all the regions accessed in an application. The region tree indexes the information about the regions accessed by an application using the low-level representation as index. Each edge is labeled with one of the possible digit values in the low-level representation, and the sequence of edge values from the root node to each leaf determines the low-level representation of the region. Given a region to look up all intersecting regions on a tree, the tree must be traversed following the edges that could lead to intersecting regions. If the region overlaps totally or partially with an existing region, it means that a dependency exists and this is updated in the task dependency graph and in the region tree.

Both the computation of the low-level representation of a region and the traversal and update of the region tree have a significant overhead. However, these overheads are compensated by the potential parallelism that can be discovered. For example, in the case of the FFT shown in Figure 5.1, in the absence of regions, the programmer would be forced to use a barrier synchronization between the transposition tasks and the FFT tasks, precluding the overlap between these phases.

5.3.4   The Scheduler Component

Once all the data dependencies are satisfied, the *work descriptor* passes to the scheduling module. The scheduling module is divided in two different parts. On one hand there are the different mechanisms like context switching, idling, blocking and queueing. On the other hand there is the scheduling policy. All mechanisms are oblivious of the actual policy in use which can be adjusted for each execution. Nanos++ supports different task scheduling policies, but we used here a locality-aware policy that minimizes the amount of data transfers in an execution environment like the GPUs, or the *cluster* version is critical to obtain good performance.

The locality-aware scheduling policy favors moving code to data and not data to code. A global directory stores a map with the location of all data in the system. When a new task is ready, the scheduler computes an affinity score for each device based on the data that the task will use and the size of that data. This score is used to place the *work descriptor* in the queue of the device with the highest affinity. If no device has the highest affinity, it is placed in a global queue which is accessed by all devices and the main host.

When a thread looks for work, it looks first into its device queue. If the queue is empty, then it looks into the global queue. If also empty, it tries to steal work from the queues of the other devices to prevent the load imbalance of the execution. Also, when the execution of a *work descriptor* finishes, the scheduler tries to select first a successor in the dependency graph before looking in the ready queues. The idea behind this is that it will further improve data locality. Ready queues are implemented using spinlock synchronization.

The scheduler component is also responsible for deciding the device best suited to execute the task (if it can run in more than one). Different policies can be implemented, including simple ones based on the order in the **device** clause, based on the availability of the device, based on performance predictions for each device or, for example, based on the current location of the data accessed by the task.

5.3.5 Memory Consistency Component

Once the scheduler selects which thread (and device) should run a task, the runtime calls the memory coherence subsystem to ensure that the data specified by the programmer is available in the device (or host). To do this, the runtime maintains a directory with information about where data is in the system and its status (this is similar to that used for the locality scheduling). For efficiency reasons this directory is implemented in a hierarchical fashion where each *work descriptor* knows about the data referenced by its children. Using this directory, the runtime decides if for the *work descriptor* to be executed data needs to be moved or not. The directory is also used at **flush** points to invalidate the data (and thus force a flush to main memory if it is dirty) on the different devices. Because of the hierarchical design of the directory, we are able to flush only the dirty contents of each *work descriptor* context, without needing to flush all the devices memory which would result in too many memory transfers. It is important to notice that the coherence mechanisms assume program correctness. Applications where tasks write the same data simultaneously without specifying the correct synchronization (e.g. by means of dependencies) result in an undetermined behavior.

If data needs to be moved, it calls the architecture-dependent copy mechanisms. This allows to use optimized data movement and caching techniques for every device while the general coherence logic is shared across all devices. For most devices Nanos++ maintains a cache with the data that is currently alive in the device, along with its location in the device and a version number. This version number is matched against the version number of the same data in the directory to check if the data on the device is still valid.

For example, in the implementation for Nvidia GPUs, the runtime maintains two per-GPU structures: a GPU memory arena and a data cache. The memory arena is created at the beginning of the execution by calling *cudaMalloc* to obtain a large chunk of GPU memory.[3] Afterward, instead of using the slow CUDA calls for allocation/deallocation, our simpler (and faster) routines are used. They are lock-free because each GPU has a single host thread acting as representative, and only this thread can allocate and deallocate memory from the GPU. The data cache is invoked every time data is supposed to go into the device. If the data already exists in the device, then a pointer to it is returned. Otherwise, storage is allocated if necessary (storage can be reused even if the data is no longer valid) and the data transferred into the device. This step may involve communication with another device if that device holds the latest version of a piece of data. The cache ensures that this device-to-device communication is done correctly. The cache will also decide, depending on the configured policy, whether to synchronize the GPU data after each *work de-*

---

[3]We reserve 80% of the memory by default. The remaining allows user applications to still use CUDA on their own up to a point.

scriptor finish (write-through policy) or delay it as much as possible (write-back policy).

For clustered architectures, there exists as well a cache per node and a preallocated arena of remote memory to be used as the cache storage. As in the GPU case, the cache is invoked when data needs to go into the device. The cache manages the transfers from main memory to the remote nodes, memory, avoiding unnecessary data movement and implementing different cache policies. By the default, the node caches use a *write-back* policy to avoid usage of the network as much as possible.

Note that even *work descriptors* that are going to execute in the host need to check the coherence mechanisms as the last valid version of the data it is going to use could be in a GPU or a remote node. Therefore, it needs to be transferred back to main memory and invalidated in the corresponding device.

5.3.6 Task Execution on the Target Device

Finally, the *work descriptor* is passed down the architecture-dependent thread layer that extracts the device-dependent information of the *work descriptor* and executes it. Architecture-specific optimizations are performed at this level.

For example, the execution of work for GPUs in its most basic form consists of only invoking the CUDA kernel that is contained in the device-dependent data of the *work descriptor* and calling *cudaThreadSynchronize* to ensure the kernel has finished. The Nanos++ runtime, between these two actions, can also prefetch the next *work descriptor* and start transferring the data it may need or overlap the output data of a previously executed *work descriptor*. These optimizations are disabled by default as our experience indicates that in most applications and modern GPUs, there is a penalization in the kernel execution time when prefetch or double buffering techniques are used (resulting in a slowdown of the total execution time).

In the cluster architecture, besides the *master* image, there is a *slave* image in each remote node. A special communication thread handles the execution of *work descriptors* in the remote nodes. The remote execution of tasks is a straightforward process. The *master* image sends a control message with the task information to the remote node that just needs to execute it. The slave images are constantly waiting for upcoming requests, and they will start the execution of the task as soon as the request arrives. When the task finishes, another message is sent back to the master to notify about the completion of the task. All low-level communications for control information and data transfers are implemented using *active messages*. We used GASNet [4] for this functionality since it offers a network-independent API with native support for various network technologies.

Tasks executed in a remote node can create new tasks that use the data transferred or created by their parent task. Local task creation improves scalability by distributing the overhead across remote nodes. Tasks created locally will be executed by any thread available in the node, before searching for work on the master node.

5.3.7   Handling Communication Tasks

With the encapsulation of MPI communication primitives in OmpSs tasks, the scheduler is able to reorder the execution of communication tasks relative to the computational tasks, just guaranteeing that the dependences are fulfilled. In this way, the programmer is relieved from the responsibility to schedule the communication requests. At the global application level, MPI imposes synchronization between matching communication tasks. The fact that each of these tasks can be reordered with respect to the computation tasks enables the propagation of the asynchronous dataflow execution within each node to the whole MPI application.

Tasks that encapsulate blocking MPI calls have an unpredictable execution time (depending on the MPI synchronization with the matching call in the remote process). This may cause deadlock if we actually devote processors to these tasks and not to advance computational tasks. In order to solve this problem, we need to ensure that every process can always devote resources to the computational task such that local progress is guaranteed. A second effect of communication tasks is that they do not make an efficient use of processor time, wasting resources while they are blocked. It would be interesting to maximize the amount of actual computation performed while the data transfer activities are overlapped with it.

The implementation in [7] instantiates as many threads as cores in the node to execute computational tasks plus one additional thread that only executes tasks that encapsulate MPI calls. When the MPI call blocks, the thread releases the core and thus as many computation threads as cores can be active during most of the time (if the applications has sufficient parallelism at the node level). When the blocking of MPI call completes, the blocked thread will wake up and thus contend for a core with the other threads. It is important to minimize such contention and also accelerate the execution of the communication threads as this would free local dependences, progress to the next communication task and block again. The sooner these activities are done, the faster the application will be able to progress globally. An easy solution to achieve this is to reduce the priority of the computing threads (through a *setpriority* call at initialization time) and leave the communication thread at a higher priority. In this way, when the communication thread blocks, all computation threads can proceed. When the communication thread unblocks, it gets to execute rapidly.

5.4   TASK GRANULARITY

Task granularity presents a fundamental trade-off between performance and programmability. While smaller tasks could be more intuitive to the programmer, the overhead of decoding task dependencies can prevent models such as OmpSs from scaling. Following the creation of a task, its data dependencies must be identified, so it can be added to the task graph. Effective utilization of resources thus requires that detecting those dependencies is done faster than they are consumed by the devices. As a baseline, we have measured the average decode rate for a highly tuned decoder of OmpSs, to be just over 700 ns, running on a 2.66 GHz Intel Core Duo. We consider this a performance indicator for software-based task decoders as other

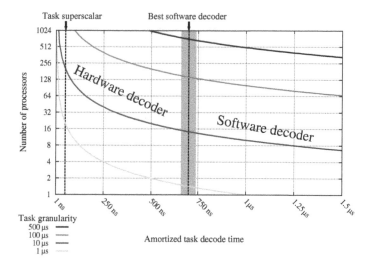

Figure 5.9 Scalability projections of hardware and software task decoders for various task granularities. The grey region in the middle of the figure indicates the scalability limitations of software-based task decoders, based on the highly tuned software decoder of OmpSs running on a modern architecture.

configurations incurred higher overheads. For example, the CellSs implementation of OmpSs incurs a task decode overhead of 2.5 µs. To make numbers simpler, if we assume a task runtime of 100 µs, a 1 µs decoding overhead would not allow the system to utilize more than 100 processors since after sending a task to the first processor, the decoder must be able to send work to all other 99 processors before the first one finishes. More formally, given a task runtime T and an amortized task decode overhead D, the number of processors that can be utilized[4] is $P = \frac{T}{D}$. Therfore, the conclusion is that minimizing the task decode overhead is crucial for system scalability, particularly when targeting medium- to fine-grain tasks.

The trade-off between performance and programmability advocates research in designing hardware-based dependency decode mechanisms can reduce the overhead of decoding tasks dependencies by over an order of magnitude, thereby supporting fine-grain, easy to program tasks. Figure 5.9 illustrates this trade-off. The figure shows the number of processor cores that can be utilized by a task decoder as a function of the decode overhead, for various task granularities, with the overheads measured for the OmpSs software decoder serving as an indicator for the scalability of software-only decoders. For example, a software decoder serving fine-grain 10 µs tasks cannot support more than 16 processor cores. In contrast, employing explicit hardware support for task decoding can potentially provide much greater scalability. One such example is that of *task superscalar* [6].

---

[4]For brevity, this calculation assumes optimal conditions in the sense of ignoring intertask data dependencies.

Task superscalar is an abstraction of an instruction-level out-of-order pipeline that operates at the task level. Like ILP pipelines, which uncover parallelism in a sequential instruction stream, the proposed task superscalar architecture uncovers task-level parallelism among tasks generated from an annotated OmpSs application. As done by its software counterpart, the task superscalar pipeline dynamically detects intertask data dependencies, identifies task-level parallelism and executes tasks out of order. In [6] the design for a distributed task superscalar pipeline front end, which can be embedded into any many-core fabric and manages cores as functional units, is proposed. The mechanism is capable of driving hundreds of cores simultaneously with nonspeculative tasks, which allows the pipeline to sustain work windows consisting of tens thousands of tasks (for a 7 MB of on-chip eDRAM). Such a large task window enables the pipeline to uncover distant parallelism and manage large multicores as a unity. Furthermore, results in that paper show that task superscalar provides fast decoding of data dependencies and adds new tasks to the task window in less than 60 ns on average. As shown in Figure 5.9, this decode rate enables programs employing fine-grain $10 \mu s$ task to scale up to ~ 256 processor cores.

Finally, other architectural parameters may impose secondary effects on the execution model. For example, if the task runtime is shorter than the time required to transfer the task data and code to the designated device, overlapping communication with computation becomes impossible as memory latencies prevail, thereby imposing a minimal task granularity.

5.5 RELATED WORK

Current hardware designs targeting from embedded products to high-performance computing incorporate multi- and many-core processors. Both homogeneous processors and heterogeneous solutions (Cell/B.E., GPUs) are presented in this book (chapter 'Multi- and Many-cores, Architectural Overview for Programmers'). In parallel, a growing number of programming and execution environments are being proposed to reduce the productivity gap between the possibilities available from the hardware and their reasonable exploitation from the programmer side. The chapter on programming models for many cores presents a useful classification of parallel programming models and environments, some of them related to our OmpSs proposal.

5.6 FUTURE WORK

We are currently porting a number of production applications and benchmarks to OmpSs. The goal is to learn what are the current limitations of the OmpSs programming model and the ability it has to better exploit the parallelism available on them. Regarding the runtime implementation, we are currently exploring novel scheduling policies (e.g. locality aware) and the use of autotuning to decide the appropriate mapping of tasks to resources available in the target architecture. Fault tolerance is a feature being included in the OmpSs runtime; transactional memory support is being leveraged to support this new feature and to provide speculative task execution.

The potential of modern parallel programming models, and specifically that of OmpSs, in alleviating much of the programming burden imposed by existing parallel programming models, should serve as a catalyst to explore novel control mechanisms for emerging multiprocessors and identify new programming abstractions that must be explicitly supported by the hardware, in order to overcome both programmability and scalability facing the parallel programming landscape.

5.7 CONCLUDING REMARKS

This chapter has presented one of the novel programming models that has been proposed to address the productive exploitation of parallelism in heterogeneous architectures. The proposal is based on a few extensions to the OpenMP 3.0 programming and execution models. In terms of programming model, a clean way to express the dataflow requirements for tasks is the basis for deriving task dependencies at run time and to implement locality-aware dataflow scheduling policies, in which data movement between different levels of the memory hierarchy or different address spaces is optimized. Also, the programming model allows a portable and incremental specification of architecture heterogeneity which provides enough information to the runtime to take scheduling decisions with different trade-offs in mind. We believe that the proposal is sufficiently generic to cover current homogeneous and heterogeneous architectures but also future ones. Finally, OmpSs easily leverages current practices based on the use of MPI and low-level extensions for specifying optimized kernels relieving the programmer from injecting computation and communication/data movement scheduling decisions.

The chapter describes the implementation of the proposed OmpSs programming model, backed up by previous proof-of-concept implementations for different target architectures. A unified runtime architecture provides support for clusters composed of heterogenous accelerator and multicore nodes. Although visible overheads are introduced when supporting all OmpSs features, we have observed that the potential parallelism that can be discovered and the better resource utilization easily compensate them.

ACKNOWLEDGMENTS

We thankfully acknowledge the support of the European Commission through the ENCORE project (FP7-248647), the TERAFLUX project (FP7-249013), the TEXT project (FP7-261580) and the HiPEAC-2 Network of Excellence (FP7/ICT 217068); the support of the Spanish Ministry of Education (TIN2007-60625 and CSD2007-00050) and the Generalitat de Catalunya (2009-SGR-980 and 2009-SGR-1372); and the BSC–IBM MareIncognito project. Ioanna Tsalouchidou, from National Technical University of Athens (NTUA), is supported by the Erasmus student exchange programme. Yoav Etsion is supported by a Juan de la Cierva Fellowship from the Ministry of Science and Innovation of Spain.

REFERENCES

1. E. Ayguade, R. M. Badia, D. Cabrera, A. Duran, M. Gonzalez, F. Igual, D. Jimenez, J. Labarta, X. Martorell, R. Mayo, J. M. Perez, and E. S. Quintana-Orti. A proposal to extend the OpenMP tasking model for heterogeneous architectures. In *IWOMP: Evolving OpenMP in an Age of Extreme Parallelism*. LNCS, volume 5568, pages 154–167, June 2009.

2. E. Ayguadé, R. M. Badia, F. Igual-Pe na, J. Labarta, R. Mayo, and E. Quintana-Orti. An extension of the StarSs programming model for platforms with multiple GPUs. In *Euro-Par 2009*, 2009.

3. R. D. Blumofe, C. F. Joerg, B. C. Kuszmaul, C. E. Leiserson, K. H. Randall, and Y. Zhou. Cilk: an efficient multithreaded runtime system. *SIGPLAN Notices.*, 30(8):207–216, 1995.

4. D. Bonachea. GASNet Specification, v1.1. Technical report, U.C. Berkeley, October 2002.

5. A. Duran, J. M. Pérez, E. Ayguadé, R. M. Badia, and J. Labarta. Extending the OpenMP tasking model to allow dependent tasks. In *IWOMP: OpenMP in a New Era of Parallelism. LNCS,* volume 5004, pages 111–122, 2008.

6. Y. Etsion, F. Cabarcas, A. Rico, A. Ramirez, R. M. Badia, E. Ayguadé, J. Labarta, and M. Valero. Task superscalar: an out-of-order task pipeline. In *43rd International Symposium on Microarchitecture (MICRO-43)*, 2010.

7. V. Marjanovic, J. Labarta, E. Ayguadé, and M. Valero. Overlapping communication and computation by using a hybrid MPI/SMPSs approach. In *24th ACM International Conference on Supercomputing (ICS-2010)*, 2010.

8. J. M. Perez, R. M. Badia, and J. Labarta. A dependency-aware task-based programming environment for multi-core architectures. *IEEE International Conference on Cluster Computing*, pages 142–151, September 2008.

9. J. M. Perez, R. M. Badia, and J. Labarta. Handling task dependencies under strided and aliased references. In *Proceedings of the 24th ACM International Conference on Super-computing*, ICS '10, pages 263–274, 2010.

10. J. M. Perez, P. Bellens, R. M. Badia, and J. Labarta. CellSs: making it easier to program the Cell Broadband Engine processor. *IBM Journal of Research and Development*, 51(5):593–604, September 2007.

CHAPTER 6

SKELETON PROGRAMMING FOR PORTABLE MANY-CORE COMPUTING

CHRISTOPH KESSLER, SERGEI GORLATCH, JOHAN ENMYREN, USMAN DASTGEER, MICHEL STEUWER AND PHILIPP KEGEL

6.1 INTRODUCTION

The general trend toward multi- and many-core-based systems constitutes a disruptive change in the fundamental programming model in mainstream computing and requires rewriting of sequential application programs into parallel form to turn the steadily increasing number of cores into performance. Worse yet, there are a number of very different architectural paradigms such as homogeneous SMP-like multicores, heterogeneous multicores like Cell Broadband Engine™ or hybrid CPU/GPU systems, sometimes with a very high complexity of programming such systems efficiently. Moreover, we observe a quick evolution process on the hardware side, pushing new architecture generations and variations on the market with short time intervals. The lack of a universal parallel programming model immediately leads to a portability problem. OpenCL™ is an attempt to establish portability across a larger scope of architectures, but it works at a very low level of abstraction.

Programming Multicore and Many-core Computing Systems,
First Edition. Edited by Sabri Pllana and Fatos Xhafa.

In this chapter we show that *skeleton programming* can, to a large degree, solve the portability problem and also raise the level of abstraction in multi-and many-core programming.

We first revisit the concept of algorithmic skeletons in Section 6.2. Sections 6.3 and 6.4 give a detailed description of two recent approaches for programming emerging heterogeneous many-core systems, namely, SkePU and SkelCL. Basic concepts of these frameworks are presented as well as some application examples. Section 6.5 summarizes some other skeleton programming frameworks, which share some ideas with SkePU and SkelCL but address a more narrow range of architectures or are used in industrial application development.

6.2   BACKGROUND: SKELETON PROGRAMMING

Skeletons are predefined generic components derived from higher-order functions that can be parameterized in sequential problem-specific code and for which efficient implementation for a given target platform exists. *Skeleton programming* constrains the programmer to using only the given set of skeletons for the code that is to be parallelized or ported automatically – computations that do not fit any predefined skeleton (combination) still have to be rewritten manually. In turn, parallelism and synchronization, as well as leveraging the target architectural features, come almost for free for skeleton-expressed computations: skeleton instances can easily be expanded or bounded to equivalent expert-written efficient target code that encapsulates all low-level platform-specific details such as managing parallelism, load balancing, communication, utilization of SIMD instructions, etc. Hence, as long as a computation can be expressed in terms of the available skeletons, parallel programming is not harder than well-structured sequential programming.

Based on the main source of parallelism to be exploited, skeletons can be classified into *data-parallel* and *task-parallel* skeletons. In the following, we introduce a few important representatives of each category, including those that we will use later in example codes. We put more emphasis on the data-parallel skeletons here because our skeleton systems described later mainly target GPU-based systems, which traditionally only support data parallelism.

6.2.1 Data-Parallel Skeletons

Data-parallel skeletons operate on sequences of data structures in a parallel manner. While existing language-specific data types such as arrays or lists could be applied, these aggregated operands are technically often represented in generic container data types such as `vector` that can hide implementation details internally and improve portability. The data-parallel skeletons draw their main source of parallelism from applying the same function in an element-wise manner. The most fundamental and well-known data-parallel skeletons are Map, Reduce, Scan and variations and combinations of these.

In the Map skeleton, every element in the result vector v_0 is a function f of the corresponding elements in one or more input vectors $v_1 \ldots v_k$. Formally, $v_0[i] =$

$f(v_1[i], \ldots, v_k[i])$ $\forall i \in \{0, \ldots, N-1\}$ where the k input vectors $v_1, \ldots, v_k$ and the output vector v_0 are assumed to all have the same *length* N, that is, number of elements. An example of the Map skeleton in SkelCL is shown in Listing 6.3. Some skeleton frameworks use different skeleton names for Map with different arity, and most frameworks limit the number of operands to a small constant.

The *MapOverlap* skeleton is a generalization of Map where each element $v_0[i]$ of the result vector is a function of several adjacent elements of one input vector v that reside at a certain constant maximum distance d from i in that input vector. Formally, $v_0[i] = f(v[i-d], v[i-d+1], \ldots, v[i+d])$ $\forall i \in \{0, \ldots, N-1\}$. Image filters such as convolution are examples for calculations that fit into this pattern. An example for such a function f for a Gaussian blur filter used with a MapOverlap skeleton in SkePU is shown in Figure 6.2. Especially for nonshared memory systems, the (maximum) value for the overlap d is an important design parameter because it implies the required amount of temporary buffering for data to be communicated at boundaries between regions of v that are mapped to different execution units.

By using additional arguments in SkelCL (see Listing 6.4), the MapOverlap skeleton can also be implemented using the Map skeleton.

Reduction is another common data-parallel pattern. The scalar result r is computed by applying a commutative associative binary operator $\oplus$ across all N elements of the input vector v: $r = v[0] \oplus v[1] \oplus \cdots \oplus v[N-1]$. A reduction using + as operator would, for example, yield the global sum of the input vector elements. Such an instantiation of the *Reduce* skeleton in SkePU is shown in the first line of Figure 6.4.

Different skeleton instances can be composed serially in a straightforward way using data flow, by feeding the result value of one skeleton invocation as an input argument of a subsequent one. In certain cases it makes sense to define new skeletons for frequently occurring combinations, because the computation and buffering of intermediate results can be specially optimized and internal synchronization constraints can be relaxed. For instance, when executed on an accelerator such as a GPU, intermediate results could be kept in device memory, and the combined skeleton computations could share the same computation kernel, leading to reduced overhead. A typical example of such a combination is the *MapReduce* skeleton, whose behavior is the same as if one would first apply a Map on one or more input vectors to produce an intermediate result vector and then do a reduction on that intermediate vector.

Formally, $r = f(v_1[0], \ldots, v_k[0]) \oplus \cdots \oplus f(v_1[N-1], \ldots, v_k[N-1])$. An example of MapReduce in SkePU is shown in Listing 6.1 which, instantiated with f =mult for mapping and $\oplus$ =plus for reduction, computes the dot product of two vectors.

Scan or *prefix sums* is a generalization of reduction where the partial sums of the first i elements, for all $i = 0, \ldots, N-1$, should be returned in a vector. For a binary associative operation $\oplus$, the prefix-$\oplus$ vector v_0 of operand vector v_1 is thus defined by $v_0[i] = \bigoplus_{j=0}^{i} v_1[j]$ $\forall i \in \{0, \ldots, N-1\}$. Scan is an important building block of scalable parallel algorithms such as parallel integer sorting.

6.2.2 Task-Parallel Skeletons

A *task farm* is a set of independent tasks that are to be executed. Generally, the computational load of the tasks may vary and is not known before runtime, which requires parallel implementations that apply dynamic load balancing to map the tasks to execution resources. A common special case of task farming holds if the task code is the same for all task instances. A typical case is a parallel loop, that is, a loop that has no interiteration dependences. Skeleton programming frameworks sometimes provide a parallel loop skeleton such as *Forall* for this important special case.

Pipelining denotes a task-parallel pattern that operates on one or several input streams, where tasks are generally dependent for the same input element but independent for different input elements. Pipelines of tasks are represented by task graphs where edges show the forwarding of intermediate results from producing to consuming tasks in the pipeline. For frequent cases such as a linear pipeline, some skeleton frameworks provide a specific `pipe` construct.

6.3 SKEPU: A TUNABLE SKELETON PROGRAMMING LIBRARY

SkePU [6] is a skeleton programming framework for multicore CPU and multi-GPU systems. It currently provides six data-parallel algorithmic skeletons, two container types, and support for execution on multi-GPU systems both with CUDA™ and OpenCL™. SkePU is a C++ template library that provides a simple and unified interface for specifying data-parallel computations with the help of skeletons on GPUs using CUDA and OpenCL. The interface is also general enough to support other architectures, and SkePU implements both a sequential CPU and a parallel OpenMP™ backend.

As a simple way of defining functions that can be used with the skeletons regardless of the target architecture, SkePU provides a *macro language* where preprocessor macros expand, depending on the target selection, to the right kind of structure that constitutes the function. The SkePU user functions generated from a macro-based specification are basically a `struct` with member functions for CUDA and CPU and strings for OpenCL. Figure 6.1 shows one of the macros and its expansion.

6.3.1 Skeletons and Containers

6.3.1.1 Skeletons SkePU provides `Map`, `Reduce`, `MapReduce`, `MapOverlap`, `MapArray` and `Scan` skeletons with sequential CPU, OpenMP, CUDA and OpenCL implementations. A program using SkePU needs to include SkePU header file(s) for skeleton(s) and container(s) used in the program that are defined under the namespace `skepu`.

In the object-oriented spirit of C++, the skeleton functions in SkePU are represented by objects. By overloading `operator()`, they can be made to behave in a way similar to regular functions. All of the skeletons contain member functions representing each of the different implementations, CUDA, OpenCL, OpenMP and CPU. The member functions are called CU, CL, OMP and CPU, respectively. If the

```
BINARY_FUNC(plus, double,
a, b, return a+b; )


         ⇓ EXPANDS TO: ⇓


struct plus
{
skepu::FuncType funcType;
std::string func_CL;
std::string funcName_CL;
std::string datatype_CL;
plus()
{
funcType = skepu::BINARY;
      (continues in right column)
```

```
       (continued from left column)
funcName_CL.append("plus");
datatype_CL.append("double");
func_CL.append(
"double plus(double a, double b)\n"
"{\n"
"    return a+b;\n"
"}\n");
}
double CPU(double a, double b)
{
return a+b;
}
__device__ double CU(double a,
double b)
{
return a+b;
}
};
```

Figure 6.1   User function, macro expansion.

skeleton is called with `operator()`, the library decides which one to use depending on the execution plan used (see Section 6.3.3). In the OpenCL case, the skeleton objects also contain the necessary code generation and compilation procedures. When a skeleton is instantiated, it creates an environment to execute in, containing all available OpenCL or CUDA devices in the system. This environment is created as a singleton so that it is shared among all skeletons in the program. As an example,

```
skepu::Reduce<plus> globalSum(new plus);
```

creates a skeleton instance called `globalSum` by instantiating the Reduce skeleton with the user function `plus` (as described in Fig. 6.1) as a parameter. In the current version of SkePU, it needs to be provided both as a template parameter and as a pointer to an instantiated version of the user function (remember that the user functions are in fact `structs`).

6.3.1.2 Multi-GPU Support   SkePU has support for carrying out computations with the help of several GPUs on a data-parallel level. By default, SkePU will utilize as many GPUs as it can find in the system; however, this can be controlled by defining `SKEPU_NUMGPU`. Setting it to 0 makes it use its default behavior. Any other number represents the number of GPUs it should try to use.

6.3.1.3 Containers   In addition to the skeletal functions, SkePU also includes an implementation for the containers `Vector` and `Matrix` (where `Matrix` currently does not yet support all six skeletons).

The skeletons can be called with whole containers as arguments, doing the operation on all elements of the container, or with *iterators* specifying start and end of an access range, which allows to apply the skeleton on parts of a vector.

The `Vector` container represents a vector/array type, designed after the STL container `vector`. Its implementation uses the STL `vector` internally, and its interface is mostly compatible with STL `vector`. For instance,

```
skepu::Vector<double> input(100,10);
```

creates a vector of size 100 with all elements initialized to 10.

`Matrix` is a 2D container that internally uses a 1D container (`std::vector`). Its interface and behavior are similar to the SkePU `Vector` but with some additions and variations. It provides methods to access elements by row and column index and is resizable. Furthermore, it provides an iterator for row-wise access, while for column-wise access, matrix transpose is to be used to provide read-only access.

6.3.1.4 Lazy Memory Copying   The SkePU containers hide GPU memory management and internally use lazy memory copying to avoid unnecessary memory transfer operations between main memory and device memory. A SkePU container keeps track of which parts of it are currently allocated and uploaded to the GPU. If a computation is done, modifying the elements in a container in the GPU memory, these are not immediately transferred back to the host memory. Instead, the container waits until an element is accessed on the host side before any copying is done (eg., through the [] operator for `Vector`). This lazy memory copying is of great use if several skeletons are called one after the other, with no modifications of the container by the host in between. In that case, the payload data of the containers is kept on the device (GPU) through all the computations, which greatly improves performance. Most of the memory copying is done implicitly, but the containers also contain a `flush` operation which updates a container from the device and deallocates its memory.

6.3.1.5 A Small Example   Listing 6.1 shows a complete example using SkePU using the MapReduce skeleton. The MapReduce skeleton is instantiated with two user functions, one for the mapping part and one for reduction. Two parameters are needed at instantiation time: first the function for mapping and then the function for reduction. Here, a MapReduce skeleton is created which will map two vectors with `mult` and then reduce the result with `plus`, thus implementing the dot product of the two vectors. The result value computed in this example is 4000.

6.3.2   Application Examples

We present two example applications implemented with SkePU: a Gaussian blur filter and a Runge–Kutta ODE solver.

6.3.2.1 Gaussian Blur Filter   The Gaussian blur filter is a common operation in computer graphics that convolves an input image with a Gaussian function, producing a new smoother and blurred image. The method basically calculates the new value of each pixel based on its own and its surrounding pixels' values.

```
1 #include <iostream>
2 #include "skepu/vector.h"
3 #include "skepu/mapreduce.h"
4
5 BINARY_FUNC(plus, double, a, b,
6 return a+b;
7 )
8
9 BINARY_FUNC(mult, double, a, b,
10 return a*b;
11 )
12
13 int main()
14 {
15 skepu::MapReduce<mult, plus> dotProduct( new mult, new plus );
16
17 skepu::Vector<double> v0(1000,2);
18 skepu::Vector<double> v1(1000,2);
19
20 double r = dotProduct(v0,v1);
21
22 std::cout<<"Result: " <<r <<"\n";    return 0;
23 }
```

Listing 6.1   A MapReduce example that computes the dot product.

```
1 OVERLAP_FUNC(blur_kernel, int, 19, a,
2 return (a[-9] + 18*a[-8] + 153*a[-7] + 816*a[-6] + 3060*a[-5]
3 + 8568*a[-4] + 18564*a[-3] + 31824*a[-2] + 43758*a[-1]
4 + 48620*a[0] + 43758*a[1] + 31824*a[2] + 18564*a[3]
5 + 8568*a[4] + 3060*a[5] + 816*a[6] + 153*a[7]
6 + 18*a[8] + a[9])>>18;
7 )
```

Listing 6.2   User function used by MapOverlap when blurring an image.

It can be done either in two dimensions, for each pixel accessing a square halo of neighbor pixels around it, or in one dimension by running two passes over the image: one row-wise and one column-wise. For simplicity, we use here the second approach, which allows to use Vector as container for the image data. When calculating a pixel value, the surrounding pixels are needed but only within a limited neighborhood. This fits well into the calculation pattern of the MapOverlap skeleton. MapArray (a variant of MapOverlap without the restriction to a constant-sized overlap) was also used to restructure the array from row-wise to column-wise data layout. The blurring calculation then becomes a MapOverlap to blur horizontally, then a MapArray to restructure the image and another MapOverlap to blur vertically. The image was first loaded into a vector with padding between rows.

Timing was only done on the actual blur computation, not including the loading of images and creation of vectors. For CUDA and OpenCL, the time for transferring the image to the GPU and copying the result back is included. The filtering was done with two passes of a 19-value filter kernel which can be seen in Listing 6.2. For simplicity, only grayscale images of quadratic sizes were used in the benchmark.

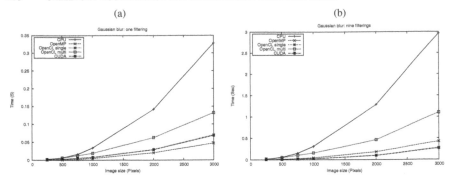

Figure 6.2   Average (100 runs) time of blurring quadratic grayscale images of different sizes. (a) Gaussian kernel applied *once* to the image. (b) Gaussian kernel applied *nine* times to the image.

Figure 6.2(a) shows the time when applying the filter kernel *once* to the image, and Figure 6.2(b) when applying it nine times in sequence, resulting in heavier blur. We see that while faster than the CPU variant, CUDA and OpenCL versions are slower than the one using OpenMP on 8 CPU cores for one filtering. This is due to the memory transfer time being much larger than the actual calculation. In Figure 6.2(b), however, filtering is done nine times which means more computations and less memory I/O due to the lazy memory copying of the vector. Then the two single GPU variants outperform even the OpenMP version.

Since there is a data dependency in the MapOverlap skeleton when running on multiple GPUs, we also see that running this configuration loses a lot of performance when applying MapOverlap several times in a row because it needs to transfer data between the GPUs, via the host.

6.3.2.2 ODE Solver   A sequential Runge–Kutta ODE solver was ported to GPU using the SkePU library. The original code used for the porting is part of *LibSolve*, a library of various Runge–Kutta solvers for ODEs by Korch and Rauber [15]. LibSolve contains several Runge–Kutta implementations, iterated and embedded ones, as well as implementations for parallel machines using shared or distributed memory. The simplest default sequential implementation was used for the port to SkePU; however other solver variants were used unmodified for comparison. One of the ODE test sets provided in LibSolve, BRUSS2D-MIX, was used for evaluating SkePU.

Four different grid sizes (problem sizes) were evaluated: 250, 500, 750 and 1000.

The porting was fairly straightforward since the default sequential solver in Lib-Solve is a conventional Runge–Kutta solver consisting of several loops over arrays sized according to the problem size. These loops were replaced by calls to the Map, Reduce and MapReduce skeletons. The right-hand-side evaluation function was implemented with the MapArray skeleton. In all tests the integration interval was 0–4 ($H=4$), and time was measured with LibSolve internal timer functions, which on UNIX systems use `gettimeofday()`. The different solver variants used in the testing were the following:

ls-seq-def: The default sequential implementation in LibSolve.

ls-seq-A: A slightly optimized variant of ls-seq-def.

ls-shm-def: The default shared memory implementation in LibSolve. It uses Pthreads and was run with 8 threads, one for each core of the benchmarking computer.

ls-shm-A: A slightly optimized variant of ls-shm-def, using Pthreads and run with 8 threads.

skepu-CL: SkePU port of ls-seq-def, OpenCL as backend, running on *one* Tesla™ C1060 GPU.

skepu-CL-multi: SkePU port of ls-seq-def, using OpenCL as backend, running on *two* C1060 GPUs.

skepu-CU: SkePU port of ls-seq-def, CUDA as backend, running on *one* Tesla C1060 GPU.

skepu-OMP: SkePU port of ls-seq-def using OpenMP as backend, using 8 threads.

skepu-CPU: SkePU port of ls-seq-def using the default CPU backend.

CU-hand: A 'hand'-implemented CUDA variant, similar to the SkePU ports, but no SkePU code was used. Instead, CUBLAS functions were used where applicable, and some handmade kernels.

The result can be seen in Figure 6.3. The two slowest ones are the sequential variants (ls-seq-def and ls-seq-A), with ls-seq-A of course performing slightly better due to the optimizations. LibSolve shared memory solvers (ls-shm-def and ls-shm-A) show a great performance increase compared to the sequential variants, being almost five times faster for the largest problem size ($N=1000$).

We also see that the SkePU CPU solver is comparable to the default LibSolve sequential implementation and the OpenMP variant is similar to the shared memory solvers. The SkePU OpenCL and CUDA ported solvers are however almost 10 times faster than the sequential solvers for the largest problem size. The reason for this is that all the calculations of the core loop in the ODE solver can be run on the GPU, without any memory transfers except once in the beginning and once at the end. This is done implicitly in SkePU since it is using lazy memory copying. However, the SkePU multi-GPU solver does not perform as well; the reason here also lies in the memory copying. Since the evaluation function needs access to more of one vector than what it has stored in GPU memory (in multi-GPU mode, SkePU divides the vectors evenly among the GPUs), some memory transfers are needed: first from one GPU to host and then from host to the other GPU; this slows down the calculations considerably.

Comparing the 'hand'-implemented CUDA variant, we see that it is similar in performance to skepu-CU with CU-hand being slightly faster ($\approx 10\%$). This is both due to the extra overhead when using SkePU functions and some implementation differences.

There is also a start-up time for the OpenCL implementations during which they compile and create the skeleton kernels. This time (≈ 5–10 s) is not included in the times presented here since it is considered an initialization which only needs to be done once when the application starts executing.

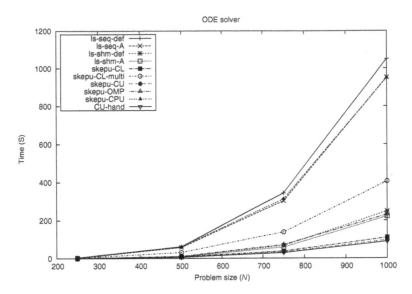

Figure 6.3   Times for running different LibSolve solvers for N =250,500,750 and 1000 with the BRUSS2D-MIX problem.

```
skepu::Reduce<plus> globalSum(new plus);
skepu::ExecPlan plan;
plan.add(1,3500, skepu::CPU_BACKEND);
plan.add(3501,3200000, skepu::OMP_BACKEND);
plan.add(3200001,5400000, skepu::CL_BACKEND);
plan.add(5400001,skepu::INFTY, skepu::CLM_BACKEND);
globalSum.setExecPlan(plan);
```

Figure 6.4   Defining an execution plan and applying it to a Reduce skeleton.

6.3.3 Tuning Potential

SkePU contains multiple backend implementations for each skeleton definition, including CPU, multi-CPU, GPU and multi-GPU backends. Tuning which backend to use for which problem sizes is supported in SkePU by the concept of an *execution plan* [5]. An *execution plan* is an object containing different parameters that will affect the execution time of a skeleton. The parameters include a list of vector sizes[1] and adjoining backends, which is used to decide which backend to use at certain input sizes. Other tuning parameters are group and grid size for the GPU backends.

All skeletons include an execution plan and also support for changing it manually. A default execution plan is created at skeleton instantiation time, containing default parameters chosen by the implementation. Figure 6.4 shows how to define an execution plan and apply it to a skeleton.

---

[1] At the time of writing, execution plans are configured to be used with SkePU Vector, as the corresponding support for Matrix is not implemented yet.

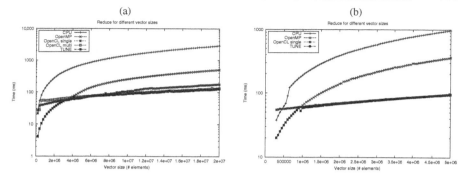

Figure 6.5   Vector sum with Reduce on target architecture 1 (a) and architecture 2 (b). TUNE uses an empirically determined execution plan for each architecture.

6.3.3.1 A Tuning Example   To explain tunability support in SkePU, we consider a simple vector sum computation, expressed by a single Reduce skeleton instance, which is repeated 100 times for the measurements. We consider two different GPU-based target architectures to demonstrate performance portability[2] that can be achieved with SkePU just by configuring the execution plan for each new target. The first one is a dual-quadcore Intel® Xeon® E5520 server clocked at 2.27 GHz with 2 NVIDIA® GT200 (Tesla C1060) GPUs. For this platform, the following empirically determined execution plan was used:

```
skepu::ExecPlan plan;
plan.add(1,3500, skepu::CPU_BACKEND);
plan.add(3501,3200000, skepu::OMP_BACKEND);
plan.add(3200001,5400000, skepu::CL_BACKEND);
plan.add(5400001,INFTY, skepu::CLM_BACKEND);
```

Figure 6.5(a) shows the behavior on the dual-quadcore Xeon server with 2 T C1060 GPUs. Here, OpenMP generally uses 8 threads. Note that, for technical reasons, it is not possible (without major effort) to mix OpenCL and CUDA code within the same program. Here we decided to use OpenCL as it allows better support for multi-GPU computing. The tunable version (TUNE) selects the OpenMP Reduce for small problem sizes, OpenCL on a single GPU for medium sizes and OpenCL on two GPUs for large sizes.

We now consider a different target system, an Intel® Core® 2 Duo E6600 with one GeForce™ GTS250 GPU, to demonstrate the potential for performance portability. For this platform, we preset the following execution plan:

```
skepu::ExecPlan plan;
plan.add(1,3500, skepu::CPU_BACKEND);
plan.add(3501,900000, skepu::OMP_BACKEND);
plan.add(900001,INFTY, skepu::CL_BACKEND);
```

[2] A mechanism for automated tuning of skeleton programs toward a given target architecture or system configuration extends portability to *performance portability*, that is, a best-effort adaptation for performance optimization for a new target system without touching the source code.

Note that the plan does not contain an entry for dual-GPU computing because the target system only has a single GPU. Figure 6.5(b) shows the resulting performance with the new plan on the new target architecture.

6.4   SKELCL: A LIBRARY FOR HIGH-LEVEL MULTI-GPU PROGRAMMING

SkelCL [26] is a high-level programming framework for single- and multi-GPU systems. It greatly simplifies the development of real-world applications while providing high performance close to optimized OpenCL implementations. SkelCL is built on top of OpenCL and provides a C++ API that shields the programmer from boilerplate code (e.g. for program initialization) and recurrent tasks such as explicit data transfer between CPU and GPU. GPU programming is simplified by using algorithmic skeletons and a container data type that allows for high-level memory management. For maximal flexibility, SkelCL can also be used in combination with low-level OpenCL code.

6.4.1   Skeletons and Containers

6.4.1.1 Skeletons   There are four basic skeletons provided by SkelCL: Map, Zip, Reduce and Scan. To instantiate a skeleton, a customizing kernel function is specified and passed to it. The kernel must match the selected skeleton: for example, a unary function is specified for a Map skeleton as shown in line 1 of Listing 6.3. Instead of providing the kernel as a string, the user may also load the source code from a file.

```
1 Map<float> neg("float main (float in) { return -in; }");
2 Vector<float> a(ptr, size);
3 Vector<float> b = neg(a); // execute skeleton 'neg'
```

Listing 6.3   Creation of a simple Map skeleton in SkelCL.

An arbitrary OpenCL code can be used within the kernel function, including multiple function definitions or include statements. This allows for sharing common header files between the host application and the device code. The only prerequisite is that the function called by the skeleton is named main. It is not required to declare the kernel with a special OpenCL qualifier like __kernel. A skeleton is executed like an ordinary function: the user specifies the input arguments in parentheses, thus passing them to the skeleton. The skeleton calculates the result and returns it.

The kernel function is used by the SkelCL implementation to generate a valid OpenCL kernel and merge it with preimplemented skeleton code. The resulting OpenCL code is compiled at runtime by OpenCL and can be executed on arbitrary devices. To reduce the time for compiling OpenCL kernels, SkelCL saves already compiled kernels on disk and loads them later if the same kernel is used again.

6.4.1.2 Vectors   To free the user from the low-level memory management of traditional GPU computing, SkelCL offers the container type Vector that provides a unified memory abstraction, that is, a vector is accessible by both host and device. Data is exchanged implicitly between host and device, freeing the user from low-level memory operations. Vectors are the input and output of all skeletons, except for the `Reduce` skeleton which returns a scalar. In Listing 6.3, a vector is created and passed to the skeleton. When executed, a skeleton ensures that all input vectors' data is available on the device. This may result in implicit data transfers from host to device memory. After execution, the calculated data resides in the device memory and is not copied back to the host. SkelCL performs data exchanges in a lazy manner: it keeps track if a vector's data is up to date on the host and device side. Thereby, it avoids redundant data transfers: for example, if an output vector is used as the input of another skeleton, no further data transfer is performed.

6.4.1.3 Additional Arguments In general, a skeleton implies a fixed arity for its customizing kernel function, for example, a `Map` skeleton requires a unary kernel. To loose this restriction, SkelCL allows the user to pass an arbitrary number of arguments directly to the kernel. For this, the function definition is changed to expect the additional arguments; these arguments are prepared and passed to the skeleton upon execution Listing 6.4 shows the `Map` skeleton using one additional argument to specify the scalar of a scalar multiplication.

```
1 Map<float> smult("float main(float in, float num){ return in * num; }");
2 Arguments arguments; arguments.push(2.5); // prepare additional arguments
3 smult(input. arguments);                  // execute skeleton
```

Listing 6.4   Implementation of a scalar multiplication using a `Map` skeleton and additional arguments.

The additional arguments (e.g. vectors) are collected in an `Arguments` object which is passed to the skeleton. Arbitrary types can be passed by providing a pointer and the size of the.type. The arguments are passed to the skeleton in the order of the function definition.

6.4.1.4 Multi-GPU Support SkelCL has been particularly designed for multi-GPU systems, to free the user from the additional challenges that arise in low-level programming environments, like CUDA or OpenCL, which handle multiple devices manually. For managing memory on multiple devices, SkelCL offers the concept of *distribution*: either SkelCL automatically sets the distribution of the input and output vectors or the user selects a distribution to optimize performance. SkelCL provides three distributions: `single`, `block` and `copy`. With `single` distribution, only one device stores the vector's data; this device can be specified or the first device is taken as default. The `block` distribution splits and distributes the vector evenly among all available devices. The `copy` distribution copies the entire vector to all devices.

It is possible to change a distribution at runtime: either implicitly by a skeleton or explicitly by the programmer. This triggers a data exchange between multiple devices: data is downloaded to the host and then, according to the new distribution,

```
1 SkelCL :: init ();
2 Complex *plane = new Complex[WIDTH * HEIGHT];  // create complex numbers
3 SkelCL :: Vector<Complex>  in (plane , WIDTH * HEIGHT);
4 SkelCL :: Vector<RGBColor> out(WIDTH * HEIGHT);
5 SkelCL :: Map<Complex , RGBColor> mandelbrot(kernel_stream);
6 mandelbrot(in , out);                            // execute map skeleton
7 write_image(out);
```

Listing 6.5   Computing a Mandelbrot fractal using SkelCL.

redistributed among the devices. The upload to the devices is performed lazily, that is, it is deferred until the data is actually needed on the devices.

The number and activity of devices that are used for a skeleton execution depend on the distribution of the input vectors. For example, if the input vector of a Map skeleton is block distributed, the skeleton is executed in parallel by multiple devices: each device processes a chunk of the input vector's data.

The Map skeleton selects the block distribution by default. The distribution of the output vector is determined from the input vectors' distribution. For the Reduce and Scan skeletons, special multidevice implementations are implemented and used instead of the single-device implementation if the input vector is block distributed.

6.4.2   Application Examples

We present two example applications to demonstrate the flexibility of SkelCL. While the first example – calculation of a Mandelbrot fractal – is a rather simple, embarrassingly parallel benchmark, the second one is a real-world application for medical imaging that requires the use of almost all of SkelCL's features.

6.4.2.1 *Mandelbrot Fractals*   The computation of a Mandelbrot fractal is a popular benchmark for embarrassingly parallel computations as all fractal's pixels can be computed independently [27]. Since the Map skeleton naturally supports this kind of parallelism, a parallel SkelCL implementation for computing a Mandelbrot fractal is simple (see Listing 6.5). After initializing SkelCL, we put a set of complex numbers into a Vector that is used as input for a Map skeleton; we also create an empty output Vector for the skeleton. The Map skeleton is instantiated with an input file stream, from which it reads a customizing kernel function. This function takes a complex number as input, performs an iterative calculation for this number and returns the color of the Mandelbrot fractal's corresponding pixel. For execution, the input and output vectors are passed to the Map skeleton. The computed Mandelbrot fractal resides in the output vector and can, for example, be written to a file.

6.4.2.2 *Medical Image Reconstruction*   list-mode ordered subset expectation maximization (LM OSEM) [21] is a compute-intensive algorithm for image reconstruction in positron emission tomography (PET). During a PET scan, a huge data set of "so-called"*events* is acquired and has to be processed to reconstruct a 3D image of the patient. With LM OSEM, the data set is split into equally sized *subsets* that are processed successively. The following steps are performed iteratively for each subset: (i) read a subset, (ii) compute an error image from the subset's events and (iii) update the reconstruction image using the error image.

While LM OSEM cannot be parallelized as a whole because of its iterative structure, the processing of subsets is well parallelizable. LM OSEM has been ported to different parallel architectures including GPUs [19, 25, 24] using low-level programming models like MPI, OpenMP and CUDA. Most implementations exploit two partitioning strategies: partitioning the subset and partitioning the image; sticking to a single partitioning approach leads to performance decrease [2].

To implement LM OSEM with SkelCL, we parallelize the computation of the error and reconstruction image using a Map and a Zip skeleton, respectively (see Listing 6.6). SkelCL's Vector data type is used to save the error and the reconstruction image, as well as the subset which is read at the beginning of each iteration. In a straightforward implementation, one could apply a Map skeleton to the subset to process all its events in parallel. However, such an implementation is not feasible on GPUs, as it would exceed the capacity of the GPU's memory (e.g. 4.4 GB for a typical subset containing 10^6 events). To avoid this memory bottleneck, we use a modified approach: we create an index Vector, with each element corresponding to a sub-subset of events. Moreover, we create a kernel function for the Map skeleton that processes one such sub-subset given by its index. With these preparations, we compute the error image by passing an index vector to the Map skeleton; the size of the index vector limits the number of GPU threads and thus the number of concurrently processed events.

Our SkelCL program remains unchanged for single- and multi-GPU cases. We use this feature by distributing the subset block-wise to all devices (line 11 in Listing 6.6), such that each device computes a local error image. We copy the reconstruction and the (empty) error image to all devices by setting the copy distribution. The Map skeleton only passes an index from the index vector to its kernel. However, the kernel also accesses the subset, the reconstruction image (input arguments) and the error image (output argument): these arguments are passed using SkelCL's additional arguments feature. The skeleton has no output but returns the error image via side effect, such that SkelCL is not able to detect these modifications of the error image. Therefore, we explicitly indicate this using the dataOnDevicesModified method.

In order to employ all available devices for updating the reconstruction image, we distribute both error and reconstruction image to all devices. With SkelCL we can easily change the images' distribution. In particular, we specify a merging operation (add in line 25) for the local error images to obtain a global error image before distributing it to the devices. Finally, we call the Zip skeleton to update the reconstruction image with the error image.

```
 1 std :: ifstream  err_proj_knl("err_proj.cl");
 2 std :: ifstream  update_knl("update.cl");
 3 SkelCL :: Map<unsigned> err_proj(err_proj_knl , SCL_INPLACE);
 4 SkelCL :: Zip<float>     update  (update_knl);
 5
 6 for (l=0; l<num_subsets; ++l) {
 7 Vector<Event>      subset      = Vector<Event>(read_subset());
 8 Vector<unsigned> index_vector = Vector<unsigned>(indices);
 9
10 /* distribute subset to devices */
11 subset . setDistribution(Distribution :: block);
12 /* copy index vector and images to all devices */
13 index_vector . setDistribution(Distribution :: copy);
14 image . setDistribution(Distribution :: copy);
15 error . setDistribution(Distribution :: copy);
16
17 /* prepare arguments and compute error image */
18 Arguments arguments;
19 arguments . push(subset); arguments . push(subset . size());
20 arguments . push(image); arguments . push(error);
21 err_proj(index_vector , arguments); // compute error image (map skeleton)
22 error . dataOnDevicesModified();      // mark error image as modified
23
24 /* merge and re—distribute */
25 error . setDistribution(Distribution :: block , add);
26 image . setDistribution(Distribution :: block);
27
28 /* update reconstruction image (zip skeleton) */
29 update(image , error , image);      }
```

Listing 6.6   Implementation of LM OSEM using SkelCL.

6.4.2.3 Experimental Results
In order to show the impact of using skeletons and implicit data management on programming effort, we compare the SkelCL-based implementations of our example applications with OpenCL and CUDA versions.

Regarding lines of code (LOC; see Figures 6.6 and 6.7), the Mandelbrot application requires most programming effort with OpenCL (host: 90, kernel: 28), while CUDA (21, 28) and SkelCL (31, 26) require a smaller number of LOC. For the LM OSEM example, SkelCL is most efficient requiring only 283 LOC (kernel: 248, host: 35), while the CUDA and OpenCL require 335 or even 510 LOC, respectively.

We measured the runtime of all implementations on a quad-core Intel Xeon E5520 server clocked at 2.26 GHz, connected to an NVIDIA Tesla S1070 computing system with four GPUs. The Mandelbrot application computed a fractal of 4096×3072 pixels. Its runtime results are shown in Figure 6.6. We observe that when using only one GPU, the OpenCL-based implementation (25 s) is slightly faster than the one based on SkelCL (26 s). The CUDA-based implementation (18 s) provides the best performance. However, the SkelCL-based implementation can directly use multiple GPUs of our test system, such that we achieved speedups of 1.5 or 2.2 when using two and four GPUs, respectively.

For LM OSEM, we compared our SkelCL implementation to implementations based on OpenCL and CUDA for multiple GPUs (see Figure 6.7). We measured the average runtime of a single iteration of the algorithm when processing a small but representative PET data set of about 10^7 events obtained by scanning a mouse. The

(a)

(b)

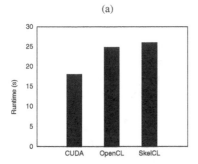
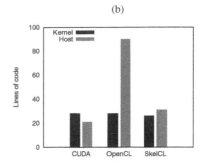

Figure 6.6 Mandelbrot example: comparison of runtime (a) and lines of code (b) of implementations using OpenCL, CUDA and SkelCL on a platform with one GPU.

(a)

(b)

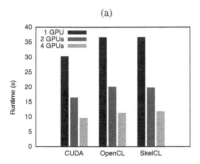
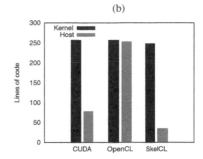

Figure 6.7 LM OSEM example: comparison of runtime (a) and lines of code (b) of implementations using OpenCL, CUDA and SkelCL on a platform with four GPUs.

CUDA-based implementation performs best, while the OpenCL- and SkelCL-based implementations are about 20% slower. However, the OpenCL version is only 5% faster than the SkelCL version. These results also hold for two and four GPUs: we obtained speedups of about 1.84 and 3.15, respectively.

Our application examples demonstrate that SkelCL shields the application developer from the low-level details of GPU programming and requires considerably less boilerplate code. As compared to implementations of the same applications using CUDA or OpenCL, SkelCL provides competitive performance and scalability.

6.5 RELATED WORK

Introduced by Cole for the purpose of structured parallel programming [3], the skeleton programming approach has been intensively developed in the 1990s and 2000s, mainly in Europe, to provide higher-level abstractions for parallel and distributed programming. Surveys are provided, for example, in books by Pelagatti [18] and Rabhi and Gorlatch [20]; for a recent survey and classification of skeleton programming frameworks, we refer to González-Vélez and Leyton [8].

Parallel programming with skeletons has been successfully applied to various architectures and with different libraries as backends [17, 7, 16, 4]. With the appearance of multicore CPUs in mainstream computing systems, skeleton programming concepts are, since the early 2000s, also being increasingly adopted by software industry in the form of new language constructs in concurrent, parallel and distributed programming frameworks.

Threading Building Blocks (TBB) is a library developed by Intel® for programming multicore processors. It extends C++ with a task-based parallel programming model including high-level parallel algorithm templates, concurrent containers, mutexes and atomic operations (see a comparison to OpenMP in [13]). TBB is based on a sophisticated task scheduling mechanism, which completely shields the programmer from threads. Unlike other parallel programming models, for example, Pthreads, parallelism is expressed by fine-grained tasks rather than threads. At runtime, TBB creates tasks and assigns them to threads which are scheduled to cores by the operating system.

On top of its scheduling mechanism, TBB offers parallel algorithm templates, similar to skeletons, which can be nested to increase parallelism.

Besides task-parallel templates such as `pipeline`, TBB also provides data-parallel templates which resemble the skeletons presented in Section 6.2, for example, `parallel_for` is similar to a `map` or `zip` skeleton.

The body objects of TBB are more coarse-grained than GPU kernels to better fit the capabilities of general-purpose cores.

TBB is also used for implementing Intel's new OpenCL SDK [12].

Thrust is a C++ template-based library developed at NVIDIA® Research [10]. It enables the programming of GPUs using an interface similar to the C++ Standard Template Library (STL). As dynamic containers, a `host_vector` and a `device_vector` are provided, which reside in host memory and in GPU device memory, respectively. Both types can be used like an STL vector: elements can be accessed directly using the standard bracket notation or using iterators.

By assigning a `host_vector` to a `device_vector`, the `host_vector`'s data is copied all at once to the GPU device memory.

Besides the dynamic containers, Thrust offers common parallel algorithms with implementations for host and device. They include searching, sorting, reordering, reductions, prefix sum calculations (a. k. a. scans) and transformations.

Some algorithms accept functions as arguments, similar to algorithmic skeletons. For instance, the `transform` algorithm (a. k. a. map) applies an unary or binary functor to an input range or a pair of input ranges, respectively. So far, Thrust supports single-GPU systems only and makes no use of multiple GPUs. Thrust is based heavily on CUDA, which restricts the user to GPUs of NVIDIA®.

CUDPP is a library of data-parallel algorithm primitives such as parallel prefix sum (scan), parallel sort and parallel reduction [9]. However, it does not provide higher-order functions that could take user-defined functions as input.

Sato and Iwasaki [23] describe a more generic skeleton framework for GPGPU programming. Instead of providing a library, they introduce the skeletons as functions in C; these skeletons are transformed to CUDA code by a precompiler and so, in a way, constitute a new programming language. The compiler can also generate equivalent C code using macros and is therefore entirely C compatible. One advantage of using a separate compiler is that optimizations can be built in.

Kirschenmann *et al.* [14] describe an implementation of the `Parallel_for` skeleton designed to work on both CPU and GPU.

BlockLib [1] is a C-based skeleton programming library for simplifying Cell/B.E.™ programming by encapsulating memory management, doubly buffered DMA communication, SIMD optimization and parallelization across the SPE cores in skeletons.

Map, MapOverlap, Reduce and MapReduce have been implemented.

The library consists of compiled code and macros and requires no extra tools besides the C preprocessor and compiler.

The parameterization in problem-specific user code can be done in different ways that, on Cell, differ very much in performance and ease of use.

BlockLib provides the user with a simple *function definition language*, implemented as C preprocessor macros, which generates SIMD-optimized inner loops.

Many macros have a close mapping to one or a few Cell SIMD instructions or to functions in the IBM SIMD Math library [11].

A skeleton library for Cell/B.E. based on C++ templates, called *Skell BE*, was proposed by Saidani et al. [22].

6.6 CONCLUDING REMARKS AND FUTURE WORK

We have presented two recent skeleton programming frameworks, SkePU and SkelCL, that can provide portability across a range of multi- and many-core platforms including multi-GPU systems. We also demonstrated tunability for performance portability.

The systems and examples considered in this chapter focus on data-parallel skeletons as data parallelism is the main source of parallelism provided by current GPU systems. However, recent GPUs such as NVIDIA Fermi™, multi-GPU systems and GPU clusters allow to also exploit task parallelism at a much larger extent in the near future. Adding support for portable task parallelism, such as `farm` skeletons, will thus be an important issue for future work.

REFERENCES

1. M. Ålind, M. Eriksson, and C. Kessler. Blocklib: a skeleton library for cell broadband engine. In *Proc. ACM Int. Workshop on Multicore Software Engineering (IWMSE-2008) at ICSE-2008, Leipzig, Germany*, May 2008.

2. P. Ciechanowicz, P. Kegel, M. Schellmann, S. Gorlatch, and H. Kuchen. Parallelizing the LM OSEM image reconstruction on multi-core clusters. In B. Chapman, F. Desprez, G. R. Joubert, A. Lichnewsky, F. Peters, and T. Priol, editors, *Parallel Computing: From*

Multicores and GPU's to Petascale, volume 19 of *Advances in Parallel Computing*, pages 169–176. IOS Press, 2010.

3. M. Cole. *Algorithmic Skeletons: Structured Management of Parallel Computation*. MIT Press, 1989.

4. M. Cole. Bringing skeletons out of the closet: a pragmatic manifesto for skeletal parallel programming. *Parallel Computing*, 30:389–406, 2004.

5. U. Dastgeer, J. Enmyren, and C. Kessler. Auto-tuning SkePU: a multi-backend skeleton programming framework for multi-GPU systems. In *Proc. Int. Workshop on Multicore Software Engineering (IWMSE-2011), Hawaii, USA*. ACM, May 2011.

6. J. Enmyren and C. Kessler. SkePU: a multi-backend skeleton programming library for multi-GPU systems. In *Proc. 4th Int. Workshop on High-Level Parallel Programming and Applications (HLPP-2010)*, Baltimore, MD, USA, September 2010. ACM.

7. J. Falcou, J. Sérot, T. Chateau, and J. T. Lapresté. QUAFF: efficient C++ design for parallel skeletons. *Parallel Computing*, 32:604–615, 2006.

8. H. Gonzalez-Velez and M. Leyton. A survey of algorithmic skeleton frameworks: high-level structured parallel programming enablers. *Software – Practice and Experience*, 40:1135–1160, 2010.

9. M. Harris, J. Owens, S. Sengupta, Y. Zhang, and A. Davidson. CUDPP: CUDA data parallel primitives library. http://gpgpu.org/developer/cudpp, 2009.

10. J. Hoberock and N. Bell (NVIDIA® Research). Thrust: a parallel template library. http://thrust.googlecode.com/, 2010. Version 1.3.0.

11. IBM. developerworks: Cell Broadband Engine resource center. http://www.ibm.com/developerworks/power/cell, 2008.

12. Intel Corporation. *Intel® OpenCL SDK – Intel® Software Network*, January 2011-01-06.

13. P. Kegel, M. Schellmann, and S. Gorlatch. Using OpenMP vs. Threading Building Blocks for medical imaging on multi-cores. In *Euro-Par*, pages 654–665, 2009.

14. W. Kirschenmann, L. Plagne, and S. Vialle. Multi-target C++ implementation of parallel skeletons. In *POOSC '09: Proc. 8th workshop on Parallel/High-Performance Object-Oriented Scientific Computing*, pages 1–10. ACM, 2009.

15. M. Korch and T. Rauber. Optimizing locality and scalability of embedded Runge–Kutta solvers using block-based pipelining. *Journal of Parallel and Distributed Computing*, 66(3):444–468, 2006.

16. H. Kuchen. A skeleton library. In *Proc. Euro-Par 2002 Parallel Processing*, pages 85–124, 2002.

17. M. Leyton and J. M. Piquer. Skandium: Multi-core programming with algorithmic skeletons. In *Euromicro Conf. on Parallel, Distributed, and Network-Based Processing*, pages 289–296, 2010.

18. S. Pelagatti. *Structured Development of Parallel Programs*. Taylor & Francis, 1998.

19. G. Pratx, G. Chinn, F. Habte, P. Olcott, and C. Levin. Fully 3-D list-mode OSEM accelerated by graphics processing units. In *Nuclear Science Symposium Conference Record*, volume 4, pages 2196–2202. IEEE, October 2006.

20. F. A. Rabhi and S. Gorlatch, editors. *Patterns and Skeletons for Parallel and Distributed Computing*. Springer-Verlag, 2003.

21. A. J. Reader, K. Erlandsson, M. A. Flower, and R. J. Ott. Fast accurate iterative reconstruction for low-statistics positron volume imaging. *Physics in Medicine and Biology*, 43(4):823–834, April 1998.

22. T. Saidani, C. Tadonki, L. Lacassagne, J. Falcou, and D. Etiemble. Algorithmic skeletons within an embedded domain specific language for the CELL processor. In *Proc. 18th Int. conf. on Par. Architectures and Compilation Techniques (PACT-2009)*. IEEE Computer Society, 2009.

23. S. Sato and H. Iwasaki. A skeletal parallel framework with fusion optimizer for GPGPU programming. In *APLAS'09: Proc. 7th Asian Symposium on Programming Languages and Systems*, pages 79–94. Springer, 2009.

24. M. Schellmann, S. Gorlatch, D. Meiländer, T. Kösters, K. Schäfers, F. Wübbeling, and M. Burger. Parallel medical image reconstruction: From graphics processors to grids. In Victor Malyshkin, editor, *Parallel Computing Technologies*, volume 5698 of *Lecture Notes in Computer Science*, pages 457–473. Springer Berlin/Heidelberg, 2009.

25. M. Schellmann, J. Vörding, and S. Gorlatch. Systematic parallelization of medical image reconstruction for graphics hardware. In *Euro-Par 2008 - Parallel Processing*, volume 5168 of *LNCS*, pages 811–821. Springer, 2008. ISBN 978-3-540-85450-0.

26. M. Steuwer, P. Kegel, and S. Gorlatch. SkelCL – A Portable Skeleton Library for High-Level GPU Programming. In *Proceedings of the 16th International Workshop on High-Level Parallel Programming Models and Supportive Environments*, May 2011.

27. B. Wilkinson and M. Allen. *Parallel Programming*. Pearson Education, second edition, 2005.

CHAPTER 7

DSL STREAM PROGRAMMING ON MULTICORE ARCHITECTURES

PABLO DE OLIVEIRA CASTRO, STÉPHANE LOUISE AND DENIS BARTHOU

7.1   INTRODUCTION

The advent of multicore processors raises new programmability challenges. Complex applications are hard to write using threads, since they do not guarantee a deterministic execution, and are difficult to optimize because the programmer must carefully tune the application by hand.

Stream languages are a powerful alternative to program multicore processors for two main reasons: (i) they offer a deterministic execution based on a sound mathematical formalism (synchronous data flow (SDF) [21]), and (ii) the expression of the parallelism is implicitly described by the stream structure, which leverages compiler optimizations that can harness the multicore performance without having to tune the application by hand.

The stream programming model emphasizes the exchange of data between filters. To properly express and optimize stream programs, it is crucial to capture the

Programming Multicore and Many-core Computing Systems,
First Edition. Edited by Sabri Pllana and Fatos Xhafa.
© 2017 John Wiley & Sons, Inc. Published 2017 by John Wiley & Sons, Inc.

```
1  float –>float pipeline MatrixMultiply (int x0, int y0,
       int x1, int y1) {
2    add splitjoin {
3      split roundrobin(x0 * y0, x1 * y1);
4      add DuplicateRows(x1, x0);
5      add pipeline {
6        add Transpose(x1, y1);
7        add DuplicateRows(y0, x1*y1);
8      }
9      join roundrobin;
10   }
11   add MultiplyAccParallel(x0, x0);
12 }
13 float –>float splitjoin Transpose(int x, int y) {
14   split roundrobin;
15   for (int i = 0; i < x; i++) add Identity<float>();
16   join roundrobin(y);
17 }
18 float –>float splitjoin DuplicateRows(int t, int l) {
19   split duplicate;
20   for (int i = 0; i < t; i++) add Identity<float>();
21   join roundrobin(l);
22 }
23 float –>float splitjoin MultiplyAccParallel(int x, int
       n) {
24   // Omitted ... realises the dot product of
25   // the rows of A and the columns of B in parallel.
26 }
```

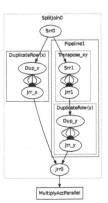

Figure 7.1   Excerpt of a StreamIt program for matrix multiplication.

data access patterns in the stream model. We can distinguish two families of stream programming languages:

- Languages in which the data access patterns are explicitly described by the programmer through a set of reorganization primitives

- Languages in which the data access patterns are implicitly declared through a set of dependencies between tasks

We present in the following a brief overview of related works concerning these language families and then expose the principle of a two-level approach combining the advantages and expressivity of both types of languages.

7.1.1   Explicit Manipulations of Streams

7.1.1.1   StreamIt   StreamIt [4] is both a streaming language and a compiler for RAW and SMP architectures. StreamIt revolves around the notion of filters. A filter takes a stream of input elements, performs a computation and produces the result of the computation on an output stream, thus capturing the producer–consumer pattern often used in signal applications.

Filters are assembled in a flow graph by using a set of connectors: pipes form chains of consumers and producers, split/joins allow to dispatch the elements inside a stream to a group of filters (parallelizing the computation) and reassemble the results, and feedback loops allow to introduce cycles in the flow graph. Using these connectors constraints the structure of the StreamIt graphs to a series–parallel hierarchical organization. This is a conscious design choice of the StreamIt designers [27] since it simplifies the textual description of the graph. The use of these connectors is demonstrated in Figure 7.1 where a program implementing the matrix multiplication in StreamIt is provided.

StreamIt adapts the granularity and communication patterns of programs through graph transformations [17], belonging to one of these three types: fusion transformations cluster adjacent filters, coarsening their granularity; fission transformations parallelize stateless filters, decreasing their granularity; and reordering transformations operate on splits and joins to facilitate fission and fusion transformations. Complementary transformations have also been proposed. For example, optimizing transformations proposed in [1] take advantage of algebraic simplifications between consecutive linear filters. On cache architectures, fusion transformations proposed in [25] optimize filters to instruction and data cache sizes.

7.1.1.2 Brook   Brook is a stream programming language that targets different architectures: Merrimac, Imagine, and graphic accelerators. The Brook syntax is inspired by the C language and implements many extensions for stream manipulation. Streams are typed and possess an arbitrary high number of dimensions. To the best of our knowledge, current Brook compilers are limited to primitive types on streams (no composite or arrays types).

Filters in Brook are normal C functions but preceded with the keyword `kernel` which indicates they accept streams as parameters. Side effects between filters must be strictly confined to stream communications. The access rights of kernels to stream parameters can be specified as write only, read only or random access, which allows the compiler to optimize memory handling.

To express data reorganizations, Brook introduces a set of functions that reorder the elements within a stream:

- `streamStencil` extracts blocks of data inside a stream by moving a *stencil* inside its shape.

- `streamStride` allows to select the elements in a stream that are separated with a given stride factor.

- `streamRepeat` allows to duplicate elements in a stream.

- `streamMerge` combines elements from multiple streams.

In [22] an optimization method is proposed to leverage the affine partitioning framework. To do this it translates the aforementioned data reorganization functions into a set of dependences that can be optimized in the polyhedral model. The dependence equations are not necessarily affine, but according to the authors, in many cases they can be reduced to a set of equivalent affine equations.

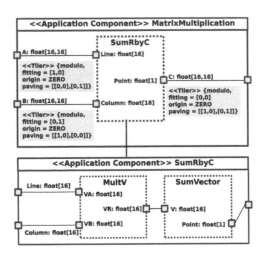

Figure 7.2   Matrix multiplication in Array-OL as viewed in the IDE Gaspard2 [8].

7.1.2   Expressing Streams through Dependencies

7.1.2.1   *Array-OL*   Array-OL [16] is a language that specifically targets signal applications. Data is represented using multidimensional arrays which can have one infinite dimension (e.g. to represent time). Arrays are toroidal avoiding border effects in many applications.

In Array-OL, programs are composed of filters that can exchange data arrays through streams. The program description is done at two levels:

- *The global level* describes connexions between filters using an oriented acyclic graph. A filter can have multiple input and output streams. The absence of cycle forbids feedback loops but simplifies scheduling.

- *The local level* describes dependences between filter inputs and outputs. Each input has an associated *tiler* describing the order in which the filter consumes its elements. A tiler is composed of an origin point, a shape, a paving matrix and a fitting matrix. Each time the filter is executed, it consumes a stencil of elements inside the input arrays, determined by the tilers, *shape*. The stencil is then translated according to the origin point and paving and fitting matrix. Just like a tiler determines the dependences for each input stream, each output stream also possesses a tiler describing the order of the elements produced by the filter.

Array-OL programs can be developed in a visual IDE called Gaspard [12] which eases the visualization of the local and global model. Figure 7.2 shows a matrix multiplication program as seen in Gaspard.

Array-OL programs can be transformed into a Kahn process network [3] which enables a concurrent execution of the tasks. Recent works on Array-OL compilation propose a set of optimizations that fusions Array-OL filters to coarsen the grain of parallelism and factor producer–consumer dependencies to increase reuse in pipelines [13, 15]. But to the best of our knowledge, there is no automatic framework to decide when these transformations should be applied.

7.1.2.2 Block Parallel   Block Parallel [6] also targets signal applications. The author argues that the multidimensional formulations proposed, for example, by Array-OL are difficult to optimize since each new dimension increases the number of possible data traversals. He pushes for a compromise between expressivity and ease of compilation by allowing only data shapes of one or two dimensions and restricting the input programs to acyclic graphs. He combines the input and output filter dependencies proposed by Array-OL with the splitter and joiners proposed by StreamIt (used to introduce data parallelism in the application). The author proposes a set of optimizations to increase reuse in the filters and optimize the order of access. Yet these transformations are very limited since they only work on the programs that can be expressed using Block Parallel filter dependencies. For example, matrix multiplication of fast Fourier transformation are out of the scope of Block Parallel optimizations.

7.1.3 A Two-Level Approach

Brook and StreamIt propose a low-level language to manipulate streams: StreamIt uses joiners and splitters that route and copy data through the graph, while Brook manipulates the streams using primitives that reorder and select elements on streams. StreamIt and Brook propose efficient optimizations. StreamIt uses fusion, fission and reordering transformations to optimize the throughput, and Brook leverages the optimizations offered by affine partitioning [22]. Array-OL and Block Parallel on the other hand propose a high-level description of data dependences [6, 16]. Nevertheless the high-level description comes at a price: optimizations in these languages are harder to implement, in particular optimization regarding the routing of data through the application. As pointed in [14, 15], the formalism underlying Array-OL dependences (ODT) makes difficult to express some transformations: since the result of the optimizations must be a valid ODT Array-OL dependence set, the palette of available transformation is limited.

Instead of using a single language to both describe and optimize the application, we propose a two-level language approach. A high-level typed DSL, called SLICES, is used to describe the data dependencies. SLICES is then converted to an intermediary stream language, SJD, which can be efficiently optimized with a set of semantically preserving stream graph transformations. The use of different levels of abstraction allows a clean separation of concerns and a modular compilation chain. The expressivity problematic is addressed by a domain-specific high-level typed language which can grow more complex to accommodate the users' demands. The optimization problematic is addressed by a simple and restricted language easier to optimize.

Recent works have also considered intermediary stream representation to capture the parallelism and flow of data information. Erbium [24] proposes a data flow intermediary representation enabling mainstream compilers to better optimize stream

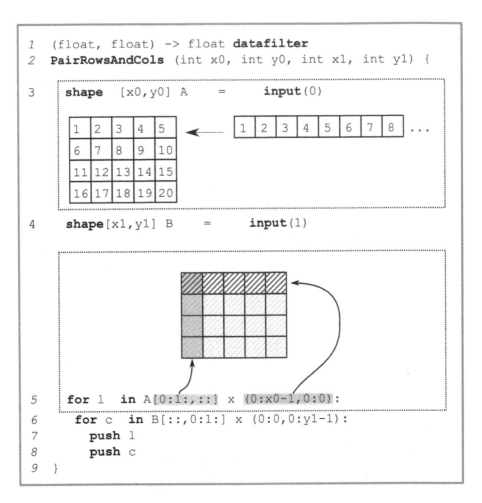

```
1   (float, float) -> float datafilter
2   PairRowsAndCols (int x0, int y0, int x1, int y1) {
3       shape  [x0,y0] A    =    input(0)
```

```
4       shape[x1,y1] B      =    input(1)
```

```
5       for l  in A[0:1:,::] x  (0:x0-1,0:0):
6           for c  in B[::,0:1:] x (0:0,0:y1-1):
7               push l
8               push c
9   }
```

Figure 7.3 SLICES program that captures a matrix multiplication communication pattern. First the raw stream inputs are casted to shape to view them as matrices. Then the rows of A are paired with the columns of B in the iterator loop and pushed to the output. In the graphical examples we have chosen x0 = 5 and y0 = 4.

applications. FastFlow [2] is a parallel programming runtime based on skeletons that also advocates a multilayered approach. The high-level layer is a library of very general parallel patterns (Farm, Pipeline, etc.) that are build upon the simple but efficient lock-free queues of the lower layers.

7.2 A HIGH-LEVEL DSL: SLICES

The high-level *domain-specific language* SLICES enables to model the multidimensional data dependencies of filters in signal applications. For this, the domain of each filter is described as a combination of multidimensional slicings over the input streams. The language is built around five concepts: shapes, grids, blocks, iterators and zippers. We are going to present the language through a practical example: the data dependencies of a matrix multiplication filter. To multiply two matrices, as in $C_{y0,x1} = A_{y0,x0} \times B_{y1,x1}$, we must extract the lines of A and pair them with the columns of B, before processing them through a dot-product filter.

Lines *1 and 2* of the program in Figure 7.3 instantiate a datafilter embedding SLICES code. The filter has two stream inputs with `float` values containing the elements of each matrix and is parametrized with the matrix dimensions.

7.2.1 Shapes

SLICES allows us to restructures input streams into multidimensional views using *shape* types. In line *3*, we cast the raw input of the first matrix to a type `shape` `[x0,x1]`. This produces a view A, where `input(0)` is seen as a stream of matrices. In practice we can use an arbitrary number of dimensions in a *shape* type.

7.2.2 Blocks

Blocks are used to select a set of elements inside a *shape* view. A block is defined by a d-dimensional box parametrized by its min and max coordinates on each dimension: $(a_1:b_1, \ldots a_d:b_d)$ with $a_i, b_i \in \mathbb{Z}$. In our example we want to extract from view A each horizontal line. To achieve this we define in line *5* the block `(0:x0-1, 0:0)`.

7.2.3 Grids

To select *each and every* horizontal line from A, we must apply the previous block to each row. To define a set of anchor points where a block is applied, SLICES provide the grid constructor. A grid is defined by three parameters for each dimension i: the lower bound of the grid l_i, the upper bound of the grid h_i and the stride δ_i. This triplet describes for each dimension i, the set of points $G_i = \left\{ \delta_i.k.\vec{e_i} : \forall k \in \left[\left[\frac{l_i}{\delta_i}; \frac{h_i}{\delta_i} \right] \right] \right\}$. The elements of a grid are constructed by computing the Cartesian product of the G_i in lexicographical order. The grid operator uses a standard slicing notation where l_i, h_i, δ_i are separated by colons and each dimension is separated by commas. For example, `V[0:10:2]` would describe the points in V that are between position 5 and 10 with a stride of 2. Out of simplicity, it is possible to omit one or more values of the triplet; missing values are replaced by sensible default values (0 in place of l_i, the size of the dimension in place of h_i, 1 in place of δ_i). For instance, the previous example could be rewritten `B[:10:2]`.

A block can be applied upon a grid with the *grid* × *block* operator. This returns the set of points produced by centering the block around each point of the grid. For example, to extract the rows of A, we must apply the previous block to every point in the first column of A in line *5*. Indeed the grid `A[0:1:, 0:y0:1]` defines the first column as a set of anchor points and is combined with the `(0:x0-1, 0:0)` block.

When applied to a grid, successive blocks may overlap which is convenient to write filters working on sliding windows of data (e.g. FIR or Gauss filter). Blocks may also partially fall outside of the view *shape* to handle border effects.

7.2.4 Iterators

shape, grid and block return instances of the *iterator* type that we can interleave using nested 'for v in *iterator*' loops. A loop iterates over the elements of the given iterator, binding each returned set of points to the variable v. In lines *5 and 6* we iterate over the rows of A and the columns of B and produce each pair to the output using the push keyword.

For a complete presentation of the language and of its underlying type system, please refer to [10]. SLICES is able to capture frequently used data reorganization patterns in signal applications: de Oliveira Castro [9] presents the design with SLICES of a Sobel filter, a Gauss filter, a Hough filter and the odd–even mixing stage of a fast Fourier butterfly transformation.

7.3 INTERMEDIARY REPRESENTATION SJD

The intermediary representation must provide a framework for the efficient optimization of applications. To accomplish this objective, two requirements must be satisfied: first, the representation must be simple enough to enable a well-understood set of optimizations, and second, the representation should capture all the possible static data reorganizations (we cannot optimize what we cannot model). A high-level multidimensional representation like Array-OL and Block Parallel does not satisfy the first requirement, since the optimization complexity grows with the number of dimensions [6]. A simple graph language like StreamIt is much easier to optimize. Nevertheless, by design StreamIt imposes a hierarchical series–parallel structure on the application graphs that cannot model all the possible static data reorganization. As a simple example, [27] shows that StreamIt can never alter the position of the first element of a stream. Therefore, in StreamIt to reverse the order of a vector of elements, we cannot use splitters and joiners and must hide the communication pattern inside a filter. Another limitation of the hierarchical graph restriction is that it cannot capture all the optimizing transformations we propose (UnrollRemove or BreakJS in Section 7.4.2 cannot be expressed with a series–parallel graph). To build our intermediary representation, we have removed the hierarchical restriction from StreamIt graphs that hampers the expressivity of the language.

Source (I) and **Sink (O)** nodes model the program inputs and outputs, respectively. The source produces a stream of inputs elements, while the sink consumes all the elements it receives. A source producing always the same element is a *constant* source **(C)**. If the elements in a sink are never observed, it is a *trash* sink **(T)**.

Functions in the imperative programming paradigm are replaced by **filter** nodes $(\mathbf{F}(\mathbf{c_1}, \ \mathbf{p_1}))$. Each filter has one input and one output and an associated pure function f (i.e. with no internal state). Each time there are at least c_1 elements on the input, the filter is fired: the function f consumes the c_1 input elements and produces p_1 elements on the output.

Another category of nodes dispatch and combine streams of data from multiple filters, routing data streams through the program and reorganizing the order of elements within a stream.

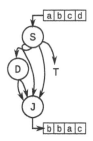

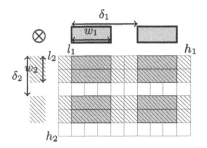

Figure 7.4 Example of data reorganizations enabled by SJD. (The split and join consumptions and productions are always 1 in this graph.)

Figure 7.5 Multidimensional grids and blocks extraction.

Join J(c_1 ... c_n): A join node has n inputs and one output. Each time it is fired, it consumes c_i elements on every i^{th} input and concatenates the consumed elements on its output.

Split S(p_1 ... p_m): A split node has m outputs and one input. A split consumes $\sum_i p_i$ elements on its input and dispatches them on the outputs (the first p_1 elements are pushed to the first output, then p_2 elements are pushed to the second, etc.).

Dup D (m) has one input and m outputs. Each time this node is fired, it takes one element on the input and writes it to every output, duplicating its input m times.

By breaking the hierarchical constraint of StreamIt and introducing trash nodes, SJD is able to capture all the finite static data reorganizations in the application: for example, a vector can be easily reversed without using filters. In [9] we prove the following result.

Theorem 7.1 (Expressivity) *SJD graphs without filters exactly capture the reorganizations* $[i_{\phi(1)}, \dots, i_{\phi(m)}]$ *where* $[i_1, \dots, i_n]$ *are the elements being reorganized and ϕ is an application from* $[1, \dots, m]$ *to* $[1, \dots, n]$.

In other words, SJD graphs enable any finite permutation, reordering, duplication or pruning of elements. Figure 7.4 demonstrates those features on a simple example.

Like StreamIt, our intermediate representation is built upon the SDF computation model [21] where nodes are actors that are fired periodically and edges represent communication channels. We can schedule an SDF graph in bounded memory if it has no deadlocks and is consistent. A *consistent SDF graph* admits a repetition vector $\vec{q}_G = [q_1, q_2, \dots, q_{N_G}]$ where q_N is the repetition number of node N. A schedule where each actor N is fired q_N times is called a *steady-state* schedule. Such a schedule is rate matched: for every pair of actors (U, V) connected by an edge e, the number of elements produced by U on e is equal to the number of elements consumed by V on e during a steady-state execution (data dependencies are satisfied). The number of elements exchanged in a steady state through edge e is noted $\beta(e)$.

7.3.1 Compiling SLICES to SJD

To be able to optimize programs written using SLICES, we must compile SLICES programs to the intermediate representation SJD. A detailed description of the

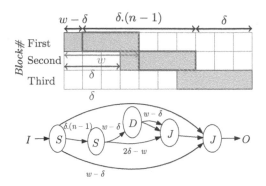

Figure 7.6 Compiling 1D blocks that partially overlap $(1 < \frac{w}{\delta} < 2)$.

compilation process is outside the scope of this chapter, (please see [10]); however, the main steps are as follows:

1. Each SLICES datafilter is parsed and type checked. For every SLICES program that type checks, the compiler is able to generate a correct reentrant SJD graph without deadlocks.

2. Multidimensional grids and blocks are by construction Cartesian products of their 1D counterparts. For instance, the following grid and block 2D expression,

$$[l_1 : h_1 : \delta_1, l_2 : h_2 : \delta_2] \times (a_1 : b_1, a_2 : b_2),$$

can be decomposed as shown in Figure 7.5 into

$$([l_1 : h_1 : \delta_1] \times (a_1 : b_1)) \otimes ([l_2 : h_2 : \delta_2] \times (a_2 : b_2))$$

3. We compile each 1D constituent to an equivalent SJD graph using a set of simple patterns. As an example, in the case of partial overlapping blocks $(1 < \frac{w}{\delta} < 2)$, the SJD graph produced is given in Figure 7.6.

4. Our compiler analyzes the nested for loops, duplicates and reorders (inserting appropriate Dup and Join nodes in the final graph) according to the iterators length and the nesting depth of push instructions.

We prove in [9] that the number of nodes in the SJD graph produced by this compilation process is $\mathcal{O}(p.d.w)$, where p is the number of push instructions, d is the maximum number of dimensions used and w is the largest width in any dimension of the extracted blocks. Thus the complexity of the generated graphs is independent of the size of the input shapes. This means that working on large sets of data will not increase the number of nodes in the intermediate representation.

When we compile the SLICES program from matrix multiplication of Figure 7.3, our compiler generates the SJD graph in Figure 7.7. The matrix B is transposed using the first S–J pair and then the rows of A and columns of B are duplicated with the

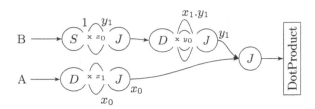

Figure 7.7 Intermediate SJD representation equivalent to the SLICES matrix multiplication program (Fig. 7.3). The intermediate representation was automatically generated by our SLICES to SJD compiler.

D–J pairs and paired together with the final J node, before being sent through the dot-product filter.

7.4   OPTIMIZING THE INTERMEDIATE REPRESENTATION

The way we optimize the intermediate representation is through a set of transformations of the program. These transformations alter the communication patterns and the degree of parallelism in the SJD representation of the original program while preserving its semantics.

We follow the formulation given in [5]: a transformation T applied on a graph G, generating a graph G', is denoted $G \xrightarrow{T} G'$. It is defined by a matching subgraph $L \subseteq G$ and a replacement graph $R \subseteq G'$. It operates by deleting the match subgraph L from G and replacing it by the replacement subgraph R. The part of graph that remains untouched $(G \setminus L)$ is called the *context* of the transformation.

7.4.1   Soundness of Transformations

An optimizing transformation can only be applied if it preserves the semantics of the original program, preserves consistency and does not introduce deadlocks.

In [9] we prove the following sufficient condition where $L(I)$ are the output traces of subgraph L for given input traces I and $\overline{L(I)}$ is the length of the output traces. For simplicity we consider that L and R have only one input and output, but the sufficient condition stands for multiple input/output subgraphs.

Lemma 7.1 (Local correction) *If a transformation* $G \xrightarrow{T} G'$ *satisfies*

$$\forall I \quad \Rightarrow \quad L(I) \text{ is a prefix of } R(I)$$
$$\exists b \in \mathbb{N}, \forall I \quad \Rightarrow \quad \overline{R(I)} - \overline{L(I)} \leq b$$
$$L \text{ is consistent} \quad \Rightarrow \quad R \text{ is consistent}$$

then the transformation T *is correct.*

This lemma establishes the correction of a transformation independently of the context. A transformation that verifies Lemma 7.1 can be applied to any input SDF program. In particular such a transformation is legal inside a feedback loop in the SJD graph without introducing deadlocks or breaking consistency.

7.4.2 Transformations

Using the previous lemma we have constructed a set of *correct* transformations on SJD graphs. In Figure 7.8 a subset of these transformations is presented. The transformations split or reorder the streams of data and modify the expression of concurrency, and they can be separated in three groups according to their effect.

7.4.2.1 Node Removal   These transformations rewrite communication structures that use less nodes, for example, by removing nodes whose composed effect is the identity.

> **RemoveJS/RemoveSJ/RemoveD** These transformations (not shown in the figure) are very simple and remove nodes whose composed effect is the identity: a Split and a Join of identical consumption and productions, a single branch Dup, a single branch Split, etc.
>
> **CompactSS/CompactDD/CompactJJ** (Fig. 7.8(f)) CompactSS (resp. JJ, DD) fuses together a hierarchy of Split (resp. Join, Dup) nodes.

7.4.2.2 Synchronization Removal   These transformations remove synchronization points inside a communication pattern, usually by decomposing it into its smaller constituents.

> **Constant propagation**(Fig. 7.8(e)) When a constant source is split, we can eliminate the Split duplicating the constant source.
>
> **Dead code elimination**(Fig. 7.8(g)) This eliminates nodes whose outputs are never observed.
>
> **BreakJS**(Fig. 7.8(i)) This breaks join–split junctions into smaller constituents, and it often triggers **Synchronization Removal** (Fig. 7.8(h)) which tries to find two matching groups in the productions/consumptions of the junction. This allows to break a join–split junction into two smaller junctions.

7.4.2.3 Restructuring   These transformations restructure communication patterns. They find alternative implementations which may be more efficient in some targets and sometimes trigger some of the previous transformations.

> **SplitF** (Fig. 7.8(a)) This transformation splits a filter on its input. SplitF introduces split–join parallelism in the programs. Because filters are pure, we can compute each input block on a different filter concurrently.
>
> **InvertDN** (Fig. 7.8(d)) This transformation inverts a duplicate node and its children, if they are identical. This transformation eliminates redundant computations in a program.

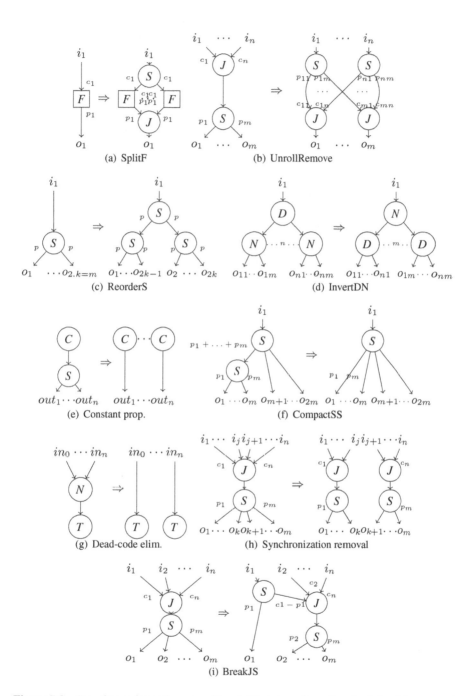

Figure 7.8   Set of transformations considered. Each transformation is defined by a graph rewriting rule. Node N is a wild card for any arity compatible node.

UnrollRemove (Fig. 7.8(b)) This transformation inverts the order between join and split nodes. The transformation is admissible in two cases:

1 - Each p_j is a multiple of $C = \sum_i c_i$, and the transformation is admissible, choosing $p_{ij} = c_i . p_j / C$, $c_{ji} = c_i$.

2 - Each c_i is a multiple of $P = \sum_j p_j$, and the transformation is admissible choosing $p_{ij} = p_j$, $c_{ji} = p_j . c_i / P$.

ReorderS/ReorderJ (Fig. 7.8(c)) ReorderS (resp. ReorderJ) creates a hierarchy of Split (resp. Join) nodes. In the following we will only discuss SplitS. The transformation is parametric in the Split arity f. This arity must divide the number of outputs, $m = k.f$. In the figure, we have chosen $f = 2$. As shown in Figure 7.8(c), the transformation works by rewriting the original Split using two separate stages: odd and even elements are separated; then odd (resp. even) elements are redirected to the correct outputs. We have omitted some more complex transformations for simplicity sake. For an in-depth description of the transformation set, please see [9, 11].

7.5   REDUCING INTERCORE COMMUNICATION COST

The previous set of transformations change the degree of parallelism and the communication patterns of the original program. In this section we will demonstrate how they can be used to reduce the intercore communication cost in a parallel program.

7.5.1   Measuring Intercore Communication Cost

To execute an SJD program on a multicore target, we partition the nodes in the SJD graph among the available cores. For a given partitioning $\mathcal{P}$ of G, we define *inter*$(G, \mathcal{P})$ as the set of edges that connect nodes in different partitions.

The Hockney [18] model distinguish two cost factors in a point-to-point communication: (i) a fixed cost equal to the latency c_0 and (ii) a variable cost that increases with the number of streamed elements and depends on the bandwidth bw. The communication cost during a steady-state schedule execution is noted $c_e = c_0 + \frac{\beta(e).s(e)}{bw}$, where $\beta(e)$ is the number of elements exchanged during a steady state and $s(e)$ is the size in bytes of each element. The intercore communication cost is computed by aggregating the costs of all the edges that link different cores, $C(G, \mathcal{P}) = \sum_{e \in inter(G, \mathcal{P})} c_e$.

7.5.2   Exploring the Optimization Space

We can improve the intercore communication cost by optimizing two factors: partitioning of the SJD nodes among the processors and the communication patterns between filters.

To partition the SJD nodes among the processors, we solve the following optimization problem: (i) reduce the intercore communication cost C and (ii) under the constraint that the *work imbalance* among the cores is less than a small threshold (5% in our setup). The work imbalance is the difference of load between the core which

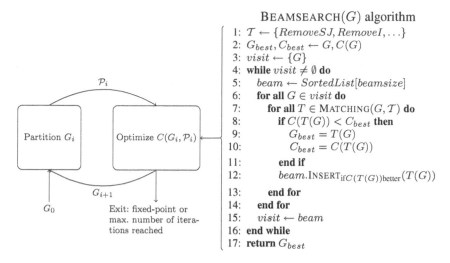

BEAMSEARCH(G) algorithm

```
 1: T ← {RemoveSJ, RemoveI,...}
 2: G_best, C_best ← G, C(G)
 3: visit ← {G}
 4: while visit ≠ ∅ do
 5:     beam ← SortedList[beamsize]
 6:     for all G ∈ visit do
 7:         for all T ∈ MATCHING(G, T) do
 8:             if C(T(G)) < C_best then
 9:                 G_best = T(G)
10:                 C_best = C(T(G))
11:             end if
12:             beam.INSERT_{ifC(T(G))better}(T(G))
13:         end for
14:     end for
15:     visit ← beam
16: end while
17: return G_best
```

Figure 7.9   Reducing the intercore communication through an iterative process.

is busiest and the core with the less work. To solve this problem we use the graph partitioner METIS [19]. The threshold makes the balancing constraint a bit more flexible, opening opportunities for the partitioner to improve the communication cost.

To optimize the communication patterns between filters, we use the set of transformations presented in Section 7.4.2. Given an SJD graph G_0, a derivation is a chain of transformations that can be successively applied to $G_0 : G_0 \xrightarrow{T_0} G_1 \cdots \xrightarrow{T_n} \cdots$. Each derivation produces a new variant, semantically equivalent to G_0 but with different communication patterns. Given an initial graph G_0, the number of derivations that exist is very large, how should we pick one? In [9] we prove that for any given graph there are no infinite derivations, that is to say, the optimization space is bounded. To choose which transformations to apply, we use the BEAMSEARCH [23], search heuristic which is tuned with a constant parameter $beamsize \in \mathbb{N}$. The algorithm explores the optimization space recursively by applying all the possible transformations to the initial graph G_0, sorting the produced first-generation variants by their intercore communication costs and discarding all but the first $beamsize$ ones. The algorithm is then applied recursively on the selected best first generation variants. BEAMSEARCH is guaranteed to terminate since the optimization space is finite. These two passes, partitioning and communication optimization, are interleaved in an iterative process, depicted in Figure 7.9, similar to [7].

7.6 EVALUATION

We have evaluated the intercore communication reduction technique on two sets of signal application benchmarks: a first set of SLICES programs, matrix multiplication, Gauss filter and Sobel filter which are first compiled to the SJD intermediate representation and a second set of programs from the StreamIt benchmarks [26], Bitonic sort, FFT, DES and DCT which are directly translated to the SJD representation.

Table 7.1 Intercore communication cost reduction. 'original' and 'optimized' represent the intercommunication volume per steady state for the original program and the optimized program in Bytes. 'C reduction' is the reduction percentage of intercore communications computed as $\frac{C_{original} - C_{optimized}}{C_{original}} \times 100$.

	MM-COARSE	GAUSS	BITONIC	HOUGH	FFT	DES	DCT
Original (B)	18,864	10,563,200	384	48,480,000	384	192	3072
Optimized (B)	6624	7,340,000	256	401,624	192	192	1956
C reduction (%)	64.9	30.5	33.4	99.2	50	0	36.3
Opt. cost (s)	5	18	925	411	10	66	10

'opt. cost' is the time spend optimizing the SJD representation in seconds.

The target architecture is quadcore SMP Nehalem (Xeon© W3520 at 2.67 GHz) with 256 KB of L2 cache and a shared 8MB L3 cache. The communications between cores happen through the L3 cache with a very low latency (here we suppose that $c_0 = 0$).

We have measured the communication cost for two versions of the programs: the *original* one is mapped with METIS to reduce the communication cost but graph transformations are *not* applied to it; the *optimized* one is mapped with METIS *and* optimized using the graph transformation set.

Table 7.1 summarizes the intercore communication reductions achieved by our optimization framework. The mean percentage of reduction among all the programs is 49.9%, and the mean time spend optimizing the programs is 3.4 min.

The DES encryption program shows no gains at all: the program admits very few graph transformations that have no impact on the global layout of communications.

The gains in MM-COARSE can be attributed to several transformations of the flow graph that can be seen in Figure 7.10. After optimization, the synchronization bottlenecks (nodes J 8 and S15) have been removed. The transposition of matrix B has been decomposed in blocks and distributed among the four cores. Finally, duplications are made locally which reduce the volume of intercore communications.

The GAUSS filter is a bidimensional sliding-window filter that extract overlapping 3×3 windows of data from the input image. Our transformations are able to break the sliding-window extraction among the different cores and reorganize the Split, Join and Dup nodes to increase the horizontal reuse of data among filters, reducing intercore communication.

The HOUGH filter computes the Hough transformation in a tight loop. Our optimization framework breaks this loop in three smaller loops that are distributed among the cores, making the state in the loop local to each processor.

The FFT and DCT filters possess many synchronizations points that are removed by our transformation process allowing a better partitioning among the cores.

7.6.1 Impact on the Execution Time

We have implemented [9] a complete backend that compiles the intermediate SJD representation to C code running on an SMP architecture. The compilation process

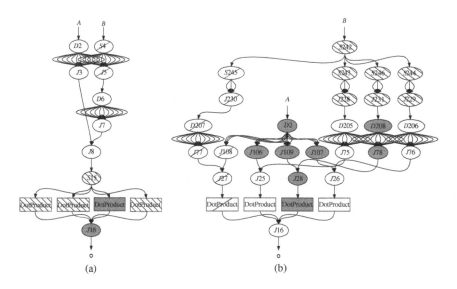

Figure 7.10   Optimizations applied to MM-COARSE. In the original program the inter-core communication cost is high since the program presents many synchronizations points: for example, at runtime J 8 and S15 quickly become communication bottlenecks. After optimization, J 8 and S15 have been split; the transposition of matrix B has been divided in blocks and distributed among the four cores; duplicate nodes (nodes D205, D208, etc.) have also been distributed among the cores; since the consumers of the duplicate streams are all in the same core, duplications can be compiled to multiple reads to the same buffer and are not added to the intercore traffic (a) Partitioning of original MM-COARSE on 4 cores, (b) Partitioning of optimized MM-COARSE on 4 cores.

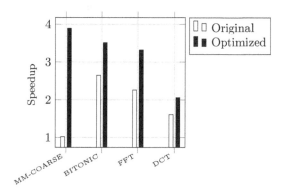

Figure 7.11   Impact of the communication reductions on the performance: speedups of the original program and the optimized program on an SMP Nehalem quadcore. The executions times are normalized to the reference (StreamIt original program execution time on a single core).

can be broken in a series of steps: partitioning, scheduling, task fusion, communication fusion and code generation.

Our compiler takes into account two types of parallelism: (i) task or data parallelism which is explicit in the SJD graph and (ii) pipeline parallelism which allows to overlap successive executions of consumers and producers in a Stream Graph Modulo scheduling [20]. In the Stream Graph Modulo scheduling, a node execution can be overlapped with its communications, hiding the cost of the cheaper operation. In this context, the performance of a program is determined by the maximum between: (i) the time needed to complete a schedule tick of a node execution and (ii) the time needed to copy the productions of the node to the consumer.

Reducing the intercore communication cost should therefore have an impact on performance on communication-bound programs. To verify this hypothesis we have selected among the previous benchmarks the programs for which we had a reference implementation (StreamIt) and for which our intercore communication reduction was successful.

Our baseline is the execution time of the StreamIt version of the program compiled on **a single core** with the command `strc -O3`. The speedups presented are normalized by the StreamIt single-core performance. Then we have measured the execution time of the SJD original program and the SJD optimized program using our backend on **four cores**. Figure 7.11 presents the results obtained. The mean speedup without applying optimizations is $\times 1.85$, while the mean speedup with intercore communication reductions is $\times 3.2$.

7.7 CONCLUSION

The challenge for stream programming on multicore architectures is to describe stream manipulation, dependent on the application, and adapt this stream to complex and changing multicore architectures. In particular, the program has to adapt to the parallelism of the target architecture and to the bandwidth limitation and limited cache (or buffer) sizes.

Stream transformations and optimizations are the key to this adaptation, and both parallelism and communication metrics can be evaluated on a flow graph describing the stream. Being able to explore different stream formulation according to the metrics to be optimized is essential to obtain high-performance stream programs. So far, research efforts in stream-specific languages have focused on two language categories: languages such as Array-OL and Block Parallel describe streams through dependences between filters, and languages such as StreamIt and Brook explicitly manipulate stream operators. While it is more natural to the developer to describe its program as a set of filters communicating through dependences, stream optimizations are hampered by the strong constraints imposed by the underlying dependency model. For languages explicitly manipulating stream objects, the range of possible optimizations is larger but suffers from the difficulty to describe complex flows.

We have presented in this chapter a novel approach for stream programming. Based on the fact that the description of the stream and its optimization are separate concerns, we proposed an approach based on two domain-specific languages, one for each concern. This approach retains both the expressivity of high-level languages such as Array-OL and Block Parallel and the rich optimization framework, similar to StreamIT and Brook.

SLICES manages to retain a high-level multidimensional expression of programs while enabling an efficient compilation to the intermediary language. The SJD intermediary language extends the expressivity of StreamIt by allowing nonhierarchical graphs, extending the range of possible optimizations. We introduce a formal framework for building correct transformations of SJD programs and an iterative exploration algorithm to optimize a program according to a metric. This method achieves a mean 49.9% reduction of the intercore communication cost among a set of significant benchmarks. We expect our results to be even more relevant as the number of cores increases, but this will be shown as future work. A limited exploration of the space of solutions seems to be difficult to overcome so far: the metrics such as intercore communication or memory consumption are nonlinear metrics.

REFERENCES

1. S. Agrawal, W. Thies, and S. Amarasinghe. Optimizing stream programs using linear state space analysis. In *Proceedings of the 2005 international conference on Compilers, architectures and synthesis for embedded systems*, pages 126–136. ACM, 2005.

2. M. Aldinucci, M. Danelutto, P. Kilpatrick, M. Meneghin, and M. Torquati. Accelerating sequential programs using FastFlow and self-offloading. Technical Report TR-10-03, arXiv:1002.4668, Universita di Pisa, 2010.

3. A. Amar, P. Boulet, and P. Dumont. Projection of the Array-OL specification language onto the Kahn process network computation model. In *Proc. Parallel Architectures, Algorithms and Networks, 2005*, page 6, 2005.

4. S. Amarasinghe, M. Gordon, M. Karczmarek, J. Lin, D. Maze, R.M. Rabbah, and W. Thies. Language and compiler design for streaming applications. *International Journal of Parallel Programming*, 33(2):261–278, 2005.

5. M. Andries, G. Engels, A. Habel, B. Hoffmann, H. J. Kreowski, S. Kuske, D. Plump, A. Schürr, and G. Taentzer. Graph transformation for specification and programming. *Science of Computer Programming*, 34(1):1–54, 1999.

6. D. Black-Schaffer. *Block Parallel Programming for Real-Time Applications on Multicore Processors*. PhD thesis, Stanford University, 2008.

7. P. M. Carpenter, A. Ramirez, and E. Ayguade. Mapping stream programs onto heterogeneous multiprocessor systems. In *CASES '09: Proceedings of the 2009 international conference on Compilers, architecture, and synthesis for embedded systems*, pages 57–66, New York, NY, USA, 2009. ACM.

8. A. Charfi, A. Gamatié, A. Honoré, J.L. Dekeyser, and M. Abid. Validation de modèles dans un cadre d'IDM dédié à la conception de systèmes sur puce. *4èmes Jounées sur l'Ingénierie Dirigée par les Modèles (IDM 08), Mulhouse, France*, 2008.

9. P. de Oliveira Castro. *Expression et optimisation des réorganisations de données dans du parallélisme de flots*. PhD thesis, Université de Versailles Saint Quentin en Yvelines, 2010.

10. P. de Oliveira Castro, S. Louise, and D. Barthou. A multidimensional array slicing DSL for stream programming. In *2010 International Conference on Complex, Intelligent and Software Intensive Systems*, pages 913–918. IEEE, 2010.

11. P. de Oliveira Castro, S. Louise, and D. Barthou. Reducing memory requirements of stream programs by graph transformations. In *High Performance Computing and Simulation (HPCS), 2010 International Conference on*, pages 171–180. IEEE, 2010.

12. F. Devin, P. Boulet, J.L. Dekeyser, and P. Marquet. GASPARD: a visual parallel programming environment. In *Proceedings of International Conference on Parallel Computing in Electrical Engineering, 2002. PARELEC'02*, pages 145–150, 2002.

13. P. Dumont. *Spécification Multidimensionnelle pour le traitement du signal systématique*. PhD thesis, Université des sciences et technologies de Lille, 2005.

14. C. Glitia. *Optimisation des applications de traitement systématique intensives sur system-on-chip*. PhD thesis, Université des Sciences et Technologies de Lille, 2009.

15. C. Glitia and P. Boulet. High level loop transformations for systematic signal processing embedded applications. In *Proc. of the 8th international workshop on Embedded Computer Systems: Architectures, Modeling, and Simulation*, pages 187–196. Springer-Verlag, 2008.

16. C. Glitia, P. Dumont, and P. Boulet. Array-OL with delays, a domain specific specification language for multidimensional intensive signal processing. *Multidimensional Systems and Signal Processing*, 21:105–131, June 2010.

17. M. I. Gordon, W. Thies, M. Karczmarek, J. Lin, A. S. Meli, A. A. Lamb, C. Leger, J. Wong, H. Hoffmann, D. Maze, and S. Amarasinghe. A stream compiler for communication-exposed architectures. In *Int. Conf. on Architectural Support for Programming Languages and Operating Systems*, pages 291–303. ACM, 2002.

18. R. W. Hockney. The communication challenge for mpp: Intel paragon and meiko cs-2. *Parallel Comput.*, 20(3):389–398, 1994.

19. G. Karypis and V. Kumar. A fast and high quality multilevel scheme for partitioning irregular graphs. *SIAM Journal on Scientific Computing* 20(1):359–392, 1998.

20. M. Kudlur and S. Mahlke. Orchestrating the execution of stream programs on multicore platforms. In *Proc. of the SIGPLAN conf. on Programming Language Design and Implementation*, pages 114–124. ACM, 2008.

21. E. A. Lee and D. G. Messerschmitt. Synchronous data flow. *Proceedings of the IEEE*, 75(9):1235–1245, 1987.

22. S.-w. Liao, Z. Du, G. Wu, and G.-Y. Lueh. Data and computation transformations for brook streaming applications on multiprocessors. In *Int. Symp. on Code Generation and Optimization*, Washington, DC, USA, 2006. IEEE.

23. B. T. Lowerre. *The Harpy Speech Recognition System*. PhD thesis, Carnegie Mellon University, Pittsburgh, PA, USA, 1976.

24. C. Miranda, P. Dumont, A. Cohen, M. Duranton, and A. Pop. ERBIUM: a deterministic, concurrent intermediate representation for portable and scalable performance. In *Conf. Computing Frontiers*, pages 119–120, 2010.

25. J. Sermulins, W. Thies, R. Rabbah, and S. Amarasinghe. Cache aware optimization of stream programs. *ACM SIGPLAN Notices*, 40(7):126, 2005.

26. StreamIt Group. Streamit benchmarks. `http://groups.csail.mit.edu/cag/streamit/shtml/benchmarks.shtml`.

27. W. Thies. *Language and Compiler Support for Stream Programs*. PhD thesis, Massachusetts Institute of Technology, 2009.

CHAPTER 8

PROGRAMMING WITH TRANSACTIONAL MEMORY

Vincent Gramoli and Rachid Guerraoui

8.1 INTRODUCTION

The transactional memory (TM) paradigm simplifies concurrent programming by hiding all synchronizations from the standpoint of the application programmer. Basically, it relieves the programmer of the lock management burden; therefore the programmer does no longer have to explicitly acquire and release locks but simply has to delimit regions of sequential code that should appear as atomic, the *transactions*.

Transactions cannot block each other, hence guaranteeing deadlock-free executions. In contrast, purely lock-based systems are known to be complex, and, for example, in [4] the authors identified that 34% of Linux bugs [4] were due to synchronization, while in [9] the authors thought having found eight potential deadlock bugs in the Linux kernel v2.5. TM provides a transaction abstraction appealing for it remedies numerous concurrency problems.

It is the role of the TM to execute transactions concurrently yet guaranteeing that their execution is equivalent to an execution in which they would be serialized. The synchronization mechanics are thus still present but transferred to the TM program underlying the applications. TM greatly simplifies concurrent programming by hiding these complex mechanics from the application programmer.

More specifically, the TM program provides a basic high-level interface for the programmer to convert a sequential program into a concurrent one: `begin`, `read`, `write`, `commit`. The `begin` and `commit` delimit the *transaction*, that is, the region of code that should appear as being executed atomically in isolation from the rest of the system. The `read` and `write` calls are wrappers to usual memory accesses that are used to redirect memory loads and stores that belong to a transaction. Besides making sure that the transaction executes the corresponding `load` (resp. `store`), the `read` (resp. `write`) maintains the metadata defining the transaction state.

This chapter sheds some light on the current programming advances in the context of TM and describes how a programmer can exploit them to write simply efficient concurrent programs. For more general concepts on TM, the interested reader may refer to [14, 17]. Section 8.2 illustrates the simplicity of transactions to solve a common concurrency problem. Section 8.3 summarizes TM support in existing programming languages and presents the transactional constructs for C, C++ and Java. Section 8.4 introduces TM implementations by discussing hardware support and presenting a running example for software support. Section 8.5 outlines causes for performance limitations TMs may suffer from, and Section 8.6 introduces recent solutions to cope with these limitations.

8.2 CONCURRENCY MADE SIMPLE

The TM paradigm initiated a complexity shift between the development of the concurrent applications and the development of the TM programs. This section illustrates the simplicity of writing a TM-based concurrent program with the dining philosopher problem.

The dining philosopher problem is a common concurrency control problem proposed by Dijkstra and reformulated by Hoare [23], in which five philosophers sitting around a table with a rice bowl in front of each of them and a single chopstick between each pair of consecutive bowls (see Fig. 8.1) alternate between thinking and eating. A philosopher can eat only if he acquires the two chopsticks near his bowl; hence not all philosophers can eat at the same time. Solving the dining philosopher problem relies in designing an algorithm that avoids *starvation* so that each philosopher is guaranteed to eat eventually.

Figure 8.1 The five chopsticks shared by the five dining philosophers to eat rice.

A naive spinning lock-based solution that consists of acquiring the left chopstick before trying to acquire the right one suffers from *deadlocks*, as all philosophers could potentially acquire the left one and wait forever for the right one to be released by his right neighbor. Djikstra solution consists of acquiring and releasing all chopsticks in a predetermined order; however, if the placement of the chopstick is not adequate, then the solution may be very costly forcing many philosophers to release their chopstick to let a single one eat. Other deadlock-free solutions are not starvation-free as they may suffer from *livelocks*, where philosophers keep acquiring and releasing chopstick without being able to eat.

Algorithm The try-to-eat procedure of the dining philosopher i.

```
 1: try-to-eat()ᵢ:
 2:    begin()                              ▷ transaction starts
 3:      pickup(chpks[i])
 4:      pickup(chpks[i + 1 mod 5])
 5:    commit()                             ▷ transaction ends
 6:    eat()
 7:    begin()                              ▷ transaction starts
 8:      putdown(chpks[i + 1 mod 5])
 9:      putdown(chpks[i])
10:    commit()                             ▷ transaction ends

11: pickup(chpk)ᵢ:
12:    chpk.owner = i                       ▷ write memory

13: putdown(chpk)ᵢ:
14:    chpk.owner = ⊥                       ▷ write memory
```

This algorithm depicts a transaction-based try-to-eat procedure that shows how TM can simply solve the dining philosopher problem. Let us focus on the first transaction – the second transaction is simply used to ensure that safety is preserved even though transactions do not execute in isolation from nontransactional accesses. The all-or-nothing transaction semantics guarantees that the transaction either acquires both chopsticks or none of them. If the transaction commits, the philosopher can eat. Conversely, if the transaction aborts, then the philosopher does not prevent another philosopher from eating, granting additional time to his neighbors to finish eating. Note that another solution would be to write a transaction that wraps the whole try-to-eat procedure. Although it would be perfectly correct, the resulting program would have enabled less concurrency. A general guideline for programmers is to write transactions that are as short as possible. If the transactions are too long, then it is likely that one of them may have to abort and restart. A separate contention manager plays the role of avoiding livelocks in which a transaction gets repeatedly aborted. For instance, contention managers either map a high priority to aborting transactions [32] or make aborting transactions back off some time before restarting [21].

The simplicity comes from the fact that synchronization complexities are transferred to the TM itself and are hidden from the programmer. In fact, the exposed synchronization is reduced to begin and commit delimiters, the rest being bare sequential code. No locking primitives are exposed to the programmer, and deadlock freedom is inherently guaranteed by the hidden TM. TM implementations are detailed in Section 8.4.

8.3   TM LANGUAGE CONSTRUCTS

Several compilers support transaction language constructs. For instance, there exist at least three compilers that compiles transactions in C at the time of writing: the proto-type DTMC,[1] the TM branch of gcc,[2] and the Intel® C++ STM compiler (icc).[3] The Glasgow Haskell Compiler provides support for transactions in Haskell [18]. Multi-verse offers support for TM in Java and has been used in Scala [2]. Fortress supports transactional language constructs, and Pugs compiles and interprets transactions in Perl 6. .NET Framework 4 supports software transactional memory (STM). Multi-ple third-party programs allow also to support transactions in other languages, like STMlib for OCaml and Durus for Python.

8.3.1   C/C++ Programming Languages

The first attempts to support TM in production compilers led to the definition of dedicated transactional language constructs in a C++ specification draft [34], resulting originally from the collaboration of Intel®, IBM® and Sun® Microsystems (Oracle®). This draft describes the constructs to delimit a compound statement that is identified by the compiler as a transaction, in addition to several subtleties we list here. For several years now, this specification has been reviewed and discussed by academicians and other industrials on the TM-language mailing list,[4] for the sake of language expressiveness and compliance with existing TM systems and other languages.

In C, a transaction is simply delimited using the block

$$\texttt{\_\_tm\_atomic\{ ... \}}$$

while in C++ a transaction is delimited by a `__transaction{ ... }` block where `__transaction{` (or equivalently `__transaction [ [atomic] ] {`) indicates the point in the code where the corresponding transaction `begin` should be called. The closing bracket `}` indicates the point in the code where the corresponding transaction `commit` should be called. Within this block, memory accesses are instrumented by the compiler to call the transactional `read` and `write` wrappers. More precisely, the binary files produced by the compiler call a dedicated TM runtime library through an appropriate application binary interface (ABI) specified in [24]. This ABI is used for both C and C++ and has been optimized for the Linux OS and x86 architectures to reduce the overhead of the TM calls and to allow fast accesses to thread-specific metadata shared by existing TMs.

---

[1]http://www.velox-project.eu/software/dtmc.
[2]http://www.velox-project.eu/software/gcc-tm.
[3]http://software.intel.com/en-us/articles/intel-c-stm-compiler-prototype-edition/.
[4]http://groups.google.com/group/tm-languages.

Transaction nesting, which consists in encapsulating a transaction block into another, is allowed, and the [[outer]] keyword is explicitly used to indicate that a transaction cannot be nested inside another. Generally, it is not allowed to redirect the control flow to some point in the context of a transaction, but exceptions can be raised within the context of transaction to redirect the control flow outside the transaction context by propagating the exception.

Irrevocable transactions do not execute speculatively and are used to execute actions that cannot be rolled back once executed; this is typically necessary in cases where an action has some external side effects like I/O have. Attribute in C++1x-style indicates whether the transaction executes speculatively as by default __transaction[[atomic]]{} or has to execute without being aborted __transaction[[relaxed]]{}, say, in *irrevocable* mode. Only irrevocable transactions can execute calls with irrevocable side effects, and, for example,

```
[[transaction_unsafe]] void fire_missile{};
```

declares a fire_missile function that can only be called in an irrevocable transaction. The attribute [[transaction_safe]] void do_work{}; is especially used to indicate the opposite – that function do_work does not have to be called in an irrevocable transaction and can execute speculatively as part of a transaction prone to abort.

8.3.2 Java™ Programming Language

In Java, TM supports has been initially proposed using the combination of Java annotations for identifying transactional accesses and a corresponding bytecode instrumentation framework that instruments transactional accesses either at load-time or statically prior to execution. Multiverse[5] and Deuce [26] are two such JVM agents that instrument transactional accesses of the annotated bytecode resulting from a concurrent program.

Multiverse distinguishes @TransactionalObject and @TransactionalMethod annotations that apply, respectively, to Java objects and methods. All instance methods of an annotated object are thus instrumented transactions, and annotated methods allow to specify which methods of a non-annotated object are transactions. Additionally, annotating a method of an already annotated objects allows to differentiate explicitly read-only methods from update methods using @Transactional (readonly = true). Such differentiation is useful for the underlying TM to optimize the validation of a read-only transaction that commits.

Deuce instruments methods annotated with the @Atomic keyword and uses a clear interface a TM should provide: begin (viz. init), read (viz. onReadAccess), write (viz. onWriteAccess) and commit methods and additional beforeReadAccess and abort (viz. rollback) methods. The

---

[5]http://multiverse.codehaus.org.

current distribution features classical transactions of state-of-the-art software TMs developed collaboratively like TL2 [7], LSA [30], NOrec [5] and $\mathcal{E}$-STM [10] that combine classical and elastic transactions, as described in Section 8.6.2.2.

Unlike C/C++ compilers, the aforementioned bytecode instrumentation frameworks cannot consider an arbitrary compound statement as a transaction because they rely on annotation mechanisms. The Java precompiler TMJava[6] remedies this limitation by extending Java with transactional blocks. More specifically, TMJava supports the `__transaction{ ... }` language construct in Java and outputs a purely Java annotated program whose bytecode can be instrumented with Deuce.

It is noteworthy that TMs have recently found other applications in Java, including coordinated exception handling [16]. In this case, the failure atomicity guaranteed by transactions is useful for recovering from an inconsistent state even in a concurrent environment.

8.4 IMPLEMENTING A TM

Programming with transactions shifts the synchronization complexity from the application to the TM. This section discusses the TM implementations in hardware and then in software, illustrating different design choices.

8.4.1 Hardware Support

Hardware transactional memory (HTM) has already shown promising results for leveraging parallelism in the Linux OS [31] where transactions are combined with spinlocks. HTMs scale better than locks in some scenarios. For example, if a single lock is protecting multiple elements of a data structure, then concurrent transactions accessing these elements may not abort each other. Finally, transactions are inherently compositional and deadlock-free, an additional reason for using HTMs over locks.

The scheme of the MetaTM [31] is similar to LogTM [27]. When a thread executing a transaction executes a modification, the modification becomes immediately visible, and the old value is recorded into an undo-log. If the transaction aborts, it then rolls back by reverting the value to the old value. A thread can stop a transaction and restart it afterwards which facilitates interrupt handling. HTMs have been applied to bus-based systems in which the network-on-ship communications have to be diminished. In [25], the authors propose an HTM that targets object-oriented programming. This object-aware HTM attempts to avoid the high abort ratio induced by considering conflicts at the level of objects that can be arbitrarily large. The key idea is to provide an object cache with object address and field offset that are cached.

HTMs suffer, however, from some limitations. For example, some HTMs require transactions to be of limited size [19] because of the limited hardware resource, like bounded cache size. Some HTMs require specific system events or instructions

[6]http://tinystm.org/tmjava.

to be executed outside transactions [6, 27]. Despite being dedicated to OSes, some others cannot support transaction suspension, migration or context switches [15, 25]. Finally, transactions must be small enough to provide responsive irrevocable I/O despite their speculative behaviors. The development of the Rock processor [6], which provided a best-effort HTM, has been canceled. This processor used aggressive speculation to provide high single-thread performance in addition to high system throughput. For these reasons, it is unlikely that future TM implementations will be purely hardware, and upcoming TMs are expected to contain a software component.

8.4.2 Software Support

We present a running example of STM that does not need special hardware support – it is implemented in software. First, we present a 2-phase-locking STM by giving the pseudocode of its `begin`, `read`, `write` and `commit` functions, and then we derive four variants that enable greater concurrency among transactions.

8.4.2.1 *Two-Phase Locking*
We first present a naive STM algorithm whose transactions use two-phase locking. Each read and write access of a transaction t tries to acquire a lock on the accessed memory location. If t succeeds in acquiring all the locks, t is granted an exclusive access to these locations, and t commits. If t cannot acquire a lock, it detects a conflict and may abort. Upon commit or abort, t releases all the locks it acquired. The TM presented in the algorithm in the following serializes transactions that access common locations as its transaction semantics is two-phase locking with no distinction on the type of accesses: acquiring locks on all accessed locations (first phase) and releasing them all in a row (second phase).

This algorithm depicts the pseudocode of the 2-phase-locking TM algorithm that lets a transaction commits only if it obtains exclusive accesses. Such a transaction is likely to detect a conflict preventing it from committing. As the contention management policy simply aborts and restarts the transaction upon conflict detection (Lines 8 and 15), the same scenario will likely occur later. For brevity, we omitted the description of the `abort-and-restart()` procedure that consists of resetting the shared locations and thread-private metadata to their default value (abort) and redirecting the control flow to the `begin()` of the transaction (restart). In the following text, we explore several modifications of such naive TM algorithm that leads to better performance.

8.4.2.2 *Read Sharing*
For the previous TM to enable greater concurrency, one can allow *read sharing* to let concurrent transactions read the same memory location.

This algorithm presents the modifications to obtain a TM with read sharing. The idea is simply to change the mutex locks into read/write locks. The read operation acquires a read lock on location x only if the write lock on x is not acquired, that is, $lock(x)$ is w-unlocked (Line 7); the write operation acquires a write lock on x only if neither the read nor the write lock on x is acquired, that is, $lock(x)$ is unlocked (Line 3).

Algorithm Naive TM for transaction t.

```
 1: begin()_t:
 2:    r-set ← ∅
 3:    w-set ← ∅
 4:    w-log ← ∅

 5: write(x, v)_t:
 6:    if ⟨x, v'⟩ ∉ w-set then
 7:       while !cas(lock(x), unlocked, locked) do
 8:          abort-and-restart()                              ▷ contention mgmt
 9:       w-log = w-log ∪ {⟨x, store(x, v)⟩}
10:       w-set = w-set ∪ {⟨x, v⟩}
11:    return(ok)
12: read(x)_t:
13:    if ⟨x, *⟩ ∉ w-set then
14:       while !cas(lock(x), unlocked, locked) do
15:          abort-and-restart()                              ▷ contention mgmt
16:       v = load(x)
17:       r-set = r-set ∪ {⟨x, v⟩}
18:    else let v be such that ⟨x, v⟩ ∈ w-set
19:    return(v)

20: commit()_t:
21:    for ⟨x, *⟩ ∈ w-set do unlock(x)
```

Algorithm Read sharing TM for transaction t.

```
 1: write(x, v)_t:
 2:    ...
 3:    while !cas(lock(x), unlocked, w-locked) do
 4:    ...
 5: read(x)_t:
 6:    ...
 7:    while !cas(lock(x), w-unlocked, r-locked) do
 8:    ...
```

8.4.2.3 Time of Update

The previous TM algorithms execute update *in-place*, meaning that each modification of a write access is immediately reported in memory. Another approach, called *deferred* update, aims at recording each write access into a redo-log and to report their logged modifications to the memory at commit time. The algorithm in the following presents the changes to make to the previous one to obtain a TM with deferred update transactions. Note that by postponing the time of memory update, there is no need to maintain an undo-log with the old version, *w-log* (Line 5), as no value has to be reverted in case of abort.

In-place update transactions have a lightweight commit phase but a costly abort phase. They require to record all their write accesses into an undo-log to revert the memory appropriately upon abort. Moreover, they have to protect their modifications until commit time to preserve their isolation. Otherwise the TM could suffer from *cascading aborts*: a transaction t that aborts forces the transactions that have read t's modifications to abort as well, provoking, in turn, additional aborts.

Problems due to the lack of isolation can be even more dramatic: division by zero, infinite loops, etc. A TM copes with these issues if it ensures opacity [14], that is, any execution it produces is equivalent to an execution where transactions

---

Algorithm Deferred update TM for transaction t.

```
 1: write(x, v)_t:
 2:   if ⟨x, v'⟩ ∉ w-set then
 3:     while !cas(lock(x), unlocked, w-locked) do
 4:       abort-and-restart()
 5:       w̶-̶l̶o̶g̶ ̶=̶ ̶w̶-̶l̶o̶g̶ ̶∪̶ ̶{̶⟨̶x̶,̶ ̶s̶t̶o̶r̶e̶(̶x̶,̶ ̶v̶)̶⟩̶}̶
 6:     w-set = w-set ∪ {⟨x, v⟩}
 7:   return(ok)
 8: commit()_t:
 9:   for ⟨x, v⟩ ∈ w-set do store(x, v)
10:   for ⟨x, *⟩ ∈ w-set do unlock(x)
```

---

execute sequentially, respecting the order of nonconcurrent transactions in the original execution, and where all transactions, including aborting ones, do not observe a noncommitted state.

Deferred update transactions have to replay the redo-log at commit time but do have a lightweight abort phase as no modifications have to be reported in memory in case the transaction aborts. Additionally, a deferred update transaction may make its modifications invisible from concurrent transactions until it commits, which may represent a waste of effort as running transactions that will eventually abort keep cores busy. Invisible write transaction t has, however, the advantage of letting other transactions access same locations and commit before t reaches its commit phase. We discuss in the next section how to make write invisible.

8.4.2.4 *Write Invisibility*
A TM with in-place updates cannot have invisible writes, as by modifying the shared location before it commits; other concurrent transactions accessing the same location are guaranteed to see the modification. Conversely in a deferred update transaction, the writes can be invisible until commit time. Deferred update transactions can also have visible writes, by changing the metadata associated with some locations. For example, the TM resulting from modifications of the previous algorithm have visible writes as it locks a location x at the time the write on x is executed and before commit time. While accessing the same location x, concurrent transactions detect that the lock on x has been acquired.

Algorithm Invisible write TM for transaction t.

```
 1: write(x, v)_t:
 2:   if ⟨x, v'⟩ ∉ w-set then
 3:     while !̶c̶a̶s̶(̶l̶o̶c̶k̶(̶x̶)̶,̶ ̶u̶n̶l̶o̶c̶k̶e̶d̶,̶ ̶w̶-̶l̶o̶c̶k̶e̶d̶)̶ do
 4:       a̶b̶o̶r̶t̶-̶a̶n̶d̶-̶r̶e̶s̶t̶a̶r̶t̶(̶)̶
 5:     w-set = w-set ∪ {⟨x, v⟩}
 6:   return(ok)
 7: commit()_t:
 8:   for ⟨x, v⟩ ∈ w-set do
 9:     while !cas(lock(x), unlocked, w-locked) do
10:       abort-and-restart()
11:     store(x, v)
12:   for ⟨x, *⟩ ∈ w-set do unlock(x)
```

As illustrated in the algorithm earlier, the TM has simply to postpone the locking of x from the write time to the commit time to make writes invisible from concurrent transactions.

8.4.2.5 Time-Based Implementations
In 2006, time-based TM algorithms [7, 30] were suggested as an alternative to purely lock-based TMs.

The aforementioned lock-based TM implementations rely on locks that simply indicate whether a memory location is protected. Typically, a transaction t_1 locks a memory location between the time it reads it and the time it commits preventing a concurrent transaction t_2 from overwriting the read value during this time interval. This prevention is however restrictive as t_1 could still be serialized before t_2 even if t_2 is allowed to write. An alternative is to use a global counter so that each transaction and each memory location get assigned an associated version, whose comparison indicates whether memory locations can be read by the transaction.

Algorithm Time-based TM for transaction t.

```
 1: begin()_t:
 2:     ...
 3:     ts ← counter                                              ▷ read global counter

 4: commit()_t:
 5:     t ← counter++                                             ▷ set a new version
 6:     for ⟨x, v, t⟩ ∈ w-set do
 7:         while !cas(lock(x), unlocked, w-locked) do
 8:             abort-and-restart()
 9:         store(x, v, t)                                        ▷ record new version
10:     for ⟨x, *, *⟩ ∈ w-set do unlock(x)
11: read(x)_t:
12:     if ⟨x, *, *⟩ ∉ w-set then
13:         while !cas(lock(x), w-unlocked, r-locked) do
14:             abort-and-restart()
15:         ⟨v, t⟩ = load(x)                                      ▷ get version
16:         if (t > ts) then try-update()                        ▷ validate
17:         r-set = r-set ∪ {⟨x, v, t⟩}
18:     else let v be such that ⟨x, v, *⟩ ∈ w-set
19:     return(v)
```

Transaction t calls try-update when it reads a memory location whose version t is more recent than the time ts the transaction started, indicating that the location has been concurrently updated. The try-update tries to update ts by checking if all previously read locations have not been overwritten since t has started. Upon failure, the transaction aborts.

8.4.2.6 Read Invisibility
A TM that executes *invisible read* transactions ensure that no transactions can detect read accesses of pending transactions. If transaction t executes invisible reads, then no concurrent transactions can detect related conflicts; thus it is the role of t to validate its set of read accesses, *r-set*, at commit time to make sure that all these remain consistent. Although a monomorphic TM algorithm with exclusive read accesses cannot have invisible reads, allowing shared read accesses from two concurrent transactions, as we did in modifications of Section 8.4.2.2,

permits having invisible reads. (Transaction monomorphism and polymorphism are discussed in Section 8.6.2.) We now present the additional modifications necessary to obtain a TM with invisible reads.

Algorithm Invisible read TM for transaction t.

```
1:  read(x)_t:
2:     if ⟨x, *, *⟩ ∉ w-set then
3:        while !cas(lock(x), w-unlocked, r-locked) do
4:           abort-and-restart()
5:        ...

6:  commit()_t:
7:     for ⟨x, v, t⟩ ∈ r-set do
8:        if v ≠ load(x) then abort-and-restart()
9:     ...
```

The read no longer acquires locks so that concurrent transactions cannot observe that a location has been read-locked. The reading transaction could check that the current location is locked by updating transactions and abort if so, but it does not have to check whether its read is consistent at the time it reads, if all transactions have invisible writes. The validation of an invisible read transaction is done at commit time by checking that all its read accesses are still valid at the commit time, if not a conflict is detected (Line 8).

8.5 PERFORMANCE LIMITATIONS

TM has become very popular these past ten years. Few years ago however, several researchers expressed their skepticism about this programming paradigm. This tendency follows the well-known Gartner Hype Cycle and seems to indicate that TM, after having been on the peak of inflated expectations, is reaching the trough of disillusionment. This reveals a critical period after which TM becomes a mature idea.

8.5.1 Trough of Disillusionment

This disillusionment was expressed in an experimental paper, invited for publications in the October 2008 issue of CACM, questioning the capability of STM-based concurrent applications to even speedup the performance one could obtain from a single-threaded sequential application [3]. Differing results [8], which appeared recently also in CACM, state that STM is finally a mechanism that scales significantly the performance of various applications as the level of parallelism increases, provided that the underlying multicore machine features enough hardware parallelism.

A more theoretical paper shed some light on some formal appealing properties, like read invisibility and strict disjoint-access parallelism, TM implementations fail in guaranteeing [1]. Disjoint-access parallelism properties may present a lighter impact when placed in the shared memory context where accessing shared data is fast and where the TM bottleneck is more susceptible to come from the lack of concurrency

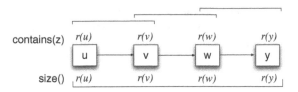

Figure 8.2   Sorted (lexicographically) linked list example in which two operations with same accesses have distinct semantics: contains (z) is a parse operation whereas size () is a snapshot operation.

or the ignorant contention management policy than the sharing of centralized counter metadata. Recently, a workshop outlined a potential gap between recent theoretical concerns about TM and its practical concerns [29].

To conclude, as TM has become more and more popular for the challenging goal of simplifying concurrent programming, several researchers expressed their skepticism about the adoption of such paradigm mainly due to the overhead of their software implementations. After this trough of disillusionment, TM have finally won its spurs, perhaps already reaching the slope of enlightenment that is common to mature ideas.

8.5.2   Classical Transactions Limit Concurrency

In a concurrent environment, two operations may look very similar even though they do not share the same semantics as explained in [13]. For example, this is the case for a contains(z) operation parsing a linked list of data structure and failing in finding element z and another operation size() capturing an atomic snapshot of the number of elements of this data structure. Both operations have the same sequence of read/write accesses, yet they have distinct semantics. Figure 8.2 depicts the read $r(*)$ and write $w(*)$ of these operations.

The contains(z) is consistent even though y is concurrently inserted after $r(x)$ occurs. Identifying the modification of the next pointer of x to insert y as a conflict with $r(x)$ would unnecessarily limit concurrency: we thus refer to such a conflict as a *false-conflict*. Conversely, the size() requires, for example, that x and y, which are both counted, be both present in the linked list at the same time. Hence, contains(z) enables theoretically more concurrency than size () as it tolerates concurrent updates, and a fine-grained locking technique (e.g. hand-over-hand locking) could naturally exploit this additional concurrency. To implement these two different operations with transactions, the programmer encapsulates all accesses within transaction delimiters. The semantics of the transactions has of course to be strong enough to support both semantics. The drawback is that transaction-based contains does not enable greater concurrency than size; thus classical transactions abort in an overconservative manner.

Despite having the appealing property of composition, transaction-based algorithms are known to execute generally slower than lock-based and lock-free alternatives, in part for this aforementioned reason. In the next section we present how an average programmer can use a TM library to implement a concurrent application that overcomes these issues.

8.6   RECENT SOLUTIONS

We describe two different techniques: exposing commutativity and using transaction polymorphism. The former technique exploits concurrency between operations by letting the expert programmer explicitly ignore ordering constraints between commutative operations. The latter technique exploits operation concurrency by using polymorphic transactions for various operation semantics.

8.6.1   Exposing Commutativity

Novel TM models [10, 20, 28] have been proposed to overcome the lack of concurrency. The idea common to these models is to let the TM ignore the false read–write conflicts when executing high-level operations that are commutative. As a drawback of exploiting commutative operations, delimiting transactions within a sequential program is no longer sufficient to obtain a concurrent program.

8.6.1.1   Open Nesting   The open nesting model [28] allows a transaction to commit and report its changes to the memory while being nested inside a transaction that has not committed yet. The key idea is to enable higher concurrency by splitting high-level operations into transactions and to define appropriate abort handlers that would compensate the effect of committed inner transactions if their parent transaction aborts. To enable higher concurrency, each transaction keeps track of the high-level operations that they have executed. In some cases though, they also have to keep track of lower-level operations to be able to compose.

8.6.1.2   Transactional Boosting   Transactional boosting [20] aims at transforming a linearizable object into a transactional object by implementing transactions that call the high-level operations from an external thread-safe library. These operations do not have to execute speculatively, and can, for example, be implemented using lock-free primitives. As the library operations apply directly their low-level changes in memory without keeping track of them, the library can only provide invertible operations and must accordingly provide their respective inverses.

The commutativity-based transaction models are more complex to use than other transaction models as a sequential program cannot be converted into a concurrent program by simply using transaction delimiters. The application programmer has to identify the pairs of commutative operations and must implement specific compensating actions or complex abort handlers for each transaction.

8.6.2   Transaction Polymorphism

A recently suggested synchronization technique, called *transactional polymorphism* [13], provides transaction control to the average programmers to improve performance of their concurrent applications. The key idea is to provide transactions of distinct semantics that can execute concurrently while preserving their respective semantics.

The average programmer can exploit these various semantics to implement high-level linearizable operations without annihilating their concurrency, whereas the novice can ignore these semantics and use the default transaction semantics for all operations. Although the programmer needs to have some understanding of the various transaction semantics to enhance concurrency of all operations, the novice programmer can straightforwardly implement a potentially slower but safe concurrent program using only transactions with default semantics.

We present how the average programmer can enable greater concurrency by implementing `contains(z)` and `size()` operation presented in Figure 8.2 using transaction polymorphism. First we present two potential relaxed transaction semantics, early release and elastic transaction, and then present complementary form of transactions.

8.6.2.1   *Early Release*   The early release mechanism extends the traditional TM interface with a release action. The release [22] is the action of forgetting past reads during the execution of their transaction. This mechanism enhances concurrency by decreasing the number of low-level conflicts for some pointer structures: some of the unnecessary low-level conflicts involving `contains(z)` can thus be ignored. As opposed to the explicit `Select For Update` that strengthens snapshot isolation in database systems, early release provides an explicit `release` that weakens serializability. It requires the programmer to carefully determine when and which objects in every transaction can be safely released [33]: if an object is released too early, then inconsistencies may happen.

Such a technique exposes additional calls to the programmer; hence to benefit from early release the programmer cannot simply delimit regions of a sequential program to obtain a concurrent one. The simple TM interface as well as the ABI mentioned in the introduction do not support such explicit calls.

8.6.2.2   *Elastic Transactions*   Elastic transactions enable transaction polymorphism without the need to change the TM interface. The programmer simply has to delimit regions of sequential code to obtain a concurrent program.

Syntactic Sugar   Elastic transaction [10] is a transactional model that respects the classical ABI but enables greater concurrency than classical transactions. Two versions (in C and Java) of $\mathcal{E}$-STM, combining elastic and classical transactions, have been released,[7] and the Java version is currently part of the distribution of Deuce [26], the bytecode instrumentation framework described in Section 8.3.2.

---

[7]http://lpd.epfl.ch/gramoli/php/estm.php.

The key idea is that an elastic transaction is a particular form of transaction that executes `begin/read/write/commit` events differently from classical transactions. The programmer has simply to add a parameter to the `begin` delimiter to differentiate an elastic transaction from a classical transaction. As the `begin` delimiters already support parameters in icc and gcc, there is no need to change the ABI to support elastic transactions. Similarly, the Deuce bytecode instrumentation framework also supports metainformation given as parameters to `begin` delimiters. As an example Deuce annotates methods that represent transactions with parameterized annotations and supports elastic transactions. As an example the following `addAll` method adds multiple elements to a `Collection`, atomically:

```
———————————— Deuce support for elastic transactions ————————————
@Atomic(metainf="elastic")
public void addAll(Collection c) {
        for (x : c) this.add(x);
}
```

Semantics   We now present the semantics of elastic transactions. An elastic transaction executes its read-only prefix in a hand-over-hand style by recording the ith, $i + 1$st, ..., $i + k$th read locations before discarding the ith one. In the linked list example of Figure 8.2, if p_1 executes the `contains`(z) operation in an elastic transaction with $k = 1$, then a concurrent transaction can execute $w(x)$ between $r(y)$ and $r(z)$ as the potential conflicts involving the $r(x)$ start being ignored. An elastic transaction executes the accesses following its read-only prefix as in a default transaction, keeping track of all conflicts with its read accesses for later validation. In Section 8.6.2.2, all modifications performed by the series of `add` are hence part of the same default transaction.

Elastic transactions are compatible with classical transactions, in the sense that the TM providing elastic transactions also provides classical transactions that can all run concurrently while preserving their respective semantics. Due to this polymorphism, the elastic transaction model allows composition as opposed to usual relaxed transaction models.

For example, one could try to reuse `contains` and `add` operations by composing them to implement an `addIfAbsent`(x, y) operation, which inserts x given that y is absent. However, because the relaxed `contains` ignores some low-level conflicts to enhance concurrency, the concurrent execution of `addIfAbsent`(x, y) and `addIfAbsent`(y, x) leads to an inconsistent state where both x and y are present. The elastic transaction model solves this issue by letting an elastic transaction check whether it is nested inside another transaction and if so determines the type of its enclosing transaction to determine its own type. Hence, if the enclosing transaction is regular, it can switch its type to regular to prevent inconsistencies. If the enclosing transaction is elastic, then the nested one does not have to change its type.

8.6.2.3   *Other Aspects*   Transaction polymorphism has been shown to enable more concurrency than monomorphic STMs in [13], hence conveying the intuition that transactions may achieve comparable performance to other synchronization

techniques. Experimentations have confirmed these thoughts by showing that transaction polymorphism is more efficient than lock-based and lock-free synchronization techniques to implement atomic `Collections` in Java [12], where snapshot operations and parse operations use distinct forms of transactions. Finally, other appealing features of transaction polymorphism lies in the way the contention manager could associate priority to each transaction depending on their form.

8.7 CONCLUDING REMARKS

After years of investigation, TM has become a mature technique that allows to greatly simplify concurrent programming. A complete TM stack has been released [11]; it features TM-based applications, TM language extensions for Java, C and C++, ×86 instruction set extension[8] for TM support in hardware as well as hybrid mechanisms that combine both software and hardware mechanisms. The major limitations having caused skepticism of users have been addressed: I/O are now supported by compilers, and with polymorphism a TM compensates its performance limitations at high level of parallelism.

Building on top of the current advances on the topic of TM, the notions we have presented here aim at giving any programmer of concurrent applications the possibility to exploit the power of TM. As opposed to other concurrent programming paradigm, TM does not require specific programming skills. Expert programmers could certainly extend polymorphic TMs with very specific forms, average programmers could adequately choose the right form of transaction to improve the performance of their applications, but novice programmers will always be able to exploit the default TM settings to write easily safe and live concurrent programs.

ACKNOWLEDGMENTS

The research leading to some results presented in this chapter has received funding from the European Community's Seventh Framework Programme (FP7/2007–2013) under grant agreement numbers 216852 and 248465.

REFERENCES

1. H. Attiya. The inherent complexity of transactional memory and what to do about it. In *Proceedings of the 29th annual ACM symposium on Principles of distributed computing (PODC)*, 2010.

2. N. G. Bronson, J. Casper, H. Chafi, and K. Olukotun. Transactional predication: high performance concurrent sets and maps for STM. In *Proceedings of the 29th Annual ACM Symposium on Principles of Distributed Computing (PODC)*, 2010.

[8]AMD ASF. http://developer.amd.com/cpu/asf/pages/default.aspx.

3. C. Cascaval, C. Blundell, M. M. Michael, H. W. Cain, P. Wu, S. Chiras, and S. Chatterjee. Software transactional memory: why is it only a research toy? *Communications of the ACM*, 51(11):40–46, 2008.

4. A. Chou, J. Yang, B. Chelf, S. Hallem, and D. Engler. An empirical study of operating systems errors. In *Proceedings of the 18th ACM Symposium on Operating systems principles (SOSP)*, 2001.

5. L. Dalessandro, M. F. Spear, and M. L. Scott. Norec: streamlining STM by abolishing ownership records. In *Proceedings of the 15th ACM SIGPLAN Symposium on Principles and Practice of Parallel Programming (PPoPP)*, pages 67–78, New York, NY, USA, 2010. ACM.

6. D. Dice, Y. Lev, M. Moir, and D. Nussbaum. Early experience with a commercial hardware transactional memory implementation. In *Proceedings of the 14th International Conference on Architectural Support for Programming Languages and Operating Systems (ASPLOS)*, 2009.

7. D. Dice, O. Shalev, and N. Shavit. Transactional locking II. In *20th International Symposium on Distributed Computing (DISC)*, 2006.

8. A. Dragojević, P. Felber, V. Gramoli, and R. Guerraoui. Why STM can be more than a research toy. *Communications of the ACM*, 54:70–77, April 2011.

9. D. Engler and K. Ashcraft. Racerx: effective, static detection of race conditions and deadlocks. In *Proceedings of the 19th ACM Symposium on Operating Systems Principles (SOSP)*, SOSP '03, pages 237–252, New York, NY, USA, 2003. ACM.

10. P. Felber, V. Gramoli, and R. Guerraoui. Elastic transactions. In Proceedings of the 23rd International Symposium on Distributed Computing (DISC), *volume 5805 of* LNCS, pages 93–107. Springer-Verlag, September 2009.

11. P. Felber, E. Riviere, W. M. Moreira, D. Harmanci, P. Marlier, S. Diestelhorst, M. Hohmuth, M. Pohlack, A. Cristal, I. Hur, O. S. Unsal, P. Stenström, A. Dragojevic, R. Guerraoui, M. Kapalka, V. Gramoli, U. Drepper, S. Tomic and, Y. Afek, G. Korland, N. Shavit, C. Fetzer, M. Nowack, and T. Riegel. The velox transactional memory stack. *Micro, IEEE*, 30(5):76–87, September–October 2010.

12. V. Gramoli and R. Guerraoui. Technical Report EPFL-REPORT-163379, EPFL, 2011.

13. V. Gramoli and R. Guerraoui. Brief announcement: transaction polymorphism. In *Proceedings of the 23rd ACM Symposium on Parallelism in Algorithms and Architectures (SPAA)*, 2011.

14. R. Guerraoui and M. Kapalka. *Principles of Transactional Memory*. Morgan & Claypool, 2010.

15. L. Hammond, V. Wong, M. Chen, B. D. Carlstrom, J. D. Davis, B. Hertzberg, M. K. Prabhu, H. Wijaya, C. Kozyrakis, and K. Olukotun. Transactional memory coherence and consistency. In *Proceedings of the 31st International Symposium on Computer Architecture (ISCA)*, 2004.

16. D. Harmanci, V. Gramoli, and P. Felber. Atomic boxes: coordinated exception handling with transactional memory. In *Proceedings of the 25th European Conference on Object Oriented Programming (ECOOP)*, 2011.

17. T. Harris, J. Larus, and R. Rajwar. *Transactional Memory*. Morgan & Claypool, second edition, 2010.

18. T. Harris, S. Marlow, S. Peyton-Jones, and M. Herlihy. Composable memory transactions. In *Proceedings of the 10th ACM SIGPLAN Symposium on Principles and Practice of Parallel Programming (PPoPP)*, pages 48–60, New York, NY, USA, 2005. ACM.

19. M. Herlihy and J. E. B. Moss. Transactional memory: architectural support for lock-free data structures. *SIGARCH Computer Architecture News*, 21(2):289–300, 1993.

20. M. Herlihy and E. Koskinen. Transactional boosting: a methodology for highly-concurrent transactional objects. In *Proceedings of the 13th ACM SIGPLAN Symposium on Principles and Practice of Parallel Programming (PPoPP)*, 2008.

21. M. Herlihy, V. Luchangco, and M. Moir. Obstruction-free synchronization: double-ended queues as an example. In *Proceedings of the 23rd International Conference on Distributed Computing Systems (ICDCS)*, pages 522–529, Washington, DC, USA, 2003. IEEE Computer Society.

22. M. Herlihy, V. Luchangco, M. Moir, and W. N. Scherer, III. Software transactional memory for dynamic-sized data structures. In *Proceedings of the Proceedings of the 22nd Annual ACM Symposium on Principles of Distributed Computing (PODC)*, 2003.

23. C. A. R. Hoare. Communicating sequential processes. *Communications of the ACM*, 21:666–677, August 1978.

24. Intel Corporation. Intel transactional memory compiler and runtime application binary interface, May 2009.

25. B. Khan, M. Horsnell, I. Rogers, M. Lujan, A. Dinn, and I. Watson. A first insight into object-aware hardware transactional memory. In *Proceedings of the 20th ACM Symposium on Parallelism in Algorithms and Architectures (SPAA)*, 2008.

26. G. Korland, N. Shavit, and P. Felber. Deuce: noninvasive software transactional memory. *Transactions on HiPEAC*, 5(2), 2010.

27. K. E. Moore, J. Bobba, M. J. Moravan, M. D. Hill, and D. A. Wood. LogTM: Log-based transactional memory. In *Proceedings of the 12th International Symposium on High-Performance Computer Architecture (HPCA)*, 2006.

28. J. E. B. Moss. Open nested transactions: semantics and support. In *Workshop on Memory Performance Issues (WMPI 2006)*, February 2006.

29. S. Ravi, V. Gramoli, and V. Luchangco. Transactional memory, linking theory and practice. *SIGACT News*, 41:109–115, December 2010.

30. T. Riegel, P. Felber, and C. Fetzer. A lazy snapshot algorithm with eager validation. In *Proceedings of the 20th International Symposium on Distributed Computing (DISC)*, 2006.

31. C. J. Rossbach, O. S. Hofmann, D. E. Porter, H. E. Ramadan, B. Aditya, and E. Witchel. TxLinux: using and managing hardware transactional memory in an operating system. In *Proceedings of the 21st ACM Symposium on Operating Systems Principles (SOSP)*, 2007.

32. W. N. Scherer III and M. L. Scott. Advanced contention management for dynamic software transactional memory. In *Proceedings of the 24th Annual ACM Symposium on Principles of Distributed Computing (PODC)*, pages 240–248, New York, NY, USA, 2005. ACM.

33. T. Skare and C. Kozyrakis. Early release: friend or foe? In *Workshop on Transactional Memory Workloads*, June 2006.

34. Transactional Memory Specification Drafting Group. Draft specification of transactional language constructs for C++, 2009. `http://software.intel.com/file/21569`.

CHAPTER 9

OBJECT-ORIENTED STREAM PROGRAMMING

FRANK OTTO AND WALTER F. TICHY

This chapter presents an approach unifying the concepts of object-orientation (OO) and stream programming. OO provides a high degree of modularity and reusability, which makes it the de facto standard in mainstream software development. However, OO languages such as C++ or Java address parallelism at an abstraction level that is too low. Programmers have to create and manage threads and synchronize accesses to shared resources. This is an error-prone process that may result in hard-to-find synchronization bugs such as data races or deadlocks. In addition, programmers have to consider performance aspects and make applications adaptable to different platforms. In sum, programming parallel mainstream applications significantly increases complexity and work for developers.

The arising question is: How can the OO model be extended to simplify general-purpose parallel programming, aiming for both better programmability and performance gains? The model should provide straightforward syntax that is capable of easily implementing parallel design patterns. Synchronization and performance tuning should happen automatically wherever possible. Object-oriented stream programming (OOSP) can serve as a solution.

Programming Multicore and Many-core Computing Systems,
First Edition. Edited by Sabri Pllana and Fatos Xhafa.
© 2017 John Wiley & Sons, Inc. Published 2017 by John Wiley & Sons, Inc.

9.1   STREAM PROGRAMMING

Stream programming follows a paradigm exposing parallelism in a way that is suitable for multicore architectures. A stream program consists of interconnected computational units, also called *actors* or *filters*, that process a large (theoretically infinite) sequence of data items. The connected filters form a *stream graph*, describing how data flows through actors.

In contrast to thread-based languages, the stream programming model allows for efficient implementations of different types of parallelism:

- *Pipeline parallelism.* A pipeline is a chain of actors $a_1, \ldots, a_n$ that are directly connected in the stream graph. Each pair (a_i, a_{i+1}), $i \in \{1, \ldots, n-1\}$ has a producer/consumer relationship, that is, a_i consumes items produced by a_{i-1} and produces items that serve as input for a_{i+1}.

- *Task parallelism.* Two actors a_1, a_2 are task parallel if they are on different branches of the stream graph. In contrast to pipelines, there are no input/output dependences between a_1 and a_2.

- *Data parallelism.* The stream programming domain defines data parallelism as the property of an actor to have no dependences between one execution and the next. If this property holds, the actor is stateless and thus can be replicated. Data parallelism uses multiple instances of an actor.

Figure 9.1 shows a stream graph for a simple equalizer based on band-pass filters. A stream of input signal values is passed to different band-pass filters; the resulting values are added and form the output signal stream. Each dimension corresponds to one type of parallelism, that is, data, task or pipeline parallelism. In the example, there are three types of actors: *duplicate*, *bandpass(i)* and *add* (in the following denoted as d, b_i, a). As illustrated, d, $(b_1, \ldots, b_n)$, a build a pipeline. $b_1, \ldots, b_n$ are task parallel

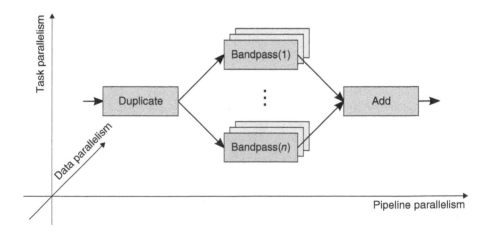

Figure 9.1   A stream graph.

since they do not depend on each other. The actors b_i are stateless and thus can run in data parallel mode by replicating them.

A characteristic of the stream programming paradigm is that input/output dependences between actors are modeled explicitly. Actors are typically lightweight components that can execute independently from each other due to data locality. The stream graph of a program with compute and communication estimates for each actor enables compilers to determine and optimize schedules of execution.

9.2   OBJECT-ORIENTED STREAM PROGRAMMING

The synthesis of object-orientation and stream programming is a programming model suitable for mainstream software development [13–15]. It provides intuitive syntax for parallelism based on stream concepts while preserving the flexibility and expressiveness of object-orientation. The benefits are:

1. Higher productivity and lower risk for bugs through abstraction

2. Code that is easier to understand and maintain

3. What-you-see-is-what-you-get parallelism through an appropriate syntax for expressing parallel patterns such as pipelines, master/worker or divide and conquer

4. Significantly reduced need for platform-specific performance tuning, leading to higher performance portability

The following sections illustrate these benefits from the perspectives of language, compiler and runtime system concepts.

9.3   XJAVA

XJava is a prototype OOSP language and a superset of Java. It consists of a compiler *xjavac* and a runtime system *xjavart*. *xjavac* transforms XJava to Java code (either source code or bytecode), generates code variants and inserts parameters and context information for performance tuning (cf. Section 9.4.3). *xjavart* executes that generated code and adjusts runtime parameters according to the target platform (cf. Section 9.4.4).

Syntactically, the two central extensions are tasks and parallel statements. Tasks are basically OO actors; they are specialized methods that define potentially parallel activities. Parallel statements finally create parallelism by combining task calls with operators.

Before going into details, Example 9.1 illustrates these basic language features with a simple file indexing application as it could be used for desktop search. The program employs a pipeline indexing text files in a given directory, accordingly updating a global index. This first example will be extended in the course of this chapter to introduce more language concepts.

■ **EXAMPLE 9.1** **File indexing in XJava**

```
1 class Index {
2   public static Set<String> computeIndex(File f) {...}
3   public update(Set<String> s) {...}
4 }
5
6 public class Indexer {
7   protected Index index = new Index();
8
9   public void => File read(Directory dir) {
10    Iterator<File> i = dir.getFiles().iterator();
11    while(i.hasNext()) { push i.next(); }
12  }
13
14  public File => Set<String> index() {
15    work(File f) { push Index.computeIndex(f); }
16  }
17
18  public Set<String> => void update() {
19    work(Set<String> s) { index.update(s); }
20  }
21
22  public static void main(String[] args) {
23    Indexer i = new Indexer();
24    ...
25    i.read(dir) => i.index() => i.update();
26    System.out.println("Done!");
27  }
28 }
```

The program's main class `Indexer` declares three tasks `read`, `index`, `update`. `read` produces a stream of files contained in a given directory `dir`. `index` accepts a stream of files and produces a stream of word sets. Finally, `update` accepts a stream of word sets and accordingly updates the global index.

Inside the `main` method, parallelism is introduced by calling these tasks and combining them with the pipeline operator =>. This expression abstracts from threads, synchronization and the actual execution behavior. After the pipeline statement, there is an implicit barrier. That is, the 'Done!' message is printed when all data in the pipeline has been processed. Now, after the introducing example, we approach the extensions more formally.

9.3.1 Tasks

Tasks are specialized methods and are declared in classes or interfaces. Tasks and methods have several things in common. A task declaration consists of a signature (i.e. name and parameters) and a body. Properties can be specified with modifiers such as `public`, `final`, `static` or `abstract`. A task can be inherited or overridden.

9.3.1.1 Input and Output Types In contrast to methods, tasks do not have a return type, but input and output types. These define the types of stream elements the task expects and produces. If there is no input or output, the corresponding type is void. In Example 9.1, the update task's output type is void since it only receives a stream of Set objects and updates the index, producing no output stream.

9.3.1.2 Task Bodies Unless a task is declared abstract, it has a body. In general, the body may contain any regular Java code. In order to receive and produce data streams according to the task's specified input and output types, there are work blocks and push statements.

Work blocks. A work block is a loop defining how to process the incoming stream elements. It is repeatedly executed as long as there is input available at the task's input port. Before each iteration, the received stream element is assigned to a local variable declared after the work keyword. The compiler ensures that the type of that local variable matches the task's input type. In Example 9.1, the index task assigns the current stream element to the local variable f of type File.

Push statements. A push statement puts a value or object reference on the output stream. The type of that value or reference must match the task's output type. In Example 9.1, the read task repeatedly pushes File objects to the output stream; the update task does not contain a push statement since its output type is void.

9.3.2 Parallel Statements

In order to create parallelism, tasks need to be called and connected with operators to parallel statements. There are operators for pipeline and task parallelism.

Example 9.1 already showed how to create pipelines using the pipeline operator '=>'. The operator connects tasks via their input/output ports. The compiler checks if the corresponding input and output types match.

The task parallel operator '| | |' creates task parallel statements. Other than for pipeline statements, there are no input/output dependences between the called tasks. We extend Example 9.1 by assuming two different implementations to compute indices in the Index class. That is, the stream of File can be indexed by either computeIndexA or computeIndexB. These methods could use different algorithms, data structures or handle different file formats such as text or PDF files. Then, the main class Indexer can be extended by two corresponding tasks indexA and indexB:

```
1 class Index {
2   public static Set<String> computeIndexA(File f) {...}
3   public static Set<String> computeIndexB(File f) {...}
4   public update(Set<String> s) {...}
5 }
6
7 public class Indexer {
8   ...
9   public File => Set<String> indexA() {
10     work(File f) { push f.computeIndexA(); }
11   }
12
13   public File => Set<String> indexB() {
14     work(File f) { push f.computeIndexB(); }
15   }
16
```

```
17   public File => Set<String> index() {
18     indexA() ||| indexB();
19   }
20   ...
21
22   public static void main(String[] args) {
23     Indexer i = new Indexer();
24     ...
25     i.read(dir) => i.index() => i.update();
26     System.out.println("Done!");
27   }
28 }
```

In order to concurrently apply both tasks indexA and indexB, the index task's body uses the corresponding task parallel statement instead of a work block. Parallel statements inside task bodies allow for (arbitrary) parallel nesting and refinement of parallel structures. The input and output types of a nested parallel statement must match the input and output types of its surrounding task. The index task's input and output types are File and Set<String>. Therefore, both tasks in the nested task parallel statement, indexA and indexB, must match the input and output types of the surrounding task index.

9.3.3 Variants of Task Calls

As we have seen, tasks are basically called like methods. They can be combined with operators to create pipeline and task parallelism. In addition, there are variants of task calls to enable data parallelism as well. Given a task t, it can be called in the following ways:

- t(): Using the standard call will create exactly one instance of t.

- t():[n]: Combining the call with some integer expression n will create *n* instances of t. That is, the expression t(): [3] is equivalent to t() ||| t() ||| t().

- t():[+]: Using the '+' wild card will create at least one instance of t. The number is constant and determined at runtime.

- t()+: This expression also creates a certain default number of instances of t but allows for dynamically adjusting this number, depending on workload distribution in the whole application. This is a feature relevant for online performance tuning that will be discussed in Section 9.4.4.

For illustration, to fully automate the replication of the indexA and indexB tasks, we can modify the index task in the following way:

```
public File => Set<String> index() {
    indexA()+ ||| indexB()+;
}
```

In this case, it will be determined at runtime how many replica to use for each task.

9.3.4 Splitting and Joining Streams

Whenever a data stream is split according to task or data parallelism, we need to specify splitting and joining semantics, that is, the logical order in which stream elements have to be distributed and merged. By default, this is done in a round-robin fashion to keep the stream's original order. Sometimes the order in which stream elements are processed is not important, or elements need to be broadcasted to all following tasks. For these situations, the pipeline operator '=>' can be further refined in the way J =>S, where $J := \{?\}$ and $S := \{?, *\}$ are optional join and split modifiers according to Table 9.1.

Table 9.1 Splitting and joining streams.

Split modifier	Usage	Semantics
None	... => t() : [3] ...	Round-robin
?	... =>? t() : [3] ...	First come–first serve
*	... =>* t() : [3] ...	Broadcast

Join modifier	Usage	Semantics
None	... t() : [3] => ...	Round-robin
?	... t() : [3] ?=> ...	First come–first serve

9.3.5 Implementing Parallel Patterns

When developing software systems, the use of design patterns is essential. Design patterns provide concepts and solutions to recurring design problems, thus increasing productivity and maintainability. In the context of parallel programming, several parallel design patterns help implement parallel code for specific problem structures. This section shows with the example of XJava how OOSP can simplify implementing parallel patterns.

9.3.5.1 Pipeline One important pattern is the pipeline, which has already been discussed in the file compression example. As a chain of interconnected tasks, we distinguish linear and nonlinear pipelines. A pipeline is nonlinear if at least one stage is task or data parallel, requiring the stream to be split and joined. Both types of pipelines can be efficiently implemented with OOSP in general and XJava in particular. Using abstract tasks in classes or interfaces or refinement by inheritance allows for defining flexible pipelines in an elegant way.

9.3.5.2 *Producer/Consumer*

A producer/consumer configuration can be seen as a nonlinear pipeline with two stages: a producer stage and a consumer stage. The following generic class declares the tasks produce and consume:

```
1  class ProducerConsumer<E> {
2    void => E produce() {
3      while (cond) {
4        E item = ...
5        push item; // produce item
6      }
7    }
8
9    E => void consume() {
10     work (E item) {
11       ... // consume item
12     }
13   }
14 }
```

Given an object pc of type ProducerConsumer, a configuration with *p* producers and *c* consumers can be written as

$$pc.produce\ ():[p]\ =>?\ pc.consume\ ():[c]$$

Note that both tasks can be arbitrarily refined by overriding. The order in which items are consumed is typically not important in the producer/consumer pattern, so we use the variant '=>?' of the pipeline operator.

9.3.5.3 *Master/Worker*

The master/worker pattern is a widely used pattern for distributing and concurrently processing work units. This pattern can be implemented in XJava by combining two task calls with variants of the '=>' operator. Assume a class declaring master and worker tasks:

```
1  class MasterWorker<E> {
2    void => E master() {
3      while (cond) {
4        E workUnit = ...
5        push workUnit; // send workUnit
6      }
7    }
8
9    E => void worker() {
10     work (E workUnit) {
11       ... // do work
12     }
13   }
14 }
```

Then, given a `MasterWorker` object mw, a master/worker pattern can be implemented by

```
mw.master() => mw.worker()+;
```

In this context, the number of workers is set dynamically; this number may increase and decrease with the workload. To make the number of workers (1) constant or (2) set it to a concrete number *n*, we can write

```
mw.master() => mw.worker():[+]; // (1)
mw.master() => mw.worker():[n]; // (2)
```

Using the '=>' operator feeds the workers in a round-robin fashion with elements from the stream. Alternatively, the '=>?' operator variant distributes elements dynamically on a first-come–first-serve basis. If each element should be sent to all workers, we use the '=>*' operator instead.

9.3.5.4 *Divide and Conquer* Divide-and-conquer algorithms offer parallelization potential by solving subproblems concurrently. XJava can exploit this potential in a simple way. For example, consider a sequential merge sort algorithm:

```
1  void mergesort(int first , int last) {
2    if (last − first > threshold) {
3      int mid = first + (last − first) / 2;
4      mergesort(first , mid);
5      mergesort(mid + 1, last);
6      merge(first , mid + 1, last);
7    } else sort(first , last);
8  }
```

In order to parallelize this algorithm with XJava, two small changes are required. First, the method `mergesort` is made a task. Then, to make the recursion step parallel, we use a concurrent statement combining the calls of `mergesort` with the '|||' operator:

```
1  void => void mergesort(int first , int last) {
2    if (last − first > threshold) {
3      int mid = first + (last − first) / 2;
4      mergesort(first , mid) ||| mergesort(mid + 1, last);
5      merge(first , mid + 1, last);
6    } else sort(first , last);
7  }
```

This implementation abstracts from synchronization, the number of threads used for execution and the question when to switch from parallel to sequential execution. Note that this example does not necessarily need to operate on streams. A fully stream-based alternative would be the following:

```
1 void => int arrayToStream(int[] a) {...}
2 int => int sort(int n) {...}
3 int => int merge(int n) {...}
4 int => void streamToArray(int[] b) {...}
5
6 int => int msort(int n) {
7   if (n < threshold) sort(n) => merge(n);
8   else msort(n/2):[2] => merge(n);
9 }
```

We assume `arrayToStream` converts an array to a stream while `streamToAr-ray` does the opposite. In addition, `sort (int n)` receives and sorts a stream of n elements; `merge (int n)` merges two 'sorted' streams of size n/2 each to a sorted stream of size n. Finally, to sort an array a and write the result to array b, we use the nonlinear, recursive pipeline:

`arrayToStream(a) => msort(a.length) => streamToArray(b)`

9.4 PERFORMANCE

The previous sections focused on programmability aspects when developing general-purpose software. This section addresses aspects of performance tuning. We first approach these aspects from a more general perspective. Then we describe the potential of OOSP with respect to performance tuning, including compiler and runtime system concepts.

Adapting parallel applications to the underlying hardware is crucial to achieve good performance. A large number of performance-relevant program parameters need to be considered, for example, how many threads are used for calculation, how to set the size of data partitions, how many stages a pipeline requires or how to accomplish load balancing for worker threads. These parameters are called *tuning parameters*.

Consider a parallel program $P(p_1, p_2, \ldots, p_n)$, where $p_1, \ldots, p_n$ are tuning parameters with possible value domains $dom(p_1), \ldots, dom(p_n)$. The challenge is to find a configuration $(x_1, \ldots, x_n) \in dom(p_1) \times \cdots \times dom(p_n)$ that provides the best performance for a specific target platform.

9.4.1 Search-Based Auto-Tuning

Manual optimization is hard and time consuming due to large parameter search spaces. Therefore, search-based approaches for automatic performance tuning (auto-tuning) [1, 18, 20, 22] have been developed to automate optimization. The auto-tuning process consists of several tuning iterations. Each iteration can be divided into three basic steps: (i) applying a parameter configuration to the program, (ii) program execution and performance monitoring and (iii) generation of a new parameter configuration. The new parameter configuration can be computed by optimization algorithms such as hill climbing or simulated annealing.

Since multicore systems differ in many respects (e.g. in number or type of cores, cache architecture, available memory or operating system), there is a diversity of

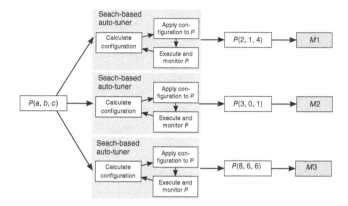

Figure 9.2   Search-based auto-tuning of a program *P* for three different machines *M*1, *M*2, *M*3.

targets to optimize for. Optimizations for one machine cannot generally be ported to another machine. That is, a program usually has to be retuned for each platform. Figure 9.2 illustrates auto-tuning of a program *P* with tuning parameters *a, b, c* for three different machines.

A very simple example is a parallel program with one tuning parameter *t* that adjusts the number of concurrent threads. The best configuration for *t* on a quadcore machine is most likely a value close to 4. However, this value seems to be a bad choice when using a machine with 16 cores. For the auto-tuner, *t* is nothing more than a variable associated with a set of values to choose from. However, if the purpose of *t* was known, *t* could be directly set according to the number of available cores.

OOSP can simplify the whole performance tuning process [15]: the compiler can infer tuning parameters and context information from code, which provides a higher level of abstraction for the programmer. The knowledge of parameters and their semantics and contexts enables the concept of parameter prediction, achieving a high degree of performance portability by reducing the need for platform-specific retuning (cf. Fig. 9.3).

9.4.2   Essential Tuning Parameters

This section describes important types of tuning parameters that are of special relevance for parallel applications in general and streaming applications in particular. One application can contain several parameters of the same type.

Thread count (*TC*). The performance of a parallel application is strongly affected by the total number of threads used for computations. An insufficient number might result in idle cores, thus limiting the speedup. Using too many threads might add too much synchronization overhead and memory consumption, causing slowdowns.

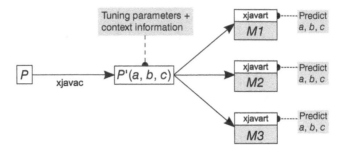

Figure 9.3   Inferring tuning parameters and context information to enable parameter prediction on different machines.

Load balancing strategy (*LB*). The load balancing strategy decides how to distribute workload to execution threads or CPU cores. Strategies can be static, for example, performing round-robin distributions, or dynamic, for example, first-come–first-serve policies or work stealing.

Cutoff depth (*CO*). Complex parallel applications often make use of parallelism on different abstraction levels. Especially low-level parallel code sections may cause slowdowns if synchronization costs outweigh the possible speedup. That is, there is a level where sequential execution is preferable to parallel execution. The cutoff depth denotes this level.

Stage replica (*SR*). The bottlenecks of pipelines are slow stages, limiting throughput and therefore the overall speedup. If a stage is stateless, it can be safely executed by more than one thread. Stage replication creates several instances of the same stage. The number of instances is defined by the parameter *SR*.

Stage fusion (*SF*). Given a pipeline consisting of n stages $s_1, \ldots, s_n$, the standard way of execution is to assign each stage one thread. However, it can be worthwhile to fuse some stages to reduce the overhead for buffering data. That is, stage fusion represents functional composition of stages. The parameter *SF* defines whether to fuse a stage with the previous stage.

Data size (*DS*). When parallel applications process a large amount of data, it often needs to be decomposed into smaller data partitions. The sizes of the partitions usually influence performance.

9.4.3 XJava Compiler

Based on high-level OOSP syntax, the XJava compiler infers tuning parameters, their semantics (i.e. their purpose) and information about the contexts they refer to. In addition, tunable code alternatives are generated. The XJava extensions conceptually compile as follows:

- A task declaration *task* compiles to a class c_{task} as well as a method sm_{task} for sequential execution.

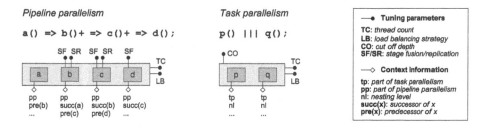

Figure 9.4   Inferring tuning parameters and context information from XJava code.

- Parallel statements basically consist of a set of task calls. A call of a task *task* compiles to:

    1. The creation of an instance of c_{task} that is enriched with context information and passed to the runtime system *xjavart*, which is responsible for handling parallelism

    2. A call of the corresponding sequential method sm_{task}

    With each call of *task* at runtime, it is determined whether to use the parallel version c_{task} or sequential version sm_{task} to cut off parallelism (cf. Section 9.4.4).

9.4.3.1   *Inferring Tuning Parameters*

The XJava compiler generates Java code and adds relevant tuning parameters. Each parallel statement is instrumented with parameters *thread count* (*TC*) and *load balancing strategy* (*LB*). In addition, task parallel statements get another parameter *cutoff depth* (*CO*) indicating whether to execute that statement in parallel or sequentially. A pipeline statement consisting of n stages $s_1, \ldots, s_n$ is instrumented with *stage fusion* parameters $SF_i, i \in \{2, \ldots, n\}$, where SF_i indicates whether to fuse stages s_{i-1} and s_i. Finally, the parameter *stage replica* (*SR*) is added to each replicable stage.

Figure 9.4 illustrates inferred tuning parameters and context information for a pipeline and a task parallel statement.

- A pipeline a () => b () + => c () + => d () compiles to a set of four task instances *a*, *b*, *c* and *d* that build the pipeline stages. Stages *b* and *c* are replicable, so a tuning parameter *SR* is added to both. Then, *b*, *c* and *d* get a Boolean parameter *SF* defining whether to fuse that stage with the previous one.

- A task parallel statement p () ||| q () is instrumented with a parameter *CO*. This statement executes concurrently if the cutoff depth has not been reached. Otherwise, *p* and *q* run sequentially.

9.4.3.2   Inferring Context Information   In addition to tuning parameters, the XJava compiler exploits context information for tasks and associated parameters. This knowledge is used by *xjavart* for adequately setting tuning parameters while the program executes. Important context information is the following:

1. **Purpose.** Is the task call part of a pipeline or a task parallel section?

2. **Periodicity.** Does the task perform a single operation or repeated work? The latter case enables measurement loops for online tuning, allowing to vary parameters and observe performance impacts.

3. **Dependences.** Which input/output dependences to other tasks are known?

4. **Level of parallelism.** On which level of parallelism does the task call happen? This information is needed for setting cutoff parameters (CO).

5. **Workload.** Monitoring the current workload of a task helps avoiding bottlenecks by preferably executing tasks with more workload. Currently, the workload is approximated by the number of elements at the task's input port.

Context information can be static or dynamic. For example, a task's purpose is constant, while its workload may change over time. Figure 9.4 illustrates context information for pipelines and task parallelism.

9.4.4   XJava Runtime System

Object-oriented stream programs can be efficiently executed on multicore systems. *xjavart* uses an executor service for tasks to control the number of threads and enable workload-aware scheduling, that is, tasks with higher workload have a higher priority.

To ensure performance portability, *xjavart* uses the concept of context-based parameter prediction. Beyond that, OOSP enables on-the-fly auto-tuning, that is, dynamic adjustments of parameters.

An auto-tuner typically has a black-box view of an application, only knowing adjustable parameters and their value range. With OOSP, context information can be extracted and used for suggesting good values for those parameters. If the *purpose* of a parameter is known as well as the *context* it refers to, its value range can be drastically reduced, leading to a high probability that a chosen value will be close to optimum. XJava can currently infer and predict five essential types of parameters:

- **Thread count** (TC). *xjavart* employs a number of executor threads and monitors the numbers of running and idle threads at any time. The total number of threads is initially set $1.5 \cdot n$, where n is the number of CPU cores on a system. TC may increase during execution. In particular, tasks that perform blocking operations due to I/O or lock acquisition may be assigned to separate executor threads in order to reduce the overall blocking time and avoid deadlocks.

- **Load balancing** (LB). Based on available context information, *xjavart* provides different load balancing strategies. For nested task parallelism such as

(a)   (b)

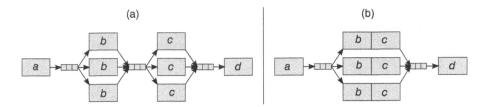

Figure 9.5   Fusing replicable stages of a pipeline reduces the overhead for splitting and joining data streams. (a) Stage replication without fusion. (b) Fusing replicable stages.

divide-and-conquer algorithms, *xjavart* applies work stealing, similar to the Java fork/join framework [9]. For pipelines, *xjavart* uses a dynamic load balancing strategy that prioritizes stages with higher workloads.

- **Cutoff depth** (*CO*). The cutoff depth for nested parallelism is determined dynamically. Assume that a parallel statement S has to be executed on nested level l. If idle executor threads are available, *xjavart* sets $CO = \infty$. That is, S will be executed in parallel mode. On the other hand, if there are no idle executor threads, the cutoff depth is set to $CO = l$, that is, the level on which S appears. In this case, S is executed sequentially. However, it is possible to switch back from sequential to parallel execution to avoid load imbalances.

- **Stage replica** (*SR*). If a task is declared replicable, *xjavart* sets $SR = i$ for that task, where i is the number of idle executor threads. That is, i instances of that task will be initially created. This number may be adapted during program execution.

- **Stage fusion** (*SF*). The more stages a pipeline consists of, the more buffer operations between stages are required. Especially subsequent replicable stages introduce overhead for splitting and joining streams. Therefore, *xjavart* identifies chains of replicable stages and fuses them into a single replicable stage. Figure 9.5 illustrates this heuristic for a pipeline a() => b() + => c() + => d() : the longest chain of replicable stages is (b, c), which is converted into a single replicable stage *bc*.

9.4.4.1 Online Adaption of Parameters

Although heuristics for tuning parameter prediction lead to good performance results, it may be necessary to adjust them during execution. Parameter prediction alone can result in performance that is close to optimum, but it can be further improved. An even more interesting case where parameter adjustment might be useful is changing workload.

Figure 9.6 illustrates a scenario with two master/worker configurations MW_1 and MW_2 running in parallel. For each configuration, we focus on the tuning parameter SR_1 and SR_2 indicating the number of workers. Using parameter prediction, that number is initially set to a default value $SR_1 = SR_2 = 3$ (Scenario S0). After some time, the workload may have changed, since the work units passed to workers

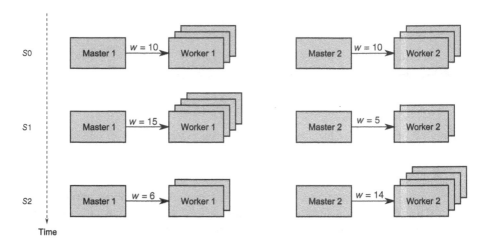

Figure 9.6   Tuning two master/worker configurations depending on workload w.

may have different complexities, requiring different amounts of time to complete. In Scenario $S1$, the workload w_1 of MW_1 has increased to 15, while w_2 has decreased to 5. Given that context information, the runtime system knows that MW_1 is obviously currently more complex than MW_2 and can adjust the values to $SR_1 = 4$ and $SR_2 = 2$. In Scenario $S2$, the situation may have changed again, resulting in new parameter configurations $SR_1 = 2$ and $SR_2 = 4$.

9.5   EXPERIENCES

XJava has been evaluated with applications of different sizes and from different domains, for example, algorithms, the JavaGrande benchmark suite [19], applications for video processing and cryptography as well as different desktop search engines [12]. Smaller programs such as sorting algorithms or single JavaGrande benchmark programs mostly employ simple task parallelism, divide and conquer or master/worker patterns. These programs expose two or three relevant tuning parameters each. More realistic applications such as video processing, cryptography and desktop search consist of more complex, often nonlinear pipelines. For these applications, we identified up to 14 relevant tuning parameters.

We compared XJava with threaded Java with respect to code structure and performance. The code structure was measured in terms of lines of code, the amount of manual synchronization needed and the number of tuning parameters that have to be declared and tuned manually. In order to quantify the effectiveness of context-based parameter prediction, we compared the achieved performance to the best known static parameter configuration found by an offline auto-tuner. Experiences can be summarized as follows:

- Code is up to 40% shorter compared to threaded Java and contains 80–100% fewer synchronization primitives such as locks, joins or wait–notify operations. However, some applications contained a few shared variables that had to be locked in order to prevent data races.

- Exposing parallel patterns results in code that is easier to implement and understand and less error prone.

- On average, 90% of the relevant tuning parameters can be inferred and set automatically and therefore are invisible to the programmer. The only parameter type that had to be optimized manually was the size of data blocks passed between pipeline stages.

- The need for auto-tuning can be considerably reduced. On three different platforms, the performance of XJava applications was only 5–9% lower on average than the best solution found by an auto-tuner. The lower performance typically was due to suboptimal numbers for threads or stage replicas, resulting in either throughput bottlenecks or inefficient cache usage. However, we plan to further improve performance by incorporating more efficient feedback-driven run time tuning mechanisms.

9.6 RELATED WORK

XJava is mainly inspired by the pure stream-based language StreamIt [7, 21]. We extended its concepts and adapted them for object-oriented programming. Other examples for stream languages are Brook [2] and Cg [11], mainly targeting GPUs. The application domain of stream languages is data-centric computations such as signal processing or graphics. This class of programs typically operates on primitive data types and homogeneous data streams. In addition, stream languages do not provide the power and expressiveness of OO features.

Aside from stream languages, there is a large body of work on parallel programming models in general. Libraries such as java.util.concurrent [10] or TBB [17] have been developed to provide constructs for high-level parallelism in Java or C/C++. Chapel [3], Cilk [16] and X10 [4] are parallel languages that focus on fine-grained task and data parallelism and numerical computations.

In contrast to the aforementioned languages and models, XJava incorporates auto-tuning as a key component of the programming language and runtime system. Auto-tuning as a stand-alone tool has mainly been studied in the context of numerical algorithms and high-performance computing. For example, FFTW [6] employs auto-tuning specifically tailored to Fourier transformations. Datta et al. [5] introduce optimization strategies for stencil computations. Active Harmony [20] is an automated runtime tuning system targeting program algorithmic libraries.

9.7   FUTURE WORK

XJava is a prototype OOSP language demonstrating the usefulness of streaming concepts in general-purpose programming languages. Current and future research topics address runtime performance tuning and correctness issues.

Although the concepts of parameter inference and context-based parameter prediction show promising results, we plan to support user-defined tuning parameters in addition to the parameters mentioned in Section 9.4.4. Also, we are currently integrating a runtime kernel auto-tuner [8] into XJava, allowing for interprocess application optimization and faster parameter adjustments.

Since OOSP allows for shared variables among tasks, data races may occur. Therefore, we are investigating ways to prevent these defects. Currently, the XJava compiler employs static analysis determining potential conflicts between tasks and gives warnings to the programmer. Alternatively, this information can be used to automatically protect critical code with locks or software transactional memory.

9.8   SUMMARY

Integrating the concepts of stream programming into the object-oriented paradigm offers great potential for both programmability and performance of parallel applications. The intuitive stream syntax provides an elegant way to express different types of parallelism on different layers. Important parallel patterns such as pipelines, master/worker or divide and conquer can be efficiently implemented. The stream-based syntax abstracts from threads, most synchronization, and performance-critical parameters. This chapter illustrated these benefits with the example of XJava, a prototype OOSP language extending Java.

In terms of the average programmer, OOSP reduces the risk of hard-to-find synchronization bugs as well as the need for performance optimizations while improving productivity and code maintainability. OOSP compilers can generate code alternatives and, as they know the language features' semantics, infer tuning parameters and context information about the parallel application. Thus, a runtime system has a more transparent and detailed view of the applications and its structure. Tuning parameter values can be predicted and dynamically adjusted, allowing for efficient execution on multicore systems.

REFERENCES

1. K. Asanovic et al. *The Landscape of Parallel Computing Research: A View from Berkeley.* Technical Report, University of California, Berkeley, 2006.

2. I. Buck et al. Brook for GPUs: Stream Computing on Graphics Hardware. ACM SIG-GRAPH 2004 Papers, ACM, 2004.

3. B. Chamberlain, D. Callahan, and H. Zima. Parallel programmability and the Chapel language. *International Journal of High Performance Computing Applications*, 21(3), 2007.

4. P. Charles et al. X10: an object-oriented approach to non-uniform cluster computing. *In Proceedings of the OOPSLA '05*, ACM, 2005.

5. K. Datta et al. Stencil computation optimization and auto-tuning on state-of-the-art multicore architectures. *In Proceedings of the Supercomputing Conference*, 2008.

6. M. Frigo and S. Johnson. FFTW: an adaptive software architecture for the FFT. *In Proceedings of the ICASSP, volume 3*, 1998.

7. M. Gordon, W. Thies, and S. Amarasinghe. *Exploiting coarse-grained task, data, and pipeline parallelism in stream programs*. In *Proceedings of the ASPLOS-XII*, ACM, 2006.

8. T. Karcher and V. Pankratius. *Run-time automatic performance tuning for multicore applications*. In *Proceedings of the Euro-Par*, Springer, 2011.

9. D. Lea. A java fork/join framework. *In Proceedings of the Java Grande '00*, ACM, 2000.

10. D. Lea. The java.util.concurrent synchronizer framework. *Science of Computer Programming*, 58(3): 2005.

11. W. Mark et al. Cg: a system for programming graphics hardware in a C-like language. *ACM Transactions on Graphics*, ACM, 2003.

12. D. Meder and W. Tichy. *Parallelizing an Index Generator for Desktop Search*. Technical Report, University of Karlsruhe, Germany, 2010.

13. F. Otto, V. Pankratius, and W. Tichy. High-level multicore programming with XJava. *In Comp. ICSE '09*, New Ideas And Emerging Results, ACM, 2009.

14. F. Otto, V. Pankratius, and W. Tichy. *XJava: exploiting parallelism with object-oriented stream programming*. In *Proceedings of the Euro-Par*, Springer, 2009.

15. F. Otto et al. *XJava: a language-based tuning mechanism for task and pipeline parallelism*. In *Proceedings of the Euro-Par*, Springer, 2010.

16. K. Randall. Cilk: *Efficient Multithreaded Computing*. PhD thesis. Dep. EECS, MIT, 1998.

17. J. Reinders. *Intel Threading Building Blocks*. O'Reilly Media, Inc. (2007).

18. C. Schaefer, V. Pankratius, and W. Tichy. Engineering parallel applications with tunable architectures. *In Proceedings of the ICSE*, ACM, 2010.

19. L. Smith, J. Bull, and J. Obdrzalek. A parallel java grande benchmark suite. *In Proc. Supercomputing Conference*, 2001.

20. C. Tapus, I.-H. Chung, J. Hollingsworth: active harmony. towards automated performance tuning. *In Proceedings of the Supercomputing Conference*, 2002.

21. W. Thies, M. Karczmarek, and S. Amarasinghe. StreamIt: a language for streaming applications. In R. N. Horspool, editor, CC, volume 2304 of Lecture Notes in Computer Science, Springer, 2002.

22. O. Werner-Kytola and W. Tichy. Self-tuning parallelism. *In Proceedings of the 8th International Conference on High-Performance Computing and Networking*, 2000.

CHAPTER 10

SOFTWARE-BASED SPECULATIVE PARALLELIZATION

Chen Tian, Min Feng and Rajiv Gupta

10.1 INTRODUCTION

Extracting thread-level parallelism from sequential programs is very important for improving their performance on widely available multicore processors. Since manual code parallelization by programmers is a time-consuming and error-prone process, compiler-based parallelization techniques have drawn much attention of researchers. Many early works on DOALL parallelism [9, 12] focus on identifying loops without cross-iteration dependences and executing their iterations in parallel. However, most sequential programs cannot be parallelized using the previous approach by the compiler due to the potential presence of cross-iteration dependences. To handle such dependences, DOACROSS parallelism techniques [1, 13] have been considered. Using explicit communication operations (i.e. sends and receives), values are passed between threads, and cross-iteration dependences are correctly enforced. However, due to the high communication costs and the serialization resulting from communication operations, the benefits of DOACROSS parallelism are quite limited.

Programming Multicore and Many-core Computing Systems,
First Edition. Edited by Sabri Pllana and Fatos Xhafa.

Thread-level *Speculative Parallelization* (SP) is another approach that has been proposed for parallelizing sequential programs. It allows dynamic parallelism that may be present in a sequential program to be aggressively exploited. The idea behind this technique is as follows. Let P denote a sequential program containing a pair of subcomputations C and C' such that the execution of C precedes the execution of C' during P's sequential execution (e.g. C and C' may represent consecutive iterations of a loop). Thus, the results computed during the execution of C are available during the execution of C'. The goal of SP technique is to relax the strict ordering imposed on the execution of C and C' by speculatively executing C' while C is still executing. During the speculative execution of C', if a data value is read prematurely (i.e. it is read before it has been computed by C), then *misspeculation* occurs, and thus the results computed during speculative execution of C' must be discarded and C' must be nonspeculatively reexecuted. On the other hand, if misspeculation does not occur, the execution time of the program is reduced due to parallel execution of C and C'. Of course, speculative execution is only beneficial if the misspeculation occurs *infrequently*. Opportunities for speculative execution arise because the dependences from C to C' may arise from infrequently executed code, or even if they do arise, they may be deemed harmless (e.g. dependences may arise due to silent stores). The aforementioned approach naturally extends to multiple levels of speculation. Given a series of dependent computations $C_1 \rightarrow C_2 \rightarrow \cdots C_n$, while C_1 executes nonspeculatively, C_2 through C_n can be speculatively executed in parallel with C_1 on additional cores.

SP is usually applied to loops and performed at compile time. The compiler ignores cross-iteration dependences and optimistically parallelizes sequential loops. When the speculatively parallelized program is executed, the runtime system or specialized hardware is used to detect misspeculation (i.e. manifestation of ignored dependences) and recover from it. While hardware-based techniques have been extensively researched, the specialized hardware structures (e.g. versioning cache [6], versioning memory [5], etc.) on which these techniques rely have not been incorporated in commercial multicore processors. On the other hand, software-based techniques have also drawn attention from researchers, and they have the advantage that they can be used to exploit the multicore systems available today.

SP techniques require minimal help from the programmer who may be required to identify loops to which SP is to be applied. An alternative is to profile the program and identify loops that are found to contain significant levels of parallelism due to infrequent occurrences of cross-iteration dependences. The compiler performs the tedious task of generating parallelized code, and the runtime system ensures the correctness of speculative execution. The main challenge of employing this approach is designing and implementing a sound and efficient runtime system to support SP.

To design and implement an SP system, several issues need to be addressed. A computation model that supports speculative execution and allows for misspeculation detection and recovery capabilities must be designed. Efficient techniques for handling misspeculations must be developed; otherwise, when the misspeculation rate is high, the performance achieved through parallelism will be nullified. Programs that make extensive use of pointer-based dynamic data structures pose additional challenges to SP systems. However, for wide applicability of SP, these challenges must be addressed. Finally, techniques for identifying parallelizable regions must be developed. The rest of the chapter addresses the aforementioned issues. Some ongoing projects that focus on SP techniques are also briefly discussed followed by future work and conclusions.

10.2 SPECULATIVE EXECUTION IN CORD

During the execution of a sequential program, only a single execution entity, a process or a thread, exists. However, when the SP technique is used, multiple execution entities must be employed to aggressively exploit parallelism. Different design decisions can be made. For example, should threads or processes be used? How should the created processes or threads coordinate their execution?

This section presents the copy-or-discard (CorD) execution model [18] which supports speculative execution. CorD is a thread-based model which employs one main thread and multiple speculative parallel threads. The advantage of using threads is that the entire memory space is accessible for all threads within the process. Thus, thread interactions are lightweight in comparison to the process-based model.

A computation is divided into sequential (nonparallelized) regions and speculatively parallelized regions. The main thread and multiple parallel threads execute these regions as follows. The main thread executes all sequential regions, and when it reaches a speculatively parallelized region, it spawns a number of speculative threads and assigns a piece of work taken from the parallelized region to each of them. After task assignment, it simply waits for the speculative threads to finish their assigned tasks. When a speculative thread finishes a task, it notifies the main thread so that the main thread can detect misspeculations and ask the speculative thread to redo the same task or assign a new task to it. This pattern continues until the entire parallelized region has been executed. After that, if the next region is sequential, the main thread executes it; otherwise, all existing speculative threads are reused to perform the computation in the next parallel region. These speculative threads will terminate when the last parallel region has finished executing. Thus, while the speculative threads perform computations in speculatively parallelized regions, the main thread executes all sequential regions, coordinates activities of speculative threads, detects misspeculations and so on.

10.2.1 State Separation

One of the key issues of the SP technique is to distinguish the speculative results from nonspeculative results. In SP techniques, there are two typical schemes to update the computation results, *eager update* and *lazy update*. In the *eager update* scheme, each speculative thread commits its results before the speculation check. If a misspeculation is detected at a later point, the system must have the ability to *roll back* to an earlier correct state. This requires a design that allows the system to distinguish speculatively committed results. In contrast, *lazy update* does not allow any speculative results to be committed unless they pass the misspeculation check. Therefore, *state separation* is employed to maintain nonspeculative state separately from the speculative state of the computation. Most existing SP techniques adopted the lazy update scheme because the execution of each thread (or process) is isolated from execution of all other threads (or processes). Thus, if the execution of one thread results in misspeculation, it does not necessarily force the reexecution of all other threads.

To achieve state separation, CorD divides the entire memory space of a speculatively parallel execution into three disjoint partitions <D, P, C> such that each partition contains a distinct type of program state (see Fig. 10.1).

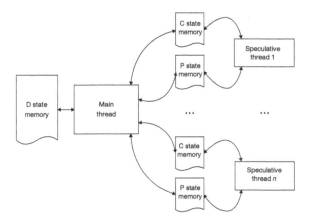

Figure 10.1   Maintaining memory state.

10.2.1.1 *Nonspeculative State*   D memory is the part of the address space that reflects the nonspeculative state of the computation. Only the main computation thread Mt performs updates of D. If the program is executed sequentially, Mt performs the entire computation using D. If speculative threads are used, then Mt is responsible for updating D according to the results produced by the speculative threads.

10.2.1.2 *Parallel or Speculative State*   P memory is the part of the address space that reflects the parallel computation state, that is, the state of the speculative threads Ts created by Mt to boost performance. Since speculative threads perform speculative computations, speculative state that exists is at all times contained in P memory. The results produced by the speculative threads are communicated to Mt that then performs updates of D. Note that P memory is further divided into a number of disjointed spaces. Each speculative thread uses one of these spaces as its own P Space. To avoid execution interference, a speculative thread is not allowed to access any other speculative thread's P Space.

10.2.1.3 *Coordinating State*   C memory is the part of the address space that contains the coordinating state of the computation. Since the execution of Mt is isolated from the execution of speculative threads Ts, mechanisms are needed via which the threads can coordinate their actions. The coordinating state provides memory where all state needed for coordinating actions (e.g. actions in *control* component) is maintained. Similar to P memory, C memory is further divided into a number of C spaces, each corresponding to one speculative thread.

10.2.2 Copying Operations

When a speculative thread starts a speculative computation, it requires the input data and the values of context variables (i.e. variables that are used before being defined) to be present in its P space. When a parallel thread finishes a speculative computation and the results are validated, all produced data needs to be moved back to D space. Therefore, a mechanism is needed to transfer data between D space and P space. This mechanism is implemented through a copying operation in CorD. In particular, *copy in* refers to the operation that copies data values from D space to a P space and *copy out* refers to the operation that copies data values from a P space to D space.

When copying operations are performed to transfer data, certain information has to be maintained for consistency. In particular, when a data value is copied in, both its source and destination address have to be remembered. Thus, when this value is changed by a speculative thread, copy-out operation can update the correct memory location in D. To achieve this, the mapping table is required for the copying operation. It is allocated by the main thread for every speculative thread. As shown in the following, an entry in the mapping table contains five fields.

D_Addr	P_Addr	Size	Version	WriteFlag

The D_Addr and P_Addr fields provide the corresponding addresses of a variable in the D state and P state memory, while Size is the size of the variable. Version is the version number of the variable when the value is copied from D state to P state memory. It is used during misspeculation detection which will be described later. The WriteFlag is initialized to *false* when the value is initially copied from D state to P state memory. However, if the parallel thread modifies the value contained in P_Addr, the WriteFlag is set to *true* by the speculative thread. During the result-committing stage, this flag is examined to determine which variables need to be copied out.

Note that copying operations can be highly optimized [18]. The main idea is to identify the access patterns of data values by combining dynamic and static analysis. For example, if a data is read only or thread local, no copying operations should be performed. The optimization can greatly reduce copying operations and thus improve the performance.

10.2.3 Misspeculation Detection and Recovery

A misspeculation occurs when a speculative computation reads a data value before it is produced by an earlier computation. The misspeculation check is performed by the

```
1:    foreach variable v that has an entry e in the mapping table {
2:        if (e.version != v.global_version){
3:            discard all results and ask t to reperform the task;
4:            return SpeculationFail;
5:        }
6:    }
7:    foreach variable v that has an entry e in the mapping table {
8:        if (e.WriteFlag){
9:            copy-out v;
10:           v.global_version++;
11:       }
12:   }
13:   return SpeculationSuccess;
```

Figure 10.2   Misspeculation detection.

main thread in sequential order. In particular, the main thread performs the misspeculation check for a speculative thread performing the earliest task among all tasks being currently performed by all the speculative threads.

Misspeculation detection algorithm considers each data value speculatively read by a committing speculative thread. The main thread examines if any such value is updated during the execution of an earlier committed task to detect misspeculation. Thus, a *global version* of each variable in D state memory that is potentially read and written by speculative threads needs to be maintained. This version is incremented every time the value of the variable in D state memory is modified during the committing of results produced by speculative threads. For each variable in D state memory, if it is copied into a speculative thread's P space, its global version is also copied into the *version* field of the corresponding entry in the mapping table.

When a speculative thread t informs the main thread that it has completed a speculative task, the main thread performs the misspeculation check by consulting the *mapping table* and accordingly taking the actions shown in Figure 10.2. The main thread compares the current version numbers of variables with the version numbers of the variables in the mapping table. If a version number does not match, then the main thread concludes that misspeculation has occurred (lines 1–5). It discards the results and asks the speculative thread to reperform the task. If all version numbers match, then speculation is successful. Thus, the main thread commits the results by *copying* the values of variables for which the WriteFlag is true from P state memory to D state memory by using P_Addr and D_Addr stored in the mapping table. The global version of the copied variable is also incremented by one (lines 6–12). Note that if the WriteFlag is not true, then there is no need to copy back the result as the variable's value is unchanged.

Note that the results produced by speculative threads are also committed in sequential order. If a misspeculation occurs for a thread, the main thread waits for this thread to finish the nonspeculative reexecution before committing the correct results to D space. Next, the main thread moves to the misspeculation check for the next speculative thread. This is important for eliminating the need for extra synchronizations on shared data structures and ensuring that the results of the parallelized program are consistent with the results of the sequential program.

10.2.4 Identifying Parallelizable Regions

*10.2.4.1 **Program Profiling*** Offline profiling can be used to identify the parallelizable regions of a program. The high-level loop structures of the program can be first identified. Then the dynamic dependence graph, which represents the runtime dependences of the variables used within loops, is constructed through profiling run. This graph is used to determine if a loop is a good candidate for SP. The original proposal of CorD system follows this approach. It requires a loop iteration to be partitioned into the prologue, speculative body and the epilogue. In CorD, prologue and epilogue are executed by the main thread, and the speculative body is executed by speculative threads.

The algorithm for performing the partitioning first constructs the prologue, and then the epilogue and finally everything that is not included in the prologue or the epilogue is placed in the speculative body. The construction of the prologue and the epilogue is as follows:

- (Prologue) The prologue is constructed such that it contains all the input statements that read from files. This is because such input statements should not be executed speculatively. In addition, an input statement within a loop is typically dependent *only* upon its execution in the previous iteration – this loop-carried dependence is needed to preserve the order in which the inputs are read from a file. Therefore input statements for multiple consecutive loop iterations can be executed by the main thread before the speculative bodies of these iterations are assigned to speculative threads for execution. Loop index update statements are also included into the prologue, as the index variables can be considered as the input of each iteration and hence should be executed nonspeculatively.

- (Epilogue) The epilogue is made up of two types of statements. First the output statements are included in the epilogue because output statements cannot be executed speculatively. If an output statement is encountered in the middle of the loop iteration or it is executed multiple times, then the code is transformed so that the results are stored in a memory buffer and the output statements that write the buffer contents to files are placed in the epilogue which is later executed nonspeculatively by the main thread. Second a statement that *may depend* (i.e. determined by profiling results) upon another statement in the preceding iteration is placed in the epilogue if the probability of this dependence manifesting itself is above a threshold. In addition, any statements that are control or data dependent upon statements already in the epilogue via an intraiteration dependence are also placed in the epilogue.

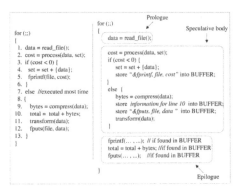

Figure 10.3   Partitioning a loop into prologue, speculative body and epilogue.

Figure 10.3 illustrates the partitioning of a loop body. In the *for* loop shown on the left, the first statement is a typical input statement as it reads some data from a file and stores it into a buffer. Hence, it is placed into the prologue. Then the epilogue of this loop is constructed. First, all output statements (lines 5 and 12) are included. Since the profiling information reveals that a loop dependence at line 10 is exercised very often, this statement is also put into the epilogue. Otherwise, all speculative executions of iterations will fail because of this dependence. Thus, the epilogue of this loop has three statements, as shown by the code segment to the right in Figure 10.3. Note that in this example, all three statements appear in the middle of the loop. Thus, a buffer is used to store the information of epilogue statements such as the PC of statements and values of the arguments. When the epilogue is executed by the main thread, the information stored in this buffer is referenced.

10.2.4.2 Language Support   Another approach to identify parallelizable region is to use language support. Recent work [4] has proposed a portable standard for writing parallel programs while hiding the complexity of parallel programming from developers. The standard contains a set of directives. The compiler directives enable the programmer to mark and parallelize a section of code that is meant to be run in parallel just as is the case in OpenMP [2]. A compiler directive in C/C++ is called a pragma. Compiler directives specific to CorD model in C/C++ start with #pragma. The compiler directives are summarized as follows:

   #pragma parallel CorD is used to specify the potential parallel region of the program. The parallel region must be a loop, written in for, while or do ... while form. The specified region will be used CorD model.

   #pragma subregion [name] [order] [speculative] is used to specify a subregion in the parallel region. Developers can assign a name to the subregion and specify the execution order of different instances of the sub-region or different subregions. A subregion can be specified to be executed speculatively. By default, the whole loop body of the parallel region is one subregion.

#pragma commit [order] is used to call the commit operation, which commits all variables that are updated in the subregion to the D space. Developers can specify whether to perform misspeculation check before the commit operation. If the misspeculation check fails, the subregion is reexecuted. Developers can also specify the execution order of the commit operation which can be used to enforce the sequential semantics of the parallel region. In particular, [order] specifies execution order between execution instances of code regions and commits. The format [order] is order_after(ITER-NUM, REGION)), where ITER is a keyword, NUM is a positive integer and REGION is the name of a user-defined subregion. It means that the execution of the associated region/commit of iteration 'i' must wait until the execution of subregion REGION of iteration 'i-NUM' is finished.

Figure 10.4 shows the kernel of benchmark telecomm-CRC32 in MiBench suite. The program calculates 32-bit error-detecting code of cyclic redundancy check (CRC) for a set of strings and put the results into the error variable. The update of error depends on the value of error from previous iterations. Therefore, the subregion R2 has a cross-iteration dependence on itself. However, since the function calculate_crc usually returns 0 that represents success in real runs, the cross-iteration dependence is rarely manifested. The program can be parallelized by *speculating* on the absence of the dependence. In the example, the program is parallelized using CorD. The loop body is divided into two subregions. The subregion R1 is executed sequentially since there is a cross-iteration dependence due to the file pointer in the read function. The subregion R2 is executed in parallel but the commit operation in R2 is performed sequentially to ensure the sequential semantics of the loop. Before the commit operation, a misspeculation check is performed to detect if the cross-iteration dependence occurred. If the dependence

```
error=0;
i=0;
#pragma parallel CorD {
    for(i=0;i<n;i++) {
        #pragma subregion R1 order_after(ITER-1, R1) {
            string = read();
            #pragma commit
        }
        #pragma subregion R2 no_order speculative {
            ret = calculate_crc(string);
            if (ret != 0)
                error |= ret;
            #pragma commit order_after(ITER-1, R2)
        }
    }
}
```

Figure 10.4   Kernel of benchmark telecomm-CRC32.

is detected, then the whole subregion R2 is reexecuted. Otherwise, R2 can commit its results safely. Subregion is designed for programmers to specify synchronization (i.e. execution order) between execution instances of code regions.

10.2.5 Experimental Results

To demonstrate the potential of SP techniques, experiments are presented. The results of an experiment that uses four *SPEC* programs [21] and one MiBench program [7] are presented. The main loops in these programs, which contain cross-iteration dependences, were successfully parallelized by CorD. Since these dependences infrequently manifest themselves at runtime, they cannot be embarrassingly parallelized and have to use the speculation feature provided by CorD [18].

In the experiment, the baseline which is the sequential execution time is first measured. Then the time of executing this loop in the model with different numbers of speculative threads is measured. Figure 10.5 shows the speedups. Figure 10.5 shows when the number of speculative threads increases, the speedup for all benchmarks goes up linearly. The highest speedup achieved ranges from 4.1 to 7.8 across the benchmarks when 8 speculative threads are used. The misspeculation rates observed in this experiment are less than 10%. More experimental results and detailed discussions can be found in [18].

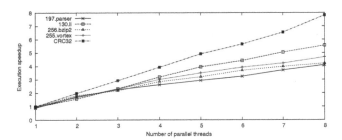

Figure 10.5 Execution speedups for SPEC and MiBench programs on a dual quadcore 3.0 GHz Xeon server.

10.3 ADVANCED FEATURES OF CORD

10.3.1 Handling High Misspeculation Rate

10.3.1.1 Multiple Speculations   The presence of cross-iteration dependences in a sequential loop causes misspeculations when loop iterations are speculatively executed in parallel. If such dependences frequently take place at runtime, the speculations fail very often and thus benefits of parallelism are wiped out.

To address this problem, the frequent cross-iteration dependences must be resolved. A typical solution is to use value prediction. Specifically, the values of live-in variables (i.e. variables involved in cross-iteration dependences) can be predicted in a later iteration before they are produced by an earlier iteration. If the prediction is correct, these two iterations can still be executed in parallel. To increase the accuracy of predictions, the predictions can be performed in a path-sensitive manner, that is, the values of live-ins can be predicted in different ways for different paths. By assigning different prediction methods to different control flow paths, high prediction accuracy is achieved.

Figure 10.6 shows a SP example where the loop iterations can be speculatively executed in parallel. Specifically, there is a cross-iteration dependence on variable *latest_config* between statements at lines 1 and 9. If the condition *cond1* is always or frequently true at runtime, using SP technique cannot speed up the execution as misspeculations occur frequently. The dependence carried by variable *latest_config* causes the loop iterations to be executed sequentially. Moreover, the overhead of the technique such as isolating speculative states and dealing with misspeculation could make the performance even worse.

This problem can be addressed by using the *multiple speculations* technique [16]. In particular, if both *cond1* and *cond2* are always true, then predicting *latest_config* to be *config[var1]* enables SP to succeed and leads to a better performance. However, a single predicted value may not be very accurate. For instance, consider the scenario for Figure 10.6 in which *cond1* and *cond2* keep evaluating alternately to true and false. Thus, a single prediction for the value of *latest_config* is not effective as it is not frequently successful. To solve this problem, multiple predictions are employed, each giving rise to a distinct version of the second iteration. The idea is that among all predictions that are chosen, it is highly likely that one prediction will turn out to be correct and the corresponding version will generate the correct result. More importantly, the correct result is computed in parallel with the execution of the first iteration. In other words, parallelism is exploited by executing two consecutive iterations in parallel.

Figure 10.7 shows the thread execution model. The original sequential execution, which consists of 4 iterations, is shown on the left. The corresponding parallel

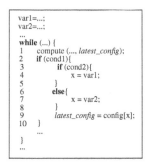

```
var1=...;
var2=...;
...
while (...) {
1    compute (..., latest_config);
2    if (cond1){
3        if (cond2){
4            x = var1;
5        }
6        else{
7            x = var2;
8        }
9        latest_config = config[x];
10   }
     ...
}
...
```

Figure 10.6   A speculation example.

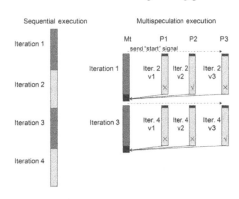

Figure 10.7   Thread execution model.

execution is shown on the right. There is one main thread and multiple speculative threads. The main thread executes iteration 1 and 3 while speculative threads execute different versions of the iterations 2 and 4. The speculative thread that generates the correct result is also called the *winner*. Figure 10.7 shows that speculative threads P2 and P3 are the winners for iterations 2 and 4, respectively. In this execution model, every two dependent iterations can be executed in parallel, and hence the theoretical speedup for the parallel execution is 2.

Generating Multiple Versions   To construct a speculative version of the second iteration, the value prediction code of live-in variables needs to be inserted before the original loop iteration code. The most accurate value prediction for a variable is to compute the value by executing its *full slice* extracted from the first iteration. However, the size of the full slice (i.e. including all control and data dependences) can be as large as the computation of the whole iteration. Using such a slice to obtain the value is the same as executing the two iterations sequentially.

To construct small prediction code and take advantage of the multiple value prediction model, the following steps are used to generate multiple versions of the second iteration. First, only the *backwards data slices* of a live-in variable needs to be computed. All the control dependences and the dependence chains of predicates are removed. Since different control flow paths may be taken in the first iteration, the data slice is computed on each *different path*. Consequently, multiple data slices are obtained for a live-in variable. At this point, multiple versions can be created for the second iteration based on different control flow paths taken by the first iteration. Specifically, each path corresponds to one version, and the data slice on that path is used to predict the live-in variable. The data slice and path information can be computed based on the profiling trace.

Note that when certain paths are seldom taken, the possibility of the corresponding version being correct is also very low. In that case, the versions that correspond to the hot paths for the third iteration or even later iterations should replace those versions that are unlikely to be correct. As a result, the speedup can exceed two in the best case.

The effectiveness of multiple speculations technique has been evaluated by using a set of SPEC 2000 benchmarks. Experimental results show that 1.7x speedup can be achieved across all used benchmarks. More benchmark descriptions and experimental results are presented in [16].

10.3.1.2 Incremental Recovery   Although the previous section proposes a value-prediction-based approach to deal with high misspeculation rate, its effectiveness is determined by the accuracy of value prediction. The fundamental reason for the performance loss upon a misspeculation is that all results generated are assumed to be incorrect and hence discarded. However, it is observed that a misspeculation on a live-in variable may not necessarily cause all speculatively computed results to be incorrect. Based on this observation, this section describes an approach for *Incremental Recovery* that mitigates the performance loss caused by high misspeculation rate [19].

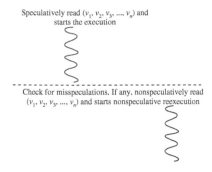

Speculatively read $(v_1, v_2, v_3, ..., v_n)$ and starts the execution

Check for misspeculations. If any, nonspeculatively read $(v_1, v_2, v_3, ..., v_n)$ and starts nonspeculative reexecution

Figure 10.8 Discard-all recovery.

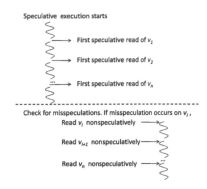

Speculative execution starts

First speculative read of v_1

First speculative read of v_2

First speculative read of v_n

Check for misspeculations. If misspeculation occurs on v_i,

Read v_i nonspeculatively

Read v_{i+1} nonspeculatively

Read v_n nonspeculatively

Figure 10.9 Incremental recovery.

In the basic CorD model, recovery from misspeculations is achieved by discarding all speculatively computed results. This process is shown in Figure 10.8. Before starting speculative execution of a computation (e.g. a loop iteration), the input values or *live-ins* needed for its execution are speculatively read from nonspeculative state and copied into the speculative state for the thread. The reads of values (v_1, v_2, v_3, ..., v_n) are speculative because the values are read while execution of one or more earlier iterations is in progress; if any of these values is changed by these earlier iterations, then misspeculation occurs. After reading, the computation is performed, and then the misspeculation check is executed. If the check fails, misspeculation occurs. To recover from misspeculation, the values of *live-ins* are now read again, this time nonspeculatively, and the entire computation is repeated. This strategy for recovery is called *discard-all* as all results computed are discarded, and computation is performed again in its entirety.

It should be noted that even if the misspeculation occurs due to *any* one of the live-ins, *all* results are discarded. While this approach is simple to implement, discarding all speculatively computed results is a suboptimal solution. It is possible that a subset of speculatively computed results may be correct, and thus there may not be a need to perform the entire computation again. Discarding all results can be very wasteful, especially when the misspeculation rate is relatively high because the cost of recovery begins to add up.

Achieving Incremental Recovery   To efficiently support the speculation system, an *incremental recovery* technique is proposed. As shown in Figure 10.9, the key idea is to delineate the computation into many sections according to the points at which the *earliest reads* of the *live-ins* are encountered. In the figure it is assumed that the first speculative read of v_i appears before the first speculative read of v_{i+1} for all i. Therefore, the live-ins (v_1, v_2, ..., v_n) cause the computation to be divided into $n + 1$ sections. Now let us assume that of all the values among (v_1, v_2, ..., v_n) that cause misspeculation, v_i is the one that is read the earliest. In this case the entire computation performed by the sections of code preceding the first read of v_i can

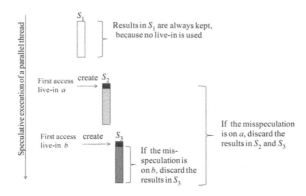

Figure 10.10   Decoupling space allocation from thread creation.

be certainly reused. Thus, the recovery can be performed by simply repeating the execution of code starting from the point at which v_i was first read. If v_i happens to be v_1, the reuse achieved is minimum. On the other hand, if v_i happens to be v_n, the reuse is the maximum.

To achieve the incremental recovery, the creation of a speculative thread that performs speculative execution needs to be decoupled from the creation of the speculative space that it uses for saving results. At each point which represents a first read of a speculative value, a *new version* or *copy* of the speculative space is created. Figure 10.10 illustrates the idea. In the figure, a speculative thread creates three speculative spaces S_1, S_2 and S_3 instead of just one space during the speculative execution. Space S_2 is created when the first access of live-in variable a is encountered, and S_3 is created when the first access of live-in variable b is encountered. If a misspeculation is found to have occurred due to a, the results stored in S_2 and S_3 are discarded and recomputed using the correct value of a. However, if the misspeculation is caused by b, only the results in S_3 are recomputed. The results in S_1 are only computed once and are never discarded during recovery because the computation does not use any speculative variable.

Experiments have been conducted to evaluate incremental recovery technique in prior work [19]. The results show that for a set of programs with inputs causing around 40% and 80% misspeculation rates, applying incremental recovery technique can achieve 1.2–3.3× and 2.0–6.6× speedups, respectively, in comparison to the original discard-all recovery scheme. More evaluation results are described in work [19].

10.3.2   Handling Dynamic Data Structures

A dynamic data structure consists of large number of nodes such that each node contains some data fields and pointer fields. The pointer fields are used to link together the nodes in the data structure (e.g. link lists, trees, queues etc.). Such data structures are also called dynamic data structures because the shape and size of the data structure can change as the program executes.

Applying SP technique in applications that make extensive use of dynamic data structures is much more challenging than in those using scalar variables or static data structures such as arrays, because complexities of pointer analysis make it difficult to identify the portion of the dynamic data structure that is referenced by the speculative computation. Moreover, if a large number of nodes are referenced, tracking the copying operations (also referred to as *access check*) using a mapping table is very expensive. To address these challenges, two different schemes, namely, *metadata storage* and *fat pointer* have been proposed lately [4, 17].

10.3.2.1 *Metadata Storage*

When a data item is first accessed by some speculative thread, an entry is setup in this thread's mapping table so that future reference in the speculative execution does not invoke duplicated copies of the same data. However, this requires a walk through the entire table. To efficiently perform the access checks metadata can be associated with each node that tracks certain information related to accesses of the node. This metadata is called *heap prefix*.

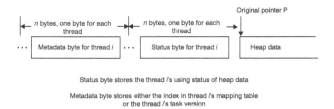

Status byte stores the thread *i*'s using status of heap data

Metadata byte stores either the index in thread *i*'s mapping table
or the thread *i*'s task version

Figure 10.11   Heap prefix format.

For each memory chunk allocated on the heap, $2 * n$ additional bytes are allocated in front of it where n is the total number of speculative threads. These bytes are called *heap prefix* and used to store important information to assist in access checks. The format of the heap prefix is shown in Figure 10.11. The first n bytes immediately before the program's original heap data are the *status bytes*. The additional n bytes are *metadata bytes*. In the status byte, byte i represents the status for speculative thread i, and it can represent four different possible status values. Status NOT_COPIED means the heap data has not been copied into thread i's speculative state. Status ALREADY_COPIED means the heap data has been copied into thread i's speculative space, and the index of this entry in thread i's mapping table is stored in the corresponding metadata byte. Status ALREADY_READ means the heap data has been read by thread i, and the corresponding metadata bytes store the *task ID* of thread i. Status INTERNAL indicates that the node is already in the speculative state. Therefore, status NOT_COPIED, ALREADY_COPIED and ALREADY_READ only appear in heap elements of nonspeculative state, and status INTERNAL only appears in heap elements in speculative state. In the metadata bytes, metadata byte i stores either an index number of the mapping table of thread i or the *task ID* of thread i.

With the status bytes and metadata bytes in the heap prefix, the *access check* for a heap node access in thread i can be implemented as follows. First, the thread i's status s in the node 's prefix is examined. If s is NOT_COPIED and the access is a read, s will be updated to ALREADY_READ, and the task ID of thread i is stored in the metadata byte i.

If the access is a write, s is updated to ALREADY_COPIED. A new local copy of the node is then created with the corresponding status byte to be set to INTERNAL. After that, a mapping entry is added into the mapping table to reflect this copy operation, and the index of the entry is stored in the metadata byte i. Finally, the pointer is pointing to the newly created node.

If s is ALREADY_COPIED, then that means the node has been copied, so address translation is needed. Fortunately, the mapping entry can be quickly located through metadata byte i, and there is no need to adjust the pointer to point to the address of the local copy. Finally, if s is ALREADY_COPIED and the access is a write, then the copy-in operation is performed as when s is NOT_COPIED. Otherwise, the access would be a read or s is INTERNAL. In both cases, no further actions are required.

In summary, there are two main advantages of using heap prefix to implement access checks. First, the status byte can tell the access checks whether or not a node has been copied. Second, the metadata bytes allows the speculative thread to find the mapping entry in O(1) time, which can speed up the process of address translation for copy-in operations.

10.3.2.2 *Fat Pointer*

Different from *metadata storage*, the *fat-pointer* scheme presents an augmented representation for pointers because the nodes in dynamic data structures are always referenced via pointers. To enable fast access checks for dynamic data structures, the current pointer representation is extended with four fields: D space address of the data structure, P space address of the data structure; thread ID and iteration ID. In the sequential region of the program, only D space address field is used. When an extended pointer in the parallel region is being dereferenced, it has to be checked whether the P space address field is valid (i.e. whether the dynamic data structure has a copy in the P space at the specified address). This is done by checking whether the pointer's thread ID and iteration ID fields match the current thread and iteration. If they match, the P space address is valid, and it can be directly used. Otherwise, the P space address stored in the pointer is invalid. In this case, it has to be further checked whether the pointed to data structure has been copied into the P space due to the dereference of other pointers.

When a dynamic data structure and its pointers in the P space are committed to the D space, all these pointers need to be redirected to the copy of the dynamic data structure in the D space. This usually results in high runtime overhead for searching the pointers and translating the addresses. The *fat-pointer* scheme eliminates the need for altering pointers during the commit procedure. The extended pointer contains two address fields: one for D space address and the other for P space address. The D space address field always contains the D space address of the data structure no matter in which space the pointer is. When a pointer is assigned to another pointer, both address fields are copied. The D space address field of a pointer is used when the copy of the data structure in the D space is referred to. Therefore, there is no need to translate the addresses.

Experiment shows that these techniques can significantly improve the performance of the programs that make extensive use of heap-based dynamic data structures. In prior work [17], seven benchmarks are used to make quantitative evaluation, and maximum speedups from 1.56 to 3.2 can be observed. More experimental results about these techniques can also be found in [4].

10.4 RELATED WORK

This section gives a brief introduction to other parallelization projects. All of these projects mainly employ compiler-based techniques for parallel region identification, loop transformation and misspeculation check. Some techniques rely on hardware or OS support for better performance.

10.4.1 Process-Based Speculation

While CorD is a thread-based software SP system, there also exist process-based systems such as behavior-oriented parallelization (BOP) [3, 8]. Similar to CorD, BOP is also based on state separation. In other words, speculative computations are performed in a separate memory space. The results are not committed to the nonspeculative space until the speculation succeeds. BOP provides simple programming constructs for specifying possible parallel region. Due to the use of processes, data copying operations can be performed at page level. In particular, speculative writes can be captured and tracked by OS and customized page fault handler. However, the disadvantage is that significant amount of memory pages need to be copied when speculation succeeds. The execution model of BOP is different from CorD. In BOP the work is assigned to the cores round by round, and the next round cannot start until all work in the previous round is finished successfully. If speculation with respect to a process fails, the work by following processes in the same round is completely discarded. BOP uses nonspeculative understudy to guarantee its basic efficiency.

10.4.2 Worklist-Based Speculation

The Galois system [11] is a parallelization system to exploit the data parallelism in applications with irregular parallelism. It mainly features two programming constructs called optimistic iterators for expressing worklist-based data parallelism. It is supported by a runtime system that performs parallelization of these iterators, misspeculation checks and rolling back operations as needed. Parallelization requires speculation with respect to data dependences. The Galois system allows users to specify the commutativity of the method invocations in a loop. When speculation fails, user supplied code is executed to perform rollback. The Galois system has been extended to use data partitioning for optimizing worklist-based parallelism [10].

It requires the data partition to be known before starting a computation. Computations are distributed to threads based on the data partition. This increases the data locality and reduces the chances of data conflicts. Based on the data partition, lock coarsening is used to further reduce the parallelization overhead.

10.4.3 Speculative Software Pipelining

One commonly used approach for parallelization of loops is software pipelining. This technique partitions a loop into multiple pipeline stages where each stage is executed on a different processor. Decoupled software pipelining (DSWP) [14, 15, 20] is a technique that targets multicore processors. DSWP partitions a loop based on its dependence graph. Each pipeline stage of the loop is a strongly connected subgraph of the dependence graph. The loop code is split into different threads based on the pipeline stages. DSWP hides the communication latency by overlapping communication with computation. Speculative DSWP [20] adds speculation to DSWP. It allows partitioning a strongly connected dependence graph into multiple stages by speculating on certain dependence edges. Speculative DSWP makes pipelining applicable to more loops and allows more balanced loop partitioning. The proposed DSWP techniques require two kinds of hardware support that is not commonly supported by current processors. First, hardware support is used to achieve efficient message passing between different cores. Second, hardware support is versioned memory which is used to support speculative DSWP parallelization. Since DSWP requires the flow of data among the cores to be acyclic, in general, it is difficult to balance the workloads across the cores. Raman et al. [15] address this issue by parallelizing the workload of overloaded stages using DOALL techniques. This technique achieves better scalability than DSWP but it does not support SP which limits its applicability.

10.5 FUTURE WORK

10.5.1 Energy Consumption

This chapter mainly focuses on improving performance of sequential program by exploiting multiple cores. While performance is important for computing, power consumption may become a big concern in resource-constrained environment. In the future work, SP technique should address the energy consumption issue. In particular, the number of speculative tasks should be controlled so that a balance between performance improvement and energy consumption can be better achieved.

10.5.2 Parallelization Enhancement

The parallelization algorithm proposed in this chapter is based on the profiling results or language supports. In the former case, the accuracy of profiling largely affects the performance of software TLS. Since the input of the profiling run and the input of the real run are different, the information gathered in the profiling run may not lead to efficient parallelization. To address this problem, future work should consider online profiling. Based on the results, the code should be re-transformed to better exploit frequently observed parallelism.

If parallelization is performed by using new language extensions, the performance and correctness will rely on how well programmers use these extensions. Future work should consider new compiler analysis to avoid possible errors introduced by programmers.

10.5.3 Emerging Architectures

This work considers the multicore processors of today as the target architecture. In the future, heterogeneous processors and 3D multicore processors may become prevalent. Future work should consider adapting software TLS system to such new architectures.

10.6 CONCLUDING REMARKS

This chapter discusses several design principles and issues of software-based TLS system. A thread-based speculative execution model called CorD is proposed. It contains one main thread and several speculative threads, and the main thread controls the entire execution. The memory state is divided into three disjoint partitions such that the execution of each thread is isolated. In particular, the main thread maintains the nonspeculative state, and speculative threads perform speculative computations on the speculative state. Coordinating state provides memory for bookkeeping important information needed to support speculation. In CorD the data communications between the main thread and speculative threads are performed through copying operations. The misspeculation is checked by the main thread, which also commits the speculatively computed results if the speculation is successful. If a misspeculation is detected, the speculative results are simply discarded, and the failed task is performed again.

This chapter also presents several advanced features of CorD. To deal with high misspeculation rate, two different approaches, multiple speculations and incremental recovery, are proposed. In the first approach, the values of live-in variables are predicted, and multiple speculative versions of the same task are created and executed with a nonspeculative task in parallel. If one of these versions is correct, parallelism between these two tasks is achieved. The second approach decouples the creation of each parallel thread from the creation of its speculative state. It allows speculatively computed results to be reused as long as they are not using the live-in variables that are the cause of misspeculations. Finally, challenges of applying CorD in the presence of dynamic data structures are addressed.

REFERENCES

1. M. G. Burke and R. K. Cytron. Interprocedural dependence analysis and parallelization. In *SIGPLAN '86: Proceedings of the 1986 SIGPLAN symposium on Compiler construction*, pages 162–175, 1986.

2. L. Dagum and R. Menon. Openmp: an industry-standard api for shared-memory programming. *IEEE Computational Science and Engineering*, 5(1):46–55, 1998.

3. C. Ding, X. Shen, K. Kelsey, C. Tice, R. Huang, and C. Zhang. Software behavior oriented parallelization. In *PLDI '07: Proceedings of the 2007 ACM SIGPLAN Conference on Programming Language Design and Implementation*, pages 223–234, 2007.

4. M. Feng, R. Gupta, and Y. Hu. SpiceC: scalable parallelism via implicit copying and explicit commit. In *PPoPP'11: 16th ACM SIGPLAN Annual Symposium on Principles and Practice of Parallel Programming*, 2011.

5. M. J. Garzarán, M. Prvulovic, J. M. Llabería, V. Viñals, L. Rauchwerger, and J. Torrellas. Tradeoffs in buffering speculative memory state for thread-level speculation in multiprocessors. *Transactions on Architecture and Code Optimization*, 2(3):247–279, 2005.

6. S. Gopal, T. N. Vijaykumar, J. E. Smith, and G. S. Sohi. Speculative versioning cache. In *HPCA '98: Proceedings of the 4th International Symposium on High-Performance Computer Architecture*, pages 195–205, 1998.

7. M. R. Guthaus, J. S. Ringenberg, D. Ernst, and R. B. B. Todd M. Austinand Trevor Mudge. Mibench: A free, commercially representative embedded benchmark suite. In *IEEE 4th Annual Workshop on Workload Characterization*, Austin, TX, USA, 2001.

8. K. Kelsey, T. Bai, C. Ding, and C. Zhang. Fast track: a software system for speculative program optimization. In *CGO '09: Proceedings of the 2009 international Symposium on Code Generation and Optimization*, pages 157–168, 2009.

9. K. Kennedy and J. R. Allen. *Optimizing compilers for modern architectures: a dependence-based approach*. Morgan Kaufmann Publishers Inc., San Francisco, CA, USA, 2002.

10. M. Kulkarni, K. Pingali, G. Ramanarayanan, B. Walter, K. Bala, and L. P. Chew. Optimistic parallelism benefits from data partitioning. In *ASPLOS XIII: Proceedings of the 13th International Conference on Architectural Support for Programming Languages and Operating Systems*, pages 233–243, 2008.

11. M. Kulkarni, K. Pingali, B. Walter, G. Ramanarayanan, K. Bala, L. P. Chew. Optimistic parallelism requires abstractions. In *PLDI '07: Proceedings of the 2007 ACM SIGPLAN conference on Programming Language Design and Implementation*, pages 211–222, 2007.

12. L. Lamport. The parallel execution of do loops. *Communication of the ACM*, 17(2):83–93, 1974.

13. A. W. Lim and M. S. Lam. Maximizing parallelism and minimizing synchronization with affine partitions. *Parallel Computing*, 24(3–4):445–475, 1998.

14. G. Ottoni, R. Rangan, A. Stoler, and D. I. August. Automatic thread extraction with decoupled software pipelining. In *MICRO 38: Proceedings of the 38th annual IEEE/ACM International Symposium on Microarchitecture*, pages 105–118, 2005.

15. E. Raman, G. Ottoni, A. Raman, M. J. Bridges, and D. I. August. Parallel-stage decoupled software pipelining. In *CGO '08: Proceedings of the 2008 International Symposium on Code Generation and Optimization*, pages 114–123, 2008.

16. C. Tian, M. Feng, and R. Gupta. Speculative parallelization using state separation and multiple value prediction. In *ISMM '10: Proceedings of the 2010 International Symposium on Memory Management*, 2010.

17. C. Tian, M. Feng, and R. Gupta. Supporting speculative parallelization in the presence of dynamic data structures. In *PLDI '10: Proceedings of the 2010 ACM SIG-PLAN conference on Programming language design and implementation*, pages 63–73, 2010.

18. C. Tian, M. Feng, V. Nagarajan, and R. Gupta. Copy or discard execution model for speculative parallelization on multicores. In *MICRO '08: Proceedings of the 2008 41st IEEE/ACM International Symposium on Microarchitecture*, pages 330–341, 2008.

19. C. Tian, C. Lin, M. Feng, and R. Gupta. Enhanced speculative parallelization via incremental recovery. In *PPoPP'11: 16th ACM SIGPLAN Annual Symposium on Principles and Practice of Parallel Programming*, 2011.

20. N. Vachharajani, R. Rangan, E. Raman, M. J. Bridges, G. Ottoni, and D. I. August. Speculative decoupled software pipelining. In *PACT '07: Proceedings of the 2007 International Conference on Parallel Architectures and Compilation Techniques*, pages 49–59, 2007.

21. http://www.spec.org.

CHAPTER 11

AUTONOMIC DISTRIBUTION AND ADAPTATION

Lutz Schubert, Stefan Wesner, Daniel Rubio Bonilla and Tommaso Cucinotta

11.1 INTRODUCTION

It has been noted multiple times in this book how the future development trend of processor architecture goes toward heterogeneous mixed many-/multicore systems, such as already demonstrated by IBM's Cell processor[1] or the OMAP5 by Texas Instruments.[2] It is thereby also obvious that future software (and implicitly software developers) has to exploit parallelism in order to improve the efficiency of execution or even just to enable additional features and functions. The main problem however consists in the complexity of the according programming models and the degree of knowledge required about program behavior for its effective parallelization. In order to execute tasks and functions in parallel, their dependencies have to be identified

---

[1]http://www.research.ibm.com/cell/.
[2]http://www.ti.com/ww/en/omap/omap5/omap5-platform.html.

Programming Multicore and Many-core Computing Systems,
First Edition. Edited by Sabri Pllana and Fatos Xhafa.
© 2017 John Wiley & Sons, Inc. Published 2017 by John Wiley & Sons, Inc.

and work or data segmented in a fashion that improves rather than reduces the overall execution performance.

Most programming models originate however from the purely sequential computing area and offer little support for writing parallelized applications. With the rise of high-performance computing (HPC) and hence heavily parallel environments, these classical models were extended with features to offer some support for parallelism that mostly consist of explicit or implicit means for controlling communication. As the HPC domain has so far been a restricted usage area, compared with common day-to-day programming and application development, developers in this domain typically pursue(d) a very specific interest and therefore spend the time and effort on learning dedicated programming extensions and in particular on parallelizing their code and taking additional precautions to achieve maximum performance. With the entry of parallelism into the desktop domain, this additional effort is however no longer justifiable, and more usable models are required in order to enable 'mainstream parallelism'.

This chapter describes an approach for increasing the scalability of applications by exploiting inherent concurrency in order to parallelize and distribute the code. We thereby focus specifically on concurrency in the sense of reduced dependencies between logical parts of an application. Concurrency forms a crucial part in any parallelization approach, as the degree of dependencies across potential threads defines the delay due to messaging and synchronization overhead. For example, loop unrollments show best performance improvement if they are highly concurrent and thus vectorizable.

What is even more important, though, is the fact that concurrency can be exploited for parallel execution of *sequential* (i.e. unparallelizable) code logic. In other words, if multiple, independent sequential segments can be identified, they can be executed in parallel to each other. Thus concurrency exploitation directly affects the limiting factor of Amdahl's [1]. We will show how graph analysis methods can be employed to assess the dependencies on code level, so as to identify concurrent segments and to relate them to the specific characteristics of the (heterogeneous, large-scale) environment.

11.2 PARALLEL PROGRAMMING MODELS

As the need for parallel applications increases, so does the demand for efficient and yet easy to use programming models and languages that enable scalable and – in the long run – portable behavior over heterogeneous infrastructures. In the following, we will provide an overview over some of the existing parallel programming models and their strengths and weaknesses with respect to the following specific goals.

11.2.1 Explicit Communication and Synchronization

The most classical approach to parallelization consists in enabling the development (and parallel execution) of 'threads', for example [6]. Like processes, threads are effectively nothing else but independent applications that however can identify each other in order to exchange data through dedicated communications. As the description indicates, the classical thread enhancements do not offer an explicit means for data synchronization or sharing. In other words, the developer has to identify communication points in his program and explicitly specify the data to be transmitted – in order for one thread to share data with a second thread, it is therefore necessary for the first thread to explicitly select and send the respective data set to the second thread which in turn will have to wait for reception of this data. In the case of explicitly shared data, this means furthermore that the according data set will have to be send back and forth in order to maintain consistent state. Accordingly it is easy to introduce synchronization and hence performance issues.

It can therefore be generally noted that thread-based programming models are only efficient given the right expertise of the developer and a use case where data needs only be shared at clear, discrete points in time. If the according knowledge is missing, or should the synchronization points not be obvious enough, this approach can lead not only to significant performance losses but also to locking and unpredictable behavior. Many parallelization methods can raise this condition, such as write before read across iterations in a parallelized loop. What is more, the approach as such does not support addressing the heterogeneity issue of computing systems, which not only affects how these threads need to be compiled but in particular also leads to deviations in the synchronization behavior, if, for example, the execution speed between resources deviates from one another.

With the introduction of the **Message Passing Interface**[3] (MPI), an attempt was made to standardize the communication between threads (and processes) in order to principally allow message-based data synchronization across infrastructures. Using MPI it is thus possible to execute different threads and/or processes in different environments and nonetheless communicate with each other, as long as all involved systems share information about the thread IDs. Since MPI promotes a specification and therefore a general strategy rather than an explicit execution model or framework, it could be easily integrated into existing programming models and compiler models.

MPI provides all the essential capabilities needed to deal with large-scale and heterogeneous infrastructure. However, its efficiency depends almost completely on the capabilities of the developer. Furthermore, MPI was developed for multiprocessor systems with an explicit communication framework between these units – in other words, MPI does not cater for indirect communication or shared memory systems. Most modern multicore processors however build on some form of hardware-based cache coherency (ccNUMA) for which MPI is not suitable or at least generates unnecessary overhead. Even though future many-core systems will most likely not share memory across all processing units, we must nonetheless assume that at least some cores will share memory across or at least grant remote access to this memory [8].

---

[3]See http://www.mpi-forum.org/.

As opposed to real distributed systems, where each processing unit/node contains its own full environment, machines in which multiple units share a common memory – either physically or through a hardware-based protocol – are comparatively easy to program for. This is simply due to the fact that the developer does not explicitly have to cater for sharing and distributing state-related data but instead can assume 'global' state across all threads so that all processes can handle the data as if local. The simplest example to parallelizing work in a shared-memory environment therefore consists in loop unrollments where the individual iterations of a loop are executed in parallel. Notably, the loops may not have any dependencies across iterations, that is, no access to previous values $n[i] = f(n[i-1])$ as this will cause conflicts if $n[i]$, $n[i+1]$, ... $n[i+j]$ are calculated in parallel. The **Open Multi-Processing**[4] (OpenMP) API is the classical programming extension to develop such shared-memory applications.

However, OpenMP does not cater for heterogeneous architectures as they actually may arise in future multicore systems, even if it is not necessarily to be expected that cores of different types will not directly share cache or memory. As different cores will have different execution performance with respect to the same tasks, even in a straightforward work segmentation, such as in the aforementioned loop unrollment, the individual processes may deviate, leading to similar locking and read–write issues as in the thread-based case.

As noted, future processors will not solely rely on shared- or cache-coherent memory architectures, as these approaches do not scale to the degree needed and cause performance loss due to the maintenance overhead. Instead, the microarchitecture will have to rely on combined models of shared-memory tiles connected with other tiles over a network-on-chip communication infrastructure – in principle very similar to modern days' cluster architectures that effectively integrate a large amount of processors with multi-cores in a high-performance network environment. Accordingly, most modern day HPC developers already employ a mixture of OpenMP and MPI programming models to realize large-scale applications that scale across the heterogeneous hierarchical infrastructure.

Obviously, this makes usage just more complicated for the average developer. What is more, the heterogeneity of future systems is expected to increase even beyond the point where it can still be handled with this approach.

11.2.2   Implicit Communication

Rather than having the user/developer deal directly with the specifics of the hardware, most modern programming models approach the problem by abstracting the system and having the middleware and the compiler deal with the actual architectural details: for example, the **partitioned global address space**[5] (PGAS) model builds on the simplicity of programming shared-memory machines and therefore exposes capabilities of (virtually) shared-memory spaces that the API converts into message

---

[4]http://openmp.org/wp/.
[5]http://www.pgas-forum.org/.

calls or actual shared-memory usage, basing on the specifics of the architecture. However, this requires that the according infrastructure information is provided to the compiler – as we will discuss later, this is currently not generally possible, and compilers will instead base on generic assumptions about the infrastructure characteristics.

Even though the PGAS approach has the big advantage of being comparatively easy to use, in particular for more skilled developers, most actual implementations of PGAS still suffer from performance issues. This is due to the fact that the compiler effectively still converts the shared-memory access requests into a set of message-based transactions, disregarding the infrastructure. As noted, currently hardware descriptions are not used for the purposes of steering compilation though. Without this, even the PGAS model cannot avoid running into similar problems as the OpenMP and MPI combined approach, that is, the inability to handle the large scope of heterogeneity we are about to face in day-to-day development.

It should not be disregarded thereby that even shared-memory programming is still too complicated for many developers and in particular is not applicable to all development and use cases. In fact, most applications do not even execute complex algorithms that would benefit from the shared-memory approach a require complete rethinking on the developer's side. Accordingly, many manufactures pursue a more user-centric approach which essentially tries to take over parallelization tasks for the developer. However, optimal parallelization actually belongs to the class of NP complete problems [3] so that the 'automagic' parallelization can (and should) not be expected. On the other hand, suboptimal parallelization still can improve performance of common code and thus provide an acceptable solution for the average developer.

11.2.3 Automated Parallelization

The main goal of modern programming models consists in simplifying usage of the increasingly complex modern infrastructures – in particular in order to overcome the problems of scale and heterogeneity. As it cannot be expected that developers deal with all types of future infrastructures by themselves, the programming model has to abstract from the hardware and still make best use of it in terms of performance – most current approaches thereby base on some form of virtualization technique in order to hide the infrastructure complexity.

The general principle behind these approaches consists in identifying algorithmic patterns which indicate parallelizable functions, such as loops, queries, etc. Similarly, some libraries offer functionalities which are implemented in a parallel fashion, thereby replacing the sequential implementation as provided by the standard extensions. The latter approach is particularly popular for mathematical libraries in HPC environments. The main problem with both approaches however consists in potential errors introduced through parallelizing an otherwise sequential invocation, for example, by neglecting time-dependent read–write operation on a specific memory space. To reduce this problem, almost all models require the developer to provide additional information or, more frequently, to explicitly invoke parallel versions of the according functionalities, such as 'Parallel.For'. The parallel .NET extensions, for example, provide a series of parallel database queries and functions as part of the LINQ instruction set.

This approach essentially leaves all performance-related decisions to the developer, that is, whether to use a parallel or sequential implementation of a specific functionality. Inexperienced developers will, for example, often select a parallel loop even for simple computational tasks, thus creating overhead for thread instantiation, distribution and communication that reduces performances below the pure sequential execution. In large-scale systems, such a degradation of performance can easily arise due to the high communication overhead introduced by wide distributions of code. What is more, due to the nature of this approach, only specific parts of the code can be parallelized in the first instance, leaving many parts of the code sequential. The performance gain therefore strongly depends on the type of algorithms to be executed and the expertise of the developer.

11.3   CONCURRENT CODE

The keyword for further parallelization, in particular of common work tasks that do not adhere to the typical parallel patterns mentioned earlier, is therefore 'concurrency'. It also determines whether a loop or a pattern can be effectively executed in parallel in the first instance.

Concurrency in this specific context reflects the dependencies of a given code segment or function on other functions or parts of the code. The higher the degree of concurrency, that is, the less dependencies exist, the more effective is its parallel execution and the less likely delays occur due to synchronization overhead. In the ideal case, such as in embarrassingly parallel tasks, the concurrency reaches a maximum that implies that there are virtually no dependencies between the processes.

Obviously, a high degree of concurrency does not necessarily imply that the according segment can be executed in full parallel. A single shared variable can stall the full execution, if the seemingly concurrent code has to wait for the first thread to finish its calculation before the variable is free for access. At the same time, this obviously depends on the read–write order of the respective segments. Accordingly, and as discussed in more detail later, it is difficult to automatically identify concurrency in a given code efficiently. More realistic approaches, such as the **Star Superscalar** programming model, [7] therefore require the developer to explicitly annotate data dependencies across their code and functions. This information can then be exploited by the compiler to generate a dependency graph which provides implicit information about the execution order and potential points for parallelization and task distribution.

Star Superscalar is thereby still very coarse granular and expects specific function calls to exhibit concurrency rather than, for example, direct workload in a loop. It furthermore does not assess the execution speed of individual function blocks so that resources may not be used to their full optimum – nonetheless the model provides an easy method to increase the overall execution performance.

Essentially, even classical parallelization measurements base on the principle of maximizing concurrency between threads, so as to minimize dependencies and thus communication and synchronization overhead. Concurrency identification can therefore be regarded as the key factor in (semi-)automated parallelization and in addressing the requirements for future programming models. As indicated, however, concurrency cannot be reliably identified automatically.

11.3.1 Concurrency Analysis and Exploitation

There is an extensive literature on automated parallelization which deals with multiple aspects of concurrency analysis in order to identify dependencies. In general, the stronger such a dependency, the less parallelizable the according function. However this furthermore depends on the sequence of read–write statements in the code and on frequency of such occurrences. As a rule of thumb, the gain achieved through the concurrent execution must be higher than the loss introduced this way. While this may sound trivial, it has multiple implications.

The major performance loss occurs by latency introduced through any delays – the most obvious are (i) waiting for data to become available and (ii) passing it to the respective thread and returning results. Similarly, additional delay arises through access to shared-memory spaces. Less obvious however is the fact that many implicit operations will cause additional delays – this ranges from the overhead for creating the thread to executing system calls. In the first case, additional operations need to be executed in order to perform a seemingly simple task – this however involves a high degree of additional message passing. In the latter case, the major reason for delay is not so much the communication overhead but the fact that in all setups limited resources exist. This includes not only exclusive devices (such as hard drive or keyboard) but also the operating system – most modern OS architectures are monolithic and hence centralistic in nature (see e.g. [4]). System calls will build up with the increasing number of threads, and processes being executed concurrently, thus affecting the scalability of the operating system drastically.

A particularly relevant limited resource is the underlying network itself: not only does it introduce physical limitations in term of bandwidth and latency, but also more importantly, it will also be used by multiple processes at the same time, thus leading to further reduction of the bandwidth and implicitly to further delays. ccNUMA architectures particularly suffer from this reduction of bandwidth introduced by the consistency maintenance tasks of the cache coherency protocol. In other words, concurrency analysis must respect the dependencies not only within the code but also across the infrastructure, and in order to achieve efficient execution, this system information must be fed back to the mechanisms for thread distribution and instantiation.

The most general approach to identifying concurrency in a given code consists in analyzing variable usage throughout the code logic and all its invocations. If two segments share a parameter, they become codependent according to the type of actions executed on the variable (i.e. read or write actions). The main problems consist obviously in reassigning the same variable name in different contexts and in passing the content to other variables. Similarly, we need to distinguish between global and local usage scope, as well as between references and copied instances.

Most strategies focus less on individual variables, as their impact is comparatively low, rather than larger data or address spaces, that is, memory ranges. In most programs, they are represented as arrays over which the algorithm acts. Arrays and in particular indexes of arrays are thus the primary interest of most concurrency analysis mechanism. The principle itself is straightforward: depending on the access pattern and in particular the index relationships across iterations; specific parallelization techniques can be employed. For example:

- No dependencies:
  S: $A(i) = A(i) + C(i)$
  T: $B(i) = B(i) - C(i)$

- True dependency (same iteration):
  S: $A(i) = A(i) + C(i)$
  T: $B(i) = B(i) - C(i) + A(i)$

- True dependency (with previous iteration):
  S: $A(i) = A(i) + C(i)$
  T: $B(i) = B(i) - C(i) + A(i - d)$

- Antidependence (WAR):
  S: $A(i) = A(i) + C(i) - B(i)$
  T: $B(i) = B(i) + C(i)$

- Antidependence (WAR) (with increased index):
  S: $A(i) = A(i) + C(i)$
  T: $B(i) = B(i) - C(i) + A(i + d)$

Obviously this approach concentrates on concurrency in loops rather than general occurrences of concurrent segments. The principle nonetheless may also be applied across different logical segments, given that the parameters, that is, the array, in question can be uniquely identified.

This **source code level analysis** however neglects two crucial aspects: (i) most code behavior depends on the data, that is, the concurrency may alter given a specific data set, and (ii) the execution speed and actual memory usage of the code cannot be assessed correctly so that potential synchronization issues cannot be detected, unless the concurrent segments are essentially uniform, as is the case in loop unrollment.

What is more, the analysis is generally restricted to the source code at hand, leaving aside aspects of implicit dependencies that arise, for example, from system calls, resource access and similar.

In other words, the approach is comparatively restrictive in comparison to the techniques and means applied by expert parallel developers. Accordingly, there is

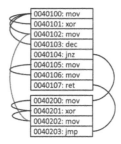

Figure 11.1   A dependency graph derived from code behavior analysis. Edges on the left denote dataflow and on the right workflow (simplified).

no guarantee for improved execution performance following this approach, even if resources are generally exploited better (Fig. 11.1).

An alternative to source code level analysis consists in monitoring the actual execution behavior of a program on **machine code level**. The Service-oriented Operating Systems project[6] (S(o)OS) promotes this approach to gain more fine-granulated data-specific information about not only the actual dataflow but also the workflow of the code. The (runtime) behavior provides additional information about the actual connectivity between the individual segments and thus its require-ments toward the communication model, that is, the relationship of latency versus bandwidth.

Implicitly, runtime behavior effectively provides more information about the potential code distribution than the programmer can currently encode in the source code. This is simply due to the fact that this is not in-line with our current way of writing programs and is implicitly not directly supported by programming models. The foundation is however laid out by integration of remote processes (web services) and dedicated synchronization points in parallel processes, and this does not always reflect the best distribution though, as the according invocations are mainly functionality – rather than communication driven.

By integrating a memory monitor into the kernel, the operating system can acquire information about the memory access behavior of the full scope of the code, that is, including jumps, data access and, interestingly, system calls. Like in the source code model, the system can use this information to generate a dependency graph, not unlike the one generated in Star Superscalar (see previous text). Accordingly, the information can be used in a similar fashion by analyzing this dependency graph with respect to the concurrent segments and potential parallel execution.

Due to the nature of runtime code analysis, however, the dependency information is much more fine granulated, leaving little room for 'obvious' concurrency. Instead, the graph has to incorporate additional information that, for example,

[6]http://www.soos-project.eu.

the Star Superscalar model and the source code level analysis do not consider, in particular:

- Access frequency (of invocations or read/write actions)

- Type of action (jump, read, write)

- Access order in time

- Size of the code/data accessed

With this information, we can derive a graph where the strength of the relationship and the size of the underlying code/data is encoded as weights (or distances) of vertices and edges. The dependency information in this graph can be used to extract different segments in the form of subgraphs according to nearness (connection strength) and combined size, in other words, according to the number of memory accesses with fewer accesses implying a potentially good cutting point. Segmenting the graph is thereby similar to the problem of identifying the maximum flow in a flow network and thus the max-flow min-cut theorem which is often also applied for segmentation purposes in image analysis (see e.g. [5]). The minimum cut in our case therefore reflects the segments that share the least dependencies. This means that the created segments can principally be distributed over multicores, if the timing dependencies (i.e. synchronization delays) between the individual functions are respected (Fig. 11.2).

Figure 11.2   Potential segmentation of the reduced graph (simplified).

Dependent segments thereby can nonetheless still be executed in parallel if the according communication and synchronization means are provided, as discussed earlier. The maximum execution speedup through this form of parallelization is thereby directly related to the maximum degree of execution overlap that can be achieved without affecting consistency of the program. The overlap should thereby be ideally identical to the maximum delay created by communication.

What is more, by applying similar pattern analysis approaches as in the source code analysis, potential points for parallelization rather than just concurrent execution can be identified. As such, it can be, for example, shown that the graph of an antidependence loop iterates across memory in line with the index and that the cross dependency between S and T is depicted by a read access prior to a write access on the same memory space so that both S and T can execute in full parallel by overwriting memory (for B) from S with data from T after execution or by first executing S in full parallel before unrolling T.

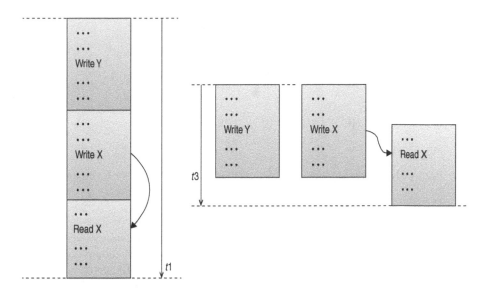

Figure 11.3   Code to infrastructure mapping principles.

While the benefits of this approach are obvious, the method nonetheless suffers from two strongly related issues: as the code behavior may be impacted by the environmental conditions, ranging from dynamic sources (such as a keyboard) to data-specific behavior (e.g. reacting to specific occurrences in a data stream), the actual dependencies may alter over time. Accordingly, the segmentation at a given point in execution may not be static itself but subject to changes over execution time (Fig. 11.3).

11.3.2   Mapping and Adaptation

It was already mentioned in the beginning of this chapter how the architecture of future processors is going to change and deviate drastically from today's more or less homogeneous and uniform setups. Already setups such as Intel's Many Integrated Core[7] (MIC) architecture clearly show the tendency toward nonuniform connectivity between processing units, that is, network-on-chip connections between cores. Texas Instrument and IBM on the other hand show how future processors will integrate various processing types in a single chip.

Accordingly, it will become more than ever important to respect the actual hardware specifics for parallel code distribution. In particular, this relates to the following main criteria (Fig. 11.4):

- Cache size
- Connectivity (bandwidth and latency)
- ISA/capabilities

---

[7]http://www.intel.com/technology/architecture-silicon/mic/index.htm.

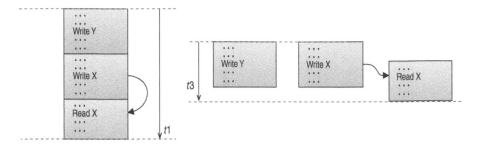

Figure 11.4   Rearrangement of concurrent logical segments for maximum speedup.

These criteria specify how individual code segments should be deployed relative to one another within a single processor so as to reduce unnecessary overhead and exploit the given specifics to their most. For example, many applications contain logical parts that can be easily vectorized or at least executed efficiently on a single instruction, multiple data (SIMD) unit, such as stream processing tasks. If such a unit is available in the processing infrastructure, it should therefore ideally be exploited for the according logic. Similarly, two threads communicating frequently should be placed next to each other in a network-on-chip structure, so as to exploit the communication linkage between the two rather than far apart with multiple concurring threads in between which will lower the bandwidth and increase latency.

The according information for exploiting code specifics can be easily derived from the code analysis as described earlier. For example, the best communication layout relates directly to the connectivity weight between code segments in the behavior graph. Mapping this relationship information to the network layout is obviously an NP complete tasks, yet classical graph matching strategies can be applied to this problem (see e.g. [9]).

More problems however are posed by the specific capabilities of a given processing unit: in order to fully exploit (and to cope with) the heterogeneity of the infrastructure, compiler and ideally execution manager (such as the operating system) of the respective code should be capable of identifying, interpreting and using the hardware-specific characteristics. In the example provided earlier, this would mean that the SIMD core is retrieved and the specific criteria and capabilities toward the code are identified. It would furthermore mean that the infrastructure uses this information to prepare the code accordingly.

As long as the processing units in question adhere to the same instruction set architecture (ISA), conversion (in the sense of potential rearrangement of code) can be easily adhered to. It must be expected however that future models will not even maintain compliant ISAs anymore – accordingly, a porting request of a specific code segment to a noncompliant unit will implicitly require conversion of the underlying ISA. Obviously, this is easily achieved at source code level by providing the according compiler directives – on machine code level, this however is nearly impossible without major loss of efficiency. Implicitly, the information gained from machine code monitoring can only be indirectly be exploited, by feeding it back to the source code level and hence the compiler.

What is more, however, is that no current hardware description method allows to identify capabilities in the required fashion. The most widely used description language for hardware – the Very High Speed Integrated Circuit Hardware Description Language[8] (VHDL) – is too detailed to allow such information extraction and is furthermore too complicated for easy adaptation to the arising scope of new infrastructures. Baaij et al. therefore promote a hardware description language basing on functional declarations that would allow more abstract queries over the structure so as to derive capability information, such as processor type (cf. [2]).

11.4 CONCLUSIONS

The advances in heterogeneous multicore systems has taken the software industry and the programming language community essentially unprepared. Already the advances made on hardware level progress faster than the ones on software and programming level so that by now processor architectures start to offer more capabilities than a developer can sensibly exploit. Within this chapter we have highlighted which specific obstacles hinder the developer from making use of such new systems and which specific obstacles are yet to overcome in order to enable the broad scope of developers that will have to make use of these systems in the near future.

A promising approach thereby consists in exploitation of concurrency rather than 'automagic' parallelization which can only lead to very suboptimal solutions. Concurrency can be analyzed on multiple code levels, thus providing information of different granularity – however, all approaches so far still base on the programmer providing the according dependency information. So far this information cannot even be properly validated against the code, thus making it error prone.

What makes the exploitation of concurrency so specifically interesting in this context is not only its ability to support the developer though. Even more important is the capability that proper exploitation of concurrency can further reduce the limitations posed by Amdahl's law: next to the classical means of parallelization (segmentation of work or data), it can also affect the 'unparallelizable' part of the code, that is, which is denoted as 'sequential part' in Amdahl's law. This is achieved by executing multiple sequential logical parts at the same time rather than parallelizing the respective code itself. Due to the nature of this type of parallelization, however, the scalability is restricted not only by the number of available processing units but also by the number of concurrent segments that can be identified. In other words, if only 10 concurrent segments can be identified, the maximum theoretically possible speedup is 10 – even if more processing units are available.

Not only the high degree of scalability will pose issues to future programming models but also in particular the large variance of processor architectures with increasing deviations even on the ISA level. So far, the developer must be well aware

[8]http://www.vhdl-online.de/.

of these differences in order to give according compiler instructions. To enable compilers or even the execution infrastructure to automatically detect and exploit the hardware specifics, new description languages are needed that can expose the respective unit's characteristics and capabilities in a fashion that can be interpreted according to the infrastructure's needs. Functional languages thereby show high promise, as they are more intuitive and flexible than traditional models and enable abstract queries from which additional information about the specifics can be derived.

REFERENCES

1. G. Amdahl. Validity of the single processor approach to achieving large-scale computing capabilities. *In AFIPS Conference Proceedings*, volume 30, pages 483-485, 1967.

2. C. P. R. Baaij, M. Kooijman, J. Kuper, W. A. Boeijink, and M. E. T. Gerards. CÎżash: structural descriptions of synchronous hardware using haskell. In *Proceedings of the 13th EUROMICRO Conference on Digital System Design: Architectures, Methods and Tools, 1-3 Sep 2010, Lille, France.*, pages 714–721. IEEE Computer Society, 2010.

3. C. Backstrom. Finding least constrained plans and optimal parallel executions is harder than we thought. In *Proceedings of the 2nd European Workshop on Planning*, 1994.

4. A. Baumann, P. Barham, P.-E. Dagand, T. Harris, R. Isaacs, S. Peter, T. Roscoe, A. SchÃijpbach, and A. Singhania. The multi-kernel: a new os architecture for scalable multicore systems. In *SOSP*, 2009.

5. Y. Boykov and G. Funka-Lea. Graph cuts and efficient n-d image segmentation. *International Journal of Computer Vision*, 70:109–131, 2006. 10.1007/s11263-006-7934-5.

6. IEEE Standard for Information Technology. Portable operating system interface (posix). Technical report, IEEE Std 1003, 2004.

7. J. M. Perez, R. M. Badia, and J. Labarta. A dependency-aware task-based programming environment for multi-core architectures. In *Proceedings of the 2008 IEEE International Conference on Cluster Computing*, pages 142–151, 2008.

8. F. Petrot, A. Greiner, and P. Gomez. On cache coherency and memory consistency issues in noc based shared memory multiprocessor soc architectures. In *Proceedings of the 9th EUROMICRO Conference on Digital System Design*. IEEE Computer Society, 2006.

9. D. B. West. *Introduction to Graph Theory*. Prentice Hall, second edition, 1999.

PART III

PROGRAMMING FRAMEWORKS

CHAPTER 12

PEPPHER: PERFORMANCE PORTABILITY AND PROGRAMMABILITY FOR HETEROGENEOUS MANY-CORE ARCHITECTURES

SIEGFRIED BENKNER, SABRI PLLANA, JESPER LARSSON TRÄFF,
PHILIPPAS TSIGAS, ANDREW RICHARDS, GEORGE RUSSELL,
SAMUEL THIBAULT, CDRIC AUGONNET, RAYMOND NAMYST,
HERBERT CORNELIUS, CHRISTOPH KELER, DAVID MOLONEY AND
PETER SANDERS

PEPPHER takes a pluralistic and parallelization agnostic approach to programmability and performance portability for heterogeneous many-core architectures. The project develops *methodology*, *framework* and *guidelines* for constructing software (including paths to migration of existing, parallel software) that can be ported between different, possibly in themselves, heterogeneous many-core systems under preservation of specific quantitative and qualitative performance aspects.

PEPPHER introduces a flexible and extensible compositional metalanguage for expressing functional and nonfunctional properties of software components, their resource requirements and possible compilation targets, as well as providing abstract specifications of properties of the underlying hardware. This enables the PEPPHER framework to compile variants of the software components and direct the supporting, adaptive libraries. It furthermore provides handles for the PEPPHER run-time system to schedule the components well on the available hardware resources. Performance predictions can be (automatically) derived by combining the supplied performance models. Performance portability is aided by guidelines and requirements to ensure

Programming Multicore and Many-core Computing Systems,
First Edition. Edited by Sabri Pllana and Fatos Xhafa.
© 2017 John Wiley & Sons, Inc. Published 2017 by John Wiley & Sons, Inc.

that the PEPPHER framework at all levels chooses the best implementation of a given component or library routine among the available variants, including settings for tunable parameters, prescheduling decisions and data movement operations.

12.1   INTRODUCTION AND BACKGROUND

With the proliferation of multi-/many-core architectures,[1] as the design space for efficient and programmable parallel processors is being explored, application portability is evidently one of the major challenges facing the software industry. To address the problem, which is intimately linked to the problem of multicore programmability in general, several (new) factors have to be taken into account:

- Many-core architectures are parallel architectures that need to be programmed as such. Even within the same architecture class, key characteristics can be different from one instance to the next, for example, number of cores, size of caches and structure of memory system. Manageable and efficient parallel programming model, adequate compiler support and adaptive support libraries that can statically or dynamically adjust to the concrete architecture characteristics are some of the means to cope with these factors.

- The spectrum of multicore architectures is large, spanning general- and special-purpose processors, shared or distributed memory architectures and MIMD to SIMD, each of which call for their own programming model, language, methodology and library support. An abstract model covering even a part of this spectrum and allowing for efficient compilation to such different target architectures may not be feasible or even desirable.

- Heterogeneous multicore architectures consisting of cores of such different architecture types are already prominent in many application domains where extreme performance and/or low-power consumption for dedicated subtasks is called for. For general-purpose computing, striving to exploit the potential of heterogeneous multicore designs, difficult load balancing, scheduling and memory management problems arise.

- Efficiency criteria are changing from pure concerns with processor utilization, scalability and throughput, towards best overall, most *power-efficient* utilization of available resources.

A few examples substantially illustrate these observations: Intel's Larrabee (cache-coherent, shared-memory, homogeneous general-purpose many-core) [30] and SCC (homogeneous, general purpose, many-core for on-chip message-passing, CPU power domains) [19] architectures; Tilera's embedded, mesh-connected many cores [7]; Sun's Niagara processors (homogeneous, simultaneous multi-threading) [22]; the IBM/Sony/Toshiba Cell processor (general-purpose, heterogeneous, local memory cacheless multicore) [21]; NVIDIA Tesla/Fermi and AMD ATI

---

[1] The terms multi- and many-core are used interchangeably.

(special-purpose, highly parallel, idiosyncratic processors with general-purpose processing appeal); and ClearSpeed CSX700 (special-purpose numerical accelerator). Also in the embedded space, heterogeneous multicore processors are prevalent, for example, Texas Instruments' OMAP ARM/DSP, Qualcomm's Snapdragon ARM/DSP and Movidius SABRE RISC/VLIW multimedia coprocessor. See Ref. [8] for an extended overview.

We expect that this architectural diversity will prevail, for better or for worse, for the coming years. There is therefore an acute need to develop means to port code developed for one type of parallel multicore architecture as seamlessly as possible to any or another type of architecture and especially to understand how performance characteristics are affected in this process. The latter is captured in the vague concept of *performance portability*. Performance portability could mean that ways of characterizing and translating performance aspects of algorithms and code between different architectures are provided. This *descriptive* approach can take the form of traditional performance models but could also include higher level, more qualitative properties of implementations and their inputs. On the other hand, a *prescriptive* approach to performance portability would pose requirements to applications, language and library implementations and the run-time that would guarantee that certain performance aspects are preserved when porting code between different architectures. Such requirements would be partly fulfilled by calibration and algorithmic autotuning in a setup phase. The prescriptive approach aims to ensure a 'best possible' performance of any supported architecture relative to the available basic libraries and run-time.

Rather than suggesting a uniform programming model and rely on compiler, library and run-time support to ensure portability and performance, PEPPHER takes a pluralistic approach to the programmability and performance portability challenges. Many-core applications are viewed as collections of components [34] that can be be written in different styles for different target architectures, with explicit or implicit dependencies. Performance and other properties of components are expressed using PEPPHER's flexible and extensible annotation metalanguage and are used to guide both the compilation process and the run-time responsible for scheduling the compiled components to the available resources according to given performance requirements. The richer the set of components and the more informative the annotations, the better the quality of the code that can be generated (including code variants for different types of architectures) and the better the scheduling decisions that can be made. In the following we outline this approach in more detail.

12.1.1 Related Work

A large number of projects are currently concerned with aspects of multicore programmability as mentioned earlier. In contrast to many of these (e.g. HyVM, SARC, AppleCore), PEPPHER is not focusing on providing a common programming model or portability layer. Instead the application programmer provides performance information by annotating components and describing characteristics of the actual environment/architecture. Likewise PEPPHER is not concerned with automatic parallelization per se. PEPPHER will extend work on algorithmic autotuning by considering algorithms' libraries for different types of architectures.

The overall project goals are somewhat similar to those of the Merge project, although this project was focused on using MapReduce [12] as the programming model [25, 37].

A related, ambitious autotuning project is PetaBricks [1], which by autotuning provides (performance) portability across different, mainly homogeneous, parallel architectures. In contrast, PEPPHER aims to support also heterogeneous architectures with different parallelization models, which requires run-time support in addition to what can be achieved by algorithmic autotuning.

A longrunning effort in adaptive algorithm selection is STAPL [35, 39]. An interesting aspect of STAPL is that algorithms and implementations are classified by more qualitative properties that can be matched at run-time against similar properties of the input to select the best performing implementation variant [39] and is thus not relying on a traditional, input-oblivious performance models.

12.2 THE PEPPHER FRAMEWORK

The PEPPHER framework consists of three main parts:

- A flexible and extensible composition metalanguage for describing performance and other (functional and nonfunctional) properties of components. By a *component* we mean an implementation of a specific algorithmic solution for a well-defined functionality. Components may be parameterized with tunable parameters such as blocking factors or buffer sizes, allowing multiple component variants to be generated from the same (generic) component, even for the same target architecture.

- Adaptive algorithm libraries that implement the same basic functionality [26, 31, 32] across different architectures. Autotuning techniques are used at PEPPHER installation and calibration time and even dynamically to generate the best possible library for each target architecture.

- An efficient run-time that schedules compiled component variants (so-called *codelets*) across the available resources, using performance information provided by the components layer as well as other execution history-based performance information.

The challenge of the project is to make these linguistic, algorithmic and run-time elements fit together to provide for efficient portability across a variety of typical heterogeneous and homogeneous multicore architectures. The PEPPHER framework is sketched in Figure 12.1.

A new or existing application is described as a collection of components with either implicit (program order) or explicit interactions and dependencies. This purely functional interface is extended in PEPPHER by metadata (annotations) to capture important nonfunctional component properties (e.g. information and qualitative

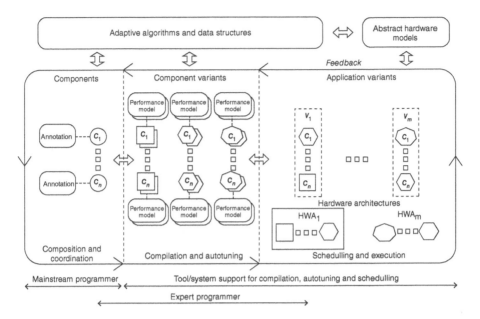

Figure 12.1   The PEPPHER framework for creating performance portable software across a variety of heterogeneous many-core systems. The application is described as a set of (generic) components with annotations specifying performance and other nonfunctional properties (left). A set of component variants is generated (e.g. by source-to-source transformation) or chosen (from expert-written libraries) for different architectures and configurations (middle). For each concrete, heterogeneous architecture, appropriate component variants are selected and compiled into codelets that are scheduled efficiently at run-time (right) using static and dynamic performance information. Performance models are derived from abstract hardware descriptions and component annotations.

descriptions of input and output data distribution) and may be coupled with a parameterized performance model. The annotation framework is extensible, and absence of information is handled by default rules (sequential composition, no specialization, no performance information for the run-time system). For each component C_i different variants $C_i', C_i'', C_i''', \ldots$ tailored for specific architectures (general-purpose cores, different types of specialized accelerator cores) and environments (number of cores, memory system) and/or specialized for specific input data are compiled automatically, guided by the supplied metainformation. Functionally equivalent but algorithmically different, variants C_i'''' can in addition be provided by the expert programmer.

Components will typically make use of expert-written libraries of algorithms and data structures that at configuration time (but also dynamically) are adapted to the given set of target architectures. The component metadata that is usually not available in conventional component frameworks allows for automatic generation of dispatch code that at run-time selects the most appropriate compiled component.

The automatic generation of such executables is guided by performance models, meta-data information on application input and dynamic feedback from hardware captured during execution, and the resulting *codelets* contain this information in a form that can be used by the PEPPHER run-time system. Components can implement parallel algorithms and be expressed with any convenient parallelization model/interface, for example, OpenMP, native threads, Threading Building Blocks, Cilk, Ct, a message-passing framework, OpenCL or other. Obviously, the chosen framework may make a given component instance unsuitable for some target architectures and would limit portability. A reasonable completeness requirement to parallel PEPPHER components is therefore that a sequential variant can always be generated, either by enabling execution on a single core or providing explicitly a functionally equivalent sequential component. Parallelism in the PEPPHER framework arises from parallel (malleable) components, independent components that may be scheduled simultaneously (perhaps on different resources) and parallel libraries, for example, parallel STL [32]. At the user level, PEPPHER is in this sense substrate agnostic.

As described the PEPPHER framework provides a path for gradually paralleliz-ing legacy C++ codes (use of components, annotation, automatic code generation) and making such codes (performance) portable to completely unforeseen classes of new architectures. Components and application code are compiled to a set of sup-ported target architectures $HWA_1, \ldots, HWA_m$, for instance, by compiling to OpenCL that is likely to be supported by a large set of (somewhat similar) architectures. Compilation to other low-level substrates is also possible, though. The amount of performance portability between the supported architectures depends on the qual-ity of the decision/glue code binding the components together and the quality of the compilation process. However, for very different architectures where different algorithmic approaches are needed, additional support is required. This is provided by a set of basic algorithms and data structures, as used widely in high-level appli-cation development [26, 31]. Application portability is enhanced by relying exten-sively on standard library algorithms, and performance portability can therefore be gradually improved by enhancements (some of which can be automatic) to the algo-rithms' layer. Finally, the PEPPHER run-time is responsible for choosing among the possible codelets at execution time for the most efficient execution at the avail-able cores under the given load of the multicore processor. Orchestration of data transfers between different memory systems is required and also handled by the PEPPHER run-time. The run-time relies on synchronization mechanisms and data structures suitable to the supported target architectures. To support new architec-tures that may emerge in coming years, the algorithms and run-time layers of PEP-PHER have to be likewise augmented. This is done gradually following the PEPPHER methodology.

The PEPPHER framework is in principle language independent but focuses on supporting C++ code with PEPPHER-specific annotations as pragmas or external annotations. The framework is open and extensible; the PEPPHER methodology details how new architectures are incorporated.

```
1        template<typename T>
2        PEPPHER_interface Sorting {
3              void sort (inout T *a,
4              in problemsize unsigned int n);
5        }
```

Figure 12.2   Generic PEPPHER component interface for a sorting component.

12.2.1   An Example of Component-Based PEPPHER Programming

As an initial example of the PEPPHER framework in action, we consider sorting. The functionality is declared in a generic PEPPHER interface Sorting as shown in Figure 12.2 and can be implemented by different components each realizing a particular sequential or parallel sorting algorithm. Components adhering to the interface in question are considered functionally equivalent and have the same input/output behavior. For clarity we have here used pseudocode and assumed convenient language extensions for C++. The final PEPPHER framework strives for a more nonintrusive style to better facilitate migration of legacy code.

As shown in Figure 12.2, an interface declaration can contain information on what is considered a problem size, which is important for building performance models for the different components.

The optimization goal is chosen at component deployment time. Here we simply assume an optimization for expected execution time (time), but other objectives are possible and relevant, for example, energy. Furthermore, time is an appropriate measure only if execution resources, especially processor cores, are managed explicitly at user level, as is the case in many SPMD programming frameworks [28, 29]. If this is not the case, PEPPHER delegates resource management to the run-time system, in which case total work may be a more suitable objective. Sorting components can announce their expected time behavior by a prediction function time_sort with the same parameters as sort and additional parameters for resource usage such as the number of cores p to be used on, for instance, a homogeneous, NUMA multicore architectures; see Figure 12.3. If no such prediction function is given, PEPPHER uses a default function.

A specialized sorting component for GPU architectures, for example [9], also implementing the component interface, is finally shown in Figure 12.4. Such specialized components that cannot be derived automatically from the base component implementations are likely to be contributed by expert programmers.

By adding metainformation about target machine usage, the component becomes *resource aware*. By adding metacode for microbenchmarking code segments on the target machine (not shown here) and for time prediction (the time function), the component becomes *performance aware* [15, 29]. In this sorting example there are no tunable component parameters; more complex components would typically have such parameters.

```
1  template <typename T>
2  PEPPHER_component ParMS implements Sorting<T>
3  requires Merging<T> uses HOM, NUMA
4  // uses/requires homogeneous NUMA architecture
5  // not applicable e.g. to GPU since
6  // implementation is recursive
7  {
8  void sort (T *a, unsigned int n)
9  {  ...  // many details omitted
10 @PEPPHER_taskgraph {
11 // composition point: pre-scheduling/resource pre-allocation
12 @PEPPHER_task (T1, Sorting<T>, sort (a, n/2));
13 @PEPPHER_task (T2, Sorting<T>, sort (a+n/2, n-n/2));
14 // no precedence constraints given - the tasks are independent
15 }
16 @PEPPHER_task (T3, Merging<T>, merge (a, n));
17 ...  // many details omitted
18 }
19
20 // The following code is used at deployment time:
21 float time_par1;  // some basic timing param. for time_sort
22 ...
23 void perf_calib (void) { ... } // Basic performance param.:
24 // time, energy comsumption, ...
25 // Time prediction function for ParMS<T>::sort:
26 float time_sort (unsigned int n, unsigned int p)
27 {  ...   // simplified
28 float tmrg = @PEPPHER_lookup(Merging<T>, merge(n, p));
29 float trec =
30 (p>1) ? @PEPPHER_lookup(Sorting<T>, sort(n/2, p/2))
31 : 2 * @PEPPHER_lookup(Sorting<T>, time_sort(n/2, 1));
32 return  time_par1 + tmrg + trec;
33 }
34 }
```

Figure 12.3 Implementation of a PEPPHER sorting component by a merge sort algorithm. The pseudocode notation with C++ language extensions used in this example is one of several possibilities considered for the PEPPHER annotation framework. Alternatives keep the annotations separate to the actual code.

```
1 template<typename T>
2 PEPPHER_component GPUsort implements Sorting<T>
3 uses GPU
4 { ... // host code with CUDA code encapsulated here,
5      details omitted.
6      // No further component calls inside
7      ... // perf_calib(), time_sort() etc. omitted
8 }
```

Figure 12.4 A specialized GPU sorting component.

A two-stage approach is adopted for performance prediction:

1. To keep the prediction cost at a moderate level and controlled by the component programmer, a hybrid approach is used for static performance prediction which allows to use microbenchmarking for calibrating parameters in the programmer-supplied prediction functions. Predictions are used in the deployment phase to initialize time and dispatch tables as described later.

2. At run-time table entries are refined with actually measured values and can thus automatically adapt to typical workload situations.

At deployment time the component variants are processed by the PEPPHER composition tool, which has access to (performance models of) the target machine. Nonapplicable components are automatically discarded. The composition tool first derives the dependence graph between the interfaces from the union of the implementing components' `requires` relations. All components implementing the same interface are processed together in reverse topological order. In the example in Figure 12.3, the `Merging` components must be processed before the `Sorting` components, etc. Microbenchmarking on the target machine to gather basic prediction parameters for a component, such as `time_par1` used in `ParMS<T>::time_sort`, is done before evaluating `time_sort` for the first time and is factored out into a separate `perf_calib` routine.

For each processed interface, the composition tool inspects all components and from interpreting their `time` functions builds (sparse) data structures that can be indexed by problem sizes and resources:

- A *time table*, for example, T_{sort}, that lists for selected call contexts consisting of a problem size (n) and resource configuration (p) the predicted expected execution time ($T_{sort}[n, p]$)

- A *dispatch table*, for example, V_{sort}, that lists for selected call contexts a reference to the expected fastest component

Finally, the composition tool patches the marked-up composition points in the component implementations (such as the *@PEPPHER_task* and *@PEP-PHER_taskgraph* constructs in Figure 12.3, lines 8–11) by dispatch code that at run-time uses the *V* table to call the expected fastest variant, as dispatch as outlined here is done by table lookup run-time overhead will be low.

The patched component code is processed further by native compilers for the target systems.

12.3   THE PEPPHER METHODOLOGY

The PEPPHER methodology consists of rules for how to extend the framework for new architectures. This mainly concerns adaptivity and autotuning for algorithm libraries, the necessary hooks and extensions for the run-time system and any supporting algorithms and data structures that this relies on. The methods for annotation and composition, automatic generation of glue code and so on as described earlier are also used when augmenting the supporting layers of the PEPPHER framework. To aid performance portability it is important that performance requirements and guidelines are followed. The methodology also gives rules and advice to the mainstream programmer for how to write new and port existing code to PEPPHER.

12.4   PERFORMANCE GUIDELINES AND PORTABILITY

One conception of performance portability is that no (high-level) application restructuring is necessary when porting code from one architecture to another [20]. This is of course untenable for radically different architectures where different algorithms are called for, but for algorithms that can be constructed from standardized library functionality, it is a reasonable approach to try to delegate the performance portability requirements to such libraries. Requirements, constraints and guidelines on building blocks are defined towards this goal.

Such (meta)requirements and guidelines would for instance prescribe that no building block (library component) can be improved just by expressing the same functionality by means of other related library components. This would also imply that the PEPPHER framework does the best possible selection among different available implementations of a library component, a highly nontrivial guarantee in a heterogeneous, dynamic setting which would relieve the user from the temptation to try and do better and write such selection code himself. Similar *monotonicity* metarules govern the use of annotations: the more (noncontradictory) information is provided, the better PEPPHER can do at all levels; providing more information must not worsen the resulting performance. If no information is provided for the components, the PEPPHER framework produces default code (that maybe only runs on a single processor). There is thus an incremental road to performance (portability). PEPPHER will explore in detail the formalization and implementation of such performance requirements, such that they could ideally be verified and enforced during the calibration phase for each new architecture. For more specific performance prediction, user and framework-supplied performance models can be automatically composed (when available) and possibly be verified against historical performance data gathered at run-time [27, 28].

12.5 FURTHER TECHNICAL ASPECTS

12.5.1 Compilation Techniques and Parallel Language Extensions

As shown in Section 12.2.1, a PEPPHER (sub-)component may benefit from the explicit use of specialized, nonportable code to provide an implementation for a specific platform. Such specialized components are typically provided (gradually) by expert programmers and further contribute to the overall performance portability of the given application.

Offloading is a specific technique for programming heterogeneous platforms that can sometimes be applied with high efficiency. Offload as developed by the PEPPHER partner Codeplay [10, 14] is a particular, nonintrusive C++ extension allowing portable C++ code to support diverse heterogeneous multicore architectures in a single code base. Compile-time techniques using automatic call-graph duplication and pointer-type inference allow compilation of portable, nonannotated code on heterogeneous multicore architectures with distinct memory spaces. The compiler generates routines appropriate for the used target processor and memory space combination. Essentially, offload blocks embedded in host code are compiled into kernels (e.g. OpenCL kernels) to run on accelerator processors. At run-time upon entering such a block, an instance of the corresponding kernel is created and subsequently invoked by the PEPPHER run-time facilitating its wealth of performance features, advanced scheduling strategies and supported hardware. The availability of the PEPPHER run-time for various platforms and the integration with the offload system enable the prompt adoption of portable programming models across a wide range of different heterogeneous processors.

Specialized components written explicitly using Offload C++ support a variety of parallel implementation strategies, from multithreading on shared-memory homogeneous multiprocessors to offloaded threads across accelerators in heterogeneous multiprocessors with private memory and execution on both accelerator and host cores. Sequential execution can also be supported, either on a host or accelerator core.

The run-time system may invoke and schedule appropriately compiled component implementations on various subsets of the available hardware resources, for example, single or multiple accelerators, accelerators and host processors combined or host CPUs alone.

12.5.2 Algorithmic Support

The PEPPHER framework is supported by algorithm libraries capturing essential, frequently used functionality. Libraries with standardized interfaces enhance code portability across different architectures and since typically developed by expert programmers can contribute significantly also towards *performance portability*. The parallel, multicore MCSTL library [32], for instance, contains parallel implementations where applicable of the C++ STL algorithms and data structures, tuned toward efficient execution on standard multicore architectures. MCSTL is part of the g++ system. This approach will be extended with autotuning techniques for improved automatic (static and dynamic) adoption to parameterized classes of multi-core architectures, which extends conventional work on autotuning for numerical kernels [16, 24, 38]. Complementing the example in Section 12.2.1, the first case study will be sorting [9, 23, 36].

Other essential types of algorithmic (library) support consist in lock-free algorithms and data structures for efficient concurrent interprocess synchronization, especially when generalized to different types of architectures [17, 18]. A rich library of fundamental nonblocking algorithms and data structures that can be used in the PEPPHER framework is NOBLE [33].

Further, essential algorithmic support for the PEPPHER framework consists in methods for efficient dispatch and online algorithm selection, construction of dispatch tables as outlined in Section 12.2.1 and efficient run-time scheduling strategies.

12.5.3 The PEPPHER Run-Time System

For exploiting the potential of hybrid systems consisting of general-purpose multi-core processors and special-purpose accelerators, offloading approaches alone will not suffice to utilize the available resources concurrently. Instead, application sub-tasks must be scheduled at run-time across the various resource. The PEPPHER run-time system which constitutes an essential part of the framework is based on the StarPU task-scheduling engine [3, 5], initially developed by the PEPPHER partner INRIA.

The compiled version of a PEPPHER component is a set of *codelets* which the run-time can dynamically assign as appropriate to the available compute units. In addition to performance estimations and other information generated from component annotations and static machine performance models, codelets contain explicit references to their input and output. This enables the scheduler to automatically fetch the input data of a task before execution. To minimize data transfers data are kept where last used, and multiple (read-only) copies on different memory systems are allowed. StarPU implements a relaxed consistency model with data replication capabilities.

The scheduler uses performance prediction models as provided by the compositional layer to estimate the completion time of each ready task over each computing unit. In addition to or absence of explicit component performance models, the run-time can attempt performance prediction based on codelet performance history. For some applications this has been shown to quickly achieve useful performance estimations when the granularity of codelets remains constant [4] and can sometimes even outperform *a priori* performance models.

We now use LU decomposition of dense matrices to illustrate how these techniques can exploit heterogeneous hardware efficiently. We consider a *blocked LU decomposition* with TRSM and GEMM BLAS3 kernels. Our experiments were performed on an E5410 quadcore 2.33 GHz Xeon with 4 GB of memory equipped with an NVIDIA Quadro FX 5800 graphics card with 4 GB of memory. We used the ATLAS3.6 and CUBLAS2.3 implementations of the BLAS kernels. Performance is given in GFlops.

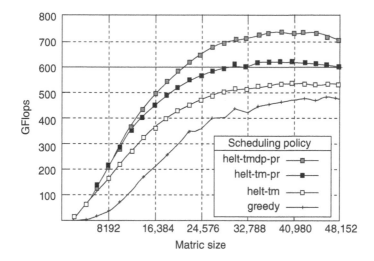

Figure 12.5 Impact of different StarPU scheduling policies (greedy, heft-tm, heft-tm-pr and heft-tmdp-pr) on the LU decomposition example.

Results are given in Figure 12.5 for varying problem size and different scheduling policies. The greedy strategy simply assigns the codelets to the available computing units in FIFO order. The heft-tm strategy is an implementation of the *Heterogeneous Earliest Finish Time* algorithm using the aforementioned history-based performance prediction mechanism. One can observe that it significantly outperforms the greedy strategy and thus illustrates the benefits of using carefully tuned performance models on such hardware. The heft-tm-pr policy is a further enhancement that masks the cost of memory transfers by overlapping them with computations by use of aggressive prefetching. Finally, the heft-tmdp-pr strategy further penalizes nonlocal data accesses and thus favoring data locality. This has a strong impact on the total amount of data transfers which drops almost by half.

More interestingly, Table 12.1(a) shows that the speed achieved by our scheduling policy on a hybrid platform exceeds the sum of the speeds of the components of the system and demonstrates a *superlinear efficiency*. This is possible because the LU decomposition is composed of different types of tasks, with different relative speedups between their ATLAS/CPU and their CUBLAS/GPU implementations. The second column of Table 12.1(b) shows that the different tasks of the LU decomposition do not perform equally: matrix products (GEMM) are particularly efficient on the GPU, while the pivoting is quite inefficient with a mere speedup of 1.2. The use of per-task performance models allows the heft-tm strategy to distribute tasks with respect to their actual efficiency on the different types of compute units (third and fourth column of Table 12.1(b)).

The efficiency of such run-time techniques depends not only on the quality of codelets generated from the component and algorithm layers (and their associated scheduling hints) but also on the tight cooperation between the run-time and upper

Table 12.1 Example of acceleration on a double precision LU
decomposition with partial pivoting (DGETRF) on a 3.2 GB matrix.

(a) Performance of DGETRF on a 3.2 GB problem

	(3CPUs + 1GPU)	3 CPUs	1 GPU
GFlop/s	79.5 ± 0.4	17.4 ± 0.3	61.0 ± 0.1
efficiency (%)	$101.4 = 79.5/(17.4 + 61.0)$		

(b) Relation between speedup and task distribution

Kernel	Relative speedup	Task balancing (%)	
	(1 GPU vs 1 CPU)	3 CPUs	GPU
Pivot	1.2	94.7	5.3
DGETRF	6.7	0.0	100.0
DTRSM (lower)	6.0	46.3	53.7
DTRSM (upper)	6.2	45.3	54.7
DGEMM	10.8	21.7	78.3

layers in order to dynamically adjust task granularity. Experiments showing that task
granularity should vary dynamically even for regular applications such as LU decomposition have been conducted. Autotuning of such parameters in a heterogeneous
context is one of the most challenging aspects of PEPPHER.

12.6   GUIDING APPLICATIONS AND BENCHMARKS

Eventually the feasibility of the PEPPHER approach will be demonstrated by
applying the methodology and framework to real-world applications and/or kernels
abstracting properties of applications from various computing domains. More
concretely, application kernels will be taken from the following domains:

- CFD simulations, as an example using OpenFOAM (see `www.openfoam`
  `.com`)

- Iterative solvers [6]

- Weather and climate simulation, for example, ECHAMP5 or WRF (see
  `www.wrf-model.org`)

- GROMACS for molecular dynamic simulation (see `www.gromacs.org`)

- Game AI (e.g. line-of-sight calculations; see `aigamedev.com`, route planning [13]).

- Physics engine (e.g. Tokamak, see `www.tokamakphysics.com` or ODE;
  see `www.ode.org`)

- Visual computing, for example, ray tracing and volume rendering

These cover applications from technical (high-performance) computing, multimedia (embedded) computing and consumer and commercial enterprise computing.

As the project progresses we will validate and showcase the PEPPHER framework for different types of parallelism such as data parallelism, task parallelism, dataflow, dispatcher–worker and MapReduce. Here mainly common basic kernels and industry benchmarks will be utilized, for example, common basic BLAS operations, signal/image processing operations, network-edge processing, sorting, kernels from the heterogeneous computing platform benchmark [11] and the Berkeley dwarfs [2].

As part of the PEPPHER-supported parallel and heterogeneous many-core platforms, we will establish baseline references for all applications and kernel implementations and tests based on industry standard x86 multicore systems to act as a validation, development, portability and many-core proxy system and platform vehicle.

12.7 CONCLUSION

We motivated the PEPPHER approach to performance portability and programmability for heterogeneous many-core architectures and described some of the initial steps that have been taken in the project. We think the approach is unique and promising, combining a compositional software framework, algorithmic autotuning, specific compilation techniques and an efficient run-time and thereby maintaining independence of specific programming models, virtual machines and architectures. The combination of component-based adaptation with a run-time system provides for flexibility not found in many other autotuning projects, where scheduling decisions are hard coded at an early stage. In addition to the main thrust as described here, PEPPHER aims at generating feedback on enhanced hardware support for performance portability and parallel algorithmics.

REFERENCES

1. J. Ansel, C. P. Chan, Y. L. Wong, M. Olszewski, Q. Zhao, A. Edelman, and S. P. Amarasinghe. PetaBricks: a language and compiler for algorithmic choice. In *Proceedings of the 2009 ACM SIGPLAN Conference on Programming Language Design and Implementation, PLDI 2009*, pages 38–49. ACM, 2009.

2. K. Asanovic, R. Bodík, J. Demmel, T. Keaveny, K. Keutzer, J. Kubiatowicz, N. Morgan, D. A. Patterson, K. Sen, J. Wawrzynek, D. Wessel, and K. A. Yelick. A view of the parallel computing landscape. *Communications of the ACM*, 52(10):56–67, 2009.

3. C. Augonnet and R. Namyst. A unified runtime system for heterogeneous multi-core architectures. In *Euro-Par 2008 Workshops – Parallel Processing*, volume 5415 of *Lecture Notes in Computer Science*, pages 174–183. Springer, 2008.

4. C. Augonnet, S. Thibault, and R. Namyst. Automatic calibration of performance models on heterogeneous multicore architectures. In *Euro-Par Workshops 2009 (HPPC 2009)*, volume 6043 of *Lecture Notes in Computer Science*. Springer, 2009.

5. C. Augonnet, S. Thibault, R. Namyst, and P.-A. Wacrenier. StarPU: a unified platform for task scheduling on heterogeneous multicore architectures. In *Euro-Par 2009 Parallel Processing, 15th International Euro-Par Conference*, volume 5704 of *Lecture Notes in Computer Science*, pages 863–874. Springer, 2009.

6. R. Barrett, M. Berry, T. F. Chan, J. Demmel, J. Donato, J. Dongarra, V. Eijkhout, R. Pozo, C. Romine, and H. V. der Vorst. *Templates for the Solution of Linear Systems: Building Blocks for Iterative Methods*. SIAM, second edition, 2000.

7. S. Bell, B. Edwards, J. Amann, R. Conlin, K. Joyce, V. Leung, J. MacKay, M. Reif, L. Bao, J. Brown, M. Mattina, C.-C. Miao, C. Ramey, D. Wentzlaff, W. Anderson, E. Berger, N. Fairbanks, D. Khan, F. Montenegro, J. Stickney, and J. Zook. Tile64 processor: A 64-core SoC with mesh interconnect. In *IEEE International Solid-State Circuits Conference (ISSCC)*, pages 88–89, 598, 2008.

8. G. Blake, R. G. Dreslinski, and T. Mudge. A survey of multicore processors. *IEEE Signal Processing Magazine*, 26(6):26–37, 2009.

9. D. Cederman and P. Tsigas. GPU-quicksort: a practical quicksort algorithm for graphics processors. *ACM Journal of Experimental Algorithmics*, 14, 2009.

10. P. Cooper, U. Dolinsky, A. F. Donaldson, A. Richards, C. Riley, and G. Russell. Offload – automating code migration to heterogeneous multicore systems. In *High Performance Embedded Architectures and Compilers, 5th International Conference (HiPEAC 2010)*, volume 5952 of *Lecture Notes in Computer Science*, pages 337–352. Springer, 2010.

11. A. Danalis, G. Marin, C. McCurdy, J. S. Meredith, P. C. Roth, K. Spafford, V. Tipparaju, and J. S. Vetter. The scalable heterogeneous computing (SHOC) benchmark suite. In *3rd Workshop on General-Purpose Computation on Graphics Processing Units (GPGPU)*, pages 63–74, 2010.

12. J. Dean and S. Ghemawat. MapReduce: simplified data processing on large clusters. *Communications of the ACM*, 51(1):107–113, 2008.

13. D. Delling, P. Sanders, D. Schultes, and D. Wagner. Engineering route planning algorithms. In *Algorithmics of Large and Complex Networks – Design, Analysis, and Simulation*, volume 5515 of *Lecture Notes in Computer Science*, pages 117–139. Springer, 2009.

14. A. F. Donaldson, P. Keir, and A. Lokhmotov. Compile-time and run-time issues in an auto-parallelisation system for the cell be processor. In *Euro-Par 2008 Workshops - Parallel Processing*, volume 5415 of *Lecture Notes in Computer Science*, pages 163–173. Springer, 2008.

15. T. Fahringer, S. Pllana, and J. Testori. Teuta: tool Support for Performance Modeling of Distributed and Parallel Applications. In *International Conference on Computational Science (ICCS 2004)*, volume 3038 of LNCS, pages 456–463. Springer, 2004.

16. M. Frigo and S. G. Johnson. The design and implementation of FFTW3. *Proceedings of the IEEE*, 93(2):216–231, 2005. Invited paper, Special Issue on "Program Generation, Optimization and Platform Adaptation".

17. P. H. Ha, P. Tsigas, and O. J. Anshus. Wait-free programming for general purpose computations on graphics processors. In *22nd IEEE International Symposium on Parallel and Distributed Processing (IPDPS 2008)*, pages 1–12. IEEE, 2008.

18. P. H. Ha, P. Tsigas, and O. J. Anshus. NB-FEB: a universal scalable easy-to-use synchronization primitive for manycore architectures. In *Principles of Distributed Systems, 13th International Conference (OPODIS 2009)*, volume 5923 of *Lecture Notes in Computer Science*, pages 189–203. Springer, 2009.

19. J. Howard, S. Dighe1, Y. Hoskote, S. Vangal, D. Finan, G. Ruhl, D. Jenkins, H. Wilson, N. Borkar, G. Schrom, F. Pailet, S. Jain, T. Jacob, S. Yada, S. Marella, P. Salihundam, V. Erraguntla, M. Konow, M. Riepen, G. Droege, J. Lindemann, M. Gries, T. Apel, K. Henriss, T. Lund-Larsen, S. Steibl, S. Borkar, V. De, R. V. D. Wijngaart, and T. Mattson. A 48-core IA-32 message-passing processor with DVFS in 45nm CMOS. In *IEEE International Solid-State Circuits Conference (ISSCC)*, pages 19–21, 2010.

20. D. Jiang, H. Shan, and J. P. Singh. Application restructuring and performance portability on shared virtual memory and hardware-coherent multiprocessors. In *ACM SIGPLAN Symposium on Principles and Practice of Parallel Programming (PPoPP)*, pages 217–229, 1997.

21. J. A. Kahle, M. N. Day, H. P. Hofstee, C. R. Johns, T. R. Maeurer, and D. J. Shippy. Introduction to the cell multiprocessor. *IBM Journal of Research and Development*, 49(4–5):589–604, 2005.

22. P. Kongetira, K. Aingaran, and K. Olukotun. Niagara: a 32-way multithreaded sparc processor. *IEEE Micro*, 25(2), 2005.

23. N. Leischner, V. Osipov, and P. Sanders. GPU sample sort. In *24th IEEE International Parallel and Distributed Processing Symposium (IPDPS)*, 2010.

24. Y. Li, J. Dongarra, and S. Tomov. A note on auto-tuning GEMM for GPUs. In *Computational Science, 9th International Conference (ICCS 2009)*, volume 5544 of *Lecture Notes in Computer Science*, pages 884–892. Springer, 2009.

25. M. D. Linderman, J. D. Collins, H. Wang, and T. H. Y. Meng. Merge: a programming model for heterogeneous multi-core systems. In *Proceedings of the 13th International Conference on Architectural Support for Programming Languages and Operating Systems, (ASPLOS 2008)*, pages 287–296. ACM, 2008.

26. K. Mehlhorn and S. Näher. *Leda: A Platform for Combinatorial and Geometric Computing*. Cambridge University Press, 2000.

27. S. Pllana, S. Benkner, F. Xhafa, and L. Barolli. Hybrid performance modeling and prediction of large-scale computing systems. In *International Conference on Complex, Intelligent and Software Intensive Systems (CISIS 2008)*, pages 132–138. IEEE, 2008.

28. S. Pllana, S. Benkner, E. Mehofer, L. Natvig, and F. Xhafa. Towards an Intelligent Environment for Programming Multi-core Computing Systems. In *Euro-Par 2008 Workshops*, volume 5415 of LNCS, pages 141–151. Springer, 2008.

29. S. Pllana and T. Fahringer. On customizing the UML for modeling performance-oriented applications. In ≪*UML*≫ *2002*, volume 2460 of LNCS, pages 259–274. Springer, 2002.

30. L. Seiler, D. Carmean, E. Sprangle, T. Forsyth, P. Dubey, S. Junkins, A. Lake, R. Cavin, R. Espasa, E. Grochowski, T. Juan, M. Abrash, J. Sugerman, and P. Hanrahan. Larrabee: A many-core x86 architecture for visual computing. *IEEE Micro*, 29(1):10–21, 2009.

31. J. G. Siek, L.-Q. Lee, and A. Lumsdaine. *The Boost Graph Library: User Guide and Reference Manual*. Addison-Wesley, 2002.

32. J. Singler, P. Sanders, and F. Putze. MCSTL: The multi-core standard template library. In *Euro-Par 2007, Parallel Processing, 13th International Euro-Par Conference*, volume 4641 of *Lecture Notes in Computer Science*, pages 682–694. Springer, 2007.

33. H. Sundell and P. Tsigas. NOBLE: non-blocking programming support via lock-free shared abstract data types. *SIGARCH Computer Architecture News*, 36(5), 2008.

34. C. Szyperski. *Component Software: Beyond Object-oriented Programming*. Addison-Wesley/ACM Press, second edition, 2002.

35. N. Thomas, G. Tanase, O. Tkachyshyn, J. Perdue, N. M. Amato, and L. Rauchwerger. A framework for adaptive algorithm selection in stapl. In *Proceedings of the ACM SIG-PLAN Symposium on Principles and Practice of Parallel Programming (PPoPP) 2005*, pages 277–288. ACM, 2005.

36. P. Tsigas and Y. Zhang. A simple, fast parallel implementation of quicksort and its performance evaluation on SUN enterprise 10000. In *11th Euromicro Workshop on Parallel, Distributed and Network-Based Processing (PDP)*, pages 372–381. IEEE Computer Society, 2003.

37. P. H. Wang, J. D. Collins, G. N. Chinya, H. Jiang, X. Tian, M. Girkar, N. Y. Yang, G.-Y. Lueh, and H. Wang. EXOCHI: architecture and programming environment for a heterogeneous multi-core multithreaded system. In *Programming Language Design and Implementation (PLDI)*, pages 156–166. ACM, 2007.

38. R. C. Whaley, A. Petitet, and J. Dongarra. Automated empirical optimizations of software and the ATLAS project. *Parallel Computing*, 27(1–2):3–35, 2001.

39. H. Yu, D. Zhang, and L. Rauchwerger. An adaptive algorithm selection framework. In *13th International Conference on Parallel Architectures and Compilation Techniques (PACT 2004)*, pages 278–289, 2004.

CHAPTER 13

FASTFLOW: HIGH-LEVEL AND EFFICIENT STREAMING ON MULTICORE

MARCO ALDINUCCI, MARCO DANELUTTO, PETER KILPATRICK AND
MASSIMO TORQUATI

Computer hardware manufacturers have moved decisively to multicore and are currently experimenting with increasingly advanced many-core architectures.

In the long term, writing efficient, portable and correct parallel programs targeting multi- and many-core architectures must become no more challenging than writing the same programs for sequential computers. To date, however, most applications running on multicore machines do not exploit fully the potential of these architectures.

This situation is in part due to the scarcity of good high-level programming tools suitable for multi- /many-core architectures and in part to the fact that multicore programming is still viewed as a kind of exotic branch of high-performance computing (HPC) rather than being perceived as the *de facto* standard programming practice for the masses.

Some efforts have been made to provide programmers with tools suitable for mapping data-parallel computations onto both multicores and GPUs – the most popular manycore currently available. Tools have also been developed to support stream parallel computations [28, 30] as stream parallelism *de facto* represents a pattern

Programming Multicore and Many-core Computing Systems,
First Edition. Edited by Sabri Pllana and Fatos Xhafa.

characteristic of a large class of (potentially) parallel applications. Two major issues with these programming environments and tools relate to programmability and efficiency. Programmability is often impaired by the modest level of abstraction provided to the programmer. Efficiency more generally suffers from the peculiarities related to effective exploitation of the memory hierarchy.

As a consequence, two distinct but synergistic needs exist: on the one hand, increasingly efficient mechanisms supporting correct concurrent access to shared memory data structures are needed; on the other hand there is a need for higher level programming environments capable of hiding the difficulties related to the correct and efficient use of shared memory objects by raising the level of abstraction provided to application programmers.

To address these needs we introduce and discuss FastFlow, a programming framework specifically targeting cache-coherent sharedmemory multicores. FastFlow is implemented as a stack of C++ template libraries.[1] The lowest layer of Fast-Flow provides very efficient lock-free (and memory fence-free) synchronization-based mechanisms. The middle layer provides distinctive communication mechanisms supporting both single-producer–multiple-consumer and multiple-producer–single-consumer communications. These mechanisms support the implementation of graphs modeling various kinds of parallel/concurrent activities. Finally, the top layer provides, as programming primitives, typical streaming patterns exploiting the fast communication/synchronizations provided by the lower layers and supporting efficient implementation of a variety of parallel applications, including but not limited to classical streaming applications.

In our opinion the programming abstractions provided by the top layer of Fast-Flow represent a suitable programming model for application programmers. The efficient implementation of these programming abstractions in terms of the lower layers of the FastFlow stack also guarantees efficiency. Moreover, the possibility of accessing and programming directly the lower layers of the FastFlow stack to implement and support those applications not directly supported by the FastFlow high-level abstractions provides all the processing power needed to efficiently implement the most existing parallel applications.

In this Chapter we adopt a tutorial style: first we outline FastFlow design and then show sample use of the FastFlow programming environment together with performance results achieved on various *state-of-the-art* multicore architectures. Finally, a related work section concludes the Chapter.

13.1 FASTFLOW PRINCIPLES

The FastFlow framework has been designed according to four foundational principles: *layered design* (to support incremental design and local optimizations); *efficiency in base mechanisms* (as a base for efficiency of the whole framework);

---

[1]FastFlow is distributed under LGPLv3. It can be downloaded from SourceForge at http://sourceforge.net/projects/mc-fastflow/.

support for *stream parallelism* (intended as a viable solution for implementing classical stream parallel applications and also data parallel, recursive and Divide & Conquer (D&C) applications); and a programming model based on *design pattern/algorithmic skeleton* concepts (to improve the abstraction level provided to the programmer).

Layered Design   FastFlow is conceptually designed as a stack of layers that progressively abstract the shared memory parallelism at the level of cores up to the definition of useful programming constructs supporting structured parallel programming on cache-coherent shared-memory multi- and many-core architectures (see Fig. 13.1). These architectures include commodity, homogeneous, multicore systems such as Intel core, AMD K10, etc. The core of the FastFlow framework (i.e. *run-time support* tier) provides an efficient implementation of single-producer-single-consumer (SPSC) first in, first out (FIFO) queues. The next tier up extends from one-to-one queues (SPSC) to one-to-many (SPMC), many-to-one (MPSC), and many-to-many (MPMC) synchronizations and data flows, which are implemented using only SPSC queues and arbiter threads, thus providing lock-free and wait-free arbitrary dataflow graphs (*arbitrary streaming networks*). These networks exhibit very low synchronization overhead because they require few or no memory barriers and thus few cache invalidations. The upper layer, that is, *high-level programming*, provides a programming framework based on parallel patterns (see Section 13.1). The FastFlow pattern set can be further extended by building new C++ templates. Programs written using the abstractions provided by the FastFlow layered design may be seamlessly ported across the full range of architectures supported. The run-time tier has specific conditional compilation parts targeting the different shared memory and cache architectures in the various target architectures. Extra fine-tuning possibilities will be provided in future FastFlow releases, in particular, to allow users to allocate memory

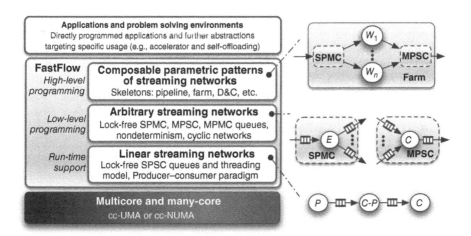

Figure 13.1   FastFlow-layered architecture with abstraction examples at the different layers of the stack.

Table 13.1   Average latency time and standard deviation (in nanoseconds) of a push/pop operation on a SPSC queue with 1024 slots for 1M insert/extractions, on the Intel 8 core 16 context and on AMD 48 core.

	Same core and different contexts		Same CPU and different cores		Different CPUs	
	8 core	48 core	8 core	48 core	8 core	48 core
Average	14.29	–	11.23	19.73	9.6	20.21
standard deviation	2.63	–	0.29	2.23	0.1	1.9

in one of the 'banks' sported by the target architecture. This, along with the possibility offered to pin a thread to a specific core, will provide the user full locality control.

Efficiency of Base Mechanisms   FastFlow SPSC queues represent the base mechanisms in the FastFlow framework. Their implementations are lock-free and wait-free [16]. They do not use interlocked operations [13]. Also, they do not make use of any memory barrier for total store order processors (e.g. Intel core) and use a single memory write barrier (in the push operation) for processors supporting weaker memory consistency models (full details on FastFlow SPSC can be found in [31]). The SPSC queue is primarily used as a synchronization mechanism for memory pointers in a consumer–producer fashion. SPSC FIFO queues can be effectively used to build networks of communicating threads which behave in a dataflow fashion. The formal underpinning of these networks dates back to Kahn process networks (KPNs) [18] and dataflow process networks [19]. Table 13.1 shows the average latencies involved in the use of the SPSC queues on different configurations of producers and consumers on state-of-the-art Intel and AMD multicore architectures.

Stream Parallelism   We chose to support only stream parallelism in our library for two basic reasons: (i) supporting just one kind of parallelism keeps the Fast-Flow implementation simple and maintainable, and (ii) stream parallel patterns, as designed in FastFlow, allow different other parallelism forms to be implemented (see following text), including simple data parallelism, parallelism in recursive calls and D&C. *Stream parallelism* is a programming paradigm supporting the parallel execution of a stream of tasks by using a series of *sequential* or *parallel* stages. A stream program can be naturally represented as a graph of independent *stages* (kernels or filters) that communicate explicitly over data channels. Conceptually, a streaming computation represents a sequence of transformations on the data streams in the program. Each stage of the graph reads one or more tasks from the input stream, applies some computation and writes one or more output tasks to the output stream. Parallelism is achieved by running each stage of the graph simultaneously on *subsequent* or *independent* data elements. Local state may be either maintained in each stage or distributed (replicated or scattered) along streams.

Streams processed in a stream parallel application are usually generated (input streams) and consumed (output streams) externally to the application itself. However, streams to be processed may also be generated *internally* to the application. For example, an embarrassingly data-parallel application may be implemented as a pipeline with three stages: the first generates a stream of tasks, each representing one of the data-parallel tasks that can be independently processed to compute a subset of the application results; the second processes in parallel this input stream of tasks, producing an output stream of results; and the last stage processes the output stream to rebuild the final (nonstream) result. We refer to the first kind of streams – those produced/consumed outside the application, as *exo-streams* – and the second, those produced/consumed internally, as *endo-streams*.

Parallel Design Patterns (algorithmic Skeletons)   Attempts to reduce the programming effort by raising the level of abstraction date back at least three decades. Notable results have been achieved by the *skeletal* approach [10, 11] (a.k.a. *pattern-based* parallel programming). This approach appears to be becoming increasingly popular after being revamped by several successful parallel programming frameworks [8, 12, 30, 32].

Algorithmic skeletons capture common parallel programming paradigms (e.g. MapReduce, ForAll, D&C, etc.) and make them available to the programmer as high-level programming constructs equipped with well-defined functional and extrafunctional semantics [2]. Some of these skeleton frameworks explicitly include stream parallelism as a major source of concurrency exploitation [2, 17, 30, 32]: rather than allowing programmers to connect stages into arbitrary graphs, basic forms of stream parallelism are provided to the programmer in high-level constructs such as *pipeline* (modeling computations in stages), *farm* (modeling parallel computation of independent data tasks) and *loop* (supporting generation of cycles in a stream graph and typically used in combination with a farm body to model D&C computations). More recently, approaches such as those followed in algorithmic skeletons but based on *parallel design patterns* have been claimed to be suitable to support multi- and many-core programming [8, 21]. Differences between algorithmic skeletons and parallel design patterns lie mainly in the motivations leading to these two apparently distinct concepts and in the research environments where they were developed: the parallel programming community for algorithmic skeletons and the software engineering community for parallel design patterns.

In FastFlow we chose to adopt an algorithmic skeleton/parallel design-pattern-based approach to address the problems outlined in the introduction, and we restricted the kind and the number of skeletons implemented to keep the size of the implementation manageable while providing a useful skeleton set. This choice allows us to provide full support for an important class of applications, namely, *streaming applications* [7, 28].

13.2   FASTFLOW μ-TUTORIAL

The FastFlow parallel programming framework may be used in at least two distinct ways. A first classic usage scenario is related to development 'from scratch' of brand new parallel applications. In this case, the application programmer logically follows a workflow containing the following steps:

STEP 1   Choose the most suitable skeleton nesting that models the parallelism paradigm that can be exploited in the given application

STEP 2   Provide the parameters needed to correctly instantiate the skeleton(s), including the sequential portions of code modeling the sequential workers/stages of the skeleton(s)

STEP 3   Compile and run the resulting application code, consider the results and possibly go back to step 1 to refine the skeleton structure if it becomes apparent that there is a better combination of skeletons modeling the parallelism exploitation paradigm in mind

The workflow just mentioned can be used also to parallelize existing applications. In this case, rather than choosing the most suitable skeleton nesting for the *whole* application, the programmer will analyze the application, determine which kernels are worth parallelizing and finally enter the aforementioned three-step process, with step one being performed only on targeted portions of the code. As a result, the sequential flow of control of a given kernel will be substituted by the parallel flow of control expressed by the skeleton nesting.

A second scenario, relating to the use of *software accelerators*, is particularly targeted to low-effort parallelization of existing applications.

In this case programmers identify independent tasks within the application. Then they choose a representation for the single task, declare a FastFlow accelerator – for example, a farm accepting a stream of tasks to be computed – and use the accelerator to offload the computation of these tasks, much in the sense of OpenMP tasks being executed by the thread pool allocated with the scoped `#pragma parallel` directive. This scenario is distinct from the first in that the application programmer using FastFlow in this way does not necessarily need any knowledge of the skeleton framework implemented in FastFlow. Tasks to be computed are simply sent to a generic 'parallel engine' computing some user-supplied code. Once the tasks have been submitted, the program can wait for completion of their computation while possibly performing other different tasks needed to complete application execution.

13.2.1 Writing Parallel Applications 'From Scratch'

When designing and implementing new parallel applications using FastFlow, programmers instantiate patterns provided by FastFlow to adapt them to the specific needs of the application at hand. In this section, we demonstrate how the principal FastFlow patterns may be used in a parallel application.

13.2.1.1 Pipeline   A very simple FastFlow pipeline code is sketched in Figure 13.2. A FastFlow pipeline object is declared in line 4. In line 5 and 6 nStages objects of type `Stage` are added to the pipeline. The order of the stages

```
  #include <ff/pipeline.hpp>
2 using namespace ff;
  int main() {
4   ff_pipeline pipe;
    for(int i=0;i<nStages;++i)
6     pipe.add_stage(new Stage);
    if (pipe.run_and_wait_end()<0)
8     return -1;
    return 0;
10 }
   class Stage: public ff_node {
12   int svc_init () {
       printf("Stage %d\n",get_my_id());
14     return 0;
     }
16   void * svc(void * task) {
       if (ff_node::get_my_id()==0)
18       for(long i=0;i<ntasks;++i)
           ff_send_out(i);
20       else printf("Task=%d\n",(long)task);
       return task;
22   }
   };
```

Figure 13.2   Hello world pipeline.

in the pipeline chain is given by the insertion order in the pipe object (line 6). The generic Stage is defined from line 11 to line 23. The Stage class is derived from the ff_node base class, which defines three basic methods, two optional, svc_init and svc_end and one mandatory svc (pure virtual method). The svn_init method is called once at node initialization, while the svn_end method is called once when the end of stream (EOS) is received in input or when the svc method returns NULL. The svc method is called each time an input task is ready to be processed. In the example, the svc_init method just prints a welcome message and returns. The svc method is called as soon as an input task is present and prints a message and returns the task which will be sent out by the FastFlow runtime to the next stage (if present). For the first stage of the pipeline, the svc method is called by the FastFlow runtime with a NULL task parameter. The first node (the one with id 0 in line 17) generates the stream sending out each task (in this simple case just one long) by using Fast-Flow's run-time method ff_send_out (line 19). The ff_send_out allows for queueing tasks without returning from the svc method. The pipeline can be started synchronously as in the example (line 7) or asynchronously by invoking the method run without waiting for the completion, thus allowing overlap with other work. It is worth noting that the ff_pipeline class type is a base class of ff_node type, so a pipeline object can be used where an ff_node object has to be used.

13.2.1.2 Farm   A farm paradigm can be seen as a two- or three-stage pipelines, the stages being an ff_node called the *emitter*, a pool of ff_nodes called *workers*, and – optionally – an ff_node called the *collector*. A FastFlow farm pattern can be declared using the ff_farm<> template class type as in Figure 13.3 line 4. In line

```
   #include <ff/farm.hpp>
 2 using namespace ff;
   int main() {
 4   ff_farm<> farm;
     std :: vector<ff_node*> workers;
 6   for(int i=0;i<nWorkers;++i)
       workers.push_back(new Worker);
 8   farm.add_workers(workers);
     farm.add_emitter(new Emitter(nTasks));
10   farm.add_collector(new Collector);
     if (farm.run_and_wait_end()<0)
12     return -1;
     return 0;
14 }
   struct Emitter: public ff_node {
16   Emitter(int ntask):ntask(ntask){}
     int svc_init () {
18     printf ("Work Start\n");
     }
20   void * svc(void *) {
       long task = new task_t(ntask--);
22     return (void*)task;
     }
24   long ntask;
   };
26 struct Worker: public ff_node {
     void * svc(void * task) {
28     // do something useful with the task
       return task;
30   }
   };
32 struct Collector: public ff_node {
     void * svc(void * task) {
34     printf ("Task=%d\n",(long)task);
       delete task;
36     return GO_ON;
     }
38   void svc_end() { printf ("Done!\n");}
   };
```

Figure 13.3   Hello world farm.

6 and 7, a vector of nWorkers objects of type Worker is created and added to the farm object (line 8). The *emitter* node, added in line 9, is used in the example code to generate the stream of tasks for the pool of *workers*. The svc method is called by the FastFlow runtime with a NULL task parameter (since, in this case, the *emitter* does not have any input stream) each time a new task has been sent out and until a NULL value is returned from the method. Another way to produce the stream without entering and exiting from the svc method each time would be to use the ff_send_out to generate all the tasks.

The *emitter* can also be used as sequential preprocessor if the stream is coming from outside the farm, as is the case when the stream is coming from a previous node of a pipeline chain or from an external device.

The farm skeleton must have the *emitter* node defined: if the user does not add it to the farm, the run-time support adds a default *emitter* which acts as a stream filter and schedules tasks in a round-robin fashion toward the *workers*. In contrast, the *collector* is optional. In our simple example, the *collector*, added at line 10, gathers the tasks coming from the *workers*, writes a message and deletes the input task allocated in the *emitter*. Each time the `svc` method is called and the work completed, the *collector*, being the last stage of a three-stage pipeline, returns the tag GO_ON task which tells the run-time support that further tasks must be awaited from the input channel and that the computation is not finished. The GO_ON tag can be used in any `ff_node` class. Finally, as for the pipeline, the farm base class is `ff_node`.

13.2.1.3 *Farm and Pipeline with Feedback*

In the farm paradigm the *collector* can be connected with a feedback channel to the *emitter*. It is also possible to omit the *collector* by having, for each worker thread, a feedback channel toward the *emitter*. For the pipeline paradigm it is possible to link the last stage of the chain with the first one in a ring fashion. In general, several combinations and nestings of farm, pipeline, and feedback channels are possible without any particular limitations to build complex streaming networks. For example, it is possible to have a farm skeleton whose *workers* are pipelines or a farm skeleton whose *workers* are other farms, each with a feedback channel.

When a feedback channel is present in the farm paradigm, the performance may strongly depend on the scheduling policies of tasks. FastFlow offers two predefined scheduling policies: dynamic round robin (DRR) and on demand (OD). The DRR policy schedules a task to a worker in a round-robin fashion, skipping workers with full input queue. The OD policy is a fully dynamic scheduling, that is, a DDR policy where each worker has an input queue of a predefined small size (typically 1 or 2 slots). Furthermore, in the farm skeleton, the *emitter* may also be used to implement user-defined scheduling policies, that is, it is possible to add new scheduling policies tailored to the application behavior by subclassing the `ff_loadbalancer` and redefining the method `selectworker`. The new scheduling class type should be passed as template parameter to the farm object. In this way it is possible, for example, to define weighted scheduling policies by assigning weights to tasks and to schedule the tasks directly to the worker that has the lowest weight at scheduling decision time (i.e. `ff_send_out`).

13.2.2 Using FastFlow as an Accelerator

FastFlow can also be used as a *software accelerator* to accelerate existing sequential code. An accelerator is defined by a skeletal composition augmented with an input and an output stream that can be, respectively, pushed and popped directly from the sequential code. Accelerating sequential code differs slightly from plain parallelization of existing code such as that sketched at the end of Section 13.2.1. In that case, more extensive application knowledge is needed in order to choose the most suitable parallel pattern composition for the whole application. Instead, when the accelerating methodology is used, programmers have to identify potentially concurrent *tasks* and request their execution (by explicit task offloading) onto the FastFlow skeletal composition in order to let those tasks be computed in parallel. As a consequence, the programmer has only to identify the concurrent tasks in the code and provide a suitable representation of those tasks to be submitted through the accelerator input stream. A detailed description of the FastFlow software accelerator and its usage can be found in [5].

13.3 PERFORMANCE

The FastFlow framework has been validated using a set of very simple benchmarks, starting from low-level basic mechanisms up to the simplest FastFlow patterns: farm and pipeline. Furthermore, a brief description of some significant real-world applications is reported pointing out, for each application, the kind of parallelization used.

Two platforms are used in the evaluation: *8-core*: Intel workstation with $2 \times$ quad-core Xeon E5520 Nehalem (16 HyperThreads) @2.26 GHz; *48-core*: AMD Magny-Cours 4×12-core Opteron 6174 @2.2 GHz. Both run Linux $\times$ 86_64.

13.3.1 Base Mechanism Latencies

Table 13.1 shows the results obtained when running a synthetic microbenchmark consisting in a simple two-stage pipeline in which the first stage pushes 1 million tasks into a FastFlow SPSC queue (of size 1024 slots) and the second stage pops tasks from the queue and checks for correct values. In the table are reported three distinct cases obtained by changing the physical mapping of the two threads corresponding to the two stages of the pipeline: (i) the first and second stages of the pipeline are pinned on the same physical core but on different HW contexts (only for the Intel 8-core architecture), (ii) are pinned on the same CPU but on different physical cores (for the AMD 48-core architecture we pinned the two threads on 2 cores of the same die), and (iii) are pinned on two cores of two distinct CPUs. On the 8-core box (Intel), Fast-Flow's SPSC queue takes on average 9.6–11.23 ns per queue operation with standard deviations of less than 1 ns when the threads are on distinct physical cores. Since threads mapped on different contexts of the same core share the same ALUs, the performances are a little bit worse in this case. On the 48-core box (AMD), Fast-Flow's SPSC queue takes on average 19.7–20.2 ns per queue operation with standard deviations around 2 ns.

It is well known that dynamic memory allocation and deallocation can be very expensive, especially for the management of very small objects. The FastFlow framework offers a lock-free dynamic memory allocator specifically optimized for the allocation/deallocation of small data structures. It is used to allocate FastFlow's tasks (which are usually small) flowing through the FastFlow network, which are frequently allocated and deallocated by different nodes. Figure 13.4 reports the execution time, on both architectures, of a very simple farm application where the *emitter* allocates 10 million tasks each of size 32 bytes (4 long) and the generic worker deallocates them after a synthetic computation of $1 \mu s$. We compare the standard libc-6 allocator (glibc-2.5-42), TBB's scalable allocator v.3.0 (30_20101215) and FastFlow's allocator. FastFlow's allocator achieves the best performance for all numbers of threads on the 8-core box (Intel), whereas on the 48-core machine, FastFlow's allocator and

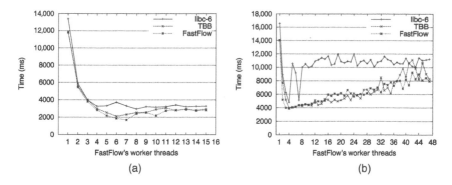

Figure 13.4 Execution time of the farm pattern with different allocators: libc versus TBB versus FastFlow allocator on 8-core Intel (a) and 48-core AMD (b) using a computational grain of 1 μs.

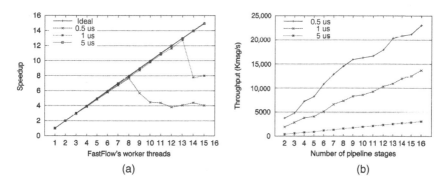

Figure 13.5 Speedup of the farm (a) and throughput in thousands of messages per second (Kmsg/s) of the pipeline (b) paradigms for several computational grains.

TBB's allocator achieve almost the same performance, much better than the standard libc-6 allocator which performs poorly on this architecture.

13.3.2 Efficiency of High-level Streaming Abstractions

To evaluate the overhead of the communication infrastructure for the FastFlow farm and pipeline paradigms, we developed two simple synthetic microbenchmark tests. In the microbenchmarks neither dynamic memory allocation nor access to global data is performed.

For the farm paradigm, the stream is composed of a sequence of 10 million tasks which have a synthetic computational load associated. By varying this load it is possible to evaluate the speedup of the paradigm for different computation grains. Figure 13.5(a) shows the results obtained for three distinct computation grains: 0.5, 1 and 5 μs. The speedup is quite good in all cases. We have almost linear speedup starting from a computation grain of about 1 µs. Larger computation grains give better results, as expected.

For the pipeline paradigm, the test consists in a set of N stages where the last stage is connected to the first, forming a ring. The first stage produces 1 million tasks in batch mode, that is, apart from the first 1024 tasks sent out at starting, for each input task received from the last stage, it produces a batch of 256 new tasks. Each task has a synthetic computational load associated, so that the throughput expressed in thousands of messages per second (Kmsg/s) for the entire pipeline can be evaluated using different computational grains. The results obtained are sketched in Figure 13.5(b).

13.3.3 Real-World Applications

Several real-world applications have been developed using the FastFlow framework. Here we report some of them: the Smith–Waterman biosequence alignment, the parallelization of the YaDT decision tree builder, the parallelization of a stochastic simulator, an edge-preserving denoiser filter and an extension of the pbzip2 parallel compressor. Table 13.2 summarizes the types of FastFlow patterns and streams used in these applications.

Biosequence Alignment: SWPS3-FF Biosequence similarities can be determined by computing their optimal local alignments using the Smith–Waterman algorithm [27]. SWPS3 [29] is a fast implementation of the Striped Smith–Waterman algorithm extensively optimized for Cell/BE and ×86/64 CPUs with SSE2 instructions. SWPS3-FF is a porting of the original SWPS3 implementation to the FastFlow framework [4]. The pattern used in the implementation is a simple farm skeleton without the *collector* thread. The *emitter* thread reads the sequence database and produces a stream of pairs: ⟨query sequence, subject sequence⟩. The query sequence remains the same for all the subject sequences contained in the database. The generic *worker* thread computes the Smith–Waterman algorithm on the input pairs using the SSE2 instruction set in the same way as the original code and produces the resulting score. Figure 13.6 reports the performance comparison between SWPS3 and the FastFlow version of the algorithm for ×86/SSE2 executed on the Intel test platform. The scoring matrix used is BLOSUM50 with 10–2k gap penalty.

Table 13.2 Patterns and streams used in real-world applications.

	BioAlign	DecTreeBuild	StocSimul	Denoiser	File compressor
Pattern(s)	Farm	Farm + Loop	Farm	Farm	Pipe(farm)×2
Stream(s)	Exo	Endo	Endo	Endo	Exo + Endo
Tasks from	DB	Recursive calls	sim no.	DP tasks	shell+file chunks

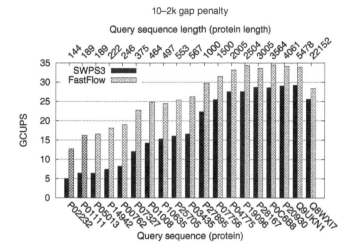

Figure 13.6 SWPS3 versus SWPS3-FF performance for $102k$ gap penalties evaluated on release 57.5 of UniProtKB/Swiss-Prot.

As can be seen, the FastFlow implementation outperforms the original SWPS3 ×86/SSE2 version for all the sequences tested.[2]

Decision Tree Builder: YaDT-FF   Yet another Decision Tree (YaDT) builder implementation [25] is a heavily optimized, efficient C++ version of Quinlan's C4.5 entropy-based algorithm [24]. It is the result of several optimizations and algorithm redesigns with respect to the original C4.5 induction algorithm and represents an example of extreme sequential algorithmic optimization. YaDT-FF is the porting of YaDT onto general purpose multicore architectures.

The decision tree growing strategy is a top-down breadth-first tree visit algorithm. The porting consists in the parallelization of the decision tree visit by exploiting stream parallelism, where each decision node is considered a task of the stream that generates a set of subtasks corresponding to the child nodes. In order to obtain additional parallelism, the computation of the information gain of attributes associated with each node has also been parallelized. The overall parallelization strategy is described in detail in [6].

The pattern used is a *farm-with-feedback* skeleton which implements the D&C paradigm.

Initially the computation is started by off-loading the tree root node task so that the stream can be initiated. The *emitter* gets as input the root node task and produces as output the subtasks corresponding to the children of the node, scheduling those tasks to a number of worker threads using an application-tailored scheduling policy.

---

[2]The Giga-Cell Updates Per Second (GCUPS) is a commonly used performance measure in bioinformatics and is calculated by multiplying the length of the query sequence by the length of the database divided by the total elapsed time.

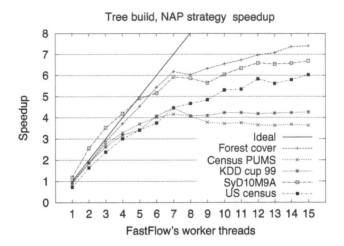

Figure 13.7   YaDT-FF speedup using several standard training sets. Superlinear speedup is due to the fact that the farm emitter performs a minimal amount of work contributing to the final result, but the parallelism degree given is related to the worker threads only.

The *workers* process the tasks independently and in parallel and eventually return the resulting tasks to the *emitter*.

The speedup of YaDT-FF is shown in Figure 13.7 for a set of reference datasets that are publicly available from the UCI KDD archive, apart from *SyD10M9A* which is synthetically generated using function 5 of the QUEST data generator.

Stochastic Simulator: StochKit-FF   StockKit [23] is an extensible stochastic simulation framework developed in the C++ language. It aims at making stochastic simulation accessible to practicing biologists and chemists while remaining open to extension via new stochastic and multiscale algorithms. It implements the popular Gillespie algorithm, explicit and implicit tau-leaping and trapezoidal tau-leaping methods.

StockKit-FF extends StockKit version 1 with two main features: support for the parallel run of multiple simulations on multicores and support for the on-line parallel *reduction* of simulation results, which can be performed according to one or more user-defined associative and commutative functions. StockKit-FF exploits the FastFlow basic *farm* pattern. Each farm worker receives a set of simulations and produces a stream of results that are gathered by the farm *collector* thread and reduced into a single output stream. Overall, the parallel *reduction* happens in a systolic (tree) fashion via the so-called *selective memory* data structure, that is, a data structure supporting the on-line *reduction* of time-aligned trajectory data by way of user-defined associative functions. More details about StockKit-FF and the *selective memory* data structure can be found in [1].

As shown in Figure 13.8, StockKit-FF exhibits good scalability when compared with the sequential (one-thread) version of StockKit.

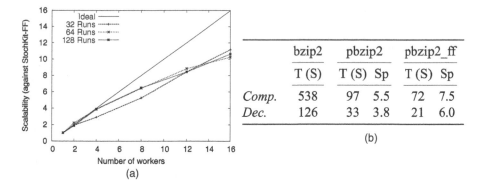

Figure 13.8 (a) scalability of StockKit-FF(n) against StockKit(1), where n is the number of worker threads. (b) execution time (T) and speedup (Sp) over bzip2 in the case of a stream of 1078 files: 86% small (0–1 MBytes), 9% medium (1–10 MBytes), 4% large (10–50 MBytes) and 1% very large (50–100 MBytes). pbzip2 uses 16 threads. pbzip2_ff uses 16 threads for each accelerator. *Comp* stands for compression and *Dec* for decompression.

Stream File Compressor: pbzip2-FF   This application is an extension of an already parallel application: *pbzip2* [14], that is, a parallel version of the widely used sequential *bzip2* block-sorting file compressor. It uses pthreads and achieves very good speedup on SMP machines for large files. Small files (less then 1 MB) are sequentially compressed. We extend it to manage streams of small files, which can be compressed in parallel. The original pbzip2 application is structured as a farm: the generic input file is read and split into independent parts (blocks) by a splitter thread; then each block is sent to a pool of worker threads which compress the blocks. The farm is hand coded using pthread synchronizations and is extensively hand tuned.

The FastFlow port of pbzip2 (*pbzip2_ff*) was developed by taking the original code of the *workers* and including it in a FastFlow farm pattern. Then, a second Fast-Flow farm, whose *workers* execute the file compression sequentially, was added. The two farms are run as two accelerators and fed by the main thread which selectively dispatches files to the two accelerators depending on the file size. Logically the application is organized as two 2-stage pipelines.

The table in Figure 13.8 compares the execution times of sequential bzip2, the original pbzip2 and pbzip2_ff on files of various sizes showing the improved speedup of pbzip2_ff against pbzip2. Compression and decompression performance for a single large file show no performance penalty for pbzip2_ff against hand-tuned pbzip2.

Edge-Preserving Denoiser   We also implemented an edge-preserving denoiser, a two-step filter for removing salt-and-pepper noise, which achieved good performance on the 48-core platform (AMD). Sequential processing for the test images grows linearly with noise ratio: from 9 to 180 s with 10% to 90% noise ratio. The parallel version speeds them up to a range of 0.4–4 s (further details may be found in [5]).

13.4 RELATED WORK

Structured parallel programming models have been discussed in Section 13.1. Fast-Flow high-level patterns appear in various algorithmic skeleton frameworks, including Skandium [20], Muesli [9] and Muskel [3]. The parallel design patterns presented in [21] also include equivalents of the FastFlow high-level patterns. These programming frameworks, however, do not specifically address stream programming and so FastFlow outdoes them in terms of efficiency. Also, most of the algorithmic skeleton frameworks afore mentioned and in Section 13.1, with the exception of Skandium, were designed originally to target cluster and networks of workstations, and multi-core support has been–in some cases, for example, in Muesli and Muskel–only a later addition.

Stream processing is extensively discussed in the literature. Stream languages are often motivated by the application style used in image processing, networking and other media processing domains.

StreamIt [30] is an explicitly parallel programming language based on the synchronous data flow model. A program is represented as a set of filters, that is, autonomous actors (containing Java-like code) that communicate through FIFO data channels. Filters can be assembled as a *pipeline*, possibly with a *FeedbackLoop*, or according to a *SplitJoin* data-parallel schema. S-Net [26] is a coordination language to describe the communications of asynchronous sequential components (a.k.a. boxes) written in a sequential language (e.g. C, C++, Java) through typed streams. The overall design of S-Net is geared toward facilitating the composition of components developed in isolation. Streaming applications are also targeted by TBB [17] through the *pipeline* construct. However, TBB does not support any kind of nonlinear streaming network, which therefore has to be embedded in a pipeline with significant programming and performance drawbacks.

OpenMP is a very popular thread-based framework for multicore architectures. It chiefly targets data-parallel programming and provides means to easily incorporate threads into sequential applications at a relatively high level. In an OpenMP program data needs to be labeled as shared or private, and compiler directives have to be used to annotate the code. Both OpenMP and TBB can be used to accelerate serial C/C++ programs in specific portions of code, even if they do not natively include farm skeletons, which are instead realized by using lower-level features such as the *task* annotation in OpenMP and the *parallel_for* construct in TBB. OpenMP does not require restructuring of the sequential program, while with TBB, which provides thread-safe containers and some parallel algorithms, it is not always possible to accelerate the program without some refactoring of the sequential code.

FastFlow falls between the easy programming of OpenMP and the powerful mechanisms provided by TBB. The FastFlow accelerator allows one to speed up execution of a wide class of existing C/C++ serial programs with just minor modifications to the code.

The use of the lock-free approach in stream processing is becoming increasingly popular for multicore platforms. The FastForward framework [13] implements a lock- and wait-free SPSC queue that can be used to build simple pipelines of threads that are directly programmed at low level; arbitrary graphs of threads are not directly supported. The Erbium [22] framework also supports the streaming execution model with lock- and fence-free synchronizations. Among cited works, Erbium is the only framework also supporting the MPMC model. In contrast to FastFlow, scheduling of tasks within MPMC queues is statically arranged via a compilation infrastructure. The trade-off between overhead and flexibility of scheduling is as yet unclear. González and Fraguela recently proposed a general schema (i.e. a skeleton) for D&C implemented via C++ templates and using as synchronization library the Intel TBB framework [15].

13.5 FUTURE WORK AND CONCLUSIONS

The FastFlow project is currently being extended in several different directions. Fast-Flow currently supports cyclic graphs, in addition to standard, noncyclic streaming graphs. We are using a formal methods approach to demonstrate that the supported cyclic graphs are deadlock-free, exploiting the fact that each time a loop is present, unbounded queues are used to implement point-to-point channels. A version of FastFlow running on standard windows framework is being finalized.

We are currently planning further developments of FastFlow: (i) to increase memory-to-core affinity during the scheduling of tasks in order to be able to optimize consumer–producer data locality on forthcoming many-core architectures with complex memory hierarchy; (ii) to provide programmers with more parallel patterns, including data-parallel patterns, possibly implemented in terms of the stream parallel patterns already included and optimized; and (iii) to provide simpler and more user-friendly accelerator interfaces.

The emergence of the so-called power wall phenomenon has ensured that any future improvements in computer performance, whether in the HPC center or on the desktop, must perforce be achieved via multiprocessor systems rather than decreased cycle time. This means that parallel programming, previously a specialized area of computing, must become the mainstream programming paradigm. While in the past its niche status meant that ease of development was a secondary consideration for those engaged in parallel programming, this situation is changing quickly: programmability is becoming as important as performance. Application programmers must be provided with easy access to parallelism with little or no loss of efficiency. Traditionally, for the most part, abstraction has been bought at the cost of efficiency and vice versa. In this work we have introduced FastFlow, a framework delivering both programmability and efficiency in the area of stream parallelism.

FastFlow may be viewed as a stack of layers: the lower layers provide efficiency via lock-free/fence-free producer–consumer implementations; the upper layers deliver programmability by providing the application programmer with high-level programming constructs in the shape of skeletons/parallel patterns. FastFlow is applicable not only to classical streaming applications, such as video processing, in which the stream of images flows from the environment, but also applications in which streams are generated internally – covering areas such as D&C, data-parallel execution, etc. While FastFlow has been created primarily to target developments from scratch, provision has also been included for a migrating existing code to multicore platforms by parallelizing program hot spots via self-offloading using the FastFlow accelerator. The applicability of FastFlow has been illustrated by a number of studies in differing application domains including image processing, file compression, and stochastic simulation.

REFERENCES

1. M. Aldinucci, A. Bracciali, P. Liò, A. Sorathiya, and M. Torquati. StochKit-FF: efficient systems biology on multicore architectures. In *Euro-Par '10 Workshops, Proc. of the 1st Workshop on High Performance Bioinformatics and Biomedicine (HiBB)*, volume 6586 of *LNCS*, pages 167–175. Springer, Ischia, Italy, September 2010.

2. M. Aldinucci and M. Danelutto. Skeleton based parallel programming: functional and parallel semantic in a single shot. *Computer Languages, Systems and Structures*, 33(3–4):179–192, October 2007.

3. M. Aldinucci, M. Danelutto, and P. Kilpatrick. Skeletons for multi/many-core systems. In *Parallel Computing: From Multicores and GPU's to Petascale (Proc. of PARCO 2009, Lyon, France)*, volume 19 of *Advances in Parallel Computing*, pages 265–272. IOP Press, September 2009.

4. M. Aldinucci, M. Danelutto, M. Meneghin, P. Kilpatrick, and M. Torquati. Efficient streaming applications on multi-core with FastFlow: the biosequence alignment test-bed. In *Parallel Computing: From Multicores and GPU's to Petascale (Proc. of PARCO 09, Lyon, France)*, volume 19 of *Advances in Parallel Computing*, pages 273–280. IOP press, September 2009.

5. M. Aldinucci, M. Danelutto, M. Meneghin, P. Kilpatrick, and M. Torquati. Accelerating code on multi-cores with FastFlow. In *Proc. of 17th Intl. Euro-Par '11 Parallel Processing*, *LNCS*. Springer, Bordeaux, France, August 2011. To appear.

6. M. Aldinucci, S. Ruggieri, and M. Torquati. Porting decision tree algorithms to multicore using FastFlow. In *Proc. of European Conference in Machine Learning and Knowledge Discovery in Databases (ECML PKDD)*, volume 6321 of *LNCS*, pages 7–23. Springer, Barcelona, Spain, September 2010.

7. S. Amarasinghe, M. I. Gordon, M. Karczmarek, J. Lin, D. Maze, R. M. Rabbah, and W. Thies. Language and compiler design for streaming applications. *International Journal of Parallel Programming*, 33(2):261–278, 2005.

8. K. Asanovic, R. Bodik, J. Demmel, T. Keaveny, K. Keutzer, J. Kubiatowicz, N. Morgan, D. Patterson, K. Sen, J. Wawrzynek, D. Wessel, and K. Yelick. A view of the parallel computing landscape. *CACM*, 52(10):56–67, 2009.

9. P. Ciechanowicz and H. Kuchen. Enhancing Muesli's data parallel skeletons for multi-core computer architectures. In *Proc. of the 10th Intl. Conference on High Performance Computing and Communications (HPCC)*, pages 108–113. IEEE, Los Alamitos, CA, USA, September 2010.

10. M. Cole. *Algorithmic Skeletons: Structured Management of Parallel Computations*. Research Monographs in Par. and Distrib. Computing. Pitman, 1989.

11. M. Cole. Bringing skeletons out of the closet: a pragmatic manifesto for skeletal parallel programming. *Parallel Computing*, 3(30): 389–406, 2004.

12. J. Dean and S. Ghemawat. MapReduce: Simplified data processing on large clusters. In *Usenix OSDI '04*, pages 137–150, December 2004.

13. J. Giacomoni, T. Moseley, and M. Vachharajani. Fastforward for efficient pipeline parallelism: a cache-optimized concurrent lock-free queue. In *Proc. of the 13th ACM SIG-PLAN Symposium on Principles and practice of parallel programming (PPoPP)*, pages 43–52, New York, NY, USA, 2008.

14. J. Gilchrist. Parallel data compression with bzip2. In *Proc. of IASTED Intl. Conf. on Par. and Distrib. Computing and Sys.*, pages 559–564, 2004.

15. C. H. Gonzalez and B. B. Fraguela. A generic algorithm template for divide-and-conquer in multicore systems. In *Proc. of the 10th Intl. Conference on High Performance Computing and Communications (HPCC)*, pages 79–88. IEEE, Los Alamitos, CA, USA, September 2010.

16. M. Herlihy. Wait-free synchronization. *ACM Transactions on Programming Languages and Systems*, 13(1):124–149, 1991.

17. Intel *Threading Building Blocks*, 2011. http://www.threadingbuildingblocks.org/.

18. G. Kahn. The semantics of a simple language for parallel programming. In J. L. Rosenfeld, editor, *Information processing*, pages 471–475, Stockholm, Sweden, Aug 1974. North Holland, Amsterdam.

19. E. Lee and T. Parks. Dataflow process networks. *Proceedings of the IEEE*, 83(5):773–801, May 1995.

20. M. Leyton and J. M. Piquer. Skandium: multi-core programming with algorithmic skeletons. In *Proc. of Intl. Euromicro PDP 2010: Parallel Distributed and network-based Processing*, pages 289–296. IEEE, Pisa, Italy, February 2010.

21. T. Mattson, B. Sanders, and B. Massingill. *Patterns for Parallel Programming*. Addison-Wesley Professional, first edition, 2004.

22. C. Miranda, P. Dumont, A. Cohen, M. Duranton, and A. Pop. Erbium: a deterministic, concurrent intermediate representation to map data-flow tasks to scalable, persistent streaming processes. In *Proc. of the 2010 Intl. Conference on Compilers, Architecture, and Synthesis for Embedded Systems (CASES)*, pages 11–20. ACM, Scottsdale, AZ, USA, October 2010.

23. L. Petzold. *StochKit: stochastic simulation kit web page*, 2009. http://www.engineering.ucsb.edu/~cse/StochKit/index.html.

24. J. Quinlan. C4.5: Programs for Machine Learning. Morgan Kauffman, 1993.

25. S. Ruggieri. YaDT: yet another decision tree builder. In *16th IEEE Int. Conf. on Tools with Artificial Intelligence (ICTAI 2004)*, pages 260–265. IEEE, 2004.

26. A. Shafarenko, C. Grelck, and S.-B. Scholz. Semantics and type theory of S-Net. In *Proc. of the 18th Intl. Symposium on Implementation and Application of Functional Languages (IFL'06)*, TR 2006-S01, pages 146–166. Eötvös Loránd Univ., Faculty of Informatics, Budapest, Hungary, 2006.

27. T. F. Smith and M. S. Waterman. Identification of common molecular subsequences. *Journal of Molecular Biology*, 147(1):195–197, March 1981.

28. R. Stephens. A survey of stream processing. *Acta Informatica*, 34(7):491–541, July 1997.

29. A. Szalkowski, C. Ledergerber, P. Krähenbühl, and C. Dessimoz. *SWPS3 – fast multi-threaded vectorized Smith-Waterman for IBM Cell/B.E. and x86/SSE2*, 2008. http://www.scientificcommons.org/39542148.

30. W. Thies, M. Karczmarek, and S. P. Amarasinghe. StreamIt: a language for streaming applications. In *Proc. of the 11th Intl. Conference on Compiler Construction (CC)*, pages 179–196, London, UK, 2002.

31. M. Torquati. Single-Producer/Single-Consumer Queues on Shared Cache Multi-Core Systems. Technical Report TR-10-20, Dept. Comp. Science, Univ. of Pisa, Nov. 2010. http://compass2.di.unipi.it/TR/Files/TR-10-20.pdf.gz.

32. M. Vanneschi. The programming model of ASSIST, an environment for parallel and distributed portable applications. *Parallel Computing*, 28(12):1709–1732, December 2002.

CHAPTER 14

PARALLEL PROGRAMMING FRAMEWORK FOR H.264/AVC VIDEO ENCODING IN MULTICORE SYSTEMS

Nuno Roma, António Rodrigues and Leonel Sousa

14.1 INTRODUCTION

Among the several multimedia applications that have emerged along the past decade, video encoding has gained a particular relevance in a vast set of domains, however, it is also one of the most computational demanding. In particular, the recognized success of the latest generation of video standards, such as the H.264/MPEG-4 Part 10 (or AVC), is mainly due to its remarkable encoding performance in what concerns the relation between the output video quality and resulting bit rate, at the cost of a significant increase of the computational complexity. As a consequence, real-time encoding by exploiting the whole set of offered encoding mechanisms is still far beyond the capabilities of most computational systems.

To cope with such difficulties, several approaches have been proposed that try to take advantage of current parallel platforms to accelerate the encoding [5, 6, 10, 18]. Nevertheless, most of such proposals represent specific optimizations to the

Programming Multicore and Many-core Computing Systems,
First Edition. Edited by Sabri Pllana and Fatos Xhafa.

considered platforms, requiring the rewrite of the encoder software (SW) whenever a new target hardware (HW) platform or parallelization model is considered.

To circumvent such limitations, a new parallel programming framework is presented. This framework allows to easily and efficiently implement high-performance H.264/AVC video encoders in a wide set of different parallel platforms. The offered modularity and flexibility make this framework particularly suited for efficient implementations either in homogeneous or heterogeneous parallel platforms, providing a suitable set of fine-tuning configurations and parameterizations that allow a fast prototyping and implementation, thus significantly reducing the developing time of the whole video encoding system.

14.1.1 H.264/AVC Video Standard

The H.264/AVC standard has been widely adopted by most recent video applications to address the consumers' needs and the most demanding encoding requirements. The standard is divided in several profiles to define the applied encoding techniques, targeting specific classes of applications. For each profile, several levels are also defined, specifying upper bounds for the bit stream or lower bounds for the decoder capabilities, such as processing rate, capacity of multipicture buffers, video rate, motion vector range, etc. [21].

To achieve the offered encoding performance, this standard incorporates a set of new and powerful techniques (see Fig. 14.1), namely, 4×4 integer transforms, variable block-size inter-frame prediction, quarter-pixel motion estimation (ME), in-loop deblocking filter, improved entropy coding based on context-adaptive variable-length coding (CAVLC) or on content-adaptive binary arithmetic coding (CABAC), and new intraframe prediction modes. Moreover, the adoption of bipredictive frames (B-frames), along with the previous features, provides a considerable bit rate reduction with negligible quality losses. As a result, when compared with other previous standards (such as H.263, MPEG-1/2 Video or MPEG-4 Visual), the H.264/AVC has proved to provide greater coding efficiency levels, with an excellent trade-off between the output video quality and bit rate.

However, the simultaneous exploitation of those new features significantly increased the encoder computational cost. As an example, a direct execution of a straight compilation of the JM reference SW [14] in a latest generation processor (running at 2.7 GHz), leads to frame-rate performance levels as low as a single or at most a couple of 4CIF frames per second. At this respect, several complexity analyses have shown that the *Inter prediction* module is usually the most time consuming—about 80%–followed by the *Interpolation* module [1].

14.1.2 Parallel Architectures and Platforms for Video Coding

To account for the complexity problem of the H.264/AVC video standard, several different approaches have been adopted, either from the SW point of view (e.g. application of low-complexity ME algorithms [13]) or from the HW point of view. In particular, with the vast set of parallel processing platforms that are now available,

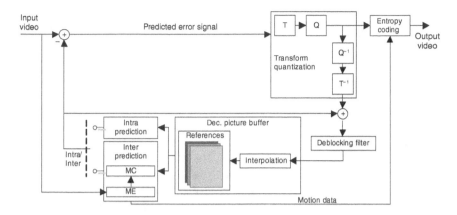

Figure 14.1   H.264/AVC encoding loop.

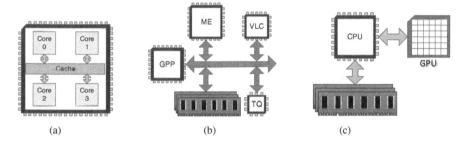

Figure 14.2   Parallel video coding architectures. (a) Homogeneous. (b) Heterogeneous, with embedded accelerators. (c) Heterogeneous, with GPU accelerators.

further levels of parallelism are now worth exploiting, either on *homogeneous* parallel platforms composed by multicore processing systems with several identical CPUs sharing the same chip (see Fig. 14.2(a)) or on *heterogeneous* platforms [12]. These last alternatives are often implemented either with dedicated processing structures integrated in an embedded system on chip (SoC) [8] (see Fig. 14.2(b)) or even with accelerators composed by graphics processing units (GPUs) interconnected to off-the-shelf general purpose processors (GPPs) (see Fig. 14.2(c)).

In the particular domain of video coding, *homogeneous* parallel platforms are usually applied in the exploitation of data-level parallelism techniques, by distributing the video data to be encoded/decoded across several similar parallel computing nodes. Moreover, with the advent of single-instruction multiple-data (SIMD) vector extensions to the ISA of current processors, these techniques have been even complemented with the exploitation of a subword parallelism level, by simultaneously processing several data elements with a single instruction. In contrast, *heterogeneous* platforms often adopt functional/task parallelism techniques, where the several modules of the video encoder/decoder are independently implemented by the different parallel computing nodes. In particular, many of such architectures adopt a pipeline processing scheme, where the video data is sequentially processed by the several different and independent stages of the pipeline.

Until very recently, most parallelization efforts around the H.264 standard have been mainly focused on the *decoder* implementation [2, 3, 5, 20], where the complex data dependencies that characterizes the encoding loop are not observed. When the most challenging and rewarding goal of parallelizing the *encoder* is concerned, it has been observed that a significant part of the efforts were devised in the design of specialized and dedicated systems [9, 15, 16]. Most of these approaches are based on parallel or pipeline SoC topologies, using dedicated HW structures to implement some of the most demanding parts of the encoder and leaving the remaining sequential and less complex code to be executed in a GPP. In most of such implementations, the corresponding segments of the original SW code are simply replaced by instantiations of the accelerated procedures in the proper HW structures. Other similar approximations make use of heterogeneous structures composed by digital signal processors (DSPs) or very long instruction word (VLIW) processors to accelerate the implementation of the encoding procedure. Some examples of such approach are the TriMedia processors from NXP Semiconductors (former Philips Semiconductors™) [20] and the OMAP processors from Texas Instruments™ [3]. Nevertheless, independent of the adopted accelerating structure, difficult challenges still often arise in what concerns the transfer of the processed data, as well as the concurrent access to the shared frame memory by the GPP and the several accelerators, usually requiring complex and platform-specific implementation issues and optimizations.

On the other hand, when *pure-SW* approaches are considered, fewer parallel solutions have been proposed. Most of them are based on the exploitation of data-level parallelism, in order to simplify the schedule and the synchronization of the several processing cores. One popular parallelization approach is based on the massive use of similar and concurrent threads, by exploiting the several CPUs that are currently available in multicore chips [5]. As it will be seen in Section 14.2.1, frames can be divided in several independent slices, and an individual thread is assigned to each slice. Some of such strategies even make use of Intel™hyper-threading (HT) technology to increase the number of concurrent threads [6, 10]. Furthermore, some proposals have even complemented the exploited parallelization by also using SIMD multimedia vector instructions currently available in MMX and SSE extensions [5]. Other parallelization approaches based on a heavy exploitation of similar and concurrent threads make use of the OpenMP pragmas for their implementation [19]. They mostly combine the use of thread queues to process the several segments of pixels, together with the exploitation of HT to further speed up the encoding.

Another approach is based on the use of message passing communication protocols (e.g. MPI), namely, on clusters composed by several independent computers [18]. One common strategy is to implement the encoder architecture in parallel, where an independent group-of-pictures (GOP) can be assigned to each cluster node.

Furthermore, each node can even be implemented by a multicore CPU, allowing further parallelization. However, these solutions often present, as their main disadvantage, significant communication overheads that can even surpass the computation time. Moreover, they also require greater amounts of memory to accommodate the several encoded sub-streams at the same time.

Meanwhile, other parallelization approaches have also arisen by exploiting some recent heterogeneous architectures that emerged in the market [11, 17]. One of such proposals includes the implementation of a pipeline encoding structure in the Cell Broadband Engine [11]. In such implementation, the SPEs are used to exploit both slice-level and macroblock (MB)-level (see Section 14.2.1) parallelism, achieving real-time processing for high-definition image formats.

Other acceleration approaches have also emerged by using the capability of current GPUs to speed up certain parts of the encoder with data-level parallelism [7]. As an example, in [4] the implementation of the ME module by using the GPU support and providing a speedup of about 12 is presented.

Independent of the adopted strategy, the innumerous data dependencies imposed by this complex video standard frequently inflict a very difficult challenge to efficiently take advantage of the several possible parallelization strategies that may be applied. Moreover, the use of the vast set of powerful parallel platforms that are now available has been often refrained by the absence of a unified parallel encoding framework that easily adapts to and efficiently exploits the set of variable resources offered by such concurrent platforms. In this scope, a flexible and highly modular parallel programming framework for *pure-SW* or *HW-accelerated* H.264/AVC encoders is now presented. The aimed challenge is to speed up the encoding procedure without sacrificing the output video quality or increasing the resulting bit rate. The conducted evaluations, by using different instantiations of the framework, have shown that linear and close to optimal speedup values, in what concerns the achieved frame rate, can be obtained in current homogeneous parallel platforms. Moreover, the provided modularity and flexibility attested its configurable attributes, in order to easily and better adapt it to the targeted parallel platform.

14.2 PARALLEL PROGRAMMING FRAMEWORK FOR H.264/AVC VIDEO ENCODING

To circumvent the recognized need for a generic and highly modular SW architecture that can be used to efficiently implement H.264/AVC encoders in a vast set of different parallel structures, an innovative parallel programming framework is presented. With such framework, the programmer or system integrator is given the capability to easily configure and adapt the SW architecture to several different platforms, ranging from the *homogeneous* solutions composed by several GPPs that extensively exploit data-level parallelism to distinct *heterogeneous* solutions where functional-level concurrency can be exploited in different pipeline/data-flow topologies (see Fig. 14.2).

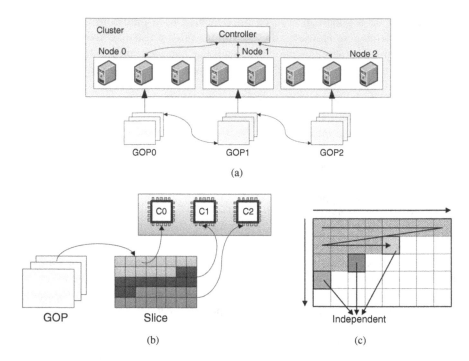

Figure 14.3 Exploited data-level parallelism models. (a) Frame level. (b) Slice level. (c) Macroblock level.

14.2.1 Data-Level Parallelism

Several parallelization models have been considered to improve the performance of H.264/AVC encoders [5, 10, 18]. Due to the encoder's nature, many of these parallelization approaches exploit concurrent execution at *frame level*, *slice level*, and *MB level*. However, careful design methodologies in what concerns its parameterization and modularity have to be considered, in order to avoid the introduction of performance losses in terms of the final bit rate and peak signal to noise ratio (PSNR).

At *frame level*, the input video stream is usually divided in GOPs. Since GOPs are usually made independent from each other, it is possible to develop a parallel architecture where a controller is in charge of distributing the GOPs among the available cores (see Fig. 14.3(a)). The advantages of this model are clear: PSNR and bit rate do not change, and it is easy to implement, since GOPs' independency is assured with minimal changes in the SW code. However, the memory requisites significantly increase, since each encoder must have its own decoded picture buffer (DPB), where all GOPs' references are stored. Moreover, real-time encoding is hard to implement using this approach, making it more suitable, for example, for video storage purposes. As a consequence, this solution has been mainly used in cluster systems [18]. Other parallelism levels usually have to be exploited in order to further improve the speedup.

In *slice-level* parallelism, frames are divided in several independent slices, making the processing of MBs from different slices completely independent (see Fig. 14.3(b)). In the H.264 standard, a maximum of sixteen slices are allowed in each frame. This approach allows to exploit parallelism at a finer granularity, which is suitable, for example, for multicore computers where parallel encoding of the several defined slices may be concurrently executed in multiple threads for each individual frame [10]. Moreover, the resulting increase of the allocated memory is smaller, because only one DPB is required. The main issues of this alternative are concerned with the limited number of slices per frame (sixteen in the H.264 standard), together with a greater parallelization effort in order to ensure a good performance and the need to redesign some data structures and algorithms in order to avoid caching of unnecessary data. Furthermore, this model often restricts the exploited spatial prediction within a frame, thus leading to a moderate increase of the resulting bit rate.

The parallelism at *MB level* allows independent MBs to be encoded at the same time [2]. According to the standard, a given MB is predicted using its left and upper three neighbors, which can be performed by following a wave-front approach, as depicted in Figure 14.3(c). Any two MBs are said to be *independent* if there isn't any data dependency in their prediction. As it will be seen in Section 14.4.3, this strategy may be used as a viable alternative to complement the exploited parallelism level. The main design issues of this approach are concerned with the need of a centralized control, to guarantee that only independent MBs are processed in parallel, and with the nonuniform distribution of the computational weight that may arise among the cores. However, in middle- and high-resolution video sequences, as well as when a great number of processors is available, this model may be preferable to the slice level, since the parallelism is only limited to $\lceil N/2 \rceil$, where N denotes the number of MBs in the diagonal of the frame/slice (see Fig. 14.3(c)).

14.2.2 Functional-Level Parallelism

To ensure the maximum flexibility of the framework, several modules of the encoder were carefully structured and implemented in independent routines. With such approach, it becomes possible to easily exploit functional-level parallelism, by using pipeline or data-flow topologies where each available core/accelerator may implement a different encoder module. Such feature is particularly important in heterogeneous configurations, where distinct parts of the encoder may be easily migrated to dedicated or specialized architectures.

With such SW architecture, three different topologies are made available:

- *Pipeline*
- *Straight parallel*
- *Mixed*

In the *pipeline* topology, illustrated in Figure 14.4(a), the encoding procedure is divided in several different stages. Each of these stages implements an individual or a particular set of encoding modules. The number of concurrent stages is determined

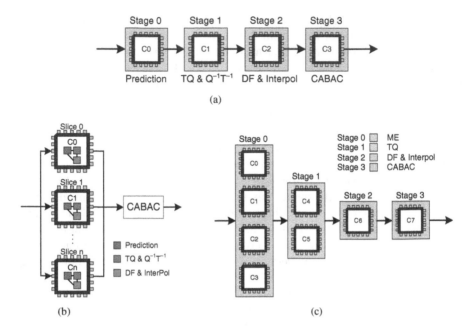

Figure 14.4   Parallel topologies to implement the encoding modules depicted in Figure 14.1 by using functional-level parallelism. (a) Pipeline. (b) Straight parallel. (c) Mixed.

by the number of cores/accelerators available in the system. Nevertheless, for each specific concretization of this topology, three main issues need to be carefully analyzed: how the stages communicate, how they are synchronized, and how the several modules are distributed among the stages.

Since it is impossible to guarantee that all stages have the same processing time, it is important to ensure that this SW pipeline only advances when all stages have finished their processing. To achieve this synchronization, barrier instances have been adopted in the SW architecture. As soon as all parallel execution flows reach these barriers, they resume executing in parallel the code that follows the barrier. Hence, to better balance the pipeline stages, it is also important to evaluate the processing time corresponding to all subfunctions. Only then should they be grouped in pipeline stages.

Table 14.1 depicts one example configuration. Considering that *interframe prediction* represents the most demanding part of the encoder, this example illustrates one possible configuration where the ME corresponding to the eight possible prediction modes were implemented in a homogeneous architecture using a pipeline topology, by considering the usage of 2, 3, 4, 6, and 8 cores.

The design principle corresponding to the *straight parallel* topology is particularly targeted for the exploitation of data-level parallelism, where the slices are assigned to similar concurrent threads that are independently executed. By assuming that slices

Table 14.1 Example configuration using a pipelined architecture to implement the eight interprediction modes in a variable number of cores.

Number of cores	Number of pipeline stages							
	1	2	3	4	5	6	7	8
2	16 × 16 16 × 8 8 ×16 *DIR*	8 × 8 8 × 4 4 × 8 4 × 4						
3	16 × 16 16 × 8	8 × 16, *DIR*, 8 × 8 8 × 4	4 × 8, 4 × 4					
4	16 × 16	16 × 8 8 × 16 *DIR*	8 × 8, 8 × 4	4 × 8, 4 × 4				
6	16 × 16	16 × 8	8 × 16	*DIR*, 8 × 8	4 × 4 4 × 8			
8	16 × 16	16 × 8	8 × 16	*DIR*	8 × 8	8 × 4	4 × 8	4 × 4

approximately have the same size, it can be expected that all threads finish their tasks at the same time in homogeneous systems.

Figure 14.4(b) illustrates one possible configuration of this topology. In this setup, each available core implements the whole encoding loop, in order to process one particular slice of the video frame. Subsequently, all slice buffers are joined together to supply an external entropy encoding (CABAC/CAVLC) module, in order to form the output stream packet.

The *mixed* topology can be seen as an extension of the pipeline solution, where more than one single core is assigned to implement the most demanding modules of the encoder. Figure 14.4(c) illustrates one hypothetical configuration of this topology. In this setup, the eight available cores were distributed among the several modules of the encoder, according to their relative computational requirements: 4 cores to implement the *prediction* module, 2 cores to compute the *transform* and *quantization* (and their corresponding inverses), 1 core to implement the *deblocking filter* and *interpolation* modules and 1 core to implement the *entropy encoding* (CABAC) module.

14.2.3 Scalability

As it was referred before, while pipeline topologies can be particularly adapted to heterogeneous architectures, straight parallel configurations, based on a massive exploitation of *slice-level* parallelism, are often more suited to be implemented in homogeneous systems, composed by several identical CPUs. Nevertheless, according to the H.264/AVC standard, such parallelism is limited by a maximum of 16 slices (threads). Hence, to further increase the exploited concurrency, this SW framework allows to complement the applied *slice-level* parallelism with a simultaneous exploitation of *MB-level* parallelism. In such configuration (illustrated in Fig. 14.5(a)), a *team of threads* is allocated to the processing of each slice. For each team, independent MBs are distributed among the set of cores that were assigned to the processing of that slice. At the end, entropy coding is performed separately and at slice level.

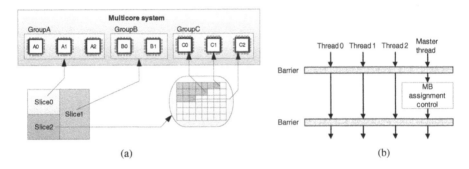

(a)   (b)

Figure 14.5   Simultaneously exploitation of slice and macroblock parallelism levels. (a) Thread allocation. (b) Thread synchronization.

The synchronization between the several concurrent threads is guaranteed by using appropriate synchronization barriers. Only threads belonging to the same team are blocked in these barriers. This mechanism is used before and after the execution of the control mechanism that assigns the set of MBs processed by each slice (Fig. 14.5(b)). While the first barrier guarantees that all threads have finished their tasks, the last barrier assures the correct MB assignment. Only after the team master thread has executed the assignment procedure that controls the set of MBs that will be processed in the next run can the rerunning threads of the team start executing. No further synchronization is needed.

Another considered option to increase the exploited concurrency is to adopt *slice scattering*, where slices are divided into several subslices located in nonadjacent areas of the frame (see Fig. 14.6). The application of this technique introduces an added level of data independency among the MBs of different subslices, allowing them to be processed in different threads. When compared with the previously referred approaches, the extra parallelization level provided by slicescattering is offered at the cost of an eventual degradation characterized by a slight increase of the resulting bit rate and a reduction of the output PSNR levels (due to the presence of more blocking effect). As a consequence, this parallel approach is regarded to be more appropriate to encode higher video resolutions, where the spatial redundancy can be exploited without seriously compromising the resulting encoding efficiency.

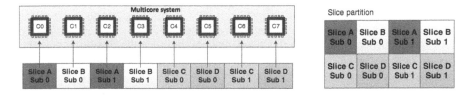

Figure 14.6 Possible slice-scattering distribution in a multi-core architecture.

14.2.4 Software Optimization

The presented parallel SW framework is based on JM [14] reference SW, thus maintaining full compliancy with the original encoder. In order to achieve an efficient parallel execution, the conducted research was focused on (i) code profiling, (ii) performance improvement through structural redesign and code optimization, (iii) definition of the concurrent modules set and (iv) parallelization.

Code profiling was extensively performed in the first step, in order to identify the most time-consuming operations. Several 4CIF standard test video sequences were used for more accurate results (see Fig. 14.7): *Soccer* and *Crew*, characterized by higher amounts of movement; and *Harbour* and *City*, with a higher spatial detail. As expected and according to the results presented in Table 14.2, *Inter Prediction* is the

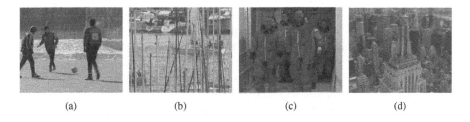

(a)   (b)   (c)   (d)

Figure 14.7 Considered set of test video sequences. (a) Soccer. (b) Harbour. (c) Crew. (d) City.

Table 14.2 `gprof` profiling results of the H.264/AVC reference SW.

Function	Video sequences (4CIF)			
	Soccer	Harbour	Crew	City
Inter prediction (%)	89.1	86.0	88.4	87.7
Intra prediction (%)	0.9	1.1	0.9	1.1
Transf. & quant. (%)	1.4	1.7	1.6	1.7
Interpolation (%)	2.3	2.9	2.4	2.7
Deblocking filter (%)	0.4	0.7	0.5	0.5
CABAC (%)	0.4	0.8	0.6	0.3
Others (%)	6.9	8.5	7.2	7.8

most computational demanding component of the encoder [1], making it the must suited target for parallelization.

An important step to increase independency and improve the flexibility was the redesign of the original data structures, not only to provide more efficient ways to manipulate and correlate information but also to save time when fetching them from the memory system, by efficiently exploiting the cache access patterns. On one hand, spatial locality can be further exploited by appropriately resizing the structures, since the probability to store the whole processed data in cache is higher, thus reducing the conflict and capacity misses. On the other hand, temporal locality can also be exploited by data resizing and by joining together the information needed to process wide data sets in each particular module of the encoder. Such resizing was mainly accomplished by removing nonused or duplicated parameters in certain modules and by adjusting their size to their effective range. As it will be seen in Section 14.4, when compared with the original data structures, the mutual combination of the conducted optimizations allows a reduction of the required memory space as high as 85.5%.

The conducted code optimization also took into account that many signal processing functions of the encoder can be decomposed into a set of vector operations [5], where the same operation is simultaneously applied to several data elements. By considering that most current processor families and embedded cores already include some multimedia extensions to the instruction set (e.g. MMX, SSE1, SSE2, SSE3, etc.), such optimization allows to exploit an added degree of SIMD parallelization. In the presented framework, the optional usage of SSE2 SIMD instructions can be activated through a simple compilation option. The usage of these instructions was mainly exploited in the implementation of the most demanding modules, namely, the computation of the sum of absolute differences (SAD) in MB prediction by ME, the Transformation-Quantizer (and corresponding inverses) modules and the Interpolation module (see Fig. 14.1).

To allow the implementation of the presented framework in HW-restricted platforms, some additional optimizations and optional configurations were also made available. In this scope, all data structures were statically allocated in memory, allowing this framework to be easily executed in embedded systems that do not necessarily include a dynamic memory allocation system. Furthermore, to ease the implementation in systems with strict memory restrictions, another optimized configuration was also made available, which interchanges the order of the DPB and the Interpolation modules (see Fig. 14.1) for the half-pixel resolutions (keeping the original order for the quarter-pixel resolution frames), thus conferring an extra configurable trade-off between the required memory resources and the involved computational cost. Such option is particularly suited for pipeline topologies implemented with dedicated accelerators in heterogeneous platforms.

14.3 PROGRAMMING PARALLEL H.264 VIDEO ENCODERS

14.3.1 Framework Parameterization

The modularity and flexibility provided by this framework allows an easy customization in order to suit it to distinct types of multicomputer, multicore, or even embedded systems. Such customization can be easily accomplished during source compilation (through the supplied Makefile) by properly choosing the most suitable options to the target system. As an example, the following parameters define the type of data-level parallelism that is exploited:

- CORES—number of considered parallel slices
- NESTED_CORES—number of considered parallel MBs within each slice

Likewise, the desired optimization can be selected by the following options:

- SSE_SUPPORT—enables the exploitation of SIMD SSE instructions
- LOW_MEMORY—enables low memory usage

Furthermore, thanks to the performed code simplification and division of the encoder into functional modules, the end user can still easily add, remove, and modify the sources with minimum effort.

14.3.2 Implementation Platforms and APIs

The main aim of the presented framework was to develop a highly modular SW architecture to implement parallel encoders of the latest generation of video standards. To achieve such objective, the several modules of the encoder were implemented with "objects" of self-contained code segments and data structures, in order to provide an easy and efficient migration of such "objects" to several homogeneous or heterogeneous parallel platforms.

A direct consequence of such strict premise is the provided easiness to implement a vast set of different parallel video encoding structures, by using any of the several parallel application programming interfaces (APIs) currently available, such as MPI, POSIX Threads, OpenMP, OpenCL, and CUDA.

Hence, after selecting the data-level and functional-level parallel topology that is most suitable for the considered HW platform, the programmer only has to take care of the migration of the parallelized modules and of the data transfer mechanisms, according to the selected API. Then, proper concretizations of the restricted set of adopted communication structures should be selected. At this respect, several alternatives can be adopted, such as explicit shared memory systems with uniform memory access (UMA) (e.g., homogeneous multicore systems implemented either with POSIX Threads or OpenMP), distributed memory systems with nonuniform

Table 14.3   Specifications of the considered parallel computational platform.

Platform	Intel™	AMD™
Processor	2 × Intel Xeon Quad-Core E5530	8 × AMD Quad-Core 8384
#Cores	8	32
Frequency	2.40 GHz	2.7 GHz
Caches	Individual L1 with 128 KB	Individual L1 with 512 KB
	Individual L2 with 256 KB	Shared L2 with 6 MB
	Shared L3 with 8 MB	–
Memory	24 GB	64 GB
O.S.	64-bits SuSE Linux	64-bits Ubuntu Linux
API	OpenMP	OpenMP

memory access (NUMA) (e.g., cluster encoding systems implemented with MPI), heterogeneous or nonshared memory systems (e.g., GPU accelerating systems implemented with CUDA or OpenCL), or even dedicated embedded architectures, implemented with specialized HW structures. Finally, all implicit synchronization mechanisms that are integrated within the framework should be implemented according to the adopted API.

14.4   EVALUATION OF PARALLEL H.264 VIDEO ENCODERS

To demonstrate the feasibility and the advantages provided by the presented framework, several parallel instantiations based on currently available multicore structures were considered and compared with a sequential implementation of the reference SW running in one core. In particular, considering the specificity and the wide variability presented by most heterogeneous architectures, eventually composed by possibly different accelerating structures, it was decided to adopt a homogeneous structure to demonstrate the performance offered by the proposed framework in an easily reproducible parallel platform. Table 14.3 depicts the characteristics of the considered computational systems. Furthermore, considering that most SW-based and nondedicated parallel encoders that have been presented up until now make use of homogeneous solutions implemented with POSIX Threads or OpenMP APIs [5, 6, 10, 19], it was decided to evaluate the proposed framework by using a similar environment, in order to achieve fair and correlatable comparisons. As such, *straight-parallel* configurations, exploiting either *slice-level* and *MB-level* parallelism will be considered. The whole evaluation procedure was conducted by considering the encoding parameters presented in Table 14.4.

To achieve the most efficient parameterization of the framework, the time consumption profiling results presented in Table 14.2 were carefully considered. From such analysis, it was clear that the *Inter Prediction* module, which includes ME and motion compensation functions, represents the most computational demanding block. As a consequence, the conducted parallelization approach primarily focused on this

Table 14.4   Considered H.264/AVC encoding parameters.

Parameter	Value
GOP structure	One I frame followed by thirty B-B-P frames
Intra prediction	All prediction modes
Inter prediction	All prediction modes
Reference frames	3 backward and 1 forward references
ME search algorithm	Simplified UMHexa
ME precision	Quarter-pixel precision
ME error metric	SAD
Entropy coding	CABAC
In-loop deblocking filter	Enabled

particular module. Nevertheless, the whole end-to-end encoder structure was implemented in each instantiation.

14.4.1 Baseline Optimizations

As it was referred in Section 14.2.4, extensive SW optimizations were considered in order to increase the efficiency of the presented framework. When the memory resources of a particular instantiation of the presented H.264 parallel framework are compared with those of the reference (original) SW, the result of such code improvements becomes clear, leading to a global memory usage reduction of about 93% (see Table 14.5). Such reduction is particularly important when the encoding system is implemented in embedded systems with memory and power consumption restrictions, as well as in parallel configurations that require replication of data in the memory system. Moreover, such optimizations (including the conducted cleaning of the code, reutilization of shared functions, and static allocation of data structures) provided a baseline speedup by a factor of 2, even without the exploitation of any level of parallelism.

Besides such optimizations, some of the most computational intensive modules were wholly redesigned in order to also exploit an SIMD parallelism level, by simultaneously processing several data elements with a single instruction. As an example, the application of MMX vector instructions to the ME (SAD) and the transform modules (DCT) led to partial speedup values of about 1.56 and 1.54, respectively.

14.4.2 Exploiting Slice-Level Parallelism

To evaluate the performance that is offered by the presented framework when *slice-level* parallelism is exploited, each frame of the video sequence under processing was divided into several slices, which were subsequently assigned to an individual core, as described in Figure 14.4(b).

The results obtained with the Intel platform are illustrated in Figure 14.8 for the several different parameterizations that are offered by this framework. With

Table 14.5 Memory allocation for the reference and optimized SW versions.

Data structure	Reference software	Optimized software	
		Regular	Low memory
Image parameters	82433 B	248 B	248 B
Input parameters	5.9 kB	6.1 kB	6.1 kB
Picture parameters set	248 B	152 B	152 B
Sequence parameters set	2.1 kB	1.7 kB	1.7 kB
Slice	2.3 MB	2.4 MB	2.4 MB
Macroblock	171.7 kB	74.3 kB	74.3 kB
Decoded picture buffer	203.1 MB	22.4 MB	6.6 MB
Intra processing	–	2.0 MB	2.0 MB
Inter processing	–	2.8 MB	2.8 MB
Total	205.7 MB	29.7 MB	13.9 MB
Memory saved	–	85.5%	93.2%

the exception of the setup that made use of 16 threads, all the considered cases evidence a speedup gain very close to the theoretical optimal acceleration. In fact, considering that this platform only incorporates 8 independent CPUs, the observed exception corresponds to a particular setup where the number of running threads was extended by using the HT technology. Nevertheless, all the observed results are entirely similar to those that were also obtained with dedicated SW frameworks [6, 10].

In the whole, it is observed that the slice independency allows a parallel execution with little data sharing between the several threads, thus minimizing the inherent segmentation and scheduling overheads. However, since the H.264 standard limits this frame division to a maximum of 16 slices, other levels of parallelization will have to be applied in order to avoid this constraint and allow greater levels of scalability.

14.4.3 Exploiting Macroblock-Level Parallelism

As it was observed by Gerber et al. [10], the data independency that is achieved by dividing the frame into several slices often introduces a negative impact on the amount of spatial prediction that is exploited within a frame, with a consequent decrease of the resulting encoding efficiency. A direct consequence of such effect is a natural increase of the output bit rate and a subsequent decrease of the resulting video quality, as a result of the application of the output buffer control mechanism. According to Gerber et al. [10], such effect is particularly observed as soon as the number of slices is greater than 4 (see Fig. 18.6 of [10]). Hence, not only is the maximum number of independent slices low but also its increase gives rise to a consequent decrease of the encoding efficiency (see shaded region in Fig. 14.8).

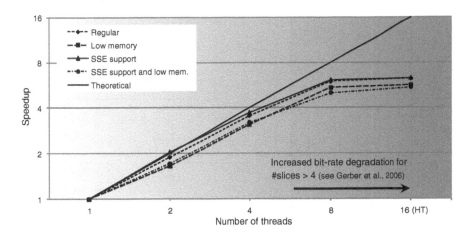

Figure 14.8   Provided speedup in Intel platform using *slice-level* parallelism.

To circumvent such undesirable effect, the added level of parallelism at MB level (see Fig. 14.5(a)) that is also offered by the presented framework allows the several cores from the same group to cooperate in the concurrent processing of independent MBs, in order to further accelerate the encoding of the same slice without sacrificing the resulting bit rate and encoding quality.

In the presented evaluation of this topology, this extra level of concurrency was implemented with nested threads. As soon as the slices are assigned to the primary threads, they are responsible to create other threads, in order to form *teams of threads*. Then, the set of independent MBs within each slice is distributed among the remaining available cores in each team. At the end, entropy encoding is performed separately and at *slice level*, to avoid memory bottlenecks and the usage of shared data.

The results presented in Table 14.6 illustrate the speedup levels that can be obtained either by an isolated or mutual exploitation of the *slice* and *MB* parallelism levels. Contrasting with the close-to-optimal results that were obtained with the *slice-level* model, the speedup values that are provided with an exclusive exploitation of the *MB level* (Slice = 1) are somewhat more modest, achieving a maximum value of about 4.4 and 3.2 when using 8 threads in Intel's platform and 32 threads in AMD's platform, respectively. Data sharing between the several cores of these multiprocessors is the main reason for this limitation, leading to a memory bottleneck and higher latency times.

An evaluation of the conceived capability to enhance the scalability of the parallel framework is also presented in Table 14.6. The simultaneous exploitation of *slice* and *MB* parallelism levels was assessed by using a set of configurations characterized by a different (but fixed) amount of threads: 1, 2, 4, 8, ... When compared with the previous results, it can be observed that the *MB* parallelism level, that is now possible to exploit as a complement to the *slice-level* parallelism,

Table 14.6 Provided speedup using *slice* and *macroblock* parallelism levels, by considering a maximum of 4 slices (to avoid bit-rate degradation [10]).

			Number of concurrent macroblocks within each slice			
			1	2	4	8
Intel™	Number of	1	1.0^1	1.7^2	3.0^4	4.4^8
E5530	concurrent	2	1.9^2	3.3^4	5.0^8	4.6^{16}
(8 cores)	**slices**	4	3.6^4	5.3^8	6.3^{16}	–
AMD™	Number of	1	1.0^1	1.6^2	2.5^4	3.2^8
8384	concurrent	2	2.3^2	4.1^4	3.7^8	4.5^{16}
(32 cores)	**slices**	4	3.7^4	4.6^8	5.3^{16}	6.8^{32}

NOTES:
Number of concurrent threads represented in superscript, above the speedup value; Intel's configurations using 16 threads make use of hyper-threading technology.

provides an extra speedup space beyond the *slice-level* baseline. Contrary to other highly specific and dedicated SW implementations [5, 6, 10, 18], such capability is now easily exploited by simply parameterizing the presented SW framework.

14.5 CONCLUDING REMARKS

A new open-SW framework to implement parallel H.264/AVC encoders was presented in this chapter. Such framework significantly eases the exploitation of the parallel processing capabilities offered by current homogeneous and heterogeneous multicore architectures, as an efficient means to increase the resulting encoding performance.

Three different *functional-level* topologies are supported and easily parameterized by the presented SW framework: pipeline, straight parallel, and mixed. In what concerns the exploitation of *data-level* parallelism, two models are particularly supported, besides the trivial frame-level partition model: slice level and macroblock level.

Despite the limitations imposed by the H.264 standard, *slice-level* parallelism proved to be the most efficient approach, with speedup gains quite close to the theoretical maximum. On the other hand, the *macroblock-level* parallelism model has shown to offer an extra and quite viable speedup margin that can be exploited as a complement to the *slice-level* parallelism, in order to improve the scalability of the parallel implementation, in particular, when the number of available cores is greater than 16.

ACKNOWLEDGMENTS

This work was supported by FCT (INESC-ID multiannual funding) through the PID-DAC Program funds.

REFERENCES

1. M. Ali Ben Ayed, A. Samet, and N. Masmoudi. H.264/AVC prediction modules complexity analysis. *Wiley InterScience on European Transactions on Telecommunications*, 18:169–177, March 2007.

2. A. Azevedo, B. H. H. Juurlink, C. H. Meenderinck, A. Terechko, J. Hoogerbrugge, M. Alvarez, A. Ramirez, and M. Valero. A highly scalable parallel implementation of H.264. *Transactions on High-Performance Embedded Architectures and Compilers (HiPEAC)*, September 2009.

3. J. Bae, Y. Soh, D. Kim, and M. Lee. A programmable multi-format video decoder. In *Proceedings of International Conference on Intelligent Computation Technology and Automation (ICICTA'09)*, volume 4, pages 25–28, 2009.

4. W.-N. Chen and H.-M. Hang. H.264/AVC motion estimation implementation on Compute Unified Device Architecture (CUDA). In *Proceedings of IEEE International Conference on Multimedia and Expo (ICME'2008)*, pages 697–700, 2008.

5. Y.-K. Chen, E. Q. Li, X. Zhou, and S. L. Ge. Implementation of H.264 encoder and decoder on personal computers. *Journal of Visual Communications and Image Representations*, 17(2):509–532, April 2006.

6. Y.-K. Chen, X. Tian, S. Ge, and M. Girkar. Towards efficient multi-level threading of H.264 encoder on Intel hyper-threading architectures. In *Proceedings of International Parallel and Distributed Processing Symposium*, pages 63–72, April 2004.

7. N.-M. Cheung, X. Fan, O. C. Au, and M.-C. Kung. Video coding on multicore graphics processors. *IEEE Signal Processing Magazine*, 27(2):79–89, March 2010.

8. T. Dias, N. Roma, and L. Sousa. H.264/AVC framework for multi-core embedded video encoders. In *Proceedings of International Symposium on System-on-Chip (SOC'2010)*, pages 89–92, September 2010.

9. T. Dias, N. Roma, L. Sousa, and M. Ribeiro. Reconfigurable architectures and processors for real-time video motion estimation. *Journal of Real-Time Image Processing*, 2(4):191–205, 2007.

10. R. Gerber, A. J. C. Bik, K. Smith, and X. Tian. *The Software Optimization Cookbook*, chapter 18 – Case Study: Threading a Video Codec, pages 323–343. Intel Press, second edition, 2006.

11. X. He, X. Fang, C. Wang, and S. Goto. Parallel HD encoding on CELL. In *Proceedings of International Symposium on Circuits and Systems (ISCASâĂŹ2009)*, pages 1065–1068, May 2009.

12. M. Herlihy and N. Shavit. *The Art of Multiprocessor Programming*. Morgan Kaufmann, March 2008.

13. S. Hiratsuka, S. Goto, and T. Ikenaga. An ultra-low complexity motion estimation algorithm and its implementation of specific processor. In *Proceedings of IEEE International Symposium on Circuits and Systems (ISCAS'2006)*, 2006.

14. *JM H.264/AVC Reference Software*. http://iphome.hhi.de/suehring/tml/, 2011.

15. S. Kim and M. Sunwoo. ASIP approach for implementation of H.264/AVC. *Journal of Signal Processing Systems*, 50(1):53–67, January 2008.

16. H. Mizosoe, D. Yoshida, and T. Nakamura. A single chip H.264/AVC HDTV encoder/decoder/transcoder system LSI. *IEEE Transactions on Consumer Electronics*, 53(2):630–635, May 2007.

17. S. Momcilovic and L. Sousa. Modeling and evaluating non-shared memory CELL/BE type multi-core architectures for local image and video processing. *The Journal of Signal Processing Systems*, 62(3):301–318, March 2010.

18. A. Rodríguez, A. González, and M. P. Malumbres. Hierarchical parallelization of an H.264/AVC video encoder. In *International Conference on Parallel Computing in Electrical Engineering*, pages 363–368, 2006.

19. X. Tian, Y.-K. Chen, M. Girkar, S. Ge, R. Lienhart, and S. Shah. Exploring the use of hyper-threading technology for multimedia applications with Intel OpenMP compiler. In *Proceedings of International Parallel and Distributed Processing Symposium*, pages 1–8, April 2003.

20. S.-W. Wang, Y.-T. Yang, C.-Y. Li, Y.-S. Tung, and J.-L. Wu. The optimization of H.264/AVC baseline decoder on low-cost TriMedia DSP processor. In *Proceedings of SPIE*, volume 5558, pages 524–535, 2004.

21. T. Wiegand, Gary J. Sullivan, G. Bjontegaard, and A. Luthra. Overview of the H.264/AVC video coding standard. *Transactions on Circuits and Systems for Video Technology*, 13:560–576, July 2003.

CHAPTER 15

PARALLELIZING EVOLUTIONARY ALGORITHMS ON GPGPU CARDS WITH THE EASEA PLATFORM

OGIER MAITRE, FREDERIC KRUGER, DEEPAK SHARMA,
STEPHANE QUERRY, NICOLAS LACHICHE AND PIERRE COLLET

15.1 INTRODUCTION

Artificial evolution algorithms raise great interest in their ability to find solutions that are not necessarily optimal, but adequate for complex problems. The quality of obtained results depends on various factors, including the available computing power. Increasing this power is interesting, as it would allow to explore usually immense search spaces more widely and deeply, for better results.

In 2004, massively parallel general-purpose graphics processing unit (GPGPU) processors became available, with hundreds of cores and very fast memory. In 2011, these processors typically offer 1 teraflop for a couple hundred dollars.

Evolutionary algorithms (EAs) are inherently parallel, because they evolve a population of distinct individuals in a generational loop. These algorithms are therefore very good candidates to be ported on massively multicore architectures. Indeed, many works take this direction, but in order to obtain good results, the user must be an expert both in EAs and in GPGPU programming.

Programming Multicore and Many-core Computing Systems,
First Edition. Edited by Sabri Pllana and Fatos Xhafa.

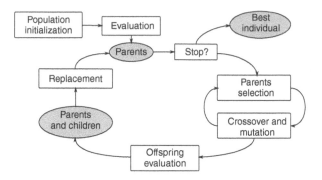

Figure 15.1   Basic evolutionary algorithm.

EAsy Specification of Evolutionary Algorithm (EASEA) is a software platform dedicated to EAs that allows to exploit parallel architectures, which range from a single-GPGPU equipped machine to multi-GPGPU machines and, to a cluster or even several clusters of GPGPU machines. The EASEA software is available on Source-Forge or on the dedicated EASEA platform web site.[1]

Parallel algorithms implemented by the EASEA platform are presented in this chapter for EAs and evolution strategies, genetic programming (GP) and multiobjective optimization (MOO). Finally, a set of problems is presented that contains artificial and real-world problems. These approaches were tested and presented in different papers [18, 21, 23, 24].

15.1.1 Evolutionary Algorithms (EAs)

An EA optimizes a problem by successively evolving generations of populations of potential solutions to a given problem. The initial population is usually created at random by the initialization function, and all individuals are evaluated in order to determine how well they solve the problem. Parents are selected (with a bias toward the best) to create children by applying crossover and/or mutation operators. This offspring population is then evaluated, and a replacement operator gets the temporary population (parents + offspring) back to the original population size (cf. Fig. 15.1). For a more thorough description of EAs and GP, please refer to [4, 6, 7].

From a parallelization point of view, these algorithms are very interesting, because many computations are applied to independent objects. There are two main ways to parallelize EAs: parallelization of one EA over several cores (or even several machines) and getting several interconnected EAs to run in parallel (island model).

15.1.2 Some Hardware Considerations

Compute Unified Device Architecture (CUDA) is the first released framework for the exploitation of a unified GPU architecture that was supplied by the NVIDIA

---

[1]http://lsiit.u-strasbg.fr/easea.

manufacturer in 2004. CUDA abstracts GPGPU architecture to allow portability between different models of the brand. For further information, the reader is invited to refer to the official CUDA documentation [25].

CUDA views a GPGPU processor as a set of cores (called SPs for *streaming processors*) grouped together in a single-instruction, multiple-data (SIMD) bundle of 8 or 32 *multiprocessors* (MPs). An MP decodes and executes an instruction on 32 threads, which are always performed together. This bundle of threads is called a *warp*. The cores of an MP access a private extremely fast shared memory, whose size varies between 16 and 64 KB. Then, each core can access a large global memory (up to 6 GB), whose bandwidth is high, but suffers from high latency.

Shared memory can be used to replace the L1 cache (absent from the first models and implemented in the fast 64 KB on the new ones) where data reuse avoids reloading. On memory stalls, MPs implement a hardware scheduler similar to a hyper-threading mechanism, which exchanges the warp with another one that is ready for execution. This mechanism allows to hide memory latencies, if enough threads are loaded on an MP and if hardware constraints (such as free registers) are met.

15.2 EASEA PARALLELIZATION OF EA ON GPGPU

The approach used in the EASEA platform has been more deeply presented in [21, 23]. Although different trends exist in EAs, in [8, 9] the authors propose a unified vision, focusing on common points and differentiating evolutionary engines thanks to parameters only. Deeper differences are embedded in individual representation (as in the case of GP) or special ranking mechanisms (as in MOO, for instance).

The EASEA platform was initially designed to assist users in the creation of EAs [5]. It is designed to produce an EA from a problem description. This description is written in a C-like language, which contains code for the genetic operators (crossover, mutation, initialization and evaluation) and the genome structure. From these functions, written into a .*ez* file, EASEA generates a complete EA with potential parallelization of evaluation over GPGPUs, or over a cluster of heterogeneous machines, thanks to the embedded island model discussed in the following text.

The generated source file for the EA is user readable. It can be used as is, or as a primer, to be manually extended by an expert programmer.

For single-objective algorithms, it was chosen to parallelize the evaluation step only, because this phase is often the most time consuming in the whole algorithm. It means that the parallel and sequential versions of an algorithm can be completely identical for the evaluation step.

For multiobjective evolutionary algorithms (MOEAs), a specific stochastic ranking method has been developed, which can be parallelized without impacting quality.

An EASEA EA is defined by problem-specific pieces of code provided by the user. The genome structure is, of course, the first piece that is needed, followed by genetic operators such as the initialization operator (which constructs a new individual), the crossover operator (which creates a child out of two parents), the mutation operator and finally the evaluation function that returns a value proportional to how well an individual does on the problem to be solved (fitness). An EASEA source code (.ez file) consists in several sections, many of which are dedicated to these problem-specific operators. Different papers explain how this is done, including [5, 18, 21–23].

15.2.1 EASEA Parallelization Standard EAs

Various attempts at porting EAs onto GPGPU have been made. All these implementations were done early in the maturity cycle of these cards [12, 20, 31] using graphical programming languages and showing poor performance. EASEA uses more standard C/C++ syntax and benefits from the CUDA sdk.

15.2.1.1 EASEA Implementation of Evolutionary Algorithms For single-objective EAs, it was decided to use GPGPUs for population evaluations only for several reasons:

1. Porting the whole code on a GPGPU multicore architecture is quite complex and would result in an algorithm that would behave differently than standard EAs implemented on CPUs.

2. In most cases, population evaluation is considered to be the most computationally intensive part of an EA.

3. Keeping the evolutionary engine on the host machine allows to access individuals in the GPU in read only: the new population needs to be transferred to the GPU at each generation, but only fitness values need to be copied back.

The population to be evaluated is distributed into blocks that are assigned to all MPs. In order to ensure good load balancing and efficient scheduling, some hardware constraints must be respected (no block should use more registers than available on an MP). The following algorithm distributes the population onto the card:

Algorithm 15.1

Input: N: PopulationSize, w: WarpSize, M: number of MPs, s: max number of schedulable tasks, e: max number of tasks **Output :** b: number of blocks, t: number of threads per block
Repeat $\quad b := b + M \quad\quad t := \lceil \mathrm{Min}(s, e, N/(b \times M)))/w \rceil \times w$; **until** $b \times t$ $> N \wedge e > t \wedge s > t$

The number of blocks should be $\geq M$ (number of MPs). Then, the minimum number of threads per block is w (the minimum number of SIMD threads), or the thread limit (e,s) that is given by the maximum scheduling capacity (s) or the number of tasks that an MP can execute (e). The last limit is related to task complexity (the number of registers used by a thread and the number of available registers per MP). As the number of threads that are really executed is a multiple of w, the first multiple of w which is greater than this minimum is taken.

For evaluation, the population is sent to the GPGPU memory, and the evaluation function is applied, using the distribution mechanism described in the preceding text. Finally fitness values are returned to the CPU memory, so that the standard algorithm can continue.

To avoid multiple memory transfers between the card and the host system, individuals are collected in a single buffer before being transferred to the memory card.

15.2.1.2 *Evaluation Step*   In the general case, the evaluation of individuals is done independently and can therefore be parallelized. Each evaluation takes place in a thread and all threads execute the same function. Thus, threads running at the same time on a set of SIMD processors do not suffer from divergence (SIMD means that all processors must execute the same instruction at the same time).

15.2.2   EASEA Implementation of Genetic Programming

GP [4] typically evolves functions represented by trees that are evaluated on all points of a training set.

It is interesting to note that where EAs execute an identical evaluation on different data (different individuals), GP does the opposite: different individuals are executed on identical data (the training set). In order to evaluate different individuals in an efficient way on SIMD hardware, it is therefore necessary to think differently.

15.2.2.1 *Related Works*   To our knowledge, the first work on GP was published in 2007 by Chitty [2]. This implementation evaluates a population of GP-compiled individuals, using the Cg (C for graphics) programming language.

Then, Harding and Banzhaf published a first implementation of interpreted GP in 2007 [16], where they use the GPU card to evaluate a single individual on every core.

Another implementation of interpreted GP is done by Langdon et al. [19] where the authors use RapidMind to do a complete implementation of a GP population evaluation. Each core runs an individual and the interpreter computes all the operators contained in the function set for every node, picking up the interesting result and discarding the others. This is equivalent to assuming the worst divergence case for each node and to using the GPGPU card as a fully SIMD processor (which it is not).

In 2008 and 2009 [26, 27], Robilliard et al. present an implementation using CUDA that takes into account the hardware structure of NVIDIA cards by conducting the evaluation of several individuals over several fitness cases at the same time. But some hardware tools are left unused, in particular the MP scheduling capability.

15.2.2.2 *EASEA Implementation of GP*   The approach used in EASEA was published in [22, 24]. As with the implementation of Robilliard *et al.*, individuals are trees that are flattened in reverse Polish notation (RPN) before they are transferred on the GPGPU for evaluation.

15.2.2.3 Evaluation Step In GP, the fitness of an individual is generally a sum of errors, obtained when comparing the values produced by the individual with an expected value on a training set element. The execution of individuals on these training cases is an independent task. Only the sum of errors for all training cases requires a synchronization.

The RPN interpreter presented here is inspired from Robilliard's paper [26], but a special emphasis has been put onto maximizing the number of tasks assigned to MPs. This difference allows to benefit from the MP hardware scheduler, which allows to overlap memory latencies.

It is necessary to load $k/4$ MP tasks in order to maximize scheduling ability ($k = 768$ or 1024 depending on the GPGPU version) and to use $k/4$ training cases in parallel in order to assign one case to each thread.

However, if the warps are executed in SIMD, it is possible to execute different instructions in each warp [25], which allows to evaluate different individuals simultaneously and to maximize scheduling, if the training set contains more than 32 cases.

An interpreter stores the results of the nodes in a stack stored in global memory that cannot be shared between tasks.

15.2.3   Island Model

The island model is a well-known way to parallelize EAs [1], as it often allows to obtain superlinear speedup over one machine and linear speedup over several machines. On a cluster of computers, every node runs a complete EA, which can be seen as an island. A migration mechanism is added that allows to periodically export some individuals to other nodes.

The island model thus allows to parallelize an EA on several machines. Exchanges between nodes are limited to the migration of one individual every n generations, which is a very lightweight asynchronous communication.

EASEA implements islands using a loosely connected model based on UDP, which allows to parallelize over neighbor or distant machines (cluster or grid computing).

15.2.4   Multiobjective Evolutionary Algorithm

Real-world problems often need to optimize multiple different goals simultaneously. This can be done either by converting these goals into a single objective or by using MOO techniques, among which MOEAs are very efficient, as they can find (*Pareto optimal* solutions) in one run [3, 10]. Interesting MOEAs are designed on the concept of dominance which can be categorized as dominance rank, dominance count and dominance depth. NSGA-II [11] sorts individuals according to dominance depth, using the concept of nondominated sorting [15], and SPEA2 [32] assigns rank based on dominance depth and dominance count, where the count of dominated individuals by an individual is used. These efficient dominance-based methods evaluate rank serially in a deterministic way (except NPGA), with a quadratic ranking complexity on the population size ($O(mn^2)$ for NSGA-II, where m is the number of objectives and n is the population size).

15.2.4.1 *Related Works*

A large population is often required when solving many-objective problems [3, 10] or GP with more than one objective (error minimization and parsimony) in which case MOEAs become computationally expensive. The first appreciable effort of parallelizing MOEA on GPUs is shown in [30]. In this study, the dominance comparison of NSGA-II has been implemented on GPU, but the sorting of individuals in different fronts is still done on CPU.

This chapter presents the Archive-based Stochastic Ranking Evolutionary Algorithm (ASREA) [28], which has been developed for MOO with an $O(man)$ ranking complexity (where a is the size of an archive that depends on the number of objectives m) which breaks the $O(mn^2)$ complexity while yielding improved results over NSGA-II (discussed in Section 15.3.3). Furthermore, ASREA has been designed so that the ranking and function evaluations can be done in parallel on GPGPUs [29].

15.2.4.2 *Implementation*

Figure 15.2 shows the flowchart of G-ASREA, which starts with evaluating a random initial population (**ini_pop**) on GPGPUs. An archive is maintained in G-ASREA according to an archive updating algorithm

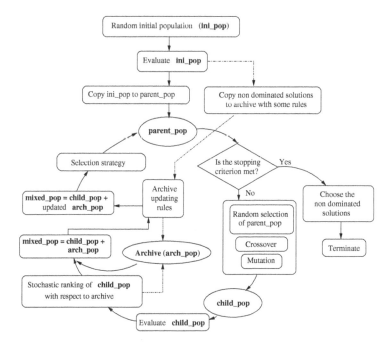

Figure 15.2   ASREA flowchart.

15.2.4.2 where the distinct nondominated individuals of **ini_pop** are copied. Before starting the standard EA loop, **ini_pop** is copied to **parent_pop** and a termination criterion is then checked. If the criterion is not met, then **child_pop** is created by repeatedly selecting *randomly* two parents from the **parent_pop** and creating children through a crossover, followed by a mutation, after which the **child_pop** is evaluated on GPGPU.

Algorithm 15.2

If Number of non-dominated solutions $\leq$ archive size Copy distinct non-dominated solutions to archive **else** Copy the extreme solutions of non-dominated front to archive and evaluate crowding distance (CD [11]) of rest of the non-dominated solutions. Fill the remaining archive with the sorted CD-wise individuals in descending order

---

G-ASREA now ranks the **child_pop** on GPGPU by comparing individuals of **child_pop** with the members of the archive. The rank of individual (A) of **child_pop** is calculated on the following dominance rank criterion:

$$\text{rank}(A) = 1 + \textit{number of } \textbf{\textit{arch\_pop}} \textit{ members that dominate } A \qquad (15.1)$$

Note that in G-ASREA, the lower rank is better, with best rank = 1.

To perform the ranking on GPGPU, *CR*, an integer array of size n (allocated in the global GPU memory) is used for storing the rank of **child_pop**. Suppose the thread processor *idx* computes the rank of a **child_pop** individual using equation (15.1); then it stores the calculated rank at position *idx* of *CR*.

During the ranking on GPU, each thread processor also keeps track of the domination count of **arch_pop**, independently. For this, another single integer array *AR* of size $a \times n$ is allocated in the global GPU memory before execution. Note that the array is initialized to value 1 because all members of **arch_pop** are rank 1 solutions. When an individual of thread processor *idx* dominates the Kth member of **arch_pop**, then the thread processor increments $AR[(a \times idx) + k]$ by 1. This dominance check information is used later to update ranks in the archive.

After parallel stochastic ranking is finished on the GPU, ranks of the **child_pop** are updated by copying *CR* back to the CPU. The rank of the archive is also modified using array *AR* in the following manner: suppose that the modified rank of the Kth member of the archive is evaluated. Then, for $i = 0$ to $n - 1$, the integer value of every $AR[(i \times a) + k]$ is added and finally subtracted by n. If the Kth member is still nondominated, then its modified rank is 1. Otherwise, the rank of the Kth member depends on the number of **child_pop** individuals who dominated it.

The next step of ASREA is then to update the archive and propagate good individuals to the next generation. First, the ranked **child_pop** and **arch_pop** with modified ranks are mixed together to form **mixed_pop**. Now, the archive is updated from the set of nondominated solutions (*rank* = 1) of **mixed_pop** as given in algorithm 15.2.

Algorithm 15.3

```
Copy the extreme solutions of updated arch_pop to the parent population.
Fill 20% of parent_pop from the updated arch_pop in the following way:
While (20% of parent_pop is not filled)
    Pick randomly two individuals of updated arch_pop
    If Crowding distances are different
        Copy the individual with larger crowding distance into parent_pop
    else Copy any individual randomly
Fill rest of parent_pop from child_pop in the following way:
While (rest of parent_pop is not filled)
    Pick two individuals randomly from child_pop without replacing them
    If Ranks are different
        Copy the individual with smaller rank into parent_pop
    else-if Copy the individual with larger crowding distance into parent_pop
    else Copy any individual randomly
```

The next generation (new parent population) is also selected from **mixed_pop** according to the strategy discussed in Algorithm 15.3. Here, 20% of the new parent population is filled from the updated archive with randomly picked members. The rest of **parent_pop** is filled from **child_pop** individuals using tournament selection. The EA loop is then completed and can start again by checking whether a termination criterion is met (e.g. number of generations) as in Figure 15.2.

15.3 EXPERIMENTS AND APPLICATIONS

15.3.1 Weierstrass/Mandelbrot

To evaluate the ES/GA implementation, it was chosen to minimize the Weierstrass/ Mandelbrot function, which is a difficult problem because it has a very irregular fitness landscape. It has parameters that can increase the irregularity of its fitness landscape (Hölder coefficient h) and its computation time (the approximation of the

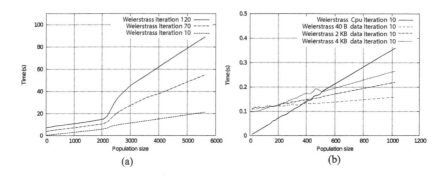

Figure 15.3 Impact of population size, number figure of iterations and dimensions on execution time and overhead. (a) Impact of population size and evaluation complexity on execution time. (b) Impact of individual size on transfer time overhead.

infinite sum is done by a number of iterations that can be modified). Finally, the number of dimensions can also be increased, in order to test larger genome sizes:

$$W_{b,h}(x) = \sum_{j=0}^{n} \sum_{i=1}^{iteration} b^{-ih} \sin(b^i x_j)$$

with $b > 1$ and $0 < h < 1$

These experiments were performed with the EASEA platform on an old Pentium IV 3.6GHz computer with an early 8800GTX card of the same era, running under Linux. Different population sizes are tested along with different iteration values (10, 70 or 120) and with different individual sizes (10–1000 dimensions).

Figure 15.3(a) shows that under 2000 individuals, the computing time does not increase linearly (even though it should, as it should take twice more time to evaluate 2000 individuals than 1000). This means that the increase in computation time comes from the sequential part of the algorithm (evolution engine without the evaluation step). Evaluations are done in parallel as the card is being loaded. Beyond 3000 individuals, evaluation time becomes linear with the population size. It is interesting to note that the slope for 10 iterations is virtually identical under 2000 individuals and beyond 3000 individuals, meaning that evaluation time is negligible. This is ideal to test parallelization overhead, which is studied in Figure 15.3(b) where one sees that even with a huge genome size corresponding to 1000 parameters to optimize (4 KB), parallelization overhead is overcome for population sizes beyond 600 individuals. Transfer time plus initiation of the computation on the GPU takes 0.12 s only (Fig. 15.4).

For speedup measurements, the EASEA platform has been used to create a (standard) sequential algorithm to be run on a very fast core of an Intel i7-950 processor and check the speedup obtained with different generation cards (from a 2006 8800GTX to a 2010 GTX480). The architecture of the cards is different, but EASEA performed the load balancing automatically using the algorithm presented in Section 15.2.1.1.

Finally, evolution of the fitness of the best individual is observed on 1, 5, 10 and 20 machines using the embedded EASEA island parallelization. It is interesting to

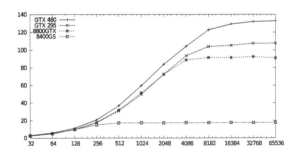

Figure 15.4   Speedup on an average of 10 runs for several GPGPUs cards versus an Intel i7-950 on a 10-dimension 120-iteration Weierstrass benchmark.

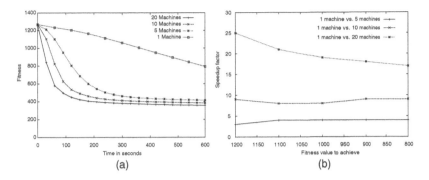

Figure 15.5 Speedup obtained with the island model on Weierstrass 1000 dimensions, h = 0.35 for 81200 individuals.

note that the same population size was used for the different runs, that is, 81,920 individuals on one machine, 16384 individuals on each of the 5 machines, 8192 on each of the 10 machines and 4096 individuals on each of the 20 machines. Speedup is roughly linear with the number of machines until the single-machine implementation gets stuck in a local optimum (after value 500). Speedup then becomes superlinear with reference to one machine but still roughly linear between multi-island configuration (Fig. 15.5).

The cluster of machines used for this test being equipped with GTX275 cards yielding a speedup of around 100× over a Core-i7-950, the speedup for 20 machines is therefore of about 2000×, meaning that a one hour run on this cluster is equivalent to a 83-days run for a similar sequential algorithm on a top-notch workstation.

15.3.2   Symbolic Regression

To test the EASEA implementation of Genetic Programming on GPGPU, we used a symbolic regression benchmark from Koza's book [24]: $x^3 - 3x^2 + x$. Several learning set sizes have been tried as well as several tree sizes to find out what kind of speedup factors could be obtained.

Figure 15.6(a) shows the speedup obtained between an Intel Quad Core Q8200 and a GTX275 card on the evaluation function implementation described in Section 15.2.2.3.

A first point that can be seen from this figure is that the speedups reach a plateau fairly quickly, with only 32 fitness cases, confirming that scheduling is a real gain. Secondly, in terms of speedup, the influence of tree size is much less important than the fact that the number of fitness cases is greater than 32.

A second parameter that can influence the speedup is the computational intensity of the function set used in the tree construction. Two function sets are listed with different intensities: $F1 = \{+, -, /, \times\}$ and $F2 = \{+, -, /, \times, \cos, \sin, \log, \exp\}$. Using $F2$ increases the *computation/memory access* ratio and improves the speedup as shown in Figure 15.7. Furthermore, it is possible to use special function units (SFU) in the card in order to compute approximations for trigonometric functions, which

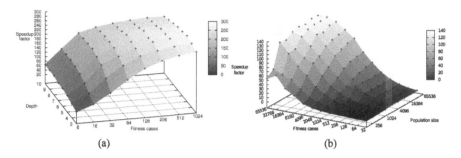

(a)   (b)

Figure 15.6 Speedup factor for symbolic regression wrt different parameters. (a) Speedup wrt tree depth and learning set size, for the evaluation function only. (b) Speedup wrt number of fitness cases.

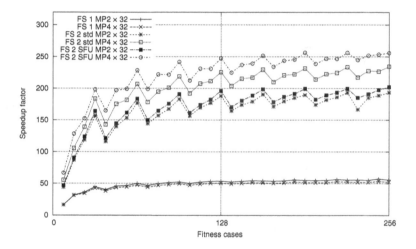

Figure 15.7 Influence of function set computational intensity.

further reduces the evaluation time for populations containing SFUs at the cost of reduced computing accuracy. Using different function sets, speedups range between 50× and 200× and up to 250× using SFUs.

Figure 15.6(b) shows the speedup achieved on the complete regression algorithm using the $F2$ function. Even if the speedup is much larger than 1 on the evaluation function only, even with a small number of training cases, it is to be noted that the speedup of the complete algorithm is lower. Indeed, the volume of data is quite high here compared to the cost of the population evaluation. For a large number of training cases, speedup becomes more attractive especially on a large population. This can also be attributed to the overhead of the tree flattening step, which is more easily overcome in these extreme cases.

It is nice to see that speedup for GP is greater than for other EAs. This comes from the fact that GP is very computation intensive and parallelizing evaluation of the same individual over different test cases in SIMD mode is very efficient.

15.3.3 Performance of G-ASREA on Multiobjective Test Functions

Paper [28] compares the behavior of ASREA on several Zitzler–Deb–Thiele (ZDT) test functions [33] with other MOEAs on CPU. ZDT functions are executed with identical parameters of MOEAs on Intel(R) Core(TM)2 Quad CPU Q8200 @ 2.33 GHz computer with one of the 2 GPUs of a GTX295 card.

15.3.3.1 *Solution Performance* Nondominated fronts of ASREA, NSGA-II and SPEA2 are compared for the ZDT3 function. For 25 different runs, MOEAs start with a population of 100 and terminate after 500 generations. 0% attainment plots [13, 14] are shown in Figure 15.8 for MOEAs at different function evaluation stages.

Initially (10^3 EVAL), ASREA shows the closest proximity to the front and maintains a very good spread. At (10^4 EVAL), ASREA and NSGA-II have converged on the theoretical Pareto front, while SPEA2 is lagging behind (see [28] for tests and curves on more functions).

On 100 individuals, the O(mn^2) ranking complexity of most MOEAs is not an issue. However, this is not the case on population sizes that must be used for massive parallelism to be effective.

Figure 15.9 shows that for 100 individuals, a speedup of 4.95 is obtained by ASREA ranking over NSGA-II ranking and only 4.14 by G-ASREA (the parallel version) over NSGA-II, because of the parallelization overhead.

Things are different for 1000, 10,000 and 100,000 population sizes, where NSGA-II uses 3.8910^{-2} s, 4.54 s and 19 h, respectively, where ASREA takes 1.01 10^{-3} s, 9.97 10^{-3} s and 9.86 10^{-2} s and where G-ASREA 1.62 10^{-4} s, 8.34 10^{-4} s and 7.11 10^{-3} s.

For 1 million individuals, ASREA takes 0.992 s and G-ASREA 0.0661 s for ranking, where NSGA-II and other deterministic ranking MOEAs would take days, if not years, to compute, this time not even including evaluation time of the individuals.

Overall, the advantage of CPU and GPGPU versions of ASREA over other algorithms is twofold: a first speedup comes from the smaller ranking complexity, and another one comes from GPU parallelization.

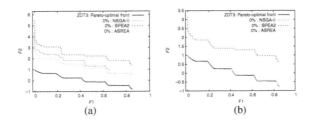

Figure 15.8 Attainment surface plots of ASREA, NSGA-II and SPEA2 for ZDT functions. (a) ZDT3 at 1000 EVAL. (b) ZDT3 at 10,000 EVAL.

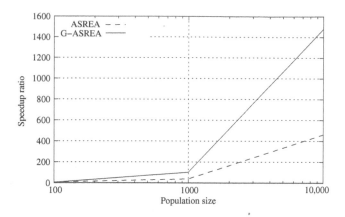

Figure 15.9   Speedup for ZDT3 function on population sizes 100, 1000 and 10000.

15.3.4   Real-World Problem: Aircraft Model Regression

Finally, benchmark testing is great but rarely reflect real-world problems where things never work as planned. Here is an example taken from automation science, whose principle is to describe the evolution of a controlled system using first-order differential equations, which are function of physical variables and control inputs.

Systems can have different complexities, and so the number of physical variables (called state variables) which are necessary to describe the evolution of the complete system can vary. In a similar way, the number of control inputs which are used for the purpose of proper system control can be different.

Usually, state variables cannot be directly measured, and system outputs correspond to installed sensor measurements. In such cases, state estimators (or observers) are used to estimate the state variable values from the sensor output values.

In multi-input, multioutput (MIMO) systems, a control vector contains several elements, meaning that several equations for what is called a state-space representation that can use linear or nonlinear representations.

Most of the automation tools are designed to be used with a linear representation (matrix products) for which a linearization is performed around the equilibrium point. Unfortunately, nonlinear systems controlled by a linear state-space representation do not perform very well, as the system diverges quite fast. It would be much better to use equations representing a nonlinear state space, but unfortunately, such equations are much more difficult to determine and to use.

If we consider the following state vector X and control vector U:

$$x^T = [x_1 x_2 x_3 \ldots x_n] \quad u^T = [u_1 u_2 u_3 \ldots u_m]$$

Then, the nonlinear state-space representation is

$$\begin{cases} \dot{x}_1(t) = f_1(t, x_1(t), \ldots, x_n(t), u_1(t), \ldots, u_m(t)) \\ \ldots \\ \dot{x}_n(t) = f_n(t, x_1(t), \ldots, x_n(t), u_1(t), \ldots, u_m(t)) \end{cases}$$

For aircraft control, the state variable vector contains 14 elements, and the control input vector contains 4 elements. All the state variables are supposed to be known, due to the proper application of an extended Kalman filter (EKF) dedicated to navigation.

The choice of the state vector is

$$x^T = [V, \alpha, \beta, p, q, r, q_1, q_2, q_3, q_4, N, E, h, T]$$

where V is the airspeed, α the angle of attack, β the heeling angle, p the x-axis rotation rate, q the y-axis rotation rate, r the z-axis rotation rate, q_1 q_2 q_3 q_4 the attitude quaternions, N the latitude, E the longitude, h the altitude and T the real thrust.

The choice of the control vector is $u^T = [T_c\ \delta_e\ \delta_a\ \delta_r]$, where T_c is the commanded throttle, δ_e the commanded elevator, δ_a the commanded ailerons and δ_r the commanded rudder. The nonlinear state-space representation then becomes

$$\begin{cases} \dot{V}(t) = f_1(t, V(t), \alpha(t), \dots, T(t), T_c(t), \dots, \delta_r(t)) \\ \dot{\alpha}(t) = f_2(t, V(t), \alpha(t), \dots, T(t), T_c(t), \dots, \delta_r(t)) \\ \dots \\ \dot{q}_1 = f_7(t, V(t), \alpha(t), \dots, T(t), T_c(t), \dots, \delta_r(t)) \\ \dot{q}_2 = f_8(t, V(t), \alpha(t), \dots, T(t), T_c(t), \dots, \delta_r(t)) \\ \dot{q}_3 = f_9(t, V(t), \alpha(t), \dots, T(t), T_c(t), \dots, \delta_r(t)) \\ \dot{q}_4 = f_{10}(t, V(t), \alpha(t), \dots, T(t), T_c(t), \dots, \delta_r(t)) \\ \dots \\ \dot{h}(t) = f_{13}(t, V(t), \alpha(t), \dots, T(t), T_c(t), \dots, \delta_r(t)) \\ \dot{T}(t) = f_{14}(t, V(t), \alpha(t), \dots, T(t), T_c(t), \dots, \delta_r(t)) \end{cases}$$

A model is necessary for the development of an autopilot system. Some experts are often required to determine this model. But from a telemetry file, recorded during a human commanded flight, a GP algorithm might be able to find such equations, sufficiently accurately for the autopilot to fly the aircraft.

15.3.4.1 *Considered Functions* The attitude quaternions are the 4 functions which are more often used in the navigation field, because they cover the entire angle domain, without exception. As a real-world application, it was chosen to try to regress the 4-quaternion equations, which are given by the following system:

$$\begin{cases} \dot{q}_1 = f_7 = 0.5(q_4 p - q_3 q + q_2 r) \\ \dot{q}_2 = f_8 = 0.5(q_3 p + q_4 q - q_1 r) \\ \dot{q}_3 = f_9 = 0.5(-q_2 p + q_1 q + q_4 r) \\ \dot{q}_4 = f_{10} = 0.5(-q_1 p - q_2 q - q_3 r) \end{cases}$$

A telemetry file, containing the necessary $[V, \alpha, \beta, p, q, r, q_1, q_2, q_3, q_4, N, E, h, T]$ state variables as well as the $u^T = [T_c\ \delta_e\ \delta_a\ \delta_r]$ and time) control variables, has been created through a nonlinear state-space system of a small F3A airplane performing a simulated flight of several minutes. The learning set contains 51,000 points, that is, around 8 min of flight.

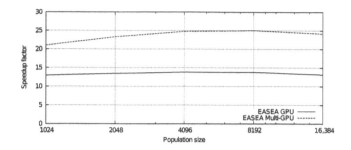

Figure 15.10   Speedup obtained on the airplane problem with EASEA tree-base GP implementation.

Four EASEA GP runs have been launched in order to find the equations for the four quaternions.

Figure 15.10 shows the obtained speedups for a population size of 40,960 individuals over 100 generations, F1 function set, $x[1] \ldots x[17]$, $[ERC]\{0, 1\}$ terminal set and 51,000 values in the training set. In this case, the time spent in the evolution engine is negligible compared with evaluation time. Because of the simple $F1$ function set, the speedup is lower than shown in Section 15.3.2 for more complex function sets. In the current experiment, the terminal set is larger (random constant and 17 variables), meaning that the GPU interpreter has to perform more memory accesses than on the test bench, where the only variable can be stored in a register by the optimizer. These drawbacks, as well as the evolutionary process, can be blamed for the drop in speedup.

However, the obtained speedup on one machine is still very nice given the size of the problem. A real run takes hours of computation on CPU, but just several minutes on GPU. This is very important, because 14 different functions need to be found to solve the complete problem.

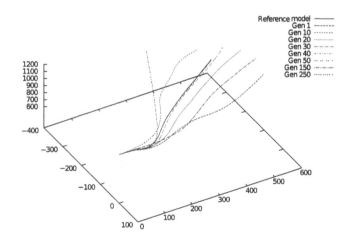

Figure 15.11   Difference between original and reconstructed trajectory.

Figure 15.11 shows the original trajectory and trajectories obtained by evolved quaternions at different generations. The original and last trajectory shows a negligible difference.

15.4 CONCLUSION

Tianhe-1A is currently the most powerful supercomputer on Earth, with a peak performance of 4.7 petaflops. It is made of 112 clusters of GPU computers, which are horrendously difficult to use efficiently, unless one uses several levels of parallelization, such as described in this chapter.

The EASEA platform can efficiently parallelize generic evolutionary optimization problems at a very low level on one GPU card or at a slightly higher level on several cards in one computer (by dividing the population to be evaluated among the cards). Then, it can also parallelize at a higher level between machines of a same cluster using an island model and even over several clusters by exchanging individuals between clusters (runs have been made using 20 machines in Strasbourg, France, and 32 machines in St John's, Newfoundland, Canada).

By their parallel and independent nature, EAs are perfectly suited to run on current petaflop machines and future exaflop machines, provided that all levels of parallelism are efficiently mastered, which is what the EASEA platform attempts to do.

REFERENCES

1. E. Alba and M. Tomassini. Parallelism and evolutionary algorithms. *IEEE Transactions on Evolutionary Computation*, 6(5):443–462, October 2002.

2. D. M. Chitty. A data parallel approach to genetic programming using programmable graphics hardware. In *Proceedings of the 9th Annual Genetic and Evolutionary Computation Conference (GECCO)*, pages 1566–1573. ACM, New York, NY, USA, 2007.

3. C. A. C. Coello, G. B. Lamont, and D. A. Van Veldhuizen. *Evolutionary Algorithms for Solving Multi-Objective Problems*. Springer-Verlag, New York, Inc., 2007.

4. P. Collet. Genetic programming. In J.-P. Rennard, editor, *Handbook of Research on Nature-Inspired Computing for Economics and Management*, volume I, chapter V, pages 59–73. Idea Group Inc., 1200 E. Colton Ave, 2007.

5. P. Collet, E. Lutton, M. Schoenauer, and J. Louchet. Take it easea. In *Proceedings of the 6th International Conference on Parallel Problem Solving from Nature*, PPSN VI, pages 891–901. Springer-Verlag, London, UK, 2000.

6. P. Collet and J.-P. Rennard. Evolutionary algorithms. In J.-P. Rennard, editor, *Handbook of Research on Nature-Inspired Computing for Economics and Management*, volume I, chapter III, pages 45–58. Idea Group Inc., 1200 E. Colton Ave, 2007.

7. P. Collet and J.-P. Rennard. Stochastic optimization algorithms. In Jean-Philippe Rennard, editor, *Handbook of Research on Nature-Inspired Computing for Economics and Management*, volume I, chapter III, pages 28–44. Idea Group Inc., 1200 E. Colton Ave, 2007.

8. P. Collet and M. Schoenauer. Guide: unifying evolutionary engines through a graphical user interface. In P. Liardet, P. Collet, C. Fonlupt, E. Lutton, and M. Schoenauer, editors, *Artificial Evolution*, volume 2936 of *Lecture Notes in Computer Science*, pages 203–215. Springer, 2003.

9. K. De Jong. Evolutionary computation: a unified approach. In *Proceedings of the 10th Annual Genetic and Evolutionary Computation Conference (GECCO)*, GECCO '08, pages 2245–2258. ACM, New York, NY, USA, 2008.

10. K. Deb. *Multi-Objective Optimization using Evolutionary Algorithms*. Chichester, UK: Wiley, first edition, 2001.

11. K. Deb, S. Agrawal, A. Pratap, and T. Meyarivan. A fast and elitist multi-objective genetic algorithm: NSGA-II. *IEEE Transactions on Evolutionary Computation*, 6(2):182–197, 2002.

12. K.-L. Fok, T.-T. Wong, and M.-L. Wong. Evolutionary computing on consumer graphics hardware. *IEEE Intelligent Systems*, 22(2):69–78, 2007.

13. C. M. Fonseca, V. G. Fonseca, and L. Paquete. Exploring the performance of stochastic multiobjective optimizers with the second-order attainment functions. In *Proceedings of the Third Evolutionary Multi-Criterion Optimization (EMO-05) Conference*, pages 250–264, 2005.

14. V. G. Fonseca, C. M. Fonseca, and A. O. Hall. Inferential performance assessment of stochastic optimizers and the attainment function. In *Proceedings of the First Evolutionary Multi-Criterion Optimization (EMO-01) Conference*, pages 213–225, 2001.

15. D. E. Goldberg. *Genetic Algorithms in Search, Optimization and Machine Learning*. Addison Wesley, 1989.

16. S. Harding and W. Banzhaf. Fast genetic programming on GPUs. In M. Ebner, M. O'Neill, A. Ekárt, L. Vanneschi, and A. Esparcia-Alcázar, editors, *10th European Conference on Genetic Programming (EuroGP)*, volume 4445 of *Lecture Notes in Computer Science*, pages 90–101. Springer-Verlag, Berlin, Heidelberg, 4 2007.

17. J. R. Koza. *Genetic Programming: On the Programming of Computers by Means of Natural Selection (Complex Adaptive Systems)*. MIT Press, Cambridge, CA, 1992.

18. F. Krüger, O. Maitre, S. Jiménez, L. Baumes, and P. Collet. Speedups between× 70 and× 120 for a generic local search (Memetic) algorithm on a single GPGPU chip. *Applications of Evolutionary Computation*, pages 501–511, 2010.

19. W. B. Langdon and W. Banzhaf. A SIMD interpreter for genetic programming on GPU graphics cards. In M. O'Neill, L. Vanneschi, S. Gustafson, A. I. Esparcia Alcazar, I. De Falco, A. Della Cioppa, and E. Tarantino, editors, *11th European Conference on Genetic Programming (EuroGP)*, volume 4971 of *Lecture Notes in Computer Science*, pages 73–85. Springer-Verlag, Berlin, Heidelberg, 3 2008.

20. J.-M. Li, X.-J. Wang, R.-S. He, and Z.-X. Chi. An efficient fine-grained parallel genetic algorithm based on GPU-accelerated. In *IFIP International Conference on Network and Parallel Computing Workshops (NPC)*, pages 855–862. IEEE Computer Society, Los Alamitos, CA, USA, 9 2007.

21. O. Maitre, N. Lachiche, P. Clauss, L. Baumes, A. Corma, and P. Collet. Efficient parallel implementation of evolutionary algorithms on GPGPU cards. In H. Sips, D. Epema,

and H.-X. Lin, editors, *Euro-Par 2009 Parallel Processing*, Lecture Notes in Computer Science, pages 974–985. Springer-Verlag, Heidelberg, Berlin, 8 2009.

22. O. Maitre, S. Querry, N. Lachiche, and P. Collet. EASEA parallelization of tree-based Genetic Programming. In *IEEE Congress on Evolutionary Computation (CEC)*, pages 1–8, 7 2010.

23. O. Maitre, L. A. Baumes, N. Lachiche, A. Corma, and P. Collet. Coarse grain parallelization of evolutionary algorithms on gpgpu cards with easea. In Franz Rothlauf, editor, *Proceedings of the 11th Annual conference on Genetic and evolutionary computation (GECCO)*, pages 1403–1410. ACM, New York, NY, USA, 2009.

24. O. Maitre, N. Lachiche, and P. Collet. Fast evaluation of GP trees on GPGPU by optimizing hardware scheduling. In A. Esparcia-Alcázar, A. Ekárt, S. Silva, S. Dignum, and A. Uyar, editors, *Genetic Programming*, volume 6021 of *Lecture Notes in Computer Science*, pages 301–312. Springer Berlin / Heidelberg, 2010.

25. NVIDIA. *NVIDIA CUDA Programming Guide 2.0*. 2008.

26. D. Robilliard, V. Marion-Poty, and C. Fonlupt. Population parallel GP on the G80 GPU. In M. O'Neill, L. Vanneschi, S. Gustafson, A. I. Esparcia Alcázar, I. De Falco, A. Della Cioppa, and E. Tarantino, editors, *11th European Conference on Genetic Programming (EuroGP)*, volume 4971, pages 98–109. Springer-Verlag, Berlin, Heidelberg, 2008.

27. D. Robilliard, V. Marion, and Cy. Fonlupt. High performance genetic programming on GPU. In *Workshop on Bio-inspired algorithms for distributed systems*, pages 85–94, Barcelona, Spain, 2009. ACM, New York.

28. D. Sharma and P. Collet. An archived-based stochastic ranking evolutionary algorithm (ASREA) for multi-objective optimization. In *GECCO '10: Proceedings of the 12th annual conference on Genetic and evolutionary computation*, pages 479–486. ACM, New York, NY, USA, 2010.

29. D. Sharma and P. Collet. Gpgpu-compatible archive based stochastic ranking evolutionary algorithm (g-asrea) for multi-objective optimization. In R. Schaefer, C. Cotta, J. Kolodziej, and G. Rudolph, editors, *PPSN (2)*, volume 6239 of *Lecture Notes in Computer Science*, pages 111–120. Springer, 2010.

30. M. L. Wong. Parallel multi-objective evolutionary algorithms on graphics processing units. In *GECCO '09: Proceedings of the 11th Annual Conference Companion on Genetic and Evolutionary Computation Conference*, pages 2515–2522. ACM, New York, NY, USA, 2009.

31. Q. Yu, C. Chen, and Z. Pan. Parallel genetic algorithms on programmable graphics hardware. In *First International Conference on Natural Computation (ICNC)*, volume 3612 of LNCS, pages 1051–1059. Springer-Verlag, Heidelberg, Berlin, 8 2005.

32. E. Zitzler, M. Laumanns, and L. Thiele. SPEA2: improving the strength pareto evolutionary algorithm for multiobjective optimization. In K. C. Giannakoglou et al., editors, *Evolutionary Methods for Design, Optimisation and Control with Application to Industrial Problems (EUROGEN 2001)*, pages 95–100. International Center for Numerical Methods in Engineering (CIMNE), 2002.

33. E. Zitzler, K. Deb, and L. Thiele. Comparison of multiobjective evolutionary algorithms: empirical results. *Evolutionary Computation Journal*, 8(2):125–148, 2000.

PART IV

TESTING, EVALUATION AND OPTIMIZATION

CHAPTER 16

SMART INTERLEAVINGS FOR TESTING PARALLEL PROGRAMS

Eitan Farchi

16.1 INTRODUCTION

In this chapter we consider the problem of testing programs that execute several parallel tasks. We'll refer to all such programs as parallel programs. Parallel programs might be distributed on different machines and synchronize through some message passing mechanism, or they might reside on a single machine and communicate through shared memory. In order to synchronize tasks and protect shared data, parallel programs might use different flavors of synchronization primitives such as locks, conditional variables, wait-on-event and compare-and-swap. These primitives provide different guarantees on synchronization between the tasks and different atomicity guarantees. The tasks themselves might come in different flavors such as threads and processes.[1] Regardless of the type of task, allocation of tasks to machine and

---

[1] Many good textbooks on concurrent and distributive programming [1] cover the construction of parallel programs.

Programming Multicore and Many-core Computing Systems,
First Edition. Edited by Sabri Pllana and Fatos Xhafa.
© 2017 John Wiley & Sons, Inc. Published 2017 by John Wiley & Sons, Inc.

synchronization primitive used, parallel programs suffer from similar testing challenges. We will tackle these challenges in this chapter.[2] In what follows we'll assume familiarity with parallel programming paradigms and will use the terms threads, processes and tasks interchangeably. For our purpose, distinguishing between these terms will not be necessary.

Parallel programs are hard to test. Given a set of inputs to a parallel program, many orders of task execution are possible. Moreover, because program tasks are not executed atomically, many orders of program execution are possible as well. To thoroughly test a parallel program, the set of possible orders of program execution needs to be covered. Different environment events, such as node or network failures, should be covered as well, and their timing may influence the result of the program execution. Thus, the challenge of parallel program testing includes the definition and coverage of this huge space of possible orders of tasks and environment events. In what follows, for a parallel program P and for a given set of P's inputs, we refer to the space of possible orders of task execution and environment events as the space of program interleavings, $I(P)$. As we'll see shortly, the number of possible orders of execution grows quickly with the number of tasks, making testing even more difficult in modern many-core environments.

This chapter is organized around the process of developing parallel programs with a focus on their testing. Once a program is defined, it can be reviewed to validate its correctness. Classical review techniques are at a loss when it comes to handling the review of parallel programs. Instead, parallel bug pattern-based reviews and distributed reviews are introduced. The review stage enables the design of a test plan for the parallel program that is then implemented in unit testing. Thus, the parallel program is well tested when it reaches function and system test (with some exceptions that are discussed in what follows), and many of the problems related to the testing of such programs are eliminated.

16.2 REVIEWS OF PARALLEL PROGRAMS

Reviews are known to be an effective way to find defects early in the development process. Review techniques were originally developed for sequential programs. In a typical review meeting, the code is projected on the screen, and the owner paraphrases the code and explains what it is doing and why. The reviewers ask questions, raise concerns and find problems in the code. Several inherent parallel program traits hinder the effectiveness of this approach. Given that many tasks are executing in parallel, the state of the program includes each task's program counter, each task's state, the global state of the memory and the state of the messages sent from one task to another. As a result, it is much harder to understand the parallel program's behavior from a paraphrase that is (necessarily) associated with a single program location. In other words, the state of a parallel program is not localized and is much harder to grasp and review. In addition, the space of possible interleavings is huge. The reviewer's

---

[2]We don't tackle the challenge of debugging parallel programs.

challenge is to identify a problematic interleaving out of this huge space. Doing so is also hard because the program is nondeterministic: at each stage of the execution, any active task that is not blocked can advance.

Two approaches are used to overcome this challenge. The first approach is to expose developers to parallel bug patterns [8], that is, types of parallel bugs that occur repeatedly but never in exactly the same way. The developers will look for signs of these bugs that will facilitate their identification in reviews. The second approach is the *distributive review* approach [7], in which a special new role called the devil's advocate is introduced. The devil's advocate is familiar with parallel bug patterns. As a suspect scenario is reviewed, the devil's advocate maximizes the chance that a problem will be identified by advancing the tasks that are most likely to cause a parallel bug to occur. The two approaches are complementary.

We proceed as follows. We first introduce a set of parallel bug patterns. This set is not meant to be comprehensive. In practice, the bug patterns that are applicable to one given environment and program paradigm might not be applicable to another, and customization is required to arrive at the optimal set. For example, under one programming paradigm, a lock can be obtained within its own scope, something that is not possible under another programming paradigm. One environment might use a reliable message passing mechanism and another an unreliable one. Another environment might have several layers of memory, so that a write to memory by one task may not be immediately visible to another task. These differences naturally lead to different types of bugs. Nevertheless, parallel bugs have a commonality that is independent of the programming paradigm. It is this commonality that we will attempt to highlight here.

After discussing parallel bug patterns, we will present the distributive review technique. It will then be much easier to explain the decisions made by the devil's advocate using the set of parallel bug patterns. We will also touch briefly on the test design review activity, which leads to the choice of a particular scenario to review.

16.2.1 Parallel Bug Patterns

Some definitions are required to facilitate the discussion. One way of viewing a parallel bug pattern of a given concurrent program P is to look at the relationship between the space of possible interleavings, $I(P)$, and the maximal space of inter-leavings for P under which the program is correct, $C(P)$. A parallel bug pattern can be viewed as defining interleavings in $I(P) - C(P)$. We will sometimes refer to $C(P)$ as the programmer view of the program P and to $I(P) - C(P)$ as the bug pattern gap.

As an example, consider n threads executing $x++$ in parallel on a shared variable that is initialized to 0. We assume that the intended result of the program is n. Further assume that each thread i executes $x++$ by copying the value of x to a memory location x_i that is only manipulated by that thread, incrementing the value in the local copy, x_i, by one and then copying the value back to the shared location x. Thus, each thread, i, executes, in sequence, the following operations: $x_i = x; x_i + +; x = x_i$. An interleaving in $I(P)$ is any permutation of $x_i = x; x_i + +; x = x_i, i = 1 \ldots n$ that respects the order of operations $x_i = x$, then $x_i + +$ and then $x = x_i$. Thus, for $n = 3$, the following is a legal interleaving in $I(P)$, $x_1 = x$; $x_2 = x$; $x_3 = x$; $x_1 + +$; $x_2 + +$; $x_3 + +$; $x = x_1$; $x = x_2$; $x = x_3$. The result of the program execution in this case is 1, while the intended result is 3. Thus, the previously mentioned interleaving is in $I(P)$ $- C(P)$. We recommend that the reader now attempt to solve Problem 16.1 at the end of this chapter.

An operation or set of operations is atomic if it appears to the rest of the system to occur instantaneously. A parallel bug pattern occurs when an operation or set of operations is incorrectly assumed to be atomic. This is the first category of bug patterns that we consider. Our previous example is an instance of this bug pattern. Indeed, the source of the programmer's mistake in our previous example is the erroneous assumption that $x + +$ is an atomic operation. If $x + +$ were an atomic operation, only interleavings in $C(P)$ would have been possible (i.e. only atomic execution of $x++$ by each thread in any order), and the only possible outcome of the program would have been n. As $x + +$ is not atomic, a bug pattern is created and more interleavings are possible.

There are two additional categories that create a bug pattern gap in $I(P) - C(P)$. One is an incorrect assumption that a certain execution order of concurrent events is impossible, and the other is an incorrect assumption that a code segment is non-blocking. In what follows we provide examples of parallel bug patterns to highlight these general categories. The list is not intended to be complete, but the three general categories mentioned earlier probably are.

16.2.1.1 *Atomicity Bug Patterns*   The most trivial instance of this bug pattern occurs, as we said, when an operation is incorrectly assumed to be atomic. A harder-to-spot problem occurs when the scope of atomicity defined by the program is incorrect. Naturally, the correct scope of atomicity could be longer or shorter than the one defined by the programmer. For example, adding and removing operations are performed concurrently by first accessing a database table to translate from *key*1 to *key*2. Then *key*2 is used to access another table and add or remove the data. Accesses to both tables are implemented atomically (possibly using a lock). However, the code segment that accesses the two tables is left 'unprotected' between the access to the first and the second table. This causes a parallel bug. After a thread obtained *key*2 from the first table, and before the second table is accessed, other threads may access and change the two tables, making *key*2, obtained in the first table access, obsolete. An interleaving that makes *key*2 obsolete after it was obtained was not intended by the programmer and resides in $I(P) - C(P)$.

Atomicity is typically implemented through some access protocol. An access protocol mandates that some code will be executed before and after the set of operations that should be executed atomically. An instance of this could be that a lock is obtained before the operations are executed and then released afterward. Another instance could be that a transaction, distributive or not, is started before the set of operations is executed and committed at the end of the execution of that set. Regardless of the access protocol, it must be followed by all tasks; otherwise, atomicity will be broken.[3] Consider, for example, a case in which the even threads in our previous example obtain a lock, execute $x + +$ and then release the lock while the odd threads continue to execute $x + +$ as before. The program remains incorrect as thread one may perform $x_1 = x$, wait until all other threads terminate and then execute $x_1 + +$; $x = x_1$. The end result of this execution is $x == 1$ and not n. Naturally we assume that n > 1. The reader can now attempt to solve Problem 16.2 at the end of this chapter.

The concept of high-level data races [2] is noteworthy in this context. To define a high-level data race, a *view* is introduced. For a given program run and a given thread, a view is a set of variables that were accessed under the scope of a lock. For example, the following thread execution

$lock(m);\ x = y;\ z = x;\ unlock(m);\ lock(m);\ z = t;\ unlock(m);$

has two views, $\{x, y, z\}$ and $\{z, t\}$. A high-level data race exists if a view indicated by one thread is broken into several views by another thread. This can be seen in the following example, where another thread executing

$lock(m);\ x = y;\ unlock(m);\ lock(m);\ z = x;\ unlock(m);$
$lock(m);\ z = t;\ unlock(m);$

will break the view $\{x, y, z\}$ created by the first thread into two views, $\{x, y\}$ and $\{x, z\}$. Runtime identification of high-level data races can be used to identify some of the atomicity bug patterns discussed in this section. We recommend attempting problem 16.3 at the end of this chapter.

16.2.1.2 Some Interleavings Can Never Occur
In this bug pattern, the programmer assumes that a certain interleaving never occurs because of the relative execution length of the different threads or because of some assumptions on the underlying hardware or some order of execution 'forced' by explicit delays, such as *sleep*()s, introduced in the program. In other words, interleavings in $I(P) - C(P)$ are considered impossible in practice, or not considered at all, by the programmer.

Imagine, for example, that the programmer assumes network operations are always slower than I/O operations on the current hardware. As a result, the programmer assumes that a write to a local disk will complete before a remote write to another node's disk is performed over the network when the local and remote writes are preformed in parallel. This works for a few years, but then the hardware changes, and the network remote write operation becomes faster than the local disk write operation. The original assumption about the hardware's relative speed is no longer correct, and a new interleaving occurs in which a write to the disk completes after the remote write to another node completes. The application is now broken.

Another instance of this bug pattern occurs when a parent process spawns several child processes and needs to wait until they complete their operations before it

[3]This requirement can be mitigated if an atomicity primitive is available.

inspects the result. To ensure that the child processes completed their operations, the programmer introduces a long enough delay in the parent process before the result is inspected. Instead the programmer should have introduced a barrier that waits for the child threads to complete. The delay might work in a certain environment, but be sensitive to any change in the software stack or hardware configuration. Thus, changes to the software stack or hardware configuration may result in the parent inspecting the result before it is ready for inspection. This interleaving is considered impossible by the programmer during program design.

Yet another problem might occur in the implementation of the read–copy–update (RCU) lock. In this case, writers to the shared data update all the global references to the updated data with a new copy and use the callback scheme to free the old copy after all the CPUs have lost local references to it. If this is not done in the right order or some mistakes are made about memory update visibility, the implementation of the RCU lock will have a bug.[4]

16.2.1.3 Blocking Threads
In this bug subcategory, some interleaving in $I(P) - C(P)$ contains a blocking operation that blocks indefinitely. There may be several reasons for this:

- A classic *cyclic dependency deadlock* occurs when a task that blocks and waits for another task to complete some operation is part of a cycle of such blocking dependencies. Say, for example, that the first thread obtains lock m and then the second thread obtains lock n, after which the first thread tries to obtain lock n but blocks because that lock is held by the second thread, while the second thread tries to obtain lock m but blocks because it is held by the first thread. The program will thus halt indefinitely. The cyclic dependency here is of length two: thread one is waiting for thread two to complete the lock operation, but thread two will never complete its lock operation as it is waiting for thread one to do the same! Environments may assist in debugging such problems. For example, the Linux kernel *DEBUG_RT_MUTEXES, DEBUG_SPINLOCK, DEBUG_MUTEXES* and *PROVE_LOCKING* configuration options will help detect such cycles.

- A task may terminate unexpectedly, leaving the system in an inconsistent state. Let's say some event should have been but wasn't triggered by a task. Other tasks will thus wait indefinitely for this event to occur. If, for example, a thread obtains a lock and then takes an exception, it is, under certain programming paradigms, the programmer's responsibility to release this lock. But if the programmer forgets to do so, the lock is never unlocked, and waiting threads will wait on that lock forever.

- A task is assumed to eventually return control, but it blocks and never does. This situation may occur in a critical section protocol. The requirement of

---

[4]In the Linux kernel environment, the *CONFIG_RCU_TORTURE_TEST* can be used to test the implementation of the RCU lock.

a critical section protocol is to have only up to a predefined n tasks execute some code segment in parallel. A task enters the critical section by starting to execute the critical section code and is assumed to eventually exit it by completing the execution of that section. But if the task executing within the critical section performs some blocking I/O operation (file, socket or GUI interface waiting for an event), it may never exit. As a result, the system may hang or its performance degrade as fewer tasks are allowed in the critical section in parallel. If the critical section is executed in kernel mode, the Linux *CONFIG_DETECT_SOFT_LOCKUP* and *CONFIG_DETECT_HUNG_TASK* configuration options may help detect this bug as it will print the stack when the task stays in the kernel for more than some threshold or in the interruptible 'D' state indefinitely. In addition, if the *CONFIG_DEBUG_SPINLOCK_SLEEP* Linux kernel configuration option is turned on, routines that may block and are called under the scope of a spin lock will notify the programmer.

Another instance of this bug pattern occurs when a server receives requirements for operations from a queue. The server's main loop repeatedly removes a requirement for an operation from the queue and then executes it by calling a service. A service called in the same thread is assumed to eventually return, but again, for the reasons mentioned earlier, this might never happen and the server will hang as a result. Another variation of this bug pattern occurs when a server's service method, known to be nonblocking, is overwritten by the incorrect use of inheritance with a blocking method. In addition, service methods can be long or written by different project members (or by a third party, which is even worse from a testing perspective). Thus it is hard to guarantee that the service method is nonblocking.

- A task may wait for an event that happened in the past but was not registered. As a result, the task will block indefinitely. This bug actually occurs in Java if a *notify*() on an object occurs before a *wait*() on that object. In this case the object notification is lost, and the *wait*() will not return as a result of the object notification.

What all of the aforementioned cases have in common is a thread waiting for an event that never occurs. This thread is blocking, and the fact that it is blocking might cause the system to hang or its performance to degrade.

16.2.2 Distributed Desk Checking

Equipped with an understanding of parallel bug patterns, we turn our attention to distributed reviews. As mentioned in the beginning of this section, the distributed review method assists in dynamically and efficiently exploring the space of possible program interleavings. This is done through appropriate test design of the high-level scenarios to be reviewed and the detailed exploration of a given scenario or interleaving to review through the introduction of a new role: the devil's advocate. The devil's advocate has to be an expert in parallel bug patterns. He or she increases the chance a problem will be found when reviewing a specific interleaving by making appropriate scheduling decisions according to this expertise.

Next we briefly review the desk checking review technique and then extend it to obtain the distributive review technique and handle the review of parallel programs.

16.2.2.1 *Desk Checking*   Desk checking of sequential programs consists of selecting the input test data and manually executing the program. There is a large body of work on test data selection (e.g. Chapter 23 on defect selection in [15]). We will thus assume that some appropriate input was chosen. Next, a review meeting is set, and the selected input (or inputs) is manually exercised. Naturally, a debugger may be used if available to alleviate some of the tediousness of the process. In addition, assumptions are made on the behavior of parts of the program that are assumed to be correct in order to keep the review process at the intended abstraction level. For example, as the program is manually executed in the review meeting, we might assume that when a certain function is called with a given input, it will return the expected output that it was designed to return. Manual execution of the function body can thus be skipped, meaning that we are not concerned that this function will exhibit incorrect behavior in the current scenario being reviewed.

As the manual desk checking progresses, the reviewers record the following:

- Input data as it is read

- Successive values of the variables

- Results as they are generated

- Program conditions as they are evaluated

- Faults found

The following program segment is used to give an example of desk checking[5]:

```
while(x > 0)
{
  x = obtainNextNumber();
  if(x%2 = 0)
    print(" even");
  else
    print(" odd ");
}
```

We assume that $x = 2$ at the beginning of the execution of the program and that *obtainNextNumber*() will alternate returning 1 and then 2. Note that we can conduct this type of review even if the function *obtainNextNumber*() has not yet been implemented (or is an interface to hardware that is not yet available). A clear advantage

---

[5]Code samples are given in self-explanatory, high-level imperative language pseudocode.

of desk checking is that it can be used to dynamically review the behavior of code whose environment is not yet available or whose environment behavior is hard to set up (pooling of a plug or a certain network failure behavior). In the review meeting, the code is manually executed using the aforementioned assumed inputs, and the following program intermediate states are recorded:

program state - $x = 2$
control - $while(x > 0)$ condition evaluates to true
control - $x = obtainNextNumber()$;
program state - $x = 1$
control - $if\,(x\%2 = 0)$ condition evaluates to false
$print("\,odd\,")$;
control - $while(x > 0)$ condition evaluates to true
control - $x = obtainNextNumber()$;
program state - $x = 2$
control - $if\,(x\%2 = 0)$ condition evaluates to true
$print("\,even")$;

and so on and so forth. The reviewers will quickly see that the program segment contains an infinite loop that is probably unintentional.

16.2.2.2 *Distributed Desk Checking*   But desk checking parallel programs is not so simple: reviewing a single interleaving associated with the run of a concurrent program P with input I in order to determine the correctness of P with I is not enough. To make things worse, the number of possible interleavings can, as already discussed, be very large. Given N processes, each executing M concurrent events in some fixed order, the number of possible interleavings is exponential in $N * M$. See Section 16.2.1 for an example that illustrates the size of the interleaving space.

The distributed desk checking methodology includes methods for the selection of the interleavings to be reviewed, the formal review procedure and the participants' roles. Like sequential desk checking, distributed desk checking requires no preparation other than the selection of inputs and interleavings to review and the assignment of roles to review participants. The assigned roles are the *program counter, devil's advocate* and *stenographer*. The program counter is responsible for determining the control flow of the program during the review process. Usually this role is given to the program owner unless the interleaving being reviewed is owned by more than one person. The devil's advocate is responsible for making choices about the schedule, network delays and environment behavior, in order to maximize the probability that bugs will be found in the review. In other words, for a given input, the devil's advocate chooses an interleaving to review. That choice is based on knowledge of parallel bug patterns. The stenographer is responsible for the clear and concise representation of system states during the review. As a parallel program execution description includes timing dependencies between different tasks, the representation is more complicated than in the sequential case. This is why a separate role is designated. Various standard representation schemes, such as sequence or time diagrams and tools that support their representation, may be used.[6] As in sequential desk checking, here too the formal review protocol includes the manual execution of the chosen program input and interleaving. We next discuss the selection of input and interleaving.

The parallel program might not exhibit any external parallel behavior. For example, the program may perform matrix multiplication. Externally, the *sequential* operation of matrix multiplication is performed while internally parallelism is used to increase the speed of the multiplication operation. In that case, standard test design techniques are applied for the design of the program inputs to be reviewed. We'll thus focus on the case in which the parallel program exhibits external parallel behavior and illustrate how test design is conducted in this case. As an example of such a parallel program, consider a multiple-reader/single-writer protocol in which we are given a critical section[7] and two types of tasks, readers and writers. Several reader tasks can access the critical section simultaneously, but only one writer task can access it at any given time and only when no readers are present in the critical section. The protocol will typically manipulate two variables, one that counts the number of readers, c_r, and another that counts the number of writers, c_w. In addition, the protocol has an entry and exit section to be executed by readers and writers before entering the critical section and when exiting it. The protocol entry and exit sections manipulate the readers' and writers' counters to reflect the number of tasks currently in the critical section. This is typically done in a nonatomic manner to improve the performance of the protocol.[8] The entry and exit protocols are typically exposed to the protocol user through a read/write lock. We will use this example to illustrate the process of test selection for parallel programs that exhibit parallelism externally.

The first step in the design of interleavings to review, as in any testing design activity, is based on specific concerns about the correctness of the programs. For parallel programs, typical concerns pertain to parallel bug patterns. In general, we would like to see appropriate contention on resources, synchronization of interleavings exercised and interface agreements met. These three broad concerns correspond to the three parallel bug pattern categories introduced previously, in Sections 16.2.1.1–16.2.1.3, respectively. Each concern leads to a different choice of interleavings to review. We will briefly discuss the type of interleavings typically designed as a result of each concern. We will then focus on the atomicity concern for an in-depth illustration of how to design interleavings for review.

Interleavings that contend on resources are introduced to determine if atomicity is handled correctly. The synchronization concern typically leads to the design of specific interleavings in which critical events such as message sending/receiving and shared memory access occur in a certain order. For example, in the case of message sending, we would like to review an interleaving in which the message is sent before a thread is there to receive it and an interleaving in which it is sent after another thread

---

[6] Any Unified Modeling Language (UML) reference may be reviewed to get ideas on how to represent timing relations.
[7] A code section designated as a critical section.
[8] See Nancy A. Lynch's book on distributed algorithms [12].

is there to receive it (see Section 16.2.1.2). The third concern leads to a review of whether or not users of the protocol meet the protocol assumptions. For example, do tasks using a critical section eventually return control to the critical section? This type of review is sometimes referred to as a contract review and leads to specific interleaving to review, as explained next.

In contract reviews you define the obligation that needs to be met after a certain program location is executed and check that it is met along any possible execution path of the program after that program location was executed. For example, if memory is allocated at a certain program location, we check that it is freed along any path that can occur after that program location was executed. In our case, once a task is in the critical section, regardless of whether it is a reader or a writer, it is obligated to eventually exit the critical section and return control to the exit protocol of the critical section. This should occur along any possible path in the critical section, including error paths and paths that are taken by the program due to an arriving exception or signal. In such an event, control might change to an exception or signal handler or be altered in some other way, depending on the particular programming paradigm. Thus, checking that obligations are met suggests particular interleavings to review. For example, the following interleaving checks whether running the exit protocol is met by the task in the critical section. A writer obtains entrance to the critical section, a reader attempts to obtain entrance to the critical section but is correctly blocked, and then a signal arrives and is handled by the writer in the critical section. If the code handling the signal exits the critical section, it is obligated to call the exit protocol of the critical section. If this is not done, the reader is blocked indefinitely, and we have found a bug (see Section 16.2.1.3 for detailed discussion of this bug type).

Next we focus on the atomicity concern and analyze the interleaving test design process in detail. Our reader/writer protocol handles the shared access of tasks of different types to a shared resource, the critical section. As the readers' and writers' counters are accessed nonatomically to facilitate performance, contention on resources might occur. To address this concern, we want readers' and writers' tasks to access the critical section in parallel, thus creating the appropriate contention. Note that requiring that two writers enter the critical section simultaneously may not be enough to identify a bug in the entrance protocol. It is the role of the devil's advocate to further specify the exact interleaving being executed during the actual review and thus actually reveal the bug. Consider the following buggy entrance protocol. The protocol is clearly buggy as no synchronization is applied when accessing the readers' and writers' counters:

```
// Critical section entrance protocol
   while(true){
   if (c_w = 0) {
      c_w + +
      exit the while loop and enter the critical section
   }
   }
```

The test design choice of two writers entering the critical section in parallel may lead to the review of an interleaving that is perfectly correct. For example, the following (correct) interleaving has two writers enter the critical section in parallel. Indeed, one writer is blocked as the result of the other writer entering the critical section:

program state - $c_r = c_w = 0$
first writer - *while*(*true*) condition evaluates to true
first writer - *if* ($c_w = 0$) condition evaluates to true
first writer - $c_w + +$
program state - $c_r = 0$ and $c_w = 1$
first writer - enters the critical section
second writer - *while*(*true*) condition evaluates to true
second writer - *if* ($c_w = 0$) condition evaluates to false
second writer is blocking until first writer leaves the critical section (i.e. until c_w is set to 0)

It's an easy exercise in this case to find an interleaving in which both writers enter the critical section at the same time. The devil's advocate role is to further guide the review during the review session so that this possibility is indeed revealed. At this point the reader may choose to stop reading and attempt to find an interleaving that lets both writers enter the critical section simultaneously. In addition, before reading the next paragraph, the reader may choose to try and define the different reader and writer contentions that should be reviewed as a result of the atomicity concern.

With regard to the contention concern, we can intuit that the following interleavings are of interest:

1. Several writers arrive and attempt to enter the critical section concurrently.

2. Several readers arrive and enter the critical section concurrently.

3. Several readers arrive and enter the critical section; a writer attempts to enter the critical section but waits; several readers arrive, attempt to enter the critical section and wait; eventually the writer enters the critical section and exits.

4. Several writers arrive and one enters the critical section; several readers arrive, attempt to enter the critical section and wait.

The Cartesian product technique is used to determine whether there are other interesting interleavings to review. For instance, in the aforementioned example, we define two attributes, *readerIn* and *writerIn*, which indicate whether a reader or a writer is attempting, not attempting or currently accessing the critical section.[9] We assume two

---

[9]Can you suggest another attribute value?

readers and two writers and thus have four cases to consider. A typical element in the considered Cartesian product is

(*attempting, attempting, not attempting, not attempting*),

which means that two readers are attempting to access the critical section and two writers are not attempting to access it. This event will probably occur at least in the previous scenario two. We thus obtain 3*3*3*3 = 81 possible events in the Cartesian product that we would like to observe when reviewing the selected set of interleavings. Note that some of these events, for example, any event where two writers simultaneously access the critical section, should turn out to be impossible. Some of the 81 events are not interesting as they do not contend for the critical section:

(*not attempting, not attempting, not attempting, not attempting*),

for example. Next, the aforementioned 81 combinations are systematically reviewed to see whether they are covered by at least one of the four scenarios mentioned earlier, or do not represent contention on the critical section, or are considered impossible. To facilitate the process, tools such as FoCuS[10] can be used. The reader may pause at this stage to consider some of the 81 combinations and determine whether they are possible, whether they represent contention and whether they are covered by the four scenarios mentioned earlier.

This Cartesian product is sometimes referred to as a functional coverage model. It can be further utilized during the testing phase to check that the parallel program is tested. Out of the 81 combinations previously mentioned, all of the events that are possible and represent contention should occur, and none of those that break the critical section requirements and have more than one writer in the critical section simultaneously should occur. Thus, a by-product of the distributed review is a test design for the parallel program, utilized in the testing phase. In the next section we will see how the testing task of parallel program is approached and the test design we just completed is utilized.

16.3 TESTING OF PARALLEL PROGRAMS

This section will describe how to test parallel programs and the state-of-the-art techniques that make their testing possible. Testing parallel programs is like finding a needle in a haystack if not done skillfully. Imagine that one task is executing 100,000 instructions, one of which is a load followed immediately by a store and a second task is executing a load. Further assume that the first task should have executed the consecutive pair of load and store instructions atomically. For the program to exhibit an incorrect behavior, the load of the second task should occur after the load of the first task and before the store of the first task. This is only one out of 100,000 possible schedules, and the probability that the program will exhibit wrong behavior is slim. Thus, a fundamental objective of parallel program test design is to reduce the space of possible interleavings that needs to be tested.

---

[10]See www.alphaworks.ibm.com/tech/focus.

Contrary to the common practice of parallel bug removal by stress testing of the parallel program at system test, we reduce the space of possible interleavings by moving the parallel program testing activity to as early as possible in the development cycle. This means that the ideal time for testing parallel programs is, whenever possible, at unit test. The space of possible interleavings is further reduced by isolating the *business code*, that is, code not related to synchronization, from the code that handles synchronization. The program thus obtained is referred to as the *isolated parallel program*. For example, in our single-writer/multiple-reader running example, we could test the atomicity (Section 16.2.1.1) and synchronization concerns (Section 16.2.1.2) by removing the business code and having the readers and writers do nothing when they enter the critical section. This will not address the interface concern (Section 16.2.1.3), and problems may still arise from tasks not meeting the contract by not executing the exit protocol eventually once they obtained entry to the critical section. But it will serve to further reduce the space of possible interleavings to be tested. This example is characteristic of the situation in general. Typically, only testing for atomicity and synchronization can be moved up to the unit test stage. The interface concern can only be tested later on in the development cycle, when the system is integrated and the interfaces are exercised. Thus, the application of the contract review is the most effective approach for early detection of interface issues.

Next, we reuse the test designed during the distributed review stage (Section 16.2.2.2) and create tests for the isolated parallel program. In order to determine if the test is strong enough, we use an *empty implementation* of the parallel program under test. An empty implementation is an implementation of the parallel program interfaces that manipulates shared resources and synchronization messages but drops any synchronization guarantees. We next illustrate the concept of removing the business code and the empty implementation using our multiple-reader/single-writer running example. Assume the writer is buggy and is implemented as follows:

```
//c_w counts the number of writers in the critical section
//c_r counts the number of readers in the critical section

//writer calls the critical section writer entrance protocol
   while(true){
   if (c_w = 0 && c_r = 0) {
      c_w + +
      //exit the while loop and enter the critical section
}
}
//writer enters the critical section

//writer add an entry to some shared structure
//For example, add new employees to an employ table.
//Another example, is to add a file representation to a
//kernel table of current files being accessed.
//This is referred to as the business code−
```

```
//although it deals with shared resources it
//does not handle their protection
if(insertNewRecord(new record) == failed)
 reportInsertFailure();
```

```
//writer exit the critical section by calling the exit protocol
c_w − −
//end of writer exit protocol
```

As mentioned earlier, we drop the business code and create an empty implementation for the protocol. In addition, in order to check the protocol, we print the number of readers and writers in the critical section. We thus obtain the following program which we run our tests against. The empty implementation is buggy and we expect to see readers and writers in the critical section at the same time. This will give us an indication that the tests are strong enough:

```
//writer calls the critical section writer entrance protocol
 c_w + +
//writer enters the critical section
```

```
//print number of readers and writers
print(x_w, x_r);
```

```
//writer exit the critical section by calling the exit protocol
c_w − −
//end of writer exit protocol
```

The reader is encouraged at this stage to define the empty and isolated reader implementation and implement five readers and five writers accessing the critical section in parallel. This can be done using any programming language. To the surprise of many, in some environments we will never observe, even after repeating the test many times, writers and readers in the critical section simultaneously. The following heuristic is now applied to make the test stronger. We examine critical events, that is, events used to synchronize between processes such as access to shared variables and message passing, and randomly add delays before and after the critical events to increase the chance that the interleavings we are concerned about will occur. This activity is similar to what the devil's advocate does during a distributed review (Section 16.2.2.2) and is done using knowledge of parallel bug patterns. In the aforementioned isolated empty implementation example, the introduction of a delay after a writer enters the critical section will increase the chance that other writers or readers enter the critical section while that writer is still in it. Once this delay is introduced and we manage to fail the isolated and empty implementation using our tests, we reinstate the implementation and repeat the aforementioned heuristic. The reader may choose to do exactly that with his/her tests and see that he/she can fail an erroneous implementation of the reader/writer protocol. If the tester is lucky and working with Java, the ConcurrentTesting[11] tool can be used instead to automate this stage. The ConcurrentTesting tool automatically instruments the critical events and randomly introduces delays before and after the critical event in a biased manner, using knowledge of parallel bug patterns. We'll cover the ConcurrentTesting tool in the next section.

At this stage the tests are run many times (e.g. overnight). We measure that the functional coverage model developed during the distributed review stage (Section 16.2.2.2) actually occurs. For instance, we make sure that many readers and a single writer access the critical section simultaneously and so on for the rest of the possible events previously defined during the review stage. As the tests are going to be run many times, it's a best practice to implement the protocol invariant so that we will get a failure message only if the test failed. In our case we would substitute the following count of the number of readers and writers in the critical section:

//*print number of readers and writers*
print(x_w, x_r);

with

//*print number of readers and writers*
//*only if the protocol failed*[12] —
if not (($c_r = 0 \parallel c_w = 0$) && $c_w <= 1$) *print*(x_w, x_r);

If the aforementioned steps are followed, the parallel program is probably bug-free, at least with regard to bugs of the atomicity (Section 16.2.1.1) and synchronization (Section 16.2.1.2) category. Interface concerns might still surprise us but can be mitigated through appropriate contract reviews. With respect to the later stages of testing, there is another technique worth mentioning. Synchronization coverage [5] is a general coverage model aimed at measuring contention on resources. For example, we want to see that each lock in the system is contended on (i.e. that there are two processes attempting to obtain the lock at a given program location simultaneously, one task obtaining it and the other waiting for the lock to be released). Note that this meets the requirements of a coverage model because we can enumerate the coverage tasks (one task for each program location that attempts to obtain a lock), and we expect all coverage tasks to be possible during some execution of the program. If a coverage task cannot occur during a run of the program, then the lock is redundant as it is impossible to contend on it. Such general-purpose coverage models are useful at later stages of testing, as it is interesting to determine which locks are not contended on in system test.

---

[11] See www.alphaworks.ibm.com/tech/contest.
[12] Can you spot what might be wrong with this statement?

16.3.1 Smart Interleaving Testing

In this section we describe the basic ideas that underline the Java-based concurrentTesting[13] tool [6]. The objective of the tool is to explore the space of possible interleavings and thus increase the probability that a parallel bug materializes. In addition, such a technology is required to avoid false alarms and not produce impossible interleavings. As a result, all interleavings created by the tool should be possible in some legal environment of the parallel program being tested. To meet these requirements, the following design guidelines are followed:

- The testing tool should, in principle, be able to create any possible interleaving. Thus, the tool must be able to intercept critical events that otherwise could have been used to replay[14] [10] a parallel program before and after their execution. Critical events include all program events that have to do with synchronization, such as shared memory access, locking and message passing. The exact set of critical events will change from one programming paradigm to another and is expected to evolve over time.

- As mentioned before, the testing tool should only produce legal interleavings. That typically boils down to the testing tool code executing before and after critical events not having any side effects. For example, the testing tool should never consume signals [10].

- Synchronization coverage captures contention on resources. The testing tool strives to make this contention occur [5]. As such, the tool can be viewed as a test generation tool. Test generation is a subject of a long line of research.[15] The objective of a test generation problem is often a coverage model, such as statement coverage, requiring that each statement in the program be exercised, and the tests are generated on the set of possible program inputs. In contrast, the objective of the test generation problem in the parallel program case is to cover the synchronization coverage model, and the explored space is the space of possible interleavings. The same techniques used for classical test generation might be applicable. Note that the exact definition of the synchronization coverage model will differ according to the programming model.

- The number of critical events that produce a parallel bug is small [3, 4, 16]. As a result, the testing tool should focus on identifying events related to a known bug pattern and changing the order in which these events occur by introducing delays.

- The tool should strive to minimize the intercepted critical events. Static analysis may sometimes be used to minimize the number of events that are intercepted.

[13] See www.alphaworks.ibm.com/tech/contest.
[14] By replay we mean capturing the temporal dependences of the program in such a way the program can be deterministically rerun, producing the parallel bug in each run.
[15] Review the International Symposium on Software Testing and Analysis (ISSTA) and other such venues for literature on test generation.

For example, variables that are not on the stack may be shared by more than one thread. Static analysis may help avoid intercepting more heap variables than necessary by identifying heap variables that are actually shared by more than one thread.

The aforementioned general design guidelines may be applied whenever the implementation of a testing environment similar to the ConcurrentTesting tool for Java is attempted.

16.4 RELATED WORK

This work tackles the problem of testing concurrent programs through specialized review and test techniques. Others have attempted to define a set of reusable concurrent design patterns [11] and thus avoid the problem of testing concurrent programs altogether. Still others have formally approached the problem through modeling and manual or automatic verification of the correctness of the concurrent program [1, 12, 14]. The reusable concurrent design pattern approach is challenged when the off-the-shelf design pattern does not readily apply to the problem at hand while the formal approach, although making great steps forward in the automatization of formal verification [9, 13], is severely challenged by its scalability and the skill set it requires from the programmer.

16.5 FUTURE WORK

Current commercial systems include hundreds or thousands of clients interacting with several servers. The servers run databases and interact with storage components. Many-core architectures are used by the different system nodes. Thus, correctly constructing concurrent programs on an unprecedented scale is becoming an urgent need. Future work will further develop the techniques defined in this chapter to deal with the scaling challenge. How do you review and test when there are thousands of interacting tasks expected to run a multitude of environments? Clustering approaches are called for. One must be able to reason about a small set of tasks and have the result apply to the large scale as well. Similarly, in order to make the testing feasible, one should be able to simulate, in its entirety, the typical complex commercial system with its thousands of clients and expensive server and storage components. The current state of the art needs to grow to meet these challenges.

16.6 CONCLUDING REMARKS

A fundamental principle of software engineering is *hiding*. Typically it applies to the hiding of data manipulated by a given interface from the rest of the system. The system design process is thus simplified in that only a small set of data needs to be considered at any given time. In the context of the design of concurrent programs, a simpler principle applies, but it does not necessarily apply to the hiding of data. Rather, you want to 'hide' concurrency from the rest of the system. One way of doing so is by using an interface that provides concurrency guarantees such as atomicity to the rest of the system. Otherwise, it is very hard to create a correct system that uses concurrency.

Once such an interface is designed, its validation begins. If the test planning and review techniques outlined in this chapter are applied from day one and the reviewed test scenarios are then tested, we can be confident that the interface does not have concurrency bugs. Debugging such bugs when the interface is integrated with the entire system is incredibly hard, and thus the extra effort incurred by following this chapter approach is worthwhile.

REFERENCES

1. G. R. Andrews. *Concurrent Programming*. The Benjamin/Cummings Publishing Company, Inc., 1991.

2. C. Artho, K. Havelund, and A. Biere. High-level data races. *Software Testing Verification and Reliability*, 13(4):207–227, 2003.

3. Y. Ben-Asher, Y. Eytani, E. Farchi, and S. Ur. Producing scheduling that causes concurrent programs to fail. PADTAD 2006: 37–40.

4. Y. Ben-Asher, E. Farchi, Y. Eytani, and S. Ur. Noise makers need to know where to be silent – producing schedules that find bugs. ISoLA 2006: 458–465.

5. A. Bron, E. Farchi, Y. Magid, Y. Nir, and S. Ur. Applications of synchronization coverage. PPOPP 2005: 206–212.

6. O. Edelstein, E. Farchi, E. Goldin, Y. Nir, G. Ratsaby, and S. Ur. Framework for testing multi-threaded Java programs. Concurrency and Computation: Practice and Experience 15(3–5): 485–499 (2003).

7. E. Farchi, A. Hayardeny, and S. Fienblit. Distributed desk checking. *Concurrency and Computation: Practice and Experience*, 19(3):295–309, 2007.

8. E. Farchi, Y. Nir, and S. Ur. Concurrent bug patterns and how to test them. IPDPS 2003: 286.

9. G. Holzmann. *Design and Validation of Computer Protocols*. Prentice Hall, 1991.

10. R. B. Konuru, H. Srinivasan, and J.-D. Choi. Deterministic replay of distributed java applications. In *IPDPS*, pages 219–228, 2000.

11. D. Lea. *Concurrent Programming in Java*. Addison-Wesley, 2004.

12. N. A. Lynch. *Distributed Algorithms*. Morton Kaufmann Publishers, Inc, 1996.

13. Z. Manna and A. Pnueli. *Temporal Verification of Reactive Systems*. Springer, 1995.

14. A. W. Roscoe. *The Theory and Practice of Concurrency*. Prentice Hall, 1997.

15. I. Sommerville. *Software Engineering*. Addison Wesley Longman Publishing Co., Inc., Redwood City, CA, USA, fifth edition, 1995.

16. E. Trainin, Y. Nir-Buchbinder, R. Tzoref-Brill, A. Zlotnick, S. Ur, and E. Farchi. Forcing small models of conditions on program interleaving for detection of concurrent bugs. PADTAD 2009.

PROBLEMS

16.1   Given a parallel program with n threads, each executing $x + +$, and an intended result at the end of its execution of n, characterize the interleavings in $C(P)$ and $I(P) - C(P)$ and determine if any value between 1 and n can be obtained as an end result of the program execution.

16.2   Given a parallel program with n threads where an even thread obtains a lock, execute $x + +$ and release the lock and an odd thread executes $x + +$, determine the possible end result of the program execution.

16.3   Give an example of an atomicity bug pattern that is not a high-level data race.

CHAPTER 17

PARALLEL PERFORMANCE EVALUATION AND OPTIMIZATION

Hazim Shafi

Improving application performance is the *raison d'être* of parallel programming on shared-memory multicore processor systems. Unfortunately, achieving good speedup and scalability on such systems can be challenging for all but a small class of relatively simple applications. These challenges are usually the result of some well-understood phenomena such as cache coherence overheads and delays due to contention for synchronization objects. In this chapter, we will cover the most important aspects of shared-memory parallel programming that impact performance. We will also give guidance for diagnosing such issues in order to assist in performance tuning. By paying attention to the main impediments to performance during application design, developers can increase the chances of achieving good performance.

Although parallel program performance is also governed by the same issues that affect serial programs, such as choice of algorithm and instruction and data locality, we limit our discussion to topics that are specific to parallel programs. The parallel performance advice presented here is applicable to a large spectrum of shared-memory multicore programs and is not limited to a single application domain.

Programming Multicore and Many-core Computing Systems,
First Edition. Edited by Sabri Pllana and Fatos Xhafa.

Our goal is to introduce all the important concepts and lead the reader to learn more details about specific topics. Although many references are made to Windows®APIs, the concepts described are applicable to many platforms, and readers are encouraged to find the equivalent APIs for their specific parallel programming environment.

17.1   SEQUENTIAL VERSUS PARALLEL PERFORMANCE

There are many issues affecting performance that are different between a parallel implementation and a sequential one. In this chapter, when we refer to a sequential implementation, we imply an application running with a single thread of execution. Conversely, a parallel implementation refers to an application written to run on a multicore processor-based system with shared-memory support in order to leverage all its processor cores to improve performance.

First, to ensure correctness in the presence of hardware caches, modern multi-processors implement a cache coherence mechanism. Cache coherence results in additional memory latency due to coherence cache misses. These overheads are incurred when memory locations – or more accurately, cache lines – are shared among processors in the system. This sharing can be *true when memory locations are shared among threads or* false when different threads access different locations that happen to reside on the same cache line. We will discuss the implications of cache coherence in more detail in Section 17.3. Second, many shared-memory programming models use the abstraction of a thread to allow developers to express parallelism in their applications. Operating systems schedule these threads on a system's processor cores. Threads come with some inherent costs including memory resources and context switch overheads. These costs can have a detrimental impact on performance. We will discuss these costs and possible mitigations in Section 17.2. Third, when a sequential application is parallelized, synchronization has to be added to enforce data dependences and resolve data race conditions. Synchronization introduces overheads that do not exist in the serial implementation, resulting in potential performance degradation. We will discuss synchronization in more detail in Section 17.4. Fourth, memory latency is one of the primary performance bottlenecks in computers today. Although caches, simultaneous multithreading and hardware- or software-controlled prefetching mechanisms have been used extensively to reduce or hide memory latency, reducing memory latency remains a very effective performance optimization. Many multicore processor-based systems today implement nonuniform memory access (NUMA) memory hierarchies. This means that memory latency as measured at a processor core can vary depending on the physical memory location being accessed and the topological relationship between the processor performing the access and the memory controller that owns the memory address. We will cover NUMA issues in Section 17.5. Fifth, latency hiding and asynchronous programming can be valuable tools for improving parallel application performance because they allow an increase in the degree of concurrency and processor efficiency for an application. We cover this topic in more detail in Section 17.6.

An important component of performance optimization is diagnostic tools. Section 17.7 gives an overview of some tools and techniques that are effective for identifying parallel performance bottlenecks.

17.2 THREAD OVERHEADS

Threads are similar to lightweight processes in the sense that they represent a processor core context (e.g. register contents), an area of memory used as a stack, and access to resources owned by its parent process, such as file handles and the process's memory address space. Many modern operating systems support kernel-level threads. This means that the kernel is responsible for managing thread state and the scheduling of threads on processor resources. This allows a single process to instantiate multiple threads that execute in parallel in a multiprocessor system to improve performance. When the kernel stops one thread running on a processor core and replaces it with another, we refer to that as a context switch operation.

17.2.1 The Cost of Context Switches

A context switch involves saving an executing thread's processor context and restoring another thread's context on the processor core on which the operation is taking place. On architectures that have virtually indexed and tagged caches, a context switch may also need to flush the caches to avoid threads from accessing cache lines belonging to other processes. In addition, since a context switch may involve switching process address spaces, again depending on the architecture, cached page table entries in translation lookaside buffers (TLBs) may also need to be flushed.[1] The direct performance cost of a context switch is usually pretty small – on the order of a few thousand CPU cycles. The direct costs can often be dwarfed by indirect costs. Indirect costs of context switches include the following:

1. **Memory latency:** If a thread is switched out for a long period of time or migrated to another processor core, then it will incur additional cache misses when it is switched in. This is a natural consequence of other threads running on the core and bringing in their working sets into the cache hierarchy, potentially replacing the cache lines of threads that previously ran there. When a thread is migrated, these effects are usually exacerbated since the thread's working set may not have been loaded into the caches to begin with. The degree of cache miss increases, and the resulting memory latency is a function of many variables, including the system topology, the identity of the threads sharing the processor cores and the degree to which the threads share data and instructions. For example, a thread that is migrated to a core that shares a cache with the thread's previous core might incur less cache miss latency overheads

---

[1]Cache and TLB flushes on context switches are rare on modern systems. This information is included for completeness.

compared to being migrated to a core that shares no caches with the previous core.

2. **Address translation:** Just as caches keep recently accessed memory locations close to the processor to reduce memory latency, TLBs keep address translation entries close to the processor to reduce the latency of translating virtual addresses to physical addresses. This address translation has to happen on every load or store instruction that is issued by the processor and often needs to complete before the access may be presented to the cache hierarchy because many modern caches are physically tagged. When a thread is switched out, the address translation entries belonging to it (or more precisely, to its process address space) may be replaced by those of the incoming threads. The degree to which this occurs is a function of many variables, such as whether previously running threads shared memory with the incoming thread, but the likelihood that more TLB entries will be missing in the TLB usually increases when a thread is migrated across cores or sockets. When a TLB lookup fails to find an entry for a virtual address, a time-consuming page table walk has to take place to find the correct entry. This page table walk, which may be performed by the hardware or software, may involve multiple memory accesses, each of which, assuming that page tables are cacheable, may result in a cache miss. This makes TLB misses particularly costly to performance.

3. **Interference with power management:** Excessive context switches, especially those that transition a core to and from the idle state, can be even more expensive. That is because it is often more energy efficient to switch a core to a lower power state when it is idle or to even turn it off completely in certain cases. When a core in a low power state has to transition back to running a thread at full speed, there is extra latency in that transition. Reducing the number of executing threads to the minimum necessary increases the opportunities for power reduction.

Because of the costs of context switches, it is recommended that developers avoid situations that increase the number of context switches in their applications.

17.2.2 Guidance and Mitigation Techniques

This section describes suggested best practices to reduce context switch overheads. We will not cover all techniques, rather, we will attempt to summarize those that we believe are the most important based on experience:

- **Create only the number of threads that are necessary to achieve best performance.** This may sound somewhat nebulous but is an extremely important concept in many scenarios. The simplest example to illustrate this point is a CPU-intensive application that is parallelized by partitioning its dataset across n threads, where n is the number of cores in the system. This guideline suggests that you should not create $> n$ threads when this application executes. The reasoning is simple: creating additional threads does not improve performance since you can only run n threads at a time in parallel on the system, but you are introducing more overheads due to an increase in context switches. In fact, you might degrade performance significantly due to load balancing and non-determinism introduced by the operating system's scheduler. For example, if the size of the dataset is p and you divide it equally among n threads, assuming a linear relationship between data size and execution time, the algorithm should complete in $O(p/n)$; however, if you divided the data across $n + 1$ threads, the execution time, depending on scheduling, could become as high as $O(2p/(n + 1))$ because only n threads may execute simultaneously, and all of them will have to wait for the last thread to complete before the program may terminate. A common class of programs where introducing more threads can degrade performance due to context switch overheads is server applications that use threads to hide latency. In such applications having more threads than the number of cores makes sense if threads often block (e.g. due to input/output (I/O)) while handling requests. In order to increase CPU utilization, programmers typically inject more threads to keep the processor cores busy. But, if this is not done carefully, performance can degrade when more threads than necessary to maximize CPU utilization are introduced. In such a case, context switch overheads, including cache and TLB effects, may reduce the CPU time used to execute the workload and throughput degrades. In addition, synchronization overheads may increase due to higher contention (see Section 17.4). Many server applications of this ilk use thread pool abstractions to dynamically manage the number of threads. Unless the pool implementation monitors the right performance metrics for a given application (e.g. throughput or latency) to ensure that adding threads is improving performance, thread injection may result in worse performance.

- **Avoid excessive thread creation/destruction.** Thread creation and destruction can be time consuming because the kernel has to create and tear down thread-related data structures. Whenever possible, threads created to execute a task should be reused and assigned additional tasks rather than terminated.

- **Watch out for thread memory usage.** Each thread owns a private stack that consumes process address space. For example, the default stack size for a Windows Win32 or .NET user application thread is 1 MB. Although the system is clever about committing memory for the thread's stack, 1 MB of virtual address space will be reserved to ensure that the stack resides in contiguous addresses. When hundreds of threads are created, hundreds of megabytes of address space are consumed. One way to mitigate this cost is to tune the stack size, but this can be tricky and stack overruns may be difficult to diagnose.

- **Carefully use thread affinity to minimize thread migration overheads.** Operating system schedulers may implement policies to minimize thread migration penalties by restricting specific threads to execute on a specific set of processor cores. Even when a thread needs to be migrated, the scheduler might attempt to minimize the penalty by using another core on the same die or socket; however, the scheduler usually does not know the relationship among threads and data, so it can easily choose a suboptimal core. One way of mitigating this is to inform the operating system of the set of cores that a thread's execution should be constrained to in order to optimize performance. The operating system treats such instructions as a contract, meaning that it will not schedule a thread on a core that is not specified in that thread's set of cores as specified by the programmer. The reason why we caution against the widespread use of thread affinity is that applications are often not aware of the resource requirements of other workloads running on the system. If all applications request thread affinity on a certain set of cores while other cores are idle, performance can degrade. That is why we typically discourage the use of processor affinity unless the application in question has full knowledge of the load on the system and the distribution of resources. In practice, this implies that affinity should only be considered in server-like or high-performance computing environments. Using affinity for client applications should be avoided. Another drawback of affinity is that it can introduce load-balancing problems where some cores are oversubscribed while others are experiencing significant idle periods. Since the operating system's scheduler is aware of resource utilization in the whole system, it can often do a better job distributing work across the system's processors. Finally, thread affinity can also prevent the system from distributing work in a manner that reduces energy consumption by putting one or more cores into low power states.

17.3   CACHE COHERENCE OVERHEADS

Before discussing the performance implications of cache coherence, it is worthwhile to introduce the motivation for implementing cache coherence.

Table 17.1   Example of cache coherence problem.

Time	Core 0	Core 1
$t = 0$	$ld\ r0,\ [x]$	$ld\ r0,\ [x]$
$t = 1$	$incr\ r0$	
$t = 2$	$st[x],\ r0$	
$t = 3$		$ld\ r1,\ [x]$

Table 17.1 illustrates a simple cache coherence problem using pseudoassembly code. Assume that memory location x contains 0 at time $t = -1$ and that both cores contain private caches that are empty. At $t = 0$, two threads from the same process (i.e. sharing the same address space) load the contents of address x into their respective caches. The thread on Core 0 proceeds to increment the value and store it back to the same memory location. This store overwrites the previous cached value of x in Core 0's cache. When Core 1 performs a read of location x at $t = 3$, in the absence

of a cache coherence mechanism, it will read the old cached value of 0 instead of 1. Most developers would rather program on a machine where a load always returns the last value written. That is what cache coherence provides, namely, ensuring that *a load from a memory location returns the last value written to it*. Note that for this to work, the memory operation has to be seen by the cache subsystem, so stores that are buffered within the core are not subject to cache coherence mechanisms.

The performance implications of cache coherence become obvious when we study how it is achieved. Most systems today implement a form of invalidation-based cache coherence [5]. In such systems, each cache line implements a state machine based on activity by the owning core(s) and memory transactions involving the cache line in the system. When a processor performs a write to a cache line, that operation is delayed until all other copies of the target cache line are invalidated in all other caches in the system, ensuring that subsequent reads will have to wait to fetch the up-to-date version of the cache line. So, in our example shown in Table 17.1, when the store operation is performed on Core 0 at $t = 2$, it will only proceed after the copy of the cache line in Core 1's cache is invalidated. This ensures that Core 1 will see the new value at $t = 3$ since the read will miss in the cache due to the invalidation and the latest copy of the cache line will be fetched in. This additional cache miss due to invalidation is referred to as a *coherence miss* and is the primary performance impact of cache coherence. The delay incurred by Core 0 as the invalidation of Core 1's cache line takes place may also degrade performance, but many techniques are implemented in hardware to minimize the impact of write latency [2].

17.3.1 Guidance and Mitigation Techniques

Now that we have given an overview of the performance impact of cache coherence, we present the following guidelines for minimizing these overheads:

- **Minimize write sharing.** From the aforementioned description of cache coherence mechanisms, it becomes clear that one primary goal of parallel performance tuning is to avoid coherence misses. Coherence misses only occur as a result of cache line invalidations triggered by store operations. Loads due to read-only sharing do not cause coherence overheads. So, minimizing the negative impact of cache coherences implies reducing the number of stores to shared data structures that are followed by load misses at other processors that would otherwise be cache hits. This optimization requires a careful choice of algorithms, data partitioning and data layout strategies to minimize these shared read–write access patterns.

- **Avoid false sharing.** The worst scenario related to cache coherence overheads is when applications suffer the penalty of cache coherence misses on data structures that are not shared. This can occur when thread-private data structures from multiple threads happen to reside on the same cache line. Store operations to the cache line by one or more of the threads causes excessive coherence misses. This problem can be identified by observing excessive cache misses on accesses to private (nonshared) data structures. Avoiding false sharing requires identifying the data structures that can reside on the same cache line and may require padding, alignment and/or restructuring of data structures to eliminate this behavior. A similar problem occurs when multiple contended-for shared structures reside on the same cache line (e.g. multiple locks), which exacerbates contention and degrades performance further.

17.4 SYNCHRONIZATION OVERHEADS

Synchronization is one of the main causes of performance and scalability degradation in shared-memory parallel programs because it introduces serialization and CPU overheads. Serial code is detrimental to scalability as illustrated by Amdahl's law [3]. Synchronization is required by parallel applications to ensure correctness for two primary reasons. First, when serial programs are parallelized, a mechanism is needed to ensure that all data dependences that exist between memory operations performed by different threads are enforced. This mechanism comes in the form of explicit synchronization APIs that are inserted by the application developer. Second, when two or more threads may simultaneously access the same memory location and at least one of these accesses is a store, it is necessary to serialize accesses to ensure correctness. This is addressed using either locks or atomic fetch-and-op operations. In both cases, ensuring correctness through synchronization primitives or atomic operations introduces execution time overheads. The main sources of synchronization overheads are:

1. Cache coherence traffic on the data structures of the synchronization object itself, which causes an increase in memory latency delays experienced by the application program.

2. Contention for synchronization objects introduces queuing delays and exacerbates cache coherence overheads due to contention on cache lines containing those synchronization objects. The nature of contention can vary depending on the usage of the synchronization operation, its frequency, duration for which a primitive is held by a thread and the number of threads/cores participating in computation.

3. Fairness of the synchronization primitive's implementation plays an important role in synchronization object acquire time distribution which may impact load balancing.

4. Interactions with the operating system scheduler can also increase the overheads of synchronization. For example, if a thread is preempted while holding a synchronization object, all other threads waiting on that object will incur longer synchronization acquire overheads. When threads of varying priority synchronize, a low-priority thread that is holding a lock can delay the execution of higher-priority threads, especially when the low-priority threads are preempted. This phenomenon is often referred to as *priority inversion*. On MS Windows operating system, priority inversion may occur as a result of implicit

priority boosts when certain synchronization events (see the documentation for the Win32 SetThreadPriorityBoost() function for more information).

5. Interactions with memory ordering optimizations implemented by the processor can increase synchronization delays. This is because synchronization operations typically include either memory serializing or barrier/fence instructions. Such instructions reduce the processor's ability to hide memory latency. For example, a memory barrier/fence might cause the processor to wait for any buffered store operations to become globally visible before the synchronization memory operation can complete. This adds more memory latency costs to the application and may increase the effective synchronization object's hold time.

17.4.1   Types of Synchronization Primitives

Synchronization operations fall into four categories:

1. **Locks:** These are constructs used to ensure mutual exclusion or serialize access to shared objects, typically for solving race conditions. Win32 critical sections, slim reader/writer locks, mutexes, and semaphores are examples.

2. **Flags:** These are primitives used to preserve data dependence constraints, for example, in a producer–consumer relationship among threads. Win32 events and condition variables are examples of flag synchronization objects.

3. **Barriers:** These are primitives used to ensure that multiple threads have reached a certain point in their execution and to notify all participating threads of that fact. There are no barrier synchronization objects in Win32. A slightly different form of a barrier, often called a *join*, allows a thread to wait for other threads to terminate. This is accomplished by waiting on thread handles using the WaitForMultipleObjects() API in Win32. The use of joins is discouraged because it relies on threads terminating. It is more efficient to reuse threads when possible across barrier synchronization operations.

4. **Atomic or interlocked operations:** These are a set of atomic operations on memory locations that provide serialization without needing locks. They are implemented using atomic instructions such as compare and exchange or load linked/store conditional in the processor's instruction set. They require special hardware support to ensure atomicity. The InterlockedCompareExchange() and InterlockedIncrement() APIs in Win32 are examples.

17.4.2   Guidance and Optimizations

Before providing guidance on the choice of primitives, it is important to discuss some of the performance aspects of synchronization object implementations that will inform the guidance provided in the following text. There are four things to consider: waiting mechanism, kernel-mode versus user-mode actions, fairness and reader versus writer differentiation. We describe these aspects next.

17.4.2.1 Blocking versus Spin-Waiting An important decision when choosing or implementing a synchronization primitive is the mechanism used for waiting when a thread cannot immediately acquire the object. There are two basic choices: either to block the thread or to spin-wait (poll). A potential third alternative is to provide a nonblocking means of checking whether the object is free or can be acquired without blocking. That gives the thread the option of doing other useful work while the object is busy. Blocking usually implies that the thread will cease execution and block either in the kernel or in a user-mode threading library waiting on a signal to awaken it. The advantage of this option is that the thread does not consume any CPU cycles while waiting, allowing other threads with useful work to proceed. A blocking thread will also not constantly read the cache line containing the object, which reduces contention, memory interconnect bandwidth and energy consumption. The disadvantage is that additional latency will be incurred from the time that a synchronization object becomes free until the thread is awakened and rescheduled, so it can acquire the object. In fact, depending on the fairness of the implementation (see following text) the thread may not wake up in time to successfully acquire the object. The alternative, which is spin-waiting, affords the minimum latency between a synchronization object freeing up and the waiting threads being notified. Unfortunately, spin-waiting comes with many disadvantages. The obvious one is that spin-waiting wastes CPU cycles and memory interconnect bandwidth that can be used to perform work, so it can degrade performance. It also increases the energy consumption of the system. When there is no other useful work that can be scheduled, spin-waiting prevents the CPU from switching to a low power state. Some efficient synchronization implementations use a short spin-waiting loop before blocking a thread to capture cases where acquisition delays are usually very short, thereby capturing the benefits of spin-waiting while avoiding the negative side effects just mentioned. This is the strategy employed by critical sections in Win32, for example. Some synchronization operations use sleeps or yields in the spin-wait loop. A sleep usually blocks a thread for a given period of time. Using sleeps while spinning is almost never wise because it causes context switches while not ensuring the low latency benefits of spin-waiting. In contrast, yields (e.g. using the SwitchToThread() API in Win32) are operations that invoke the operating system's scheduler to preempt the executing thread if other threads are ready to run. Although this might mitigate some of the bad effects of spin-waiting by allowing other threads to perform useful work, it does not negate the power management concerns since it will keep the spin-waiting thread running when there is no other work pending. Some architectures include special instructions that improve the performance and reduce the power consumption of spin-wait loops. For example, the Intel x86 architecture defines the PAUSE instruction for this purpose.

17.4.2.2 Kernel Mode versus User Mode In the previous section, we discussed how hybrid short spin and block implementations of some synchronization variables can be an effective compromise to achieve short acquire latencies while minimizing wasted CPU cycles and energy consumption. When synchronization primitives implement blocking through operating system calls, the kernel has to be invoked, which is an expensive operation. One way of reducing kernel involvement is to use user-mode threading libraries such as the Concurrency Runtime (ConcRT) or the user-mode scheduling (UMS) packages from Microsoft®. Such user-mode runtime systems reduce the need to invoke the kernel by allowing a transition from a blocking thread (or a task in ConcRT terminology) to another task that is ready to execute without involving the kernel. This reduces overheads while allowing the running process to use its complete scheduling quantum which is another benefit of such techniques.

Some synchronization primitives allow synchronization across processes. The mutex and semaphore objects in Win32 are examples of such synchronization primitives. In order to support interprocess synchronization, the kernel has to play a role in communicating across the different address spaces. This makes such primitives expensive compared to others that do not support interprocess synchronization, such as the Win32 critical sections. Lightweight synchronization primitives like critical section only invoke the kernel when a thread needs to block but otherwise operate completely in user mode. Developers should be aware of these implementation details when choosing appropriate synchronization primitives for their applications.

17.4.2.3 *Fairness*
The question of fairness in synchronization primitives is an important one. Fairness in this context refers to whether a synchronization primitive implements provisions to ensure that the thread that has been waiting the longest to acquire a synchronization object will be given priority to acquire it when it becomes free. The concern here is whether some threads can starve others, which can eventually lead to load imbalance and performance degradation. In other cases, starvation can ruin the user experience if the thread being starved is the user interface (UI) thread for instance. So, the fairness of synchronization primitives used by an application is another important characteristic that one should keep in mind when implementing parallel programs.

Fairness usually requires implementing a queue abstraction that tracks the order in which threads block waiting on a synchronization object. When the synchronization object is released, the thread at the head of the queue is awakened, allowing it to acquire the object and make forward progress. When blocking is used, this unfortunately introduces a source of inefficiency due to the delay between the object being freed and the thread getting scheduled in order to acquire the object. This delay can be significant and results in exacerbating queuing delays and contention for the object in question. This is the strongest reason for not implementing high levels of fairness. For spin locks, it is possible to implement fairness while minimizing scheduling delays and contention for the spin variable as is the case with MCS locks [6]. In Windows Win32, critical sections do not implement fairness, thus reducing scheduling delays, but one needs to be careful if starvation can be detrimental to performance in the particular use cases. Win32 mutexes and semaphores are fair.

17.4.2.4 *Reader versus Writer Differentiation*
Generic lock implementations do not differentiate between threads that acquire a lock to read memory locations protected by it and others that write to the same locations. Since race conditions

require at least one writer to exist, it is perfectly legal to allow multiple reader threads to acquire a lock simultaneously while requiring writers to obtain exclusive access to the lock. This is the motivation for using so-called reader–writer locks. Implementing such locks efficiently is nontrivial because of certain challenges that arise. For example, the lock has to implement a policy with respect to writer threads to avoid starving them when a constant stream of readers continuously acquires the lock. Addressing these concerns results in reader–writer lock implementations that are inherently more time consuming than generic locks. This implies that one needs to use such locks with care by ensuring that the ratio of readers to writers is high enough to reap the benefits of the increase in concurrency despite the increase in lock acquire and release overheads.

17.4.2.5 Synchronization Guidelines   Here are some rules that can help improve the performance of your parallel algorithm by reducing synchronization overheads:

- **Avoid synchronization when possible.** The best way to minimize synchronization overhead is to avoid synchronization altogether. This often means thinking about your algorithm and finding ways of reducing or eliminating synchronization. Data privatization is often very useful for this. This refers to a class of transformations that allow multiple threads to compute and update partial results that are frequently generated in thread-private memory while minimizing the frequency that such results get reflected in globally shared data structures. Careful design and consideration prior to implementation can greatly reduce the need for synchronization.

- **Avoid spin-waiting.** Pure spin-waiting synchronization primitives almost never make sense unless you are dealing with low-contention environments or operating system operations where blocking is not allowed. The costs in terms of wasted CPU cycles and power consumption usually far outweigh any responsiveness benefits. Hybrid spin-wait then block implementations are often a good compromise.

- **Use reader–writer locks when effective.** If the sharing pattern for variables protected by a lock exhibits a high reader to writer thread ratio, you should consider using reader–writer locks. The exact ratio of readers to writers beyond which such locks improve performance is implementation dependent, so you should guide your decision by measurements. Beware that such optimizations only benefit situations with lock contention.

- **Understand fairness requirements.** Synchronization primitives may or may not guarantee fairness, and you should consider to what degree fairness is required for your application. Beware that fairness often comes at a performance penalty, so you should only strictly enforce it when necessary.

- **Cautiously consider lock-free algorithms.** Lock-free algorithms attempt to improve performance by replacing high-level synchronization objects such as locks with atomic (interlocked) operations. This exposes such algorithms to memory ordering issues, potentially requiring the insertion of memory barrier/fence instructions. In addition, such algorithms may result in performance degradation if excessive interlocked operations are required for correctness. In general, lock-free algorithms are considered difficult to program and verify to be correct, so one needs to be careful before considering them.

17.5   NONUNIFORM MEMORY ACCESS

Memory latency continues to be a major performance bottleneck for CPU-bound application phases. Many modern multicore processor implementations integrate memory controllers on chip, reducing the latency to main memory. To support multisocket multiprocessors, systems today implement point-to-point interconnection networks that allow any thread running on any socket to access physical memory attached to either the local memory controller or a controller on a remote socket while supporting cache coherence. In multisocket systems, this configuration unfortunately results in variable memory latencies depending on the source of the data. Further, the ratio of latency differences can vary depending on the system topology and identity of communicating sockets. Performance measurements on an Intel Nehalem-EX-based two-socket system show approximately a 50% increase in memory latency when accessing a remote cache line. Systems that exhibit this phenomenon are referred to as cache-coherent non-uniform memory access (ccNUMA) systems. We will use NUMA for short. Most modern multisocket computer systems today fall into this category. One or more memory controllers on a single package in a NUMA system are often referred to as a node. A node usually has a group of processor cores associated with it, but that is not necessarily the case (i.e. there can be nodes that do not contain processor cores).

NUMA systems present a challenge to application performance because, depending on where a thread is running and which memory address it's accessing, the performance of the application may vary. This presents developers with the additional burden of ensuring that their applications do not suffer from NUMA latency effects. This section describes how this may be accomplished.

Optimizing performance on NUMA systems is simple in principle. To improve performance, threads should access data that is allocated from the memory controller that is closest in latency to the processor core(s) on which they execute. Achieving this simple task can be difficult in practice, but the next section presents some useful guidance.

17.5.1   Guidelines and Optimizations

This section gives an overview of NUMA-specific optimizations to improve application performance on such systems.

17.5.1.1   *Data Partitioning and Allocation*   When designing a parallel program that runs on a NUMA system, care must be taken to ensure that private or

shared-memory data structures that are mostly accessed by a thread or groups of threads running on a given node are allocated from the nearest memory controller. Data structures shared equally among threads on different nodes should be distributed among the nodes in order to achieve reasonable average latency behavior.

In order to accomplish the aforementioned, the operating system's memory manager and the programming APIs need to implement NUMA support. Standard heap managers usually provide a means for allocating and freeing *virtual* addresses; however, here we are concerned with *physical* memory allocation. Often, when a portion of a process' address space is touched for the first time, the memory manager allocates physical memory (usually at the granularity of a page) and creates a corresponding address translation entry. Unless the programmer provides the memory manager with a hint to ensure that physical memory is allocated from a specific node, the memory manager will use its own heuristics for allocation which might not be ideal for the application. As of Windows Vista and Windows Server 2008, there are APIs that allow applications to request that physical memory be allocated from a specific node. The memory manager does its best to comply with the request when allocating physical pages to back the requested virtual addresses.

One complicating factor is the degree of NUMA awareness in runtime systems and operating systems. For example, the standard C/C++ heap manager is usually not NUMA aware. The same applies to the .NET Framework and Java, although there has been some recent work to improve this. Operating system memory managers try to compensate for this by implementing heuristics such as a first-touch physical memory allocation policy where a page is allocated from the node on which a memory address was accessed first. Although such heuristics help, they do not replace intentional actions by the developers who best understand application behavior. It will take some time for NUMA awareness to permeate all systems, programming languages, libraries and runtimes. In the meantime, you should leverage whatever support exists to improve memory allocation locality.

17.5.1.2 *Computational Affinity*   Ensuring that memory is allocated from a specific node will not improve performance unless some assurances are in place that the thread(s) accessing that memory will run on cores in the same node. This requires a means of conveying this requirement to the operating system's scheduler. In Section 17.2, we discussed setting thread affinity in the context of techniques to reduce thread migration. We also discussed that setting affinity may interfere with power management or cause interference or conflict when different applications affinitize many threads on the same core while other cores are idle or lightly loaded. The type of affinity we were assuming in that section is referred to as *hard* affinity because the scheduler will always schedule a thread on a core that is in that thread's specified affinity set. The same arguments against hard affinity apply here, except for very specific environments such as high-performance computing or server applications where a single process effectively has full ownership of all compute and memory resources in the system. In contrast, *soft* affinity is a compromise that provides reasonable guarantees for computational locality while reducing bad effects. This form of affinity allows the developer to specify a *preferred* core as a hint to the operating system scheduler,

but it allows the scheduler to override that hint based on the load on the system and current resource utilization. The scheduler may also exercise some NUMA awareness by trying to keep a thread on cores that share the same NUMA node – often a multicore processor – as the preferred core. This minimizes thread migration overheads while keeping the thread close to its preferred memory controller. If cores in a NUMA node share a cache, the overhead incurred by migrating a thread to a core on the same node is further reduced.

17.5.1.3 Understanding System Topology The previous advice regarding computation and memory allocation locality implicitly requires a good understanding of system topology. In addition, it requires a good understanding of processor and memory utilization across NUMA nodes. The Windows operating system includes provisions for retrieving the topology of the system in terms of the number of cores, whether the system supports simultaneous multithreading on each core, the cache hierarchy, how each cache level is shared as well as the socket and node that each core and cache belongs to. It also includes APIs to query the amount of free memory on each NUMA node. By using these APIs in conjunction with the memory management and thread affinity APIs, good performance can be achieved on a NUMA system.

17.6 OVERLAPPING LATENCY

I/O latency can be a major source of serialization in a parallel application. The best way to deal with I/O is to overlap it with other work when possible. Modern operating systems include support for overlapped (or asynchronous) I/O. This support often eliminates the complexity of creating dedicated application I/O worker threads in order to overlap I/O latency to avoid blocking. Overlapped I/O minimizes the resource and context switch overheads associated with threads covered previously. In Windows, for example, the I/O completion port facility can be used to support asynchronous I/O. This is a construct that allows programmers to manage I/O intensive application phases while providing reasonable bounds on the number of threads simultaneously handling I/O completions. For example, imagine an application that receives requests from a network. At any given point in time, the application needs to post receive buffers on a socket and perform work on the data received while minimizing thread context switches. An I/O completion port delivers I/O completion notifications to threads waiting on the port and allows the specific degree of thread concurrency indicated by the developer to limit the number of threads actively working at a given point in time. You should familiarize yourself with such asynchronous I/O facilities in your runtime environment if your application's concurrency is affected by serialization due to disk or network I/O. A key to success is to achieve the right balance between fully utilizing the bandwidth of I/O devices by generating a sufficient number of concurrent I/O requests and finding enough CPU-intensive work to hide the latency resulting from the I/O requests.

Just as I/O latency can be hidden, so too can memory latency. This is done through software- [8] or hardware-controlled [4] prefetching. The former is usually performed by hand or through compiler optimizations. Special instructions are inserted into the instruction stream by the compiler in order to prefetch cache lines in anticipation of future reads or writes. Hardware-controlled prefetching is performed by the cache hierarchy of the processor when cache misses with detectable patterns are identified. The interested reader should refer to the following reference for more information on this topic [5].

17.7   DIAGNOSTIC TOOLS AND TECHNIQUES

Diagnostic tools are critical to achieving good performance in parallel applications. That is borne out of the significant cognitive load necessary to track the complex interactions between hardware and software that can affect performance in a multi-core processor-based computer system. In this section, we give a brief description of tools used in many aspects of parallel performance tuning.

17.7.1   Synchronization Overheads

The techniques used to understand synchronization overheads depend on the waiting mechanism used. For spin-waiting synchronization primitives, the best tool is usually a profiler. There are various profilers that may be used with varying degrees of runtime overhead and fidelity of data. Some Microsoft Visual Studio editions include one profiler based on sampling and another based on instrumentation. In order to identify whether synchronization overheads are high, it is possible to search for the signature of the synchronization function in the output of the profiler. We usually recommend starting with the sampling profiler in order to catch obvious issues. Switch to the instrumentation profiler for detailed analysis of specific binary objects. If you use the instrumentation profiler across an entire application, it is likely that the output data, analysis time and runtime overheads will become excessive. The instrumentation profiler provides function call counts and other more fine-grained metrics about synchronization routines. Note that the Win32 API set does not offer a user-mode spin lock, so analysis of spin-waiting is usually related to a user's own synchronization library. However, contention for some system structures that may use spin locks may be exposed and solved using such profilers.

For analysis of blocking synchronization APIs, including critical sections, events, condition variables, mutexes, slim reader–writer locks and semaphores, we suggest using the Concurrency Visualizer (CV) tool that first appeared in Visual Studio®2010 Premium and Ultimate [11]. This tool is based on Event Tracing for Windows (ETW) [9] and was designed for performance analysis of multithreaded applications. Using this tool, one can determine the amount of time spent by threads waiting for synchronization objects as well as the resulting impact on CPU utilization or effective thread concurrency during an application's execution. The tool relates synchronization delays to application source code, thereby enabling efficient performance tuning through integration with the editor and compiler in the Visual Studio integrated development environment.

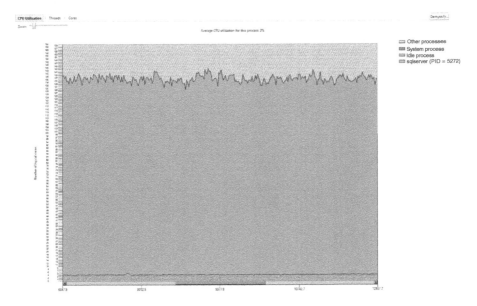

Figure 17.1   CPU Utilization view in CV showing poor concurrency in execution.

Here's an example illustrating how CV can be used to discover and fix synchronization issues in a commercial workload. In this case, the throughput and CPU utilization of the benchmark was very low, so we used the CV to analyze performance. Figure 17.1 shows the CPU Utilization view in CV. The graph shows time on the x-axis and the number of cores on the y-axis. There are three shaded areas. The bottom area shows the average number of cores being utilized by the process under analysis (SQL Server in this case) on a system with 160 logical cores. The middle region corresponds to average number of idle cores at a given time. The top area shows cores being utilized by other processes (predominantly an application server process in this case). To understand the root cause of the lack of CPU utilization by the database system, we switched to the Threads View shown in Figure 17.2. In this figure, thread states are depicted using colors in horizontal channels representing time. In the figure, you will notice that most threads spend a significant amount of time blocked on synchronization (black areas), while a single thread is always running (light-shaded line near the top). By clicking on one of the black blocking segments for a given thread, the blocking segment highlighting (wider middle-shaded rectangle) the application call stack where the current thread is blocked is shown in the window at the bottom. A white arrow (hard to see in the figure) connecting to another thread shows the thread that was holding the synchronization object, and another report tab (not shown) can show the call stack of that thread when it released the synchronization object. Using such tools, it was easy to determine that most threads were blocked on a single CPU-bound thread, and we were able to address this bottleneck in the application.

Another powerful ETW-based tool is the Windows Performance Analyzer (WPA) [7]. WPA is a free tool that can be used to perform blocking analysis similar

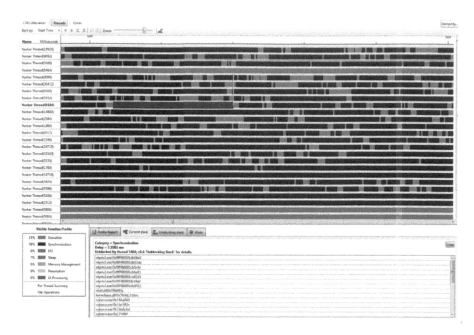

Figure 17.2 Thread synchronization analysis using the Concurrency Visualizer.

to CV. Both tools support an ETW-based sample profiler, which makes them a good starting point for both spin-waiting and blocking synchronization analysis. However, the Visual Studio profiler has more fine-grained control of parameters such as the sampling rate.

17.7.2 Thread Context Switches and Migration

Both CV and WPA provide excellent information about thread context switches via the ETW context switch provider in the Windows kernel. CV has a specific visualization and set of statistics to illustrate thread migration issues (not shown here). The Windows Performance Monitor (perfmon.exe) tool also has per-thread context switch rate counters (located under the Thread performance counter object), but we recommend an ETW-based approach because it can provide call stacks at context switches, making the data more actionable by the developer.

17.7.3 Processor and Memory Utilization

Per-core processor utilization information is provided by the Processor Information performance counter object in the Windows Performance Monitor. These counters may be interrogated by application programs to dynamically assess processor utilization. The Win32 APIs include support for determining the amount of memory available per NUMA node. The WPA tool has good support for computing and displaying CPU utilization versus time based on kernel context switch information. WPA allows filtering data by specific segments of time and generation of reports for various events of interest during specific time periods.

17.7.4 Caching, Sharing and NUMA Effects

The best tools to reason about cache effects as well as the impact of NUMA memory access delays require accessing hardware-specific performance counters. Current processors include a significant amount of performance instrumentation for tracking a wide variety of events, such as cache misses. Some processors also include sophisticated instrumentation to determine the latency of cache misses, which is highly valuable for NUMA system analysis.

Since hardware vendors know the details of their hardware well before external tool developers, the hardware vendor tools are often the first to adopt new performance instrumentation features. For Intel®IA32 or IA64, Intel®'s VTune™ [10] and the Performance Tuning Utility (PTU) tools are probably your best option. For AMD®processors, we recommend using CodeAnalyst™ [1]. There is also a large set of utilities that performance engineers have built and shared, so it is worth doing a quick tool search on the internet.

When looking for a good tool, you should choose one that not only informs you of the count of events, but also provides the instruction and data addresses when appropriate. At the very least, the tool should be able to resolve symbols to correlate instruction pointer values to your source code. Without this information, such tools may still be useful for self-relative comparisons during performance tuning, but they are not nearly as valuable as tools that can pinpoint specific application constructs that cause performance issues.

17.7.5 Input/Output Overheads

The Windows operating system includes a significant amount of instrumentation for I/O operations. Both WPA and CV have good support for analyzing disk I/O overheads, including latencies, associated thread delays, file names accessed, reads versus writes and I/O sizes. That's a great starting point for understanding the impact of I/O. Because the tools can provide call stacks, they can greatly assist in correlating performance bottlenecks to the responsible source code.

17.8 SUMMARY

In this chapter we gave a summary of many issues that can limit the performance and scalability of shared-memory parallel programs. We also provided guidance to aid programmers in making good choices to improve the performance of their applications. Finally, we provided some pointers to performance analysis tools that can significantly reduce the burden of identifying and understanding performance bottlenecks. We hope that you will find enough guidance here to navigate some of the challenges of designing and implementing efficient parallel programs.

REFERENCES

1. Advanced Micro Devices, Inc., *AMD CodeAnalyst Performance Analyzer*, `http://developer.amd.com/cpu/CodeAnalyst/Pages/default.aspx`

2. S. Adve and K. Gharachorloo. Shared memory consistency models: a tutorial. *IEEE Computer*, 29.12: 66–76, 1996.

3. G. M. Amdahl. Validity of the single processor approach to achieving large-scale computing capabilities. In *AFIPS Conference Proceedings*, pages 483–485, 1967.

4. T.-F. Chen and J.-L. Baer. Reducing memory latency via non-blocking and prefetching caches. In *Proceedings of the Fifth International Conference on Architectural Support for Programming Languages and Operating Systems*, pages 51–61, 1992.

5. D. E. Culler, J. Pal Singh, and A. Gupta. *Parallel Computer Architecture: A Hardware/Software Approach*. Morgan Kaufmann Publishers, Inc., San Francisco, 1999.

6. J. M. Mellor-Crummey and M. Scott. Algorithms for scalable Synchronization on shared-memory multiprocessors. *ACM Transactions on Computer Systems*, 9.1: 21–65, 1991.

7. Microsoft Corporation, Windows Performance Analysis Tools, January 2011. `http://msdn.microsoft.com/en-us/performance/cc825801.aspx`

8. T. C. Mowry. Tolerating Latency through Software-Controlled Data Prefetching. Ph.D. dissertation, Computer Systems Laboratory, Stanford University, 1994.

9. I. Park and R. Buch. Improve debugging and performance tuning with ETW. *MSDN Magazine*, April, 2007.

10. J. Reinders. *VTune Performance Analyzer Essentials: Measurement and Tuning Techniques for Software Developers*. Intel Press, 2005.

11. H. Shafi. Performance tuning with the concurrency visualizer in visual studio 2010. *MSDN Magazine*, 2010.

CHAPTER 18

A METHODOLOGY FOR OPTIMIZING MULTITHREADED SYSTEM SCALABILITY ON MULTICORES

NEIL GUNTHER, SHANTI SUBRAMANYAM AND STEFAN PARVU

18.1 INTRODUCTION

The ability to write efficient multithreaded programs is vital for system scalability, whether it be for parallel scientific codes or large-scale web applications. Scalability is about guaranteeing sustainable size, so it should be incorporated into initial system design rather than retrofitted as an afterthought. That requires a complete methodology which combines controlled measurements of the multithreaded platform together with a scalability modeling framework within which to evaluate those performance measurements.

In this chapter we show how scalability can be quantified using the *universal scalability law* (USL) [9, 10] by applying it to controlled performance measurements of memcached (MCD), J2EE and WebLogic. Commercial multicore processors are essentially black boxes, and although some manufacturers do offer specialized registers to measure individual core utilization [14, 25], not just overall processor utilization, the most accessible performance gains are primarily available at the application level. We also demonstrate how our methodology can identify the most significant performance tuning opportunities to optimize application scalability and provide an easy means for exploring other aspects of the multicore system design space.

The typical performance focus is on tools and techniques to profile and compile fine-grained parallel codes for scientific applications executing on many-core and multicore processors. Here, however, we shall be concerned with performance at the other end of that spectrum, namely, *system performance* of concurrent, multithreaded applications as employed by commercial enterprises and large-scale web sites. Economies of scale dictate that these systems eventually be migrated to many-core and multicore platforms.

Why is the emphasis on system performance important? Whatever the performance gains attained at the individual processor level, the impact of those gains must also be evident at the integrated system level so as to justify the cost of the effort. A fortiori, optimizing a local processor subsystem does not guarantee that the total system will also be optimized.

The claimed benefits of the various tools used for programming multicore applications [15, 17, 22] need to be evaluated *quantitatively*, not merely accepted as qualitative prescriptions [16, 18]. It often happens that applications which are heralded as being multithreaded and scalable turn out not to be when measured correctly [11]. To avoid setting incorrect expectations, system performance analysis should be incorporated into a comprehensive methodology rather than being done as an afterthought. We provide such a methodology in this chapter.

The organization of this chapter is as follows: In Section 18.2 we establish some of the terminologies used throughout and the basic procedural steps for assessing system scalability. In Section 18.3 we review what it means to perform the appropriate controlled measurements. The design and implementation of appropriate load test workloads for such controlled measurements is discussed in Section 18.4. Section 18.5 presents the universal scalability model that we use to perform statistical regression on the performance data obtained from controlled measurements. In this way we are able to quantify scalability. In Section 18.6 we present the first detailed application of our methodology to quantify MCD scalability. In Section 18.7 we give some idea on how to extend our methodology to a multithreaded Java application. Section 18.9 discusses some ideas about quantifying GPU and many-core scalability. The importance of our methodology for the often overlooked validation of complex performance measurements is presented in Section 18.8. Finally, Section 18.11 provides a summary and possible extensions to our methodology.

Although we shall focus on the broader issues of general-purpose, highly concurrent, multithreaded, and multicore [17] applications [23], we anticipate that readers who are more involved with scientific applications will also be able to apply our methodology to their systems.

18.2 MULTITHREADING AND SCALABILITY

We begin by presenting the context and terminology for comparing multithreaded applications that either scale out or scale up.

Much of the FOSS stack used for running web applications, for example, MCD, MySQL, and Ruby on Rails, has scalability limitations that are masked by the widespread adoption of horizontal scale-out. As traffic growth forces the necessity for more and cheaper multicore servers, multithreading scalability becomes a significant issue once again.

Most web deployments have now standardized on horizontal scale-out in every tier–web, application, caching, and database–using cheap, off-the-shelf, white boxes. In this approach, there are no real expectations for vertical scalability of server applications like MCD or the full LAMP stack. But with the potential for highly concurrent scalability offered by newer multicore processors, it is no longer cost-effective to ignore the potential under utilization of processor resources due to poor thread-level scalability of the web stack.

Our USL methodology quantifies scalability using the following iterative procedure:

1. Measure the system throughput (e.g. requests per second) for a configuration where either the number of user threads is varied on a fixed multicore platform or the number of physical cores is varied using a fixed number of user threads per core.

2. Measurements should include at least half a dozen data points in order to make the regression analysis statistically meaningful.

3. Calculate the capacity ratio $C(N)$ and efficiency $E(N)$ defined in Section 18.5.

4. Perform nonlinear statistical regression [19] to determine the USL scalability parameters α and β defined in Section 18.5.

5. Use the values of α and β to predict N_c, where the scalability maximum is expected to occur. N_c may lie outside any physically attainable system configuration.

6. The magnitude of the α parameter is associated with system *contention* effects (in the application, the hardware or both), and the β parameter is associated with data *coherency* effects. This step provides the vital connection between the numerical output of the USL model and the identification of likely candidates for further performance tuning in software and hardware. See Sections 18.6 and 18.8.

7. Repeat these steps with a new set of measurements until any differences between data and the USL projections are optimized.

We elaborate on each of these steps in the subsequent sections.

18.3 CONTROLLED PERFORMANCE MEASUREMENTS

When doing scalability analysis of multithreaded applications, it is important to collect the data using controlled measurements. Controlled measurements require:

1. A controlled hardware platform that faithfully represents the real system being analyzed. The load test platform that we used to perform the measurements presented in Section 18.6 is shown schematically in Figure 18.1.

2. A well-designed workload together with tools that produce accurate data resulting in measurements that are repeatable. The workloads that we used are described in Section 18.4.

The throughput results from a typical performance test are shown in Figure 18.2. A performance test is characterized by a 'ramp-up' period in which load is increased on the system, a 'steady-state' period during which performance data is gathered, and a 'ramp-down' period as the load diminishes.

It is important to ensure that the ramp-up period is sufficiently large to get the server performing operations in a normal manner, for example, all data that is likely to be cached has been read in. This can require times ranging from a couple of minutes to several tens of minutes, depending on the complexity of the workload.

The steady-state time should be sufficiently long to include all of the activity that may occur on the system during normal operations (e.g., garbage collection, writing to logs at some regular interval, etc.)

Scalability tests should ensure that the infrastructure is well tuned and does not have inherent bottlenecks (e.g., incorrect network routes). This implies active monitoring of the test infrastructure and analysis of the data to ascertain it is accurate. Repeating the tests can also help to validate measurements.

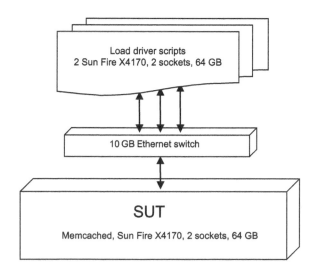

Figure 18.1   Schematic of scalability load measurement configuration.

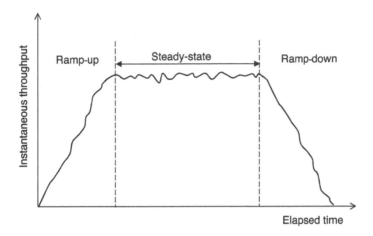

Figure 18.2 Steady-state measurement of instantaneous throughput, for a particular load value N, represented as a time series to show the ramp-up and ramp=-down phases.

18.4 WORKLOAD DESIGN AND IMPLEMENTATION

Data collected from controlled performance measurements are only as good as the workload used to run the tests. A poorly designed workload can result in irrelevant measurements and wrong conclusions [23]. A well-designed workload should have the following characteristics:

Predictability: The behavior of the system while running the workload should be predictable. This means that one should be able to determine how the workload processes requests and accesses data. This helps in analyzing performance.

Repeatability: If the workload is run several times in an identical fashion, it should produce results that are statistically identical. Without this repeatability, performance analysis becomes difficult.

Scalability: A workload should be able to place different levels of load in order to test the scalability of the target application and infrastructure. A workload that can only generate a fixed load or one that scales in an haphazard fashion that does not resemble actual scaling in production is not very useful.

These characteristics can be realized using the following design principles:

Design the interactions: Define the actors and their use cases. The use cases help define the operations of the workload. In a complex workload, the different actors may have different use cases, for example, a salesperson entering an order and an accountant generating a report. Combine use cases that are likely to occur together into a workload. For example, batch operations run at night should be a separate workload from online, interactive operations.

Define the metrics: Typical metrics include throughput (number of operations executed per unit time) and response time. Response time metrics are usually specified as average 90th or 95th percentiles.

Design the load: This means defining the manner by which the different operations associated with the metrics offer load onto the servers. This involves deciding on the operation mix, mechanisms to generate data for the requests and deciding on arrival rates or think times. This step is crucial to get right if the workload needs to emulate a production system and/or is being used for performance testing of the important code paths in the application. A slow operation that is executed only 1% of the time can sometimes be ignored, whereas even a 5% drop in performance of an operation that occurs 50% of the time may be not tolerable.

Define scaling rules: This step is often overlooked, leading to overly optimistic results during testing. Complex workloads need a means by which to scale the workload depending on the actual deployment hardware. Often, scaling is done by increasing the number of emulated users/threads. Any data-dependent application also needs to have the data set scaled in order to truly measure the performance impact of a large number of concurrent users.

With regard to workload implementation, there exist several open-source and commercial tools that aid in developing workloads and running them. Available tools vary considerably in functionality, ability to scale and their own performance overhead. Some preliminary investigations may be necessary to ensure that a given choice of tool can meet the anticipated requirements.

18.5 QUANTIFYING SCALABILITY

There are many well-known techniques for achieving better scalability: collocation, caching, pooling and parallelism, to name a few. But these are only qualitative descriptions. How can one decide on the relative merits of any of these techniques unless they can be quantified? This is clearly a role for performance modeling. Performance models are essential not only for prediction but also, as we discuss in Sections 18.6 and 18.8, for *interpreting* scalability measurements.

Many performance modeling tools, such as event-based simulators and analytic solvers, are based on a queueing paradigm that requires measured service times as modeling inputs. More often than not, however, such measurements are unavailable, thereby thwarting the use of these modeling tools. This is especially true for multi-tier, web-based applications. A more practical intermediate approach is to apply nonlinear regression [19] to performance measurements that are more accessible, the major advantage being that service time measurements are not required.

Table 18.1 Interpretation of $M/M/1/N/N$ queueing metrics.

Metric	Repairman	Multicore	Multithread
N	Machines	Virtual processors	User threads
Z	Up time	Execution period	Think time
S	Service time	Transmission time	Processing time
W	Wait time	Interconnect latency	Scheduling time
X	Failure rate	Bus bandwidth	Throughput

18.5.1 Queueing Model Foundations

The universal scalability model (or USL model) that we present in this section is a realization of the approach alluded to in the previous section. The USL is a nonlinear parametric model [9, 10] derived from a well-defined queue-theoretic model known as the *machine–repairman model* [5, 8].

Elementary $M/M/m$ queueing models [8] of multicores and multithreaded systems are too simple because they allow an unbounded number of requests to occupy the system and they cannot account for processor-to-processor interactions. Machine–repairman models, like $M/G/m/N/N$, are defined to have only a finite number of requests [8]. That constraint can be used to reflect the finite number of threads in a load test platform, as discussed on Sections 18.3 and 18.4. Alternatively, $M/G/m/N/N$ models can represent the interactions between N processors [2]. Indeed, the machine–repairman model can be further generalized in terms of queueing network models to analyze the performance of parallel systems [21], including architectures with multiple latency stages [7], provided the requisite service times can be measured.

Here, we restrict ourselves to the $M/M/1/N/N$ queueing model where the single Markovian server represents the interconnect latency between N processors and cores. Since the components of this queue have a consistent physical interpretation with respect to multicore performance metrics (Table 18.1), we also avoid mere curve-fitting exercises with ad hoc parameters.

To motivate our choice of performance model, we briefly review the key physical attributes of scalability. Referring to Figure 18.3:

1. **Ideal parallelism:** Linear scaling corresponds to *equal bang for the buck* computational capacity where each increment in the load, ΔN on the x-axis, produces a constant increment in throughput, ΔX on the y-axis, as indicated by the dashed inclined line in Figure 18.3. Such linearity in capacity can be written symbolically as

$$C(N) = N \qquad (18.1)$$

This includes scaled sizing of the workload [9].

2. **Resource sharing:** Accounts for the fallaway from linear scaling due to waiting for access to shared resources. This loss of linearity due to resource contention is associated with the USL model parameter

$$0 < \alpha < 1 \tag{18.2}$$

3. **Resource limitation:** Even if such linear scaling is achievable, it cannot exceed the finite capacity of the system resources. This is defined by an asymptotic bound from above:

$$\lim_{N \to \infty} C(N, \alpha) = \frac{1}{\alpha} \tag{18.3}$$

This saturation limit is shown as the dashed horizontal line in Figure 18.3. This bound could be lower due to execution-time skew in components of the workload [1, 6].

4. **Retrograde scaling:** Worse than saturation, this effect arises from the additional latency due to *pairwise* interprocessor communication, for example, exchange of data between caches, and is given by the binomial coefficient

$$\binom{N}{2} = \frac{N(N-1)}{2} \tag{18.4}$$

and is associated with a USL parameter β.

Another useful metric is the efficiency

$$E(N) = \frac{C(N)}{N} \tag{18.5}$$

which defines the scalability (18.11) per core or per thread. We shall apply this metric to data validation in Section 18.8.

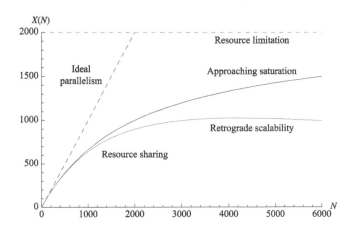

Figure 18.3 Physical components of scalability.

18.5.2   Universal Scalability Model

The following theorem allows us to combine each of the physical scalability components of Section 18.5.1 into a parametric model:

Definition 1 (Universal Scalability Law)

$$C(N, \alpha, \beta) = \frac{N}{1 + \alpha(N-1) + \beta N(N-1)} \tag{18.6}$$

where the factor of 2 in (18.4) has been absorbed into the β coefficient.

Theorem 18.1 (Queueing Bound) *The USL model (18.6) is equivalent to the synchronous bound on the throughput of a machine–repairman queueing model with a service time that is linearly load dependent on N.*

The formal proof is too long to reproduce here. A pivotal observation [9] is that for $M/M/1/N/N$, the throughput $X(N)$ is bounded below by

$$X(N) \geq \frac{N}{NS + Z} \tag{18.7}$$

in the notation of Table 18.1. It also excludes super-linear scaling [1, 21].

Proof 1 (Sketch) *When the first request is in service (at the repairman), the mean waiting time for the remaining requests is*

$$W = (N-1)S \tag{18.8}$$

where N is the number of requests in the system. Let the service time be linearly load dependent:

$$S(N) = cNS$$

with c a constant of proportionality. For synchronous queueing all requests are enqueued simultaneously, so we can rewrite (18.8) as

$$W = cN(N-1)S \tag{18.9}$$

Expressed as relative throughput, (18.9) appears in the denominator of (18.6) as the corresponding quadratic term. ∎

The interested reader is referred to Ref. [10] for details and Ref. [13] for supporting simulation results.

Perhaps the most important point for our methodology is that (18.6) is a mean value equation in the queueing variables and, in that sense, accounts for the possibility of fluctuations in the size of workload components and subtasks. In particular, the machine–repairman model has been proven to be robust to fluctuations in these queue variables [5].

Corollary 18.1 (Duality) *The scaling variable N in the parametric model (18.6) can be interpreted equally as representing a finite number of threads (software view) or a finite number of core processors (hardware view) because it is a bound on the same $M/M/1/N/N$ queueing model.*

Setting $\beta = 0$ in (18.6) produces the standard parametric version of Amdahl's law with (18.2) the *serial fraction* of the workload. However, by virtue of Theorem 18.1, Amdahl's law can be interpreted as a limiting case (zero coherency delays) of the USL.

Corollary 18.2 (Amdahl's Law) *Amdahl's law corresponds to the relative through-put (speedup) due to synchronous queueing in the standard machine–repairman queueing model with constant mean service time.*

Amdahl's law is the synchronous throughput bound on an $M/M/1//N$ queue having a load-independent mean service time S.

Proof 2 (Sketch) *The proof relies on the identity*

$$\alpha = \frac{S}{S+Z} \rightarrow \begin{cases} 0 & as \ S \rightarrow 0, with \ Z = constant \\ 1 & as \ Z \rightarrow 0, with \ S = constant \end{cases} \quad (18.10)$$

between the queueing metrics in Table 18.1 and the parameter α in (18.2). ∎

See Appendix A of Refs [9, 10] for a more detailed discussion.

An important point to note from the preceding is that Amdahl's law represents worst-case queueing effects [4, 12]. This is consistent with the notion that synchronous requests have longer delays than asynchronous requests, the latter being the mean value throughput for $M/M/1//N$. Other examples of applying (18.6) to both hardware and software scalability can be found in [9].

The capacity ratio for measured data is defined as the normalization:

$$C(N) = \frac{X(N)}{X(1)} \quad (18.11)$$

Since the capacity ratio has two definitions–one empirical (18.11) and the other analytical (18.6)–the optimization goal is to match them in such a way that the adjusted USL coefficients provide the best fit of performance data.

The key distinction is that, unlike Amdahl's law, (18.6) possesses a maximum at

$$N_c = \sqrt{\frac{1-\alpha}{\beta}} \quad (18.12)$$

the location of which is controlled by the USL coefficients according to:

(a) $N_c \rightarrow 0$ as $\alpha \rightarrow 1$

(b) $N_c \rightarrow 0$ as $\beta \rightarrow \infty$

(c) $N_c \to \infty$ as $\beta \to 0$

(d) $N_c \to \beta^{-1/2}$ as $\alpha \to 0$

The important implication for our methodology is that beyond N_c the throughput becomes *retrograde*. See Figure 18.3. This effect is commonly observed in applications that involve shared-writable data.

Summarizing the steps for application optimization:

1. Steady-state measurements of throughput $X(N)$ for each load point N.

2. At least half a dozen N values are required in order to be statistically significant for USL fitting.

3. Calculate the capacity ratio (18.11) for each N value.

4. Use nonlinear statistical regression [19] to determine the USL coefficients α and β.

5. Optimize the complete scalability function (18.6) for any desired N value.

The same methodological procedure can be applied to hardware scalability optimization although, as we had pointed out in the introduction, most commodity hardware is now a silicon black box, which means the hardware performance tuning opportunities are far fewer.

The use of the term 'universal' in this context refers not only to the general applicability of (18.6) to both multicore hardware and multithreaded software scalability but also to the fact that no more than two coefficients are needed to accommodate the possibility of reaching saturation limits (Amdahl scaling) or thrashing limits (coherency delays). In the latter case, there is little virtue on modeling such degraded performance; better try and improve it.

We now present some case studies that demonstrate how this methodology has been successfully applied.

18.6 CASE STUDY: MEMCACHED SCALABILITY

As mentioned in Section 18.2, most large-scale web sites have standardized on horizontal scale-out in every tier as a simple way to achieve high degrees of scalability. A ubiquitous application used in this context is MCD. In this section, we demonstrate how our analysis leads to improved thread scalability of MCD [10].

Figure 18.4 shows controlled MCD throughput as a function of $N \le 12$ threads for three releases: 1.2.8, 1.4.1, and 1.4.5, measured in thousands of operations/sec (KOPS). Each release has a very similar retrograde throughput profile, peaking between $N = 6$ and $N = 7$ threads.

Whereas the lines in Figure 18.4 merely associate data points belonging to the same MCD release, the curve in Figure 18.5 is generated by statistically fitting (18.6) to those data and is not required to pass through every data point.

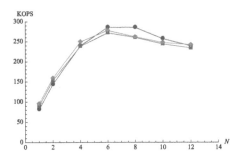

Figure 18.4   Throughput of three MCD releases up $N = 12$ threads.

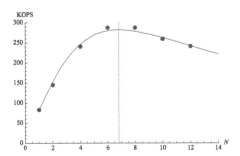

Figure 18.5   USL regression analysis of memcached 1.2.8 data (*dots*) in Figure 18.4.

Table 18.2   Memcached scalability parameters.

Version	α	β	N_c
1.2.8	0.0255	0.0210	6.8121
1.4.1	0.0821	0.0207	6.6591
1.4.5	0.0988	0.0209	6.5666

The USL regression analysis of MCD 1.2.8 reveals a contention parameter value of $\alpha = 0.0255$ and a coherency parameter value of $\beta = 0.0210$. Repeating this procedure with the other MCD versions results in the USL coefficients summarized in Table 18.2. In this way, the scalability of MCD is now fully quantified. It is also clear that it would be desirable to move the estimated maximum at $N_c \approx 6$ to a higher value.

Figure 18.6 shows how scalability improved after various code changes were applied. This is where the procedural steps of our USL methodology, outlined in Section 18.2, actually pay off.

Access to the MCD cache is controlled by a single-mutex lock. When running with greater than 6 threads, contention for this mutex increases dramatically. A partitioned cache was implemented with each partition controlled by its own mutex. In addition,

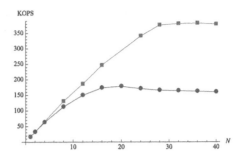

Figure 18.6 Comparison of scalability data for standard MCD (*lower curve*) and patched MCD (*upper curve*).

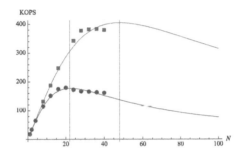

Figure 18.7 USL model of patched MCD data in Figure 18.6 extended out to $N = 100$ threads.

contention for the stats lock was identified. This lock controls access to the stats structure that is updated on every request. The stats structure was redesigned to hold stats on a per-thread basis. This fix was applied in release 1.4.5, and it greatly improved scalability.

The USL fit to the patched MCD data in Figure 18.6 is extended out to $N = 100$ threads in Figure 18.7. The original scalability peak at $N_c = 22$ threads (*lower curve*) is now moved out to $N_c = 48$ threads (*upper curve*).

At this point, the reader may be dumb struck as to how the actual changes made to the application code are determined from the seemingly abstract numerical output of the USL model. First, it is important to recall that the role of the performance analyst is to measure and validate, not to modify hardware or software for which he or she was not responsible in the first place. That is the role of the hardware engineer or the software developer.

Second, the interpretation of the USL analysis and the choice of performance tuning optimization arise from discussions between the performance analyst and the appropriate engineers. Since the latter are the real experts, it is helpful if the modeling analysis can point to specific types of effects that may be contributing to inferior scalability. This is precisely what the USL does by virtue of its parameters having explicit physical meaning, namely, the respective degrees of concurrency (N), contention (α) and coherency (β).

In this way, step 6 of the USL methodology in Section 18.2 can evoke a 'light bulb' moment for engineers. In practice, we have seen this synergy occurring time and again. Moreover, the corrective action taken is usually something we, as performance analysts, could never have foreseen because we were not in possession of the implementation details. Although we have presented an example of improvements made to MCD software, Corollary 18.1 implies it could also have been that scalability improvements came from hardware changes, such as memory resizing or more recent revisions to the multicore architecture. That said, no matter what insights are favored or what tuning actions are adopted, the ultimate arbiter is the next iteration of the USL methodology.

18.7 OTHER MULTITHREADED APPLICATIONS

We focused on MCD scalability in Section 18.6 to demonstrate how the USL methodology is applied in detail. In this section, we show how the same methodology can be applied to other multithreaded applications.

Java 2 Platform, Enterprise Edition (J2EE) applications are extremely popular in enterprises because the J2EE platform is known to be robust, secure, and scalable [24].

Figure 18.8 shows how the application throughput scales when load is added to a J2EE server. The circled and squared points show different data sets to exhibit how the USL regression values change accordingly. See Table 18.3.

When the USL is applied to the circled data points, it results in the upper curve in Figure 18.9, which indicates excellent scalability up to more than $N_c \approx 12,000$ users. This modeling result is reasonable as the initial data set shows almost linear scalability through $N = 800$ users.

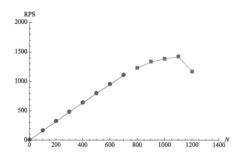

Figure 18.8 Initial J2EE throughput data (*left*) and subsequent data (*right*) measured in requests per second (RPS).

Table 18.3   J2EE application scalability parameters.

Load	α	β	N_c
Low	1.49×10^{-5}	6.7×10^{-9}	12216.90
High	0.0	2.4×10^{-7}	2041.24

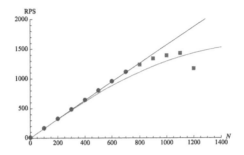

Figure 18.9   USL models of J2EE scalability for initial data (*upper curve*) and subsequent data (*lower curve*).

However, consider what happens when the data set changes. As the load was increased and the red data points in Figure 18.8 were measured, the corresponding USL parameters change accordingly resulting in the lower curve of Figure 18.9. The larger β value in Table 18.3 reflects a substantial decrease in predicted scalability. However, even that scalability is still extremely good (cf. the corresponding α and β for MCD in Table 18.2), but instead of simply appealing to qualitative descriptions like 'highly scalable', or 'great performance', the USL coefficients provide us with true quantification of J2EE scalability.

We want to underscore that what looks like a bad prediction is, in fact, precisely how our methodology should work. Based on the initial data, maximum scalability was estimated to occur at $N_c \approx 12{,}000$ user threads. Further measurements, however, show that this maximum occurs at $N_c \approx 2{,}000$ user threads instead. It is not that the original USL projections were wrong, but that those initial data did not contain any information about a subsequent scaling limitation present in the JVM. The important point is that the USL sets expectations and then forces performance engineers to explain subsequent deviations at each stage of the measurement process.

18.8   CASE STUDY: DATA VALIDATION

Another simple and immediate practical benefit of applying the methodology is *validation* of performance data.

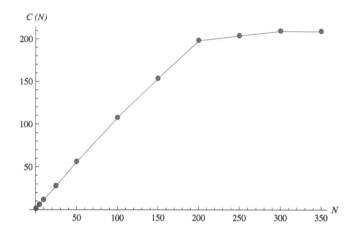

Figure 18.10   Web application scalability data.

Consider a test environment, similar to that described in Sections 18.4 and 18.7, where test scripts are developed using different test cases for a particular application. In this case, the test configuration used Apache Jakarta JMeter as a load injector for a J2EE application [23] running on Java 6 with a WebLogic application server. We are not interested in what this application was doing internally but rather in examining and validating the load testing procedure.

Several tests were run against this J2EE application, and the reported JMeter values were recorded. As usual, we were interested in the throughput and response time metrics. Following Section 18.5.2, throughput was the primary metric of interest for determining application scalability. Figure 18.10 shows an example of the throughput data. It appears acceptable because:

- The data points are monotonically increasing. A sequence of numbers is monotonically increasing if each element in the sequence is larger than its predecessor. Notice that the profile appears to decrease slightly beyond $N = 300$. The USL is designed to model such a characteristic.

- The sequence is linearly rising up to $N = 200$ virtual users.

- The throughput reaches saturation around $N = 300$. This is exactly what we expect for a closed queueing system [8] with a finite number of active requests (as is true for any load testing or benchmarking system). In this case, the onset of saturation looks rather sudden as indicated by the discontinuity in the gradient ('sharp knee') at $N = 200$. This is usually a sign of significant internal change in the dynamics of the combined hardware–software system.

These data seem to pass the visualization test, and most performance testing would stop here. Unfortunately, visualization alone is not always sufficient proof of optimal scalability. Applying our USL methodology, we modeled these data to evaluate the α and β coefficients and determine if application scalability could further be improved.

Table 18.4 Preparation for
USL analysis of the data in
Figure 18.10.

N	$C(N)$	$E(N)$
1	1.00	1.00
5	5.67	1.13
10	11.33	1.13
25	27.50	1.10
50	55.83	1.12
100	107.50	1.08
150	153.33	1.02
200	198.33	0.99
250	204.17	0.82
300	210.00	0.70
350	209.67	0.60

In setting up the USL model to perform statistical regression, we detected some efficiencies (18.5) that were greater than 100%. In particular, Table 18.4 exhibits $E(N) > 1$ for test loads in the range $N = 5$–150 virtual users.

From a logical standpoint, we cannot have more than 100% of anything. Sometimes, however, there are *conventions* in performance analysis where quantities exceeding 100% have a particular interpretation, for example, 3200% processor capacity might be shorthand for a maximal machine utilization of 32 cores running at 100% busy. Conventions notwithstanding, any numbers that are out of bounds should be flagged for explanation by performance engineers or application developers.

Axiom 18.1 *Data + Models = Insight*

All measurements contain errors, and the more complex the measurement system, the more prone it will be to generating erroneous performance data. Without a validation framework, how can it be known when the data are wrong? The USL provides a simple mathematical reference framework for detecting anomalies like those in Table 18.4. We encapsulate this observation in Axiom 18.1.[1]

So, what was causing the excessive efficiencies in this case? Since we had not even invoked statistical regression at that point, we knew that the culprit could not be the USL model. Instead, it became clear that something was amiss with the measurement process (not the usual conclusion). The performance engineers then set about eliminating one factor at a time. Eventually, it emerged that the JMeter tool itself was the only remaining explanation for the source of the erroneous measurements. Without

---

[1] A hybridization of the book *Algorithms + Data Structures = Programs* by N. Wirth and R. Hamming's observation that computing is about insight, not numbers.

being forced by the USL modeling framework to resolve this unforeseen issue, further load testing would have been a waste of time and resources.

18.9 SCALABILITY ON MANY-CORE ARCHITECTURES

Tools for writing applications for CPU–GPU many-cores are constantly improving. Measuring and quantifying many-cores scalability of such applications is the next step and that requires a methodology, not just tools. In this section we indicate how the USL methodology can be applied to workloads running on many-core architectures.

18.9.1 Trends in Multiprocessing, Multicores, and Many-cores

In recent years, vendors have been considering multicore architectures and how applications can be migrated from single processors to multiple processors. In this paradigm, the multicore forces the application programmer to focus on maintaining and maximizing execution speed of a sequential workload but replicating it across multiple processing units inside the same physical processor [15].

A different approach, using many-cores, focuses on how to maximize the aggregate throughput, an essential requirement for the gaming industry and anything else involving 3D graphics. This many-core approach deploys a much higher number of cores per physical processor unit, without the need for internal cache memories, logic control unit for executing instructions and other complexities associated with multicore processors.

These alternative paradigms allow developers to consider which is the best option for their applications. Recent improvements offer additional mechanisms to select and direct parts of the application to either CPU or GPU, depending on its intended usage. Compute-intensive sections can be dynamically directed to a many-cores processor, while single-threaded sections can be assigned to a multicore processor. Such combinations of CPU and GPU let the workloads run optimally by taking intelligent advantage of the type of processor hardware available.

However, not all applications are written to take advantage of these new architectures. For example, legacy single-threaded workloads typically cannot make use of these new options. When executed on many-core processors, such workloads will underperform.

Without significant modification and porting effort, legacy workloads cannot scale well. Testing and analyzing these workloads in a controlled fashion (see Section 18.3) is a necessity and presents another opportunity for our USL methodology.

18.9.2 USL Methodology for GPUs

Since the USL methodology is generic, it should be applicable to quantifying the scalability of many-core applications. In this vein, we have applied it to data kindly provided to us by Prof. Frank Dehne and Kumanan Yogaratnam at Carleton University [3].

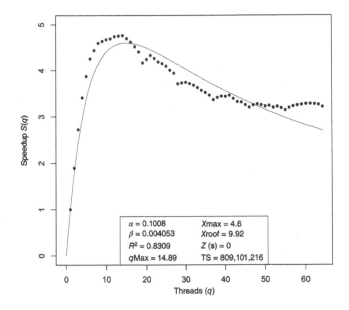

Figure 18.11   USL fit to NVIDIA Tesla GPU data.

They compare the speedup of different parallel graph algorithms running on an NVIDIA GeForce 260 with 216 2.1 GHz GPU cores and 896 MB of RAM. The parallel speedup is logically equivalent to $C(N, \alpha, \beta)$ in the USL formalism.

Their choice of parallel graphing algorithms reveals irregular data access patterns (shown as dots in Fig. 18.11) that are different from regular data access patterns found in typical parallel processing workloads for image processing, linear algebra, or scientific computing. More importantly, significant speedup degradation is observed for $N > 15$ threads.

18.10 FUTURE WORK

Applying USL regression analysis to the data in Section 18.9 produces the curve in Figure 18.11, which has a contention parameter value of $\alpha = 0.1008$ and a coherency parameter value of $\beta = 0.00405$, with an estimated maximum at $N_c = 14.89$ threads. The interpretation of these coefficients is still under investigation for potential ways to improve GPU scalability. In the meantime, the important point is that these controlled measurements are being compared with the USL performance model, thereby reinforcing Axiom 18.1.

Another avenue of research is using multicores to model multicores. The USL model is an excellent candidate for running thousands of simultaneous regressions in parallel and then selecting an optimal set of coefficients from the simulation results. Moreover, since the foundations of the USL lie in queue-theoretic models, this approach could be extended to Monte Carlo simulations [20] of Markov models.

18.11 CONCLUDING REMARKS

In this chapter, we have presented a performance methodology for quantifying application scalability on multicore and many-core systems. With potentially massive computational horsepower now being delivered in low-cost silicon black boxes, the remaining opportunities for improving performance lie mostly in the application layers.

Our methodology, based on the USL, emphasizes the importance of validating scalability data through controlled measurements that use appropriately designed test workloads. These measurements must then be reconciled with the USL performance model. It is this synergy between measuring and modeling that provides the key to achieving successful scalability on multicore platforms.

In Section 18.5 we presented the USL model and showed how it can be combined with nonlinear statistical regression to analyze controlled performance measurements. In this way, we are able to truly quantify scalability and thereby assess the cost–benefit of multithreaded applications running on multicore or many-core architectures. The USL methodology also provides data validation as a side effect of preparing for the more sophisticated regression analysis.

In Section 18.9 we presented some initial results from quantifying GPU and many-core scalability using the USL methodology. Possible confounding effects between the USL coefficients due to these fine-grained parallel workloads suggest an analysis based on the concept of *scalability zones* [13].

With ever-increasing economies of scale offered by commodity multicore to many-core systems, we anticipate that cost–benefit analysis tools, such as the USL-based methodology described here, will play an increasingly important role in the future of computing.

REFERENCES

1. K. Agrawal, C. E. Leiserson, and J. Sukha. Executing task graphs using work-stealing. In *Proceedings of the 24th IEEE International Parallel and Distributed Processing Symposium (IPDPS), Atlanta, GA, USA*, pages 1–12, April 19–23 2010.

2. M. Ajmone-Marsan, G. Balbo, and G. Conte. *Performance Models of Multiprocessor Systems*. MIT, Boston, MA, 1990.

3. F. Dehne and K. Yogaratnam. Exploring the limits of GPUs with parallel graph algorithms. arxiv.org/abs/1002.4482, 2010.

4. S. Eyerman and L. Eeckhout. Modeling critical sections in Amdahl's law and its implications for multicore design. In *Proceedings of the 37th Annual international symposium on Computer Architecture (ISCA 2010), Saint-Malo, France*, pages 362–370, June 19–23 2010.

5. D. Gross and C. Harris. *Fundamentals of Queueing Theory*. Wiley, third edition, 1998.

6. N. J. Gunther. *The Practical Performance Analyst*. iUniverse, Lincoln, NE, 2000. Chapter 14.

7. N. J. Gunther. Unification of Amdahl's law, LogP and other performance models for message-passing architectures. In *International Conference on Parallel and Distributed Computing Systems, PDCS'05, Phoenix, AZ, USA*, pages 569–576, November 14–16 2005.

8. N. J. Gunther. Analyzing Computer System Performance with Perl::PDQ. Springer, Heidelberg, 2005.

9. N. J. Gunther. *Guerrilla Capacity Planning*. Springer, Heidelberg, 2007.

10. N. J. Gunther. A general theory of computational scalability based on rational functions. arxiv.org/abs/0808.1431, 2008.

11. N. J. Gunther, S. Subramanyam, and S. Parvu. Hidden scalability gotchas in memcached and friends. In *VELOCITY Web Performance and Operations Conference, Santa Clara, California*, O'Reilly, June, 22–24 2010.

12. M. D. Hill and M. R. Marty. Amdahl's law in the multicore era. *IEEE Computer*, 41(7): 33–38, 2008.

13. J. Holtman and N. J. Gunther. Getting in the zone for successful scalability. In *34th International Computer Measurement Group Conference, Las Vegas, Nevada, USA*, pages 123–136, December 7–12 2008.

14. W. Huang, L. Cheng, M. Accapadi, and N. Keung. CPU monitoring and tuning: get rid of your CPU bottlenecks and improve performance. www.ibm.com/developerworks/aix/library/au-aix5_cpu/index.html, 2005.

15. D. Kirk and W. Hwu. *Programming Massively Parallel Processors: A Hands-on Approach*. Morgan Kaufmann, Burlington, MA, 2010.

16. R. Kumar, D. Tullsen, N. Jouppi, and P. Ranganathan. Heterogeneous chip multiprocessors. *IEEE Computer*, 38(11):32–38, November 2005.

17. Multicore programming. IEEE Computer, March 2010. Feature articles.

18. D. Patterson. The trouble with multicore. *IEEE Spectrum*, 47:28–32, July 2010.

19. C. Ritz and J. C. Streibig. *Nonlinear Regression with R*. Springer, New York, 2008.

20. C. P. Robert and G. Casella. *Introducing Monte Carlo Methods with R*. Springer, New York, 2010.

21. K. C. Sevcik. Modeling the performance of parallel computer systems. In *ACM SIG-METRICS Conference, Boulder, Colorado, USA*, pages 17–45, May 22–25 1990. Tutorial Session.

22. N. Shavit. Data structures in the mutlicore age. *Communications of the ACM*, 54(3):76–84, March 2011.

23. S. Subramanyam. Principles of good benchmark construction. In *30th International Computer Measurement Group Conference, Las Vegas, Nevada, USA*, pages 657–666, December 5–10 2004.

24. S. Subramanyam. Performance management of a J2EE application to meet service level agreements. In *31st International Computer Measurement Group Conference, Orlando, Florida, USA*, pages 327–334, December 4–9 2005.

25. R. Talashikar. Corestat: core utilization reporting tool for ultraSPARC T1. `blogs.oracle.com/travi/entry/corestat_core_utilization_ reporting_tool`, 2006.

CHAPTER 19

IMPROVING MULTICORE SYSTEM PERFORMANCE THROUGH DATA COMPRESSION

OZCAN OZTURK AND MAHMUT KANDEMIR

19.1 INTRODUCTION

As applications become more and more complex, it is becoming extremely important to have sufficient compute power on the chip. Multicore and manycore systems have been introduced to address this problem. While multicore system performance and power consumption are greatly affected by application data access characteristics, the compiler optimizations can make a significant difference. Considering that cost of off-chip memory accesses is continuously rising in terms of CPU cycles, it is critical to cut down the number of off-chip memory accesses.

Accessing off-chip memory presents at least three major problems in a multicore architecture. First, off-chip memory latencies are continuously increasing due to increases in processor clock frequencies. Consequently, large performance penalties are paid even if a small fraction of memory references go off chip. Second, the bandwidth between the multicore processor and the off-chip memory may not be sufficient to handle simultaneous off-chip access requests coming from multiple processors.

Programming Multicore and Many-core Computing Systems,
First Edition. Edited by Sabri Pllana and Fatos Xhafa.

Third, frequent off-chip memory accesses can increase overall power consumption dramatically. Note that power consumption is a critical issue for both embedded systems and large-scale high-performance server platforms.

In order to alleviate these problems, in this chapter we propose an on-chip memory management scheme based on *data compression* [5]. Our proposal compresses data in memory to (i) reduce access latencies since the compressed data blocks can be accessed faster than the uncompressed blocks; (ii) reduce off-chip bandwidth requirements since compression can allow on-chip memory to hold more data, cutting the number of off-chip accesses; and (iii) increase the effective on-chip storage capacity. A critical issue in this context however is to schedule compressions and decompressions intelligently so that they do not conflict with ongoing application execution. In particular, one needs to decide which processors should participate in the compression (and decompression) activity at any given point during the course of execution. While it is conceivable that all processors can participate in both application execution and compression/decompression activity, this may not necessarily be the best option. This is because in many cases some processors are idle (and therefore cannot take part in application execution anyway) and can be utilized entirely for compression/decompression and related tasks, thereby allowing other processors to focus solely on application execution. Therefore, an execution scheme that carefully *divides* the available computing resources between application execution and online compression/decompression can be very useful in practice.

One might envision two different strategies for such a division: *static* and *dynamic*. In the static scheme, the processors are divided into two groups (those performing compression/decompression and those executing the application), and this grouping is maintained throughout the execution of the application (i.e. it is fixed). In the dynamic scheme, the execution starts with some grouping, but this grouping changes during the course of execution, that is, it adapts itself to the dynamic requirements of the application being executed. This is achieved by keeping track of the wrongly done compressions at runtime and adjusting the number of processors allocated for compression/decompression accordingly. Our main goal in this chapter is to explore these two processor space partitioning strategies, identify their pros and cons and draw conclusions.

We used a set of five array-based benchmark codes to evaluate these two processor partitioning strategies and made extensive experiments with a diverse set of hardware and software parameters. Our experimental results indicate that the most important problem with the static scheme is one of determining the ideal number of processors that need to be allocated for compression/decompression. Our results also show that the dynamic scheme successfully modulates the number of processors used for compression/decompression according to the dynamic behavior of the application, and this in turn improves overall performance significantly.

The rest of this chapter is structured as follows: Section 19.2 gives the details of our approach. Section 19.3 presents the results obtained from our experimental analysis. Section 19.4 gives the related work and Section 19.5 describes the future work. Section 19.6 concludes the chapter with a summary of our major observations.

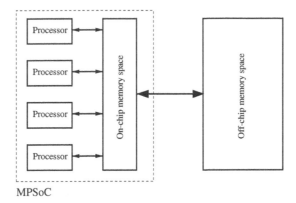

Figure 19.1 The multicore architecture considered in this chapter and the off-chip memory space.

19.2   OUR APPROACH

19.2.1   Architecture and Code Parallelization

The multicore architecture we consider in this chapter is a shared multiprocessor-based system, where a certain number of processors (typically, of the order of 4–32) share the same memory address space. In particular, we assume that there exists an on-chip (software-managed [4, 10, 12, 19]) memory space shared by all processors. We keep the subsequent discussion simple by using a shared bus as the interconnect (though one could use more sophisticated interconnects as well). The processors also share a large off-chip memory space. It should be noted that there is a trend toward designing domain-specific memory architectures [6, 8, 9, 15, 20]. Such architectures are expected to be very successful in some application domains, where the software can analyze the application code, extract the regularity in data access patterns and optimize the data transfers between on-chip and off-chip memories. Such software-managed memory systems can also be more power efficient than a conventional hardware-managed cache-based memory hierarchy [4, 6]. In this study, we assume that the software is in charge of managing the data transfers between the on-chip memory space and the off-chip memory space, though, as will be discussed later, our approach can also be used with a cache-based system. Figure 19.1 shows an example multicore with four parallel processors along with an off-chip storage. We assume that the CPUs can operate only on the data in the on-chip memory.

We employ a *loop nest-based code parallelization strategy* for executing array-based applications in this multicore architecture. We focus on array-based codes mainly because they appear very frequently in scientific computing domain and embedded image/video processing domain [6]. In this strategy, each loop nest is parallelized for the coarsest grain of parallelism where the computational load processed by the processors between global synchronization points is maximized. We achieve this as follows. First, an optimizing compiler (built on top of the SUIF infrastructure [3]) analyzes the application code and identifies all the data reuses and data dependences. Then, the loops with data dependences and reuses are placed into the inner positions (in the loop nest being optimized). This ensures that the loop nest exhibits a decent data locality and the loops that remain into the outer positions (in the nest) are mostly dependence-free. After this step, for each loop nest, the outermost loop that does not carry any data dependence is parallelized. Since this type of parallelization tends to minimize the frequency of interprocessor synchronization, we believe that it is very suitable for a multicore architecture. We use this parallelization strategy irrespective of the number of processors used for parallel execution and irrespective of the code version used. It should be emphasized, however, that when some of the processors are reserved for compression/decompression, they do not participate in parallel execution of loop nests. While we use this specific loop parallelization strategy in this work, its selection is actually orthogonal to the focus of this work. In other words, our approach can work with different loop parallelization strategies.

19.2.2 Our Objectives

We can itemize the major objectives of our compression/decompression based on the following on-chip memory management scheme:

- We would like to compress as much data as possible. This is because the more data are compressed, the more space we have in the on-chip memory available for new data blocks.

- Whenever we access a data block, we prefer to find it in an uncompressed form. This is because if it is in a compressed form during the access, we need to decompress it (and spend extra execution cycles for that) before the access could take place.

- We do not want the decompressions to come into the critical path of execution. That is, we do not want to employ costly algorithms at runtime to determine which data blocks to compress, or use complex compression/decompression algorithms.

It is to be noted that some of these objectives conflict with each other. For example, if we aggressively compress each data block (as soon as the current access to it terminates), this can lead to a significant increase in the number of cases where we access a data block and find it compressed. Therefore, an acceptable execution model based on data compression and decompression should exploit the trade-offs between these conflicting objectives.

Note that even if we find the data block in the on-chip memory in the compressed form, depending on the processor frequency and the decompression algorithm employed, this option can still be better than not finding it in the on-chip storage at all and bringing it from the off-chip memory. Moreover, our approach tries to take decompressions out of the critical path (by utilizing idle processors) as much as possible, and it thus only compresses the data blocks that will not be needed for some time. Also, the off-chip memory accesses keep getting more and more expensive in terms of processor cycles (as a result of increased clock frequencies) and power consumption. Therefore, one might expect a compression-based multicore memory management scheme to be even more attractive in the future.

19.2.3 Compression/Decompression Policies and Implementation Details

We explore two different strategies, explained below, for dividing the available processors between compression/decompression (and related activities) and application execution.

- *Static Strategy:* In this strategy, a fixed number of processors are allocated for performing compression/decompression activity, and this allocation is not changed during the course of execution. The main advantage of this strategy is that it is easy to implement. Its main drawback is that it does not seem easy to determine the ideal number of processors to be employed for compression and decompression. This is because this number depends on several factors such as the application's data access pattern, the number of total processors in the multicore and the relative costs of compression and decompression and off-chip memory access. In fact, as will be discussed later in detail, our experiments clearly indicate that each application demands a different number of processors (to be allocated for compression/decompression and related activities). Further, it is conceivable that even within an application the ideal number of processors to employ in compression/decompression could vary across the different execution phases.

- *Dynamic Strategy:* The main idea behind this strategy is to eliminate the optimal processor selection problem of the static approach mentioned above. By changing the number of processors allocated for compression and decompression dynamically, this strategy attempts to adapt the multicore resources to the dynamic application behavior. Its main drawback is the additional overhead it entails over the static one. Specifically, in order to decide how to change the number of processors (allocated for compression and decompression) at runtime, we need a metric that allows us to make this decision during execution. In this chapter, we make use of a metric, referred to as the *miscompression rate*, which gives the rate between the number of accesses made to the compressed data and the total number of accesses. We want to reduce the miscompression rate as much as possible since a high miscompression rate means that most of data accesses find the data in the compressed form, and this can degrade overall performance by bringing decompressions into the critical path.

Irrespective of whether we are using the static or dynamic strategy, we need to keep track of the accesses to different data blocks to determine their access patterns so that an effective on-chip memory space management can be developed. In our architecture, this is done by the processors reserved for compression/decompression. More specifically, these processors, in addition to performing compressions and decompressions, keep track of the past access histories for all data blocks, and based on the statistics they collect, they decide when to compress (or decompress) and when not to. To do this effectively, our execution model works on a *data block* granularity. In this context, a data block is a rectilinear portion of an array, and its size is fixed across the different arrays (for ease of implementation). It represents the *unit of transfer* between the off-chip memory and the on-chip memory. Specifically, whenever we access a data item that resides in the off-chip memory, the corresponding data block is brought into the on-chip memory (note that this can take several bus cycles). By keeping the size of the data blocks sufficiently large, we can significantly reduce the amount of bookkeeping information that needs to be maintained. A large data block also reduces the frequency of off-chip memory accesses as long as we have a reasonable level of spatial locality.

In more detail, the processors reserved for compression and decompression maintain reuse information at the data block granularity. For a data block, we define the *interaccess time* as the gap (in terms of intervening block accesses) between two successive accesses to that block. Our approach predicts the next interaccess time to be the same as the previous one, and this allows us to rank the different blocks according to their next (estimated) accesses. Then, using this information, we can decide which blocks to compress, which blocks to leave as they are and which blocks to send to off-chip memory. Note that it is possible to use various decision metrics in implementing a compression/decompression scheme, such as *usage frequency, last usage* or *next usage*. In our implementation, we use *next usage* or *interaccess time* as the main criteria for compressions/decompressions. We have also experimented with other metrics, but *next usage* generates the best results.

Consider Figure 19.2(a) which depicts the different possible cases for a given data block. In this figure, arrows indicate the execution timeline, that is, the time application spends throughout its execution. Each point in this timeline is an execution instance where various actions are being taken. Assuming the starting point of this

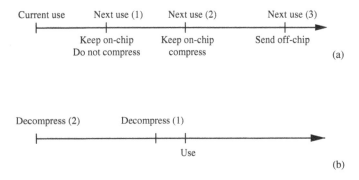

Figure 19.2   (a) Different scenarios for data when its current use is over. (b) Comparison of on-demand decompression and predecompression. Arrows indicate the execution timeline of the program.

arrow is indicating the current use of the block, we estimate its next access. If it is soon enough (relative to other on-chip blocks) – denoted Next use (1) – we keep the block in the on-chip memory as it is (i.e. without any compression). On the other hand, if the next access is not that soon (as in the case marked Next use (2)), we compress it (but still keep it in the on-chip memory). Finally, if the next use of the block is predicted to be really far (see Next use (3) in Fig. 19.2(a)), it is beneficial to send it to the off-chip memory (the block can be compressed before being forwarded to the off-chip memory to reduce transfer time/energy).

Our implementation of this approach is as follows. When the current use of a data block is over, we predict its next use and rank it along with the other on-chip blocks. Then, using two threshold values (Th_1 and Th_2) and taking into account the size (capacity) of the on-chip memory, we decide what to do with the block. More specifically, if the next use of the block is (predicted to be) T_n cycles away, we proceed as follows:

- Keep the block in the on-chip memory uncompressed, if $T_n \leq Th_1$, or else

- Keep the block in the on-chip memory compressed, if $Th_1 < T_n \leq Th_2$, or else

- Send the block to the off-chip memory, if $T_n > Th_2$.

It is to be noted that this strategy clearly tries to keep data with high reuse in on-chip memory as much as possible (even doing so requires compressing the data). As an example, suppose that we have just finished the current access to data block DB_i and the on-chip memory currently holds s data blocks (some of which may be in a compressed form). We first calculate the time for the next use of DB_i (call this value T_n). As explained above, if $T_n \leq Th_1$, we want to keep DB_i in the on-chip memory in an uncompressed form. However, if there is no space for it in the on-chip memory, we select the data block DB_j with the largest next use distance, compress it and forward it to the off-chip memory. We repeat the same procedure if $Th_1 < T_n \leq Th_2$ except that we leave DB_i in the on-chip memory in a compressed form. Finally, $T_n > Th_2$, DB_i is compressed and forwarded to the off-chip memory. This algorithm is executed after completion of processing any data block. Also, a similar activity takes place when we want to bring a new block from the off-chip memory to the on-chip memory or when we create a new data block.

While this approach takes care of the compression part, we also need to decide when to decompress a data block. Basically, there are at least two ways of handling decompressions. First, if a processor needs to access a data block and finds it in the compressed form, the block should be decompressed first before the access can take place. This is termed as *on-demand decompression* in this chapter, and an example is shown in Figure 19.2(b) as Decompress (1). In this case, the data block in question is decompressed just before the access (use) is made. A good memory space management strategy should try to minimize the number of on-demand decompressions since they incur performance penalties (i.e. decompression comes in the critical path). The second strategy is referred to as *predecompression* in this chapter and is based on the idea of decompressing the data block before it is really needed. This is akin to software-based data prefetching [16] employed by some optimizing compilers (where data is brought into cache memory before it is actually needed for computation). In our implementation, predecompression is performed by the processors allocated for compression/decompression since they have the next access information for the data blocks. An example predecompression is marked as Decompress (2) in Figure 19.2(b). We want to maximize the number of predecompressions (for the compressed blocks) so that we can hide as much decompression time as possible. Notice that during predecompression the processors allocated for application execution are not affected; that is, they continue with application execution. Only the processors reserved for compression and decompression participate in the predecompression activity.

The compression/decompression implementation explained above is valid for both the static and the dynamic schemes. However, in the dynamic strategy case, an additional effort is needed for collecting statistics on the rate between the number of on-demand compressions and the total number of data block accesses (as mentioned earlier, this is called the *miscompression rate*). Our current implementation maintains a *global counter* that is updated (within a protected memory region in the on-chip storage) by all the processors reserved for compression/decompression. An important issue that is to be addressed is when do we need to increase/decrease the number of processors allocated for compression/decompression and related activities. For this, we adopt two thresholds Mr_1 and Mr_2. If the current miscompression rate is between Mr_1 and Mr_2, we do not change the existing processor allocation. If it is smaller than Mr_1, we decrease the number of processors allocated for compression/decompression. In contrast, if it is larger than Mr_2, we increase the number of processors allocated for compression/decompression. The rationale for this approach is that if the miscompression rate becomes very high, this means that we are not able to decompress data blocks early enough, so we put more processors for decompression. On the other hand, if the miscompression rate becomes very low, we can reduce the resources that we employ for decompression. *To be fair in our evaluation, all the performance data presented in Section 19.3 include these overheads as well.*

It is important to measure miscompression rate in a low-cost yet accurate manner. One possible implementation is to calculate/check the miscompression rate after every T cycles. Then, the important issue is to select the most appropriate value for T. A small T value may not be able to capture miscompression rate accurately and incurs significant overhead at runtime. In contrast, a large T value does not cause much runtime overhead. However, it may force us to miss some optimization opportunities (by delaying potential useful compressions and/or decompressions). In our experiments, we implemented this approach and also measured the sensitivity of our results to the value of the T parameter. Finally, it should also be mentioned that keeping the access history of the on-chip data blocks requires some extra space. Depending on the value of T, we allocate a certain number of bits per data block and update them each time a data block is accessed. In our implementation, these bits are stored in a certain portion of the on-chip memory, reserved just for this purpose. While this introduces both space and performance overhead, we found that these overheads are not really excessive. In particular, the space overhead was always less than 4%. Also, all the

performance numbers given in the next section include the cycle overheads incurred
for updating these bits.

19.3 EXPERIMENTAL EVALUATION

19.3.1 Setup

We used Simics [18] to simulate an on-chip multiprocessor environment. Simics is
a simulation platform for hardware development and design space exploration. It
supports modifications to the instruction set architecture (ISA), architectural performance models and devices. This allows designers to evaluate evolutionary changes
to existing systems with a standard software workload. We use a variant of the LZO
compression/decompression algorithm [14] to handle compressions and decompressions; the decompression rate of this algorithm is about 20 MB/s. It is to be emphasized that while, in this particular implementation, we chose LZO as our algorithm,
our approach can work with any algorithm. In our approach, LZO is executed by the
processors reserved for compression/decompression. Table 19.1 lists the base simulation parameters used in our experiments. Later in the experiments we change some
of these values to conduct a sensitivity analysis.

  We tested the effectiveness of our approach using five randomly selected
array-based applications from the SpecFP2000 benchmark suite. For each application, we fast-forwarded the first 500 million instructions and simulated the next
250 million instructions. Two important statistics for these applications are given in
Table 19.2. The second column in Table 19.2 (labeled Cycles-1) gives the execution

Table 19.1 The base simulation parameters used in our experiments.

Parameter	Default value
Hardware parameters	
Number of processors	8
Clock frequency	400 MHz
On-chip memory size	128 KB
On-chip memory latency	2 cycles
Off-chip memory size	16 MB
Off-chip memory latency	100 cycles
Software parameters	
Compression/decompression algorithm	LZO
Compression/decompression rate	20 MB/s
Block size	2 KB
Th_1, Th_2	5000, 50 000 cycles
Mr_1, Mr_2	0.2, 0.6
Sampling period (T)	20 000 cycles
Starting $|C|$ value for the dynamic scheme	2

Table 19.2   The benchmark codes used in this study and important statistics. In obtaining these statistics, the reference input sets are used.

Benchmark	Cycles-1	Cycles-2
swim	91,187,018	118,852,504
apsi	96,822,310	127,028,682
fma3d	126,404,189	161,793,882
mgrid	87,091,915	96,611,130
applu	108,839,336	139,955,208

time (in terms of cycles) of the original applications. The values in this column were obtained by using our base configuration (Table 19.1) and using 8 processors to execute each application (without any data compression/decompression). In more details, the results in the second column of this table are obtained using a parallel version of the software-based on-chip memory management scheme proposed in [12]. This scheme is a highly optimized dynamic approach that keeps the most reused data blocks in the on-chip memory as much as possible. In our opinion, it represents the state of the art in software-managed on-chip memory optimization if one does not employ data compression/decompression. The performance (execution cycles) results reported in the next subsection are given as fractions of the values in this second column, that is, they are *normalized* with respect to the second column of Table 19.2. The third column (named Cycles-2), on the other hand, gives the execution cycles for a compression-based strategy where each processor both participates in the application execution and performs on-demand decompression. In addition, when the current use of a data block ends, it is always compressed and kept on-chip. The on-chip memory space is managed in a fashion which is very similar to that of a full-associative cache. When we compare the results in the last two columns of this table, we see that this naive compression-based strategy is not any better than the case where we do not make use of any compression/decompression at all (the second column of the table). That is, in order to take advantage of data compression, one needs to employ smarter strategies. Our approach goes beyond this simplistic compression-based scheme and involves dividing the processor resources between those that do computation and those that perform compression/decompression-related tasks.

19.3.2   Results with the Base Parameters

Figure 19.3(a) shows the behavior (normalized execution cycles) of the static approach with different $|C|$ values ($|C| = n$ means n out of 8 processors are used for compression/decompression). As can be seen from the x-axis of this graph, we changed $|C|$ from 1 to 7. One can observe from this graph that in general the different applications prefer different $|C|$ values for the best performance characteristics. For example, while apsi demands 3 processors dedicated for compression/decompression for the best results, the corresponding number for applu is 1. This is because each

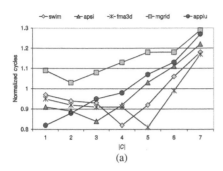 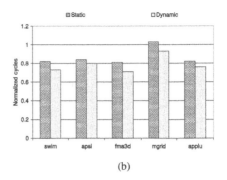

(a) (b)

Figure 19.3 (a) Normalized execution cycles with the static strategy using different $|C|$ values. (b) Comparison of the best static strategy (for each benchmark) and the dynamic strategy.

application has typically a different degree of parallelism in its different execution phases. That is, not all the processors participate in the application execution (e.g. as a result of data dependences or due to load imbalance concerns), and such otherwise idle processors can be employed for compression and decompression. We further observe from this graph that increasing $|C|$ beyond a certain value causes performance deterioration in all applications. This is due to the fact that employing more processors for compression and decompression than necessary prevents the application from exploiting the inherent parallelism in its loop nests, and that in turn hurts the overall performance. In particular, when we allocate 6 processors or more for compression and decompression, the performance of all five applications in our suite becomes worse than the original execution cycles.

The graph in Figure 19.3(b) gives a comparison of the static and dynamic strategies. The first bar for each benchmark in this graph gives the *best* static version, that is, the one that is obtained using the ideal $|C|$ value for that benchmark. The second bar represents the normalized execution cycles for the dynamic scheme. One can see from these results that the dynamic strategy outperforms the static one for all five applications tested, and the average performance improvement (across all benchmarks) is about 13.6% and 21.4% for the static and dynamic strategies, respectively. That is, the dynamic approach brings additional benefits over the static one. To better explain why the dynamic approach generates better results than the static one, we give in Figure 19.4 the execution behavior of the dynamic approach. More specifically, this graph divides the entire execution time of each application into twenty epochs, and, for each epoch, shows the most frequently used $|C|$ value in that epoch. One can clearly see from the trends in this graph that the dynamic approach changes the number of processors dedicated to compression/decompression over the time, and in this way it successfully adapts the available computing resources to the dynamic execution behavior of the application being executed.

Before moving to the sensitivity analysis part where we vary the default values of some of the simulation parameters, let us present how the overheads incurred by our

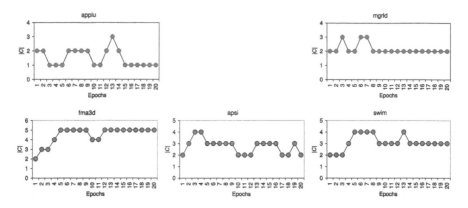

Figure 19.4   Processor usage for the dynamic strategy over the execution period.

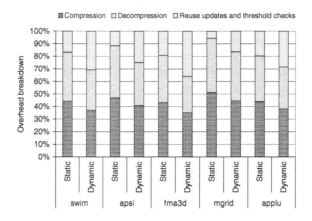

Figure 19.5   Breakdown of overheads into three different components for the static and dynamic schemes.

approach (effects of which are already captured in Figs 19.3(a) and (b)) are decomposed into different components. In the bar chart given in Figure 19.5, we give the individual contributions of three main sources of overheads: compression, decompression and reuse updates, threshold checks and other bookkeeping activities. We see from these results that, in the static approach case, compression and decompression activities dominate the overheads (most of which are actually hidden during parallel execution). In the dynamic approach case, on the other hand, the overheads are more balanced, since the process of determining the $|C|$ value to be used currently incurs additional overheads. Again, as in the static case, an overwhelming percentage of these overheads are hidden during parallel execution.

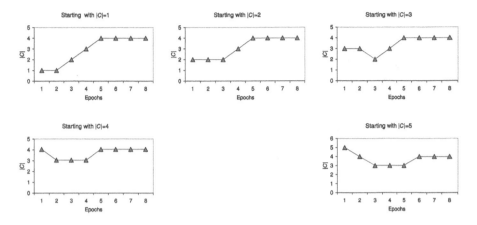

Figure 19.6 Sensitivity of the dynamic strategy to the starting $|C|$ value for the swim benchmark.

19.3.3 Sensitivity Analysis

In this subsection, we change several parameters in our base configuration (Table 19.1) and measure the variations on the behavior of our approach. Recall that our dynamic approach (whose behavior is compared with the static one in Fig. 19.3(b)) starts execution with $|C| = 2$. To check whether any other starting value would make a substantial difference, we give in Figure 19.6 the execution profile of swim for the first eight epochs of its execution. One can observe from this graph that no matter what the starting $|C|$ value is, at most after the fifth epoch all execution profiles converge. In other words, the starting $|C|$ value may not be very important for the success of the dynamic scheme except maybe for applications with very short execution times. Although not presented here, we observed a similar behavior with the remaining applications as well. Consequently, playing with the initial value of $|C|$ generated only 3% variance in execution cycles of the dynamic scheme (we omit the detailed results).

Up to this point in our experimental evaluation we have used the T, Th_1, Th_2, Mr_1 and Mr_2 values given in Table 19.1. In our next set of experiments, we modify the values of these parameters to conduct a sensitivity analysis. In Figure 19.7, we present the sensitivity of the dynamic approach to the threshold values $Th1$ and $Th2$ for two applications: apsi (a) and mgrid (b). We see that the behavior of apsi is more sensitive to $Th2$ than to $Th1$, and in general small $Th2$ values perform better. This is because a large $Th2$ value tends to create more competition for the limited on-chip space (as it delays sending data blocks to the off-chip memory), and this in turn reduces the average time that a data block spends in the on-chip memory. However, a very small $Th2$ value (12,500) leads to lots of data blocks being sent to the off-chip storage prematurely, and this increases the misses in on-chip storage. The other threshold parameter ($Th1$) also exhibits a similar trend; however, the resulting execution cycles do not range over a large spectrum. This is because it mainly influences the decision of compressing (or not

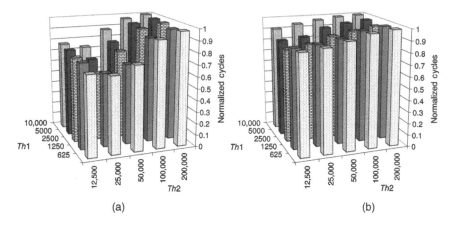

Figure 19.7   Sensitivity of the dynamic strategy to $Th1$, $Th2$ values. (a) apsi. (b) mgrid.

compressing) a data block, and since compression/decompression costs are lower than that of off-chip memory access (Table 19.1), the impact of $Th1$ on the behavior of the dynamic scheme is relatively small. Similar observations can be made with the mgrid benchmark as well. This application, however, benefits from a very low $Th2$ value mainly because of its poor data locality; that is, once a data block has been processed, it does not need to be kept on-chip.

The next parameter we study is the miscompression rate thresholds $Mr1$ and $Mr2$. Figure 19.8 depicts the normalized execution cycles for two of benchmark codes: apsi (a) and mgrid (b). Our main observation from these graphs is that the best $Mr1$, $Mr2$ values are those in the middle of the spectrum experimented. Specifically, as long as the $Mr1$ value used is 0.2 or 0.3 and the $Mr2$ value used is 0.6 or 0.7, we are doing fine, but going outside this range increases the overall execution cycles dramatically.

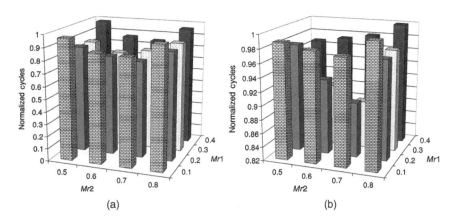

Figure 19.8   Sensitivity of the dynamic strategy to $Mr1$, $Mr2$ values. (a) apsi. (b) mgrid.

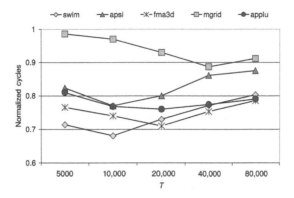

Figure 19.9 Sensitivity of the dynamic strategy to the sampling period (T).

This can be explained as follows. When the difference between $Mr1$ and $Mr2$ is very large, the dynamic scheme becomes very reluctant in changing the value of $|C|$. As a result, we may miss some important optimization opportunities. In comparison, when the difference between $Mr1$ and $Mr2$ is very small, the scheme can make frequent changes to $|C|$ based on (probably) short-term data access behaviors (which may be wrong when considering larger periods). In addition, frequent changes to $|C|$ also require frequent comparisons/checks, which in turn increase the overheads associated with our scheme.

We next study the impact on the effectiveness of the dynamic strategy when the sampling period (T) is modified. The graph in Figure 19.9 indicates that each application prefers a specific sampling period value to generate the best behavior. For example, the best T value for swim is 10,000 cycles, whereas the best value for fma3d is 20,000. We also observe that working with larger or smaller periods (than this optimum one) generates poor results. This is because if the sampling period is very small, we incur a lot of overheads and the decisions we make may be suboptimal (i.e. we may be capturing only the transient patterns and make premature compression and/or decompression decisions). On the other hand, if the sampling period is very large, we can miss opportunities for optimization. While it is also possible to design an adaptive scheme wherein T is modulated dynamically, it is not clear whether the associated overheads would be negligible.

The sensitivity of the dynamic approach to the block size is plotted in Figure 19.10. Recall that block size is the unit of transfer between the on-chip and the off-chip memory, and our default block size was 2 KB. We see from this graph that the average execution cycle improvements with different block sizes range from 18.8% (with 8 KB) to 23.3% (with 1 KB). We also observe that different applications react differently when the block size used is increased. The main reason for this is the intrinsic spatial locality (or block level temporal locality) exhibited by the application. In swim and fma3d, there is a reasonable amount of spatial locality. As a result, these two applications take advantage of the increased block size. In the remaining applications, however, the spatial locality is not as good. This, combined with the fact that

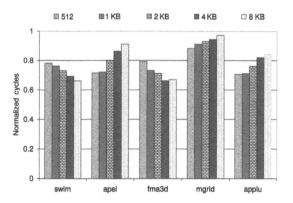

Figure 19.10 Sensitivity of the dynamic strategy to the block size.

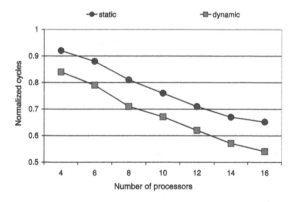

Figure 19.11 Sensitivity of the static and dynamic strategies to the processor counts.

a small block size allows our approach to manage data space in a finer-granular manner, makes a good case for the small block sizes for such applications. Therefore, we witness a reduction in the execution cycles when the data block size is decreased. We next evaluate the impact of the processor count on the behavior of the static and dynamic schemes. Recall that the processor count used so far in our experiments was 8. Figure 19.11 plots the normalized cycles for the best static version and the dynamic version for the benchmark fma3d with different processor counts. An observation that can be made from these results is that the gap between the static and dynamic schemes seems to be widening with increasing number of processors. This is mainly because a larger processor count gives more flexibility to the dynamic approach in allocating resources.

While our focus in this work is on software-managed multicore memories, our approach can work with conventional cache-based memory hierarchies as well. To quantify the impact of our approach under such a cache-based system, we performed

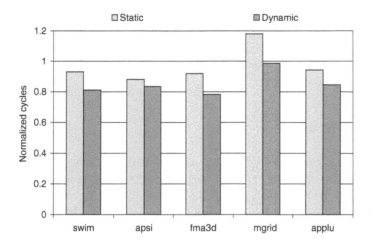

Figure 19.12   Results with a hardware-based cache memory.

a set of experiments by modeling a 16 KB two-way associative L1 cache for each
of the eight processors with a block (line) size of 128 bytes. The results shown in
Figure 19.12 indicate that our approach is successful with conventional cache memories as well. The base scheme used (against which the static and dynamic schemes
are compared in Fig. 19.12) in these experiments is from [11]. The reason that the
savings are not as large as in the software-managed memory case is twofold: First, the
unit of transfer between off-chip and on-chip is smaller with the cache-based system
(as it is controlled by the hardware). Second, it is more difficult with the cache-based
system to catch the stable values for the threshold parameters ($Th1$, $Th2$, $Mr1$ and
$Mr2$). However, we still observe average 3.1% and 14.8% reductions in execution
cycles due to the static and dynamic schemes, respectively.

19.4   RELATED WORK

Data compression has been investigated as a viable solution in the context of
scratchpad memories (SPMs) as well. For example, Ozturk et al. [17] propose a
compression-based SPM management. Abali et al. [1] investigate the performance
impact of hardware compression. Compression algorithms suitable for use in the
context of a compressed cache are presented in [2]. Zhang and Gupta [22] propose
compiler-based strategies for reducing leakage energy consumption in instruction
and data caches through data compression. Lee et al. [13] use compression in an
effort to explore the potential for on-chip cache compression to reduce cache miss
rates and miss penalties. Apart from memory subsystems, data compression has also
been used to reduce the communication volume. For example, data compression is
proposed as a means of reducing communication latency and energy consumption
in sensor networks [7]. Xu et al. [21] present energy savings on a handheld device

through data compression. Our work is different from these prior efforts as we give the task of management of the compressed data blocks to the compiler. In deciding the data blocks to compress and decompress, our compiler approach exploits the data reuse information extracted from the array accesses in the application source code.

19.5   FUTURE WORK

As has been indicated, there are many parameters that influence the performance of the memory system. In our current implementation, we explore different dimensions and different parameters manually. As the next step, we would like to extend our current approach in order to automatically find the most beneficial parameters. Toward this end, we are currently building an optimization framework to handle these parameters in the most effective way.

19.6   CONCLUDING REMARKS

The next-generation parallel architectures are expected to accommodate multiple processors on the same chip. While this makes interprocessor communication less costly (as compared to traditional parallel machines), it also makes it even more critical to cut down the number of off-chip memory accesses. Frequent off-chip accesses do not only increase execution cycles but also increase overall power consumption, which is a critical issue in both high-end parallel servers and embedded systems. One way of attacking this off-chip memory problem in a multicore architecture is to compress data blocks when they are not predicted to be reused soon. Based on this idea, in this chapter, we explored two different approaches: static and dynamic. Our experimental results indicate that the most important problem with static strategies is one of determining the ideal number of processors that need to be allocated for compression/decompression. Our results also demonstrate that the dynamic strategy successfully modulates the number of processors used for compression/decompression according to the needs of the application, and this in turn improves overall performance. Finally, the experiments with different values of our simulation parameters show that the proposed approach gives consistent results across a wide design space.

REFERENCES

1. B. Abali, M. Banikazemi, X. Shen, H. Franke, D. E. Poff, and T. B. Smith. Hardware compressed main memory: operating system support and performance evaluation. *IEEE Transactions on Computers*, 50(11):1219–1233, 2001.

2. E. Ahn, S.-M. Yoo, and S.-M. S. Kang. Effective algorithms for cache-level compression. In *Proceedings of the 11th Great Lakes symposium on VLSI*, pages 89–92, 2001.

3. S. P. Amarasinghe, J. M. Anderson, M. S. Lam, and C. W. Tseng. The SUIF Compiler for Scalable Parallel Machines. In *Proc. the Seventh SIAM Conference on Parallel Processing for Scientific Computing*, February, 1995.

4. L. Benini, A. Macii, E. Macii, and M. Poncino. Increasing energy efficiency of embedded systems by application-specific memory hierarchy generation. *IEEE Design & Test of Computers*, 17(2): 74–85, April–June, 2000.

5. L. Benini, D. Bruni, A. Macii, and E. Macii. Hardware-assisted data compression for energy minimization in systems with embedded processors. In *Proceedings of the DATE'02*, Paris, France, March 2002.

6. F. Catthoor, S. Wuytack, E. D. Greef, F. Balasa, L. Nachtergaele, and A. Vandecappelle. *Custom Memory Management Methodology – Exploration of Memory Organization for Embedded Multimedia System Design*. Kluwer Academic Publishers, June 1998.

7. M. Chen and M. L. Fowler. The importance of data compression for energy efficiency in sensor networks. In *2003 Conference on Information Sciences and Systems*, 2003.

8. CPU12 Reference Manual. Motorola Corporation, 2000. http://motorola.com/brdata/PDFDB/MICROCONTROLLERS/16_BIT/68HC12_FAMILY/REF_MAT/CPU12RM.pdf.

9. P. Faraboschi, G. Brown, and J. Fischer. Lx: A technology platform for customizable VLIW embedded processing. In *Proceedings of the International Symposium on Computer Architecture*, pages 203–213, 2000.

10. M. Kandemir and A. Choudhary. Compiler-directed scratch pad memory hierarchy design and management. In *Proceedings of the 39th Design Automation Conference*, June 2002.

11. M. Kandemir, A. Choudhary, J. Ramanujam, and P. Banerjee. Improving locality using loop and data transformations in an integrated framework. In *Proceedings of the International Symposium on Microarchitecture*, Dallas, TX, December 1998.

12. M. Kandemir, J. Ramanujam, M. Irwin, N. Vijaykrishnan, I. Kadayif, and A. Parikh. Dynamic management of scratch-pad memory space. In *Proceedings of the 38th Design Automation Conference*, Las Vegas, NV, June 2001.

13. J. S. Lee, W. K. Hong, and S. D. Kim. Design and evaluation of a selective compressed memory system. In *ICCD '99: Proceedings of the 1999 IEEE International Conference on Computer Design*, page 184, 1999.

14. LZO. http://www.oberhumer.com/opensource/lzo/.

15. M-CORE – MMC2001 Reference Manual. Motorola Corporation, 1998. http://www.motorola.com/SPS/MCORE/info_documentation.htm.

16. T. C. Mowry, M. S. Lam, and A. Gupta. Design and evaluation of a compiler algorithm for prefetching. In *Proceedings of the 5th International Conference on Architectural Support for Programming Languages and Operating Systems*, October 1992.

17. O. Ozturk, M. Kandemir, I. Demirkiran, G. Chen, and M. J. Irwin. Data compression for improving spm behavior. In *DAC '04: Proceedings of the 41st annual conference on Design automation*, pages 401–406, 2004.

18. Simics. http://www.simics.com/.

19. S. Steinke et al. Assigning program and data objects to scratch-pad for energy reduction. In *Proceedings of the DATE'02*, Paris, France, 2002.

20. TMS370Cx7x 8-bit Microcontroller. Texas Instruments, Revised February 1997. http://www-s.ti.com/sc/psheets/spns034c/spns034c.pdf.

21. R. Xu, Z. Li, C. Wang, and P. Ni. Impact of data compression on energy consumption of wireless-networked handheld devices. In *ICDCS '03: Proceedings of the 23rd International Conference on Distributed Computing Systems*, page 302, 2003.

22. Y. Zhang and R. Gupta. Enabling partial cache line prefetching through data compression. In *32nd International Conference on Parallel Processing (ICPP 2003)*, pages 277–285, 2003.

PART V

SCHEDULING AND MANAGEMENT

CHAPTER 20

PROGRAMMING AND MANAGING RESOURCES ON ACCELERATOR-ENABLED CLUSTERS

M. MUSTAFA RAFIQUE, ALI R. BUTT AND DIMITRIOS S. NIKOLOPOULOS

20.1 INTRODUCTION

Computational accelerators are positive catalysts for high-end computing systems. Heterogeneous parallel architectures that integrate general-purpose processors with computational accelerators are rapidly being established on emerging systems as the *sine qua non* for high performance, energy efficiency and reliability. Acceleration through heterogeneity has been realized in several asymmetric multicore processors, where a fixed transistor budget is distributed between many simple, specialized tightly coupled cores and few complex, general-purpose cores. The specialized cores provide custom features that enable acceleration of computational kernels operating on vector data. These cores are controlled by the relatively few general-purpose cores, which run system services and manage off-chip communication. In addition to heterogeneous processors, it is now common for processor vendors to deliver teraflop-capable, single-chip multiprocessors by integrating many simple cores with single-instruction multiple data (SIMD) or single-instruction multiple threads

Programming Multicore and Many-core Computing Systems,
First Edition. Edited by Sabri Pllana and Fatos Xhafa.
© 2017 John Wiley & Sons, Inc. Published 2017 by John Wiley & Sons, Inc.

(SIMT) datapaths. Cell [12], NVIDIA GPUs [30], Larrabee [38] and the Single-chip Cloud Computer [21] are representatives of this class of processors, both homogeneous and heterogeneous, with significant market interest and demonstrated potential [2, 6, 20, 22, 23, 33, 40]. Teraflop-capable processors accelerate computation by design, while staying within a reasonable power and cost budget. Therefore, they are considered as one of the most promising computational workhorses [5, 7, 9, 10, 13, 14, 17, 19, 26, 34] for high-performance computing (HPC).

Large-scale data centers typically employ commodity off-the-shelf components to yield a cost-efficient setup. While commodity hardware has been common place in HPC setups for almost two decades, large-scale data centers of commercial interest, for example, Google [8], Amazon's EC2 [1], etc., follow the same approach to building efficient systems at scale to meet their HPC and data processing needs. The commoditization of many-core computational accelerators renders these computational engines prime candidates for deployment in large-scale systems. Furthermore, the vector processing capabilities of accelerators makes them natural candidates for massive data processing. Although these indicators are promising, designing and programming large-scale parallel systems with heterogeneous components is an open challenge. Hiding architectural asymmetry and system scale from parallel programming models is desirable for parallel programming models [4]; however it is challenging to implement on heterogeneous systems, where exploiting the custom features and computational density of accelerators is a first-order consideration. At the same time, provisioning general-purpose resources and custom accelerators to achieve a balanced system is a nontrivial exercise.

20.1.1   Types of Accelerator-Based Systems

The asymmetry of resources on accelerator-enabled clusters introduces imbalances in resource management and provisioning. Addressing those imbalances, while hiding the associated complexity from users, is key to achieving high performance and high productivity. Although designing for all possible resource configurations and types of accelerators is very complicated, we can identify four representative design patterns for realizing asymmetric accelerator-based clusters. We characterize these patterns based on the general-purpose computing and system management capabilities of the accelerators. More specifically, we consider the following classes of accelerators:

20.1.1.1   Self-Managed Well-Provisioned Accelerators   These accelerators, shown in Figure 20.1(a), have high compute density, along with on-chip capabilities to efficiently run control code and self-manage I/O and communication. For example, an accelerator coupled with several general-purpose processor cores on the same chip falls into this category. The on-chip computational power of the general-purpose cores and the amount of memory attached to the accelerators are assumed to be sufficient for self-management, in the sense that the control code running for scheduling tasks and performing communication on the general-purpose

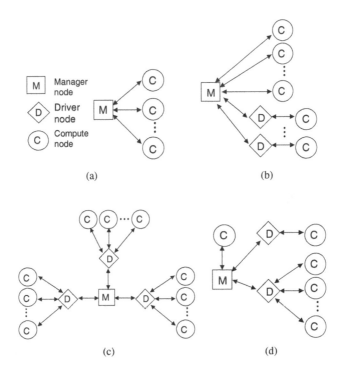

Figure 20.1 Resource configurations for enabling asymmetric clusters. (a) *Conf I:* Self-managed well-provisioned accelerators (b) *Conf II:* Resource-constrained well-provisioned accelerators (c) *Conf III:* Resource-constrained shared-driver accelerators (d) *Conf IV:* Mixed accelerators.

cores does not become the major performance bottleneck. Asymmetric multicores, such as IBM Cell [12] processors, fall under this category.

20.1.1.2 *Resource-Constrained Well-Provisioned Accelerators* These accelerators, shown in Figure 20.1(b), have high compute density but insufficient on-chip general-purpose computing capability for running control code and/or insufficient onboard memory for self-managing I/O and communication. I/O and communication are managed by an external dedicated node with general-purpose cores, which acts as a *driver* for the accelerators. Programmable FPGAs or GPGPUs, such as CUDA-enabled NVIDIA and OpenCL™ -enabled AMD/ATI GPUs, fall under this category. A conventional host processor is required in these settings to run the operating system and provide general-purpose I/O and communication capabilities to the accelerators, which communicate with the host over the I/O bus.

20.1.1.3 *Resource-Constrained Shared-Driver Accelerators* These accelerators, shown in Figure 20.1(c), are similar to the previous case; however drivers are shared among several accelerators to yield a potentially more cost-efficient design. Advanced multichip programmable GPUs, such as NVIDIA® GeForce® GTX 295 [32], or installations with multiple programmable accelerators

or FPGAs on a single driver node fall under this category. Note that the driver for these accelerators can itself support heterogeneous accelerators within a single compute node.[1] This driver organization in effect creates an additional level of asymmetry in the system.

20.1.1.4 Mixed-Mode Accelerators These accelerators, shown in Figure 20.1(d), use a mix of well-provisioned and shared-driver accelerators. A large-scale cluster using variety of accelerators, such as IBM Cell, GPUs and FPGAs, in the same setting falls under this category.

20.1.2 Challenges in Using Accelerators on Clusters

While the potential of many-core accelerators to catalyze HPC systems and data centers is clear, attempting to integrate accelerators seamlessly in large-scale computing installations raises challenges, with respect to resource management and programmability. There is an inherent imbalance between general-purpose cores and accelerators in asymmetric settings. The trend toward integrating relatively simple cores with extremely efficient vector units leads to designs that are inherently compute efficient but control inefficient. General-purpose cores are efficient in executing control-intensive code; therefore they tend to be employed primarily as controllers of parallel execution and communication with accelerators. Accelerators on the other hand are efficient in executing data-parallel computational tasks. To address this problem, large-scale system installations use ad hoc approaches to pair accelerators with more control-efficient processors, such as $\times 86$ multicore CPUs [7], whereas processor architecture moves in the direction of integrating control-efficient and compute-efficient cores on the same chip [38].

Similarly to approaches for resource provisioning, current approaches for programming accelerator-based clusters are either ad hoc or specific to an installation [1, 7], thus posing several challenges when applying to general setups. Further challenges arise because of heterogeneity, which manifest both in the programming model and in resource management. Implementing an accessible programming model on systems with many cores, many processors, multiple instruction set architectures (ISAs), and multiple compilation targets requires drastic modifications of the entire software stack. Suitable programming models that adapt to the varying capabilities of the accelerator-type components have not been developed yet. This deficit forces application writers who want to use accelerators on clusters to micromanage resources. Managing heterogeneous resources and matchmaking computations with resource characteristics is a long-standing problem. Using architecture-specific solutions is highly undesirable, as it compromises productivity, portability and sustainability of the involved systems and applications. The effects of alternative workload distributions between general-purpose processors and accelerators are also not well understood. Accelerators also typically have limited capabilities for managing external system resources, such as communication and I/O devices, thus requiring support from

---

[1] In this chapter we refer to 'accelerator-based compute node' as 'compute node'.

general-purpose processors and special consideration while designing the resource management software. To ensure overall high efficiency, resource management on accelerator-based systems needs to orchestrate carefully data transfers and work distribution between heterogeneous components.

20.2 PROGRAMMING ACCELERATORS ON LARGE-SCALE CLUSTERS

Accelerators provide much higher performance to cost ratio compared with conventional processors. Thus, a properly designed accelerator-based cluster has the potential to provide high performance at a fraction of the cost and operating budget of a traditional symmetric cluster. Unfortunately, accelerators also pose challenges to programming and resource management. Programming accelerators requires working with multiple ISAs and multiple compilation targets. Mapping a high-level parallel programming model to accelerators while hiding the details of accelerator hardware is extremely challenging and even undesirable if raising the level of abstraction comes at a performance cost. To further investigate this problem, we study the implementation of MapReduce, a high-level parallel programming model for large-scale data processing, on asymmetric accelerator-based clusters.

MapReduce is a widely used programming model for large-scale data processing on parallel architectures [15, 16, 18, 36]. A MapReduce application processes data with two simple data-parallel primitives: a *map* primitive that maps an input of (key, value) pairs to an output of intermediate (key, value) pairs- and a *reduce* primitive- that merges the values associated with each key. The runtime system partitions the output of the map stage between nodes and sorts the input to each node before applying the reduction. This programming model borrows from functional languages to provide a very high level of abstraction and hide most of the complexities of parallel programming, such as partitioning, mapping, load balancing and tolerating faults.

MapReduce is ideal for massive data searching and processing operations. It has shown excellent I/O characteristics on traditional clusters and has been successfully applied in large-scale data search by Google [16]. Current trends show that the model is considered a high-productivity alternative to traditional parallel programming models for a variety of applications, ranging from enterprise computing [1, 3] to petascale scientific computing [15, 35, 36]. Several research activities have engaged in porting MapReduce to multicore architectures [15, 18, 36], whereas recently, MapReduce has been chosen as a programming front end for Intel's Pangea architecture and Exoskeleton software environment [25, 40]. Pangea is an asymmetric multicore processor integrating Intel® Core™ Duo cores with graphic accelerators.

MapReduce typically assumes homogeneous components where any work item of map and reduce tasks can be scheduled to any of the available components. While this approach is friendly to the programmer, it adds complexity to the runtime system, if the latter is to manage heterogeneous resources with markedly variable efficiency in executing control-intensive and compute-intensive code. Recent implementations of

MapReduce do consider and address the issue of heterogeneity [1, 41]; however, they consider heterogeneity as an aftereffect of variation in external workload and not as an inherent hardware property. Inherent architecture heterogeneity remains a problem when the cluster components include specialized accelerators, as the mapping function needs to be extended to factor in differences in the individual component capabilities and limitations. Another complication arises because of the assumption that data is distributed between processors before a MapReduce computation begins execution [3]. Given limited I/O capabilities of accelerators, this assumption may not hold, thus posing the challenge of providing components with the necessary data in a distributed setting. On distributed systems with accelerators, accelerators use private address spaces that need to be managed explicitly by the runtime system. These private spaces create effectively an additional data distribution and caching layer – due to their typically limited size – which is invisible to programmers but needs to be implemented with the utmost efficiency by the runtime system.

20.3 MAPREDUCE FOR HETEROGENEOUS CLUSTERS

We introduce enhancements in three aspects of the MapReduce programming model and the associated runtime support [16]: (i) We exploit accelerators with techniques that improve data locality and achieve overlapping of MapReduce execution stages. (ii) We introduce runtime support for exploiting multiple accelerator architectures (Cell and GPUs) in the same cluster setup and adapting workload task execution to different accelerator architectures at runtime. (iii) We introduce workload-aware execution capabilities for virtualized application execution setups. The latter extension is important in data centers and clouds comprising heterogeneous computational resources, where effective and transparent allocation of resources to tasks is essential.

We arrange our resources as shown in Figure 20.2. A general-purpose well-provisioned multicore server acts as a dedicated front-end *manager* for the cluster. The server manages a number of back-end accelerator-based nodes and is responsible for scheduling jobs, distributing data, allocating work between compute nodes and providing other support services at the front end of the cluster. The brunt of processing load is carried by the Cell-based and GPU-based accelerator nodes. The manager divides the MapReduce tasks (map, reduce, sort, etc.) in small workloads and assigns these workloads to the attached accelerator-based nodes. Irrespective of the type of back-end nodes, the manager transparently distributes and schedules the workload to them. If the back end is a self-managed accelerator, its general-purpose core uses MapReduce to map the assigned workload to the accelerators. In contrast, if the back end is driver based, the driver components further distribute the assigned workload to the attached accelerator node(s). Note that the manager differs from a driver. Drivers execute control tasks for communication and I/O on behalf of accelerators, whereas the manager controls work and data distribution for the entire cluster. This model can be thought of as a hierarchical MapReduce: each level maps

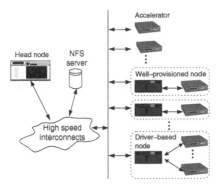

Figure 20.2   High-level overview of an accelerator-based asymmetric-distributed system.

the workload to the next level of nodes, until it reaches the compute node where the generic on-chip core maps the workload to the accelerators.

20.3.1   Extending the MapReduce Model for Heterogeneous Resources

In a typical MapReduce setting, Map and Reduce tasks are scheduled separately on potentially distinct sets of cluster nodes. In our enhanced MapReduce runtime, a data segment is assigned to a compute node, and the entire sequence of MapReduce operations on the data segment is executed on the same assigned compute node. This does not require classifying cluster resources as *mappers* or *reducers*; the data segment stays on the assigned node, and both operations (map and reduce) are performed on the data segment on the same node, thus improving data locality. One of the disadvantages of having separate mappers and reducers is that the reducers cannot start the reduce process before the completion of all mappers. In our MapReduce runtime, the manager does not wait for all nodes to complete their processing before a global merge operation is executed. Instead, the manager starts to merge the results as soon as results are received from more than one compute nodes.

Our framework uses a transparently optimized accelerator-specific binary for each type of accelerator. The runtime system hides the asymmetry between available resources. Nevertheless, a given application component will exhibit variation in performance on the different combinations of processor types, memory systems and node interconnects available on the cluster. To improve resource utilization and matchmaking between MapReduce components and available hardware resources, the runtime system monitors the execution time of tasks on hardware components and uses this information to adapt the scheduling of tasks to components so that each task ends up executing on the resource that is best suited for it. The application programmer may also guide the runtime by providing an *affinity* metric that indicates the best resource for a given task, for example, a high affinity value for a GPU implies that an application component would perform best on a GPU, whereas an affinity of zero implies that the application should preferably execute on other types of processors. The runtime system takes these values into consideration when making its scheduling decisions.

20.3.2 Execution Model for Asymmetric MapReduce

Once an application begins execution, the associated manager and accelerator software is started on the respective components, and the manager initiates MapReduce tasks on the available accelerator nodes. Once assigned, the tasks self-schedule their work by reading data from the distributed file system, processing it and returning the results back to the manager in a continuous loop. Once the manager receives the results, it merges them to produce the final result set for the application. After a particular MapReduce task has been completed by a self-managed node, the manager assigns another task to that node. This process continues until the entire input data has been processed by the accelerators. The manager handles the driver nodes similarly.

For driver-based resources, each driver loads a portion of input data into its memory, to ensure that sufficient data is readily available for the accelerator nodes. The driver then initiates the required MapReduce tasks on the accelerator nodes and sends the necessary data to the corresponding resource-constrained accelerators. When all the in-memory loaded data has been processed by the accelerators, the driver loads another portion of the input data into memory, and the whole process continues until the entire MapReduce task assigned to the particular driver has been completed by the attached resource-constrained accelerators. The driver also merges the result data produced by the accelerators, and the merged result sets are sent back to the manager.

20.3.3 Using Asymmetric MapReduce

Our framework leverages accelerator-specific tools to generate binaries that our runtime orchestrates. To facilitate automatic generation of such binaries, we develop an extended programming model based on MapReduce. From an application programmer's point of view, irrespective of the resource configuration employed, MapReduce is used on asymmetric resources as follows. The application is divided into three parts: (i) The code to initialize the runtime environment. This code runs outside of the MapReduce data processing stages and includes initialization, data distribution and finalization. This part is unique to our design and does not have a corresponding operation in prior MapReduce implementations. (ii) The code that runs on the accelerator cores and does the actual data processing for the application. This is similar to a standard MapReduce application setup running on a small portion of the input data that has been assigned to the compute node. This code includes a map phase to distribute the workload between the accelerator cores and a reduce phase to merge the data produced from accelerators. (iii) The code that runs on the manager to merge partial results from each compute node into a complete result. This code is invoked every time a result is received from a compute node and executes a global merge phase that is functionally identical to the reduce phase on each compute node.

All map, reduce and merge functions are application specific and should be provided by the programmer using the APIs exposed by our framework. Our framework requires that these operations are specified for all the accelerator types used in a particular setting, so that any given task can be executed on any available accelerator. Once identified, the binaries for the aforementioned components are generated for all the available targets (different accelerators and conventional multicore processors) in the system. The availability of these binaries enables our system to transparently schedule tasks at any time, on any type of accelerator, and hide heterogeneity and asymmetry. Furthermore, it frees the programmer from system-level details such as managing the memory subsystems of accelerators, orchestrating data transfers between the manager and the compute nodes and implementing optimized communication mechanisms between cluster nodes. Therefore, the programmer focuses exclusively on the application-specific part of code.

20.4   RESOURCE CONFIGURATION

20.4.1   Alternate Resource Configurations for Asymmetric Clusters

We consider four resource configurations for the target asymmetric clusters as shown in Figure 20.1. The configurations are driven by the type of the back-end components used as well as by economical constraints and performance goals. In all cases, the manager and all back-end nodes are connected via a high-speed commodity network, for example, Gigabit Ethernet. Application data is hosted on a distributed file system (NFS [37] in our implementation).

The first configuration (Fig. 20.1(a)) we consider is that of self-managed well-provisioned accelerators (*Conf I*), connected directly to the manager. A blade with Cell processors [28] including multigigabyte DRAM and high-speed network connectivity would fall into this category. Small-scale academic settings may also adopt such a configuration, using, for example, Cell-based Sony PlayStation® 3 (PS3™) nodes and scaling down the workload per PS3 so as to not exceed the limited DRAM capacity and not stress the limited general-purpose processing capabilities of the PS3. The compute nodes execute directly all MapReduce tasks, and the manager merges partial results from the computes nodes.

The next configuration (Fig. 20.1(b)) uses resource-constrained well-provisioned accelerators (*Conf II*). Each driver provides large memory space and communication and I/O capabilities to an individual resource-constrained accelerator, for example, a PS3. The manager distributes input data to the driver nodes in large chunks. The driver nodes proceed by streaming these chunks to the attached accelerators. Accelerators execute the MapReduce tasks; however, partial results produced by accelerators are merged at the corresponding driver nodes, and the manager executes the global merge operation on the results received from the driver nodes.

A single driver per resource-constrained accelerator is not always justifiable as one accelerator may not be able to fully utilize the driver's resources. In contrast, a single manager may not be sufficient to match the data demands of many accelerators simultaneously. We address this by using a hierarchical setup (*Conf III*) so that each driver node manages multiple accelerator nodes (Fig. 20.1(c)).

Finally, an asymmetric system may employ a mix of the aforementioned configurations based on particular requirements. We capture this mix in our last configuration (*Conf IV*) (Fig. 20.1(d)). In this case, the manager is agnostic of the class of the attached compute nodes and simply divides the input workload between available compute nodes. The execution of MapReduce tasks and merging of partial results are managed automatically at each component, while the final result is produced by the manager, which performs the global merge of the results received from the attached drivers.

20.4.2   Asymmetric Component Operations/Responsibilities

Traditional MapReduce designs do not consider individual component capabilities since they assume homogeneous components as compute nodes. An efficient design, however, has to factor in the capabilities of back-end resources when allocating tasks. For self-managed resources or drivers in other configurations, this task is straightforward. The manager divides the input data and hands it over to the nodes being directly managed. The actual assignment is done by either copying the data to the nodes' local storage or providing them with pointers to the files on the distributed file system. This approach is easy to implement and lightweight for the manager, as the manager does not need to micromanage data allocation to accelerators.

However, data handover cannot be used for resource-constrained nodes due to potential limitations such as inability to directly retrieve the data, bottlenecks on the central file system or lack of sufficient storage and memory for holding local copies. An alternative, which we adopt, is to divide the input data into chunks, with sizes based on the capabilities of compute nodes. Our runtime environment controls the size of these chunks so that each chunk can be efficiently processed at the compute nodes without overwhelming their resources, for example, without memory thrashing. Instead of a single division of data, the runtime environment streams chunks (work units) to the compute nodes until all data has been processed. The concern is that such an approach improves performance on the compute nodes at the cost of increasing the load of the manager. The runtime environment balances the load between the manager and the compute nodes, by controlling the resources dedicated to processing communication with each compute node on the manager and continuously adapting the chunk size on the compute nodes.

In addition to addressing I/O diversity, the manager faces different memory and computation pressures depending on the type of back-end resources. For self-managed nodes, the manager is also responsible for merging the results repeatedly for the entire input data. This process can be resource consuming. By contrast, for well-provisioned resources, the resource or driver does most of the merging for the accelerators, and the manager simply has to perform a global merge. These factors have to be considered when designing asymmetric clusters, taking also into account workload-specific characteristics.

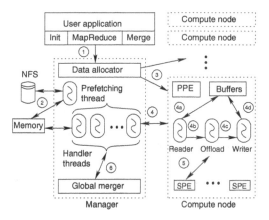

Figure 20.3 Interactions between manager and compute node components.

20.4.2.1 *Manager Operation*

The manager is responsible for job queuing, scheduling, data hosting and managing compute nodes. We assume that well-established standard techniques can be used for such manager tasks and focus on the compute node management role. Once an application begins execution (Step 1 in Fig. 20.3), the manager loads a portion of the associated input data from the file system (NFS in our implementation) into its memory (Step 2). This ensures that sufficient data is readily available for compute nodes and avoids any I/O bottleneck that can hinder performance. For well-provisioned compute nodes with drivers, this step is replaced by direct prefetching on the drivers.

Next, client tasks are started on the available compute nodes (Step 3). These tasks self-schedule their work by requesting input data from the manager, processing it and returning the results back to the manager in a continuous loop (Step 4). For well-provisioned nodes, the result data is directly written to the file system, and the manager is informed of task completion. Once the manager receives the results, it merges them (Step 6) to produce the final result set for the application. When all the in-memory loaded data has been processed by the clients, the manager loads another portion of the input data into memory (Step 2), and the whole process continues until the entire input has been consumed. This model is similar to using a large number of small map operations in standard MapReduce.

The design described so far may suffer from two potential I/O bottlenecks: the manager may stall while reading data from the distributed file system (NFS in our case), or the compute nodes may stall while data is being transferred to them either from the manager or from the file system. At both levels, we employ double buffering to avoid delays. At the manager, an asynchronous prefetch thread is used to preload data from the disk into a buffer, while the data in an already-loaded buffer is being processed, and the previously computed buffer is written back. Similarly, the driver, if used, and the compute nodes use double buffering to overlap data transfer with computation.

20.4.2.2 *Compute Node Operation* Application tasks are invoked on the compute nodes (Step 3) and begin to execute the request, process and reply (Steps 4a–4d) loop as stated earlier. We refer to the amount of application data processed in a single iteration on a compute node as a *work unit*. With the exception of an application-specific *Offload function*[2] that performs computation on the incoming data, the framework on the compute nodes provides all other necessary functions, including communication with the manager and preparation of data buffers for input and output. Each compute node has three threads that operate on multiple buffers for working on and transferring data to/from the manager. One thread is responsible for requesting and receiving new data to work on from the manager (Step 4a). The data is placed in a receiving buffer. When the thread has received the data, it hands off the receiving buffer to an offload thread (Step 4b) and then requests more data until all free receiving buffers have been filled. The offload thread invokes the Offload function (Step 5) on the accelerator cores with a pointer to the receiving buffer, the data type of the work unit (specified by the User Application on the manager node) and the size of the work unit. Since the input buffer passed to the Offload function is also its output buffer, all of these parameters are read–write parameters. This is to allow the Offload function to resize the buffer, change the data type and change the data size depending on the demands of the output. When the Offload function finishes, the recent output buffer is handed off to a writing thread (Step 4c), which returns the results back to the manager and frees the buffer for reuse by the receiving thread (Step 4d). Note that the compute node supports variable size work units and can dynamically adjust the size of buffers at runtime.

As pointed out earlier, the driver interacts with the accelerator node similarly as the manager interacts with the compute nodes. The difference between the manager and the driver node is that the manager may have to interact and stream data to multiple compute nodes, while the driver only manages a single accelerator node. The driver further splits the input data received from the manager and passes it to the compute node in optimal size chunks as discussed in the following section.

20.5   RESOURCE MANAGEMENT ON CLUSTERS WITH ACCELERATORS

20.5.1   Capability-Aware Workload Distribution Alternatives

Efficient allocation of application data to compute nodes is a central component in our design. This poses several alternatives. A straw man approach is to simply divide the total input data into as many chunks as the number of available processing nodes and copy the chunks to the local disks of the compute nodes. The application on the compute nodes can then get the data from the local disk as needed and write the

---

[2]The Offload function is a user-specified function that processes each work unit on the accelerator-type cores of the compute node. The result from the Offload function is merged by the general-purpose processor to produce the output data that is returned to the manager.

results back to the local disk. When the task completes, the result data can be read from the disk and returned to the manager. This approach is easy to implement and lightweight for the manager node as it reduces the allocation task to a single data distribution.

Static decomposition and distribution of data among local disks can potentially be employed for well-provisioned compute nodes. However, for nodes with small memory, there are several drawbacks: (i) it requires creation of additional copies of the input data from the manager's storage to the local disk and vice versa for the result data, which may quickly become a bottleneck, especially if the compute node disks are slower than those available to the manager; (ii) it requires compute nodes to read required data from disks, which have greater latency as compared with main memory or other alternatives; (iii) it entails modifying the workload to account for explicit copying, which is undesirable as it burdens the application programmer with system-level details, thus making the application nonportable across different setups; and (iv) it entails extra communication between the manager and the compute nodes, which may slow the nodes down and affect overall performance. Hence, this is not a suitable choice for use with small-memory accelerators.

A second alternative is to divide the input data as before, but instead of copying a chunk to the compute node's disk as in the previous case, map the chunk directly into the virtual memory of the compute node. The goal here is to leverage the high-speed disks available to the manager and avoid unnecessary data copying. However, for small-memory nodes, this approach can create chunks that are very large compared with the physical memory available, thus leading to memory thrashing and reduced performance. This is exacerbated by the fact that available MapReduce runtime implementations [15] require additional memory reserved for the runtime system to store internal data structures. Hence, static division of input data is not a viable approach for our target environment.

The third alternative is to divide the input data into chunks, with sizes based on the memory capacity of the compute nodes. Chunks should still be mapped to virtual memory to avoid unnecessary copying, whereas the chunk sizes should be set so that at any point in time, a compute node can process one chunk while streaming in the next chunk to be processed and streaming out the previously computed chunk. This approach can improve performance on compute nodes, at the cost of increasing the manager's load as well as the load of the compute node cores that run the operating system and I/O protocol stacks. Therefore, we seek a design point which balances the manager's load, I/O and system overhead on compute nodes and raw computational performance on compute nodes.

20.5.2 Adapting Workload Size

Efficient utilization of compute nodes is crucial for overall system performance. A key observation is that a compute node's performance can be increased manyfold by reducing memory pressure, which is in turn tied to the work unit size. The intuition is that if a smaller than optimal size is assigned to an accelerator, it would underutilize available resources and needs more scheduling iterations on the manager. In contrast, using a larger size would result in increased iteration time due to memory thrashing and resource saturation on accelerators. The challenge is to find an optimally sized work unit, which offers the best trade-off between the compute node performance and manager load.

An optimum work unit for running an application on a particular cluster can be manually determined by hard coding different work unit sizes, executing the application and measuring the execution time for each size. The best unit size is the one for which the application execution time is minimized. However, this is a tedious and error-prone process. It requires unnecessary 'test' access to resources, which may be difficult to obtain given the ever increasing need for executing 'production' tasks on a cluster to maintain high serviceability. Our framework adaptively and dynamically matches the workload assigned to a compute node to its capabilities. To this end, we define an optimal work unit size to be the largest amount of data assigned per accelerator that results in minimum execution time for a given application.

The optimal work unit size can be determined either statically or dynamically using an autotuning heuristic. We adopt an autotuning scheme where the driver or manager sends varying size work units to accelerator nodes at the start of the application and records the completion time corresponding to each size. For each size, the processing rate is calculated as the fraction (*work unit size*)/(*execution time*). The size corresponding to the maximum processing rate is selected as the optimal work unit size and is employed for the rest of the application's execution time. The same process is repeated at the drivers to find the optimal work unit size allocated from each driver to the attached compute nodes.

All available compute nodes participate in finding the optimal work unit size. Increasing work units are sent to multiple compute nodes simultaneously, although one size is sent to at least two compute nodes to determine average performance. Once an optimal work unit size is determined, it can also be reported to the application user to possibly facilitate optimization for a future run.

20.5.3 Capability-Aware Workload Distribution Algorithm

We consider two types of accelerators, Cell processors and CUDA-enabled GPUs, in designing capability-aware workload distribution schemes for multiple concurrently executing applications on heterogeneous resources. Concurrently executing applications are commonplace in virtualized execution environments, such as data centers. Our scheduler handles both stand-alone and virtualized execution of applications. In the latter case, applications share resources in space and/or time. The scheduler takes two parameters as input: (i) the number and type of compute nodes in the heterogeneous cluster and (ii) the number of simultaneously running applications on the heterogeneous cluster.

Figure 20.4 shows the different states representing the learning process and the execution flow of the scheduler. Initially, the scheduler starts with a static assignment of tasks to nodes and cores, based on the user-provided affinity metric and the performance of the resources in terms of time spent per byte of data or if no information is available, by simply dividing the tasks evenly between resources. The scheduler then

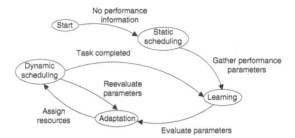

Figure 20.4 State machine for scheduler learning and execution process.

enters its learning phase, where it measures the processing times for different application components on the resources on which they are initially scheduled. Based on the processing time of the workload on each of the available compute nodes, the scheduler then computes the processing time per byte for each of the available compute nodes. Once a processing rate is known, the scheduler moves to the adaptation phase, where the schedule is adjusted to greedily maximize the processing rate. Note that, even in this phase, the scheduler continues to monitor its performance and adjust its scheduling decisions accordingly.

For multiple concurrently executing applications, the scheduler must decide which application to run on what particular accelerator. For this purpose, the scheduler tries different assignments, for example, starting by scheduling an application A on the Cell processor and application B on the GPU for a prespecified period of time T_{learn}, then reversing the assignment for another T_{learn}, then determining the assignment that yields higher throughput and finally using that assignment for the remaining execution of the application. The time to determine a best schedule will increase with the number of applications executing simultaneously; however, it can be reduced by using user input or information from past application runs. If one of the applications completes earlier than the other, the scheduler enters the learning phase and attempts to assign the recently released resources to either applications waiting in the queue or the running application if the queue is empty. It is not always possible to assign the applications to the most suitable nodes, for example, when multiple applications need the same type of accelerators and only a limited number of accelerators of the requested type is available. Nonetheless, our approach ensures that all compute nodes are kept busy and that the assignment of the applications to compute nodes is optimal in that the overall completion time for the scheduled applications is minimized for the given resources and applications.

The algorithm describes how our capabilities-aware dynamic scheduling scheme works. Since the scheduler does not have any information about how the available compute nodes perform for the given tasks, a static schedule is chosen in the beginning. The schedule is adjusted dynamically as the tasks execute, and their performance on the assigned compute nodes can be measured. Note that if there are more accelerators available than the number of applications, each application is scheduled on a separate accelerator during the learning phase. This eliminates any resource

---

Algorithm Capability-aware workload scheduling.

Input: nodeArray, appArray

  for all *node* **in** *nodeArray* **do**
    for all *app* **in** *appArray* **do**
     estArray = sendNextChunk(node, app)

    end for
  end for
  nodeAppMap = GenNodeAppComb(estArray, nodeArray, appArray)
  while *incompleteAppExist(nodeAppMap)* **do**
    for all *appNode* **in** *nodeAppMap* **do**
     app = getApp(appNode)
     node = getNode(appNode)
     if *appCompleted(app)* **then**
      nodeAppMap = GenNodeAppComb(estArray, nodeArray, appArray)
     else
      estArray = sendNextChunk(node, app)
     end if
    end for
  end while

---

conflicts between different applications and allows for determining accurate processing rates. For example, if applications A and B are assigned to a cluster with four of each of Cell- and GPU-based compute nodes, the system assigns half of the nodes (2 Cells and 2 GPUs) each to A and B during the learning phase. The assignment is then readjusted using the performance measurements to improve the overall execution time.

20.5.4 Managing Manager-Accelerator I/O Mismatch

Even with adaptive scheduling and programmer-supplied affinity metrics, the inherent asymmetry between cluster components may lead to performance degradation, especially due to communication delays associated with data distribution and collection by the manager. Thus, it is critical to handle all communication with different components of the system asynchronously. This design choice needs careful consideration. If chunks from consecutive input data are distributed to multiple compute nodes, time-consuming sorting and ordering operations would be required to ensure proper merging of the results from individual compute nodes into a consolidated result set. We address this issue by using a separate handler thread on the manager for each of the compute nodes. Each handler works with a consecutive fixed portion of the data and avoids costly ordering operations by exploiting data locality. Each handler thread is also responsible for receiving all the results from its associated compute node and for performing the application-specific merging operation on the received data. This design leverages multicore or multiprocessor head nodes effectively. Moreover, we use well-established techniques such as prefetching and double buffering to avoid I/O delays when reading data from the disks and transferring the data between manager and compute nodes.

Instead of statically dividing the input data between the available compute nodes, we adopt a streaming approach in our design. Statically allocating workloads to compute nodes, as is the case in standard MapReduce setups, may saturate the noncompute-efficient resources of accelerators that handle communication (e.g. the PowerPC® core of the Cell or the I/O bus on nodes with GPUs) and erase the performance gains that accelerators can provide. Instead, we slice the input into work units with sizes based on the memory, communication and control capabilities of the accelerators and stream the slices to compute nodes while attempting to overlap computation with data streaming.

20.5.5 Communication between Cluster Nodes

In our implementation, we have isolated the communication functionality from other functions of our framework in a custom-built communication library. This library uses LAM–MPI [11, 39] to communicate between the cluster nodes; however, it can be easily replaced with other communication libraries and primitives, such as network sockets or remote procedure calls.

In some cases applications may require setting up specific environments for their tasks to run on compute nodes. Certain parameters such as network paths or file names may need to be distributed to all compute nodes. We provide an API to add all the parameters to a special buffer. The parameters are defined in the application initialization code provided to the manager. Once execution begins, the manager broadcasts this buffer of parameters to compute nodes, allowing all compute nodes to be initialized as needed by the application.

20.6 EVALUATION

We implemented our capabilities-aware MapReduce framework in lightweight user-level libraries for each of our experimental platforms, including x86-based nodes acting as managers, nodes with IBM Cell processors where we provide libraries for the PowerPC® core and the Synergistic Processing Elements (SPEs) and heterogeneous CPU–GPU compute nodes. All our libraries are implemented for Linux-/Unix-based operating systems and use the POSIX threads [29] library. Our libraries provide programmers with all necessary MapReduce programming primitives to program a heterogeneous cluster.

We present results from an experimental test-bed using 4 Sony PlayStation® 3 (PS3™) nodes, 4 GPU-enabled Toshiba Qosmio® laptop nodes and a manager node with dual quadcore Intel® Xeon® processors. All cluster components are connected via 1 Gbps Ethernet and are arranged in the configuration shown in Figure 20.1(d) (*Conf IV*) where Cell-based well-provisioned accelerators are directly connected with the manager, and GPU-based resource-constrained accelerators are connected with the manager through general-purpose multicores in Toshiba laptops. The manager has

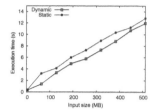

Figure 20.5   Execution time of linear regression with increasing input size.

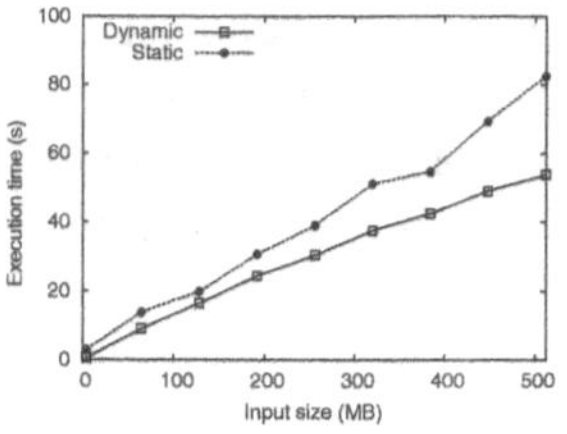

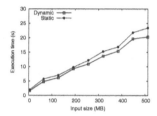

Figure 20.6   Execution time of word count while simultaneously executing histogram.

Figure 20.7   Execution time of histogram while simultaneously executing word count.

two quadcore Intel® Xeon® processors with 3 GHz clocks and 16 GB main memory and runs Linux Fedora Core 8 (kernel version 2.6.26). The PS3 has eight SPEs, out of which six are available to user-level programs [24, 26], 256 MB of main memory (of which about 200 MB is available for applications and the rest is reserved for the operating system and a proprietary hypervisor) and runs Linux Fedora Core 7 (kernel version 2.6.24). The GPU-enabled Toshiba Qosmio® laptops have one Intel dual-core processor with a 2.0 GHz clock and 4 GB of DRAM and run Linux Fedora Core 9 (kernel version 2.6.27). Each of the laptops also has one NVIDIA® GeForce® 9600M GT CUDA-enabled GPU device [31], with 32 cores and 512 MB of memory. We program the GPU using the CUDA toolkit 2.2.

In our evaluation, we use three representative MapReduce benchmarks, namely, word count, histogram and linear regression to study the effects of various design decisions on overall system performance. We compare the performance of our dynamic scheduling scheme with a static scheduling scheme. The static scheme takes into account the overall performance of the assigned workloads on Cell and GPU nodes, which in essence incorporates all the performance parameters of Cell and GPU architectures, thus providing the best static scheduling scheme for the given applications on the studied platforms. Figure 20.5 shows the execution time for the linear regression benchmark using static and dynamic scheduling schemes, while increasing the input size. Our evaluation shows an average system performance improvement of 26.9% with dynamic capability-aware scheduling over static scheduling.

We also evaluate the performance of our capability-aware scheduling scheme with multiple simultaneously running applications on available heterogeneous resources. We invoke multiple applications on the manager node to simulate a cloud computing environment where multiple applications are assigned to the cluster and computational resources are shared transparently between applications. We compare our dynamic scheduling with a static scheduling scheme that simultaneously schedules all applications to be executed on all compute nodes. The static scheduling scheme uses knowledge about how the applications would perform on each type of the compute nodes and how much data can be handled by the nodes at a time. In contrast, our dynamic scheduler has no prior knowledge of the nodes' capabilities and learns and adapts as the applications proceed in their execution. Figures 20.6 and 20.7 show the execution times of concurrent execution of word count and histogram benchmarks using the static and dynamic scheduling with increasing input sizes. For static scheduling, both benchmarks are executed on all available resources, and completion of an application does not affect the allocation of resources for other applications. For dynamic scheduling, although the benchmarks start to execute together, histogram completes quickly, leaving word count to utilize all the available resources for its remaining execution. Overall, compared with static scheduling, our dynamic scheduling scheme performs 31.5% and 11.3% better for word count and histogram, respectively.

We also observe how the performance of our benchmarks (linear regression, word count, histogram and h-means) scale with the number of compute nodes using *Conf I* [27]. Figure 20.8 shows the speedup in performance normalized to the case of 1 node in *Conf I*. Although we are only able to evaluate scaling on the relatively modest scale of 8 nodes, our results show that our framework scales almost linearly as the

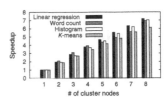

Figure 20.8 Framework scalability.

number of compute nodes increases and this behavior persists for all the benchmark. However, we observe that the improvement trend does not hold for all benchmarks when the eighth node is added. We find that the network bandwidth utilization for such cases is quite high, as much as 107 MB/s compared with the maximum observed value of 111 MB/s on our network, measured using remote copy of a large file. High network utilization introduces communication delays even with double buffering and prevents our framework from achieving a linear speedup. However, if the ratio of time spent in computation compared with that in communication is high, which is the case in scientific applications, we can obtain near linear speedup. We test this hypothesis by artificially increasing our compute time for linear regression by a factor of 10, which results in a speedup of 7.8.

20.7 CONCLUSION

This chapter explored system design alternatives for clusters with computational accelerators and capability-aware task scheduling strategies for large-scale data processing on accelerator-enabled clusters. We presented an implementation and adaptation of the MapReduce programming model for asymmetric clusters. Our contribution features runtime support for utilizing multiple types of computational accelerators in MapReduce, via runtime workload adaptation and methods for adaptively mapping MapReduce workloads to virtualized execution environments with accelerators. Based on these extensions, we were able to integrate two modern multi-/many-core accelerators, the Cell and NVIDIA GPUs, on academic-scale cost-efficient clusters, for processing realistic data-intensive applications. We find that MapReduce can effectively utilize heterogeneous clusters with multiple coexisting accelerator architectures, while preserving its transparency, simplicity and portability as a programming model. Furthermore, adaptively matching application execution properties to the computational capabilities of accelerators improves both application and system performance.

In future work, we plan to leverage the lessons learned from developing an extended MapReduce model to design generic and domain-specific programming models for accelerator-based distributed systems. Furthermore, we intend to extend our framework to develop design optimization tools and models for large-scale distributed systems, to allow future system developers to achieve performance–budget balanced configurations.

REFERENCES

1. Amazon. Amazon Elastic Compute Cloud (Amazon EC2). http://www.amazon .com/b?ie=UTF8&node=201590011.

2. AMD. The Industry-Changing Impact of Accelerated Computing. 2008.

3. Apache Software Foundation. Hadoop, May 2007. http://hadoop.apache.org/ core/.

4. K. Asanovic, R. Bodik, B. C. Catanzaro, J. J. Gebis, P. Husbands, K. Keutzer, D. A. Patterson, W. L. Plishker, J. Shalf, S. W. Williams, and K. A. Yelick. The landscape of parallel computing research: a view from berkeley. Technical Report EECS-TR-2006-183, Electrical Engineering and Computer Science Division, University of California, Berkeley, December 2006.

5. D. Bader and V. Agarwal. FFTC: fastest Fourier transform for the IBM cell broadband engine. In *Proceedings of the 14 th IEEE International Conference on High Performance Computing (HiPC), Lecture Notes in Computer Science 4873*, December 2007.

6. S. Balakrishnan, R. Rajwar, M. Upton, and K. Lai. The Impact of Performance Asymmetry in Emerging Multicore Architectures. In *Proceedings of the 32nd Annual International Symposium on Computer Architecture*, pages 506–517, June 2005.

7. K. J. Barker, K. Davis, A. Hoisie, D. J. Kerbyson, M. Lang, S. Pakin, and J. C. Sancho. Entering the petaflop era: the architecture and performance of Roadrunner. In *Proceedings of the Supercomputing*, 2008.

8. L. A. Barroso, J. Dean, and U. HÃűlzle. Web search for a planet: the google cluster architecture. *IEEE Micro*, 23(2):22–28, 2003.

9. F. Blagojevic, A. Stamatakis, C. Antonopoulos, and D. Nikolopoulos. RAxML-CELL: parallel phylogenetic tree construction on the cell broadband engine. In *Proceedings of the 21st International Parallel and Distributed Processing Symposium*, March 2007.

10. G. Buehrer and S. Parthasarathy. The potential of the cell broadband engine for data mining. Technical Report TR-2007-22, Department of Computer Science and Engineering, Ohio State University, 2007.

11. G. Burns, R. Daoud, and J. Vaigl. LAM: an open cluster environment for MPI. In *Proceedings of Supercomputing Symposium*, pages 379–386, 1994.

12. T. Chen, R. Raghavan, J. N. Dale, and E. Iwata. Cell broadband engine architecture and its first implementation – a performance view. *IBM Journal of Research and Development*, 51(5):559–572, 2007.

13. ClearSpeed Technology. *ClearSpeed whitepaper: CSX processor architecture*, 2007.

14. J. Cross. A dramatic leap forward–GeForce 8800 GT, Oct 2007. http://www.extremetech.com/article2/0,1697,2209197,00.asp.

15. M. de Kruijf and K. Sankaralingam. MapReduce for the Cell B.E. Architecture. Technical Report TR1625, Department of Computer Sciences, The University of Wisconsin-Madison, Madison, WI, 2007.

16. J. Dean and S. Ghemawat. MapReduce: simplified data processing on large clusters. In *Proceedings of the USENIX OSDI 2004*, pages 137–150, 2004.

17. B. Gedik, R. Bordawekar, and P. S. Yu. Cellsort: high performance sorting on the cell processor. In *Proceedings of the 33rd Very Large Databases Conference*, pages 1286–1207, 2007.

18. B. He, W. Fang, Q. Luo, N. Govindaraju, and T. Wang. Mars: a MapReduce framework on graphics processors. In *Proceedings of the 17th IEEE International Conference on Parallel Architectures and Compilation Techniques*, Toronto, Canada, October 2008.

19. S. Heman, N. Nes, M. Zukowski, and P. Boncz. Vectorized data processing on the cell broadband engine. In *Proceedings of the Third International Workshop on Data Management on New Hardware*, June 2007.

20. M. Hill and M. Marty. Amdahl's law in the multi-core era. Technical Report 1593, Department of Computer Sciences, University of Wisconsin-Madison, March 2007.

21. Intel. Single-chip Cloud Computer, 2010. http://techresearch.intel.com/UserFiles/en-us/File/terascale/SCC-Overview.pdf.

22. R. Kumar, K. Farkas, N. Jouppi, P. Ranganathan, and D. M. Tullsen. Processor power reduction via single-ISA heterogeneous multi-core architectures. *Computer Architecture Letters*, 2, 2003.

23. R. Kumar, D. M. Tullsen, P. Ranganathan, N. P. Jouppi, and K. I. Farkas. Single-ISA heterogeneous multi-core architectures for multithreaded workload performance. In *Proceedings of the 31st Annual International Symposium on Computer Architecture*, June 2004.

24. J. Kurzak, A. Buttari, P. Luszczek, and J. Dongarra. The PlayStation 3 for high-performance scientific computing. *Computing in Science and Engineering*, 10(3):84–87, 2008.

25. M. D. Linderman, J. D. Collins, H. Wang, and T. H. Meng. Merge: a programming model for heterogeneous multi-core systems. In *Proceedings of the 13th International Conference on Architectural Support for Programming Languages and Operating Systems*, pages 287–296, Seattle, WA, March 2008.

26. M. Mustafa Rafique, A. R. Butt, and D. S. Nikolopoulos. DMA-based prefetching for I/O-intensive workloads on the cell architecture. In *CF '08: Proceedings of the 2008 Conference on Computing frontiers*, pages 23–32, New York, NY, USA, 2008. ACM.

27. M. Mustafa Rafique, A. R. Butt, and D. S. Nikolopoulos. Designing accelerator-based distributed systems for high performance. In *Proceedings IEEE/ACM International Symposium on Cluster, Cloud and Grid Computing (CCGRID'2010)*, Melbourne, Australia, May 2010.

28. A. K. Nanda, J. R. Moulic, R. E. Hanson, G. Goldrian, M. N. Day, B. D. D'Arnora, and S. Kesavarapu. Cell/b.e. blades: building blocks for scalable, real-time, interactive, and digital media servers. *Journal of Research and Development*, 51(5):573–582, 2007.

29. B. Nichols, D. Buttlar, and J. P. Farrell. *Pthreads Programming*. O'Reilly & Associates, Inc., Sebastopol, CA, USA, 1996.

30. NVIDIA corporation. NVIDIA CUDA Programming Guide, November 2007.

31. NVIDIA corporation. GeForce 9600M GT, 2008. http://www.nvidia.com/object/product_geforce_9600m_gt_us.html.

32. NVIDIA Corporation. GeForce GTX 295 – a powerful dual chip graphics card for gaming and beyond, 2011. http://www.nvidia.com/object/product_geforce_gtx_295_us.html.

33. M. Pericàs, A. Cristal, F. Cazorla, R. González, D. Jiménez, and M. Valero. A flexible heterogeneous multi-core architecture. In *Proceedings of the 16th International Conference on Parallel Architectures and Compilation Techniques*, pages 13–24, September 2007.

34. F. Petrini, G. Fossum, J. Fernández, A. L. Varbanescu, M. Kistler, and M. Perrone. Multicore surprises: lessons learned from optimizing sweep3d on the cell broadband engine. In *Proceedings of the 21st International Parallel and Distributed Processing Symposium*, pages 1–10, 2007.

35. A. Pisoni. Skynet, Apr. 2008. http://skynet.rubyforge.org.

36. C. Ranger, R. Raghuraman, A. Penmetsa, G. Bradski, and C. Kozyrakis. Evaluating MapReduce for multi-core and multiprocessor systems. In *HPCA '07: Proceedings of the 2007 IEEE 13th International Symposium on High Performance Computer Architecture*, pages 13–24. IEEE Computer Society, Washington, DC, USA, 2007.

37. R. Sandberg, D. Goldberg, S. Kleiman, D. Walsh, and B. Lyon. Design and implementation of the Sun network file system. In *Proceedings of the Summer USENIX*, pages 119–130, Portland, OR, June 1985.

38. L. Seiler, D. Carmean, E. Sprangle, T. Forsyth, M. Abrash, P. Dubey, S. Junkins, A. Lake, J. Sugerman, R. Cavin, R. Espasa, E. Grochowski, T. Juan, and P. Hanrahan. Larrabee: a many-core x86 architecture for visual computing. *ACM Transactions on Graphics*, 27(3):1–15, 2008.

39. J. M. Squyres and A. Lumsdaine. A component architecture for LAM/MPI. In *Proceedings, 10th European PVM/MPI Users' Group Meeting*, number 2840 in Lecture Notes in Computer Science, pages 379–387, Springer-Verlag, Venice, Italy, September/October 2003.

40. H. Wong, A. Bracy, E. Schuchman, T. Aamodt, J. Collins, P. Wang, G. Chinya, A. Khandelwal Groen, H. Jiang, and H. Wang. Pangaea: a tightly-coupled IA32 heterogeneous chip multiprocessor. In *Proceedings of the 17th IEEE International Conference on Parallel Architectures and Compilation Techniques*, Toronto, Canada, October 2008.

41. M. Zaharia, A. Konwinski, and A. D. Joseph. Improving mapreduce performance in heterogeneous environments. In *Proceedings 8th USENIX OSDI*, San Diego, CA, December 2008.

CHAPTER 21

AN APPROACH FOR EFFICIENT EXECUTION OF SPMD APPLICATIONS ON MULTICORE CLUSTERS

RONAL MURESANO, DOLORES REXACHS AND EMILIO LUQUE

21.1   INTRODUCTION

The increasing use of multicore processors in high-performance computing (HPC) is evident in the top 500[1] list, in which most of today's clusters are set up with multicore nodes using a hierarchical communication architecture, which has to be handled carefully if programmers want to improve parallel application performance metrics [2]. Also, the adoption of multicore nodes in HPC has allowed more parallelism within the nodes; however, this parallelism has to be managed properly when the programmer wishes to enhance the performance metrics. The most relevant problems found on multicore nodes are related to number of cores per chip, data locality, shared cache, bus interconnection, memory bandwidth and communication congestion [13].

---

[1]TOP500: a list which provides a rank of parallel machines for HPC www.top500.org. This book chapter has been supported by the MICINN Spain under contract TIN2007-64974.

Programming Multicore and Many-core Computing Systems,   **431**
First Edition. Edited by Sabri Pllana and Fatos Xhafa.
© 2017 John Wiley & Sons, Inc. Published 2017 by John Wiley & Sons, Inc.

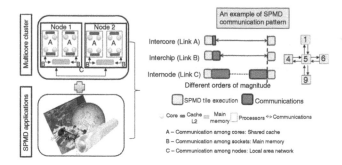

Figure 21.1   Communication and computation of SPMD tile on multicore.

The need for improving performance metrics in these hierarchical communication environments is an obstacle that parallel computing is striving to overcome. Metrics such as efficiency, speedup, execution time and strong application scalability are influenced in a different manner when parallel applications are executed in these heterogeneous environments. In this sense, we consider multicore clusters as heterogeneous due to their different communication paths, which present different speeds and bandwidths, [17] and these differences may cause degradations in the application performance [5, 9]. For example, on multicore clusters some communications are realized through network links such as local area networks (LAN), and others are established by internal processor buses, for example, intercore and interchip communication travel through the internal architecture of the node (Fig. 21.1).

Another issue that parallel programmers have to consider is that many traditional Message Passing Interface (MPI) parallel applications were designed to be executed in clusters comprised of single core nodes, in which communication within the node is not present. However, when these applications are executed on multicore clusters, the processes will be exchanging their information with other processes that are located in the same node or in different nodes. This communication exchange can generate communications imbalances that can create delays in the execution.

An additional aspect to be contemplated for an efficient execution is the parallel paradigm. Master/worker, single program, multiple data (SPMD), pipeline, divide and conquer are examples of parallel paradigms, and each of these paradigms has a different behavior and communication pattern that need to be managed properly. This chapter is mainly centered on studying applications using message passing libraries with high synchronicity through tile dependencies and communication volumes such as SPMD applications on multicore clusters. The SPMD paradigm has been selected due to its behavior, which is to execute the same program in all processes but with a different set of tiles [3]. An SPMD tile is executed in a similar computational time, but the communication processes among neighbors are performed by different links depending on the location of the SPMD processes. These communication links can vary their communication speed in an order of magnitude according to the links, and these variations are a limiting factor to improve performance.

Despite these communications issues and the behavior of MPI applications, we can take advantage of the computational power that these clusters offer with the aim of running applications faster and more efficiently [11]. The applications selected have to meet three characteristics: static, where the communication process is maintained during the entire execution; local, without collective communications; and regular, communications are repeated for several iterations. Also, the SPMD applications used are 2D grid problems with high communication volumes.

An example of the problem concerning these applications and multicore clusters is shown in Figure 21.1. This figure illustrates how a tile can be assigned to each core and what are the influences of the communication processes. The computation processes have to wait until the slowest communications link finishes receiving its information to start the new iteration. These waiting times are translated into system inefficiency.

The main objective of this chapter is focused on describing an efficient execution methodology for multicore clusters, which is based on achieving a suitable application execution with a maximum speedup achievable while the efficiency is maintained over a defined threshold. This methodology allows us to calculate the maximum number of cores that maintain strong application scalability while sustaining a desired efficiency for SPMD applications. It also calculates the ideal number of tiles that have to be assigned to each core with the objective of maintaining a relationship between speedup and efficiency.

This methodology assigns each SPMD tile of the application to a group called a supertile (ST), each of which is in turn assigned to a core. The tiles of these STs belong to one of two types: internal tiles (communication processes are made in the same core) and edge tiles (communication processes are performed with tiles allocated to other core). This division allows us to apply an overlapping method that permits us to execute the internal tiles while the edge communications are being performed. The methodology has been designed in four phases as follows: the characterization (application and environment), tile distribution (we determine the number of tile and number of cores necessary to execute efficiently and with the maximum speedup), mapping strategy (distribution of tiles over cores) and scheduling policy (define the execution order of assigned tiles). This efficient execution methodology has been tested with different scientific applications, and we have reached an improvement of around 40% in efficiency when applying our method.

This chapter is organized as follows. Section 21.2 describes the problems of SPMD applications on multicore clusters. Section 21.3 presents a methodology for efficient execution of SPMD applications on multicore clusters. Section 21.4 illustrates how to combine the efficiency and strong scalability of SPMD applications. Section 21.5 is focused on showing the improvements achieved in efficiency and speedup. Section 21.6 presents the related works, and finally, Section 21.7 summarizes and draws the main conclusions.

21.2 SPMD APPLICATIONS ON MULTICORE CLUSTERS

It is important to define the kind of SPMD applications that our methodology attempts to improve. The SPMD applications selected present a synchronicity through task or

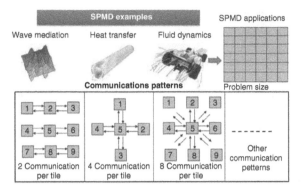

Figure 21.2 Examples of SPMD applications and communications patterns.

tile dependencies, and they do not include a process synchronicity as was established by Valiant [18] in the BSP model.

The behavior of some examples of SPMD applications can be detailed in Figure 21.2. The figure illustrates different communication patterns, which can vary according to the objective of the parallel application. In some cases, the communications can be executed in two, four, six or more bidirectional communications. These communication patterns are established at the beginning of the SPMD application execution, and these patterns are kept until the application finishes. For this reason, we have to manage the communication imbalance of the multicore architecture because it can create dramatic inefficiencies in the parallel execution that will be repeated during all the application's iterations. As mentioned previously, the applications used to apply our methodology have to be designed with static, local and regular characteristics. There are different kinds of benchmarks and applications of diverse fields that accomplish all these characteristics. One example of a suitable benchmark can be found in the NAS parallel benchmark in the CG, BT, MG, and SP applications [20]; all these benchmarks have been designed for 2D and in some case for 3D grid problem. Also, there are examples of real applications such as heat transfer and wave simulation, Laplace's equation and fluid dynamics (mpbl suite) [7]. In all these applications efficiency is mainly affected by the communications imbalances of these multicore environments.

An example of this inefficiency is illustrated in Figure 21.3, where the SPMD tiles are executed in similar time due to the homogeneity of the cores, but the communication process has different times depending on the communication links that are used between them. Also, the figure illustrates the idle time generated by slower communication links, for example, core 5 is communicating from node 1 with core 9 of node 2 through the internode link. These communications have a bigger delay than communication performed by core 5 with core 6 of the same node. The slowest communication is a limiting factor because core 5 cannot begin to calculate the next iteration as all the information transfer has not completed. These issues are translated into inefficiencies that are repeated until the application ends.

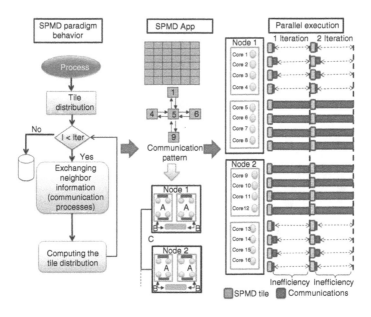

Figure 21.3 SPMD applications on multicore cluster.

However, these idle times allow us to establish suitable strategies in order to organize how SPMD tiles could be distributed on multicore clusters with the aim of managing these communications in an efficient manner. It is important to understand that the latency of the slower link will determine an SPMD iteration as is observed in Figure 21.3. For this reason, the communication inefficiencies have to be managed if we wish to execute the SPMD applications faster, while retaining efficiency and scalability. In order to solve these inefficiency problems, we use the problem size of the SPMD application that is composed by a number of tiles and we create the ST. The problem of finding the optimal ST size is formulated as an analytical problem, in which the ratio between computation and communication of the tile has to be founded with the objective of improving the relationship between efficiency and speedup. The ST is calculated maintaining the focus on obtaining the maximum speedup while the efficiency is maintained over a defined threshold. From this ST, we apply our method that is centered on characterization, mapping and scheduling strategies. The mapping strategy is focused on minimizing the communication effects, and the scheduling policy allows us to apply an overlapping strategy (Fig. 21.4).

Finally, we can use a set of tiles to form an ST of $(K * K)$. Where K is the square root of the number of tiles that has to be assigned to each core in order to maintain the relationship between efficiency and speedup. This ideal scenario is found when we apply our method to maintain the efficiency. The goal of our method is to find both the maximum number of tiles and cores that allows us to achieve the maximum speedup with a desired efficiency.

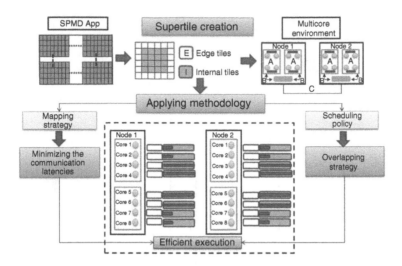

Figure 21.4   Supertile creation and methodology objective.

21.3   METHODOLOGY FOR EFFICIENT EXECUTION

This methodology is focused on managing the communications heterogeneities present on multicore clusters with the objective of improving both efficiency and speedup. This improvement process is realized through four phases (Fig. 21.5): characterization, tile distribution model, mapping strategy and scheduling policy. These phases allow us to handle the latencies and the communication imbalances generated by different communication paths [12].

21.3.1   Characterization Phase

The main objective of this phase is to gather the necessary parameters of SPMD applications and the execution environment in order to calculate the tile distribution model. The characterization parameters are classified as being part of one of three groups: application parameters, parallel environment characteristics and defined efficiency. To develop this phase, we evaluate computation and communication behavior of SPMD applications with the aim of obtaining the parameters with the closest relationship between the machine and the application.

The application parameters offer the necessary information about the application: problem size, number of tiles, iteration number, communication pattern, communication volume per tile and distribution. Also, these parameters allow us to determine, for example, if an SPMD communication pattern of a tile has been designed to communicate with one, two, three, four or more neighboring tiles. Moreover, an SPMD application can consider different distribution schemes, for example, one-dimensional and two-dimensional blocks, column based or unconstrained [14].

The environment characterizations consist of evaluating the behavior of the SPMD application on a specific multicore parallel machine. The parameters allow

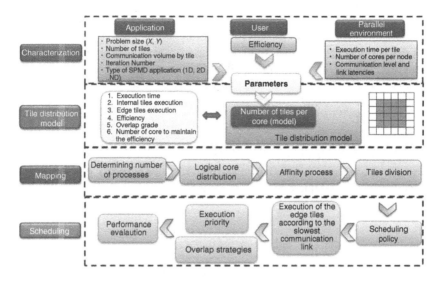

Figure 21.5 Methodology for efficient execution of SPMD applications.

us to establish the communication and computational ratio time of a tile inside the hierarchical communication architecture. This relationship values will be defined as $\lambda_{(p)(w)}$, where p determines the link where the communication of one tile to another neighboring tile has been performed, for example, links A, B or C (Fig. 21.1). The value of λ determines the communication and computation ratio of a tile, and w describes the direction of the communication processes (e.g. up, right, left or down in a four-communication pattern). This ratio is calculated with equation 21.1, where $Commt_{(p)(w)}$ determines the time of communicating a tile for a specific link p, and Cpt is the value of computing one tile on a core. This characterization process has to be done in a controlled and monitored manner:

$$\lambda_{(p)(w)} = Commt_{(p)(w)}/Cpt \qquad (21.1)$$

Finally, once all parameters have been found through the characterization phase, we have to include the efficiency value in the model. The efficiency value is given by the variable *effic* which defines the threshold for a given execution.

21.3.2 Tile Distribution Model Phase

The main objective of this phase is to determine the optimal size of the ST. The first step is to determine the behavior of the execution time of these kinds of SPMD applications. To calculate this value, we use equation 21.2. This equation represents the behavior of SPMD application using an overlapping strategy with the characteristic explained before. As can be detailed in equation 21.2, the first part calculated is the edge tile computation ($EdgeComp_i$), and then we add the maximum value between internal tile computation ($IntComp_i$) and edge tile communication ($EdgeComm_i$).

This process will be repeated for a set of iterations ($iter$). In equation 21.2, the n value determines the number of an individual iteration, and i represents the number of a specific core inside the multicore cluster. This model is only done for the communication exchanging part of the SPMD application:

$$Tex_i = \sum_{n=1}^{iter} \left(EdgeComp_{(i)} + Max \left\{ \begin{array}{l} IntComp_{(i)} \\ EdgeComm_{(i)} \end{array} \right\} \right) \qquad (21.2)$$

The values of ($EdgeComp_i$), ($IntComp_i$) and ($EdgeComm_i$) are in function of the variable K as can be observed in equations 21.3, 21.4 and 21.5, respectively. This K value represents the square root of the ideal ST size

$$EdgeComp_{(i)} = 4 * (K - 1) * Cpt \qquad (21.3)$$

$$IntComp_{(i)} = (K - 2)^2 * Cpt \qquad (21.4)$$

$$EdgeComm_{(i)} = K * Max(Comt_{(p)(w)}) \qquad (21.5)$$

In addition, the edge communication (21.5) has to be for the worst communication case. This means that we have to use the slowest communication time to estimate the number of tiles necessary for maintaining the efficiency. We chose to apply our method using the worst case because SPMD iterations are bounded by the slowest communication as was explained previously. These communications may cause other cores to have to wait until the slowest communications finish due to the data synchronization. Therefore, we have to find the maximum communications time using the maximum value of the $\lambda_{(p)(w)}$ ratio (21.1). On the other hand, the sum of the computational time of the edge and the internal computation (21.3 and 21.4) represents the total computational time of the region of K^2, that is assigned to each core.

The next step is to determine the ideal value for K which represents the conditions of our objective of finding the maximum speedup while the efficiency (*effic*) is maintained over a threshold defined by user. We start from the overlapping strategy, where internal tile computation and the edge tile communication are overlapped. Equation 21.6 represents the ideal overlapping that allows us to obtain the objective stated:

$$K * Max(Commt_{(p)(w)}) >= ((K - 2)^2 * Cpt)/effic \qquad (21.6)$$

However, this equation has to consider a constraint defined in equation 21.7. In this sense, the model can allow for $EdgeComm_{(i)}$ being bigger than $IntComp_{(i)}$ over the defined efficiency (21.6), but $EdgeComm_{(i)}$ has to be slower than the $IntComp_{(i)}$ without any efficiency definition. In this last case, when the edge communication and the internal communication are equal, the efficiency is close to the maximum value:

$$K * Max(Commt_{(p)(w)}) <= ((K - 2)^2 * Cpt) \qquad (21.7)$$

Next step is to determine the value of K from equation 21.6. To calculate the optimal value of K which represents the conditions of our objective, we start from $\lambda_{(p)(w)}$ (21.1) and solve for $Commt$, which can be calculated with respect to $\lambda_{(p)(w)}$ multiplied by computational time Cpt of a tile. This process is performed with the aim of equalizing both internal computation and edge communication equations in function of Cpt. This new value in function of Cpt is replaced in equation 21.6, and we obtain equation 21.8:

$$effic * K * Cpt * Max(\lambda_{(p)(w)}) = ((K-2)^2 * Cpt) \tag{21.8}$$

The final step is to find the value of K. To do this we divide by Cpt and set the equation equal to zero to obtain a quadratic equation that has two solutions for K (21.9). These two solutions may or may not be distinct, and for our case we have to replace these two solutions in equations 21.6 and 21.7, and we have to validate if the K value accomplishes the initial conditions:

$$K^2 - (4 + effic * Max(\lambda_{(p)(w)}) * K + 4 = 0 \tag{21.9}$$

Once the optimal value of K has been calculated, we calculate the ideal number of cores (21.10) which are needed to execute the application with the maximum speedup and with an efficiency over the defined threshold. To do this, we start with the initial consideration that establishes that one ST will be assigned to each core. For this reason, we defined the problem size as M^2, and we divided by K^2 that represent the ideal size of the ST. With equation 21.10, we can obtain the ideal number of cores that determine the inflection point up to which the application will have a strong scalability:

$$Ncores = M^2/K^2 \tag{21.10}$$

Finally, we can determine the theoretical behavior of the SPMD application for a lower number of core that the optimal calculated and predict its behavior. Equation 21.11 calculates the new values of K for a specified number of cores with the objective of determining the execution time using equation 21.2 and calculating the speedup and efficiency for these values:

$$K = \sqrt{M^2/Ncores} \tag{21.11}$$

21.3.3 Mapping Phase

The objective is to design a strategy of allocating the STs to each cores. The ST assignations are made applying a core affinity which allows us to allocate the set of tiles according to the policy of minimizing the communications latencies [10]. This core affinity permits us to identify where the processes have to be allocated and how the ST must be assigned to each core in order to create a logical distribution to identify neighbor communications.

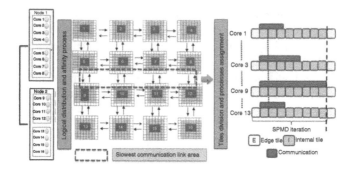

Figure 21.6   Mapping and tile distribution.

This is done using a cartesian topology of the processes that give to each process two coordinates in the grid distribution. These two coordinates identify the cores, in which the processes have to be allocated. Also, we can coordinate the communication order with the objective of minimizing the saturation of the links. For example, Figure 21.6 shows how an ST is allocated onto a multicore node; this allocation means that some processes have a different number of communication paths according to the tile distribution and core assignation.

The last step is to create and distribute the STs, where an incorrect distribution of the tiles can generate different application behaviors. One example is when the computational time of the tiles assigned is larger than the slower communication time. In this case, the SPMD application has a computation bound behavior and could improve speedup, whereas its efficiency is around the maximum value. This case allows us to add more cores to the execution. Another example is determined, when communication time bigger than computational time in this case has a communication bound behavior, and we can add more tiles to each core in order to balance the execution. Then, the model finds the ideal overlap as can be detailed in Figure 21.6, where all the cores end their execution at a similar time.

21.3.4   Scheduling Phase

The main objective of this phase is to determine the execution order of the tiles. This scheduling phase is divided into two main parts: the first is the development of an execution priority, which determines how the tile will be executed inside the core. The tile execution priority assigns to each tile the priority where the highest priorities are established for tiles which have communications through slower paths. Figure 21.7 shows the priority assignments of an ST. These assignments have the following policies: the tiles with external communications are selected with priority 1 because these can create imbalance issues when they are communicated. These edge tiles are saved in buffers with the aim of executing these first, and these buffers are updated in each iteration. The second assignation is made for internal tiles that are overlapped with the edge communications, and they have the priority 2.

The second purpose of this phase is focused on applying an overlapping strategy between internal computation and edge communication tiles. This overlapping

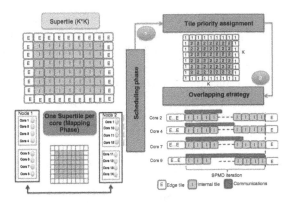

Figure 21.7   Scheduling phase.

process uses two threads, one of them to perform the internal computation and the other to establish the edge communication. We utilize asynchronous communications that enable us to perform the internal computation and the edge communication together. Both processes should finish at roughly similar time if we want to improve the application efficiency.

21.4 SCALABILITY AND EFFICIENCY OF SPMD APPLICATIONS

The efficient execution methodology attempts to find the number of core that achieves the maximum strong scalability with a defined efficiency. These performance metrics can be affected by communication heterogeneity, and our methodology includes the necessary strategies for enhancing these two metrics (scalability and efficiency).

However, an aspect to take into consideration is the scalability definition. There are two distinct definitions of scalability in HPC. One definition is weak scalability that is considered when the problem size and the number of processing elements are expanded. The main goal of this scalability is to achieve constant time to solution for larger problems, and the computational load per processor stays constant [16]. The second definition is the strong scalability in which the problem size is fixed, and the number of processing elements is increased. The goal in this scalability is to minimize the time to solution. Hence, scalability means that speedup is roughly proportional to the number of processing elements (cores or nodes) [6].

Under these two definitions, our methodology searches for a combination of strong scalability and efficiency. This combination means that our analytical model has to determine the number of cores that allows us to obtain the ideal relationship between speedup and the defined efficiency. In this sense, we must fix a specific problem, and we have to find the ideal number of cores that maintains the relationship between both metrics. This number of cores can be calculated using the model, and this number allows us to determine the maximum systems capacity growth when a problem size is fixed.

Finally, when the ideal number of core is found, we can determine the theoretical behavior of the application in speedup and efficiency with equation 21.10. This equation allows us to find the value of K that has to be assigned to each core. The analytical model only finds one ideal value to maintain the ideal overlapping. However, we can calculate values for another number of cores with the aim of evaluating the application performance.

21.4.1   A Theoretical Example

In order to understand how this methodology works, this numerical example illustrates how the efficiency and the strong scalability concept can be combined. Suppose the following application characteristics: a defined problem of $M = 1585$, a defined efficiency (*effic*) of 95% and a four-communication neighbors patterns, with three different communication links (quadcore architecture). Then, we have to determine the $\lambda_{(p)(w)}$ using equation 21.1. This ratio has to be calculated for each link, and we use the maximum value obtained. In this sense, we assume that the computational time of a tile is equal to a one unit of time, and the maximum communication time for the slowest communication link is equal to 100 time units.

Afterward, we apply our analytical model with the aim of finding the ideal number of cores and the ST size that allow us to achieve the maximum speedup while the efficiency is maintained over a defined threshold. Equation 21.9 determines the ideal ST, and equation 21.10 discovers the ideal number of cores. The number of cores calculated represents the maximum combining strong scalability and efficiency for this example. Once the analytical model has been applied, the ideal value of K is equal to 98.95, and this value is rounded to the nearest value ($K = 99$), and the number of cores for this execution is equal to 256 (21.10). The next step is to obtain the speedup and the efficiency for this point. To obtain both values, we have to determine the serial execution time of the application. This theoretical time is estimated using the multiplication of the problem size with the computational time of one tile. For this specific problem size, this example has a serial time of 2.512.225 time units; this value is for one iteration.

The analytical model results are shown in Table 21.1 where we can observe the ideal case calculated; Table 21.1 shows the result obtained for a different distribution of cores. The number of core has been increased in a logarithmical manner (Log_2) with the aim of visualizing the efficiency and speedup curve for this example. Using Equation 21.11, we can calculate K for a specific number of core.

The last step is to determine the parallel execution time of the application for a specific number of cores with the aim of calculating the speedup and efficiency for these executions. Figure 21.8 illustrates the performance behavior for different numbers of cores. As can be detailed, the ideal number of cores calculated with the model has an efficiency around the optimal value defined, and the speedup up to this point has a roughly linear growth. In this sense, this point is the maximum strong application scalability under a desired efficiency. After this ideal point, we can observe that speedup increases but not proportionally to the number of core. Also, we can see that

Table 21.1 Efficiency, speedup and scalability analysis for an SPMD app.

N cores	K	Edge Cp	Int Cp	Edge comm	Exec time	Sp	Effic (%)
16	396	1,580	155,236	39,600	156,816	16	100
32	280	1,176	77,284	28,000	78,400	32	100
64	198	788	38,416	19,800	39,204	64	100
128	140	556	19,044	14,000	19,600	128	100
(256)	**99**	**392**	**9,409**	**9,900**	**10,292**	**244**	**95**
512	70	276	4,624	7,000	7,276	345	67

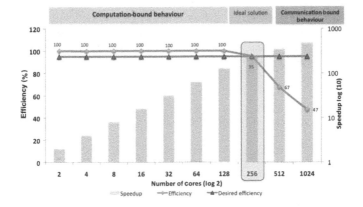

Figure 21.8 Performance evaluation theoretical example.

the efficiency begins to decrease considerably. This decrease in execution efficiency is motivated by the communication-bound behavior. This means that after this point the edge communication is bigger than internal communication (Table 21.1). In addition, we can observe in Figure 21.8 that the behavior of efficiency and speedup before the ideal point, and in these specific case the efficiency, is around the maximum values. This example is a representation of an SPMD application with four neighbors but with computational and communication values adapted for this example.

21.5 SPMD APPLICATIONS AND PERFORMANCE EVALUATION

This section explains some practical examples with the aim of validating this methodology. We have chosen the following applications: heat transfer app, Laplace application and application integrated in the MP-Labs suite (LL-2D-STD-MPI). Also, these performance evaluations have been done in a multicore DELL cluster with 8 nodes, each node having 2 Quadcore Intel Xeon E5430 of 2.66 GHz processors and 6 MB of cache L2 shared by each two core 12 GB RAM memory per blade and a gigabit Ethernet network.

21.5.1   Characterization Analysis

The first step is to analyze the different communication links present on multicore cluster. Figure 21.9 illustrates the behavior of each link when the same packet size is sent by the different communication paths present on these multicore environments. There are differences between each communication that in some cases is around one order of magnitude for the same packet size. Also, we can observe that when we increment the packet size, some links begin to become saturated and this saturation has to be considered, when we are designing our mapping strategy. Another characterization that can be studied is related to the computation and communication-bound relationship. In this sense, Figure 21.10 shows an example of how a tile behaves with respect to the computation and communication ratio. The behavior shown in this figure allows us to visualize differences in the tile behavior of each communication link. These differences enable us to design strategies for allocating more tiles with the aim of eliminating the delays generated by communications.

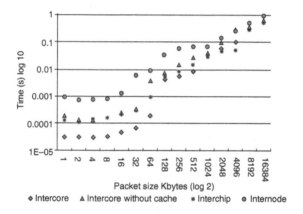

Figure 21.9   Characterization analysis for a double quadcore cluster.

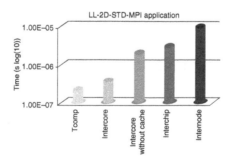

Figure 21.10   Tile computation and communication ratio characterization.

21.5.2 Tile Distribution Model Analysis

The next step is to apply the analytical model in order to find the ideal number of cores to maintain the relationship between speedup and efficiency. An example is shown in Tables 21.2 and 21.3, where the characterization and analytical values are shown for a specific problem size.

Table 21.2 Characterization values.

App.	Cpt (μs)	Commt (μs)	M (Problem size)	Effic (%)
Heat transfer	0.021	58.8	9500 × 9500	85
LL-2D-STD	0.24	60.7	1400 × 1400	95

Table 21.3 Analytical values (time expressed in seconds).

App.	K	Edge Cp	Int Cp	Edge comm	Exec T	N cores
Heat transfer	2384	$1.99E-4$	$1.18E-1$	$1.40E-1$	0.139	16
LL-2D-STD	244	$2.36E-4$	$1.44E-2$	$1.50E-2$	0.015	32

This process is carried out in a similar manner to the theoretical example that was explained before. The possible solution for K and N *cores* represents the minimum value that maintains the efficiency over the defined threshold. This solution is evaluated in order to obtain the overlap between internal computation and edge communication time. Both times have to be as close as possible with the objective of obtaining an ideal execution. As can be shown in Table 21.3, we calculate an approximate value for the edge and internal computation and the edge communication, and also, we determined the ideal values for K and N *cores* for these specific applications and problem sizes.

21.5.3 Performance Evaluation

This performance evaluation illustrates two examples using the values obtained in the characterization phase and with the analytical model (Tables 21.2 and 21.3). Then, we analyzed the efficiency and speedup between the application without using our methodology and, then again, using our methodology. Figure 21.11 shows the efficiency behavior of the heat transfer application with a specific problem size with 100 iterations. In this figure, we can detail a considerable improvement in efficiency, around 42%, when we applied our methodology. This improvement is found when we execute with the number of cores determined by our model (Table 21.3). Also, in Figure 21.11, we can observe how the application behaves similarly to the analytical model values when using our methodology. The error rate is around 5% when the number of core is below to the maximum obtained with our model.

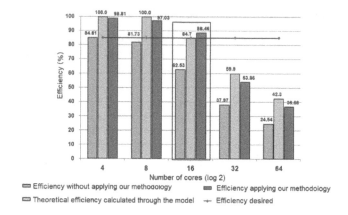

Figure 21.11   Efficiency evaluation heat transfer app.

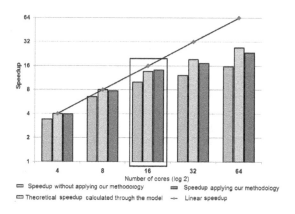

Figure 21.12   Speedup evaluation heat transfer application.

Figure 21.12 illustrates the speedup behavior. In this figure, we can see that speedup increases when we add more core, but this speedup does not scale linearly after the maximum number of core that we have determined with our model. Hence, we can observe that the number of core calculated with the model allows us to obtain the maximum speedup, the strong scalability point and the efficiency over a defined threshold for a specific problem size.

A similar example is shown in Figure 21.13, where the efficiency of LL-2D-STD-MPI is evaluated. This application is formed of three main parts, prestep, poststep and the main module where the communication and computation processes are performed. We applied our methodology to the last module, because the other two only compute and do not have any communication. This performance analysis is only for the part of the code in which the information has to be exchanged, run using 1000 iterations.

Finally, Figure 21.14 shows the behavior of speedup and strong scalability, where we can obtain a linear speedup until the number of core calculated with the model.

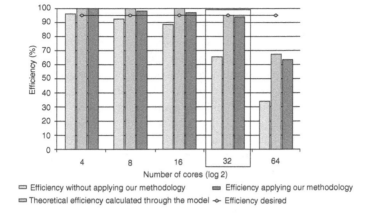

Figure 21.13 Efficiency evaluation LL-2D-STD application.

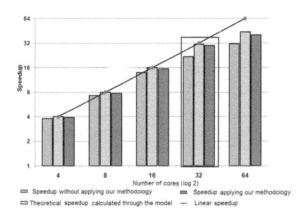

Figure 21.14 Speedup evaluation LL-2D-STD App.

This allows us to conclude that our methodology can determine the maximum strong scalability combining the maximum speedup while maintaining efficiency over a defined threshold. These two examples show an approximation of our method and how the maximum speedup is reached with a defined efficiency. The figures have shown the maximum strong scalability value with a defined efficiency. These experiments have shown how our methodology can improve the SPMD applications on multicore clusters.

21.6 RELATED WORKS

There are different works developing methodologies which are focused on improving some performance metrics in multicore environments. Mercier et al. [10] have designed a method to efficiently place MPI processes on multicore machines in order to establish an adequate placement policy to improve applications efficiency. However, this work does not include the combination of scalability that is very important when we wish to execute faster and more efficiently.

Liebrock [8] defines a method for deriving a performance model for SPMD hybrid parallel applications. This work was focused on improving three specific performance metrics: adaptability, scalability and fidelity using mapping, scheduling and synchronization of overhead strategies designed for hybrid message passing and distributed memory applications. On the contrary, our work evaluates pure MPI applications, and similarly, we develop a methodology centered on mapping and scheduling strategies, which also includes an efficient execution.

Some works have developed mapping strategy for SPMD applications, which are centered on improving the application efficiency [19]. Another technique was designed by Brehm et al. [2], in which the main objective was to map the application using its characteristics. Similarly, our mapping maintains the efficiency using the machine and application characteristics, but we add an affinity process that allows us to minimize the communication effect in multicore environments.

Moreover, there are works centered on studying and improving the efficiency [4] or enhancing the speedup on multicore clusters [19] separately. In contrast, we developed a methodology centering on mapping and scheduling strategies, and we searched for an improvement in both speedup and efficiency performance metrics on these clusters [12]. In this previous work, we have defined the methodology phases that permit us to find the number of tiles which achieves the maximum speedup while defining a desired efficiency for an SPMD application. However, this book chapter searches for a combination of strong scalability and efficiency, in which we can predict the number of core that maintains the relationship between both metrics.

Also, there are some scheduling strategies for SPMD applications [1] that are based on finding the minimum execution time, which is part of our objective. Nevertheless, we analyzed and evaluated the model defined by Panshenskov et al. [15], and we chose some characteristics such as tiles divided into blocks, asynchronous communications, and computation and communication overlapping, with the aim of minimizing the communication overhead and improving the efficiency of SPMD applications.

21.7 CONCLUSION AND FUTURE WORKS

This book chapter addresses a novel methodology for efficient execution of SPMD application on multicore clusters. This method is based on characterization, a tile distribution model, mapping strategy and scheduling policies. Our methodology is focused on determining the ideal number of tiles which has to be assigned to each ST, as well as the ideal number of cores which maintains the execution efficiency. This is performed using an efficient manner to manage the hierarchical communication architecture present on multicore clusters.

Also, this work addresses how we can combine efficiency and strong and weak scalability in parallel applications. In this sense, using our method we can observe how SPMD applications with some specific characteristics behave with a specific problem size while the number of cores is incremented. This is the main purpose of finding the maximum point that allows the SPMD application to scale linearly. On the other hand, if the problem size is increased according to the relationship of the ST, we can maintain a linear speedup while the number of cores is increased.

Experimental evaluation makes it clear that to achieve a better performance in SPMD applications, we have to manage the communication heterogeneities. In this sense, the experimentation has demonstrated that this optimal size can achieve the conditions of maximum speedup and efficiency over a defined threshold. To achieve this, we have proposed an appropriate manner to manage the inefficiencies generated by different communications links presented on multicore clusters, as was described.

Future works are focused on working with heterogeneous computation on multicore environment with the aim of executing the SPMD applications efficiently in communication and computation heterogeneous environments.

REFERENCES

1. O. Beaumont, A. Legrand, and Y. Robert. Optimal algorithms for scheduling divisible workloads on heterogeneous systems. In *Proceedings of 17th International Parallel and Distributed Processing Symposium (IPDPS)*, pages 98, 108, 2003.

2. J. Brehm, P. Worley, and M. Madhukar. Performance modeling for SPMD message-passing programs, *Journal Concurrency - Practice and Experience*, 10(5):333–357, 1998.

3. R. Buyya. High performance cluster computing: architectures and systems. *Prentice Hall PTR Upper Saddle River*, NJ, USA, 1999.

4. G. Cong and D. A. Bader. Techniques for designing efficient parallel graph algorithms for smps and multicore processors. In *Proceedings of the Fifth International Symposium on Parallel and Distributed Processing and Applications (ISPA)*, pages 137–147, 2007.

5. A. El-Mahdy and H. El-Shishiny. An efficient load balancing algorithm for image processing applications on multicore processors. In *Proceedings of the 1st international forum on Next-generation multicore/manycore technologies (IFMT)*, pages 1–2008.

6. A. Hoisie, O. Lubeck, and H. Wasserman. Performance and scalability analysis of teraflop-scale parallel architectures using multidimensional wavefront applications. *Journal of High Performance Computing App*, 14(4): 330–346, 2000.

7. T. Lee and C.-L. Lin. A stable discretization of the lattice Boltzmann equation for simulation of incompressible two-phase flows at high density ratio. *Journal of Computational Physics*, 206:16–47, 2005.

8. L. Liebrock and S. Goudy. Methodology for modelling SPMD hybrid parallel computation. *Journal Concurrency – Practice and Experience*, 20(8): 903–940, 2008.

9. M. D. Mccool. Scalable programming models for massively multicore processors. *Proceedings of the IEEE*, 96(5):816–831, 2008.

10. G. Mercier and J. Clet-Ortega. Towards an efficient process placement policy for mpi applications in multicore environments. In *Proceedings of the 16th Group Meeting on Recent Advances in Parallel Virtual Machine and Message Passing Interface (European PVM/MPI)*, pages 104–115, 2009.

11. R. Muresano, D. Rexachs, and E. luque. How SPMD applications could be efficiently executed on multicore environment. In *Proceedings of the IEEE International Conference on Cluster Computing (CLUSTER)*, pages 1–4, 2009.

12. R. Muresano, D. Rexachs, and E. Luque. Methodology for efficient execution of SPMD applications on multicore clusters. In *Proceedings of IEEE/ACM International Conference on Cluster, Cloud and Grid Computing (CCGRID)*, pages 185–195, 2010.

13. I. Nielsen and J. Curtis. Multicore challenges and benefits for high performance scientific computing. *Journal Scientific Programming - Complexity in Scalable Computing*, 16(4), 2008.

14. A. Olivier and Y. Robert. Data allocation strategies for dense linear algebra on two-dimensional grids with heterogeneus communication links. *Institut National de Recherche en informatique*, Technical Report, 2001.

15. M. Panshenskov and A. Vakhitov. Adaptive scheduling of parallel computations for spmd tasks. In *Proceedings of the International Conference on Computational Science and Its Applications (ICCSA)*, pages 38–50, 2007.

16. L. Peng, M. Kunaseth, et al. A scalable hierarchical parallelization framework for molecular dynamics simulation on multicore clusters. In *Proceedings of the Parallel and Distributed Processing Techniques and App (PDPTA)*, pages 97–103, 2009.

17. F. Trahay, E. Brunet, A. Denis, and R. Namyst. A multithreaded communication engine for multicore architectures. In *Proceedings of the IEEE International Symposium on Parallel and Distributed Processing (IPDPS)*, pages 1–7, 2008.

18. L. Valiant. A bridging model for multi-core computing. In *Proceedings of the ACM Symp. on Parallelism in Algorithms and Archict. (ESA)*, volume 5193, pages 13–28, 2008.

19. K. Vikram and V. Vasudevan. Mapping data-parallel tasks onto partially reconfigurable hybrid processor architectures. In *Proceedings of IEEE Transactions on Very Large Scale Integration Systems*, volume 14, pages 1010–1023, 2006.

20. R. der Wijngaart and H. Jin. Nas parallel benchmarks, multi-zone versions. *NASA Advanced Supercomputing (NAS) Division NASA Ames Research Center, Moffett Field, CA 94035-1000*, Technical Report, 2003.

CHAPTER 22

OPERATING SYSTEM AND SCHEDULING FOR FUTURE MULTICORE AND MANY-CORE PLATFORMS

Tommaso Cucinotta, Giuseppe Lipari and Lutz Schubert

22.1 INTRODUCTION

Computing systems are experiencing nowadays a complete paradigm shift. On the old-fashioned single-processor platforms, sequential programming used to constitute an easy and effective way of coding applications, and parallelism was used merely to easily realize independent or loosely coupled components. True parallel and distributed programming used to constitute a domain reserved to only a relatively small number of programmers dealing with high-performance computing (HPC) systems and commercial high-end mainframes. However, recently, multicore systems have become the de facto standard for personal computing and are being increasingly used in the embedded domain as well. Furthermore, in the context of servers, it is more and more common to see multiprocessor and multicore systems realizing up to 8–12 cores. The according process just continues: already experimental

Programming Multicore and Many-core Computing Systems,
First Edition. Edited by Sabri Pllana and Fatos Xhafa.

multicore processors, such as the Polaris by Intel, reach up to 80 cores and specialized processors, such as the Azul Vega, go up to 54 cores, yet the mass market commercial exploitation of these processors will still take a few years. Along that line, high-performance and massively parallel systems are undergoing a tremendous architectural shift that promises to move toward an unimaginable number of interconnected cores and other hardware elements such as local memory/cache elements, within the same chip. As a consequence, in the short future, parallel and distributed programming paradigms need to become more and more widespread and known across the whole base of developers, comprising not only the HPC domain but also the general-purpose one.

However, the entire ensemble constituting the software stack of nowadays computing systems, comprising operating systems (OSes), programming languages, libraries and middlewares, is still too much influenced by the former nonconcurrent era and is slow at adapting to the new scenario. Furthermore, when dealing with real-time and more generally time-sensitive applications, the support of a general-purpose(GP) OS suffers various drawbacks: it is often merely limited to priority-based scheduling and some kind of priority inheritance mechanism, it does not provide temporal isolation across concurrently running applications, it cannot properly deal with interactive tasks with performance and end-to-end latency requirements, etc. On the other hand, the use of a full real-time operating system (RTOS) for complex time-sensitive applications (e.g. multimedia) is prohibitive due to the lack of complex and commonly needed functionality (e.g. high-level communication protocols, middleware, encoding, etc.).

A few GP OSes (e.g. Linux) have been extended for addressing the requirements of complex, distributed real-time applications. However, being developed in the domain of real-time and embedded systems, they lack essential scalability capabilities needed for coping with large-scale systems. Also, various OS extensions and middle-ware components have been proposed to cope with large-scale distributed systems designed for Grid, high-performance or cloud computing domains. However, these approaches usually rely on traditional kernel architectures which are not capable of handling many-core nodes.

In this chapter, an overview is made on the limitations of the nowadays OS support for multicore systems, when applied to the future and emerging many-core, massively parallel and distributed platforms. Also, an overview is done of the most promising approaches which have been proposed to deal with such platforms. The discussion is strongly focused on the kernel architecture models and kernel-level mechanisms and the needed interface(s) toward user-level code.

22.1.1 Organization of This Chapter

This chapter is organized as follows: In Section 22.2, various works proposed in the literature about OS architectures and kernel models for multicore and many-core systems are overviewed. In Section 22.3, the focus is specifically on the critical problem of scheduling in multiprocessor and distributed systems, comprising scheduling of applications with precise timing requirements.

22.2   OPERATING SYSTEM KERNEL MODELS

Various models of OSes and kernels have been proposed in the literature. In what follows, an overview of the most significant works is provided.

22.2.1   Linux Scalability

It must be noted that the Linux kernel developers' community is focusing more and more on the issue of scalability of the kernel in the number of underlying cores. This is witnessed by the announcement[1] by Linus Torvalds accompanying the 2.6.35 kernel release, mentioning the imminent merge of the VFS scalability patch by Nick Piggin into the mainline kernel. This patch aims to remove many bottlenecks at the kernel level that hinder the performance of Linux file system operations when being deployed on multi-/many-core machines. Also, the scheduler subsystem is already designed since long ago with scalability in mind: distributed per-core runqueues and cpusets [22] allow for keeping a limited sharing of data among different cores.

Furthermore, there exist various projects for improving the Linux scalability of the kernel even further. The Linux Scalability Effort project,[2] running within years 2001 and 2004, aimed to improve scalability of various subsystems of the kernel. More recently, during the 2006 Kernel Summit,[3] Christoph Lameter gave a comprehensive talk about the current status of scalability issues on the Linux kernel, highlighting the importance of robustness to failures. On a related note, Deputovitch et al. [21] presented a mechanism that allows one core to recover a kernel panic occurred onto another core, with applications potentially able to recover seamlessly from kernel crashes. During the Linux Kongress 2009, Kleen [39] presented various known bottlenecks for the scalability of the kernel and workarounds for avoiding them. Boyd-Wickizer et al. [13] investigated on scalability issues of the Linux OS on a 48-core machine, identifying various related bottlenecks at the kernel level arising from the use of seven different application benchmarks. Interestingly, the authors conclude: 'a speculative conclusion from this analysis is that there is no scalability reason to give up on traditional operating system organizations just yet'. On a related note, Lelli and coworkers [25] showed how to improve the scalability of a deadline-based scheduler in Linux by using proper data structures and lock-based synchronization.

22.2.2   Microkernels

Microkernels have been proposed in the research literature as an alternative to monolithic kernels [47, 67, 80]. In this architecture, a small code base (microkernel) provides essential services, such as physical memory management and protection, interrupt handling and task scheduling. Most of the classical services provided

---

[1]More information is available at http://lwn.net/Articles/398371/.
[2]More information is available at http://lse.sourceforge.net/.
[3]More information is available at http://lwn.net/Articles/191929/.

by a monolithic OS, like network protocols, I/O device drivers, file systems and virtual memory management, are provided by special server processes running in user space. In this way, the OS is extremely modular, robust and secure. In microkernel-based OSes, all services interact with each other and with applications through message passing.

Several microkernel architectures have been proposed in the research literature, most notably the Minix system by the A. Tanenbaum Group[4] and the L4 microkernels [47]. Unfortunately, only a few researchers have investigated the performance and scalability of microkernels on multicore systems. In L4 [47], the basic IPC mechanism is designed to be highly optimized for uniprocessors. Moreover, it is not clear how to make the sharing of internal-shared data structures, namely, interrupt forwarding and virtual memory, scalable in many-core environments.

Uhlig [80] presented an adaptive mechanism for sharing data structures between microkernels running on different cores, which is a combination of coarse and fine grain locking and remote procedure call (RPC). Also, remote resources are treated differently from local resources.

The use of microkernel-based OSes has been investigated also in the domain of supercomputing on multiprocessor systems, like what happened with the Amoeba [79], Mach [67] and Chorus [68] OSes. These investigations were born from the observation that monolithic OSes used to carry on lot of unneeded functionality on each and every node of a parallel machine, introducing unneeded overheads. Also, the standard communication primitives used on traditional OSes used to be highly inefficient in the context of a multiprocessor machine. On the other hand, the approach typical of the HPC domain used to consist in not having a real OS, but rather a small run-time environment provided in the form of libraries. This was too minimalistic and used to lack potentially useful capabilities. So, the adoption of a microkernel-based OS was considered a good trade-off between these worlds [78].

A few commercial OSes were inspired by the microkernel architecture. Windows NT borrowed some of the ideas from the microkernel environment [57]; however, NT should be considered a hybrid between a monolithic kernel and a microkernel. Also, the Mac OS-X kernel, a.k.a. XNU [74], derives from the fusion of the Mach [67] and FreeBSD kernels.[5] However, only some kernel-level primitives and paradigms of Mach were kept, while the microkernel architecture has been dropped.

QNX Neutrino [65] was one of the first RTOSes to be available on embedded multicore platforms with a structure similar to a microkernel, with some of the essential scheduling services implemented directly by the kernel for efficiency reasons. OSE[6] is another microkernel-based RTOS. OSE was developed by ENEA, a spin-off of Ericsson AB. In OSE, real-time tasks are implemented as processes that communicate among them mainly through message-passing paradigm. Since memory protection is enforced between processes, the OSE kernel is known for its fault-tolerant and high-availability features, and it is widespread in telecommunication applications.

---

[4]More information is available at http://www.minix3.org.
[5]More information is available at http://www.freebsd.org/.
[6]More information is available at http://www.enea.com.

22.2.3 Single-System Image

Single-system image (SSI) OSes have been designed in the context of cluster computing for the purpose of making the usability and programmability of clusters easy. An SSI OS gives the application programmer the illusion that a cluster is a single computing system with a higher performance. The programmer writes parallel applications composed of many processes which communicate to each other by means of standard IPC mechanisms. Actually, the OS is capable of seamlessly distributing the workload over a distributed set of homogeneous machines interconnected by a network, migrating applications, and data as required in order to make an efficient use of the underlying physical resources. The SSI OS concept has been implemented, for example, in Kerrighed [59], openMosix[7] (initially based on MOSIX [5], the project was officially closed in 2008) and OpenSSI.[8] All of them constitute variants of Linux, which add to the kernel the fundamental lacking features. A comparison among these approaches can be found, for example, in [51].

SSI systems aim to realize HPC clusters preserving a local programming model that is unaware of the actual distribution of the load within the network. This allows parallel applications initially thought for multiprocessor (or multicore) systems to easily take advantage of the additional computing resources made available across the network, without any need to explicitly code the distribution logic. While being one of the main advantages of this kind of systems, it also constitutes its very limitation. The actually obtainable performance speedup depends strongly on the communication patterns among the processes composing an application. However, the assumptions of the programmer about locality of data and processes are subverted when the application is deployed in an SSI cluster. The interaction overheads (now implying networking latencies) may sometimes nullify the potential advantages due to the increased available overall computing power, unless the application is carefully coded considering the deployment environment. These kind of problems may be mitigated by proper monitoring and migration strategies at the SSI kernel level, for example, by trying to keep those processes which interact too frequently on the same machine.

It is also noteworthy to mention that there are approaches to exposing a SSI run-time to applications in a cluster which do not require any specific OS/kernel adaptation. For example, this has been done for the Java language, to allow for the seamless deployment of large parallel Java applications, with many threads but non-necessarily distributed, over a cluster of physical machines [2, 84, 85]. These approaches require the realization of proper mechanisms into the run time of the language itself, and they usually do not require any special support from the OS/kernel.

22.2.4 Operating Systems for Multi/Many Cores

Research on multiprocessor OSes is active since a long time, much before the multicore paradigm became so successful. Two broad classes of kernel organization have

---

[7]More information is available at http://www.openmosix.org.
[8]More information is available at http://www.openssi.org.

been proposed by Lauer and Needham [44]: message-based and procedure-based approaches. In a procedure-based kernel, there is no fundamental distinction between a process in user space and kernel activities: each process performs kernel operations via system calls, and kernel resources are represented by shared data structures between processes. Conversely, in a message-based kernel, each major kernel resource is handled by a separate kernel process, and typical kernel operations require message exchanges. The procedure-based approach closely mimics the hardware organization of symmetric Multiprocessors (SMP) with Uniform Memory Access (UMA): this is the basic organization underlying monolithic kernels. The message-based approach closely mimics the hardware organization of a distributed memory multicomputer, and this is the basic organization of microkernels. Chaves et al. [16] compared remote memory access versus remote invocation for kernel–kernel communication in a NUMA machine without cache coherency. In the first case, access to shared resources is performed by accessing remote memory using a remote locking mechanism; in the second case, it is achieved through invoking an operation on the remote node. The work is outdated, because of the advances in hardware architectures; however, some of the basic findings are of general validity: in particular, remote invocation is preferable for long operations, while remote memory access is preferable for short critical sections.

Many different papers [16, 44] have insisted on the tension between lock-based communication and synchronization versus remote invocation. Depending on the underlying hardware architecture and on the different structure of the OS and depending on the requirements of the applications (performance, security, scalability, etc.), sometimes the lock-based approach seems to be the most appropriate and sometimes the remote-invocation approach proves to be the best approach.

Andrew Baumann et al. recently proposed that an OS model called Multikernel [11], which advocates for independent kernel instances on the individual cores, allowed to interact solely via message passing. All kernel-level information and status data that need to be shared among multiple cores is therefore replicated between them and kept synchronized by explicit protocols. This way all communications among cores and processors need to be explicitly coded, and this naturally leads to asynchronous communication patterns, largely used in distributed systems, which enhance the possibility for the system to parallelize, and pipeline activities rather than having cores stall waiting for implicit cache coherence protocols run by the underlying hardware. Interestingly, in the Multikernel view, the fact that the OS does not rely on shared data does not preclude applications to be developed with a shared memory paradigm.

Also, Multikernel envisions a hardware-neutral OS model, where, for example, the part of a CPU driver in charge of handling the communications between different core may actually take advantage of available low-level information about the core topology and their interconnection infrastructure. For example, different hardware-level mechanisms may be exploited in order to send messages among cores sharing an L3 cache, as compared with the ones needed to send messages among cores that do not share such a cache or reside on different processors.

The Multikernel model has been implemented as the Barrelfish[9] prototype, and preliminary measurements seem promising, especially on the side of scalability of certain critical operations involving all the cores (e.g. TLB shootdown). However, the experimental results available so far are to be considered as preliminary, due to the still incomplete implementation of the Multikernel concept.

Yuan et al. proposed GenerOS [83], a variation of the Linux kernel explicitly addressing heterogeneous multicore systems. In GenerOS, the cache contention on the same core due to different types of activities going on within a system is reduced by means of partitioning the activities among the available cores: application cores, dedicated to running applications and exclusively user space code; kernel cores, dedicated to running exclusively the kernel-space part of the system calls invoked by the applications; and interrupt cores, dedicated to servicing interrupt requests. A set of modifications to the kernel are required to allow system calls to execute on a core different from the application core invoking the functionality. Also, kernel cores run one or more kernel servers. Each kernel server is dedicated to one or more system calls; it waits continuously for requests of that particular set of system calls from the application cores and serializes their execution, avoiding any context switches among requests from different applications.

The fact that kernel-space code is handed over to different cores than the ones where the main application code is running, together with the serialization of kernel-space system call executions by the kernel servers, causes a decrease of the contention in accessing the cache, when compared with a plain Linux system, as shown by the experimental results performed by the authors. However, the serialization of system calls execution is somewhat against the current trend in the Linux kernel: from the ancient ages in which the kernel-space code was nonpreemptible; in recent years a lot of effort has been dedicated just for increasing preemptibility of kernel code, which is well-known to reduce latencies and improve responsiveness of the system. Even if the presence of multiple cores may mitigate such problem, the situation is not expected to be tremendously different when high workloads are in place with a nearly saturated system. Therefore, more investigations would be needed in order to understand what is the impact of the proposed OS model on various application classes, especially on interactive and real-time ones. An issue of the GenerOS model is constituted by the proper OS configuration in terms of balancing among the various types of cores, as well as the number of kernel servers and how system calls are distributed across them. In the initial prototype, the authors used a static configuration, but they also observed that this is one of the troublesome issues to be faced in their proposed OS model.

Boyd-Wickizer et al. proposed Corey [12], an OS designed from scratch around the need for allowing applications to make an efficient use of massively parallel and multicore hardware. The authors highlight that kernel-level shared data structures may cause unneeded overheads when accessed from multiple cores, even when the applications that are being run would not need to share any data. For example, process and

---

[9]More information is available at http://www.barrelfish.org.

file descriptor tables are potentially at risk of being contended among multiple cores, even when the applications running on them are accessing independent processes and files. Therefore, it is proposed to delegate the responsibility to decide what is shared across which cores as much as possible to the application. This is done via a specialized API allowing applications to define and control three main elements: shares are areas of scope either local to a core or global for a set of identifiers; address ranges are memory segments explicitly assigned to shares; kernel cores are cores dedicated to the execution of kernel code, that is, interrupt handlers and the kernel-side part of system calls (which are handed over from the application cores to the kernel cores). Experimental results seem promising, in that a reduction of the overheads due to contentions on kernel-level data structures is achievable, at the cost of a little complexity for the application developer, who needs to properly set up shares and address ranges.

Wentzlaff and Agarwal proposed the factored operating systems (fos) [82], an OS model that builds on concepts taken from the distributed computing world, in order to reduce contention on kernel-level shared data structures. Specifically, the fos architecture foresees the partitioning of cores between applications and kernel services. Each kernel service is implemented by one or more specialized servers that run on kernel cores, and bits of service-based computing are reused for allowing each kernel service in distributing its workload to the available kernel servers, similarly to load-balancing techniques in web servers. The fos is still under development, and it is being entirely redesigned from scratch, based on a microkernel structure, where the concept of relegating OS functionality within specialized servers that communicate by message-passing mechanisms to each other and to applications is already in place. Also, in fos, each kernel core runs a single kernel server that enqueues requests in an input queue and services them in a serialized, nonpreemptible way. This removes (in the opinion of the authors of this approach) the need for having traditional temporal scheduling of kernel cores. Actually, it is foreseen to have a form of cooperative scheduling, by which a kernel core, while serving a request, can yield explicitly the core so that it can serve other requests, while it waits for some device and/or other kernel servers to respond. The way kernel servers service application requests is planned to be based on stateless protocols so that subsequent requests of the same application can be potentially handed over to different kernel servers for a better load distribution across kernel cores.

Interesting investigations in this area have also been carried out recently by Schubert et al. [69–72]. In [69], a service-oriented operating system (SOOS) model is proposed, constituting an enabling technology for future distributed collaboration scenarios called Future Workspaces. In this work, it is suggested that the OS should possess a distributed and heterogeneous nature. A main OS instance is the one offering the most complex services to applications, comprising process management, virtual memory management, I/O, networking and a graphical user interface, while other OS instances exhibit a limited set of functionality focused/specialized on the capabilities locally available on the nodes they are running on. Specifically, it is envisioned that an embedded micro OS instance should be used to directly control remote resources and devices, while a standalone micro OS instance should be used to expose access to virtualized resources made available through virtualization technology by some further OS. This structure will enable an unforeseen enhanced level of experience for mobility, where the actual resources (computational power, storage, and data) will be maintained remotely through dedicated corporate server farms, thus greatly reducing administration efforts.

One advantage of such a structure is that the OS may easily embed the additional features needed by Grid applications [70], which usually are made available today by means of specialized extensions to the OS. SOOS introduces a novel resource provisioning concept [71] that differs from existing approaches of Grids and clouds, in that it aims for making applications and computers more independent of the underlying hardware and for increasing mobility and performance.

One of the ideas that is stressed in the SOOS concept is that the programs do not necessarily need to be written in a parallel nor distributed way, like it happens in the MPI approach. Rather, it should be possible in principle to take a sequential application and automatically identify those portions of the program code that may be run remotely, then migrate them on a more powerful embedded OS instance for a faster execution. The additional latency due to the distribution of the functionality would be largely compensated by the increased performance of the code when running remotely. For example, this would be easily the case for a laptop designed for mobility running the main OS instance, whose code is partially remotely executed on a high-performance remote machine. In order to achieve this, sophisticated monitoring mechanisms will need to be built into the OS, such as monitoring the memory access patterns, building statistics on the frequency of access to the various pages, and tracking dependencies and interactions among various code segments.

Also, in a cloud environment, a vast amount of computational resources will be at reach of each process across the web or locally. Therefore, the SOOS concept calls for deep investigations into dynamic and intelligent processes (re)distribution policies according to resource availability and demand, and it proposes [72] a micro-kernel OS architecture model designed to compensate these deficits.

All these elements are under investigation in the context of the SOOS European project.[10]

All of the aforementioned approaches to the (re)engineering of the OS kernel model for dealing with massively parallel systems are extremely interesting. However, these approaches are at a quite preliminary and conceptual stage, with only some of them having experimental prototype implementations. Therefore, these do not constitute consolidated approaches proved to be industrially viable, feasible and understandable for a wide audience. More research needs to be performed on this side, addressing scalability, efficiency and programmability issues for all of the sub-components of an OS kernel and investigating on the achievable trade-offs between overall system and individual applications performance and responsiveness.

Finally, still there are researchers showing how traditional OS kernel architectures, for example, as found in Linux, can be improved from a scalability viewpoint (see Section 22.2.1).

---

[10]More information is available on the project website http://www.soos-project.eu/.

22.2.5   Operating Systems for Grids

Proposals have appeared in the literature for OSes specifically targeted at supporting Grid systems. For example, Padala and Wilson proposed [62] a Grid OS that has the goal of providing a minimum set of services which are common to all Grid middleware infrastructures, still building on a traditional OS like Linux with as few changes as possible (in fact, additional features required at the kernel level are provided through Linux loadable kernel modules). The core functionality that needs to be added to the OS, according to the authors, is high-performance I/O and networking, for example, relying on copy-free communication primitives and fine-tuning of network stack parameters such as the TCP/IP window size; communication primitives with a better support for such mechanisms as MPI; resource management features allowing for resource discovery, allocation, and monitoring; and process management capabilities supporting, for example, global identifiers for processes, which may be used in the mentioned communication primitives for distributed IPC. The point that is made by the authors, and validated by the presented experimental results, is that implementing such services merely at the middleware level, outside the kernel, as commonly done in existing Grid middleware solutions, constitutes a bottleneck in the potentially achievable performance.

More recently, Puri and Abbas conceptualized [64] a Grid OS aimed to support Grid applications, by means of embedding within the OS itself such capabilities as fault tolerance and checkpointing, transparent access to distributed resources in a location-independent fashion, load balancing by means of migration of processes and virtualization and scalability. However, the paper remains at a very abstract level, and it does not discuss practical implications of the envisioned architecture, such as what is required to be supported at the kernel level and what can be delegated to the OS middleware.

The XtreemOS European project[11] produced XtreemOS [58], a variation of the Linux OS enhanced with Grid capabilities. The XtreemOS extensions to Linux include LinuxSSI, an SSI version of Linux based on Kerrighed [59] which allows to register into the XtreemOS Grid a cluster of systems virtually seen as a single, more powerful machine; XtreemFS [35], a networked file system supporting automatic replication and high availability of data; process checkpointing, a middleware for management of Grid nodes and submission of tasks; and XOSAGA [38], an application-level API for Grid applications which constitutes an implementation of the abstract language-independent SAGA [28] specification, with some XtreemOS specific extensions.

Starting from release 10.4, the Mac OS-X embeds a simple Grid management middleware called Xgrid [56], which is immediately available on all installations of the OS, if the corresponding service is activated. Xgrid has a three-tier architecture: clients submit jobs to controllers, which in turn hand them over to agents for the actual processing. Clients may submit jobs to the Grid by means of either a command-line tool or a dedicated API which is part of the OS foundation API. In order to share

---

[11]More information is available at http://www.xtreemos.eu/.

large amounts of data among Grid tasks, it is possible to use one of the available distributed file systems, such as NFS. Xgrid is targeted to an easy setup of Grids with no strong requirements on the number of interconnected nodes and complexity of the submitted jobs. For example, only linear work flows are supported, whereas for more complex Grid settings, one can install on the OS one of the other more complex Grid management middleware solutions. Mac OS-X 10.5 introduced Xgrid 2, with some enhancements on the job scheduling decisions, such as the so-called scoreboard, that is, a customizable scoring script that may be provided by clients in order to drive the decisions made by controllers about what agent nodes to choose when multiple ones are available. The script may base its score on the availability of particular capabilities of the agent node or the connection/connectivity conditions. This is useful for increasing the performance of the deployed applications.

22.2.6 Operating Systems for HPC

As detailed in Section V on HPC, in classical cluster systems, each processor (in the sense of smallest compute unit) hosts its own OS environment. HPC jobs typically run on the system in an exclusive way, in order to achieve maximum performance. This means that the respective execution environment does not have to deal with scheduling issues, scale management, etc. Essentially, the OS therefore primarily serves the same purpose as a virtualization system, that is, it abstracts from the underlying hardware and deals with I/O of the system, in particular for accessing shared resources and communication between threads and processes. This means implicitly that many of the functions in a GP OS are obsolete for HPC usage and can (should) be removed from the kernel, in order not to produce unnecessary overhead.

As noted, it is thereby of particular relevance for efficient parallel computing that the specific characteristics of the hardware are exploited to their maximum potential, such as the memory architecture of the systems. Therefore, the OS is typically specifically adapted to the environment, so as to reduce performance loss due to misalignment.

Essentially, most HPC providers therefore reduce the OS to an essential minimum and adapt the kernel to the specific environment. Obviously, Linux is the primary choice in such cases, due to its open source nature. Microsoft Windows and even Apple Mac OS-X have been demonstrated to work for HPC clusters, too,[12] yet their performance and the overhead for adaptation typically do not fulfill the expectations – as such, there are, for example, 475 Linux-UNIX-based systems on the Top500[13] list (in which systems are ranked by their performance on the LINPACK Benchmark [24, 63]) but only 5 Windows-based ones (and none for Mac OS-X).[14] With the increasing heterogeneity and hence divergence between supercomputer setups and at the same time the growing scale of affordable high performance machines, it is likely that this distribution will change slightly in the near future.

---

[12]More information is available at http://hpc.sourceforge.net/.
[13]More information is available at http://www.top500.org/.
[14]More information is available at http://www.top500.org/stats/list/35/osfam.

Currently, the most widely used Linux distributions are probably[15] Red Hat Linux, SUSE Linux Enterprise, Scientific Linux and CentOS. Red Hat Linux[16] and SUSE Linux Enterprise[17] are widely used[18] mainly due to the range of system architectures they support (namely, x86 32 and 64 bit, Itanium IA-64, and PowerPC 32 and 64 bit), even though official Red Hat Linux releases are comparatively rare (latest official release was in 2003). The Scientific Linux[19] distribution is typically preferred over the Red Hat distribution, which is 100% compatible with Red Hat Linux. As opposed to the Red Hat version, Scientific Linux however is available for free, and adaptations to individual systems are maintained by the community rather than by Red Hat. Even though reliability is decreased this way, the distribution adapts quicker to new systems. Scientific Linux supports the following architectures: x86 32 and 64 bit and Itanium IA-64. CentOS[20] is another popular Linux distribution which bases on Red Hat Linux and is available free of charge. Like Scientific Linux it is mainly maintained by the community, yet the latest versions only support the x86 architectures thus making it less interesting in the future. At the time of writing, 7 machines in the top500 made use of CentOS.

Even UNIX-based OSes are still in use on HPC clusters, as they generally scale quite well. With a few exceptions, they are mostly commercially distributed which makes them less attractive than Linux in particular in academic circles. The number of UNIX systems in the top500 basically decreases, with the particular exception of AIX which ships with the IBM machines and supports in particular the PowerPC and the IA-64 architecture, making it attractive for the according clusters.

Though Lameter claims that Linux scales well enough for future large-scale platforms [43], it must be noted that this is mostly true for the number of processes but not the number of processors [11, 72]. The authors furthermore claim that due to messaging overhead, a microkernel approach is not a feasible alternative to Linux, yet as Barham et al. could show, the messaging approach scales better than the Linux monolithic structure [11].

22.3   SCHEDULING

One of the core features of an OS is its ability to multiplex the access to the available physical resources to multiple processes/threads that run at the same time onto the system. Some resources may be managed in an exclusive way, that is, only one application at a time is granted access to it. Other resources, and particularly processor(s) and disks, are managed in a shared way so that the competing applications alternate in accessing the resource(s) according to some scheduling policy. For the

---

[15]More information at http://www.clusterbuilder.org/software/operating-system.php.
[16]More information is available at http://www.redhat.com.
[17]More information is available at http://www.novell.com/linux.
[18]At the time of writing this, 18 machines in the top 500 use either distribution.
[19]More information is available at http://www.scientificlinux.org.
[20]More information is available at http://www.centos.org.

CPU, GP OSes usually provide round-robin-based scheduling, where the ready tasks alternate each other after a certain time slice which may be fixed or dynamically changing. GP OSes have usually scheduling policies designed so as to achieve a high overall system throughput and to serve processes on a best-effort (BE) basis, that is, no guarantees can be provided to the individual applications. On the other hand, real-time(RT) OSes have usually scheduling policies which are capable of providing precise scheduling guarantees to the competing applications. To this purpose, RTOSes undertake an *admission-control* phase, in which a new process is accepted into the system only if its timing requirements may be fulfilled, and the ones of the already accepted processes are not disrupted.

22.3.1 Scheduling on Multiprocessor

When deciding which kind of scheduler to adopt in a multiple processor system, there are two main options: partitioned scheduling and global scheduling. In a partitioned scheduler, there are multiple ready queues, one for each processor in the system, and it is possible to leave a processor in idle state even when there are ready tasks needing to be executed. The placement of tasks among the available processors is a critical step, and doing it optimally is equivalent to the bin-packing problem, which is known to be NP-hard in the strong sense [4, 42]. This complexity is typically avoided using suboptimal solutions provided by polynomial and pseudo-polynomial time heuristics (e.g. First Fit, Best Fit, etc.) [23, 45, 46, 50].

With a global scheduler, tasks are extracted from a single system-wide queue and scheduled onto the available processors. The load is thus intrinsically balanced, since no processor is idled as long as there is a ready task in the global queue. A class of algorithms, called Pfair schedulers [6], is able to ensure that the full processing capacity can be used but unfortunately at the cost of a large run-time overhead.

Complications in using a global scheduler mainly relate to the cost of inter-processor migration and to the kernel overhead due to the necessary synchronization. Even if there are mechanisms that can reduce the migration cost, it could nevertheless cause a significant schedulability loss when tasks have a large associated context (i.e. data overhead). Therefore, the effectiveness of a global scheduler is rather dependent on the application characteristics and on the architecture in use.

In addition to the aforementioned classes, there are also intermediate solutions, like hybrid- and restricted-migration schedulers [9, 14], that limit the number of processors among which a task can migrate or the possibilities that a task has to migrate (by disabling preemption). This way, fewer cache misses are expected, and the cost of migration and context changes is lower.

22.3.2 Real-Time Scheduling

The traditional real-time scheduling research area focuses mainly on hard real-time systems, where deadlines are considered to be critical, in the sense that deadline misses cannot be tolerated, because they lead to the complete system failure and possible catastrophic consequences (i.e. losses of life).

However, real-time theory and methodologies are gaining applicability in the field of soft real-time systems, where applications possess precise timing and performance requirements, but occasional failures in meeting them may be easily tolerated by the system, causing a graceful degradation in the quality of the provided service.

22.3.2.1 Scheduling Real-Time Task Sets on Multiprocessor Platforms

Only recently multiprocessing is receiving a significant attention from the real-time community, thanks to the increasing industrial interest in such platforms. While the scheduling problem for uniprocessor systems has been widely investigated for decades, few of the results obtained for a single processor generalize directly to the multiple processor case [49].

Unfortunately, predicting the behavior of a multiprocessor system requires in many cases a considerable computing effort. To simplify the analysis, it is often necessary to introduce pessimistic assumptions. This is particularly needed when modeling globally scheduled multiprocessor systems, in which the cost of migrating a task from a processor to another can significantly vary over time. The presence of caches and the frequency of memory accesses have a significant influence on the worst-case timely parameters that characterize the system. To bind the variability of these parameters, often real-time literature focuses on platforms with multiple processors but with no caches or whose cache miss delays are known. Also, the cost of preemption and migration on multiprocessor systems is a very important issue that still needs to be properly considered in real-time methodologies. Some research in the domain of hardware architectures moves toward partially mitigating such issues. Recently, a few architectures have been proposed that limit penalties associated to migration and cache misses, for example, the MPCore by ARM. Some researchers have recently proposed hardware implementations of some parts of the OS, allowing one to reduce the scheduling penalties of multiprocessor platforms [75].

22.3.2.2 Soft Real-Time Scheduling

Different scheduling algorithms have been proposed to support the specific needs of soft real-time applications. A first important class approximates the generalized processor sharing concept of a fluid flow allocation, in which each application using the resource marks a progress proportional to its weight. Among the algorithms of this class, we can cite Proportional Share [76] and Pfair [6]. Similar are the underlying principles of a family of algorithms known as resource reservation schedulers [66]. In the resource kernels project [66], the resource reservation approach has been successfully applied to different types of resources (including disk and network). The resource reservation framework has been adapted to partitioned multiprocessor systems in [7] and [8] for the Constant Bandwidth Server (CBS) and the Total Bandwidth Server (TBS) algorithms, respectively. Also, it has been proposed to let the scheduler automatically self-tune the best parameters for a running real-time application [17].

22.3.2.3 Scheduling of Distributed Real-Time Applications

The problem of designing scheduling parameters for distributed real-time applications has received a constant attention in the past few years. In [3], the authors introduce a notion of transaction for real-time databases characterized by periodicity and end-to-end constraints and propose a methodology to identify periods and deadlines of intermediate tasks. In [26], the activation periods of the intermediate tasks that comply with end-to-end real-time requirements are found by an optimization problem. In [37], the authors use performance analysis techniques to decide the bandwidth allocated to each task that attain a maximum latency and a minimum average throughput for a chain of computations.

Concerning modeling of timing requirements of real-time applications, usually models similar to synchronous data-flow networks [61] are used. As shown in [10], these models lend themselves to an effective code generation process, in which an offline schedule is synthesized that minimizes the code length and the buffer size. The models used in [19, 20] and [27] are also special cases of synchronous data-flow, but, due to the inherently distributed and dynamic nature of the considered applications, the aim is not an optimized offline scheduling of activities but rather an efficient on-line (run-time) scheduling mechanism. Finally, in [40] the problem of optimum deployment, over a physical heterogeneous network, of distributed real-time applications with computing and networking requirements subject to end-to-end response-time constraints is tackled by introducing a formalization in terms of a mixed-integer nonlinear programming optimization program, both in a deterministic and a probabilistic form.

22.3.3 Scheduling and Synchronization

Synchronization is an essential problem of concurrent programming, and it has received a great attention from the research community. The problems of concurrent access and of providing a consistent view of shared data structures can be solved in different ways, depending on the abstraction level and on the basic organization of the OS and programming paradigm. The basic properties that correct concurrent programs must possess were described by Herlihy and Wing [34], and solutions have been proposed both for shared memory and message passing. Also, synchronization is tightly coupled with scheduling.

When multiple tasks need to access a shared resource or data structure, they need to synchronize each other, in order to avoid performing the access at the same time. The basic synchronization means is constituted by a binary semaphore, which, if already taken, causes the process attempting to acquire the lock to be suspended by the scheduler and be woken up later when the lock owner exits the critical section. However, a great research effort has been done in two very important domains: in the literature of real-time scheduling, it is important to ensure that the amount of time a process has to wait before acquiring a lock may be somehow kept under control; also, in multiprocessor and multicore scheduling, if the acquired resource is held by a task on another processor and the critical section is expected to be very short (like it happens quite often in the kernel of an OS), then suspending the current task and performing a context switch might lead to unnecessary overheads, while other policies may be more convenient (e.g. spinlocking). Interestingly, the PREEMPT_RT branch of the Linux kernel has an option [52] for turning (almost) every spin-lock primitive used inside the kernel into a mutex.

In the shared-memory paradigm, all processors can access the same memory, uniformly (UMA machines) or nonuniformly (NUMA machines). A lot of work has been done to improve the basic locking mechanisms. Mellor-Crummey and Scott [55] solved the problem of reducing contention on the shared bus by using separate spin variables for each processor on which each core performed busy waiting. Many papers have proposed improvements on this basic mechanism, for example, to introduce time-out [73], to reactively change the lock behavior [48], and to balance overhead versus latency using a mixed-coarse/fine-grain locking strategy [81]. Mukherjee and Schwan [60] proposed an adaptive locking protocol that chooses between mutex locks and spin locks depending on the characteristics of the application.

A different approach consists in making a local copy of the data structure (or of part of it), modifying it and later trying to commit the changes in the global copy without disrupting the linearizability property [34]. This class of approaches is usually referred to as lock-free or nonblocking or wait-free [32]. Many wait-free algorithms have been proposed for common data structures, like priority queues [77] or stacks [31]. Transactional memory has been proposed as a hardware-level support for wait-free mechanisms [33].

For data structures where reading is more frequent than writing/updating, special mechanisms have been proposed to reduce contention, such as the read-copy-Update (RCU) mechanism [54], widely adopted within the Linux kernel for accessing critical shared lists. McKenney [53] provides a comparison of several locking techniques in the form of patterns, from different points of view: latency, memory bandwidth, memory size, granularity, fairness and read–write ratio. There is no clear winning strategy and every mechanism has its advantages and disadvantages. A similar comparison has been carried out by Anderson [1].

In the message-passing paradigm, each resource is assigned a server thread which exclusively performs operations on the data structures of the resource. Other threads (clients) must request the operation by issuing a remote invocation via an IPC. This organization mimics distributed systems where nodes do not share memory. The MPI interface [29] is based on this paradigm.

Chaves et al. [16] perform a comparison of shared-memory communication based on spin locks versus remote invocation in a NUMA multiprocessor architecture. Another comparison has been proposed by Chandra et al. [15]. They highlight that the performance is highly dependent on the underlying hardware structure and memory hierarchy (UMA or NUMA, presence of cache coherency, etc.). However, it can be generally said that message passing is more adequate for long critical operations on processors with high-memory access delay, while shared memory is preferable on short critical section on local data structures. Clearly, it is possible to mix shared-memory locking and remote invocation [30, 41]. Recently, Uhlig [80] proposed to use IPC or shared-memory locking depending on the locality of the data structure with respect to the current node and to use an adaptive locking mechanism depending on the level of contention.

Due to space reasons, we cannot overview the protocols to arbitrate the exclusive access to shared resources for real-time task sets. However, the interested reader can refer to [18] for more information.

22.3.4 Shared Resources Protocol in the Linux Kernel

The design criteria and performance metrics mainly adopted by Linux kernel developers are overall system throughput and fairness. However, although real-time behavior and predictability have not been a primary concern until now, Linux embeds a few features that are commonly included in real-time kernels, and the synchronization subsystem does not constitute an exception to that.

In a Linux system, support for mutual exclusive access to shared-memory areas is provided at both kernel and user levels. In the latter case, this is achieved by means of system libraries (e.g. the `glibc` and `pthreads` libraries).

Inside the kernel, critical sections can be protected mainly by spinlocks, mutexes and RT-mutexes. There are other means of regulating the access to sensible code, such as read–write locks and RCU locks, but describing them in details is out of the scope of this chapter.

The Linux kernel includes the POSIX [36] RT-mutexes, which support the priority inheritance (PI) protocol for avoiding priority inversion, a well-known problem of systems scheduled under priority-based policies.

In mainline Linux, the only subsystem which uses RT-mutexes is the fast userspace mutexes (`futex`) interface. A futex is a special implementation of locking primitives which, exploiting atomic instructions and memory coherence available on the underlying hardware, manages to handle the synchronization entirely at the user-space level in those cases in which there is no contention. When, instead, task blocking and unblocking is needed, then futexes involve kernel-level operations.

In PREEMPT_RT, a kernel branch maintained by a small developer group led by Ingo Molnár, with the aim of making the kernel suitable for very low latency and real-time applications, things are quite different: in fact, when this patch is applied, most of the spinlocks and mutexes are turned into RT-mutex. Basically, at the cost of sacrificing part of the overall system performance, this branch of the kernel reduces significantly the duration of nonpreemptible sections and enforces priority inversion avoidance, reducing the performance and predictability gap between Linux and classical real-time kernels.

REFERENCES

1. T. E. Anderson. The performance of spin lock alternatives for shared-memory multiprocessors. *IEEE Transactions on Parallel and Distributed Systems*, 1:6–16, January 1990.

2. Y. Aridor, M. Factor, and A. Teperman. cjvm: a single system image of a jvm on a cluster. In *Proceedings of the 1999 International Conference on Parallel Processing, ICPP '99*, pages 4–11. IEEE Computer Society, Washington, DC, USA, 1999.

3. N. C. Audsley, A. Burns, M. F. Richardson, and A. J. Wellings. Data consistency in hard real-time systems. *Informatica (Slovenia)*, 19(2): 223–234, 1995.

4. N. C. Audsley and K. Bletsas. Fixed priority timing analysis of real-time systems with limited parallelism. In *16th Euromicro Conference on Real-Time Systems (ECRTS 2004)*, pages 231–238, Catania, Italy, 2004.

5. A. Barak, S. Guday, and R. Wheeler. The mosix distributed operating system, load balancing for unix. In *Lecture Notes in Computer Science*, volume 672. Springer-Verlag, 1993.

6. S. K. Baruah, N. K. Cohen, C. G. Plaxton, and D. A. Varvel. Proportionate progress: a notion of fairness in resource allocation. In *Proceedings of the twenty-fifth annual ACM symposium on Theory of computing, STOC '93*, pages 345–354. ACM, New York, NY, USA, 1993.

7. S. Baruah and G. Lipari. Executing aperiodic jobs in a multiprocessor constant-bandwidth server implementation. In *Proceedings of the 16th Euromicro Conference on Real-Time Systems*, pages 109–116. IEEE Computer Society, Washington, DC, USA, 2004.

8. S. Baruah and G. Lipari. A multiprocessor implementation of the total bandwidth server. *Parallel and Distributed Processing Symposium, International*, 1:40a, 2004.

9. S. K. Baruah and J. Carpenter. Multiprocessor fixed-priority scheduling with restricted interprocessor migrations. *Journal of Embedded Computing*, 1:169–178, April 2005.

10. S. S. Battacharyya, E. A. Lee, and P. K. Murthy. *Software Synthesis from Dataflow Graphs*. Kluwer Academic Publishers, 1996.

11. A. Baumann et al. The multikernel: a new os architecture for scalable multicore systems. In *SOSP*, 2009.

12. S. Boyd-Wickizer, H. Chen, R. Chen, Y. Mao, F. Kaashoek, R. Morris, A. Pesterev, L. Stein, M. Wu, Y. Dai, Y. Zhang, and Z. Zhang. Corey: an operating system for many cores. In *8th USENIX Symposium on Operating Systems Design and Implementation*, 2008.

13. S. Boyd-Wickizer, A. T. Clements, Y. Mao, A. Pesterev, M. Frans Kaashoek, R. Morris, and N. Zeldovich. An analysis of linux scalability to many cores. In *Proceedings of the 9th USENIX conference on Operating systems design and implementation*, OSDI'10, pages 1–8. USENIX Association. Berkeley, CA, USA, 2010.

14. J. M. Calandrino, J. H. Anderson, and D. P. Baumberger. A hybrid real-time scheduling approach for large-scale multicore platforms. In *Proceedings of the 19th Euromicro Conference on Real-Time Systems*, pages 247–258. IEEE Computer Society, Washington, DC, USA, 2007.

15. S. Chandra, J. R. Larus, and A. Rogers. Where is time spent in message-passing and shared-memory programs? In *Proceedings of the sixth international conference on Architectural support for programming languages and operating systems*, ASPLOS-VI, pages 61–73. ACM, New York, NY, USA, 1994.

16. E. M. Chaves, P. Ch. Das, Th. J. Leblanc, B. D. Marsh, and M. L. Scott. Kernel-kernel communication in a shared-memory multiprocessor. *Concurrency: Practice and Experience*, 5(3):171–191, 1993.

17. T. Cucinotta, F. Checconi, L. Abeni, and L. Palopoli. Self-tuning schedulers for legacy real-time applications. In *Proceedings of the 5th European Conference on Computer Systems (Eurosys 2010)*, Paris, France, April 2010. European chapter of the ACM SIGOPS.

18. T. Cucinotta, G. Lipari, D. Faggioli, F. Checconi, S. Kumar, R. Aguiar, J. Paulo Barraca, B. Santos, J. Zarrin, J. Kuper, C. Baaij, L. Schubert, H.-M. Kreuz, and V. Gramoli. S(o)os project deliverable d6.1 - state of the art. Available on-line on the S(o)OS website: http://www.soos-project.eu/., 7 2010.

19. T. Cucinotta and L. Palopoli. Feedback scheduling for pipelines of tasks. In *Proceedings of the 10th international conference on Hybrid systems: computation and control*, HSCC'07, pages 131–144. Springer-Verlag, Berlin, Heidelberg, 2007.

20. T. Cucinotta and L. Palopoli. Qos control for pipelines of tasks using multiple resources. *IEEE Transactions on Computers*, 59:416–430, 2010.

21. A. Depoutovitch and M. Stumm. Otherworld: giving applications a chance to survive os kernel crashes. In *Proceedings of the 5th European conference on Computer systems*, EuroSys '10, pages 181–194. ACM, New York, NY, USA, 2010.

22. S. Derr, P. Jackson, C. Lameter, P. Menage, and H. Seto. Cpusets. Available on-line at: `http://www.kernel.org/doc/Documentation/cgroups/cpusets.txt`.

23. S. K. Dhall and C. L. Liu. On a real-time scheduling problem. *Operations Research*, 26(1):127–140, 1978.

24. J. Dongarra, J. Bunch, C. Moler, and G. W. Stewart. *LINPACK Users Guide*. SIAM, Philadelphia, 1979.

25. D. Faggioli, T. Cucinotta, J. Lelli, and G. Lipari. An efficient and scalable implementation of global edf in linux. In *Proceedings of the 7th International Workshop on Operating Systems Platforms for Embedded Real-Time Applications (OSPERT 2011)*, Porto, Portugal, 7 2011.

26. R. Gerber, S. Hong, and M. Saksena. Guaranteeing real-time requirements with resource-based calibration of periodic processes. *IEEE Transactions on Software Engineering*, 21:579–592, July 1995.

27. S. Goddard and K. Jeffay. Managing latency and buffer requirements in processing graph chains. *The Computer Journal*, 44:200–1, 2001.

28. T. Goodale, S. Jha, H. Kaiser, T. Kielmann, P. Kleijer, G. von Laszewski, C. Lee, A. Merzky, H. Rajic, and J. Shalf. Saga: a simple api for grid applications. High-level application programming on the grid. *Computational Methods in Science and Technology*, 12(1):7–20, 2006. Available online at: `Online at:http://wiki.cct.lsu.edu/saga/`.

29. W. Gropp, E. Lusk, N. Doss, and A. Skjellum. A high-performance, portable implementation of the mpi message passing interface standard. *Parallel Comput.*, 22:789–828, September 1996.

30. J. Heinlein, K. Gharachorloo, S. Dresser, and A. Gupta. Integration of message passing and shared memory in the stanford flash multiprocessor. *SIGPLAN Not.*, 29:38–50, November 1994.

31. D. Hendler, N. Shavit, and L. Yerushalmi. A scalable lock-free stack algorithm. In *Proceedings of the sixteenth annual ACM symposium on Parallelism in algorithms and architectures*, SPAA '04, pages 206–215. ACM, New York, NY, USA, 2004.

32. M. Herlihy. Wait-free synchronization. *ACM Transactions on Programming Languages and Systems*, 13:124–149, January 1991.

33. M. Herlihy and J. E. B. Moss. Transactional memory: architectural support for lock-free data structures. *ACM SIGARCH Computer Architecture News*, 21:289–300, May 1993.

34. M. P. Herlihy and J. M. Wing. Linearizability: a correctness condition for concurrent objects. *ACM Transactions on Programming Languages and Systems*, 12:463–492, July 1990.

35. F. Hupfeld, T. Cortes, B. Kolbeck, J. Stender, E. Focht, M. Hess, J. Malo, J. Marti, and E. Cesario. The xtreemfs architecture - a case for object-based file systems in grids. *Concurrency and Computation: Practice and Experience*, 20:2049–2060, December 2008.

36. IEEE standard for information technology Ãć portable operating system interface (posix), ieee std 1003.1, 2004 edition. Available online at: http://www.opengroup.org/onlinepubs/009695399.

37. D.-I. Kang, R. Gerber, and M. Saksena. Parametric design synthesis of distributed embedded systems. *IEEE Transactions on Computers*, 49:1155–1169, 2000.

38. T. Kielmann et al. Xtreemos project deliverable d3.1.6: Second prototype of xtreemos runtime engine, version 1.0.3, 1 2009.

39. A. Kleen. Linux multi-core scalability. 16th Linux Kongress. Available on-line at: http://www.linux-kongress.org/2009/abstracts.html#3_4_1., 102009.

40. K. Konstanteli, D. Kyriazis, T. Varvarigou, T. Cucinotta, and G. Anastasi. Real-time guarantees in flexible advance reservations. *Computer Software and Applications Conference, Annual International*, 2:67–72, 2009.

41. D. Kranz, K. Johnson, A. Agarwal, J. Kubiatowicz, and B.-H. Lim. Integrating message-passing and shared-memory: early experience. In *Proceedings of the fourth ACM SIGPLAN Symposium on Principles and Practice of Parallel Programming*, PPOPP '93, pages 54–63. ACM, New York, NY, USA, 1993.

42. P. Kuacharoen, M. A. Shalan, and V. J. Mooney III. A configurable hardware scheduler for real-time systems. In *Proceedings of the International Conference on Engineering of Reconfigurable Systems and Algorithms*, pages 96–101. CSREA Press, 2003.

43. C. Lameter. Extreme high performance computing or why microkernels suck. In *Proceedings of the Linux Symposium*, 2007.

44. H. C. Lauer and R. M. Needham. On the duality of operating system structures. *ACM SIGOPS Operating System Review*, 13(2):3–19, 4 1979.

45. S. Lauzac, R. Melhem, and D. Mossé. An improved rate-monotonic admission control and its applications. *IEEE Transactions on Computers*, 52:337–350, March 2003.

46. J. Liebeherr, A. Burchard, Y. Oh, and S. H. Son. New strategies for assigning real-time tasks to multiprocessor systems. *IEEE Transactions on Computers*, 44:1429–1442, December 1995.

47. J. Liedtke. On μ-kernel construction. In *15th ACM Symposium on Operating Systems Principles (SOSP)*, pages 237–250, 12 1995.

48. B.-H. Lim and A. Agarwal. Reactive synchronization algorithms for multiprocessors. In *Proceedings of the Sixth International Conference on Architectural Support for Programming Languages and Operating Systems*, ASPLOS-VI, pages 25–35. ACM, New York, NY, USA, 1994.

49. C. L. Liu and J. W. Layland. Scheduling algorithms for multiprogramming in a hard-real-time environment. *Journal of the ACM*, 20:46–61, January 1973.

50. J. M. López, J. L. Díaz, and D. F. García. Utilization bounds for edf scheduling on real-time multiprocessor systems. *Real-Time Systems*, 28:39–68, October 2004.

51. R. Lottiaux, B. Boissinot, P. Gallard, G. VallÃl'e, and C. Morin. OpenMosix, OpenSSI and Kerrighed: A Comparative Study. Technical Report 5399, INRIA, 11 2004.

52. P. McKenney. A realtime preemption overview. Available on-line at: `http://lwn.net/Articles/146861/`.

53. P. E. McKenney. Selecting locking primitives for parallel programming. *Communications of the ACM*, 39:75–82, October 1996.

54. P. E. McKenney and J. D. Slingwine. Read-copy update: using execution history to solve concurrency problems. Available online at: `http://www.liblfds.org/wikipedia/index.php/White_Papers`.

55. J. M. Mellor-Crummey and M. L. Scott. Algorithms for scalable synchronization on shared-memory multiprocessors. *ACM Transactions on Computer Systems*, 9:21–65, February 1991.

56. O. Michielin and H. Hussain-Khan. Xgrid, a "just do it" grid solution for non it's. *EMBnet.news*, 11(3), 9 2005.

57. Microsoft TechNet. Windows nt 4.0 workstation architecture. Available on-line at: `http://technet.microsoft.com/en-us/library/cc749980.aspx`.

58. Christine Morin, Yvon Jégou, Jérôme Gallard, and Pierre Riteau. Clouds: A New Playground for the XtreemOS Grid Operating System. *Parallel Processing Letters (PPL)*, 19:435–449, 2009.

59. C. Morin, R. Lottiaux, G. VallÃl'e, P. Gallard, D. Margery, J.-Y. Berthou, and I. D. Scherson. Kerrighed and data parallelism: cluster computing on single system image operating systems. In *6th IEEE International Conference on Cluster Computing*, pages 277–286, San Diego, California, 9 2004.

60. B. C. Mukherjee and K. Schwan. Improving performance by use of adaptive objects: experimentation with a configurable multiprocessor thread package. In *High Performance Distributed Computing, 1993., Proceedings of the 2nd International Symposium on*, pages 59–66, July 1993.

61. W. A. Najjar, E. A. Lee, and G. R. Gao. Advances in the dataflow computational model. *Parallel Computing*, 25:1907–1929, December 1999.

62. P. Padala and J. N. Wilson. Gridos: operating system services for grid architectures. In *Proceedings of the International Conference on High-Performance Computing (HiPC 2003)*, 2003.

63. A. Petitet, R. C. Whaley, J. Dongarra, and A. Cleary. *HPL - A Portable Implementation of the High-Performance Linpack Benchmark for Distributed-Memory Computers*, 9 2008, `http://www.netlib.org/benchmark/hpl/`.

64. S. Puri and Dr. Qamas Abbas. Grid operating system: making dynamic virtual services in organizations. *International Journal of Computer Theory and Engineering*, 2(1):96–102, 2 2010.

65. QNX Software Systems. The qnx neutrino microkernel. Available online at: `http://www.qnx.com/developers/docs/6.3.2/neutrino/sys_arch/kernel.html`.

66. R. Rajkumar, K. Juvva, A. Molano, and S. Oikawa. Readings in multimedia computing and networking. chapter Resource kernels: a resource-centric approach to real-time and multimedia systems, pages 476–490. Morgan Kaufmann Publishers Inc., San Francisco, CA, USA, 2001.

67. R. Rashid, D. Julin, D. Orr, R. Sanzi, R. Baron, A. Forin, D. Golub, and M. Jones. Mach: a system software kernel. In *Proceedings of the 34th Computer Society International Conference (COMPCON 89)*, 2 1989.

68. M. Rozier, V. Abrossimov, F. Armand, I. Boule, M. Gien, M. Guillemont, F. Herrmann, C. Kaiser, S. Langlois, P. LÃl'onard, and W. Neuhauser. Overview of the CHORUS Distributed Operating Systems. *Computing Systems*, 1:39âĂŞ–69, 1991.

69. L. Schubert, A. Kipp, B. Koller, and S. Wesner. Service oriented operating systems: Future workspaces. *IEEE Wireless Communications*, 16:42–50, 2009.

70. L. Schubert and A. Kipp. Principles of service oriented operating systems. In O. Akan, P. Bellavista, J. Cao, F. Dressler, D. Ferrari, M. Gerla, H. Kobayashi, S. Palazzo, S. Sahni, X. Shen, M. Stan, J. Xiaohua, A. Zomaya, G. Coulson, P. Vicat-Blanc Primet, T. Kudoh, and J. Mambretti, editors, *Networks for Grid Applications, volume 2 of Lecture Notes of the Institute for Computer Sciences, Social-Informatics and Telecommunications Engineering*, pages 56–69. Springer Berlin Heidelberg, 2009.

71. L. Schubert, A. Kipp, and S. Wesner. *Above the Clouds: From Grids to Service-Oriented Operating Systems*, pages 238 – 249. IOS Press, 2009.

72. L. Schubert, S. Wesner, A. Kipp, and A. Arenas. Self-managed microkernels: from clouds towards resource fabrics. In O. Akan, P. Bellavista, J. Cao, F. Dressler, D. Ferrari, M. Gerla, H. Kobayashi, S. Palazzo, S. Sahni, X. (S.) Shen, M. Stan, J. Xiaohua, A. Zomaya, G. Coulson, D. R. Avresky, M. Diaz, A. Bode, B. Ciciani, and E. Dekel, editors, *Cloud Computing, volume 34 of Lecture Notes of the Institute for Computer Sciences, Social Informatics and Telecommunications Engineering*, pages 167–185. Springer Berlin Heidelberg, 2010.

73. M. L. Scott and W. N. Scherer. Scalable queue-based spin locks with timeout. In *Proceedings of the Eighth ACM SIGPLAN Symposium on Principles and Practices of Parallel Programming*, PPoPP '01, pages 44–52. ACM, New York, NY, USA, 2001.

74. Amit Singh. What is Mac OS X? Available on-line at: `http://osxbook.com/book/bonus/ancient/whatismacosx/arch\_xnu.html.`, 12 2003.

75. J. Starner, J. Adomat, J. Furunas, and L. Lindh. Real-time scheduling co-processor in hardware for single and multiprocessor systems. *EUROMICRO Conference*, 0:0509, 1996.

76. I. Stoica, H. Abdel-Wahab, K. Jeffay, S. K. Baruah, J. E. Gehrke, and C. G. Plaxton. A proportional share resource allocation algorithm for real-time-shared systems. In *Proceedings of the 17th IEEE Real-Time Systems Symposium*, RTSS '96, pages 288–299, Washington, DC, USA, 1996.

77. H. Sundell and P. Tsigas. Fast and lock-free concurrent priority queues for multi-thread systems. *Journal of Parallel and Distributed Computing*, 65:609–627, May 2005.

78. A. S. Tanenbaum. A comparison of three microkernels. *Journal of Supercomputing*, 9, 1995.

79. A. S. Tanenbaum, M. Frans Kaashoek, R. Van Renesse, and H. E. Bal. The amoeba distributed operating system – a status report. *Computer Communications*, 14:324–335, 1991.

80. V. Uhlig. The mechanics of in-kernel synchronization for a scalable microkernel. *ACM SIGOPS Operating Systems Review*, 41(4):49–58, 2007.

81. R. C. Unrau, O. Krieger, B. Gamsa, and M. Stumm. Experiences with locking in a numa multiprocessor operating system kernel. In *Proceedings of the 1st USENIX Conference on Operating Systems Design and Implementation*, OSDI '94, Berkeley, CA, USA, 1994. USENIX Association.

82. D. Wentzlaff and A. Agarwal. Factored operating systems (fos): the case for a scalable operating system for multicores. *ACM SIGOPS Operating System Review: Special Issue on the Interaction among the OS, Compilers, and Multicore Processors*, 4 2009.

83. Q. Yuan, J. Zhao, M. Chen, and N. Sun. GenerOS: an asymmetric operating system kernel for multi-core systems. In *IEEE International Parallel & Distributed Processing Symposium*, Atlanta, USA, 4 2010.

84. H. Zhang, J. Lee, and R. Guha. Vcluster: a thread-based java middleware for smp and heterogeneous clusters with thread migration support. *Software: Practice and Experience*, 38:1049–1071, August 2008.

85. W. Zhu, C.-L. Wang, and F. C. M. Lau. Jessica2: a distributed java virtual machine with transparent thread migration support. *Cluster Computing, IEEE International Conference on*, 0:381, 2002.

GLOSSARY

Advanced Synchronization Facility (ASF)   Experimental AMD64 extension to support lock-free data structures and software transactional memory

Amdahl's law   Describes how the sequential fraction of an application limits the maximum available speedup of a parallel implementation

Auto-tuning   Automatic performance tuning of applications. Given a set of tuning parameters with corresponding value domains, the goal of auto-tuning is to find a parameter configuration that optimizes the application's performance

BlockLib   A C-based skeleton programming library for the Cell Broadband Engine

C(P)   The maximal space of interleavings for a parallel program P under which the program is correct

Cache   A component of the memory system that is located very close to the processor. It transparently stores data so that future requests for that data can be served faster

Cache line   The smallest unit of memory that can be transferred between the main memory and the cache

Cell Broadband Engine (Cell/B.E.)   A heterogeneous multicore processor developed by Sony/Toshiba/IBM

Chip multiprocessor   A processor that uses multiple processor cores on a single chip

Compare-and-swap (CAS) Atomic primitive that replaces the value of a variable iff it currently the value supplied as a parameter

Container A wrapper object of generic data type that encapsulates aggregated pay-load data such as elements of an array, stores the corresponding metadata and provides access operations

Copying-in operation Operation that transfers data from a D space to a P space

Copying-out operation Operation that transfers data from a P space to a D space

Critical event Critical events are the minimal set of program events that are needed to replay the parallel program. Examples of critical event types are shared memory access, message passing and obtaining or releasing of locks

D space Part of the address space that reflects the nonspeculative state of the computation. It is only updated by the main thread

Data interaccess time The gap between two successive accesses to the same data block

Data parallelism Parallelism that arises from the concurrent application of the same operation to the elements of a parallel data container

DCAS or CAS2 Compare-and-swap operation performed on two different words

Deadlock State of a concurrent execution where multiple processes wait for one another to release a resource, hence preventing progress

Dresden Transactional Memory Compiler (DTMC) An experimental compiler for transactional memory that supports transactional language constructs in C/C++ developed at the University of Dresden

Edge tiles Are defined as tiles that communication processes are performed with tiles allocated to other cores

Execution plan A list of expected best implementation variant and values for tunable parameters for the efficient execution of a skeleton or component invocation, depending on the actual problem size and possibly other context conditions

False conflict A conflict between two concurrent transactions that does not affect the correctness of the application

Filter Task consuming and producing elements in a stream fashion

Flynn's taxonomy A classification of computer architectures based on the concurrency of the instruction and data streams

GNU Compiler Collection (GCC) Developed by the GNU project, GCC is a compiler system for various programming languages including C

Heterogeneous multicore A processor that uses more than one type of processor core on a single chip

Homogeneous multicore A processor that uses identical processor cores on a single chip

I(P) For a parallel program P and for a given set of P's inputs, we refer to the space of possible orders of task execution and environment events as the space of program interleavings, I(P)

Internal tiles Are defined as tiles that communication processes are made in the same core

Irrevocable mode The mode of a transaction that never aborts

LAMP Stack of FOSS software based on Linux, Apache, MySQL and Perl/Python/PHP to create a web server

Livelock State of a concurrent execution where processes keep changing states without progressing

Load-linked/store-conditional (LL/SC) Two atomic primitives. Load-linked reads the value of a variable and store-conditional stores another value in the variable if it has not been changed since the read

Lock-free An algorithm is lock-free if, for all possible executions, at least one concurrent operation will succeed in a finite number of its own steps

Map A data-parallel skeleton that expresses the element-wise application of a function to each element of a collection of data elements, accessing in each element computation only a single element per operand collection

Mapping A distribution process where the tiles are assigned to each core

Mapping table A data structure that assists the result-committing stage. It is updated when a copying-in operation is performed and referred to by copying-out operations and during misspeculation check. Each speculative thread has its own mapping table

Memcached (MCD) A scalable distributed memory caching scheme to reduce backend database requests. The 'd' stands for demon

Miscompression rate The rate between the number of accesses made to the compressed data and the total number of accesses

Misspeculation check A process that detects any dependence violations that have occurred in a speculative task. It is always lazily performed (i.e. when a speculative task has finished) by the main thread

Misspeculation rate The percentage of tasks that fail to pass a misspeculation check

Moore's law Predicts that the number of transistors on a chip doubles approximately every two years

Multiprocessor A computer with two or more physical processors

Multithreading A technique that allows multiple processes or threads to share the functional units of one processor by using overlapped execution

Mutual exclusion Synchronization mechanism in which only a single processing unit may access the protected resource at any given time

MWCAS, CASN Multiword compare-and-swap operations. Compare-and-swap performed on multiple words

NOBLE Commercial library of lock-free data structures

Nonblocking full/empty bit (NB-FEB) Experimental synchronization primitive shown to be as powerful as CAS or LL/SC

Object-orientation (OO) Programming model providing a high degree of modularity and reusability. Central concepts of this model are classes, objects, fields, methods, encapsulation, inheritance, and others

Object-oriented stream programming (OOSP) Programming model unifying the concepts of stream programming and object-orientation

On-demand decompression Data block decompression per request

Open Computing Language (OpenCL) programming model A standard for portable programming of accelerator-based multi- and many-core systems, defined by the Khronos Group

Open Multiprocessing (OpenMP) A standard for portable shared memory parallel programming, defined by the OpenMP Architecture Review Board

Overlapping strategy Is to execute the internal computational tiles and the edge communications together

P space Part of the address space that reflects the state of the speculative threads. Each speculative thread has its own P space

Parallel pattern Design pattern for structuring and implementing parallelism. Important patterns are pipelines, master/worker or producer/consumer

Performance portability A property of a programming system that uses automated tuning of programs toward a given target architecture or system configuration in order to provide a best-effort adaptation for performance optimization for a new target system without touching the source code

Pipelining Assembling an object by parts such that the output of one partial assembly is fed as input to the next step

Predecompression Decompression of a data block before it is accessed

Prefetching Loading an item either by software or by hardware on the assumption that it is going to be used shortly

Process An instance of a computer program that is executed

Profiling run An execution of a program in which runtime information is collected. An instrumentation tool is usually used to gather the information

Recovery A process in which a speculative thread reexecutes its task due to misspeculation

Reduce A data-parallel skeleton that expresses reduction computations

Reduction A generic computation pattern that accumulates the elements of a collection of data into a single scalar result by applying addition or some other binary associative operation for accumulation

Result commit A process that copies out all values produced in a speculative task to D space. It must be done after misspeculation check has passed

Scalar processor A processor that operates on one computer word at a time

Scan A data-parallel skeleton that expresses prefix-sum computations

Scheduling An execution process where the tiles are executed in order to apply an overlapping strategy

Single Global Lock (SGL) A form of STM semantics which models transactional execution as critical sections protected by a single global lock

Single instruction multiple data (SIMD) Architectural paradigm of parallel execution control with a single instruction stream and multiple data streams. The same instruction is performed on multiple words concurrently.

SkelCL A C++-based OpenCL-based skeleton programming system for GPU and multi-GPU systems developed at Münster University, Germany

Skeleton A predefined generic component derived from a higher-order function that denotes a computation matching a certain data and control flow pattern, which can be parameterized in problem-specific sequential code and for which efficient implementations on various target platforms may exist

Skeleton programming Expressing the potential parallelism in a program in terms of skeletons

SkePU A C++-based multi-backend skeleton programming system for GPU and multi-GPU systems developed at Linköping University, Sweden

Speculative task A task that is executed by a speculative thread. Data values in the task may not be up to date during the execution and thus need to be verified when the task is finished

Speculative thread A thread that is created by the main thread. Several speculative threads can perform different speculative tasks simultaneously. A speculative thread is also called parallel thread or Pthread

Starvation The status of an execution in which some request (resp. transaction) may never terminate (resp. commit)

STI An alliance between Sony, Sony Computer Entertainment, Toshiba and IBM formed to develop Cell microprocessor architecture

Standard Template Library (STL) for C++ A collection of container data types and operations on them

Software transactional memory (STM) A software implementation of the transactional memory

Stream Continuous flow of data

Stream graph Graph capturing stream communications among a set of filters

Superscalar processor A processor that can issue several instructions at the same time (during one clock cycle)

Supertile A group of data that will be assigned to each core and it is composed by internal and edge tiles

Task parallelism Parallelism that arises from executing independent different parts or instances of code (e.g. function calls) in parallel

Intel Threading Building Blocks (TBB) Commercial/open-source library used to create task-based parallel applications

The main thread The default thread that executes all sequential regions. It also creates and control parallel threads

Thread   The smallest unit of processing that can be scheduled by an operating system. One or more threads run in the context of a single process

Thrust   A generic C++ library for GPU programming developed by NVIDIA Research

Tile   A unit of division of work that has communication dependency

Transactional memory (TM)   A concurrent programming paradigm consisting of delimiting regions of sequential code whose execution should look as atomic

Tuning heuristic   Approximation or model for setting a tuning parameter to an appropriate value without having to test the entire value range of that parameter

Tuning parameter   Program variable that influences the program's performance, but not its semantics. Examples are the number of threads, the number of pipeline stages or data size

Uniprocessor   A computer with only one physical processor

Vector   A container data type storing a one-dimensional array and its metadata

Warp   Number of threads that are simultaneously executed onto a multiprocessor

Zip   A data-parallel skeleton like Map with two input operands

INDEX

A

aborts, 83
adaptive locking protocol, 466
adaptive scheduling, 422
algorithmic skeleton, 263
algorithm view, 35
allocation, 418
all-or-nothing transaction, 167
Amdahl's law, 372
analytical model, 442
application-centric models, 44
array, 67
Array-OL, 146
atomicity, 84, 326
automated parallelization, 233
auto-tuning, 194–195

B

bag, 65
bandwidth, 425

benchmarks, 118, 314, 386, 425
block access, 4
BlockLib, 139
Brook, 145, 201
bus interconnection, 431

C

CABAC, 282
cache, 72, 237
cache behavior, 95
cache coherence, 348
cascading aborts, 172
CAVLC, 282
Cell/B.E. processor, 39
Cell Superscalar, 43
Charm++, 45
Cilk, 37
cloud computing, 452
cluster, 113, 311
code optimization, 292

Programming Multicore and Many-core Computing Systems,
First Edition. Edited by Sabri Pllana and Fatos Xhafa.
© 2017 John Wiley & Sons, Inc. Published 2017 by John Wiley & Sons, Inc.

Wiley Series on Parallel and Distributed Computing
Series Editor: Albert Y. Zomaya

Parallel and Distributed Simulation Systems
Richard Fujimoto

Mobile Processing in Distributed and Open Environments
Peter Sapaty

Introduction to Parallel Algorithms
C. Xavier and S. S. Iyengar

Solutions to Parallel and Distributed Computing Problems: Lessons from Biological Sciences
Albert Y. Zomaya, Fikret Ercal, and Stephan Olariu (Editors)

Parallel and Distributed Computing: A Survey of Models, Paradigms, and Approaches
Claudia Leopold

Fundamentals of Distributed Object Systems: A CORBA Perspective
Zahir Tari and Omran Bukhres

Pipelined Processor Farms: Structured Design for Embedded Parallel Systems
Martin Fleury and Andrew Downton

Handbook of Wireless Networks and Mobile Computing
Ivan Stojmenović

Internet-Based Workflow Management: Toward a Semantic Web
Dan C. Marinescu

Parallel Computing on Heterogeneous Networks
Alexey L. Lastovetsky

Performance Evaluation and Characterization of Parallel and Distributed Computing Tools
Salim Hariri and Manish Parashar

Distributed Computing: Fundamentals, Simulations, and Advanced Topics, Second Edition
Hagit Attiya and Jennifer Welch

Smart Environments: Technology, Protocols, and Applications
Diane Cook and Sajal Das

Fundamentals of Computer Organization and Architecture
Mostafa Abd-El-Barr and Hesham El-Rewini

Advanced Computer Architecture and Parallel Processing
Hesham El-Rewini and Mostafa Abd-El-Barr

UPC: Distributed Shared Memory Programming
Tarek El-Ghazawi, William Carlson, Thomas Sterling, and Katherine Yelick

Handbook of Sensor Networks: Algorithms and Architectures
Ivan Stojmenović (Editor)

Parallel Metaheuristics: A New Class of Algorithms
Enrique Alba (Editor)

Design and Analysis of Distributed Algorithms
Nicola Santoro

Task Scheduling for Parallel Systems
Oliver Sinnen

Computing for Numerical Methods Using Visual C++
Shaharuddin Salleh, Albert Y. Zomaya, and Sakhinah A. Bakar

Architecture-Independent Programming for Wireless Sensor Networks
Amol B. Bakshi and Viktor K. Prasanna

High-Performance Parallel Database Processing and Grid Databases
David Taniar, Clement Leung, Wenny Rahayu, and Sushant Goel

Algorithms and Protocols for Wireless and Mobile Ad Hoc Networks
Azzedine Boukerche (Editor)

Algorithms and Protocols for Wireless Sensor Networks
Azzedine Boukerche (Editor)

Optimization Techniques for Solving Complex Problems
Enrique Alba Christian Blum, Pedro Isasi, Coromoto León, and Juan Antonio Gómez (Editors)

Emerging Wireless LANs, Wireless PANs, and Wireless MANs: IEEE 802.11, IEEE 802.15, IEEE 802.16 Wireless Standard Family
Yang Xiao and Yi Pan (Editors)

High-Performance Heterogeneous Computing
Alexey L. Lastovetsky and Jack Dongarra

Mobile Intelligence
Laurence T. Yang, Augustinus Borgy Waluyo, Jianhua Ma, Ling Tan, and Bala Srinivasan (Editors)

Research in Mobile Intelligence

Laurence T. Yang (Editor)

Advanced Computational Infrastructures for Parallel and Distributed Adaptive Applicatons

Manish Parashar and Xiaolin Li (Editors)

Market-Oriented Grid and Utility Computing

Rajkumar Buyya and Kris Bubendorfer (Editors)

Cloud Computing Principles and Paradigms

Rajkumar Buyya, James Broberg, and Andrzej Goscinski (Editors)

Algorithms and Parallel Computing

Fayez Gebali

Energy-Efficient Distributed Computing Systems

Albert Y. Zomaya and Young Choon Lee (Editors)

Scalable Computing and Communications: Theory and Practice

Samee U. Khan, Lizhe Wang, and Albert Y. Zomaya (Editors)

The DATA Bonanza: Improving Knowledge Discovery in Science, Engineering, and Business

Malcolm Atkinson, Rob Baxter, Michelle Galea, Mark Parsons, Peter Brezany, Oscar Corcho, Jano van Hemert, and David Snelling (Editors)

Large Scale Network-Centric Distributed Systems

Hamid Sarbazi-Azad and Albert Y. Zomaya (Editors)

Verification of Communication Protocols in Web Services: Model-Checking Service Compositions

Zahir Tari, Peter Bertok, and Anshuman Mukherjee

High-Performance Computing on Complex Environments

Emmanuel Jeannot and Julius Žilinskas (Editors)

Advanced Content Delivery, Streaming, and Cloud Services

Mukaddim Pathan, Ramesh K. Sitaraman, and Dom Robinson (Editors)

Large-Scale Distributed Systems and Energy Efficiency

Jean-Marc Pierson (Editor)

Activity Learning: Discovering, Recognizing, and Predicting Human Behavior from Sensor Data

Diane J. Cook and Narayanan C. Krishnan